Who's Who in Military History

John Keegan taught military history at the Royal Military Academy Sandhurst from 1960 to 1986. Since then he has been Defence Editor of *The Daily Telegraph*. He is the author of many books, including *The Face of Battle, Six Armies in Normandy, The Second World War* and *A History of Warfare*, which won the 1994 Duff Cooper Prize. He is a Fellow of the Royal Historical Society at the Royal Society of Literature and was awarded the OBE in the Gulf War honours list.

Andrew Wheatcroft, who teaches at the University of Stirling, has specialized in the history of empires – what sustains them and what brings about their demise. In both cases he sees the role of the military as central. His two most recent books, *The Habsburgs: Embodying Empire* and *The Ottomans* (both Viking Penguin), have provided the first detailed analysis in English of those two great empires for more than a quarter of a century. His current work is a long-term study of relations between the Islamic and Christian worlds.

Who's Who in Military History

FROM 1453 TO THE PRESENT DAY

JOHN KEEGAN AND ANDREW WHEATCROFT

London and New York

U
51
.K43
1996
June 1998

First published by Weidenfeld & Nicolson in 1976
Second edition published in Great Britain in 1987 by Hutchinson, an imprint of
Century Hutchinson Ltd

This edition published 1996 by
Routledge
11 New Fetter Lane, London EC4P 4EE

Simultaneously published in the USA and Canada
by Routledge
29 West 35th Street, New York, NY 10001

Routledge is an International Thomson Publishing Company

© 1996 John Keegan, Andrew Wheatcroft, Janet Wheatcroft

Typeset in SABON by Datix International Limited, Bungay, Suffolk

Printed and bound in Great Britain by Clays Ltd, St Ives PLC

British Library Cataloguing in Publication Data

A catalogue record for this book is available from the British Library

Library of Congress Cataloguing in Publication Data

Keegan, John, 1934–
    Who's who in military history : from 1453 to the present day /
John Keegan and Andrew Wheatcroft.
        p.   cm.
    ISBN 0-415-12722-X. — ISBN 0-415-11884-0 (pbk)
    1. Military biography — Dictionaries. I. Wheatcroft, Andrew.
II. Title.
U51.K43 1996
355′.0092′2- -dc20
[B]
                                                                        95-40158
                                                                        CIP

ISBN 0-415-12722-X (hbk)
ISBN 0-415-11884-0 (pbk)

Contents

List of Maps   vi

Prefaces   vii

WHO'S WHO IN MILITARY HISTORY   1

Glossary   327

List of Maps

1 The Thirty Years' War 1618–48   332

2 The Dominance of France *c.* 1700   333

3 The Wars of Frederick the Great   334

4 The American War of Independence 1775–83   335

5 Europe 1789–1815   336

6 The American Civil War 1861–5   337

7 The First World War   338

8 The Western Front 1914–18   339

9 The Second World War   340

Maps drawn by Tony Garrett

Preface to the Second Edition

Who's who is a matter of which soldiers are left in little doubt. Not for their leaders the anonymity of a dark suit and an unmarked car. 'Who' can be told from all the whoms in the military world by a plethora of outward and visible signs – plumes, medals, sashes, gold lace, an attentive entourage and a row of stars on the official conveyance whose length exactly indicates the importance of the occupant. 'Mr Smith, I believe!', the deathless error of identification launched at the Duke of Wellington on the frock-coated streets of London, was not one even the village idiot could have made if the victor of Waterloo had been in uniform.

But all that glitters is not gold. Peacetime generals are often the first casualties of war. However stout the heart that beats beneath the braid, it is brain and nervous system that count when armies clash. The great panjandrums of the parade ground are frequently found to lack both when armies take the field. There have been some famous massacres of reputations as a result. Between August and September 1914, Joffre sacked one third of the generals in the French army. After the Wehrmacht's defeat outside Moscow in 1941, Hitler replaced nearly half the senior generals on the Russian front. Armies even coin words for these humiliations. 'Stellenbosched' was what the British army called generals sent to the place furthest from action in the Boer War. 'Limogé' was the French equivalent in the First World War.

'Stellenbosching' has its reciprocal effect. Men disfavoured or overlooked in peace are often proved by the test of war to be men of steel. Pétain, blocked for promotion and only a colonel in 1914 because of his unfashionable insistence on the importance of fire-power, found himself commanding a brigade at the battle of the Marne and a corps in the following year. By 1916 he was the saviour of Verdun and a national hero. Foch, too, was propelled to the heights with the same rapidity when war found in him a resilience and power to inspire that nothing in peace had called forth. Rommel, a colonel in 1939 and a simple infantryman, discovered in 1940 that he and the tank had an affinity for each other which resulted in the most brilliant display of mobile tactics seen since Sherman had marched from Atlanta to the sea in 1864.

Who's who in military history, in short, is not the same thing as archival research in dog-eared army lists. Most of yesterday's field-marshals signify no more in the history of warfare than dead Lord Mayors of London do in the history of high finance. The really significant warriors form a separate and inner group, whose reputations were made not by the bureaucratic processes that elevate workaday soldiers up the ladder of promotion but by lightning inspirations of mind and flashing strokes of action.

Who's Who in Military History is a time traveller's guide to the identity and biographies of such men. It does not claim to be exhaustive. The great captains of Antiquity and the paladins of the Feudal age are not here, because too little is known of many of them for it to be possible to construct biographies for all of uniform merit. The authors therefore decided to confine the scope of the book to the age of firearms which they decided should be taken to begin in 1453. That date is not only conventionally regarded as marking the end of the Middle Ages. It also marks the first unarguably decisive achievement of gunpowder weapons, the breaching of the walls of Constantinople by the giant cannon of the Ottoman sultan.

Within the chronology adopted, however, the book does seek to identify and characterized the most significant men of war. They fall into several categories. First and most obvious are the great commanders, land, sea and air, whose leadership won the most famous victories of the modern age. Some, perhaps the majority, were the products of an organized military system whom the outbreak of hostilities found in the ranks and who proved equal to its challenge. In the British service, Wellington was one of these, a junior officer at the outbreak of the French wars who commanded with success first a regiment, then a brigade, then a small army on colonial service, then a large army in the Peninsula, finally a great allied army in direct confrontation with the Emperor of the French himself. 'I do not think it could have been done had I not been there,' he remarked with uncharacteristic immodesty after Waterloo, but with incontestable accuracy. Only Wellington could have ensured that the line was held throughout the day of Waterloo.

A second category comprises those who, if not great commanders in the field, laid the ground for the victory of others. Moltke the Elder, though he did in fact command in Prussia's wars against Austria and France, is one of those. His real achievements were to create first a system of education which would produce professional staff offic-

ers, then a military organization that would make best use of their talents. 'No plan survives the first five minutes' encounter with the enemy', is his best-known military dictum. What his work ensured was that, when a plan foundered, his network of *Kriegsakademie* graduates were able to carry forward its purpose amid the chaos of events.

A third category is that of the military thinkers. Foremost among them is the man who furnished Moltke with his guiding military philosophy, Carl von Clausewitz. Also a Prussian, Clausewitz devoted his later life, after years spent campaigning, to the construction of a theory of war which would have universal validity. Though he died before the completion of his work, which was put into order by his widow, the book which resulted, *Vom Kriege*, quickly attained the status of a classic, was a dominating influence on the Prussian army under Moltke and, as a result of Moltke's victories, passed into currency throughout the armies of the world. It remains the most important work of military thought ever written.

A fourth category includes the great military technocrats. War is not exclusively a competition between technologies. Moral and intellectual factors also underlie the victory of one side over another. But superior weapons convey an advantage which it is rarely possible to offset by immaterial means. During much of the period the book covers, it was the quality of fortification that determined the success or failure of offensives and invasions. Outstanding among fortification engineers was Vauban in the seventeenth century and Todleben in the nineteenth. Vauban, chief engineer to Louis XIV, constructed the systems that protected France for over a century. Todleben, a tsarist engineer, developed the idea of field or 'flying' entrenchments that were to reach their culmination in the trench lines of the First World War.

Finally, war cannot work without heroes, men who count the value of their lives less than that of the cause. Often, they are humble men in whom war finds some touch of the sublime. Other times they are cavaliers, like the aces whom the aerial fighting of the First World War conjured into being. Guynemer and Richthofen might, two hundred years before their time, have been dashing but obscure cavalry captains. The aeroplane, and their skill in whirling it through the skies made them into world figures. They remain symbols of daring and romance to this day.

There is, of course, little romance to war in reality. 'Blood and iron' are its raw material and most of those who figure in this book spent blood and hammered iron with a brutality from which Bismarck would have shrunk in practice. These pages will have served their purpose if they succeed in singling out for the enquirer who really was who in the harsh and lethal business by which the world has engineered change since the inception of modern times.

JK and AW
1987

Preface to the New Edition

It would have seemed hubris twenty years ago to imagine that this volume would be appearing in a new edition. It is now published during perhaps the greatest period of military uncertainty in the last half century. In retrospect, when the second edition appeared in 1987, we were on the verge of a military transformation, an unravelling of the settled structures of Cold War military confrontation. Since then new styles of war have emerged, like 'ethnic cleansing'; or rather we have witnessed the resurgence of habits of barbarity which generals (and war artists) of earlier centuries would have recognized. Callot and Goya could find fresh horrors to record in Bosnia and Chechnia.

But in the same time-frame, as small conflicts began to proliferate, we have also seen in the Gulf War a textbook exercise in the art of war, the largest allied intervention since the Second World War. Moreover, it was presented as a model for the new moral use of force: for Good against Evil. This was just the first manifestation, we were told, of a New World Order, growing from the shards of the Cold War.

Since the Gulf War, these noble aspirations have turned to dust. The use of military power to prevent oppression, persecution or starvation, the modern equivalent of nineteenth-century *gunboat diplomacy*, is now seen to be, politically, a most dangerous option, so risky indeed, as to be avoided at almost any cost. The New World Order did not even enjoy a brief flowering. Instead, rather as Francis Fukuyama proclaimed the '*end of history*', suggesting that all that followed its termination was a random chaos of mere events, so too, perhaps the Gulf War was *the end of military history* in its traditional sense? The jury is out.

With that thought in mind, we bring this edition up to the end of the Gulf War, and find no one in the subsequent conflicts who merits inclusion in the annals of military history.

AW and JK
1996

A

Abbas (1571–1629) Persian shah and conqueror. To Shah Abbas belongs the distinction of creating a united Persian army, modelled on those of both the Ottoman Turks and the west, and of extending Persia's boundaries almost to the limits it had occupied in antiquity. For these achievements, and for the dramatic flowering of Persian culture which took place under his encouragement, he is known as Abbas the Great. Under Shah Ismail I, Persia had suffered both internal fragmentation and pressure from external enemies – Turks, the nomadic Uzbek tribes, and the Mogul rulers of India. Abbas decided to demolish his enemies piecemeal. Coming to the throne at the age of seventeen, he at once made peace with the Ottomans under Selim II, intending to concentrate on the protection of his northern frontier. But although he frustrated any major Uzbek incursion, he allowed them to erode the frontier in the ceaseless to-and-fro of border raiding, confident that he could recover all that he had lost in a major campaign.

His great imperative was to create an army both loyal to him and capable of prolonged campaigning. Traditionally, the Persians relied on tribal levies, and the army was composed almost entirely of cavalry, usually ill-disciplined and loyal only to their tribal chieftains. It was this pattern of Persian army which the Turkish Janissaries had shattered at Chaldiran (1515). Abbas's first task was to build up a sound basis of taxation to pay for his reforms. Thereafter, he constructed an army with a professional infantry and a 'tribe' of skilled cavalry: many of his reforms used the experience of the Turks, but for his artillery he had a team of expert English advisers, led by Sir Robert Shirley: their advice was also instrumental in the creation of a skilled force of musketeers. By 1600 he had the nucleus of a professional army, dependent solely on him for its support and able to undertake sustained campaigning far from home. Abbas soon threw back the Turks, extending his frontiers on the northern border into Uzbek and Turcoman territory. In 1606 he repulsed a major Turkish assault, under Sultan Ahmed II, at Sis, where his skilled and disciplined nucleus routed the Turks, who left 20,000 dead on the battlefield. Thereafter, although peace was made, war with Turkey was endemic throughout his reign. Turkish and Persian interests coincided too closely for any lasting peace to be possible.

From 1616 to 1618 and from 1623 to 1638 Persia was at war with Turkey: the armies were now well matched, but the vast distances involved made it difficult for either side to gain a decisive advantage. In 1623 they clashed over Baghdad, with the Turks advancing and besieging the city, Abbas cutting them off, and their army making a forced retreat. After his death the Turks were able to regain some lost ground, but the army which he founded provided his successors with a secure means of defence. To the north, he took Kandahar from the Moguls, although it was lost to the Uzbeks in 1630. His great achievement, however, was not on the battlefield, but in providing the sound administrative base that made possible the creation of a 'modern' army in a traditional system.

Abd el-Kader (1807–83) Algerian emir, general and resistance leader. In 1832, two years after the French capture of Algiers, and to prevent the extension of their conquests into the interior, Abd el-Kader raised the tribes around his capital, Mascara, in western Algeria (Oranie) and proclaimed a Moslem Holy War (*jihad*). This war was to last with interruptions for fifteen years and falls into three main episodes. In the first he was defeated at Oran (1832), but through the subsequent treaty which he signed with the French he was able to establish his ascendancy over numbers of western tribes. Thus reinforced he resumed his war against the French, defeating Trézel on the Macta, losing Mascara to Clauzel and again accepting French terms from Bugeaud (q.v.) at the Tafna in 1837. This treaty made Abd el-Kader effectively king of unconquered Algeria and in 1839 he raised the standard of revolt once more. The French were forced to garrison the countryside in strength and to organize large mobile columns to track down his bands. Most of the tribes quickly submitted, but he maintained a guerrilla campaign for another eight years, assisted by the sultan of Morocco, Abd er-Rahman. The sultan's invasion was defeated on the Isly in 1844 and Abd el-Kader, whose household had been captured in 1843, ultimately capitulated to Lamoricière (q.v.) in December 1847. He was interned in France until 1853 but was subsequently reconciled to his conquerors. His name, however, remained to Algerians a catchword of resistance to France throughout the colonial era.

Abd el-Krim, Mahommed ibn (1882–1963) Moroccan chieftain and partisan leader, best known for his masterly conduct of the Rif war (1921–6) against the French and Spanish. His long-held ambition was to lead Morocco to sovereign independence (it had become a French protectorate in 1912 – *see* Lyautey). During the First World War he was imprisoned by the French for communicating with the Germans. But, escaping, he raised the tribes around Ajdir, preached the Holy War and with German help armed 10,000 men. On 21 July 1921 he inflicted a major defeat on the Spanish in their enclave at Anual (12,000 dead), indirectly bringing down the government and ushering in Primo de Rivera (q.v.) as dictator. By 1924 Abd el-Krim had reduced the Spanish holding in Morocco to a coastal strip and in April 1925 he unleashed a successful offensive against the French border outposts. French and Spanish now combined their efforts, reinforced their garrisons and launched a joint counter-offensive against Targuist, his headquarters. He surrendered there to a French column on 26 May 1926 and was deported to the island of Reunion. Released for reasons of health in 1947, he made his way to Egypt where he resumed his anti-French campaign as a propagandist.

Abercromby, (Sir) Ralph (1734–1801) British general. The captor of St Lucia and Trinidad, 1795–6, and a participant in the Helder expedition of 1799, it was his army which defeated the remnant of Napoleon's garrison of Egypt at the battle of Aboukir (Alexandria), 1 March 1801, in which he was killed.

His brother **Robert Abercromby** (1740–1827) defeated Tippu Sultan (q.v.) in 1792.

Abul Hassan *see* Muley Hacen.

Akbar (1542–1605) Soldier and Mogul emperor of India. The Mogul empire, which was founded by Babur (q.v.), reached its finest flowering under his grandson Akbar. Born in exile, for his father Huma had been forced from his throne, he began his war of reconquest and acquisition at the age of fifteen, although he owed much to the advice of his guardian Bairam. In 1560 he took power for himself, and began a life which involved almost constant war. By the time of his death, his armies dominated the Indian subcontinent, from the Hindu Kush to the Godavari river in the south.

Akbar inherited a sound military system, based on strategic fortresses garrisoned by loyal troops and a largely cavalry army in the field. Much of the best cavalry in India was Hindu, and Akbar was remarkable for his ability to incorporate Hindu elements within his Moslem state. He married Rajput princesses, firstly in the early stages of his conquest of Rajputana, and secondly to consolidate their goodwill. He maintained the power structure of the Rajput kingdoms, and relied heavily on them for military support. He extended the traditional army by creating an artillery force and a regular infantry, some 12,000 strong, and armed with firearms. To support his conquests he revolutionized the tax structure of his domains, collecting taxes in cash rather than in kind. To administer his territories he introduced many of the Persian patterns and concepts of government, together with the lax Persian attitude towards the strict interpretation of Islam.

The success of Akbar as a ruler was that he recognized that India could not be ruled without the co-operation of Hindu society, and he abolished all the restraints under which Hinduism traditionally operated in Moslem states. He suffered the usual crop of revolts, the most serious by his son Salim in 1601. Akbar crushed the rebellion, but pardoned his son, a decision he was to regret when he was poisoned by Salim four years later. Akbar himself was not a great field commander, relying on his generals, especially the Rajput Raja Todar Malla.

Albert I (1875–1934) Belgian king and war leader. Born at the palace of Laeken, son of the Count of Flanders, Albert succeeded his uncle Leopold II in 1909. Faced by the German demand for free passage through Belgium (for their armies) in August 1914, he refused and put himself at the head of his own tiny army to oppose them. After its retreat to Antwerp in August, he directed its counter-offensive, 9–12 September 1914, and then its defence of the Antwerp fortress, 28 September–9 October. Overwhelmed by superior forces, the army was forced to retreat across the Yser into the north-western corner of Belgium, where Albert set up his headquarters at Furnes. There he remained for the rest of the war, in daily contact with his troops in the front line. His intelligence, regal bearing, dignity and sincerity made him one of the few genuinely and internationally popular figures of the First World War.

Albrecht, Archduke (1817–95) Austrian field-marshal, the victor of the battle of Custozza (1866) and the leading military figure in the Austro-Hungarian empire. The eldest son of the Archduke Charles (q.v.), the only Austrian general ever to defeat Napoleon (Aspern 1809), Albrecht inherited his father's mantle as a great commander. In 1848 he commanded the regiments in Vienna which, on his orders, fired on the crowds, thereby stimulating the revolutionary outbreak in the city. In the war of 1859 in Italy, Albrecht was sent to Germany to drum up support for the Austrian cause, but Prussian prevarication frustrated his efforts at gaining worthwhile military help against Italy and France. After the war ended with the loss of half of Austria's lands in northern Italy, the army was drastically reformed: Albrecht, despite his comparatively junior status, was destined for the command of the Austrian northern army in the event of a major war. However, when the Austro-Prussian war of 1866 broke out, Albrecht was suddenly shifted to the southern (Italian) front. Many reasons have been given for this sudden switch, most of them highly discreditable to the Emperor Franz Joseph and to Albrecht. More charitably, Albrecht's replacement Benedek (q.v.), who had until then been in command of the Italian army, was a much older and more experienced soldier, and the northern command was his by right and by public opinion. But the switch meant that he went down into an ignominious and catastrophic defeat by the Prussians at Königgrätz, while Albrecht reaped the benefit of his well-drilled and confident army, as well as a very expert staff, to defeat the Italian general La Marmora (q.v.) at the battle of Custozza, on 25 June 1866. It was a cautious man's battle, taking advantage of a carefully chosen strong natural site, and letting the enemy come to him. Yet the same caution stopped him from exploiting his victory, and the Italians were allowed to retire, bruised but intact.

After the war ended, despite Albrecht's victory, with the loss of the remaining province in Italy, and Austria's expulsion from Germany, the success at Custozza was the one relief to an otherwise gloomy picture. As a result, Albrecht was given an eminence which, strictly speaking, his achievement did not justify. He was created first commander-in-chief of the army, and then inspector-general of the army. He was a firm conservative in all matters, military and civil, and took to writing pamphlets lamenting the state of the army's morale, as well as fighting a fierce rearguard action against all forms of innovation. As Austria-Hungary's leading soldier his views carried great weight, and much of the Austrian failure in the First World War can be traced back to his long

period of power. He suffered from poor eyesight from his childhood; in his last years he was nearly blind. But his handicap did not deter him from exercising his powers right up to his death. Albrecht's influence came through his intransigence and supreme confidence in his role and mission. A stern and austere figure, he was a Habsburg more in the mould of the sixteenth century than of the effete and decadent nineteenth. His power was that of the bureaucrat, not the fighting soldier, and his thirty years of command over the peacetime Habsburg army made it a flabby instrument of war.

Alekseev, Mikhail Vasilievich (1857–1918) Russian general. The son of a private soldier, Alekseev succeeded in acquiring an offier's education, passed the staff college in 1890, became a general in 1904 and in 1914 went to war as chief of staff of the south-western army group. He planned the successful offensive into Galicia (4–11 September), which resulted in the fall of the great fortress of Przemysl and, but for the subordinate Russian army commanders' besetting fault of wirelessing each other *en clair* (*see* Rennenkampf and Samsonov), would have led to the annihilation of the Austrian field army. In March 1915 he moved to command the north-western army group and in August he succeeded the Grand Duke Nicholas (q.v.) as chief of staff of the army, with command of the European theatre of operations. Distressed by the tsar's interference in strategy, which he believed was helping Russia to lose the war, Alekseev attempted to limit his power by ultimatum but was forestalled and obliged to resign in the autumn of 1916. In March 1917 he helped to engineer Nicholas II's abdication and was reappointed chief of staff but resigned on 21 May in protest at Kerensky's failure to halt the dissolution of the army. He then gravitated towards Kornilov (q.v.) but, after the failure of that general's coup and the success of the Bolshevik revolution, he made his way to the Don, where he began to organize the White Army. Military command of it soon passed, however, to Kornilov, Alekseev retaining responsibility only for political affairs. He died of natural causes before the Civil War had fully broken out.

Alexander, Harold (1st Earl Alexander of Tunis; 1891–1969) British general and Allied commander-in-chief. Alex, as he was known throughout the British (and American) army, was the younger son of one of those Irish Protestant land-owning families (his father was Lord Caledon) which have produced so many of Britain's leading soldiers in the nineteenth and twentieth centuries. But he stands above and apart even among that illustrious band by his apparent possession of every military virtue: total physical and moral courage, athletic prowess, intelligence, charm amounting to real charisma and complete perfection of manners. 'The only man', said Montgomery (q.v.) – who temperamentally abhorred subordination – 'under whom ... any general ... would gladly serve in a subordinate position.'

Commissioned into the Irish Guards from Sandhurst (following Harrow) in 1910, Alexander rose quickly to command the 1st Battalion, and by the end of the war, at the cost of three wounds, had won the DSO, MC and many foreign decorations. Unwilling to surrender the pleasures of fighting, which he intensely enjoyed, he secured an attachment to the British forces in the Baltic and during 1919–20 commanded a militia of German-Latvians which he had raised. His inter-war career was conventional but successful and in 1939 he was commanding the 1st Division of the BEF. Promoted to lieutenant-general and to the command of I Corps after Dunkirk, he had a short spell of command in Burma, at an unhappy moment of the war, and then in 1942 was sent to Egypt as overall commander of British and Allied forces in the Western Desert.

The smoothness of the relationship he established with Montgomery and later with the Americans of the army which landed in North Africa made him the obvious choice for a supreme command, which he assumed (1943) over the British and American armies invading Italy. He retained the Italian command until the end of the war and with it the confidence and devotion of the most disparate of all the Allied armies, containing as it did (besides Britons) Indians, Canadians, Americans, Poles, Italians and Brazilians. After the war Alexander was appointed governor-general of Canada and was immensely successful in the post (1946–52), and then less happily minister of defence (1952–4). In 1962 he published his *Memoirs*, a disappointing book written by another hand. His reputation will rest on his achievements as an inter-Allied military diplomat, as a *beau idéal* to regular officers of his generation and as an Irish Guardsman of legendary courage.

Allen, Ethan (1738–89) American soldier and politician. Remembered as the commander of the 'Green Mountain Boys', a band of irregulars in the American War of Independence, Allen (like his men) found his loyalties torn between an intense local patriotism and a much less clearly defined duty to the new nation. But in May 1775 he and his men disobeyed orders and launched a surprise attack on Fort Ticonderoga, which they managed to capture. Shortly afterwards, his comrades voted him out of office as their commander, and his chapter of woe was completed when he was captured by the British. As the victor of Ticonderoga, he was an object of their horrified curiosity and he was shipped to England as a prisoner. However, he was eventually paroled to New

York City and was able (by devious means) to join Washington at Valley Forge. As much a politician as a soldier, Allen used his position for the benefit of his friends and his home state in quarrels with its neighbours; indeed, he soon became embroiled in a boundary dispute with the state of New Hampshire. His one contribution of any significance to military history was the capture of Fort Ticonderoga, which came at a crucial formative stage of the war when the rebels badly needed a victory.

Allenby, Edmund Henry Hynman (1st Viscount Allenby of Megiddo; 1861–1936) British field-marshal. The son of an East Anglian country gentleman, Allenby was commissioned in 1882 into the 6th Inniskilling Dragoons. In the Boer War he rose to command a cavalry column and in 1909, as major-general, was appointed inspector-general of cavalry. It was from this post that he transferred to lead the hastily formed cavalry division to France in 1914. Allenby's violent verbal outbursts had now become legendary in the army and he was one of its most detested – if grudgingly respected – generals. The conditions of trench warfare gave him little opportunity to show whether this respect was deserved, however, for as Third Army commander, which he became in October 1915, he controlled a front on which no offensive took place until the spring of 1917. The battle of Arras, which he directed, may be thought a success.

Allenby was then transferred to command the British forces in Palestine, which he found in a state of low morale. This, by his noisy visits from unit to unit, he did much to raise and under his command the army won a succession of victories over the Turks, capturing Beersheba and Gaza and, on 9 December 1917, Jerusalem. Lack of men and supplies prevented him launching a final offensive against the Turks until the fol-

lowing September when, in the battle of Megiddo, his forces and those of the sherif of Mecca under Lawrence defeated the remains of the Turkish army and captured Damascus. After the war, Allenby became high commissioner in Egypt and oversaw its translation from protectorate to nominal independence. He died in retirement. His inter-war reputation as an inspired cavalry leader appears, in retrospect, inflated, and he looks increasingly the archetype of the overbearing cavalry general whose unmindfulness of casualties was one of the most unattractive traits of British military leadership in the First World War. It is believed that Allenby was the model for the central character in C.S. Forester's remarkable novel *The General*.

Ali Arslan (1741–1822) Pasha of Jannina; Ottoman despot and soldier. Born in Albania, at Tebelen, of which his family had traditionally held the title of bey, Ali Arslan regained the title, despite a career of brigandage, by his defence of the local Ottoman borders against the Austrians and the Russians. Becoming in time pasha of Tricala, in Thessaly, in 1787 and Jannina (Epirus) in 1788, he soon established his power over the whole of Albania, at the cost of massacring the Suliots, a Christian people who had long resisted Turkish rule. Bonaparte tried unsuccessfully to make him an ally: the British succeeded by ceding him the port of Parga in 1814 and he eventually extended his power to include the whole of Epirus. Eventually judged by the Ottoman government to have become too powerful, he was besieged by a Turkish army in Jannina in 1822 and killed. His nickname Arslan means 'Lion', and he has been called 'The Mohammedan Bonaparte'.

Alva, Fernando Alvarez de Toledo, duque de (1508–83) Spanish soldier. To his many detractors, Alva is the incarnation of the most savage spirit of the

Counter-Reformation, notorious for the excessive repression of the Netherlands (1567–72), and his belief that the only good heretic was a burning one. But these events occurred at the end of a long and successful career and should not cloud an impression of his considerable abilities as a soldier. He entered the Spanish army in 1524, and served with great distinction at the repulse of the French from Fuenterabbia. As scion of one of the leading families in Castile, he was rapidly given more important commands, both in Italy and Germany. In the war of the Schmalkaldic League (1546–7), he dealt the rebellious Protestant faction a resounding defeat at the battle of Mühlberg (1547). He became the leading soldier in the imperial service, with the full trust and confidence of the Emperor Charles V (q.v.). The war with the German Protestants soon produced a renewal of conflict with France in northern Italy, for the French had entered an alliance with Maurice of Saxony. Alva was given the command in Italy. The invading French were defeated at the battle of Marciano (1553), and Alva himself, by now viceroy of Naples for Philip II, who had succeeded his father in 1556, outfought Francis of Guise in the south of Italy and forced him to withdraw. Alva stood very high in Philip's favour, and at court the faction around him stood for a ruthless, military solution to every problem. He was Philip's representative at the peace negotiations which led to the agreement of Cateau-Cambrésis (1559). Alva was now Philip's closest adviser, and although he argued against the tactless decrees which forced the Moriscos of Granada into revolt, once the outbreak had occurred, he insisted on the most draconian solution.

The problem posed by the Netherlands was a different one. It was recognized that the Netherlands were the richest lands of the Spanish crown; nevertheless, it was considered that the revenue they produced was too small. Further, the complicated skein of local privileges and the arrogance of many of the great Flemish nobles were anathema to Philip II. Worse still, the spread of Protestant heresy within the Netherlands was redeemable only in blood. Alva regarded the pretensions of the Flemish with distaste, and argued for repressive measures; and the breakdown of authority within the Netherlands, the destruction of Catholic churches and the hounding of priests and nuns by Protestant mobs gave him his chance. He brought his army of veterans up from Italy (1567): it was, in Philip's phrase, 'a Catholic army', bent on the destruction of heresy. The benign rule of Margaret of Parma as regent ended when she saw the measures which Alva intended to adopt: the field was clear for a sustained attempt to destroy the national spirit of the Netherlands and to extirpate the last traces of Protestantism. He brought to the easy-going Netherlands a harshness they had never seen before. On the day after Margaret of Parma's resignation as regent, the leading Flemish nobles, Egmont and Hoorn, were arrested, to be followed by all the natural leaders of Dutch society – magistrates, merchants, landowners. All their property was confiscated, and Alva's net was widened with information gained under torture. On 4 January 1568 eighty-four of the leading citizens of the Netherlands died on the scaffold of Brussels; they were the first of some 6000. Others, Protestants, were burned alive.

The policy of terror was initially successful: the Dutch were cowed and for a time Alva was able to finance his repression from the confiscations and forced sales, but when he tried to increase his revenues by imposing higher taxes, a movement for passive resistance developed, which made collections of taxes virtually impossible. On land, Alva was able to crush any attempts to oppose him; he and his subordinate commanders (his son Don Fadrique, and Julian Romero) were far abler soldiers than their enemies. At sea, however, he relied of necessity on Admiral Bossu and a combined Flemish–Spanish fleet. The story of the rebirth of Dutch patriotism is told elsewhere (*see* William the Silent), but the reasons for Alva's failure are instructive. Throughout his career he had displayed an absolute certainty in his decisions and policies; this had given him great force as a commander, and was a powerful factor in the morale of his men and subordinates. Passionately convinced of the rightness of his actions and that he acted as a soldier of Christ, he was incapable of seeing the most effective means of dealing with the situation. As a stiff-necked Castilian, he had no patience with Netherlanders and he alienated many of his natural supporters: not until Parma (q.v.) gained the supreme command was a more subtle policy properly instituted. Thus the very qualities which made Alva so good a soldier rendered him useless in a situation, as in the Netherlands, which required tact, diplomacy, warmth of personality, as well as an iron hand.

In November 1573 Philip, who had no patience with failure, recalled Alva, in virtual disgrace. His power at court now vanished, he retired from public life, but in 1580 he was recalled for a task for which he was entirely qualified – the conquest of Portugal, whose throne Philip had claimed. The army crossed the frontier at the end of June 1580; on 25 August Alva won a smashing victory at Alcantara, and by the end of the month Philip was king of Portugal, Alva received no gratitude and died, once more in the shadow of royal oblivion. He was one of the greatest servants of the Spanish state, and, in a century replete with great Spanish soldiers, one of her finest commanders. Only Cordoba (q.v.) and Parma (q.v.) were his superiors. In a sense the 'black legend' is correct, for he regretted none

of his savage actions in the Netherlands, believing them a harsh necessity. But he died a bitter man, for as he said, thinking of his master: 'Kings treat men like oranges. They go for the juice, and once they have sucked them dry, they throw them aside.'

Alvaredo, Pedro de (c. 1485–1541) Spanish conquistador. As one of Cortes's (q.v.) company, Alvaredo took part in the conquest of Mexico for Spain (and private gain). In 1518, commanding one of the ships sent by Juan de Grijalva from Cuba, he explored the coast of Yucatan, and when Cortes moved into Mexico in 1519, the knowledge of the coast and the local tribes which he had thus gained proved of great value. After the entry into Tenochtitlán and the seizure of the Aztec emperor Montezuma, Alvaredo was left in command of the city with a tiny Spanish detachment while Cortes left to fight off a rival Spanish force, led by Narvaez. In his absence, Alvaredo, fearful of the enormous odds against him, took stern action to prevent an uprising; but he only managed to provoke the Aztecs into attacking him. He was saved by the timely return of Cortes, who had defeated Narvaez, and acquired his men as reinforcements. In 1520 they abandoned the city of Tenochtitlán after the bitter fighting caused by Alvaredo, but Cortes returned in the following year, and after a fierce fight and a long siege, the capital was taken. The city was razed, the population massacred, enslaved or dispersed, and a new capital (Mexico City) built beside the old. Alvaredo was the first *alcalde* (mayor) of the new city.

Two years later with an independent force Alvaredo occupied what is now Guatemala, moving forward in 1524 into the territory now occupied by El Salvador. His last conquest of new territory began in 1534, when he led a new expedition into Ecuador but was bought off by a rival; he then set out in search of the fabled Seven Cities of Cibola and the riches they were reputed to contain. But he fell from his horse and died before the search was far advanced. Like many of the conquistadores, Alvaredo had a savage streak, but he also displayed the flexibility and courage which enabled them to overcome amazing odds.

Alvensleben, Gustav von (1803–81) Prussian general, Alvensleben commanded IV Corps in the wars of 1866 and 1870, in the latter playing a prominent part in the battle of Sedan and the investment of Paris.

His brother, **Konstantin von Alvensleben** (1809–82), a veteran of the wars of 1864 and 1866, commanded III Corps in 1870 at Mars-la-Tour and Gravelotte.

Alvinczy, Josef Freiherr von (1735–1810) Austrian field-marshal. Beginning his military career during the Seven Years' War (1756–63), in which he saw service against the French, and later serving against the Turks, Alvinczy came to high command during the wars of the French Revolution. In 1793, with Prince Friedrich of Saxe-Coburg, he fought Dumouriez (q.v.), the victor of Valmy, at Neerwinden and defeated him. Opposed by Napoleon in Italy in 1796, however, he was consistently outmanœuvred and was defeated at the battles of Arcola (15–17 November 1796) and Rivoli (14 January 1797).

Amherst, Jeffrey, 1st Baron (1717–97) British soldier. Most often remembered for his command of the British forces which expelled the French from Canada, Amherst's army career spanned nearly seventy years. He joined the Foot Guards in 1731, and served through the war of the Austrian Succession (1740–8); he served as ADC to Lord Ligonier and, later, to the Duke of Cumberland. In 1757 he was given the expedition sent to capture Louisburg, a command no-

table for the number of bright and aggressive young officers, including Wolfe and Howe (qq.v.); men whom Amherst actively encouraged. He was well regarded by his soldiers, and the successful capture of the fort (July 1758) gave him a resounding reputation at home. He commanded in Canada until the end of the Seven Years' War (1763), latterly as governor. The longest period of his career in a single position was as commander-in-chief of the army from 1772 to 1795. He brought no glory to the office, however, for under his control the army languished and he was finally replaced by the Duke of York. It also belied the intense activity of his early life. Amherst was a passionate advocate of high professional standards among officers, an innovator in light infantry tactics, and a solid, if somewhat pedestrian, campaigner. But he was essentially a man of action, and in the dry world of the administrators, he withered.

Anders, Wladyslaw (1892–1970) Polish general and leader of a Polish army-in-exile. Born near Warsaw, then part of the Russian empire, the son of a land agent, Anders enlisted as a cavalryman in the tsar's army at the outbreak of the First World War and fought against the Germans. But following the Bolshevik revolution he joined up in the Polish Corps, formed earlier by Pilsudski (q.v.) to fight on the side of the Central Powers against Russia, and was soon appointed chief of staff of the Poznán army, whose operations he directed in the Russo-Polish war, 1919–20. Independent Poland became closely allied with France, which had sent a strong team of military advisers to her assistance during 1919–20, and Anders was one of many Polish officers selected subsequently to train in France (he attended the 1922–4 course at the Ecole de Guerre). In 1939 he was engaged against both the German and Russian invaders of his country, was wounded, for the eighth time, taken captive by the Russians and imprisoned in the Lubianka in Moscow.

In 1941, consequent on Hitler's invasion of Russia, the Soviet government agreed to release its Polish prisoners in order to form an anti-Nazi army; Anders was named to command it. With Churchill's support he managed to transport both the soldiers and their families to Persia and there to create the force which was to be known to the Western Allies as the Polish II Corps and which was to win unperishable glory in the campaigns of the Desert and Italy. Its crowning achievement was the capture of Monte Cassino, 17–18 May 1944, after three previous assaults on the fortress by the British and Americans had failed. In the subsequent advance the II Corps cleared much of the Adriatic coast and fought in the battles of the Po valley. At the war's end Anders was acting commander of all Polish forces in the west, which included sizeable air and naval forces which had fought in the Battle of Britain, the Battle of the Atlantic and the Strategic Bombing Campaign against Germany. Few of these exiles chose to return to Communist-governed Poland and Anders became commandant of the organization formed to resettle them in the west. A man of great ability, courage and dignity, he was as widely respected by western leaders as he was honoured by his own compatriots.

Anderson, Richard Heron (1821–79) American (Confederate) general. A South Carolinan, a graduate of West Point and a veteran or the Mexican war, Anderson declared for the Confederacy at the outbreak of the hostilities and served in the Army of Northern Virginia as a brigade and divisional commander during the Peninsula and Gettysburg campaigns. On Longstreet's (q.v.) disablement during the Wilderness campaign of 1864 he succeeded to command of the 1st Corps and saved Spotsylvania from capture by a cleverly planned and executed night march, for which he was promoted lieutenant-general. He took part in the defence of Richmond and Petersburg, 1864–5, commanding the corps which bore his name.

Anson, George, Baron (1697–1762) British sailor and naval reformer. 'The father of the navy', Anson entered the navy in 1712 and was a captain by the amazingly early age of twenty-six. His service at sea in the period of peace which followed the war of the Spanish Succession (1701–14) followed the normal pattern of the service; but in 1740 he began an epic voyage around the world which was to last for four years. He raided the Spanish territories in South America and captured a great treasure galleon, which he sold for £400,000 prize money, his share of this booty making him a rich man. The voyage of his ship the *Centurion* became a legend of the navy. In 1745 he was appointed to the Board of Admiralty, which was to be, with two brief interludes, the scene of his activity for the remainder of his life. In 1747 he commanded a brilliant action off Finisterre, in which six French warships, of a total of nine engaged in the action, were captured.

At the Admiralty, Anson pushed forward at a rush with reforms long overdue. He systematized the organization and construction of ships, classified all the ships in the service into one of six rates, depending on its guns and purpose, a classification which lasted as long as the navy used sailing ships. In 1749 he revised the articles of war so effectively that they remained relatively unchanged until 1865. He introduced the standardized blue and white uniform for officers (1748) and in 1755 created a permanent corps of marines, both to maintain discipline aboard ship and to be used for land actions. Much of the improved performance of the navy in the Seven Years' War (1756–63) and the American War of Independence (1775–83) is directly attributable both to his reforms and to the new spirit which he succeeded in instilling throughout the service. As a naval strategist he anticipated many of the devices used to good effect in the Napoleonic wars: the close blockade of Brest which he instituted in the Seven Years' War was the key to British naval success in the war. On his death, William Pitt summed up his contribution thus: 'To his wisdom, to his experience, and care, the nation owes its success in the . . . war.'

Anthoine, François Paul (1860–1944) French general. Born at Le Mans, educated at Saint-Cyr, and in 1914 a member of the General Staff Committee, Anthoine played an important role as a staff officer in the First World War, on rather the same lines as Weygand and Gamelin (qq.v.). Chief of staff (*major général*) to Castelnau (q.v.) in 1914, and for a time an army commander in his own right during the offensives of 1917 on the Chemin des Dames and in Flanders, his principal wartime role was as chief of staff to Pétain (q.v.), November 1917–July 1918, during the desperate months of the great German offensives.

Apraxin, Fedor Matyeevich, Count (1661–1728) Russian admiral. The virtual creator of the Russian navy, Apraxin owed his position to his close friendship with Peter the Great (q.v.). In 1700 he was appointed governor of the important fort of Azov, at the mouth of the Don on the Black Sea, and with Peter's plans for the creation of a fleet, Azov with its dockyards became of crucial importance. Here Apraxin ordered the construction of a fleet of both river and sea-going vessels, which were an important factor in Russia's later conflict with Turkey (1736–9). In 1707 Apraxin was created admiral of the Baltic fleet, the outcome of Peter's experience in the Dutch and English shipyards. The tsar was determined that Russia should turn her face to the west and that she should acquire a powerful navy to secure her communications to the western states through the Baltic. The survival of his new city of St Petersburg depended on this fleet.

Responsible for the defence of the city when Charles XII turned on Russia in 1708, Apraxin, while the Russians were retreating before the Swedes in central Russia, drove off an invasion force under Lybecker and saved the nascent city. In 1714, after the Swedish war effort had lost much of its energy, the Russian fleet of 30 sailing ships and 180 galleys beat the Swedish fleet at Gangut, off the southern tip of Finland, thus ending Swedish domination of the Baltic. Later in the year Charles XII returned from his long stay in Turkey (where he had fled after defeat in Russia) and Sweden moved to the offensive. But Apraxin continued to expand his dominance at sea, and by 1719 the Russian navy was raiding the Stockholm peninsula, landing troops for attacks on the city itself. Apraxin's conquests in the Baltic were confirmed by the treaty of Nystadt (1721). After Peter's death in 1725 Apraxin's role declined, but the achievement of creating a secure Russian position in the Baltic could not be diminished.

Argyll, Archibald Campbell, Marquis of (1607–61) Scottish soldier. The leader of the Covenanters' armies, the great defender of the Presbyterian church against the English, and the bitter enemy of the Marquis of Montrose, Argyll was the cornerstone of Scotland's opposition to Charles I. During the English Civil War (1642–6) he held Scotland, while Leven (q.v.) with 18,000 infantry and 3000 cavalry, the flower of the Scottish army, entered England in support of

Parliament. Argyll was not a very accomplished soldier and he was beaten by Montrose (q.v.) at Inverlochy (1645) and at Kilsyth in August of the same year. Montrose occupied most of the country, although he had none of the heavy equipment needed to subdue a strongpoint. In September 1645 a Parliamentary army sent north under General David Leslie routed Montrose at Philiphaugh and left Argyll once again in a commanding position.

Despite the Scots alliance with Parliament, Argyll sought to preserve a delicate balance between king and Parliament. The Scots supported the king, upon conditions, in the Second Civil War (1648), but after the defeat at Preston where the Duke of Hamilton was beaten by Cromwell, Argyll repaired the breach with Parliament. After the execution of Charles I in 1649, Argyll negotiated with his son Charles II for Scottish support in his attempt to recover the throne. Agreement was reached, and Argyll went so far as to crown him as Charles II. But this support for Charles did not stop him from hounding Montrose, who had entered Scotland in support of Charles, beating his small force at Carbiesdale (April 1650), and then ensuring that he was executed as a traitor and rebel. Cromwell smashed the Scottish army at Dunbar (September 1650) and at Worcester (September 1651), and Argyll, turning his coat yet again, patched up peace with Parliament.

If Argyll was a poor soldier he was a skilled intriguer. He balanced public advantage with private gain, and the latter often triumphed. But he failed to achieve the great power for Scotland which he sought. The unattractive aspect of his character may be seen in his hatred for Montrose, whom he harried to his death, watching from his house in Edinburgh as he was dragged past on a hurdle to the scaffold. But ironically he met a like end in 1661, when after the Restoration his long career of tergiversation ended on the executioner's block. He died as a staunch and dangerous enemy of the king: but he was never staunch in any cause except his own.

Arnim, Hans Georg von (1581–1641) German mercenary. Born a Brandenburger, von Arnim tried to maintain the interests of the smaller German states in the confused power politics of the Thirty Years' War (1618–48). He served under Gustavus Adolphus (q.v.) in his war with Russia (1613–17), and then, successively, with the Poles against Sweden and under Wallenstein (q.v.). Although a Lutheran, he found no difficulty in serving Catholic masters, but he resigned his imperial commission in 1629 in protest against the Edict of Restitution, which overturned the long-established land settlement concerning former church lands in Protestant states. In 1631 a number of Protestant princes headed by John George of Saxony issued the Leipzig manifesto, which demanded redress of their many grievances (including the edict itself). When this brought no response from the Emperor Ferdinand, they raised an army led by Arnim.

In chaotic circumstances Arnim achieved no dramatic victories, although he did keep his army together. But in 1635 he refused to accept the conclusion of the peace of Prague between the Protestants and the emperor, and continued as an independent mercenary. In 1637 he was taken by the Swedes and was in danger of his life, for they considered him a traitor. Fortunately he managed to escape and rejoined the Saxon army in 1638 as a lieutenant-general: he began at once to prepare a campaign against the Swedes and French, now as much a threat to the independence of the German states as the Habsburgs, but he died before the attack could be mounted. In many respects Arnim was a freebooter, pursuing his own interests, but he did believe in the independence of Germany and fought to achieve it.

Arnold, Benedict (1741–1801) American soldier. Best known for the manner of his leaving American service, as the great turncoat of the American War of Independence, Arnold was a competent soldier. He gained his first military experience in the French and Indian war, and at the outbreak of hostilities with the British was a captain of militia: he attempted to take Fort Ticonderoga, but was forestalled by Ethan Allen (q.v.). He took part in the disastrous invasion of Canada (1775), but despite being wounded continued in the field. He then took a leading part in the campaign which led to Burgoyne's (q.v.) surrender at Saratoga (1777), and was crippled at the second battle of Saratoga (1777). Arnold's besetting sin was a sense of persecution and injustice, and his defection to the British achieved nothing. He died, a bitter man, in London.

Arnold, Henry Harley ('Hap'; 1886–1950) American air force commander. Born at Gladwyne, Pennsylvania, the son of a doctor and the grandson of a nail-maker who had fought at Gettysburg, Arnold was educated at West Point and commissioned in 1907 into the infantry. In 1911, however, he transferred to the air section of the Signal Corps, was taught to fly by Orville Wright and, though missing flying service in the First World War, ended it as assistant chief of the Air Service. In the early postwar years he let his enthusiasm for the ideas of General William Mitchell show too clearly and his career passed into the doldrums for a time, but in 1931 he was appointed commander of the First Wing GHQ Air Force and in 1938, following the death of General Westover in a flying accident, he was promoted to command the Air Corps. In this post Arnold devoted his extra-ordinary energies to increasing the Air Corps' budget, to persuading General Marshall (q.v.) of the Air Corps' vital role and to cultivating the leaders of the American aircraft industry. 'He was a superb fixer and his favourite description of any negotiation was that he was "doing business" with someone.' Among those on whose behalf he did business were the Western Allies, whose cause he championed throughout the period of American non-intervention. As soon as America entered the war, he embarked on a mammoth expansion of his air forces, pressing relentlessly meanwhile for their employment in a major strategic bombing campaign against the heartland of the enemy. It was that strategy which he carried in the US Joint Chiefs of Staff Committee, and which played a major, if endlessly controversial, part in the winning of the Second World War. His most cherished achievement, however, was the grant of separate and equal status to the United States Air Force in 1947, when his personal five-star General of the Army rank, which he had been granted in 1944, was changed to General of the Air Force.

Ashby, Turner (1828–62) American (Confederate) general. A Virginian planter of some wealth and political influence but little formal education. Ashby had formed a volunteer cavalry squadron from among his neighbours at the approach of war, and taken it to Harper's Ferry at the time of John Brown's raid. Appointed colonel of a larger cavalry regiment which his squadron joined in 1861, he served under Stonewall Jackson (q.v.) as his cavalry commander in the Shenandoah Valley campaign, 1862. He was killed in a rearguard action near Harrisburg in June, much missed by his men, to whom he was a hero, by Jackson, to whom he was a brilliant subordinate, and by Virginians, for whom he personified their romantic ideal of the Southern gentleman.

Atahualpa (1502–33) Inca emperor. Atahualpa entered history as he left it, a victim of Pizarro (q.v.). Succeeding to the throne of Peru in 1532 after defeating his brother Huascar in two years of war, he opposed Pizarro, who had 62 cavalry and 102 infantry, with the whole force of the Inca army, but was taken by treachery at Cajamarca and held to ransom. The ransom was paid, but despite the fulfilment of the agreement Atahualpa was put to death. The last independent emperor of the Incas, like the great nations on the east coast of South America he fell victim to the fear which the unfamiliar Spanish cavalry and the fire-power of the infantry inspired in the minds of the otherwise courageous Inca warriors.

Ataturk *see* Kemal Ataturk.

Athlone, Godard van Reede, 1st Earl of (1644–1703) Dutch soldier in the service of William III of England. One of the entourage of able Dutch soldiers who accompanied William of Orange to England in the Glorious Revolution of 1688, Athlone is best known for his success in subduing the Irish and the French expeditionary force after the battle of the Boyne (1690). His first act was to besiege the remaining Jacobite strongholds. He captured the crucial town of Athlone in 1691, and then proceeded to destroy the French-led field army (under the Marquis de Saint-Ruth) and the Irish Earl of Lucan at the battle of Aughrim. He turned the Irish flank and the rebels fled, losing 7000 men to the English army's 700. Lucan fled with the remnants of his army and immured himself in Limerick, the last Jacobite fortress. The fort was a strong one and had already withstood a determined assault in 1690. But Athlone invested the city in force, and in October, after a

lengthy siege, the garrison surrendered; under the terms of the surrender they were allowed to leave freely. After the pacification of Ireland, Athlone returned to the Netherlands to serve in William's later wars with France. He fought at Steenkirk (1692) and at the relief of Namur (1695). At the start of the war of the Spanish Succession (1701–14) he waived his right as the senior Dutch general to supreme command of the Dutch forces in favour of Marlborough, whom he served loyally until his death.

Auchinleck, Sir Claude (1884–1981) British field-marshal. Son of an Ulster Protestant family, like so many other generals of his generation, Auckinleck was commissioned, via Wellington and Sandhurst, into the 62nd Punjabis in 1904. His First World War service, by which he earned the DSO, was spent in Mesopotamia, his inter-war years on the North-West Frontier or on staff duty in India. In 1939 he was a lieutenant-general with an established reputation in the Indian army but none outside it. His arrival in England in 1940 to raise and command the new IV Corps was a surprise to British regular officers, as it was to himself, and it is evidence of his remarkable qualities – including his intellectual ability, for which he had been chosen for the post – that he succeeded in making the very difficult transition from the one army to the other, across the barrier of suspicion which traditionally existed between them.

This achievement, after a short excursion to Norway in 1940 and a return to India as commander-in-chief in 1941, was to pay off fully during his time as commander-in-chief, Middle East, in the Western Desert campaign, June 1941– August 1942. Superintending subordinates of varied character and ability at a difficult time for British armies, he rode out the worst of the Rommel offensives and, in what is now often called the first battle of Alamein, July 1942, halted the German drive on Cairo and stabilized a firm line (from which Montgomery, q.v., would later launch the decisive riposte). Differences with Churchill then led to his removal and he returned to India as commander-in-chief. In 1947 he was to have the unhappy task of presiding over the partition of the Indian army between the new dominions of India and Pakistan, one which he discharged with as much satisfaction to all parties as was possible in the circumstances. The two dominions, in token of their trust in him, accepted his appointment as supreme commander of the two new armies.

Augereau, Pierre François Charles (duc de Castiglione; 1757–1816) Marshal of France (Napoleon's marshals were officially created 'Marshal of the Empire', but all are described in this book as 'Marshal of France'). A Parisian, the son of a domestic servant, Augereau served in the ranks of the French, Prussian and Neapolitan armies, 1774–90, then joined the Paris National Guard and in 1793 was commissioned into the cavalry. He saw some fighting in the Pyrenees the following year and in 1795 joined the Army of Italy, where at Castiglione, 5 August 1796, he first prevented the army of Würmser (q.v.) from taking Bonaparte at a disadvantage, then played a major part in its defeat. When twelve years later Napoleon bestowed a dukedom on him, he was allowed to take Castiglione as his title – an unusual honour, for the emperor disliked reminders of others' contributions to his victories. Under the Empire, he commanded the left wing at Jena, 1806, the 7th Corps in Spain, 1809–10, and the 16th Corps at Leipzig in 1814. He held aloof from Napoleon during the Hundred Days.

Augustus II, Frederick (1670–1733) Elector of Saxony, king of Poland. Although his military reputation was created as king of Poland, Augustus owed his position to his wealth and power as a prince of the Wettin dynasty and as Elector of Saxony. In 1694 he succeeded to the electorate, and in 1696, after enormous efforts, he was elected king of Poland, having adopted the Catholic faith. His prize was a mixed blessing, for Poland was prey to attack from Russia, Sweden and Turkey. With the accession of the sixteen-year-old Charles XII to the Swedish throne, Augustus saw an opportunity to extend his territory: attacking the Swedish possessions on the Baltic, he besieged Riga. But he brought disaster on himself by this opportunism. Charles XII was not the easy victim he had expected. By 1702 he had lost his capital, Warsaw, and at the battle of Kliszow later in the year his field army was shattered. In the spring of 1703 Augustus made great efforts and created a new army: but his forces were shattered yet again by a much more skilful and effective Swedish army at Pultusk.

In the following year Charles replaced Augustus on the Polish throne with Stanislaus Leszczynski, without much difficulty since Augustus was unpopular with his subjects. But Augustus had some success in the civil war which followed, and Charles was forced to turn his attention to Poland once again. In 1705 he trounced Augustus at Punitz and Wszowa, but was unable to follow up his victories since he faced more dangerous enemies elsewhere. At Franstadt (1706), Augustus failed again to defeat a small Swedish army under Rehnskjold. In the autumn of 1706 Charles was able to make a final attempt to settle the Polish question. His armies invaded Saxony, the source of Augustus's troops and his wealth. Leipzig was captured and Augustus quickly sued for terms. At the treaty of Altranstadt he abdicated. But with the collapse of the Swedish hegemony after Poltava, where Charles was decisively defeated by Peter the

Great (q.v.). Augustus was restored to the Polish throne by Russian power. He remained there until his death. He was scarcely an admirable figure, and although known as Augustus the Strong, he had little success in war.

Aumale, Henri Eugene Philippe Louis d'Orléans, duc d' (1822–97) French prince, colonial soldier and administrator. The fourth son of the Duke of Orleans (later Louis-Philippe, King of the French, 1830–48), Aumale was born in Paris, educated at the Collège Henri IV and entered the army at the age of seventeen. His royal birth ensured rapid promotion. But he was also a soldier of real talent and quickly distinguished himself in the Algerian campaign against Abd el-Kader (q.v.). During the period of guerrilla operations which followed Kader's resumption of the war against the French after 1839, he emerged as an outstanding leader and was responsible in May 1843 for the capture of Kader's household. He was appointed governor-general of French North Africa in 1847. After the dethronement of his father at the revolution of 1848, he took refuge in England, but at the fall of the Second Empire (1870) was reappointed to the army as general of division. In that rank he presided over the tribunal which condemned Bazaine (q.v.).

B

Babur (1483–1530) Conqueror of northern India and founder of the Mogul empire. Succeeding his father as ruler of the khanate of Fergana in 1494, Babur tried to carve himself an empire in central Asia, as befitted a descendant of Timur and Genghis Khan. At first successful, he was beaten by the Uzbeks under Shaibani Khan in 1501 and expelled from Fergana. Three years later he settled in Kabul and sought to regain his former possessions. But by 1512 it was clear that he had no hope of establishing himself in central Asia, although he had now built up a considerable following, and he turned his eyes southwards to India and the rich pickings which lay before him.

In 1522 Babur captured Kandahar, and in 1524 invaded Lahore, but was repulsed. In the following year he returned with 10,000 men to face the 30,000 men of the sultan of Delhi, Ibrahim Lodi. Preparing a strong field fortification, Babur repulsed his attackers at the battle of Panipat. He then loosed his own semi-savage Turkic cavalry, and the Delhi army collapsed, leaving Lodi and 15,000 of his men dead on the battlefield. Babur occupied Delhi and established the foundations of the Mogul empire. In 1527 he beat the Rajputs at Khanua, where 20,000 of his men dispersed an enemy force of 100,000 under Rana Sanga. Two years later at Gogra he destroyed an Afghan threat to his new kingdom, his conquests interrupted only by his death. His empire was to be built on by his grandson Akbar (q.v.). An outstanding soldier, Babur displayed great creative and tactical imagination in defeating armies far larger than his own.

Baden-Powell, Robert Stephenson Smyth (1st Baron Baden-Powell of Gilwell; 1857–1941) Hero of Mafeking and founder of the Boy Scout movement. Seventh son of the Savilian Professor of Geometry at Oxford, born in London, educated at Charterhouse, Baden-Powell was excused the Sandhurst course because of his high placing in the competitive examination and gazetted direct to the 13th Hussars, then stationed in India. From the start he showed an aptitude for and joy in military scouting and irregular warfare of which the contemporary empire gave him his fill. He was detached for scouting service in Africa in the Ashanti (1895) and Matabele (1896) campaigns, promoted to command the 5th Dragoon Guards in 1897 and posted to South Africa to raise irregular cavalry at the outbreak of the Boer War. Commanding in Mafeking when it fell under siege, he maintained the defence for 217 days, the relief provoking scenes of public rejoicing at home whose exuberance remains legendary ('Mafeking Night'). He had been promoted major-general during the siege and was later to be appointed inspector-general of the South Africa Constabulary (which he raised), and inspector-general of cavalry. He retired from the army in 1910 as a lieutenant-general to pursue what had become his principal interest, the training of youth for citizenship through his Boy Scout and Girl Guide movements. It is for his promotion of his organization and ideals throughout the world, which loaded him with its decorations, that he is remembered, rather than for his slightly eccentric military career. He died in Africa (Kenya), where he had been happiest.

Badoglio, Pietro (1871–1956) Italian field-marshal and prime minister. A Piedmontese, like so many distinguished Italian soldiers of his generation, Badoglio joined the army of the united Kingdom of Italy as an artillery officer, fought in the disastrous Ethiopian campaign of 1896, then in the more successful Italo–Turkish war in Libya (1911–12). A colonel on Italy's entry into the First World War, he planned and executed the capture of Monte Sabotino, the highly successful prelude to the sixth battle of the Isonzo, August 1916, and was promoted to command II Corps. Later deputy chief of staff, he negotiated the armistice with Austria.

Twice chief of staff after the war, and promoted field-marshal, he was governor of Libya, 1928–33, and then in 1935 given command of the army in the invasion of Ethiopia, of which he subsequently became viceroy. Appointed chief of staff for the third time in 1940, he resigned after the miscarried invasion of Greece in December. A leading plotter of Mussolini's downfall, he signed Italy's unconditional surrender to the Allies in September 1943, and was the first prime minister of post-Fascist Italy.

Bagration, Prince Petr Ivanovitch (1765–1812) Russian general and hero of the Napoleonic wars. A member of a noble Georgian family, born at Kizlyar, north of the Caucasus, Bagration entered the army in 1782 and served first in his home area. A participant in the Polish campaign of 1794, following the Third Partition, his abilities were recognized by Suvorov (q.v.), who took him to fight in the Italian and Swiss campaigns of 1799. There he won recognition for his capture of Brescia. In the campaigns

of 1805–7 against Napoleon he gained further distinction on a number of occasions, covering Kutuzov's retreat after Hollabrunn and conducting other tenacious rearguard actions after Eylau and Austerlitz. His personal courage at the battle of Friedland has become legendary. In 1808 he led a force in a daring march across the ice of the Gulf of Bothnia to capture the Aaland Islands and in 1809 he was on campaign against the Turks in Bulgaria. His apotheosis came at Borodino whither, following his defeat at Mogilev in July 1812, he had brought his Second Army of the West and where he was given the left wing. Wounded in the thick of the fighting on 7 September, he died of a general infection at Simy on 24 September. Nicholas I erected a monument to his memory on the battlefield.

Balck, Hermann (1893–1950) German general. Born at Danzig. Balck was commissioned in 1914 into the 10th (Hanoverian) *Jäger* (which Guderian, q.v., had shortly before also joined). Distinguished for his bravery as a junior officer in the First World War, he was not to attract widespread public attention until the Second World War when, in May 1940, he had the good luck to be commanding the infantry regiment (*Schutzenregiment* I) in 1st Panzer Division, the spearhead formation of Guderian's Panzer Corps in its drive to the Meuse at Sedan. The opposite bank of the section of the river assigned to Balck was heavily defended but, taking advantage of an air attack, he got his infantry across in rubber boats without serious loss and established the bridgehead from which the German armour was to break out and win the Battle of France.

Promoted to command a division in Russia, Balck displayed during the defensive stages of the campaign a remarkable tactical flair in the handling of large formations and in fifteen months was promoted from major-general to full general. Appointed to command Army Group G in the west in September 1944, he unjustly incurred Hitler's displeasure for his conduct of the defence of Lorraine against Patton (q.v.) and was demoted to the command of an army (*Armeegruppe Balck*) in Hungary, where he finished the war. 'If Manstein was Germany's greatest strategist during World War II ... Balck has strong claims to be regarded as our finest field commander. He had a superb grasp of tactics and great qualities of leadership' (General von Mellenthin).

Banks, Nathaniel Prentiss (1816–94) American (Union) general. Like Breckinridge (q.v.), a politician rather than a soldier but without even his amateur military experience. Banks's standing in Congress none the less won him command of a corps by early 1862. Unfortunately his opponent was Stonewall Jackson (q.v.) who, though marginally defeated by him at Kernstown, completely outmanœuvred him in the subsequent course of the Shenandoah Valley campaign. In 1863 he took a command in the west and succeeded in defeating a small Confederate force in the Red River campaign. Its continuation the following year, though interesting for some remarkable feats of engineering by his subordinate, Colonel Joseph Bailey, was ultimately unsuccessful in its aim of carrying the Union presence into Texas and foundered in recriminations between the leaders.

Baraguay d'Hilliers, Achille (comte; 1795–1878) Marshal of France. Son of one of Napoleon's generals, Baraguay d'Hilliers commanded the military contingent in the Anglo-French expedition to Bomarsund in the Baltic in 1854 (*see* Admiral Napier) and won a victory over the Austrians at Melegnano in 1859.

Baratieri, Oreste (1841–1901) Italian general. One of the Thousand of Garibaldi (q.v.), Baratieri later became a regular officer of the army of united Italy and, as governor of the colony of Eritrea, a protagonist of the conquest of neighbouring Abyssinia. Largely on his own initiative, he invaded the ancient empire in 1894 and annexed some territory. But at Adowa on 1 March 1896, a day he had wrongly calculated would find the army of the Emperor Menelik II dispersed to celebrate the feast of Our Lady, he suffered a catastrophic defeat. Most of his soldiers were killed and Italy was deterred from attempts on Abyssinia for another forty years. Adowa and Isandhlwana (*see* Chelmsford) remain the most complete débâcles suffered by European armies at the hands of Africans.

Barbarossa (Khair-ed-Din; 1483–1546) Turkish admiral, pirate and Dey of Algiers. One of the great Mediterranean sailors of the sixteenth century. Barbarossa's career began as a Barbary pirate, a calling he followed with considerable success. His nickname, Barbarossa, from his red hair and his fearsome reputation, soon spread along the Christian coasts. Elected Dey of Algiers, he enlisted the support of the Turkish sultan Selim I (q.v.). in return for a declaration of loyalty to the Ottoman empire. It was a good bargain. Barbarossa spent twelve years in extending his control of territory around the city of Algiers, spreading both inland and along the coast. He fought the Spaniards, local chieftains and a rebellious population within Algiers itself, paying the considerable expenses of these internal wars with the continuing profits of piracy. He constructed a new harbour at Algiers, and systematized and controlled the Barbary pirates, uniting them under his leadership. In these early years Barbarossa achieved two great successes: first, the creation of a battle fleet, living off piracy but capable of concerted naval action. Second, he guaranteed the economic security of Algiers by establishing the city as the main port for pirated goods, slaves and ships. For his own protection he created a bodyguard of renegade Europeans which formed the nucleus of a professional army, owing its loyalty and support to him alone. With this new army he conquered the neighbouring kingdom of Tunis (1534), Algiers' greatest competitor: but the city was lost in the following year to the Emperor Charles V, who sent a large fleet to capture it.

With Algiers now securely established as the pirate capital of the Mediterranean, Barbarossa felt secure enough to obey a call to Constantinople from Suleiman I (q.v.) to take up the post of admiral of the Turkish fleet. He made substantial changes, improving discipline and seamanship, building more ships with more powerful armament. He created an efficient and flexible instrument of war, with subordinate officers of good quality under his command. From 1537 the Turkish fleet roamed the Mediterranean, raiding coastlines and terrorizing Christian shipping: it was his old technique of piracy, but on a grand scale. Most of the Venetian islands in the Aegean were captured, and in 1538 he beat the Venetian fleet under Andrea Doria (q.v.) at Preveza and St Maura. So successful was this naval campaign and the accompanying land campaign that Venice sued for peace. In 1541 Algiers itself was threatened by a large fleet and army under Charles V, but a storm destroyed much of the imperial fleet, and the staunch defence of the city meant that the imperial forces had to retreat with heavy losses.

After this débâcle Barbarossa extended his campaign into the western Mediterranean. In alliance with the French, he ravaged the coasts of Italy and Spain, as well as besieging and sacking Nice. He passed the winter in the sanctuary of a French port, then continued his conquests, taking Reggio and

Calabria in Italy, Palamos and Rosas on the coast of Catalonia. In 1544 the treaty of Crépy concluded the war, and it was to prove Barbarossa's last campaign, for he died two years after his triumphant return to Constantinople. Barbarossa was a brilliant naval tactician, extending the skills of piracy into the management of a larger fleet. His administrative talents were considerable, both in the creation of his Algerian kingdom and its army, and in his development of the Ottoman fleet. Despite the seemingly effortless success of his campaigns, it was built on hard-won discipline and the professional skills of seamanship.

Barclay de Tolly, (Prince) Mikhail Bogdanovich (1761–1818) Russian field-marshal. The son of a Scottish émigré family (Barclay of Towie), which had settled in Livonia in the seventeenth century and inter-married with its Baltic German neighbours, Barclay de Tolly, unlike so many émigrés, belonged not to the officer class but had originally enlisted (1776) in the ranks. After fourteen years' service he was still an NCO in a dragoon regiment when, during the Serbian campaign against Turkey, Prince Repuin noticed his military talents and made him his adjutant. As an officer, he fought against the Swedes (1790) and the Poles (1792–4), but really distinguished himself for the first time in Russia's 1806–7 campaign against Napoleon. His conduct in the battles of Pultusk (26 December 1806) and Eylau, where he was wounded, won him promotion to lieutenant-general: in 1808 he, with Bagration (q.v.), made the daring march across the frozen Gulf of Bothnia to capture Sweden's Aaland Islands.

When Napoleon invaded Russia in 1812, Barclay de Tolly had to combine the posts of minister of war, which he had held since 1810, and commander-in-chief of the Armies of the West (without the title as such), and the resulting division of his energies made his grasp of events less sure than it might have been. But his reputation suffered, too, from the criticism of unco-operative subordinates who represented his strategy of evasion and retreat before Napoleon's advance as cowardice. After the defeat of Smolensk (16–17 August 1812), he surrendered command to Kutuzov and at Borodino commanded only his own First West Army, but with such courage and judgement that his actions were chiefly responsible for the victory. He felt compelled to resign after the battle, since he was still calumnied, but returned to the field for the 1813 campaign, was made commander-in-chief and fought at Dresden, Kulm and Leipzig. He was in both invasions of France, 1814 and 1815, and by then a field-marshal and prince. He died at Insterburg on 26 May 1818. Though posterity denied him the heroic status accorded Kutuzov or Suvorov (q.v.), he deserved well of his country for his work as minister and his rescue the Russian army from decay and inanition.

Bart, Jean (1650–1702) French privateer and commerce raider. Born into a dynasty of Dunkirk pirates, and with an unsurpassed knowledge of the northern coast of France and the approaches through the Channel, in time of war Bart became a privateer sailing against the enemies of France. He had learned naval tactics serving under the great Dutch admiral de Ruyter (q.v.), but in Louis XIV's first war with Holland (1672–8) he turned on his former mentors and fought six actions, taking eighty-one prizes. At the outset of the war of the Grand Alliance (1688–97), he was taken in an action with the British; but he escaped, and with Claude de Forbin rowed for fifty-two hours to the safety of France. For this exploit Louis XIV appointed him a captain in the navy. He fought at the battle of Beachy Head (1690) under de Tourville (q.v.);

his *métier*, however, was not for the fleet action, but for the cut and thrust of commerce raiding.

Disliked and despised at the French court, Bart was admired by Vauban (q.v.), who consulted him when constructing the fortifications of Dunkirk, which Bart defended against the English in 1694 and 1696. His greatest exploit was against a Dutch flotilla guarding a grain fleet; smashing through the defence Bart carried eighty-one ships laden with grain into French ports, at a time when many areas of France were starving. Louis XIV raised him to the nobility for his services. By the end of the war he had destroyed 30 warships and taken 211 prizes. One of the greatest Channel seamen of all time, he was an outstanding success as a privateer, pioneering techniques of commerce raiding.

Bayazid II (1481–1512) Turkish sultan. The son of Mehmed the Conqueror, who had captured Constantinople, Bayazid was an essentially peaceful man, not concerning himself with great wars of conquest. But under him the frontiers of Islam were pushed forward in the west, though he failed to control Egypt and Asia Minor. Providing order in what had hitherto been a random pattern of border raiding along the northern frontiers, he expanded the artillery and infantry fire-power, the naval forces, and revised the training of the Janissaries, the most highly trained Ottoman infantry. These efforts produced some successes, notably the first naval battle at Lepanto (1499) against the Venetians. Against the Austrians he had less success, but his cavalry raided into northern Italy; and throughout Hungary, Bosnia and Serbia incessant border raiding brought normal commercial and peasant life to a standstill. The real threat, however, came from a renascent Persia, and although Persian expansion was contained, the problem was not resolved.

In the last years of Bayazid's reign any scheme of resolute action was vitiated by the bitter civil war between his sons, in which Selim (q.v.) finally triumphed. The old sultan retired to Demotika, the town of his birth, and was soon dead. Despite the fact that he had no list of brilliant conquests to his credit, Bayazid, by stabilizing the Ottoman state and reducing, in some measure, the capacity of the Janissaries to dominate the state, created a firm base on which the great wars of conquest undertaken by his son and grandson were built.

Bazaine, Achille (1811–88) Marshal of France. He was a self-made general. His father, chief engineer of the Seine-et-Oise, emigrated to Russia shortly after Achille's birth at Versailles, abandoning his family without financial support. Money was found for the boy's education (Bourbaki, q.v., was a classmate), but when he failed to follow his elder brother through the entrance examination to the Ecole Polytechnique none was available to establish him in a suitable career. He enlisted therefore in 1831 as a private in the 37th Infantry. His promotion was rapid. A corporal within three months, a sergeant within twelve, he was commissioned *sous-lieutenant*, having transferred to the newly raised Foreign Legion, in 1833. '*Son coup d'œil, son sangfroid et sa bravoure entraînante*', qualities which would distinguish him throughout all but the last months of his military career, accelerated his rise during the conquest of Algeria and the intervention in Spain. A captain at twenty-eight, he was on Napoleon III's accession a colonel and one of the most experienced and celebrated of French colonial campaigners. Napoleon III's little wars brought him further promotion, to the rank of general of brigade and then of division in the Crimea, where he took part in the final assault on Sebastopol, and then, after a classic display of leadership at Solferino in the 1859 campaign, supreme command of the army in Mexico. His task was to make the country safe for Maximilian to ascend its throne, which he temporarily achieved, being commended in 1864 for such victories as Puebla with the baton of marshal.

Nominated to command the Imperial Guard on the eve of the Franco-Prussian war, Bazaine was made commander of the Army of Lorraine after the early defeats of August 1870, and on 12 August commander-in-chief. He was to prove wholly deficient in the reserve and judgement necessary to the situation in which the Second Empire now found itself. Instead of maintaining his forces in contact with the main base at Châlons, as had been ordered, he clung to the forward pivot of Metz, fighting there three battles, Borny, 14 August, Vionville-Mars-la-Tour, 16 August, and Gravelotte–Saint-Privat, 18 August, which, though by no means defeats, he accepted as such, retiring accordingly inside the fortress. After a three-month siege, during which he failed to negotiate an imperial restoration, he surrendered it to the Germans. Returning to a republican France after the war, he was court-martialled for treasonable capitulation (though his excursion into anti-republican intrigue was an unwritten charge) and condemned to death in 1873. The sentence was commuted and he escaped in 1874 from the Ile Ste Marguerite to Spain, where he died. Bazaine is a classic example of the overpromoted man of action buckling under the strain of responsibilities his character and intelligence should not have been asked to bear. His name is nevertheless remembered in the Foreign Legion, which with typical perversity cherishes him as one of its heroes, and less affectionately in the French army, where the mess-sergeant (*gérant du mess*) is known still as 'Le Bazaine' ('*J'ai rendu Metz*').

Beatty, David (1st Earl Beatty; 1871–1936) British admiral. Anglo-Irish by ancestry and the son of a cavalry officer, Beatty was firm in his choice of the navy as a career from an early age. At thirteen he entered the training ship *Britannia* (forerunner of the Royal Naval College, Dartmouth) and at fifteen was at sea as a midshipman. The first ten years of his naval life were uneventful and increasingly frustrating to his impatient temperament. But at the end of the century he had the good fortune, which came rarely to seamen of the period, to be involved in a sustained bout of combat. In 1896 he was given command of a small fleet of gunboats, which was to accompany Kitchener's (q.v.) army along the Nile in its advance to recapture the Sudan. For his daring handling of his boats – at one stage he beat the army in the race to capture the important town of Dongola – he was awarded the DSO and in the following year, recalled to Egypt at Kitchener's request, he again so distinguished himself that he was promoted at the age of twenty-seven to the rank of commander, an occurrence which, in an institution given almost to worship of the principle of seniority, aroused incensed comment. Worse was to come for the naval mastodons: for his leadership of naval landing-parties in north China during the Boxer rebellion (1900) he was promoted captain – at twenty-nine, when the average age was forty-three – and in 1910, despite insufficiency of time at sea, rear-admiral, thus becoming the youngest officer of flag rank for a hundred years. By now he had two extra advantages to add to his formidable ability and thrustfulness: a very rich wife and the patronage of Winston Churchill, soon to be First Lord of the Admiralty. Churchill made him his naval secretary in 1911 and then in 1913 flag officer of the Battlecruiser Squadron of the Grand Fleet.

The squadron was the brainchild and darling of Fisher (q.v.) who had conceived the battlecruiser as the answer to a need for a ship fast enough to find the enemy's main fleet and strong enough to hold it in play while the Grand Fleet of slower battleships came up. Beatty, *prima facie*, was its natural commander and in the two minor naval engagements of the first years of the Great War, Heligoland Bight, 28 August 1914, and the Dogger Bank, 24 January 1915, his handling of it, despite an unfortunate signalling mishap during the latter, justified the belief widely held in his genius. His conduct of battlecruiser operations during the opening phase of the great battle of Jutland, 31 May 1916, however, was ever after to cast doubt on his real soundness of judgement. Beatty's instincts, as he frankly confessed, were essentially those of a *sabreur* and, carried away by the elation of being the first commander of major units to find and close with the High Seas Fleet, he concentrated on fighting it – to the exclusion of keeping his superior Jellicoe (q.v.) properly informed of his and its whereabouts and at the cost of the loss of three of his ships. The consequence was that the battleships came too late into contact with the Germans and, partly as a result, failed to win a conclusive victory. Beatty was nevertheless acclaimed at the time the hero of Jutland and at the end of 1916 succeeded to the command of the Grand Fleet. The course of the naval war gave him no further chance to prove his talents. He made, however, an enlightened postwar First Sea Lord. Nevertheless, he was a man born after his time, in spirit a Nelsonian, with much of that admiral's charm (but an arrogance he did not possess) and some of his ability, condemned to play the role of frigate captain in a technically more exigent age.

Beaulieu, Jean Pierre de (1725–1819) Austrian general. A native of the Austrian Netherlands, born at Lathuy, Brabant, Beaulieu distinguished himself as a junior officer in the Seven Years' War (1756–63) and, as a general during the wars of the French Revolution, defeated Biron (q.v.) at Valenciennes, and Jourdan (q.v.) at Arlon in 1794. He was defeated by Napoleon in Italy in 1796, when commander-in-chief of the Austrian armies there.

Beauregard, Pierre Gustave Toutant (1818–93) American (Confederate) general. Superintendent of West Point, of which he was a graduate, his undisguisably Southern sympathies led in the months before the outbreak of the Civil War to his removal and he went south (he was, as his name reveals, a 'Cajun' of Louisiana). He first directed operations which led to the fall of Fort Sumter and was then given command of the forces which fought at Manassas (First Bull Run) on 1 June 1861. Second in command to A.S. Johnston (q.v.) at Shiloh, he fell sick and into disfavour and did not meet Union force again until 1864, when he won the battle of Drewry's Bluff and took a successful part in the defence of Petersburg. Military in appearance rather than talent, he was, like so many of the generals of both armies of the Civil War, overpromoted.

Bellegarde, Henri, comte de (1756–1845) Austrian general. Originally in the service of Saxony. Bellegarde later joined the Austrians and commanded armies in all their campaigns from 1792 to 1814.

Belle Isle, Charles Louis Fouquet, duc de (1684–1761) French soldier. The son of Nicholas Fouquet, Louis XIV's first finance minister, who was imprisoned for corruption on a monumental scale. Belle Isle was none the less shown considerable royal favour. His first taste of active service was under Berwick (q.v.) in the brief Spanish campaign of 1719–20. In the war of the Polish Succession (1733–8) he served again with Berwick,

but was soon given an independent command, capturing Trier and Traerbach with his corps. After the war his activity became as much diplomatic as military, for Cardinal Fleury, the French prime minister, used him in a variety of missions, during which he constructed the series of alliances against Austria, prior to the death of the Emperor Charles VI. During the war of the Austrian Succession (1740–8), Belle Isle had little success on the battlefield (unlike his younger brother Louis-Charles I): he made some bold strategic moves, but won no victories and his reputation slumped. Late in the war, however, he was sent with an army to the relief of Genoa, under siege by an Austrian army. He quickly relieved the city and forced the Austrians back into Lombardy. This competent campaign did much to restore his stock at court.

As a battlefield commander Belle Isle was of small consequence, but his real legacy to the French army was organizational. For three years, 1757–60, he was minister of war, and set in train a series of reforms. He tackled some of the root causes of France's relatively poor performance in the recent wars. Aiming to make the army more professional, he established that all officers had to serve at least two years before promotion to captain, and at least five years as captain before promotion to colonel, an attempt to end the scandal of totally unqualified officers. Attacks were made on corruption and the excessive luxury of life in officers' quarters. He founded a military academy at Metz, and made efforts to improve the production of artillery and muskets. But many of his reforms were never implemented, as he retired prematurely through ill-health.

Benedek, Ludwig August Ritter von (1804–81) Austrian field-marshal. The son of a Protestant doctor of Ödenburg (Sopron), Hungary, Benedek entered the Wiener Neustadt academy in 1824 and in 1828 joined the 27th Regiment at Capua in Italy (where he was to spend most of his service). Appointed to the staff in 1833, he showed his promise in the suppression of the Galician insurrection of 1846 and during the Italian campaign of 1848–9. Radetzky (q.v.) made him his chief of staff (1850–7) and at Solferino (1859) in the war with France it was his generalship which allowed his chief to withdraw his army to the Mincio and won him the adulation of the empire. Promoted quarter-master-general of the army (1860) and commander-in-chief in Venetia (1861), he was extremely reluctant (*see* Albrecht) to take the supreme command when war threatened in 1866, complaining publicly that he felt ill at ease outside Italy and privately that he had little confidence in the army. His fears were justified for at Sadowa (Königgrätz) Prussia's riflemen decisively defeated his muzzle-loading battalions. He nevertheless rescued them from total destruction by his brilliant conduct of the retreat and, though subsequently court-martialled, was spared disgrace by the emperor's personal intervention. In turn a national hero and national scapegoat, for his generalship respectively at the battles of Solferino and Sadowa, his real crime was to have been an eighteenth-century general in a nineteenth-century war.

Bennigsen, Count Levin August (Leonti Leontievitch; 1745–1826) Russian general. One of the tsar's many émigré officers, Bennigsen entered Russian service in 1764 from the Hanoverian army, took part in the Turkish, Polish and Persian campaigns of the 1770s and 1790s, and was apparently implicated in the assassination of Paul I. Alexander I promoted him general and he successfully commanded at the battles of Pultusk (26 December 1806) and at Eylau, a genuine reverse for Napoleon, but was defeated at Friedland, 14 June 1807. Recalled to service in 1812, he commanded the

centre at Borodino but, having quarrelled both with Barclay and Kutuzov (q.v.), was again retired. On Kutuzov's death he was reappointed to an army and led the decisive attack at Leipzig, 19 October 1813, for which he was created count. An able but opinionated and insubordinate officer, he left Russia to spend his last years in his native Hanover.

Beresford, Charles William de la Poer (1st Baron Beresford; 1846–1919) British admiral. 'Charlie B', as he was known to the navy, was one of the most flamboyant sailors of the Victorian age. A son of the Marquess of Waterford (he was Lord Charles Beresford for most of his career), he captured the popular imagination by his handling of the gunboat *Condor* at the bombardment of Alexandria, 1882, when he laid it alongside Fort Marabout, silenced its guns, then landed a shore-party to restore order in the town. In 1884 Wolseley (q.v.) chose him to command the naval half of the expedition to relieve Gordon (q.v.) at Khartoum. He retired in 1909 as a full admiral, having held every naval command of importance. Beresford pursued a parallel political career, sitting as a Conservative MP almost continuously from 1874 to 1916 (when he entered the Lords), and whenever on half-pay used his voice in the Commons to oppose naval policies which he disfavoured – principally those of Admiral Fisher (q.v.).

Bernadotte, Jean Baptiste Jules (prince de Pontecorvo; 1763–1844) Marshal of France and later king of Sweden. Bernadotte belongs to that large group of Frenchmen whose careers were made by the Revolution, and to that smaller sub-group who founded dynasties upon their success. Born into the minor bourgeoisie of Pau, he was intended for the law but his father's early death left the family without resources and he was driven into the army – before 1791 'a career without future for those not "born"' – joining the *Régiment Royale-Marine* as a private in 1780. During the first popular outbreaks in Marseilles in 1789 he saved his colonel from a mob and was promoted lieutenant into the 36th Regiment. Swiftly advanced thereafter, for he was a genuine protagonist of the Revolution, he served at the battle of Fleurus (26 June 1794) as a battalion commander and then with the Armies of the North and of the Sambre-et-Meuse as a general. In 1796 he was posted to Bonaparte's Army of Italy, attracted his attention and married in 1798 Joseph Bonaparte's sister-in-law, Desirée Clary. In 1804 he was among the eighteen soldiers whom the emperor created marshals of the Empire, and was subsequently entrusted with important commands, that of the central reserve at Austerlitz (he was rewarded with the principality of Pontecorvo in June 1806) and of the 1st Corps in the Prussian campaign of 1806. This he handled so badly on the day of Jena that Napoleon considered having him court-martialled, but he made partial amends by his vigorous pursuit of the Prussians to the Baltic, where he took Blücher (q.v.) prisoner at Schwartau.

It was during the Baltic episode that Bernadotte unknowingly prepared the ground for his future kingship. Adept in his relations with foreigners, he treated with great courtesy a division of Swedish troops whom their government had sent to the Prussians' aid and allowed them to return home. He was shortly to be repaid. A repetition of poor generalship on the field of Wagram (5–6 July 1809) drove Napoleon to relieve him of command and in August 1810, on the Swedes electing him crown prince, to allow him to leave his service altogether. It was a curious decision on both sides, prompted in the Swedes by the belief that it would persuade France to exempt their country from the Continental De-

crees, in Napoleon that he was releasing a loyal servant to create a satrapy. Neither belief was vindicated. In 1812 Napoleon seized Swedish Pomerania and in 1813 Bernadotte (now Prince Carl Johan) brought Sweden into the Sixth Coalition against Napoleon. He fought Oudinot (q.v.) at Grossbeeren on 23 August and Ney (q.v.) at Dennewitz on 6 September, beating them both, and finally took part in the battle of Leipzig (16–19 October 1813). He apparently had hopes of succeeding Napoleon when he abdicated, but his fellow marshals not unnaturally regarded him as a traitor. He had to be content with the crown of Sweden (and of Norway, which he had annexed to Sweden in 1814), to which he succeeded on 5 February 1818. He died in Stockholm on 8 March 1844. In some ways the most interesting of the marshals, militarily he was among the less talented, his gifts being those of charm and of the narrow calculation of self-interest.

Bernhard, Duke of Saxe-Weimar (1604–39)   German general. A celebrated Protestant general of the Thirty Years' War (1618–48), he, like many of his contemporaries, reached his maturity as commander at an early age. His career began inauspiciously, for he was on the losing side at Wiesloch and Wimpfen (1622) and Stadtlohn (1623). Until the advent of the Swedes under Gustavus Adolphus (q.v.) in 1630, both superior generalship and better troops were to be found on the Catholic and imperial side. In his early battles Bernhard showed great capacity for independent command, with an ability to keep his forces together even if the Protestant army as a whole failed. As in the case of many soldiers of the Thirty Years' War, it is sometimes hard to distinguish when Bernhard was operating on his own account and when on behalf of his current paymaster. With the advent of the Swedes his career took a great step forward. Liked and trusted by Gustavus, he distinguished himself by his courage at Breitenfeld (1631), where he commanded the left wing of the army facing Wallenstein (q.v.). At Lützen, in November 1632, he took a major role in the battle. When, at the height of the fight, Gustavus was killed in a mêlée. Bernhard rallied the Protestants, and, fighting with great ferocity, drove back Wallenstein and captured the imperial artillery train. Pappenheim (q.v.), the leader of the imperial cavalry, was killed and the initiative remained with the Protestants.

After the death of Gustavus, however, the strong central direction of the Protestant cause began to slacken; despite the efforts of Axel Oxenstierna, who created the League of Heilbronn to unite Protestant resistance, the initiative began to slip back to the imperial forces. Bernhard, appointed commander of the army of the league, pursued an independent course, ravaging southern Germany. It was not until mid-1634 that the Protestant forces began to move forward in unison, but at Nordlingen in September their cause suffered a shattering defeat. Co-ordination between Bernhard and the Swedish general Horn broke down and the imperial army, led by the two young Habsburgs, Ferdinand of Hungary and his cousin Ferdinand of Spain, smashed the two halves of the Protestant army: 21,000 of a Protestant army of 25,000 were killed or captured, Horn was killed, and Bernhard with a tiny remnant of his army quit the battlefield. But he managed to reconstruct his army, and the league allied with the French who now entered the war.

Bernhard was first given command of the combined armies, but by the end of 1635 the armies of the league had been incorporated, for practical purposes, in the army of France. In 1636 his army blocked the imperial army of Gallas in their thrust into France from the east, and the following year drove back Charles IV of Lorraine from the river

Saône. Bernhard now drove forward into Alsace, and for the first time in three years his army crossed the Rhine into Germany. He consolidated his gains by victories at Rheinfelden, Breisach and Freiburg, which gave possession of three strategic towns dominating the lower Rhineland. These successes gave Bernhard and his 'Weimar army', as it was known, a virtually independent position, and he tried to create a new domain for himself, centred on Breisach (which capitulated in December 1638). But Richelieu refused to recognize a powerful independent force, even though an ally, as Duke of Alsace; Bernhard's plans were frustrated, and he turned again to the Swedes, in the vain hope of constructing a new third force in Germany. He died before he could accomplish this new goal. As a military commander he was not of the first rank, but he was one of the few soldiers of solid competence which the Protestant cause possessed from within Germany itself. In his campaign of 1637–9 he showed his skill in the normal war of siegecraft and a war of manœuvre, but the high point of his career was Lützen, where his quick thinking saved the day.

Berthelot, Henri Mathias (1861–1931) French staff officer. *Aide-majorgénéral* (assistant chief of staff) to Joffre (q.v.) in 1914, Berthelot had been closely involved in the conception and implementation of the French scheme to deal with an outbreak of war with Germany by an immediate offensive (Plan XVII). As Joffre's principal assistant he had also to make the plan work in the teeth of German resistance. He failed, but his cool and cheerful conduct of staff work at GHQ (*grand quartier général*) contributed much to the French army's survival of defeat in the battle of the Frontiers and in the Great Retreat, August–September 1914. On Joffre's removal from office in 1916, Berthelot was removed also, going to Romania as head of the military mission. He was recalled to command the Fifth Army in the Allied counter-offensive of 1918. Berthelot weighed 17 stones and, at work in his office, in his blouse and carpet slippers, made a memorably – but misleadingly – unmilitary impression.

Berthier, Louis Alexandre (prince de Neuchâtel et Valangin, prince de Wagram; 1753–1815) Marshal of France and chief of staff to Napoleon. Berthier's great reputation rests on the punctiliousness of his staff work. He was in many respects the first professional staff officer, and the smooth transition of Napoleon's plans into executive orders was his doing throughout the eighteen years they worked together. He had learnt the rudiments of his craft in the royal army, which he had entered in 1766 as an *ingénieur-géographe*, as had his father, who rose to be director of military survey and, through his work on the royal hunting maps, an intimate of Louis XVI. Patronage may, therefore, have played some part in Berthier's advancement to lieutenant-colonel at the age of thirty-six, but he had also worked hard for his promotion, serving in the Flanders Legion, the Lorraine Dragoons and on Rochambeau's (q.v.) staff in America during the War of Independence.

The coming of the Revolution, which Berthier chose to follow, did not at first interrupt his career, but in September 1792 he was suspended and not re-employed until March 1795, when he was posted as chief of staff, with the rank of *général de brigade*, to the Army of Italy. He thus automatically became the subordinate of Bonaparte on the latter's arrival as commander, and until 1814 they were separated only twice thereafter, once for a few days during the 1809 campaign and then at the end of the retreat from Moscow. In 1809 it was unfortunately Berthier, not Napoleon, who was left with the Grand Army and his mishandling of it demonstrated how

completely interpretative rather than creative were his military talents. Nevertheless these talents were almost indispensable to Napoleon (who also used him as minister of war, 1799–1807) and he took Berthier's defection to Louis XVII in 1814 badly. Berthier took his separation from Napoleon during the Hundred Days worse, his fatal fall from a window of his lodgings in Bamberg, whither he had withdrawn, apparently being a suicide (though the suspicion of assassination remains). He died one of the most decorated of the emperor's entourage: a marshal of the 1804 creation, he was also made hereditary prince of Neuchâtel. After his death the toy army he had raised for his realm was transferred to Prussian service, surviving until 1918 as the famous *Garde-Schutzen-Bataillon ('die Neuchateller')*.

Berwick, James, Duke of (1670–1734) French soldier. The illegitimate son of James II and Arabella Churchill, and thus nephew of the Duke of Marlborough, Berwick became one of the most successful French commanders in the war of the Spanish Succession (1701–14). At the age of fifteen he was apprenticed to Charles IV of Lorraine to assimilate the art of war at first hand: war against the Turk still had a romantic attraction. He served with Charles in his Hungarian campaign, distinguishing himself in the hard-fought siege of Buda and the second battle of Mohács (1688). After the Glorious Revolution of 1688, which replaced James II with William of Orange, he was summoned home and took an active part in his father's attempts to recover the throne. He was present at the battle of the Boyne (1690) but after the Irish campaign failed he took service in the French army, in common with many Irish and Scottish Catholics. He fought under Marshal Luxembourg (q.v.) at Steenkirk (1692) and Neerwinden in the following year, where he was taken prisoner by his uncle

(Marlborough), but was quickly exchanged. His success in these campaigns resulted in his promotion to lieutenant-general.

In the first stage of the war of the Spanish Succession (1701–14) Berwick served again in Flanders, but this time in the army of the incompetent Duke of Burgundy; however, his main role during the war lay in the successful attempt to establish Philip V on the throne of Spain, which was, after all, the ostensible cause of the war. After a year of fruitless campaigning in Spain, with a small army and little Spanish co-operation, he returned in despair (1704). But in 1706, after the British had intervened in Spain in force, he returned to take charge of a deteriorating situation. Now a marshal of France, he fought a brilliant campaign of manœuvre in Castile and Estremadura, which had the effect of forcing the British army under Galway (q.v.) to lose its nerve. Madrid was abandoned and the British retreated towards Valencia, where they could be supported by their fleet. At the battle of Almanza (1707) near Valencia, Berwick routed the English and Spanish forces under Galway and established control over almost the whole of Spain.

However, the threat to France from Marlborough's victorious army after the battle of Oudenarde (1708) meant that Berwick was required for the main struggle in the north. He met Marlborough again at the siege of Lille, in the French attempt to relieve the city. Again, when an emergency arose, this time in Piedmont, Berwick was sent to recover the situation. He fought a skilful campaign and kept the line of the Alps secure. His absence from Spain, however, had led to a deterioration in the French position there, and Vendôme (q.v.) was sent to recover the situation; in 1714 Berwick completed his success in Spain when he returned to conduct a brilliantly successful campaign in Catalonia, culminating in the capture of Barcelona in 1714. He

was to return, ironically, in 1719, at the head of an army to fight against Philip V, whom he had done so much to establish on the throne of Spain. It fought almost exclusively in the north, and although the Basque provinces suffered the ravages of campaigning armies, little progress was made towards Madrid.

Berwick's skill as a soldier combined the rather formal techniques of western European warfare with an experience of a more irregular approach. Thus his early career against the Turks, a campaign fought in 1705 against the irregular peasant Camisards of Languedoc, and the experience gained in Spain, all gave him an absolute pre-eminence in campaigns involving speedy manœuvre and unorthodox actions. Like his uncle Marlborough he paid scrupulous attention to the fine logistic details involved in planning a campaign, and he always ensured that his supplies could match every exigency of the plan of battle. His abilities in conventional positional warfare were also considerable, as the siege of Barcelona showed. He was killed during the siege of Philippsburg (1734), by a chance cannon ball.

Bessières, Jean Baptiste (duc d'Istrie; 1768–1813) Marshal of France. A simple fighting soldier, much of his life was spent at Napoleon's side, the two being unusually close friends. Bessières, by birth a gentleman, was promoted through the ranks of his local National Guard – he came from Prayssas in the Lot – to minor staff appointments in the regular army of the republic and then to a cavalry captaincy in the Army of Italy. There he attracted the attention of Napoleon, who made him commander of his personal escort of Guides, took him to Egypt, where he served at Acre and Aboukir, and thereafter kept him close to his person, usually as a superior officer of the Cavalry of the Guard. He fought at Austerlitz, Jena, Friedland and

Eylau, took part in the Spanish campaign of 1808, where he won two minor victories at Medina del Rio Seco and Guadalajara, and then in Germany during 1809, when he was present at Essling and Wagram. Briefly in Spain again in 1811, he rejoined the Grand Army for the Russian expedition, in which he commanded the Cavalry of the Guard. It was he who rescued the emperor from capture by Cossacks on 25 October 1812 at Gorodnaya. In April 1813 he was promoted to command the Imperial Guard, but on 1 May was killed by a cannon shot on the eve of the battle of Lützen while riding near Rippach in Saxony.

Bigeard, Marcel Maurice (1916–) French general. Unusually, in modern times, Bigeard rose from the lowest ranks of the French army, and from social obscurity, to its highest peak. The son of a railway worker, himself a bank clerk, he volunteered in 1939 for the *Corps francs* (a sort of commando force), was captured but escaped and in 1944 was parachuted back into France to lead the *maquis* of the Ariège. Commissioned an officer, he went to Indo-China at the outbreak of the war and served there from 1947 to 1954. His exploits as commander of the 6th Colonial Parachutists became legendary. In 1954 he jumped with his regiment into the besieged fortress of Dien Bien Phu, for command of which he subsequently became largely responsible. After its fall, he survived Vietnamese imprisonment to play an important part in the counter-insurrection of Algeria, 1954–60 (it is he on whom Larteguey is believed to have modelled the central figure of his famous novel *Les Centurions*), but he avoided involvement in anti-Gaullist politics. In 1975 he was appointed secretary of state at the Ministry of Defence in order to alleviate the discontent of the conscripts. Bigeard is perhaps less important for what he has done than as

an extreme example of the 'parachutist' type.

Biron, Armand Louis de Gontaut, duc de Lauzun et duc de Biron (1747–93) French general. Nephew of Louis Antoine, duc de Biron and marshal of France, who was the son of Charles Armand, duc de Biron and marshal of France, who was the great-nephew of Charles, duc de Biron, admiral and marshal of France, who was the son of Armand, duc de Biron, marshal of France and in his time the greatest and most senior of her generals. Armand-Louis's passionate adherence to the Revolution may be thought surprising. He had had, however, a wildly adventurous youth as an explorer in Senegal and in the Gambia and as an officer under Rochambeau (q.v.) in America, and he possessed an impatient, impulsive temperament, to which the excitement of the Revolution gave full scope. First appointed as chief of staff to Rochambeau's Army of the North in 1792, he subsequently became commander of the Army of the Rhine and then of the Army of Italy. Condemned under the Terror, he was guillotined in Paris, 31 December 1793.

Bishop, William Avery (1894–1956) Canadian fighter ace. Second-ranking among British aces of the First World War. Bishop shot down seventy-two enemy aircraft and was awarded the Victoria Cross and many other decorations. He did not start operational flying until March 1917, but in one twelve-day period in 1918 scored twenty-five victories. In the Second World War he served as an air marshal.

Blake, Robert (1599–1657) British soldier and sailor. One of the few military figures to have a distinguished career on both land and sea, Blake chose the Parliamentary side at the outset of the English Civil War (1646–9). He proved an extremely able soldier and organized two of the principal defences of the war, at Bristol and Lyme Regis where he outfaced Prince Rupert (q.v.) for a considerable time, and a further epic defence at Taunton, where he held out against Goring. But in 1649 he was to discover a second career when he was appointed, together with Deane and Popham, as one of three 'generals at sea'.

Blake turned out to be a seaman of extraordinary brilliance, the equal of the great Dutch admirals who had spent their whole active careers in naval service. His first naval command was the pursuit of his old opponent Prince Rupert in his flight to Portugal: when the Portuguese refused to allow him to land, he ravaged their shipping and commerce. It was Blake who provided the spark that caused the First Dutch War (1652–4), when he chastised the Dutch for failing to pay the normal courtesies due to an English fleet in its home waters. At the battle of Kentish Knock (1652), he drove off the Dutch fleet under Cornelis de Witt: but at Dungeness, two months later in November, he was badly beaten by a Dutch fleet twice his size under Tromp (q.v.). At Portland and off Beachy Head, in 1653, he met Tromp again, with complete and justified success. The war was assuming the character of a personal duel. Badly wounded at Beachy Head, Blake was forced to leave active command, and in the battle of the Gabbard Bank (later in the same year) the active leadership was being exercised by Monck (q.v.), although Blake's arrival with his ships was decisive in the English victory.

As part of the larger political plans of the Protectorate, Blake was next sent to cruise in the Mediterranean, where with twenty-four ships he harried the Barbary pirates and attacked Algiers (1655). But his most lasting influence was felt not at sea, but in the deliberations of the new Committee of Admirals. The navy grew by over 200 vessels during the period of the Commonwealth (1649–60) and Blake was instrumental in systematizing tactics and organization into forms which long outlasted the political institutions of the period. The committee revised tactics and issued fighting instructions. They pioneered the line-ahead formation, which greatly increased effective firepower, and issued articles of war to control discipline. In all these, Blake's was the leading voice, forever suggesting innovations and urging experiment. He died at sea with his fleet, only one hour before the ships entered Plymouth. But death was not the end. In 1660 his putrescent corpse was exhumed and cast into a lime pit outside Westminster Hall, together with those of other leaders of the Commonwealth. Blake was a radical – in politics, in religion, and in his attitudes towards the conduct of war at sea. He was an innovator of a high order, for (as the historian of the Civil War, Clarendon, described him) he was: 'The first man that declined the old track.'

Bloch, Ivan (Jean de; 1836–1902) Polish Jew of poor family, who made a great fortune in the Russian railway boom of 1860–80. Bloch devoted his declining years to the reconciliation of Polish with Russian interests and to writing on the futility of future warfare. His *War of the Future in its Technical, Economic and Political Aspects* (1897) (French and German editions 1900, English edition of sixth and final volume entitled *Is War Impossible?* 1899), though not greatly noticed in its time, became greatly admired after the First World War for the prescience of its warnings ('Everybody will be entrenched in the next war . . .') and encouraged seers like Liddell Hart and Fuller – the latter Bloch's chief admirer – to forecast the nature of the Second World War.

Blomberg, Werner von (1878–1943) German field-marshal. Minister of war to Hitler, by whom he was created field-marshal – the first of the regime – for his services to German rearmament (1 April 1936), Blomberg was removed from office and disgraced in the crucial episode now known as the Blomberg–Fritsch (q.v.) crisis of 1938. It had long been Hitler's ambition to bring the army to heel, which he was unable to do while it retained the right to provide the minister of war from the ranks of serving generals. Using evidence provided by Himmler that Blomberg's second marriage – to a typist in his office – was not just an old man's folly but an insult to the officer corps (the girl had been a prostitute), Hitler moved behind the shockwave this revelation caused to abolish Blomberg's post and transfer its functions to a new *Oberkommando der Wehrmacht*, of which he made himself head. Thereafter the subjection of the army to his will progressed uninterrupted.

Blücher, Gebhard Liberecht von (Prinz von Wahlstadt; 1742–1819) Prussian field-marshal and joint victor of Waterloo. Born at Rostock in Mecklenburg-Schwerin, Blücher enlisted at the age of fourteen in a Swedish cavalry regiment, from which he was taken prisoner by the Prussians in the early stages of the Seven Years' War (1756–63). Changing sides – a practice neither uncommon nor disreputable in eighteenth-century German warfare – he fought with his captors, the 8th Hussars, for the remainder of the war. Retiring to farm in Silesia, he rejoined the regiment in 1786, and in the campaign against the French of 1793 he showed himself a fanatically brave, determined and inspiring leader of cavalry in battle. He was promoted major-general in 1794, and his devoted command of the rearguard after Napoleon's victory at Jena (1806) was one of the few alleviations of Prussia's humiliation in that battle. Eventually forced to surrender at Rackau, near Lübeck, he

was subsequently kept from command by the French, who feared his abilities, and it was not until Napoleon's defeat in Russia that he properly returned to military life. He had meanwhile made the acquaintance of Scharnhorst and Gneisenau (qq.v.) and learnt from their example the value of competent staff support (with which Gneisenau was to provide him during the campaign of 1815). Blücher took a notable part in several battles of the Prussian War of Liberation against Napoleon: Lützen (2 May 1813), Bautzen (20 May 1813), Katzbach (26 August 1813) in which he defeated MacDonald (q.v.), and finally Leipzig (16–18 October 1813), for his part in which he was promoted field-marshal.

Despite the onset of winter, the Prussians, Austrians and Russians persisted in their pursuit of Napoleon from central Germany to northern France. Within France itself, Napoleon fought a series of defensive battles which demonstrated his old tactical and strategic superiority; but against the greater numbers enjoyed by the Allies and the determination and singlemindedness displayed by Blücher, it availed him little. Blücher's goal was Paris, towards which he advanced along the valley of the Marne, Schwarzenberg (q.v.), his Austrian confederate, advancing along the Seine. On five successive days, at Champaubert (10 February 1814), Montmirail (11 February), Château-Thierry (12 February) and Vauchamps (14 February), Napoleon checked Blücher and won the time to turn and defeat Schwarzenberg at Montereau (18 February). He defeated Blücher again at Craonne on 7 March, but when he attacked him at Laon two days later suffered heavy casualties and was forced to retreat. Concentrating thereafter chiefly against the Austrians, but steadily giving ground meanwhile, Napoleon's army next met Blücher outside Paris, where he had joined forces with the Austrians. Their joint defeat of it compelled Napoleon's abdication.

In the 1815 campaign, to take part in which he returned from his estates, Blücher took command of the Prussian troops in Belgium and was the first of the Allied commanders to meet Napoleon in force. Defeated at Ligny (16 June) he refused to do as Napoleon wished – retreat down his own line of communications, leaving the British to be defeated alone – but made a dangerous flank march towards Wavre and Waterloo. Entering the battlefield in the late afternoon of 18 June, his soldiers attacked Napoleon's army in flank and deprived him of the reserves he needed to break the British line at the decisive moment. In the twilight, the two Allied armies advanced, driving the French before them to destruction. Wellington and Blücher met outside La Belle Alliance inn to celebrate their victory. For his part in it, Blücher was created prince of Wahlstadt, and was loaded with other honours by the Allied states. He died at Kriblowitz, Silesia, on 19 September 1819. No military genius, his bravery, strength of character and inflexible honesty made him a superb ally and his earthy habits and indulgence in gin, rhubarb and strong tobacco endeared him to the German soldiers whom he had to lead.

Blyukher, Vasilii Konstantinovich (1889–1938) Marshal of the Soviet Union. A man of mystery, Blyukher was suspected in the months before the great purge (1937) of preparing his semi-independent Far Eastern Army for an anti-Stalin coup. He nevertheless escaped execution in the first wave of arrests and did not 'disappear' until late 1938. He had in earlier life successfully commanded the Red troops against Kolchak in Siberia and Wrangel in the Crimea (qq.v.) and led the military mission which advised Chiang Kai-shek (q.v.), 1924–7, under the pseudonym Galin. It is occasionally alleged that the name Blyukher was also adopted, because of its military associations, and that his real name was Gurov.

Bock, Fedor von (1880–1945) German field-marshal. An East Prussian aristocrat from Küstrin, the son of a general, he won the *Pour le mérite* for 'nerveless bravery' as an officer of the 5th Foot Guards during the First World War, afterwards became an assistant to Seeckt (q.v.) and rose eventually to command, with Rundstedt and Leeb (qq.v.), one of the three 'army groups' into which the peacetime army was organized up to 1938. On the formation of true Army Groups at the outbreak of war, he was appointed to command of North (later B), which he directed in the Polish campaign, 1939, against Holland and Belgium, 1940, and in 1941 (as Army Group Centre) in the invasion of Russia (*see* Guderian). Removed in the great purge of December 1941, he was reappointed to succeed Rundstedt at Army Group South, January–July 1942, but was then relieved by Manstein (q.v.), chiefly on grounds of age. 'Frederican Prussianism was deeply ingrained in his character: he was a violent nationalist, a stern disciplinarian and intent only upon strengthening the army and advancing his own military career.' He was killed in Schleswig-Holstein at the end of the war.

Boelcke, Oswald (1891–1916) German fighter ace. Though not a leader in the number of victories credited to him in aerial combat (forty), Boelcke was immensely successful in the organization of aerial fighting units and in transmitting to fledgling pilots his own warrior skills: his *Jasta Boelcke* was a nursery of many other aces. Earlier he had been a rival of the famous Max Immelmann and like him was killed early in the war.

Boisot, Louis (*d* 1576)   Dutch sailor. A
leading figure in the Dutch revolt against
the Spanish (1568–1609), Boisot
achieved greatest note as the commander
of the Sea Beggars, the small fleet of
Dutch vessels which harried Spanish sea
communications and rendered their control of the coastline precarious. Created
admiral of Zealand by William of
Orange, he dealt a shattering blow to
Spanish prestige by the destruction of
their fleet at Sud-Beveland in January
1574. This action effectively prevented
the relief of the besieged Spanish garrison of Middleburg. Later in the year he
led the heroic relief of the town of
Leyden, which was hard pressed by a
large Spanish force, crossing the flooded
fields to bring supplies and manpower
to the defenders. But a promising career
was cut short when, in command of the
island of Zielzee, he tried to stop a
surprise Spanish assault at low tide. His
great skill was impeccable seamanship
and a detailed knowledge of the coastline. But, above that, his exploits indicated qualities of inspired leadership and
tactical imagination.

Bolivar, Simon (1783–1830)   South
American soldier and statesman: the
'Liberator'. Born into a rich and aristocratic family in Caracas on 24 July 1783,
Bolivar was sent to Spain to complete
his education, where he wed a Spanish
noblewoman who died after a year of
marriage. He never remarried. Indeed
this personal tragedy seems to have been
decisive in setting him on his singleminded pursuit of Spanish-American liberation. As a boy he had been introduced to the thought of the Enlighten-
ment and during a secret visit to Europe
in 1804–7 he systematically worked his
way through its literature. He was also
present in Paris during Napoleon's coronation, which made a deep impression
on him, and there encountered Hum-
boldt, recently returned from his voyage
around South America, who told him he

thought the Spanish colonies ripe for
independence. Napoleon's deposition of
the Spanish king in 1808 gave the colonists, among whom Bolivar had now
returned, their opportunities to strike
for freedom.

The royal forces in the continent, however, moved to repress them and fighting
broke out in 1811. Successful, in part
through the treachery of one of the
rebels, in putting down rebellion in Venezuela, the Spanish army obliged Bolivar
to take refuge in adjoining New Granada (now Colombia). He had hitherto
played a subordinate role but though
without military training or experience
he now raised an army, defeated the
Spaniards in six pitched battles and in
August 1813 entered Caracas, where he
established himself as ruler with the title
of 'Liberator'. But he was not universally accepted; civil war broke out, the
Spanish forces regained the upper hand
and Bolivar was forced into exile, which
he spent in Jamaica and Haiti. The
black president of the latter republic,
which had freed itself from France, gave
him money and weapons; with these he
was able to recruit a force of foreign,
largely British, mercenaries and adventurers, and in 1819, from a base he had
established in the remote Orinoco
region, he led his little army to join the
guerrilla force of Santander in New
Granada. He had conceived the plan of
attacking the Spaniards in Venezuela
from the unexpected westerly direction
and, with less than 2500 soldiers,
brought it to a brilliant conclusion.
Taken by surprise, the Spaniards were
forced to fight in disadvantageous circumstances at Boyaca, outside Bogota,
on 7 August 1819. They were defeated,
Bolivar entered the city and thenceforth
carried the independence movement
from success to success.

In the following year Bolivar reopened
the campaign for Venezuela itself, whose
Spanish defenders, disheartened by the
restored Spanish king's concessions to

liberalism at home, were fairly easily overcome. After the victory of Carabobo, June 1821, Bolivar entered Caracas and in the following year, co-ordinating his advance with that of his gifted subordinate Sucre (q.v.), he invaded Ecuador and captured Quito. All of northern South America but Peru was now liberated and in a campaign in the mountainous regions of the interior, marked by the victories of Junin and Ayacuho, that region was conquered and the last major Spanish army in South America defeated. The campaign is remarkable for the difficulties of organization, supply and movement which the rebels overcame. By the end of 1826 the territory of the six modern states of Venezuela, Colombia, Ecuador, Peru, Paraguay and Bolivia had won their independence from Spain. The last four years of Bolivar's life were marred by disagreements between and within the new republics, which culminated in revolts and civil war. Feeling himself to be a cause of the dissensions among his followers, he decided to retire to Europe but died before he could embark on the journey.

Boroevic von Bojna, Svetozar (1856–1920) Austrian general. A Croat (the Croats prided themselves on their particular loyalty to the emperor), Boroevic was appointed to the Third Army on the outbreak of the First World War, commanded it in the battle of the Carpathians, January–March 1915, and in the breakthrough at Gorlice-Tarnow, April–June 1915. He then assumed supreme command on the Italian front (the Isonzo, then the Piave), retaining it until the end of the war.

Bose, Subhas Chandra (1897–1945) Indian nationalist and creator of the Indian National Army. One of the most brilliant products of the Bengali renaissance. Bose surrendered a career in the Indian Civil Service, into the

senior branch of which he passed fourth by competition in 1920, to take up the cause of Indian independence. By 1938 he was president of its principal organ, the Indian National Congress, but resigned from it on the outbreak of the war when its other leaders declined to take the chance he believed the emergency offered of leading India to immediate freedom. He was imprisoned by the British but escaped to Afghanistan in 1941 and thence to Germany, where he recruited Indians in the prisoner-of-war camps for the nucleus of an Indian National Army. Seeing in South-East Asia a more promising field of endeavour, he made thither a daring journey by U-boat and Japanese submarine in 1943, and from the Indians taken captive in Malaya and Burma eventually created a force of three (notional) divisions. But its performance at the side of the Japanese was disappointing, many INA soldiers deserting to the British at first contact, and he was discredited with the Japanese (though not with many Indians, who still regard him as a national hero). He died in an aircrash in Taiwan (on the way to seek asylum in Russia).

Bosquet, Pierre Joseph François (1810–61) Marshal of France. A Polytechnicien, whose early career had been daringly spent in the conquest of Algeria, under both Bugeaud and Saint-Arnaud (qq.v.), Bosquet commanded the 2nd Division in the Crimea and was severely wounded at the assault on the Malakov (*see* Todleben and MacMahon). He is remembered for his remark on the Charge of the Light Brigade, 'It is magnificent but it is not war.' In 1856 Napoleon III created him a marshal – a dignity he conferred too lightly.

Botha, Louis (1862–1919) South African general and statesman. Magnanimity in defeat was his most striking characteristic. After the peace of Vereeniging, which he signed with Roberts (q.v.) to end the Boer War, May 1902, Botha devoted himself wholeheartedly to the reconciliation of Afrikaaner to Briton in South Africa and of South Africa to Great Britain. And this came after his waging of a bitter and brilliant guerrilla campaign directed towards exactly contrary ends. A typical Boer farmer's son, Botha was one of the founders of the Transvaal and, though a political opponent of Kruger, took loyally to the field when war broke out with Britain in 1899. He helped to invest Ladysmith, captured the armoured train in which Winston Churchill (q.v.) was a passenger, defeated Buller (q.v.) at Colenso, and played a major role in the victories of Vaal Krantz and Spion Kop. Appointed commandant-general of the Transvaal, he sustained a guerrilla campaign against the British until resistance became hopeless. In his subsequent political career he became first prime minister of the new Union of South Africa, and in 1914–15, resuming military command, put down the pro-German rebellion of Beyers and de Wet (q.v.) and conquered the German colony of South-West Africa.

Boufflers, Louis François, duc de (1644–1711) French soldier. One of a galaxy of excellent French generals who rose to prominence in the wars of Louis XIV. Boufflers came from a Picard family with a strong military tradition. He entered the army in 1662 and commanded the royal dragoons most successfully during the First Dutch War (1672–8). He served with distinction in all the early wars against the Dutch and was created a marshal of France in 1693, in the midst of the war of the Grand Alliance (1688–97), and in 1694, a duke. Boufflers was expert in the formal positional warfare of the day, and his skill was well seen in his stubborn defence of Namur against the much larger army of William of Orange, now king of England. He held out for three months, losing over half his garrison of 14,000.

When the war ended in 1697, there were a few brief years of peace, until a general conflict developed once more in the war of the Spanish Succession (1701–14). Boufflers was given command over terrain he knew well, the Spanish Netherlands. This brought him into direct conflict with an allied army under Marlborough (q.v.). As a result of Dutch vacillation, Marlborough had to delay his attack on Boufflers: the outcome was a severe reverse for the Dutch armies at Nijmegen. The inability of the allies to act in effective concert allowed Boufflers to strengthen his hold on the towns of the southern Netherlands, extending fortifications and provisioning garrisons. Yet when the command problems of the allies were resolved, Marlborough waged a skilful campaign which resulted in the capture of the Meuse fortresses, and forced Boufflers to withdraw from his positions. But despite this reverse, his conduct of the campaign was creditable, and he was appointed commander of the Royal Bodyguard (1704).

The close of his career was highlighted by two acts of gallantry. In 1708, as commander of Lille, he defended the town with such success against an allied force of 110,000 under Eugen and Marlborough (qq.v.), that after three months he surrendered the town with full honours. Then, in the following year, at the battle of Malplaquet, he took over after Villars was wounded. He conducted the battle in a masterly manner, first attacking to recover his position after the allied assault, and then ensuring an orderly retreat. Malplaquet was the last great battle of the war, and Boufflers, now an old man, retired. He had displayed in his career the skill and professionalism which was the hallmark of the French generals of the epoch, but also a tenacity and determination in battle which made him an especially redoubtable enemy.

Boulanger, Georges Ernest (1837–91) French general and political adventurer. His importance post-dated his active military career (which had included experience in the conquests of Algeria and Indo-China, in the Franco-Prussian war and in the suppression of the Commune). Because he was on the staff of Saint-Cyr in 1870, he escaped capture by the Prussians, which befell so many of his contemporaries, and achieved very quick promotion. Appointed minister of war in the cabinets of Freycinet and Goblet (1886–7), he took to dabbling in the inner politics of the Third Republic and was adopted as a champion by a variety of dissatisfied factions – legitimists, Orleanists, Bonapartists, clericals, anti-clericals, patriotic republicans like Déroulède, anti-parliamentary conservatives and idealistic socialists. A popular belief was that he would lead France in a victorious war of revenge against Prussia. The truth was that he had no policy beyond egotism and, after securing a succession of triumphs with the Paris crowds (14 July 1886), at plebiscitary by-elections (27 January 1889) and having terrified the government with the spectre of insurrection, he meekly accepted its sentence of exile and retired to Brussels, where he committed suicide on the grave of his mistress. He left as his memorial a useful political expression, 'Boulangism', which denotes a phoney Caesarism, and the practice of painting sentry boxes red, white and blue, instituted by him while minister of war.

Bouquet, Henry (1719–65) British soldier serving in North America. Swiss-born, Bouquet entered English service and fought in the North American colonies during their wars with the French and their Indian allies. He commanded the Royal Americans, one of the most successful exponents of the skirmishing tactics developed during the Indian wars. The high quality of his troops, and his own abilities, became clear at the capture of Fort Duquesne (1758), an advance post of the French, where his troops rapidly cut off the French from their lines of supply, so that their retreat became precipitate. Thereafter, Bouquet was constantly engaged in the border wars, his Royal Americans the principal defence of the colonies against savage incursions by Indians. The most dangerous threat to the colonies came in Pontiac's (q.v.) Rebellion (1763), when the Ottawa Indians sacked all the posts and forts west of the Niagara river, and were set to descend on the coastal settlements. All that stood between them and the coast were Bouquet's Royal Americans and a section of The Black Watch, a 'loyal' Scottish regiment formed after the Jacobite '45'. At the battle of Bushy Run, he routed a much larger force of Indians who ambushed him. Adopting a strong defensive position around his supply wagons, he used his superior discipline and fire-power to break successive Indian assaults. After wearing them down, he managed to attack them in the flank with a small detachment: the result was a complete victory. Bouquet continued to serve with his regiment until his death.

Bourbaki, Charles Denis Sauter (1816–97) French general and hero of the Franco-Prussian war. Born of a family of Greek origin, Bourbaki was educated at the Prytanée and Saint-Cyr, was commissioned into the 59th Regiment in 1836 but soon transferred to the Zouaves. Like most French officers of his generation, he first saw action in Algeria, where he at once demonstrated the courage and powers of command which were to distinguish his career. A brigadier in the Crimea and divisional commander in the Franco-Austrian war in northern Italy (1859), he was commanding Napoleon III's Imperial Guard Corps at the outbreak of war with Prussia. He did not, in the opening campaign, play an important role, for the Guard was held throughout in reserve.

After the surrender of the field army at Sedan (2 September 1870), however, his luck changed. Making his way through the German lines, he offered his services to the Government of National Defence and, after lesser appointments, was ultimately named to command the Army of the East, operating towards Belfort (which was still in French hands). But, like all those raised in the aftermath of defeat, his army was too spontaneous a creation to stand against the seasoned Prussians and though he beat them in a minor battle at Villersexel on 9 January 1871, he was himself defeated on the Lisaine (15–17 January). His army then disintegrated and he attempted suicide. Bourbaki's unfortunate destiny was to have served the wrong Napoleon: under the first his panache would have assured him a glittering reputation.

Bourbon, Charles, duc de (1490–1527) French soldier in the Imperial service. A wayward and irascible soldier of great talent. Bourbon brought glory both to the arms of his native France and her Habsburg enemies. In 1515 he was appointed constable of France and was largely responsible for the recovery of the French after the surprise Swiss assault at the battle of Marignano (1515). He fell out of favour with his cousin, Francis I, however, who feared both his ambition and his military skill. He withdrew from active service at court, but Francis pursued him, setting in motion a legal process to confiscate his lands and fortune. Bourbon was certainly pursuing treasonable aims, for he was in secret negotiations with both the English and Emperor Charles V, with the clear objective of unseating Francis from the throne of France. But his plotting was betrayed and he was forced to flee the country closely pursued by his vengeful enemies.

He immediately entered the imperial service, a valuable asset to Charles V, for his proximity to the French throne made him an effective weapon to use against Francis. In 1524 Bourbon led an abortive invasion of the south of France from Italy with 20,000 men, but he was driven back by a prompt response from Francis who hastened down the Rhone valley with a large army. He fought the French invasion of Italy, which followed his unsuccessful invasion of southern France, and was present at the dramatic victory over the French at Pavia. Francis was captured in the battle and signed the treaty of Madrid, by which he abandoned all his claims against Charles V. But as soon as he was released, he repudiated the agreement and war began again. In May 1527 the imperial army launched an assault on Rome, led by Charles of Bourbon. He was killed in the first assault. What might have been a very promising military career was terminated at the age of thirty-seven. His qualities were great courage and furious impetuosity, much like those of his great enemy Francis.

Bradley, Omar (1893–1981) American general. Bradley, the 'GI General', rose rapidly to prominence in the Second World War as the commander of the II Corps in North Africa and Italy, then of Seventh Army in Italy, and finally of First Army and Twelfth Army Group in the invasion of North-West Europe. A man of humble background and notably homely appearance, Bradley attracted the attention of George C. Marshall, the wartime chief of staff, because of his attention to detail and efficiency as a staff officer. His simple manners and evident concern for their welfare made him trusted by his soldiers and his masterly execution of operational orders in France and Germany made him a favourite of Eisenhower, his contemporary at West Point. After the war, Bradley became chief of staff of the army and Chairman of the Joint Chiefs of Staff in the five-star rank of General of the Army.

Bragg, Braxton (1817–76) American (Confederate) general. A West Pointer who had retired to plant in Louisiana, Bragg rejoined the (South's) colours in 1861 and, as an ex-regular and veteran of the Mexican war ('Give me a little more grape, Captain Bragg' – Zachary Taylor, q.v., at the battle of Buena Vista) was promoted major-general almost immediately. He was chief of staff to A.S. Johnston (q.v.) at Shiloh, where he commanded the Confederate right, and in 1862, a full general, he relieved Beauregard (q.v.) as commander of the Army of Tennessee. This he led in an invasion of Kentucky but was defeated at Perryville and threw away the fruits of victory at Stones River. At Chickamauga, 19 September 1863, he did the same thing and, when he laid siege to Rosecrans (q.v.) at Chattanooga (October–November 1863) he was decisively defeated at Missionary Ridge. He was relieved by Joseph E. Johnston (q.v.) and returned to Richmond to act as Jefferson Davis's military adviser, a post he held almost until the end of the war. This appointment was not inappropriate, for his weakness lay not in conception but execution. He was, moreover, often ill with migraine in the field. 'He was frequently in the saddle when the more appropriate place for him would have been in bed', wrote one of his officers.

Brauchitsch, Walter von (1881–1948) German field-marshal. On the overthrow in 1938 of Fritsch (q.v.), Brauchitsch was appointed commander-in-chief of the German army. He was a compromise candidate, for Hitler would have preferred the pro-Nazi Reichenau (q.v.). In practice, he did the military establishment little good in its struggle to preserve its independence, for, though splendidly soldierly in appearance and manner, he lacked the fibre to stand up to Hitler in face-to-face argument. He was made the principal scapegoat for the failure of the battle outside Moscow in December 1941 and removed from office, which Hitler then assumed, thus becoming the first civilian ever to exercise command over the German army.

Braun, Wernher von (1912–77) Designer of military rocket missiles. As a schoolboy in Germany, Braun had written a thesis on the design of long-range rockets, a seemingly unlikely interest for a young aristocrat whose father served as von Papen's minister of agriculture, and at twenty-five he was appointed technical director of the German army's rocket research centre. By 1938 he had produced a rocket (the A-4) capable of carrying an explosive warhead for eleven miles, but it was not until he fully engaged Hitler's attention that he procured the necessary finance to develop it into the V-2. This, the first practical long-range, load-carrying missile, was used to bombard England from 8 September 1944, about 3600 being fired, though its small warhead ensured that it would not achieve the war-winning effect Hitler had hoped of it. In 1945 Braun, who had taken care to deliver himself, his team and his documents into American hands, transferred his design work to the United States, where he developed from the V-2 the family of liquid-fuelled rockets which provided his new homeland with its first intercontinental nuclear delivery system and with the rockets which carried the first men to the moon.

Breckinridge, John Cabell (1821–75) American (Confederate) general. A veteran of the Mexican war (but a volunteer, not a regular) and a successful politician – he had served as vice-president to Buchanan and as a senator and run against Lincoln for the presidency – Breckinridge went south in 1861, was declared a traitor by the Union government, appointed brigadier by the Confederacy and commanded the reserve corps at Shiloh. Subsequently he commanded divisions or corps in many of the major battles until appointed secretary of war in February 1865 by Jefferson Davis, whom he advised in the surrender negotiations at Appomattox.

Brialmont, Henry Alexis (1821–1903) Belgian military engineer. Called 'the Belgian Vauban' (q.v.), Brialmont owed the title to his conception of a system of fortification designed to resist the new long-range artillery, firing high-explosive shell. It was based upon the dispersion of heavily armoured detached forts in a circle, up to 8 miles in diameter, around the place to be protected. His system was an important influence upon French fortification, notably at Verdun, and he built three forts to his own design, at Antwerp, Liège and Namur. The Germans in response designed a siege train of super-heavy artillery which in August 1914 destroyed the defences of the last two places within ten days (*see* Ludendorff and Leman).

Broglie, Victor François, duc de (1718–1804)   French soldier. Scion of an illustrious family of French soldiers, Broglie first saw action in the Italian campaign of 1741, during the war of the Austrian Succession (1740–8). He was then sent with an army of French 'volunteers' led by his father, François de Broglie, to the aid of the Elector of Bavaria. In 1746 he was transferred to the army in Flanders and fought at Rocourt (1746) and Laufeld (1747). He fought through the Seven Years' War (1756–63) under a variety of commanders – Soubise, Clermont and Contades. With Contades, he was saved from defeat at the battle of Minden by the irresolution of Lord George Germaine, who refused to exploit the opening so brilliantly created for him by Ferdinand of Brunswick (q.v.). Broglie fought gallantly at Rossbach (1757), Sonderhausen (1758),

and at Bergen (1759) he managed to defeat Ferdinand of Brunswick. Now a marshal of France, he was given the chief command in Germany, but although he was successful at Corbach (1760), he was beaten again by Ferdinand of Brunswick at Vellinghausen (1761), and was removed from his command in disgrace. His most lasting influence on the French army was the organizational reform into a divisional structure, which established fixed proportions for artillery and infantry in a single unit, giving a commander a powerful and flexible tactical unit. After the French Revolution, Broglie lived abroad until his death, serving in both the British and Russian armies.

Brooke, Alan (1st Viscount Alanbrooke of Brookeborough; 1883–1963)   British field-marshal, principal military adviser to Churchill in the Second World War. A gunner officer, son of the Ulster house of Brookeborough, he had been educated in France before entering Woolwich, and his fluency in the language contributed to the great success he achieved during the First World War in adapting French methods of controlling the great rolling barrages to English practice. It marked him out as a coming officer and between the wars he held a succession of key appointments, including commander of the School of Artillery and Director of Military Training. In 1939 he was given II Corps in the British Expeditionary Force, which he commanded with great skill in the withdrawal to Dunkirk. In 1941, on the appointment of his old Staff College teacher, Sir John Dill (q.v.), to the Washington mission, he succeeded him as Chief of the Imperial General Staff and in that post he was at Churchill's elbow throughout the war. He modestly described his role, in the remarkable books which were made out of his diaries, as that of turning Churchill's inspirations into military sense, but at least some of the inspiration of British strategy between 1939 and 1945 came undoubtedly from him.

Brueys d'Aigaïlliers, François Paul (1753–98) French admiral. An officer of the royal navy, Brueys d'Aigaïlliers continued in service under the Revolution and it was his fleet which conveyed Napoleon's army to Egypt in 1798, taking Malta *en route*. On 1 August, while at anchor in Aboukir Bay, it was attacked by Nelson (q.v.) and completely destroyed (the battle of the Nile). Brueys, who believed that he had chosen an attack-proof position, was killed in the action.

Brune, Guillaume Marie Anne (1763–1815) Marshal of France. A native of Corrèze, but in 1789 a Parisian printer and journalist, Brune rose through the National Guard of the city to general of brigade in the Army of the North in 1793. Posted to Napoleon's Army of Italy in 1796, he served in the division of Masséna (q.v.) at Arcola and Rivoli and was promoted general of division. In 1799 he commanded against the Anglo-Russian expedition to the Helder in Holland, and in 1800 replaced Masséna as commander in Italy, waging against the Austrians a brisk campaign of nineteen days (passage of the Mincio, capture of Verona and Vicenza), which culminated in the signing of the armistice of Treviso. He was serving as ambassador to Turkey when Napoleon named him marshal in the great creation of 1804. In 1807 he commanded a corps, but offended Napoleon by a diplomatic peccadillo in negotiations with the Swedes and remained in disfavour until the first abdication in 1814. Despite his mistreatment, he rallied to the emperor during the Hundred Days but did not exercise a field command. He was assassinated by a White Terrorist gang at Avignon while making his way under arrest to Paris.

Brunswick, Karl Wilhelm Ferdinand, Duke of (1735–1806) Prussian general. A son of Frederick the Great's lieutenant, Brunswick had made a considerable reputation in Prussian service during the Seven Years' War (1756–63), in and during the interventions in the Bavarian Succession crisis of 1777–9 ('The Potato War') and the Dutch Civil War (1785–7) before he was chosen in 1792 to command the Allied Army of the First Coalition (Austrian and Prussian). It had been formed to compel the French to restore power to Louis XVI, but its function and the tone of the anti-revolutionary manifesto issued under Brunswick's name led instead to the storming of the Tuileries and to his defeat at Valmy on 20 September 1792. When Napoleon invaded Prussia in 1806, Brunswick was again in command, but was mortally wounded on the field of Auerstadt. An accomplished general of the old school, he had outlived his time.

Brusilov, Alexei Alexeevich (1853–1926) Russian general. His name is chiefly remembered for his planning and execution of the only successful Russian offensive of the First World War – the 'Brusilov Offensive' of 1916. A cavalry officer, he had entered the army through the Corps of Pages, had first seen fighting in the Caucasus campaign and had attracted attention by his boldness in action in the Russo-Turkish war of 1877–8. In 1914 he commanded the Eighth Army against the Austrians in Galicia. Not until the spring of 1916 did he achieve command of a large enough force (the Seventh, Eighth, Ninth and Eleventh armies) to undertake decisive operations on his own initiative. By careful concealment of his offensive preparations, he was able to surprise the Austrians on his front south of the Pripet marshes, break through, recapture most of Galicia and the Bukovina and take 375,000 prisoners. Lack of supplies and transport prevented him from sustaining the momentum of his advance. In the following year he was among those generals who urged Nicholas II to abdicate after the February revolution. After the October revolution he threw in his lot with the Soviets, but was not employed in command and soon retired.

Buchanan, Franklin (1800–74) American (Confederate) admiral. The first superintendent of the US Naval Academy, Annapolis, for which he had drawn up the plans, he also commanded the flagship which took Perry (q.v.) to Japan in 1852. He entered Confederate service in 1861 and commanded the *Merrimac* on its initial appearance in Hampton Roads, 8 March 1862; wounds prevented him fighting against the *Monitor* the day following. Promoted admiral, he commanded in the battle of Mobile Bay, 5 August 1864, where he was defeated by Farragut (q.v.).

Buckner, Simon Bolivar (1823–1914) American (Confederate) general. A Kentuckyan, Buckner had been retired from the army six years when the Civil War broke out, and tried at first to negotiate the neutrality of his state. When Union troops invaded it, however, he joined the Confederate army, was promoted brigadier-general (having previously been offered that rank by the Union) and was in command of Fort Donelson when it fell to Grant (q.v.), a West Point fellow-student (and lifelong friend). He was exchanged, fought at Perryville and commanded a corps at Chickamauga. He lived to be a pallbearer at Grant's funeral and to father a son, also Simon Bolivar, who was killed aged fifty-nine in command of the US Tenth Army on Okinawa, June 1945.

Budenny, Semen Mikhailovich (1883–1973) Marshal of the Soviet Union. Instantly recognizable in group photographs of Soviet leaders by his tsarist appearance – he sported a splendid curly moustache – Budenny had indeed begun his career as a trooper in the imperial cavalry. But in 1917 he took up the cause of revolution, was elected chairman of his divisional soviet and formed a cavalry unit that fought for Reds against Whites on the Don. Joining the Communist Party in 1919, he formed the First Cavalry Army with Stalin, Yegorov and Voroshilov (qq.v.), which played a dramatic but ultimately unsuccessful part in the Russo-Polish War of 1920 and a decisive role in operations against the White armies of Wrangel and Denikin (qq.v.). He held staff appointments after the Civil War and in 1937, as a favourite of Stalin's, was spared in the great purge and promoted. In 1941 he commanded the South-West Front (army group) against Rundstedt (q.v.), was relieved for incompetence and, again spared Stalin's anger, relegated to honorific duties. In 1958 he was created a Hero of the Soviet Union.

Buell, Don Carlos (1818–98) American (Union) general. A northerner (from Ohio), a West Pointer, a veteran of the Mexican war, Buell's promotion from major to brigadier-general at the outbreak of the war was therefore predestined. He commanded troops in the Henry and Donelson campaign, and arrived at Shiloh to contribute to Grant's (q.v.) victory. In 1862 he embarked on an independent campaign to capture eastern Tennessee (the Stones River campaign), but found himself forced to retreat by the skilful manœuvring of General Braxton Bragg (q.v.), and retrieved the situation only by fighting what turned into a drawn battle, Perryville. He was replaced in command by Rosecrans (q.v.), no improvement, some might think, and retired.

Bugeaud de la Piconnerie, Thomas Robert (duc d'Isly; 1784–1849) Marshal of France and conqueror of Algeria. A product of Napoleon's officer-producing unit, the *Vélites* of the Imperial Guard, his principal experience under the emperor was of guerrilla warfare in Spain. This was to prove of the greatest use to him when, in 1836, he was sent to command in Algeria. It was a mighty appointment for a man who had risen no higher than *chef de bataillon* in the Grand Army and whose only real military achievement since the Hundred Days (during which he had defeated an Austrian corps) was the suppression, unduly ruthless it was thought, of the domestic insurrection of 1834. His conduct of the Algerian conquest was, nevertheless, masterly. He transformed the morale of a dispirited army, brought an elusive enemy to battle, forced peace on Abd el-Kader (q.v.), and defeated his Moroccan allies at the Isly, 1844 (he took that title when created duke). A pacifier as well as a soldier, he worked to reconcile the tribes whose spirit he had broken by his strategy of pillage and razzia, while the ambitious programme of public works he carried through won from the white colonists whom he settled in the new dominions (many of them ex-soldiers) the soubriquet *père Bugeaud*. He was assisted in much of his Algerian work by a remarkable band of subordinates, including Aumale (to whom he surrendered the governorship in 1847) and Lamoricière (qq.v.). He died of cholera in Paris, having been first recalled by the Orleanist Chamber of Deputies, then reappointed to military command by prince-president Louis-Napoleon after the 1848 revolution. He ranks with Lyautey (q.v.) among French colonial soldiers. His name was chosen as *titre de promotion* by a Saint-Cyr class at the height of the Algerian rebellion, 1954–60.

Buller, Sir Redvers Henry (1839–1908) British general. Genuinely popular with the common soldier and highly regarded by his contemporaries, Buller was discredited by his failure in the Boer War and has been taken for a stereotype of the brainless blunderer, a notion to which his blimplike appearance – great girth, multiple chins, flushed complexion and walrus moustache – lends substance. But Buller was a brave man – he had won the Victoria Cross for rescuing wounded during the Zulu war – and had been one of the most zealous and intelligent of the 'ring' of young officers selected by Wolseley (q.v.) to help him win Britain's succession of late nineteenth-century colonial campaigns. He had also spent ten successful reforming years at the War Office as Quartermaster – and then Adjutant-General, 1887–97. None of this availed to offset the defeats – Stormberg, Magersfontein, Colenso – he and his subordinates suffered in the first months of the war in South Africa, whither he had been sent in 1899 as commander-in-chief.

Bulnes, Manuel (1799–1866) Chilean general and president. His victory at Yungay on 20 January 1839 over the Bolivian dictator Andreas Santa Cruz broke up the Bolivian–Peruvian confederation which Chile and Argentina opposed.

Bülow, Dietrich Adam Heinrich Freiherr von (1757–1807) Prussian military writer. This man of unhappy life – he was passed over for promotion in the service of Prussia, confined for insanity because of the unorthodoxy of his military writing and died eventually in Russian captivity, probably as a consequence of ill-treatment – produced some of the first perceptive military writing about the 'new warfare' of the French Revolution and Empire. His most important book was the *Geist des neueren Kriegssystems* (1799), in which he offered the first useful definition of the terms 'strategy', 'tactics' and 'base of operations'. In later writing he attempted to show that success in war was the fruit not of a sterile military theory but of the organization of the resources of the state to that end. He also attempted to prove much palpable nonsense and hence 'has been called everything from a conceited crank to the founder of modern military science'.

Burgoyne, John (1722–92) British soldier. 'Gentleman Johnny' Burgoyne was one of the more raffish and attractive of the senior officers in the British army. He entered the army in 1740, and showed his ability in the half-hearted raids on the French coast in 1758, which were finally abandoned after the repulse of the expedition against St Cas. Burgoyne now raised a regiment of light horse, which he took to fight in Portugal against the Spanish (1761). He routed the Spanish at the battle of Villa Velha (1762) and returned to England at the end of the war with a well-earned reputation for enterprise and daring. He soon found himself lionized in London society, and he became a fashionable swell, with a lucrative sideline of writing successful plays.

When the American War of Independence (1775–83) seemed imminent. Burgoyne was posted to a command in North America, and was sent with his troops to relieve the Canadian garrison under Sir Guy Carleton (1776). He returned to England in the winter of 1776 to propose a plan for united action against the rebel centres. It was strategically sound, although it did not have the wholehearted support of Howe (q.v.), the senior general in America. But the plan for joint action, difficult in any event over such great distances, was completely frustrated by the criminal incompetence of Lord George Germaine, the secretary of state for the colonies. He failed to issue proper instructions coordinating the expeditions, and allowed each commander – Burgoyne, Howe and St Leger – to manœuvre in the belief that they were acting in concert when in fact they were moving independently.

Burgoyne's southwards offensive (July 1777) was well managed and planned. He recaptured Fort Ticonderoga, which Ethan Allen's (q.v.) disreputable Green Mountain Boys had taken two years before. He moved slowly south, impeded by American harassment, and discovered to his horror early in August that Howe, instead of advancing north from New York to meet him, had turned south in pursuit of Washington. Burgoyne was in an exposed position, for new and powerful American forces now faced him, and his men were short of supplies. Cut off from hope of reinforcement, he sent out detachments to obtain new supplies, but the Americans mopped them up. Playing his last card, Burgoyne tried to defeat the main American force under General Gates (q.v.) in battle. But the American force was much larger than his shrunken command, and despite bold attacks, he was bloodily repulsed. Finally, abandoned by his fellow generals, he was forced to surrender at Saratoga (October 1777) with the remains of his force, 5700 men from the total of 7200 which left Canada. Burgoyne was released by Washington and returned to London, where he faced a maelstrom of hatred and venom, led by the government who sought to excuse their own ineptitude. The opposition supported Burgoyne. Howe put forward a different version of the story outlined above and a prolonged and unseemly pamphlet war resulted. With good sense and discretion Burgoyne washed his hands of the whole affair. He commanded in Ireland in 1782–3, but otherwise devoted himself to fathering four illegitimate children, to whom he was devoted, and writing diverting plays. Burgoyne was a good soldier and an entertaining character.

Burnside, Ambrose Everett (1824–81) American (Union) general. A retired regular, Burnside rejoined the army as a colonel of volunteers in 1861, was swiftly promoted general and at Antietam (17 September 1862) commanded the left wing – but so badly that Lee (q.v.) escaped the destruction he deserved. He was nevertheless promoted to command the Army of Potomac, through the lobbying of other generals who did not wish Hooker (q.v.) to have it. In supreme command at Fredericksburg (13 December 1862), he demonstrated how unimaginative his generalship was, publicly accepted blame for the defeat and reverted to subordinate command, principally that of IX Corps. But at Petersburg he again mishandled operations, admittedly of a very trying and unconventional sort (the great mine explosion), and was relieved. Grant (q.v.) described him as 'generally liked and respected [but] not ... fitted to command an army. No one knew this better than himself.' His splendid muttonchop whiskers perpetuate his name, in the form of 'sideburns'.

Buxhowden, Friedrich Wilhelm, Graf von (1750–1811) Russian field-marshal. A Balt, Buxhowden first achieved senior command in the Third Partition of Poland under Suvorov (q.v.), 1792–4, and was subsequently governor of the Russian share of the country. He commanded the Russian left wing at Austerlitz.

Byng, John (1704–57) British admiral. The son of Viscount Torrington (q.v.), Byng is noteworthy only for the manner of his death. Sent to secure the British island of Minorca in 1756, he found it under attack by French land and sea forces. He attacked the French fleet under La Galisonnière, but planned his battle badly, and the French fleet, which he just outnumbered, slipped away. He decided to abandon the expedition and return to Gibraltar. In England the

outcry against the Newcastle administration for the loss of Minorca and other failures grew: Byng was court-martialled, and although found innocent of cowardice, was found guilty of neglect of duty. A death sentence was mandatory under the Articles of War, but the court advised that mercy should be exercised. However, the government sought to transfer their mismanagement on to the person of Byng and insisted that justice and honour demanded that the sentence be carried out. Byng was shot on the deck of his own flagship, with a final remark which Voltaire transmuted into his famous statement that the British shot an admiral every now and again, '*pour encourager les autres*'. Like de Lally (q.v.) in France, Byng was a victim of public hysteria and governmental cowardice.

Byng, Julian Hedworth George (1st Viscount Byng of Vimy; 1862–1935) British field-marshal. The younger son of a military family (his grandfather had commanded one of the Guard brigades at Waterloo), Byng entered the 10th Hussars from Eton in 1883, via a commission in the militia. Until the outbreak of the Boer War he was chiefly distinguished in the army for his skills at polo, but in South Africa he made a fine name at the head of a regiment of light horse raised by himself. Commanding in Egypt in 1914, he was called to France in September to take over the 3rd Cavalry Division, then the Cavalry Corps, and thence was sent to supervise the evacuation of Suvla on the Gallipoli Peninsula. In May 1916 he was appointed to the Canadian Corps in France, which, under his command, achieved the often frustrated capture of Vimy Ridge, and in June 1917 to the Third Army, a command he exercised until the armistice.

C

Cabrera, Ramon (1806–77) Spanish (Carlist) general. Ferdinand VII's designation of his daughter Isabella as his heir, instead of his brother Don Carlos to whom Salic law gave the succession, provoked in Spain a succession struggle (the Carlist wars) which racked the country in 1834–9 and again in 1873–6. As a leader of Carlist bands in the first war Cabrera, a former theological student, won the soubriquet 'Tiger of the Maestrazgo' for his cruelty. Though a self-taught soldier, he won several victories over the royal army, including that of Morella (for which Don Carlos created him Count of Morella) in 1835. Eventually, dispirited by the pretender's feebleness and the movement's lack of success, he retired to England and spoke against insurrection during the Second Carlist War.

Cadorna, Count Luigi (1850–1928) Italian general. The son of one of the Piedmontese military families which supplied the army of the United Kingdom of Italy with so many of its officers – his father had fought in the wars of the Risorgimento and the Crimea – Cadorna became chief of staff in 1914 with the mission of modernizing its antiquated structure and equipment. War came before he could much advance the task, and in 1915 he began the period of command on the eastern Alpine frontier against the Austrians, which was to last until Caporetto (1917). He directed eleven battles of the Isonzo, each a more or less unsuccessful offensive, until in the twelfth the Austrians, with German assistance, forestalled his preparations

and destroyed his army. He was removed from command and, though found an anodyne post elsewhere, effectively disgraced. A perfectly competent general, his faults were those of many of the commanders of the First World War – intellectual arrogance, aloofness and a lack of understanding of and contact with ordinary soldiers.

Cambridge, George William Frederick Charles, Duke of (1819–1904) British field-marshal. A grandson of George III, he was commander-in-chief from 1856 to 1895, when he was at last succeeded by Wolseley (q.v.). His inflexibly conservative outlook was the principal brake on the reform of the British army between the Crimean and the Boer Wars.

Cambronne, Pierre Jacques Etienne (comte; 1770–1842) French general. When called upon to surrender the 'last square' of the Old Guard at Waterloo, 18 June 1815, Cambronne is officially reported to have cried, 'The Guard dies, it does not surrender,' but popularly believed to have shouted '*Merde*'. This obscenity is politely alluded to in, for example, French judicial proceedings as '*le mot de Cambronne*'.

Campbell, Colin (1st Baron Clyde; 1792–1863) British field-marshal. The son of a carpenter named Macliver, Colin assumed his mother's name when her brother, a colonel, put him to school and found him a commission in the 9th Regiment. He proved to be a fighting soldier of quite exceptional physical bravery. At the siege of San Sebastian in the Peninsular campaign, he left the bed where he was recovering from a double wound received in one assault to lead another, in which he was wounded for a third time; earlier – at Barossa, Terifa and Vittoria – he had shown extraordinary courage and leadership. When invalided home at the age of twenty-one he was a captain, with a wound pension of £100 a year – testimony, in an age parsimonious with rewards either of money or promotion to the lowly-born, of the exceptional mark he had made. It then took him twenty-five years to reach command of a regiment, despite long service abroad and financial help from friends in 'buying his steps'. In the 1840s his luck changed as campaigning called him again: for his part in the First China War (1842) he was made CB, and KCB for his role in the Second Sikh War. Promoted to command the Highland Brigade in the Crimea, his personification of its collective courage, particularly at Balaclava, made him almost overnight one of those popular heroes whom the Victorian public delighted to honour. On the news of the Indian Mutiny's outbreak reaching home in 1857, he was offered by Palmerston the command-in-chief and, though he arrived after Delhi and Cawnpore had been recovered, it was he who directed the second relief of Lucknow (1858). In 1858 his health failed and he returned home, to be loaded with honours before his briefly delayed death.

Canaris, Wilhelm (1888–1945) German admiral and chief of intelligence. A First World War U-boat commander, his reputation derives from his years as head of the *Abwehr* – the German joint services intelligence branch. The *Abwehr* was only one of several – some say thirty – intelligence organizations competing for primacy in Nazi Germany, but its aims in the competition were different from the others:

not to gain Hitler's ear but to guide Germany to a post-Nazi future. He and his agents consequently became entangled in a double game with the Allies abroad and with the opposition movement at home. His duplicity caused his removal in January 1944, his arrest after the July bomb plot and his death in Flossenburg camp in April 1945.

Canrobert, François Certain (1809–95) Marshal of France. Like so many of his generation, Canrobert made his name in the conquest of Algeria, where his dash in action, flaming locks and ready rapport with the rank and file made him an outstanding figure even among the *sabreurs* of the *Armée d'Afrique*. Louis-Napoleon made him his ADC general in 1850, and he took part in the imperial *coup d'état* of 1851. But though fearless in the face of personal danger, he shrank from responsibility and was not a success in the high command which imperial favour brought him; he actually resigned the supreme command in the Crimea in 1855, pleading incompatibility with his British opposite number. But he exercised subordinate command with great bravery at Solferino and Magenta in 1859, and, as a corps commander at Saint-Privat in 1870, inflicted on the Prussian Guards a murderous defeat. He subsequently entered politics, keeping alive the Bonapartist cause in the senate of the Third Republic.

Cardigan, Thomas James Brudenell, 7th Earl of (1797–1868) British general. A man of impossible character – stupid, overbearing, arrogant, vindictive – but ancient title and great wealth, he was appointed in 1854, despite his proven inability to sustain temperate relationships either with subordinates or superiors, to command the light cavalry brigade in the expedition to the Crimea. His immediate superior was Lord Lucan (q.v.), his estranged brother-in-law;

their estrangement was exacerbated by official quarrels in the field and culminated in Cardigan's leading of the Light Brigade to destruction at Balaclava (*see* Bosquet) through a misunderstanding of Lucan's orders.

Cardwell, Edward (1st Viscount Cardwell; 1813–86) British military reformer. Appointed secretary of state for war in Gladstone's government of 1868, he tackled the three major difficulties in the contemporary British military system – the army's unreadiness for war, its inability to provide adequate colonial garrisons and its officering by the antiquated system of the purchase of commissions. The fragmented infantry battalions of the army were grouped into double battalion regiments, one to remain at home feeding the other on imperial duty and providing, with associated militia and volunteer battalions, a home defence force and nucleus of an expeditionary corps. The institution of purchase was abolished, in the face of vociferous objections, the commission holders compensated, and entry to and promotion within the army regulated by competitive examination. Cardwell's reforms remained the most important in scope until those of Haldane (q.v.) in 1906–10.

Carnot, Lazare Nicolas Marguerite (*le grand Carnot*; 1753–1823) French general and minister of war; the 'Organizer of Victory'. A regular officer of engineers in the royal army, Carnot was an advocate of reform from the onset of the Revolution, became a member of the Legislative Assembly, then of the Convention and voted for the death of the king. Appointed a member of the Committee of Public Safety (August 1793), he became responsible for the raising of the young republic's armies (he raised fourteen in all) by combining new with old regiments in a system called *l'Amalgame*, ransacking the country for weapons to arm them and creating new arms factories. During the period of confusion and setback (April–July 1793) which followed the defection of Dumouriez (q.v.), victor of Valmy and Jemappes, to the Austrian and Prussian invaders, Carnot took effective command on the northern frontiers and won with Jourdan (q.v.) the stopgap victory of Wattignies (15–16 October 1793). The armies' success during the rest of the year and in 1794 drove the invaders back across the Rhine. But Carnot himself was under attack from politicians to his left in the Convention and the Committee. Although he escaped the Terror and was subsequently elected to the Directory, he had become isolated and between 1797 and 1799 was forced into exile. Recalled by the Consulate, he served as minister of war for six months in 1800 but was not employed by Napoleon during the Empire, the two being out of sympathy. In 1814, however, the fresh danger of invasion reawoke his patriotism and he sustained a remarkable defence of Antwerp. He served Napoleon as war minister during the Hundred Days, was condemned as a regicide at the Second Restoration and exiled, dying in Magdeburg. He bequeathed some influential works on fortification, and a grandson, Sadi, who was to become a president of the Third Republic.

Castelnau, Noel Marie Joseph Edouard de Curières de (1851–1944) French general. Just as Sarrail (q.v.) represented the anti-clerical interest in the faction-ridden army of the Third Republic, Castelnau – '*le capucin botté*' (friar in riding boots) – represented the militant Catholic. An aristocrat and a lay member of a religious order (hence his nickname), he was also a soldier of intellect and decision. Leaving Saint-Cyr to fight in the war of 1870, he was by 1914 a member of the *Conseil supérieur de la guerre*, had taken a major part in the preparation of War Plan XVII and was earmarked in case of hostilities for command of the Second Army. In August he led it into Lorraine, fighting at Château-Salins and Morhange, the only two offensive battles of the opening campaign. Forced into retreat, he successfully defended Nancy at the battle of *le Grand Couronné* and advanced the front to the line of the Franco-German frontier. Promoted commander of one of the army groups formed in 1915 (Centre) he directed the great (and partially successful) offensive in Champagne of 25 September. Out of favour during 1916–17, he resumed command of an army group in 1918 and directed the final offensive in Lorraine.

Castries, Christian Marie Ferdinand de la Croix de (1902–91). French general; the defender of Dien Bien Phu. Though much burdened by military ancestors – one a marshal of France – Castries failed to secure entry to Saint-Cyr and served as a cavalry trooper for three years. A superb horseman – he represented France, 1927–39 – and a daring pilot, he volunteered for the *Corps francs* (a sort of commando force) in 1939, fought with great dash and bravery behind German lines, but was eventually captured. Escaping at his fourth attempt, he joined the Free French forces in North Africa and distinguished himself in the invasions of Italy and southern France. In the postwar years he made a name as one of the most dashing commanders of a *groupe mobile* in Indo-China and was selected to command the aero-terrestrial base of Dien Bien Phu for a 'decisive battle' with the Vietminh in 1953. The 'decisive battle' shortly became an agonizing siege, which he lacked the qualities to manage, and command was effectively usurped by a group of parachutists which included the dynamic Bigeard (q.v.). Castries's courage and bearing throughout the siege, during

which he was promoted general, were nevertheless irreproachable.

Cavaignac, Louis Eugène (1802–57) French general. One of the notables of the conquest of Algeria – he succeeded Lamoricière (q.v.) as governor of Oran – he is remembered chiefly for his repression of the 'June Days' of 1848. That attempt by the Paris working class to transform the anti-Orleanist *coup d'état* into a genuine revolution so alarmed the Assembly that it voted dictatorial powers to the minister of war, who happened to be Cavaignac. He used them ferociously, extinguished the insurrection but relinquished his authority to stand against Louis-Napoleon in the presidential elections of December and was defeated. His father had voted in the Convention for the death of Louis XVI.

His son, **Jacques Cavaignac** (1853–1905), as minister of war also, played a central role in the prosecution of Dreyfus (q.v.).

Chanzy, Antoine Eugène Alfred (1823–83) French general. A Saint-Cyrien, he chose the Zouaves and served in Algeria for nearly thirty years, leaving it only to take part in the Franco-Austrian war of 1859 and the occupation of Rome which followed. Recalled to France by Gambetta after the defeat of the field army in 1870, he was appointed to command first the 16th Corps, then the Army of the Loire in the desperate and confused 'campaign in the provinces' over the winter of 1870–1. Michael Howard considers that 'He was incontestably the best of the French generals' of that tragic phase of the war.

Charles Albert (1798–1849) King of Sardinia (Piedmont), figurehead of the Italian national movement against Austria. Succeeding to the throne in 1832, Charles Albert was persuaded to mobilize the kingdom's forces against the Austrians during the popular uprising of

March 1848. He briefly liberated Lombardy from their control but was decisively defeated by Radetzky (q.v.) at Custozza, 22–5 July 1848, and Novara, 23 March 1849. He abdicated in favour of his son, Victor Emmanuel II, and died in exile.

Charles, Archduke of Austria, Duke of Teschen (1771–1847) Austrian field-marshal. Third son of Emperor Leopold II and brother of Emperor Francis I, Charles was adopted by the governor of the Austrian Netherlands, the Duke of Saxe-Teschen, and trained as a soldier. As a junior officer he fought at Jemappes, Neerwinden, Wattignies and Fleurus against the armies of the infant French republic. In 1796–7 he commanded the Army of the Rhine against Jourdan and Moreau (qq.v.) and won the victories of Rastadt, Amberg and Würzburg, which drove them back across the Rhine. Briefly in Italy, where he was not successful, he returned to the Rhine in 1799, beating Jourdan at Biberach and Stockach, but was himself then beaten by Masséna (q.v.) at Zurich, whither the focus of the campaign had shifted. He then fell into disfavour with the unstable Tsar Paul, retiring to Bohemia as governor but also busying himself with the reform of the army, and did not take command again until the 1809 campaign. Defeated at Eckmühl, 22 April, he inflicted on Napoleon the first serious defeat of his career at Aspern-Essling, 21–2 May, but was crushingly beaten in the great battle of Wagram, 5–6 July 1809. He must nevertheless be recognized as a really talented strategist and a serious student of the art of war.

Charles I (1600–49) King of England. When he raised his standard at Nottingham on 22 August 1642, signalling the start of the English Civil War (1642–6), Charles was a military novice. In the war which followed he revealed himself a more competent soldier than a politician or statesman. Campaigning with his armies in the field, Charles in general acted as a tempering and restraining influence upon them. On two occasions, after the battle of Edgehill (1642) and the first battle of Newbury (1643), he resisted attempts to set the Royalist army in a march on London, in an attempt to bring the war to a rapid conclusion. He learnt the arts of war quickly. At the battle of Cropredy Bridge (1644), not far from the site of Edgehill, he beat a larger Parliamentary army under Sir William Waller (q.v.), a defeat which Waller claimed 'broke the heart of his army'. He outmanœuvred the stolid Essex, and at the second battle of Newbury (October 1644) skilfully evaded the Parliamentary armies which seemed set to trap him, an evasion, again, the result of failure on the Parliamentary side. The security of the south and west for the Royalist cause were the result of his energetic campaigning. But it was Charles's choice to give battle at Naseby (1645), against Prince Rupert's (q.v.), strongest protestations: the result was a disaster for the Royalist cause. He was forced to flee the field, his standard was captured and his cause was in disarray.

In adversity, Charles continued to show both considerable determination and a reckless physical courage, which belied his reputation as an effete aesthete. Throughout his life he had a fatal propensity for taking bad advice, and in the military field he ran true to type. He allowed himself to be too much swayed both by his wife and his civilian advisers, notably Lord Digby, disregarding the advice of his professional military men. On his own behalf he waged a competent campaign, but with no flashes of inspiration.

Charles V (1500–58) Holy Roman emperor. The last Holy Roman emperor to be crowned by the Pope, Charles, from his election as emperor in 1519, was dominated by war or the threat of war.

An unmilitary figure who had the first taste of battle in 1535 at the siege of Tunis, he nevertheless spent over twenty years of his reign engaged in war. By far the greatest threat came from the Turks, who under Suleiman the Magnificent (q.v.), sultan for all save the first year of Charles's rule, had turned their attention from the east to the west. Both by land and sea the Turkish menace was ever present: in 1529 they reached the gates of Vienna, and barely a year passed without some Turkish activity in the Balkans or the Mediterranean. Charles's other enemies – the French, the Papacy of Clement VII, the German Protestants – were intermittent problems, and he was reasonably successful against all of them. Francis I was taken prisoner at Pavia (1525), Rome sacked and the Pope captured (1527), and the Protestant armies shattered at the battle of Mühlberg (1547). But no problem came singly, and he proved unable to resolve the extraordinary complexity of the difficulties which engaged him. In the end the dream which he sustained of the united empire of Christendom was found to be a vain, and ungovernable, aspiration. When he resigned as emperor in 1556 he split his territories between his son, Philip, who took the Spanish inheritance, and his brother, Ferdinand, who was elected emperor.

Charles V of Lorraine, Alexander, Prince (1712–80) Imperial soldier. Charles's fortunes were tied closely to those of his elder brother Francis, who married Maria Theresa, heiress to the Habsburg domains, in 1736. (The Lorraine family had long been connected with the Austrian Habsburgs, and the family lived in Vienna after 1723.) Charles joined the Austrian army in 1736 and took part in the unsuccessful Turkish campaign of 1737–9, which resulted in substantial Austrian losses at the treaty of Belgrade (1739). When the war of the Austrian Succession (1740–8)

broke out, in defence of Maria Theresa's inheritance of the Austrian empire, he and his brother took the field on the side of their adopted country. Charles led an army to counter the incursion by French 'volunteers' and Bavarian troops into Bohemia, although he met with little success. In 1742 he faced Frederick II, 'the Great', of Prussia, the first of many encounters. On this occasion Charles attacked at Chotusitz; but he was driven off by the Prussians after a sharp encounter. Turning again, he attacked the French who had occupied Prague. The great danger he faced for much of the war was of an attack in the flank or the rear from the enemy – French, Bavarian or Prussian – which he was not engaging. Time and again he was forced to interrupt a crucial operation by the need to face a fresh enemy. But in June 1742 the Prussians left the war by the treaty of Breslau, and Charles was able to turn his attentions to the west. For two years he operated with the allies – England, Holland, and some of the small German states – probing the enemy's lines along the Rhine. But Charles was outmanœuvred by his French opponent Coigny, and his series of attacks failed.

In 1744 Frederick the Great decided that the time was ripe to re-enter the war, and Charles moved east again to face him. The armies sparred and in June 1745, as Charles advanced into Prussian-occupied Silesia, they met for a decisive battle, at Hohenfriedburg. Here the Austrians and their Saxon allies lost 16,000 men to the Prussians' 1000. Frederick pursued the remains of Charles's army into Bohemia, but himself retreated as the Austrian relief armies hurried to fill the gap. Barely two months later, in September 1745, Frederick trounced Charles again at the battle of Sohr. Here, by a display of tactical virtuosity, he won the advantage of the ground from Charles, and with a surprise oblique attack caught the Austrians off balance. The result was 8000 Austrian dead and wounded for negligible Prussian casualties. Two months later, at Hennersdorf, Frederick caught him again, attacked and delivered another resounding defeat, turning swiftly to catch a second Austrian column at Görlitz. In their various encounters Charles was invariably confounded by the nerve and tactical genius of his opponent, and the superb discipline and fighting skill of the Prussian soldiers.

When the Seven Years' War (1756–63) broke out, Charles again faced the invading Prussians, this time in front of Prague. The battle was hard fought, each side losing about 14,000 men, troops which Frederick could ill afford to sacrifice. Displaying the full reserves of his generalship, Frederick demolished the Austrians and French at Rossbach in early November, and hastened to meet Daun (q.v.) and Charles who had defeated a Prussian army at Breslau. On 6 December 1757, in probably the greatest of his battles – Leuthen – he used every advantage of terrain, flanking assaults and surprise to destroy the Austrian army. He confused Charles into believing that the main attack was to come on his right wing, and then delivered a shattering blow, combining infantry and artillery, to the left wing. Only nightfall saved the Austrian army, completely wrongfooted despite herculean efforts by Daun and Charles to reconstruct the line of battle, and the survivors streamed back across the Schwiednitz river into Breslau. Charles had lost more than 20,000 captured, almost 7000 killed, and 116 guns: equally galling to Austrian pride was the loss of 51 colours. Victory had not been bought cheaply, and Frederick had almost as many dead as Charles. But whereas Frederick went on to further dazzling victories, Charles's career was in ruins. He was relieved of his command and returned, with some pleasure, to his position as governor of the

Netherlands, which he had held since 1744. He was an able administrator and highly respected by his subjects. As a soldier he had the misfortune to be matched time and again against a consummate military genius; it is no real discredit that he was worsted. Within the canons of the coventional warfare of the day, he was competent and conscientious. He had a good eye for terrain and considerable tenacity in battle. These were not small gifts.

Charles XII (1682–1718) King of Sweden. A character whose achievements and vices have become more mythical than real. Charles was a brilliant organizer and administrator, but a battlefield commander of lesser stature. He inherited from his father Charles XI a state and army which had been ruthlessly reformed and tested by experience; the army was without equal in Europe for its fierce offensive spirit and its preference for cold steel rather than fire-power as the decisive elements in a battle. But Charles XII's own interest in military affairs was consuming. His personal bodyguard, the *drabants*, were put through a programme of arduous training, in which he participated; the army was enlarged from 65,000 to 77,000, and the fleet much strengthened. He encouraged the successful generals whom his father had appointed, in particular Karl Gustaf Rehnskjold, as well as Horn, Stenbock and Sparre, and prepared for war against the many enemies who saw the accession of an adolescent in 1697, in succession to such a successful soldier as Charles XI, as an opportunity to pillage the Swedish empire. At the outbreak of the Great Northern War (1700–21), which was to occupy the whole of Charles's life, Sweden faced Denmark, Poland and Saxony, and, latterly, Russia. Much of the credit for the decisive Swedish moves early in the war, including the attack on the Danes in Zealand (1700) and the defeat of the

Russians at Narva in November of the same year, has been given to Charles, but it belongs to Rehnskjold. Not until the victory of Kliszow (1702), where 12,000 Swedes beat 16,000 Saxons, did Charles make a significant contribution to the military success of the Swedish army, and only in the following year did he undertake an independent action, free from the tutelage of his generals. At Pultusk (1703), he beat a Saxon army of 3500, with Saxon losses of a thousand for twenty Swedish dead. Poland fell into civil war, with Charles supporting Stanislas Leszczynski against his enemy, Augustus II of Poland (q.v.). In 1705, the Saxons were beaten again at Punitz and Wszowa, while Rehnskjold trounced a force double his size at Franstadt (1706). At the treaty of Altranstadt, after the invasion of Saxony itself had forced Augustus to negotiate, all Charles's objectives in Poland were gained: he was now determined to march east and dispose of the Russian threat. He built up his army, and in particular its supply services, for what he recognized would be an arduous and difficult campaign, and on New Year's Day, 1708, he marched into Russia with an army of almost 45,000, the largest he had ever commanded. He had little regard for the Russians as soldiers but at the battle of Holowczyn (1708), where they fought stubbornly against the more skilful Swedes, he was forced to recognize that the task before him was more fearsome than he had anticipated. Through the summer of 1708, while the Russians adopted a scorched earth policy, Charles attempted to create a co-ordinated policy of alliances against the Russians by using the Cossacks and the Tartars to attack them from the south. But Peter the Great (q.v.) immediately struck against Mazeppa, the Hetman of the Cossacks, and deposed him, thus robbing Charles of support on which he had depended. A more shattering blow came with the destruction of the Swedish supply train under Loewenhaupt (October 1708), which left the Swedes to face winter with dwindling resources. When spring came, Charles moved against the fortress of Poltava. Peter attacked him, with over 40,000 men to the Swedish 20,000; worst of all, Charles was wounded before the battle by a chance shot in the foot, which had festered, and could not maintain his usual active command. The battle was a decisive Russian victory, which was to be expected in the circumstances of their massive superiority in numbers, and Charles was hurried away on a litter to escape capture. He took refuge with the Turks, his rather wayward allies; for five years, 1709–14, he ruled Sweden from the camp at Bender, trying always to construct an effective force which would allow him to launch a new attack on Russia. Tension grew over the years with his Turkish hosts, and in 1713, he was actually besieged in his camp, New Bender, by a huge Turkish force; the siege was something of a formality, and despite the growth of the myth about it, the Swedes suffered only fourteen casualties and the Turks, forty. Eventually, the complicated negotiations for his return were concluded, and he made an epic secret dash across Europe, arriving at the Swedish outpost of Stralsund in November 1714. He now took command in person of the defence of Sweden, and began to put into effect the military and administrative reforms he had formulated at Bender. He fended off the assaults of his enemies, while forging a new army for renewed conquest: in the creation of the army for the Norwegian campaign of 1717–18, his administrative talents came to the fore. He revolutionized the artillery, making it much more mobile and faster firing, and through his active support for Carl Cronstedt, his artillery expert, made it the most effective in Europe. The Swedish army, already renowned for its power of attack, became more flexible as a result of Charles's tactical reforms, and the harmony in manœuvre between the various arms was marvelled at by contemporaries. Charles was killed by a chance enemy bullet at the siege of Fredriksten. His achievement lay not so much in the epic military encounters which were the basis for the myth, but in the effective absolutism which he established, enabling him to rule Sweden from the isolation of Bender or from his camp in the field.

Château-Renault, François Louis, marquis de (1637–1716) French admiral. Louis XIV's admirals, like many of his generals, displayed a high level of general competence, but their handicap lay in a lack of resources allocated to the navy. The navy was virtually the creation of Jean-Baptiste Colbert, Louis XIV's finance minister, and possessed some 270 vessels in 1677. The ships were well built and thoroughly provisioned, both in men and equipment. But in the latter part of the reign, after Colbert's death, his reforms began to lose their effect. Château-Renault nevertheless played an important role in the Irish campaign of 1689, for a time cutting communications between Ireland and the English mainland, blockading Londonderry, and ferrying French troops to support James II's attempt to recover his throne. He fended off an English fleet under Torrington (q.v.) at Bantry Bay (1689), and in 1690 he led the vanguard of the fleet under de Tourville (q.v.), which beat Torrington off Beachy Head. Control of the seas now passed to the French, but they failed to exploit it.

Chelmsford, Frederic Augustus Thesiger, 2nd Baron (1827–1905) British general. Commander of British troops in South Africa during the Zulu War, 1879, Chelmsford lost a major part of his army to Cetewayo's impis at Isandhlwana on 22 January, a disaster rivalled in scale among Afro-European battles only by Adowa (*see* Baratieri) and not fully offset by his subsequent victory at Ulundi, 4 July.

Chennault, Claire Lee (1898–1953) American airman. A brilliant aerobatic flyer and veteran pilot of the First World War (19th Pursuit Squadron), Chennault left the American air force in 1937. He organized an air force of American volunteer pilots to aid Chiang Kai-shek's armies in their fight with Japan before America's entry into the war. In 1942 these Flying Tigers were incorporated as the 14th (Volunteer) Army Air Force and Chennault was made a major-general. In early 1942 the force destroyed 300 Japanese aircraft, though flying only 250 itself, and blunted the Japanese offensive in Chekiang and Kiang. By July 1943 Chennault's air force commanded the Chinese skies. He resigned his command in 1945 in protest at official demands to disband the remaining American volunteer element of the Chinese air force.

Cherwell, Lord (Frederick Alexander Lindemann, 1st Viscount Cherwell; 1886–1957) Scientific adviser to Winston Churchill. Though born at Baden-Baden of an Alsatian father, 'the Prof' was British by nationality and passionately British in sentiment. An able experimental physicist and a dynamic scientific administrator (he became director of the Royal Flying Corps Experimental Physics Station at Farnborough in 1914), he explained mathematically why an aircraft got into spin, hitherto thought fatal, and how it could be got out, deliberately putting a plane into a spin to demonstrate his belief in the accuracy of his calculations. Between the wars he became a close friend of Winston Churchill (q.v.) and in 1940 his personal scientific adviser (officially paymaster-general 1942–5). As such, he was the first scientist to influence directly the conduct of a war, his belief in the efficacy of 'area' bombing being crucial to its adoption by Bomber Command, though his advice on this, and many other matters, was disputed by other government scientists. Arrogant, aloof, singleminded, crankish, Cherwell made many enemies and few friends. But Churchill believed in the soundness of his advice and the British war effort probably benefited from Churchill's listening to a single scientific voice, Hitler's listening to many being the cause of a wasteful diffusion of scientific effort in wartime Germany.

Chiang Kai-shek (1887–1975) Chinese general and head of state. Born in Feng-hwa, Chekiang, and trained as an officer in Tokyo, Chiang Kai-shek belonged to the generation of young Chinese who attempted, under the inspiration of Sun Yat-sen, to transform their decayed empire into a modern state. At Sun's bidding he became commandant of the new republic's military academy at Whampoa and in 1926 took command of the army which set out to establish the power of the central government over the war lords and the Communists, into whose hands the provinces of China had fallen. By a mixture of negotiation and military action he achieved the nominal submission of most (though not of the Communists) by 1928. From 1931 he had to deal also with the incursion of the Japanese, first in Manchuria, then from 1937 in heartland China. Their success forced him to withdraw the capital from Nanking to Chungking in the interior from which, supplied with plentiful American aid and air support after December 1941, he waged an unrelenting struggle in China and Burma until the end of the war. Acclaimed as the symbol of Chinese resistance to the Axis, and accepted as the co-equal of Stalin, Churchill and Roosevelt, he emerged from the war as Asia's leading statesman and its representative in world politics. But his failure – caused partly by his

concentration on the struggle against the Japanese – to extinguish Communist power in China led shortly to his downfall. In the civil war with the armies of Mao Tse-tung (q.v.), which broke out in 1947, his forces were overwhelmed and in 1949 he withdrew their remnants to Formosa (Taiwan), though America and many of its allies continued to recognize the legitimacy of his regime until 1972.

Ch'ien Lung (1711–99) Chinese emperor. Under Ch'ien Lung, the fourth Ching emperor, the Manchu empire of China reached its greatest extent. Coming to the throne in succession to his grandfather, K'anghsi, he extended effective Chinese control in Tibet (1751), conquered Sinkiang (1755–9), and in 1790–2 sent an expeditionary force into Nepal. The latter exploit marked the zenith of the Manchus' military power. Once more China was an effective force in central Asia, and Ch'ien Lung united territorial expansion to a period of high prosperity and economic development. Although he notionally abdicated in 1796, he in fact ruled, with the aid of his powerful minister Ho Shen, until his death.

Chodkiewicz, Jan Karol (1560–1621) Polish soldier and cavalry general. Born into a leading Ruthene family, Chodkiewicz created a 'godly army' of outstanding cavalry, effective both against the Swedes and Turks, two totally different styles of warfare. He established his reputation in a great campaign against the Turks in 1600, under the command of Jan Zamoyski, which drove back the invaders. But the real conflict was for the control of the Baltic littoral with Sweden. After the Turkish war, he turned to the battles in Livonia (where he had his family roots). The invading Swedes under Charles of Soder-mannland were well trained, but unimaginative in their tactics; in particular, they relied heavily on fire-power both for offence and defence, lacking a solid body of trained pikemen. The Polish calvary, possibly the best in Europe, shattered the Swedish ranks, charging at full tilt into the ill-protected lines. Outside formal battle, Chodkiewicz developed great skill in harrying an enemy, breaking his morale and destroying his communications. The traditional problem with many cavalry armies was discipline, but Chodkiewicz trained and controlled his men to a high degree.

He received little support, either financial or in manpower, from the Polish king Sigismund III (q.v.), but with a small army he expelled the Swedes from Riga, and took the towns of Dorpat (1601) and Reval. In 1601 he smashed the Swedish army again at Weissenstein. Charles, now Charles IX of Sweden, returned to the war with an army which had been re-equipped to withstand the Polish attack. But his men had not been properly trained in so short a time and again Chodkiewicz won a dramatic victory. At Kircholm (1604) his 4500 lancers and swordsmen destroyed a Swedish army of 14,000, by the simple expedient of drawing the Swedes into an incautious attack and then turning swiftly on them to demolish the ragged lines. Once again, cavalry, well led, could rout any infantry not well supported by pikemen. In all, the Swedes lost 9000 men. Chodkiewicz now turned into Poland again, putting down a revolt against Sigismund (1606–7). In 1609 a new Swedish attack was driven off from Riga; and after Charles's death in 1611 a truce was made with Sweden.

Chodkiewicz now turned to lead the Polish attack on Russia, which was much weakened by dynastic strife. In 1610 the Poles had taken Moscow and Chodkiewicz hoped to relieve the Polish garrisons, now hard pressed. But he was ill-supported once again, and in the vast waste of Russia his troops mutinied for lack of pay; he was forced to retreat to Smolensk. A pattern of border raiding

soon developed, with neither side gaining much of an advantage, until the treaty of Deulino (1618) established an uneasy peace and consolidated the Polish conquests. The Turks, meanwhile, had taken advantage of Poland's occupation in the east and invaded the Ukraine. Chodkiewicz turned to meet this new threat and succeeded in stemming the Turkish advance. At the battle of Chocim (1621), a Polish army of 75,000 defeated a Turkish host of 200,000 led by Sultan Osman, but Chodkiewicz was killed in the struggle. He was one of the great cavalry commanders of history, using the rough material at his disposal and moulding it into a flexible, disciplined army, capable of lightning movement and pulverizing blows in battle. He influenced the form the Swedish army adopted under Gustavus Adolphus (q.v.), for the experience of the wars with Poland changed the whole attitude of the Swedes towards cavalry.

Chuikov, Vasilii Ivanovich (1900–82) Marshal of the Soviet Union. A volunteer to the infant Red Army, Chuikov became a regular officer after the Civil War, escaped the great purge and spent 1941–2 in China as military adviser to Chiang Kai-shek (q.v.). On his return he became commander of the 62nd Army (later renamed the 8th Guards Army for its distinguished conduct), which in late 1942 found itself engaged in the defence of Stalingrad, providing the soldiers who occupied the tiny strip of ruins on the west bank of the Volga, which was all of the city that the Russians had prevented from falling into German hands. Chuikov maintained his command post on the west bank and by inspired leadership sustained the defence until Zhukov (q.v.) could organize the decisive counteroffensive. He later led his army in the recapture of Odessa and the assault on Berlin, became commander-in-chief of the Soviet occupation forces in Germany and eventually deputy minister of defence in the Russian government. He was the author of an account of the defence of Stalingrad, *The Beginning of the Road*, remarkable for the freshness of its style and the frankness of its judgements.

Chu Teh (1886–1976) Marshal of the People's Republic of China (all ranks, including that of marshal, were abolished in the PLA in 1965). The senior of the ten marshals created in 1955 and the leading Communist general of the civil war, Chu Teh was born of peasant parents in Szechwan and educated at the Yunnan Military Academy, where he joined Sun Yat-sen's revolutionary movement. In 1921 he gave up his military career and sailed for Europe, where he met Chou Enlai and joined the Chinese Communist Party. On his return to China in 1925 he became a Red Army commander in the south and in 1930 was named commander of all the Chinese Communist armies. During the civil war he commanded all the Liberation armies.

Cialdini, Enrico (1811–92) Italian general. A soldier not so much of fortune as of ideology. Cialdini's name crops up on the 'liberal' side in the minor and major wars of southern Europe, 1830–70. Born in the duchy of Modena, he took part in the revolt organized by Mazzini against the Austrian puppet government (1831) and was exiled to Portugal, where he fought for Queen Maria against the pretender Miguel, 1832–4. In 1835 he was in Spain, fighting for Queen Maria Christina against the Carlists, but returned to Italy in time for the nationalist war against the Austrians, 1848–9. Promoted general in the royal Piedmontese army, he distinguished himself in the victory of Palestro over the Austrians, 30 May 1859, and in the Piedmontese campaign to assist Garibaldi (q.v.),

when he defeated the papal forces at Castelfidardo, 18 September 1860.

Clark, Mark Wayne (1896–1984) American general. Born into a military family and educated at West Point, Clark was wounded in France in the First World War. In 1942 he was appointed commander of ground forces in Europe as Eisenhower's deputy. Prior to America's first great European military operation, the Torch landings in North Africa, he was landed in Algeria from a submarine to make contact with the Vichy French garrison; after the landings, he negotiated a ceasefire with Admiral Darlan (q.v.) and recognized him as head of state, a move not without repercussions. In the invasion of Italy he commanded the Fifth Army, directed the unsuccessful Anzio operation and was responsible for the controversial decision to bomb the monastery of Monte Cassino. He made a triumphal entry into Rome, 4 June 1944, and in December succeeded Alexander (q.v.) as Allied commander in Italy, directing the campaign to its conclusion. He was subsequently American commander in Austria and then in the Far East. On retirement he became commandant of the Citadel, a private military academy, in Charleston, South Carolina. An excellent commander of multi-national armies and an able strategist, Clark is perhaps unfairly best remembered for his photogenic good looks and flair for press relations.

Clausewitz, Karl Maria von (1780–1831) Philosopher of war. His military career was respectably successful. Born at Burg, near Magdeburg, he joined the Prussian army, fought against the French on the Rhine in 1793–4, and secured entry to the Berlin military academy. There he attracted the attention of Scharnhorst (q.v.), transferred to the staff on which he served during the 1806 campaign and was captured after Auerstadt. On his release he became an assistant to Scharnhorst in the secret reform of the Prussian army, was selected as military tutor to the crown prince (the future Wilhelm I) and in 1812 chose, like many other Prussian officers, to defect to Russia rather than serve Napoleon in the enforced collaboration between his country and France. In Russian service, he was a staff officer with Puhl and Wittgenstein (q.v.) and helped negotiate the convention of Taurrogen, which brought the army of Yorck von Wartenburg (q.v.) over to the Russian side. Readmitted to the Prussian army in 1814, he was chief of staff to Thielmann at Ligny and Wavre.

But his real and lasting achievements were of the mind. In 1818 he was promoted major-general and appointed director of the *Kriegsakademie*, the Berlin staff college, founded in 1810, which was subsequently to serve as a model for all foreign staff colleges. But curiously his post was a sinecure and he devoted his leisure to writing about war. A good deal of his writing was historical and little of this has been translated. But his philosophical work – heavily. though apparently unconsciously influenced by Kantian and Hegelian idealism – discovered after his death (in the great cholera epidemic of 1831) has been disseminated throughout the world. The delicacy of his analysis and its eclecticism defies summary. His ideals, moreover, have been as much misapplied as understood. But their main thrust was a) to depict war as 'the continuation of state (peace) policy', instead of as a disjunctive activity, and b) to make the destruction of the enemy's main force by a decisive battle (*Hauptschlacht*) the proper object of a general's strategy, rather than the seeking of advantage by manœuvre, evasion or delay. His ideas captured the mind of the Prussian army, underlying its strategy in the wars of 1866 and 1870, and were profoundly influential on all armies in the First and Second World Wars. The development

of nuclear weapons makes the *Hauptschlacht* too dangerous an object for which to play, and the Clausewitzian philosophy has, in the nuclear age, come under heavy and continuous criticism. But as a thesis in strategic dialectic it retains a permanent force.

Clerfayt, François Sebastien Charles Joseph de Croix (comte de Clerfayt; 1733–98) Austrian field-marshal. Born at Bruille in the Austrian Netherlands (Belgium), Clerfayt fought in the Seven Years' War and against the Turks, and in 1792 was given an Austro-Prussian corps which he commanded at Valmy and Jemappes. Later he raised the siege of Maastricht, took Le Quesnoy and contributed to the victory at Neerwinden. In 1795 he commanded the imperial army which recaptured Mainz from Custine (q.v.)

Clinton, Sir Henry (1738–95) British general. The only senior British general in the American War of Independence with a natural connection with North America (he was born in Newfoundland), Clinton joined the British army in 1757 and had a rapid if not meteoric rise: by 1772 he was a general and was sent as second-in-command to Sir William Howe (q.v.) at the start of the war (1775–83). In 1778 Howe resigned his command and Clinton took over. He was instrumental in developing the southern strategy which produced such dramatic results in 1780. Savannah was captured, and Clinton arrived with 14,000 to take Charleston; the city fell in May 1780 and Clinton, convinced that the southern campaign was completed, returned to his base in New York leaving Cornwallis (q.v.) with 8000 men to mop up the American remnants. But under Nathanael Greene (q.v.) the American cause rallied. Clinton soon disagreed violently with Cornwallis's assessment of the situation. As at Saratoga, confused orders and bad communications led to a disaster: Cornwallis, ordered into an untenable position, was forced to surrender to Washington at Yorktown in October 1781, the anniversary of Burgoyne's (q.v.) surrender at Saratoga. Clinton resigned his command and returned to England. Like so many generals of the American war, he hastened to exculpate himself with *A Narrative of the Campaign of 1781*, which was published in 1783. Cornwallis was not amused, for Clinton contrived to shift the blame for the disaster on to him. In 1794 Clinton was appointed governor of Gibraltar, where he died.

Clive, Robert, 1st Baron (1725–74) British soldier and administrator. In two great military enterprises – the capture of Arcot (1751) and the battle of Plassey (1757) – Clive frustrated French designs in India (*see* Dupleix) and established the foundations of secure British rule over the subcontinent. The capture of Arcot, the capital of Chanda Sahib, a leading French supporter, was maintained with a tiny garrison against an army of 10,000. But Clive survived a siege of fifty days, and Arcot remained in English hands. Six years later at Plassey, his military talents now recognized, Clive faced the army of Suraja Dowla, 50,000 strong, and a force of 53 guns under French command, with a force of 1100 Europeans, 2100 native troops and 10 guns. He relied on fire-power and a forceful attack on the shattered Indian ranks to sweep them away in confusion. He lost twenty-three men killed and gained not only Bengal, but fame and fortune for himself.

Cochrane, Thomas, 10th Earl of Dundonald (1775–1860) British admiral (admiral also in the service of Chile, Brazil and Greece). Eldest son of the ninth earl, the well-known experimental chemist, Cochrane chose the family calling and entered the navy in 1793. As captain of a sloop, 1800–1, he took over fifty prizes and in 1809, in command of a fleet of fireships, he broke into the roadsteads at Aix where the French fleet was blockaded. His superior, Gambier, was however miles away and did not come to his support, so that only four enemy ships were destroyed. For the action Cochrane was knighted and Gambier voted the thanks of Parliament – at which Cochrane protested so violently that he was court-martialled, but acquitted. He had been elected to Parliament himself in 1807 and used his seat to protest at abuses in the administration of the navy. Now on such bad terms with the Admiralty that it would not offer him suitable employment, he devoted his time to furthering the exposure in Parliament of naval malpractices, until in 1814 he was tried and imprisoned for a fraud (of which he was innocent). Dismissed from the service, degraded from his knighthood and expelled from Parliament, he was almost immediately re-elected by his constituents, who refused to believe that Cochrane was guilty. He himself always suspected that the Admiralty was responsible for implicating him and, after serving his term and paying his fine – for which public subscription reimbursed him – he returned to Parliament to carry on his campaign.

In 1818, however, Cochrane was offered by the Chilean government command of its infant navy in its war of liberation from Spain. By a campaign of blockade and raiding, he disrupted the Spanish coastal defences of Chile and then turning to Peru compelled by his almost unaided efforts – the army of San Martin (q.v.) which he had embarked playing little effective part – the capitulation of Lima, the capital (6 July 1821) and of the Spanish government of the colony. He was for a short while a hero; but, falling out with the government of liberation, accepted in 1825 an offer from the emperor of Brazil to command its navy in the war of liberation against Portugal, which he did until peace was signed between the two countries. He managed, nevertheless, to part from the Brazilians on bad terms and at once accepted command of the Greek navy – one constructed by a loan secured by British supporters of her independence – in her war of liberation with Turkey. This episode was not a fruitful one, few of Greece's ships ever appearing, though all the money evaporated.

In 1832, after much effort, Cochrane secured reappointment in the Royal Navy and devoted himself thenceforward to experiments with steam and screw propulsion, of which he was an early proponent. In 1847 he was reinstated in the Order of the Bath, in 1848 he was appointed commander-in-chief on the West Indian station, and in 1854 nominated rear-admiral of the United Kingdom (he was by then full admiral in the navy). He was not employed in the Crimean War, though much consideration was given to his 'secret war plan' (which he had been advocating since 1811) and which he declared (and the Admiralty apparently believed) provided an infallible method of overwhelming the defences of Sebastopol and Cronstadt. The Admiralty eventually rejected it on the grounds of humanity and its nature was kept secret until 1908, when it was revealed to be a scheme for the discharge of sulphur fumes – a prefiguration of poison gas warfare. Cochrane remains an enigma, frustrated genius or an embittered eccentric according to taste.

Codrington, (Sir) Edward (1770–1851) British admiral. Flag lieutenant to Howe (q.v.) at the Glorious First of June, 1794, and captain of the *Orion* at Trafalgar – in which battle Nelson had nominated him to lead the third column, were one to have been formed – Codrington went in 1827 to command the Anglo-Russo-French fleet ordered to

cruise off Greece in the course of its war of independence from Turkey. On 20 October he destroyed the Turkish fleet under Tahir Pasha at Navarino, the action which effectually decided the outcome of the war; like the Nile battle, it was fought close inshore with the ships at anchor. Codrington was held to have exceeded his instructions but vindicated himself and was later employed as commander-in-chief, Portsmouth.

Collingwood, Cuthbert (1st Baron Collingwood; 1758–1810) British admiral, Nelson's principal lieutenant. Entering the navy at eleven in his cousin's frigate *Shannon*, his first experience of action was at Bunker's Hill, where he was put ashore with a landing party of sailors. For his good service he was promoted lieutenant. Court-martialled for surliness to his captain in 1777, but acquitted, he had the good fortune in 1778 to be posted first lieutenant in the *Lowestoft*, the captain of which was Nelson, with whom his career was henceforth to be entwined. Captain of the *Barfleur* at the Glorious First of June (1794), he commanded the *Excellent* at Cape St Vincent, 14 February 1797, took two Spanish first rates and assisted the *Captain*, Nelson's ship, in the capture of a third. For the next eight years he was almost continuously employed on blockade of the French and Spanish coasts (consoled meanwhile by promotion to rear and then vice-admiral), but in 1805 was appointed to a squadron assisting Nelson to pursue the French fleet which had broken out of harbour. Under Nelson's command he led the lee division, when the combined French and Spanish fleets were brought to battle at Trafalgar at the end of the chase, and at its head broke their line. He was ennobled for his part in the battle.

Collins, Michael (1890–1922) Irish revolutionary. From humble origins, Collins rose by ability, force of character, charm and ruthlessness to leadership in the independence movement which grew out of the defeat of the Dublin rising of Easter 1916. Elected a Westminster MP in 1918, he, like the other Sinn Fein candidates, refused to sit in London, assembling in a Dail (parliament) in Ireland and creating a parallel machinery of government in which he held the post of minister of finance. He raised substantial loans at home and in America, but his main achievement was as director of intelligence and subversion, his early career as a post office clerk equipping him with a useful understanding of the (British) enemy's channels of communications. A wanted man, he eluded capture though taking little care to hide himself and organized ruthless counterblows against the British intelligence service, the most notable of which was the murder in their beds of twelve British intelligence officers on one Sunday morning. In December 1921 he was a member of the delegation which agreed in London to limited independence for an Irish Free State and, on the movement splitting over this, became chairman of the provisional government, and later, when civil war broke out, commander of the Free State army. He was killed in an ambush by republican forces on 22 August 1922. The 'Big Fellow' is an important figure in Irish revolutionary legend and has claims to be regarded as the chief pioneer of modern urban guerrilla warfare.

Condé, Louis II de Bourbon, 'The Great' (1621–86) It was remarked that on his deathbed, sparing time from a hastily made acceptance of the benefits of religion, Condé took time to write to Louis XIV reminding him of his status as premier Prince of the Blood. An overweening arrogance persisted in him from childhood, a confidence which also served to make him an extremely effective attacking soldier. He sprang into military prominence with an astonishing

victory over the Spanish at Rocroi (1643). At the age of twenty-two he smashed the *tercios* (infantry) under Francisco de Melo (q.v.) by concentrated artillery fire: but Rocroi, in keeping with his personality, was essentially a cavalry battle. The duc d'Enghien (as he was until his father died in 1646) took command over Turenne (q.v.) in the Rhineland campaign in 1644 and capped his reputation with a fine campaign in the Netherlands, although, to his fury, command was given to Gaston D'Orléans. Mazarin sent him to Spain, anxious to remove so successful a young prince from the French scene, and although he failed to take Lerida the campaign was a strategic success for France. But Condé was needed in the north, and he waged a brilliant battle at Lens (1648), defeating the imperial army under the Archduke Leopold Wilhelm. But after the close of the Thirty Years' War, Condé's close involvement in the civil wars of the Fronde (1648–53) served to breed great distrust between him and the young King Louis XIV. Although Condé stood aloof from the first Fronde and helped to suppress it, his ambition and haughty pride made Mazarin fearful: he imprisoned both Condé who had not entered the rebellion, and his brother Conti, who had, together with their brother-in-law the duc de Longueville, for thirteen months. Freed by popular pressure, he sought to dominate the court, until he overstepped his power and was forced into open rebellion, allying himself with the Spanish (1652). He was sentenced to death *in absentia* as a rebel in 1654. He fought the royal forces under Turenne with some success, but the Spanish were never willing to trust him entirely and kept him on a short rein, with few troops or support. The defeat at the battle of the Dunes (1658) at which Condé was present was not his fault, for he advised against giving battle in an exposed position, under fire from the sea and without proper artillery support. When peace was made in 1659 a general amnesty was declared, and Condé was able to return home.

Although theoretically reconciled with the king, Louis XIV never fully forgot Condé's treason and never reposed his full confidence in him, as he did in Turenne. In the War of Devolution (1667–8), and the Dutch war (1672–8), Condé commanded armies in Flanders under the watchful eye of the king. He was almost invariably successful in battle, and at Seneffe (1674) his power and audacity in attack enabled him to defeat a Dutch army of 67,000 with scarcely a third of that number. But he was hampered, as was Turenne, by Louis's interference: unencumbered by the royal presence his campaign might have achieved even greater success. With Turenne's death in 1675, Condé hurried to defend Alsace against Montecuccoli (q.v.), and completed the work of forcing the imperial army back over the Rhine. In this last campaign he was already stricken with the gout which was to make him almost totally inactive, and he retired to his house at Chantilly. Although he did not possess Turenne's subtlety as a general, he was a military commander of a high order.

Coningham, Sir Arthur (1895–1948) British air marshal. After an early military career spent with troops from New Zealand, where he had been brought up (hence his RAF nickname 'Maori'), Coningham became a specialist in long-distance flying. In 1939 commander of No. 4 Bomber Group, he took over the Desert Air Force in 1941 and directed its operations in support of the Eighth Army throughout its long fight with the *Afrika Korps*. He later commanded the Anglo-American 1st Tactical Air Force in the Tunisian and Southern Italian Company, and in 1944 took over command of the 2nd Tactical Air Force, which supported the Allied invasion of northwest Europe and the liberation campaign.

Conrad von Hötzendorf, Franz, Frhr. (1852–1925) Austrian field-marshal. The last of the *feldherrn* in the Benedek–Radetzky (qq.v.) tradition, Conrad von Hötzendorf was chief of the general staff from 1907 to 1917. Highly educated, an accomplished linguist (a difficult reputation to acquire in a polyglot state) and a man of wide political understanding, he was nevertheless an advocate before 1914 of aggressive war, either against Serbia or Italy, an initiative which he believed would stifle separatism within the multinational empire. It was his insistence on threatening Serbia with attack in July 1914 which helped to precipitate the First World War. He is usually held to have been a brilliant strategist, whose plans were frustrated by the weakness of the machine through which he had to work or, alternatively, stolen by the Germans, but that estimation must be taken largely on the say-so of his admirers. He was replaced, on the death of Franz Josef, by Arz von Straussenberg (q.v.).

Cordoba, Gonzalo Fernandez, Conde de (1453–1515) Spanish soldier. Cordoba, *el Gran Capitan*, was one of the soldiers of genius in the sixteenth century, a general whose skills embraced innovation in the organization of armies, a solid grasp of logistics, subtle diplomacy, as well as luck in battle. Born a Castilian of good family, he soon established himself at the court of Isabella of Castile. His real proving ground, however, was the long war against the kingdom of Granada, which ended in 1492 with the capture of the city of Granada from the Moors. The campaigning comprised a mixture of small, hectic cavalry skirmishes and positional warfare as the innumerable small towns and villages were taken. Thus his experience united an understanding of the demands of mobile war with the technical disciplines of siegecraft and the use of explosives.

His positions of command were minor

but he attracted the attention of the queen and her husband, Ferdinand of Aragon, and he was sufficiently high in their favour to be given in 1495 command of the expeditionary force sent to support the king of Naples against the French. His technique was to avoid pitched battles (after an initial disaster at Seminara) and to harass the enemy's long lines of communication, a technique so recently used against him in Granada. Progressively he weakened the French hold on the countryside, and then concentrated on the garrisons holding the cities of the kingdom. In the summer of 1496 he besieged and captured Atella and took the French commander, Montspensier, prisoner; the recovery of the Roman port of Ostia, at the mouth of the Tiber, earned him the gratitude of the Pope. He returned home in 1498 with an understanding of what was needed if the Spanish armies were to compete with the French.

The lesson of the war was that Spain needed a flexible infantry formation, capable of protecting and accommodating fire-power, able to move and manœuvre even over rough ground, and, most important, responsive to command and able to co-operate with artillery, cavalry and other arms. Cordoba expanded the Swiss doctrine of the use of pikemen, the most successful infantry of the day, which he had experienced in Italy, by increasing their offensive capacity: he added a group of arquebusiers to fight from within or in front of the spear wall, giving his formation a unique power to resist cavalry attacks, and a much greater shock power than opposing infantry. When next in Italy, the effectiveness of this force was demonstrated.

Facing the French again in 1502, Cordoba was, as before, heavily outnumbered. In April 1503 he brought them to battle on ground of his own choosing at Cerignola. Here he routed a larger French force, by using field fortifications

to protect his infantry, while the French destroyed themselves by assaults on his guns. Once demoralized, he completed their destruction by loosing his infantry from behind their palisade to carry the battlefield. The duc de Nemours, the French commander, was killed and the balance of power in Italy swung in Cordoba's direction. The importance of Cerignola was that it was the first battle in which small-arms played the decisive role, for Cordoba was unable to use his artillery after his explosive store had been detonated by an unlucky accident. He later demonstrated his mastery of combined operations involving all three major arms.

The winter of 1503 saw Cordoba on the Garigliano river, facing the French on the far bank. Shattering their sense of security, by stringing a pontoon bridge across the supposedly impassable river, which gave his army a huge tactical advantage in the ensuing night attack, he revealed in this operation the greatest of his capacities: an ability to co-ordinate a set of widely disparate activities, with only rudimentary communications, and to bring them together for a concerted, planned attack. It was a victory for an enterprising mind which quickly assessed the enemy's weakness, and had a real knowledge of the technical capacity at his disposal; and well-drilled troops responsive to his command. The victory at the Garigliano virtually destroyed the offensive capacity of the French; by January 1504 he had captured Gaeta, and the treaty of Blois forced the French to end their claim to Naples. But Cordoba's protector Isabella was now dead, and Ferdinand, suspicious of his growing influence in the world of Mediterranean diplomacy, recalled him. For the last eight years of his life he lived quietly in retirement.

The root cause of Cordoba's triumphs was his ability to recognize the reasons behind his success, and to take eclectically the best ideas of his opponents.

His reforms in organization and training made infantry units of 6000 men independent manœuvring bodies, capable of rapid defence or attack. The mixture of pikes and firearms, swords and javelins, provided a balance between position and manœuvre; but the emphasis was on the offensive. He saw that great battles were to be won by the infantry engaging and destroying the enemy's main force. Cavalry was to scout and skirmish; artillery to break up field formations. Infantry was the queen of the battlefield. Cordoba's victories and his scheme of organization was to give the Spanish the basis of military supremacy for over a century.

Cornwallis, Charles, Marquess (1738–1805) British soldier. The best British general in North America during the American War of Independence (1775–83), Cornwallis had distinguished himself in the Seven Years' War (1756–63). He succeeded to his father's earldom in 1762, and was one of the government's most savage critics in the House of Lords over the matter of taxing the American colonists. But despite his opposition to the policy of Lord North's administration, he was sent in 1776 to America to serve in Howe's (q.v.) command. At Trenton (1777), he was outwitted by Washington (q.v.), but gained his revenge at Brandywine (1777). He was Clinton's (q.v.) subordinate in the Southern campaign, participating in the early success at Charleston (1780), and, after the defeat of the main rebel army in the South, in charge of 8000 men to mop up final resistance. In the summer of 1780 Cornwallis mounted a campaign against the rapidly growing guerrilla movement, and beat the new American commander Gates (q.v.) at Camden (1780); yet another American commander Greene (q.v.) was appointed, and he forced Cornwallis to dissipate his troops in a number of small actions. When the British did succeed in bringing Greene to

battle, at Guilford Courthouse (1781), Cornwallis won, but with heavy losses: his weakened position forced him, to Clinton's fury, to abandon the Carolinas.

In the autumn of 1781 Cornwallis took up a strong position on the tip of the Virginia Peninsula, at Yorktown, where the British fleet provided his means of support and relief. Late in September 1781 nearly 17,000 American and French troops under Washington surrounded Cornwallis, with his 8000: the British temporarily lost control of the sea, and Cornwallis was forced to surrender when his position became untenable (October 1781). Despite the defeat, and possibly because of his opposition connections, his reputation did not suffer. In 1786 he was appointed commander-in-chief in India, where in the Third Mysore War (1789–92) he reduced the power of Tippu Sahib (q.v.), capturing his capital, Bangalore. Returning to England in 1793, he was created master-general of the ordnance and given a seat in the Cabinet, until, in 1797, he was sent to command in Ireland, where he was responsible for putting down the rebellion by Wolfe Tone. He was a popular and tolerant governor, and favoured Catholic emancipation.

Cortes, Hernan (1485–1547) Spanish conquistador. The destruction of the powerful Aztec empire, accomplished by Cortes with a tiny force of barely 600 men, 17 horses and 10 cannon, is one of the epics of conquest. Cortes landed on the coast of Mexico early in 1519, against the orders of the governor of Cuba, Diego Velazquez, under whose authority he technically came (Cortes had been appointed the *alcalde* (mayor) of Santiago, the capital of Cuba, and claimed that he was answerable only to the town authorities). On the coast near where he landed he built the town of Vera Cruz, and justified his further conquests under the authority of the town fathers. He was adept at exploiting dissensions within the subject peoples of the Aztecs, and it was in alliance with the Tlaxcalans and Totonacs that he marched against the Aztec capital, Tenochtitlán. The rumour, fostered by the Spaniards, was that they were the reincarnations of divine figures, and Cortes himself was Quetzalcoatl reborn. As such, the Spaniards were admitted to the city as friends, a trust which Cortes rapidly broke when he seized the person of Montezuma.

In 1520 news reached him that another force of Spaniards under Narvaez, sent by Velazquez, had landed at Vera Cruz. Cortes set out to rebuff them, leaving Tenochtitlán in the hands of Alvaredo (q.v.) and a tiny garrison. He returned to find Alvaredo under siege, and in hard struggle they left the city (Montezuma was killed by the Spanish during the fighting). It was now clear to the Aztecs that the Spanish were not gods but rapacious human enemies, so in 1520 they ranged the full weight of their army against them at the battle of Otumba, where after a savage struggle Cortes was completely victorious. But it was almost a year before a new expedition could be mounted against Tenochtitlán. In May 1521 Cortes's small army invested the Aztec capital, and after a bitter three-month siege captured the city and razed it to the ground. In its place he built a new capital, Mexico City, and set about the conquest of the rest of Mexico, which he accomplished by 1528. Eventually brought down by his enemies, who attacked his greed and misgovernment, he died unregarded. Cortes was a fine soldier, incomparable in his audacity and with a fine eye for a tactical opportunity.

Cotton, (Sir) Stapleton (1st Viscount Combermere; 1773–1865) British field-marshal. Commander of Wellington's cavalry in the Peninsula, 1808–12, and in the Waterloo campaign, 1815, Cotton was commander-in-chief in India, 1825–30, and in the first of those years took Bhurtpore, last stronghold of the Mahratta confederacy.

Couch, Darins Nash (1822–97) American (Union) general. A naturalist and explorer of some distinction, Couch had been educated at West Point and fought in the Mexican and Seminole wars, so was swiftly promoted to general rank on the outbreak of the American Civil War. He commanded the II Corps with considerable effect at Fredericksburg and Chancellorsville, but was so disgusted by the blunderings of Hooker (q.v.) in the latter battle that he asked to be relieved.

Courbet, Amédée Anatole Prosper (1827–85) French admiral. A Polytechnicien, Courbet unusually chose the navy as a career. In 1883 he was appointed to command the squadron on the Indo-China station and extended the French protectorate over that empire by landing at Hué and defeating the Chinese 'Black Flags' at Sontay. In the following year, when the Chinese again intervened, he bombarded and blockaded Formosa, captured the Pescadores and destroyed a Chinese squadron at Foochow. He died aboard his flagship in Asian waters shortly afterwards; with Garnier (q.v.), he is one of the heroes of the French conquest of Indo-China.

Cradock, (Sir) Christopher George Francis Maurice (1862–1914) British admiral. With an orthodox but adventurously successful career behind him (he had commanded the naval brigade at the storming of the Taku forts during the Boxer Rising), Cradock found himself in 1914 appointed to clear the western Atlantic of German commerce raiders with a squadron of old, slow cruisers. Having swept the American coast and West Indies, he informed the Admiralty that the German squadron in the southern Atlantic could be cornered only if an additional force were sent him. He nevertheless proceeded south, fell in with von Spee's (q.v.) ships on 1 November and went down in his flagship *Good Hope*, with all hands. Coronel enraged British feelings but was quickly revenged by Sturdee's (q.v.) victory off the Falkland Islands.

Crazy Horse (*c*. 1849–77) American Indian (Sioux) chief. He first fought the US Army under Chief Red Cloud in the campaign to close the Bozeman Trail into Sioux territory in 1865–8, and later led Sioux and Cheyennes in raids out of the reservations to which they were confined. He forced the army to withdraw from the river Rosebud in 1876 and later in the year caught and massacred the 7th Cavalry under Custer (q.v.) at the Little Big Horn. He was obliged to surrender the following year and died in captivity, resisting attempts to put him in close confinement.

Cromwell, Oliver (1599–1658) Lord Protector of England, soldier and statesman. It is impossible to separate Cromwell the military leader from Cromwell the political operator or Cromwell the statesman, for one great quality informed all his activities: an adamantine will which refused to accept the well-worn path, the accustomed method of achieving any end. Cromwell was an original thinker of a high order, a man capable of applying and sustaining his own originality against all odds. First and foremost, he had found his own path to God, struggled with his conscience, and confounded those who tried to turn him in a different direction. On this bedrock of faith, on this primal battle with himself, his enormous achievement was built.

Born into a prominent East Anglian family, but in a cadet branch, Cromwell served first as MP for Huntingdon, and,

latterly, for Cambridge. In Parliament he did not attract much attention as a high-flown orator: 'a very mean figure of a man in the beginning of this Parliament', a contemporary wrote of him at the outset of the Long Parliament (1640), but he was a man of power on the back benches, resolute in committee, and revealing himself as an able Parliamentary tactician. Cromwell was clearly remarkable, even in subordinate capacities, for his immense energy and clarity of purpose. While others vacillated, he acted. He prevented the colleges of Cambridge disposing of their bullion for the benefit of the king's war chest, seized Cambridge Castle when it might have been used in the Royalist interest, and began to raise a troop of horse at a time when others had little conception of the military implications of Parliament's decision to resist the king.

Cromwell came to the task of raising his cavalry in the autumn of 1642, with a clear view of what he wanted to achieve, of the standards he intended to enforce, and, although an amateur in military matters, of the model he hoped to follow in armaments and tactics. First and foremost he strove for a 'godly discipline' on and off the field of battle. His troops were to be responsive to his commands; desertion, looting, swearing and ungodliness were to be severely punished. Moral factors he rated above inherent professional skill: '... it must not be *soldiers* nor *Scots* that must do this work,' he once retorted to a critic, 'but it must be the godly.' He succeeded in recruiting upright citizens, convinced of the justice of their cause. Both men and officers had to meet the severest criteria as to character and probity: but Cromwell did not probe too deeply into their innermost religious feelings. Severely practical, he allowed none of the usual social preconceptions of the age – that only gentlemen were fit to command others – to interfere with his choice of men and their leaders. He fended off, brusquely, criticisms that he employed low-born men, schismatics or revolutionaries in his ranks: his sole consideration should be 'godly soldiers'. As he put it: 'Being well armed within by the satisfaction of their conscience, and without by good iron arms, they would as one man stand firmly and charge desperately.' But godliness was no match for the superior skill on horseback of many of the Royalist cavalry, gentlemen, almost born in the saddle, and armed with their own equipment – swords, breastplates and pistols. Cromwell worked hard to equip his men uniformly, with serviceable material, good horses and a proper commissariat for replacements.

Tactically, the 'Ironsides' as they came to be known, after the nickname for Cromwell himself, developed as they gained experience: but the essence was there from the outset. The complicated evolutions of the *caracole*, which used horsemen as pistoleers, depended on a high degree of training, and the tactic had been shown to be ineffective. Cromwell opted for the use of cold steel and shock tactics, which the Swedish cavalry had shown to be so successful. And it was easier to train men to ride in a body than to instruct them and their horses to manœuvre in close formation. Thus the Ironsides charged home, firing their pistols at close range before impact. The technique was successful. Cromwell's great quality as a commander of cavalry was that he could, on the whole, control his men and summon them back from a charge to reform and charge again. He was cautious about committing his troops and ready to withdraw them, to attack again, if they were unsuccessful. Individually (and he tried always to ensure that they fought in coherent bodies), they were probably outmatched by the best of the Royalist horse: but they did not become disorganized, or fritter their effectiveness in idle pursuits or lust for booty, as the Royal-

ists did. Cromwell's troopers were an extension of his own personality: flexible, unshakable and indomitable.

At the early battles in the east of England in which the Ironsides took part, both at the battle of Gainsborough (July 1643) and at Winceby, near Hagworthingham (October 1643), their influence was decisive. After Winceby the Royalist commander noted in his dispatch: 'Their Horse are very good, and extraordinarily [well] armed.' Although this comment also applies to Fairfax's (q.v.) men who played a crucial role in the battle, Cromwell's men fought stolidly on although their commander had been unhorsed and forced to retire temporarily from the battle at its critical juncture. At Marston Moor (July 1644), Cromwell's men received one charge, regrouped, and delivered a decisive blow to Goring's Royalist cavalry; turning their attention to the Royalist infantry, the massed Ironsides delivered a thunderous attack and drove them in disarray from the field. But after the indecisive second battle of Newbury (October 1644), Cromwell pressed hard in Parliament for the removal of those commanders, such as the Earl of Manchester and the Earl of Essex, as well as innummerable subordinate commanders, who owed their positions to their social influence rather than their military gifts.

With equal vehemence Cromwell also supported the creation of a New Model Army, which would extend the principles so amply vindicated by the performance of his Ironsides and which would comprise a force of 22,000 men, infantry and cavalry. The passage of the Self Denying Ordinance (December 1644) meant that Cromwell himself should have been barred from military office, but the threat from the Royalist army before Naseby meant that he was given a temporary commission as lieutenant-general of the Horse. And it was this temporary commission, repeatedly renewed, which allowed him to fight and to retain his seat in Parliament. The New Model was Fairfax's creation, although Cromwell's hand was often seen at work, but it was not quite the godly association which the Ironsides, now incorporated within it, had been. But Fairfax insisted on appointing his own officers, free from Parliamentary control, and followed Cromwell's practice of appointing humble, godly and competent men to his colonelcies. Until the campaign against the Scots in the Second Civil War (1648). Cromwell came under Fairfax's direct command. It was Fairfax who planned the strategy of the Naseby campaign and its successful aftermath. Not until the expedition to Ireland did Cromwell have a completely independent command. At Naseby (June 1645) the New Model Army showed its paces. Once again Cromwell's role was crucial. While Prince Rupert's (q.v.) Royalist cavalry smashed through the Parliamentary ranks and rode off in pursuit of their defeated enemies, Cromwell's cavalry accomplished their objectives, regrouped, and were launched by Cromwell with devastating effect at the Royalist infantry: by the time Prince Rupert's horse returned, the battle was lost for the king. In the battle of Preston (August 1648) Cromwell showed his great talents as a commanding general. Moving with great speed against the Scots, who outnumbered him, he defeated them in battle and ruthlessly battered them in their retreat. There was no let-up, no doubts or hesitations in his actions.

Cromwell's Irish campaign showed his precise attention to detail in the planning and provisioning of the expedition. Much criticism has been raised, fairly, about the savagery of the Parliamentary army in fulfilment of Cromwell's direct orders. But he operated strictly within the conventions of war then established, and moreover his campaign of terror had the desired effect: Ireland was brought to heel. In the Third Civil War (1650–1), Fairfax refused the command on grounds of conscience, and Cromwell was appointed captain-general, the supreme military office in the land. He fought two more battles, at Dunbar (September 1650) and Worcester (1651). On both occasions he showed his daring and willingness to take risks. At Dunbar, with an exhausted army, he feared defeat. But in a dawn attack he engaged the Scots with a first assault and smashed their exposed flank with his cavalry. A year later to the day, at Worcester, he faced a Scottish army again, this time with an overwhelming superiority of numbers on his side. He split his attack, himself crossing the river Severn with the bulk of his troops. When the Royalist cavalry under the young Charles II attacked his forces on the other bank, he was forced to make a hurried alteration to his plans. But the experience of the New Model told against the less expert Royalists, and Cromwell had won a final and decisive victory. The civil wars were over.

The seven remaining years of Cromwell's life were marked by the same firm conviction that he 'acted in the Lord's business'. The creation of a godly army and the (failed) attempt to create a godly nation were God's design, too important to be handled badly or with less than the full force of his titanic energy. As a soldier, he lacked the essential wayward genius of a Napoleon or Frederick the Great. Never except at Dunbar, where the choice was not his, did he fight a superior opponent. For Cromwell success in the great cause for which he fought was all-important, and nothing – neither individuals, human frailty or scruples, nor established institutions or attitudes – was allowed to stand in his way. Cromwell willed his way to victory, overcoming all obstacles.

Cronje, Piet (1835–1911) South African (Boer) general. Alone among Boer soldiers in having made a serious study of modern war, Cronje had had the experience during the First Boer War of 1881 of forcing the surrender of a British force at Potchefstroom, and had also taken the surrender of Jameson at Doornkop. If he rather than Joubert (q.v.) had been commandant-general, it is possible that the Boers might have achieved in 1899 the quick victory in which lay their only hope of success. As it was, he defeated Methuen (q.v.) at Magersfontein, but was eventually cornered by Roberts (q.v.) at Paardeburg and forced to surrender on 27 February 1900. It was the last major battle of the war.

Crook, George (1829–90) American (Union) general and Indian fighter. Wounded by a poisoned arrow in Indian fighting before the Civil War broke out, Crook played a most dashing role as a cavalry leader in the war itself, fighting at South Mountain, Antietam, Chickamauga, Winchester and Fisher's Hill. In independent command, he won his own minor victory over Confederate cavalry at Farmington, October 1863, in the pursuit from Chickamauga. He commanded the army of West Virginia in 1864 and in 1865 the army of the Potomac's cavalry, which he led in the pursuit from Richmond to Appomattox. After the war he reverted to fighting Indians, pacifying those of the Boise district, then the Apaches of northern Arizona. He took a major part in the Sioux war of 1876, and between 1882 and 1886 sought to pacify the Chiricahua Apaches. He respected the Indians, to whom he was known as Grey Fox, and advocated granting them full citizenship, but was regarded nevertheless by contemporaries as the greatest of the army's Indian fighters.

Cumberland, William Augustus, Duke of (1721–65) British general. Remembered by posterity as 'Butcher Cumberland' or 'Stinking Billy', his military career was inglorious save for his victory

over the Jacobite rebels at Culloden (1746). The Hanoverian royal family had a passion for military affairs, if no tradition of great practical competence, and Cumberland, the second son of George II (q.v.), gravitated to the army. In the war of the Austrian Succession (1740–8) he fought gallantly at Dettingen, 1743, after which he led an allied force of some 50,000 men (the army of the Pragmatic Sanction) against the French. At Fontenoy he was bested by the ailing Marshal Saxe (q.v.), who outmanœuvred him by using his artillery and cavalry in unison to break up the clumsily managed allied attack. But Cumberland managed to retreat in good order and the defeat did not become a rout.

In 1745 he was recalled home in haste to meet the threat of a Jacobite invasion of England from Scotland, aimed at restoring the Stuart dynasty and packing the Hanoverians back to Hanover. By December the Scottish armies had reached Derby and the court in London was in panic. But this was the high tide of their advance and they retired to Scotland closely followed by Cumberland. The two armies sparred with each other as they moved north: Charles Edward Stuart (q.v.), the 'Young Pretender' and leader of the Jacobite forces, tried and failed to capture Stirling Castle, the key to the lowlands; the English attempted to stop the Jacobites, but were beaten at Penrith and Falkirk. Finally the two armies met at Culloden, near Inverness, on 16 April 1746. Cumberland's artillery broke up the strength of the Highlanders' assault, and the remnants broke on the lines of English infantry. The Scots were routed and the English cavalry harried the survivors, committing numerous atrocities.

After Culloden, Cumberland spent three months in Scotland destroying the social base of Jacobitism. It was a campaign carried out with ruthless efficiency, proscribing the clan system, executing or transporting the leaders of the community, and building a system of military communication and garrisoned forts which subdued the countryside. This was the peak (or the nadir) of Cumberland's career: his suppression of Jacobitism was a complete success.

But when he returned to command the army in Europe, the old pattern of failure recurred: he lost again to Saxe at Lauffeld (1747); and in the Seven Years' War (1756–63), during his command of the defence of Hanover with 50,000 men, he was beaten by the French under d'Estrées. He was even forced to evacuate Hanover under the terms of the convention of Klosterzeveyen, which he was compelled to conclude although its terms were angrily renounced by George II. Recalled in disgrace to be told by the king that 'he had ruined his country and his army', Cumberland retired in high dudgeon to Windsor, whence he rarely emerged, since he grew immensely fat in his later years. His faults as a general were extreme stolidity and lack of imagination, but these were also his virtues. Faced with a good opponent he always lost; with a clear, simple plan to follow, he was capable of success.

Cunningham, Andrew Browne (1st Viscount Cunningham of Hyndhope; 1883–1963) British admiral. Born in Edinburgh and trained at Dartmouth, Cunningham won the DSO and two bars in the First World War, particularly distinguishing himself in command of the destroyer *Scorpion* in the Dardanelles. In 1939 commander-in-chief in the Mediterranean, of which he had great experience, he quickly established complete British naval superiority in the area. In November 1940 he directed the air attack on Taranto, which destroyed a large part of the Italian fleet at its moorings, and in the night battle of Cape Matapan, March 1941, he won a resounding moral and physical victory. The fighting off Crete in May was less successful, the British losing many

cruisers and destroyers to German air attack while covering the evacuation, but during 1943, when acting as naval commander-in-chief under Eisenhower, he recovered complete command of the sea. In October 1943, on the death of Admiral Pound (q.v.), he became First Sea Lord and acted as Churchill's principal naval adviser to the end of the war. A commander rather than an administrator, he was 'the outstanding British naval leader of the war'.

His brother, **General Sir Alan Cunningham**, (1887–1983) commanded the British forces in the liberation of Italian East Africa from the Duke of Aosta (q.v.) in December 1940–May 1941, and less successfully the Eighth Army in the Western Desert, August–December 1941.

Custer, George Armstrong (1839–76) American general. A West Pointer, his outstanding dash as a cavalry leader gave him promotion to brigadier-general at the age of twenty-three and he was present at all but one of the Army of the Potomac's battles during the Civil War, having eleven horses killed under him. After Appomattox (1865) he went west to fight the Indians, was gazetted colonel of the 7th Cavalry, at its head was ambushed by Crazy Horse (q.v.) at the Little Big Horn, 25 July 1876, and, with all his men, killed. The Indians testified that he died heroically, as indeed he had lived, the conscious embodiment of the *beau sabreur*. He was not a clever soldier.

Custine de Sarreck, Adam Philippe, comte de (1742–93) French general. A soldier of the *ancien régime*, whose enthusiasm for the Revolution was perhaps explained by his service in America (he made a name for himself at Yorktown, 1781), Custine de Sarreck was among the generals of 1792 who defended France against her Austrian and Prussian invaders. He himself led a successful counter-invasion, captured Mainz and reached Frankfurt. But he was forced eventually to retreat and during the Terror in the following year evidence was found of his treachery and he was executed.

D

Darlan, Jean François (1881–1942) French admiral and politician. A former chief of the naval staff, and in 1939–40 commander-in-chief of the French navy. Darlan had the difficult task of deciding how to dispose of the French fleet once defeat on land had become unavoidable. To Churchill he declared his resolve not to allow it to fall into German hands and at one stage appeared willing to sail it into British ports. But he eventually accepted office as minister of marine in the government of Pétain (q.v.) and kept the fleet in its North African harbours (where its major units were destroyed by British naval action, July 1940). In February 1941 he became Pétain's deputy and embarked on a policy of co-operation with Hitler in the hope of extracting concessions from him. Displaced on Laval's reconciliation with Pétain, he was named head of the French armed forces, of which the only sizeable remainder were in North Africa, and was present in the territory as high commissioner at the time of the Allied landings in November 1942. With Mark Clark (q.v.) he agreed on an armistice and declared himself sovereign representative of French authority, Allied acquiescence in which provoked criticism in Britain and America. He was assassinated by a young French monarchist on Christmas Eve.

Daun, Leopold Joseph, Graf (1705–66) Austrian soldier. If not the equal of Frederick the Great (q.v.) in his skill and daring, Daun at least developed some of the methods needed to counter-act a Frederickan attack. He was a thoroughgoing professional who had begun his service in the Austrian army in 1718. He fought in all the wars thereafter, including a campaign against the Turks (1737–9). Much of his most successful work came after the war of the Austrian Succession (1740–8), when he worked hard to reform the army, applying the many lessons he had learnt. In the Seven Years' War (1756–63), Daun, a field-marshal since 1754, administered the first defeat of Frederick the Great's career at Kolin (1757). Thereafter he developed a tactic of creative procrastination, refusing to be drawn by Frederick into battle save on the most favourable terms, using the advantages gained by an efficient system of replenishment to manœuvre and shadow the Prussians rather than come to grips. At Leuthen (1757) he came under the command of Charles of Lorraine (q.v.), so cannot be held responsible for the defeat. At Hochkirk (1758), although the Prussians were able to escape, success now effectively lay with the Austrians, who had fewer casualties, and captured 101 guns. And at the final great battle which Daun fought against Frederick, at Torgau (1760), where he was himself severely wounded, the Prussian victory was dearly bought.

Daun's strategic concept was much more than the avoidance of battle so prevalent in the eighteenth century. The experience of the war of the Austrian Succession had shown him that Austria's strength lay in artillery and light horse. He devised a campaign plan which utilized these resources. He preserved contact with the Prussians, using his own army and those of his subordinate commanders to act as a permanent threat to the Prussian forces, seeking to combine in overwhelming force and to give battle, preferably from a secure entrenched position. These were the tactics which won Kolin and made Daun's other encounters with the Prussians so costly for them. His success was recognized when he was made president of the *Hofkriegsrat* in 1762, the senior post in the Austrian army. He used his tenure to institute a mass of reforms, but his plans were cut short by his death. Much of the inventive and successful military education within the Austrian army owed its existence to Daun.

Davout, Louis Nicolas (duc d'Auerstadt, prince d'Eckmühl; 1770–1823) Marshal of France. Son of an officer of the *Royal-Champagne-Cavalerie*, into which he himself was commissioned in 1788, Davout, though undoubtedly noble, embraced the principles of the Revolution so ardently from the outset that he was put under military arrest. Elected lieutenant-colonel of one of the new volunteer battalions of the Yonne (his native *département*), he fought at Neerwinden, and, after a chequered passage in his career, was introduced to Napoleon who took him to Egypt and subsequently appointed him to command in the Consular (later the Imperial) Guard. He was created marshal in the great promotion of 1804 (having been a general since 1793) and in 1805–6 commanded the 3rd Corps, playing a decisive role at Austerlitz and at Eylau. He led it again in the 1809 campaign, to particular effect at Eckmühl and Wagram, where he had a horse killed under him. In 1812 he led the 1st Corps, gave Napoleon good advice, which he ignored, before Borodino, and lost two horses in the battle. His defence of Hamburg, 1813–14, during Napoleon's time of troubles, was an example of tenacity and fidelity. In 1815 he commanded

Paris, and signed the convention of occupation with the Allies. Davout never held the independent command which would have allowed him to demonstrate his real talents. He was one of the most efficient and consistent of the marshals, and, though not agreeable in manner, was much respected by Napoleon.

Dayan, Moshe (1915–81) Israeli general. Born at the first-established of the *kibbutzim* (Zionist communal settlements) of Palestine, Deganya, Dayan became a member of *Haganah*, the clandestine Zionist military force, in 1929, was second-in-command to Wingate (q.v.) in the Special Night Squads during the Arab revolt of 1936, and in 1939 was imprisoned when *Haganah* was declared illegal. He was released to serve in the British army during the Second World War and, at the outbreak of war with the Arab states in 1948, when Britain surrendered her mandate in Palestine, emerged as one of the new state of Israel's most talented military leaders. He became chief of staff in 1953 and planned the '100 hours' advance across the desert of Sinai which carried the Israeli army to the Suez Canal in 1956 (and provoked the Anglo-French invasion of Egypt). In 1959 he left the army for politics but in 1967, when Egypt menaced Israel by her concentration of armour in Sinai, was appointed minister of defence, more or less at popular insistence. The victory in the Six Day War (5–11 June) which followed is attributed largely to his boldness and powers of decision, though he must undoubtedly share much of the credit with the serving staff officers who had prepared plans beforehand, particularly for the decisive air strikes against the Egyptian and Syrian air bases with which the war opened.

Dearborn, Henry (1751–1829) American soldier and secretary of war. A volunteer in the War of Independence, present at Bunker's Hill, Saratoga and Yorktown, Dearborn entered politics in 1792 and was Jefferson's secretary of war, 1801–9. In 1812, on the outbreak of war with Britain, he was appointed senior major-general of the US Army, and drew up ambitious plans for an invasion of Canada, which came to nothing.

Decatur, Stephen (1779–1820) American naval officer. Remembered as the most dashing of the frigate captains whom the Corsair and 1812 wars produced, he was born at Sinnepuxent, Maryland, and entered the US Navy in 1798. Posted to Prebble's squadron in the Mediterranean in 1803, he brought off the audacious burning of the US frigate *Philadelphia* in Tripoli harbour after it had fallen into corsair hands and was promoted captain for it. In the war of 1812, as captain of the *United States*, he captured the British frigate *Macedonian* in single-ship action; though forced to surrender his flagship *President* in 1815, when attempting to break the blockade of New York, his reputation was not harmed. He subsequently commanded in the Mediterranean against the corsairs of Algiers, Tripoli and Tunis and held the post of navy commissioner until killed in a duel with a fellow naval officer at Bladensburg, Maryland. Three American towns, in Alabama, Georgia and Illinois, bear his name, which is perhaps best remembered for his aphorism: 'My country right or wrong.' (True context: a toast. 'Our Country! In her intercourse with foreign nations may she always be in the right; but our country, right or wrong!')

De Gaulle, Charles André Joseph Marie (1890–1970) French general and head of state. The son of a schoolmaster, de Gaulle was commissioned in 1914 into the 33rd Regiment (commanded at the time by Pétain, q.v.) and captured in 1916 at Verdun. After the war he became known as a military writer of unorthodox views (*Vers l'armée de métier*, 1933) and as an advocate of mechanization (though a much less radical one than has been made out). Appointed to command the half-formed 4th Armoured Division after the German invasion of 1940 had begun, he attempted, at Laon on 19 May, the only French counter-attack into the flank of the German 'panzer corridor'. Its failure was not his fault. He was almost immediately promoted *général de brigade*, the highest rank he ever held, and brought into the government as under-secretary for war. But he fled to England to raise the standard of resistance rather than participate in the armistice. His life then became that of a statesman rather than a soldier.

de la Rey, Jacobus Hercules (1847–1914) South African general. Arguably the most talented of Britain's opponents in the Boer War, de la Rey had no formal military training, but some experience of fighting the Bantu. Though opposed to Kruger's war policy he accepted high command in 1899 and, with Cronje (q.v.), contested Methuen's (q.v.) advance to the Modder river. His greatest successes came during the guerrilla phase of the war, when he captured Methuen, but chivalrously released him for medical care. Although he entered the political life of the postwar Union of South Africa, he never in his heart accepted the British connection and at the outbreak of the First World War he took the decision to raise a rebellion. On his way to the Transvaal he was shot dead by a police patrol, an event which precipitated the revolt he had planned to lead.

Denfert-Rochereau, Pierre Marie Philippe Aristide (1823–78) French hero of 1870. An engineer officer, educated at the Polytechnique and distinguished in the relief of Rome (1849), the Crimea and the pacification of Algeria, Denfert-

Rochereau was appointed in 1864 chief of engineers at the important border fortress of Belfort. Promoted to command it in 1870, when Prussia attacked, he sustained its defence defiantly for 105 days until his was the last force offering resistance to the invader in the whole of France. On 15 February 1871, on the orders of his government and by arrangement with the Prussians, the colonel marched his force out with the honours of war and into French lines. The region surrounding the fortress was exempted from annexation by the Prussians and raised by the French to the status of a *département* (*Territoire de Belfort*), which it retains.

Denikin, Anton Ivanovich (1872–1947) Russian (White) general. The son of a former serf, Denikin rose quickly by his natural talents to command a division and a corps in the First World War. He accepted the February revolution, becoming chief of staff to the new commander-in-chief, Alekseev (q.v.), and later commander of the western front. Imprisoned for his part in the Kornilov (q.v.) coup, he escaped to join an anti-Bolshevik army which Alekseev was forming on the Don, and in March 1918, on Kornilov's death, became commander of all the White armies in southern Russia. His anti-Bolshevik offensive, heavily supported by the French and British, who sent arms and supplies, got properly under way in 1919 and by that October had reached to within 250 miles of Moscow. His military government of the captured areas was, however, very unpopular with the inhabitants, and his personal relations with groups whose support he needed, particularly the Cossacks, were bad, he making little attempt to conceal his Great-Russian nationalism. Gradually his army dispersed and its remnants had to be evacuated across the Black Sea to the Crimea in March 1920. He retired in favour of Wrangel (q.v.) and went into exile in the west.

Desaix (des Aix), Louis Charles Antoine, chevalier de Veygoux (1768–1800) French general. One of the brightest stars of the revolutionary armies, Desaix was a brilliant subordinate of Napoleon's. An officer of the *ancien régime*, he opted for the Revolution (though he was briefly imprisoned for protesting against Louis XVI's dethronement) and commanded the rearguard for Moreau (q.v.) during the retreat from Wissemburg through the Black Forest in 1793. He was wounded at Lauterburg but stayed at his post and in 1796, again under Moreau, assisted in the passage of the Rhine and tenaciously defended the ruined fortress of Kehl against the Austrians. In 1798 Bonaparte gave him command of the advance guard of the army of the Orient. He took part in the battle of the Pyramids, defeated Murad Bey (q.v.) in an independent operation and set up a French administration of the province of Fayum, winning from his subjects the title of 'the just sultan'. After Bonaparte's departure it was he who was obliged to sign the convention of El Arish, but he rejoined Bonaparte in Italy swiftly enough to fight at Marengo, where he was killed in action, 'universally regretted'.

De Valera, Eamon (1882–1975) Irish statesman and revolutionary. Born in New York, son of a Spanish artist and an Irish mother, de Valera was brought up in Ireland, espoused the cause of Irish nationalism and the linguistic revival in early manhood, joined the Irish (Home Rule) Volunteers in 1913 and commanded one of its battalions in the abortive Easter Rising in Dublin, 1916. The last rebel commander to surrender, he escaped execution because of his American birth and, after imprisonment, was elected leader of the Sinn Fein party, which swept the polls in Ireland at the election of 1918. Abroad fund-raising during most of the Anglo-Irish war of 1919–21, he refused to accept the treaty

negotiated by the Sinn Fein plenipoten-
tiaries he had sent to London and led
what was to become its 'Republican'
wing into civil war with the new Free
State forces. Defeated and imprisoned,
he emerged to become the most important leader of independent Ireland
(whose strict neutrality he maintained
throughout the Second World War) and
eventually its president. He is a
twentieth-century archetype of the violent revolutionary turned statesman.

De Wet, Christiaan (1854–1922) South
African general. A veteran of the First
Boer War, 1880–1, de Wet took the field
again at the head of the Orange Free
State commandos in 1899. He commanded at the battle of Sanna's Post
and in the guerrilla phase of the war
proved the most elusive of all the Boer
cavalry leaders. After the surrender to
the British he entered politics, helped to
found the Nationalist Party and in 1914
took part in the pro-German rebellion.
He was quickly captured, through the
efforts of his ex-confederates, Botha and
Smuts (qq.v.), sentenced to six years for
treason but released after six months.

Dewey, George (1837–1917) American
admiral. One of the first Annapolis
graduates, Dewey served under Farragut
(q.v.) in the Civil War. In 1898 he was
appointed to command the Asiatic
Squadron and, on the outbreak of war
with Spain, entered Manila harbour and
captured the city, capital of the Philippines. His reception in New York and
elsewhere on his return home rivalled the
celebrations of the relief of Mafeking.

Diaz, Armando (1861–1928) Italian
field-marshal. Appointed director of operations on Italy's entry into the First
World War in 1915, Diaz succeeded
Cadorna (q.v.) in November 1917 as
commander-in-chief at the latter's removal consequent on the Caporetto disaster. In June 1918 he repelled the final

Austrian offensive on the river Piave, to
which the Italians had retreated after
Caporetto, and in October and November directed the counter-offensive which
culminated in the successful battle of
Vittorio Veneto and the Austrian capitulation. British and French troops contributed considerably to this achievement.
In 1920 he was created Duke of Vittorio
Veneto.

Diebitsch, Hans Karl Friedrich Anton
(called by the Russians Ivan Ivanovich;
Count; 1785–1831) Russian field-
marshal. A Prussian by birth and a product of the Berlin cadet school, Diebitsch
entered Russian service in 1801, fought at ·
Austerlitz, Eylau and Friedland, and was
promoted general for his conduct at Polotsk, 17–18 August 1812. Later in the
1812 campaign he helped, with Clausewitz (q.v.), to arrange the surrender of
Yorck von Wartenburg (q.v.) to the
Russians, and took part in the counter-
offensive which led to the battles of
Dresden and Leipzig. He became chief
of staff in 1824, suppressed the military
Decembrist rising in 1825, was created
count in 1827 and in 1829, for the success of his campaign against the Turks in
the Balkans (capture of Adrianople, 29
August) was granted the suffix 'Zabal-
kanski'. In 1830 he led the army sent to
suppress the rising in Poland, won the
battles of Grochow, 25 February, and
Ostroleka, 20 May, but then succumbed
to the pandemic of cholera, which also
killed Gneisenau (q.v.) and Clausewitz.
His paramount role in the Russian army
passed to Paskievich (q.v.).

Dill, Sir John Greer (1881–1944) British field-marshal. Highly regarded in the
British army during the 1930s for his
intellect – Dill had served both as commandant of the Staff College and director of military operations – he was
expected to become chief of the Imperial
General Staff, but on the outbreak of
war was given I Corps in France, and

did not achieve that post until the removal of Ironside in May 1940. This promotion brought him into close association during the greatest crisis of the war with Churchill, who thought his rationality and intellectual caution obstructive. In December 1941 he was replaced by Alanbrooke (q.v.) and sent as head of the military mission to Washington, where he formed a warm friendship with General Marshall (q.v.), ably representing British interests and establishing himself in Roosevelt's eyes as 'the most important figure in Anglo-American cooperation'. A man of immense charm, his death was widely mourned by official America.

Dönitz, Karl (1891–1980) German admiral and head of state. A regular officer of the imperial navy, which he entered in 1910, Dönitz was promoted rearadmiral by Hitler in 1939 and appointed head of the U-boat force, which he directed with almost unbroken success until January 1943. On the removal of Raeder (q.v.) and before the reversal of the U-boat campaign in the Allies' favour, he was appointed commander-in-chief of the navy and promoted grand admiral. His duty then was to preside over the defeat of the remnants of the German navy and, on 30 April 1945, to assume titular headship of Germany, in which capacity he negotiated unconditional surrender with the Allies. He was condemned by the Nuremberg Tribunal as a war criminal, sentenced to ten years and released in 1956.

Doolittle, James Harold (1896–1993) American airman. Though not a regular officer – he had left the US Army Air Corps, which he had joined as a pilot during the First World War, in 1930 – Doolittle was reappointed in high rank in 1940 and in April 1942 selected to lead the spectacular raid on Tokyo by land bombers launched from aircraft carriers (which precipitated the

Japanese navy's unwise decision to embark on the South Pacific campaign of mid-1942). For his part he was awarded the Congressional Medal of Honour and subsequently and successively appointed to command the 12th Air Force in North Africa, the 15th in Italy and the 8th in Britain – the latter the backbone of the strategic air offensive against Germany, which he took later to the Pacific.

Doria, Andrea (1466–1560) Italian admiral in the service of the Holy Roman empire. In his own right a powerful independent force in the Mediterranean before 1550, Andrea Doria was one of the last of the old-style *condottieri*. Born into the ruling caste of Genoa, he fought on land under a variety of leaders and in a mixture of causes. Equipping his own force of galleys, he engaged in a ceaseless freebooting campaign, both against the Turkish state and the Barbary pirates. In the Italian wars he served first the French, and latterly the Habsburgs; he remained, however, a Genoese patriot, and after capturing the city from French occupation in 1528, he ruled as a virtual autocrat. A grateful Emperor Charles V made him admiral of the imperial fleet, and his main activity after 1529 was directed to stemming the growth of Turkish naval power in the Mediterranean.

He had already won an important victory over the Turks at Pianosa (1519); now with the fleet at his disposal he carried the war into the eastern Mediterranean. In 1532 he gained the island of Coron and garrisoned Patras: the Morea became a Christian outpost. However, his hold on his conquests was tenuous, and in 1533 his great opponent Barbarossa (q.v.) began his naval war of conquest in response to the Christian threat. All Doria's conquests were lost, and the Turkish fleet raided the coasts of Italy. In 1537 the Turks settled down to besiege Corfu, until Doria arrived with a large fleet, combining the imperial and Venetian battle squadrons, and forced them to withdraw. But Doria could not prevent the privateering war which Barbarossa waged, striking swiftly along the coastline. Doria's aim was to bring him to battle, Barbarossa's to avoid it: for almost a year the fleets sparred, while the Turkish forces loosened the Venetian hold on her enclaves in Greece. In September 1538 a battle was fought, but without a decisive result: the Turkish fleet slipped away from the Christians, having inflicted considerable damage. Despite successful raiding against Turkish commerce and along the coastline, year by year Doria was forced back on to the defensive. He advised against the disastrous Algiers expedition of 1541, arguing that the fleet could not operate against so strong an enemy. Events proved him right: the city resisted stoutly and a storm destroyed much of his fleet. The advantage now rested firmly with the Turks. In 1542 the Turks swept into the western Mediterranean in force. Doria took refuge in Genoa and Barbarossa had free rein to ravage the coasts of Spain and Italy.

After Barbarossa's death in 1546 some of the energy went out of the Turkish westwards expansion, although his successor Tourghoud was active in northern Africa. In 1555 Doria relinquished command of the imperial fleet to his nephew, called Gian Andrea Doria, who was to command part of the fleet, now well drilled in united action and hardened over years of campaigning, at the decisive Turkish reverse at Lepanto (1571). Andrea Doria, like his opponent Barbarossa, had brought system to the haphazard warfare of the Mediterranean. Under his aegis a proper system of supply and replenishment was established, and the erratic supply of galley slaves somewhat improved. But he did not possess the financial and technical resources at Barbarossa's disposal; in addition the Christian powers were frequently divided among themselves. Andrea Doria was a great exponent of galley warfare in its final and most interesting phase.

Douhet, Giulio (1869–1930) Italian airman; 'the Mahan (q.v.) of air strategy'. An artillery officer, Douhet secured command before the First World War of the Italian army's first air unit (which was also the first to practise aerial bombardment, in Libya during the Italo-Turkish war of 1911–12). During the First World War he was court-martialled and dismissed from the service for his criticism of the high command, but the disaster of Caporetto (24 November 1917) vindicated him and he was reinstated in 1918. In 1921 he was promoted general but thereafter he increasingly withdrew from active duty to devote himself to his writing on the proper role of air power. His ideas, which he had formulated as early as 1915, were set out in *The Command of the Air* (*Il Dominio dell'Aria*) – the title is a direct reference to the central idea of Mahan's works on naval strategy – published first in 1921. They constellate around two main assumptions: a) that aircraft are weapons of limitless offensive power, against which no defence can be provided; b) that civilian morale can and should be shattered – and so wars won – by aerial attacks on cities. Because he wrote in Italian, his ideas were slow to circulate, and for that reason were apparently duplicated by protagonists of air power in other countries, notably General William Mitchell in America. None, however, arrived at so ambitious a strategy for the newly fledged air forces or one which, though it had to wait for the development of inter-continental missiles to substantiate its argument *in toto*, so terrifyingly anticipated the future.

Dowding, Hugh Caswell Tremenheere (1st Baron Dowding; 1882–1970) British air marshal. A Wykehamist and a regular artillery officer, Dowding transferred early to the Royal Flying Corps and from 1930 to 1936 he was research and development member of the Air Council, on which he encouraged the development of prototypes which were to become the Spitfire and Hurricane and authorized expenditure on radar experimentation. Appointed head of Fighter Command in 1936, he directed its operations during the Battle of France, his opposition to the transfer of squadrons from England being a precondition for its narrow but decisive victory under his command in the subsequent Battle of Britain. Despite his great abilities as a tactician and strategist, however, he remained a lonely figure (nicknamed 'Stuffy'), was not promoted after 1940 and retired in 1942. He was a spiritualist and wrote a book, *Many Mansions*, containing what he claimed were messages from beyond the grave from men killed in the war.

Dragomirov, Mikhail Ivanovich (1830–1905) Russian general and military theorist. A Guards officer and tutor to the imperial family, Dragomirov fought with great bravery during the Russo-Turkish war of 1877 in the Balkans. Wounded there at the head of his division, he was invalided into the directorship of the Nicholas Military Academy (staff college) where for eleven years he exercised a profound influence on the education and training of the Russian army. He believed strongly in what he claimed were 'traditionally Russian' methods and the 'ideas of Suvorov' (q.v.), using that old hero's words, 'the bullet is foolish, the bayonet is wise', to justify a tactical system based on mass charges instead of fire and movement. From 1889 to 1903 he translated his theories into direct teaching practice as commander of the Kiev Military District. The Russian army was to pay heav-

ily for them in the Russo-Japanese and First World wars.

Drake, Sir Francis (*c.* 1543–1596) British sailor. 'El Draque', who 'singed the King of Spain's beard' with his attack on Cadiz in 1587, has become a creature of legend rather than a figure of real substance. He was, in essence, a corsair, and remained so throughout his life although honours and riches were heaped upon him, and he acquired respectability in society. Born into a staunchly Puritan family, he began his maritime career on a coastal bark in Kent, where his parents had fled after persecutions of the new religion had blossomed in the West Country. His education was rudimentary; as he said himself: 'my bringing up hath not been in learning'. But he acquired a detailed and intimate knowledge of practical ship management, qualities which brought him rapid advance in a number of voyages under the command of his kinsmen, the Hawkins brothers. Relations with the Hawkinses were temporarily soured when they alleged that he left them in difficulties in an action at San Juan de Ulua (1568); in 1570, he mounted the first expedition to the West Indies under his own command, but without much success. Two more expeditions followed, and in 1573 he captured a quantity of Spanish treasure; in the following four years, numerous plans were made for voyages of exploration around the southern tip of the Americas, and a well-armed expedition was prepared with Drake in command. Its aims were uncertain, but it is clear that several of the backers expected a fine dividend in Spanish treasure, rather than the less tangible rewards of exploration.

This voyage, which developed into the epic circumnavigation of the globe (1577–80), was extremely profitable, with booty of more than 360,000 *pesos* from the treasure ship *Cacafuego*, taken off Callao, as well as other prizes. By knighting Drake, Queen Elizabeth conferred her approval on him for acts that amounted to piracy; England was set in direct conflict with Spain. In 1585, Drake, now a rich man, was given command of a substantial new expedition of twenty-two ships to raid the West Indies. His forces devastated the Spanish settlements. Santo Domingo and Cartagena were taken against heavy odds, and he returned to Plymouth with booty amounting to £60,000: this was less than his backers, including the Queen, had expected. After the West Indies expedition, Drake's activities combined privateering with more active preparations for the defence of England against Spanish invasion; he was, simultaneously, the commissioned agent of a privateering company, and the Royal admiral. In March 1587, he was commissioned to move against the Spanish forces which were being gathered for the invasion: in April, in the famous attack on the port of Cadiz, he destroyed some thirty vessels and a large quantity of stores. In other raids on the Spanish and Portuguese coasts, he upset Spanish preparations, in particular burning the timber to be used for water casks, on which the invading force would depend for its drinking water. Financially, the expedition was made worthwhile by the capture of the Spanish ship *San Felipe*, with a cargo worth £100,000.

In the long wait for the Spanish invasion, which his assaults delayed until 1588, Drake advocated a firm, attacking policy, but he was overruled. In the running fight up the Channel with the Armada, Drake in the *Revenge* captured the *Nuestra Senora del Rosario*, and led the way in the harrying tactics using long-range fire, which cost the Spanish many casualties. The main aim of the Armada was irretrievably lost when the fleet split up after an English attack with fireships on their anchorage off Gravelines (28–9 July 1588). But the defeat of the Armada was not the result of any great strategic skill displayed by the English admirals, and indeed, many of the ships lost to Spain were merchantmen rather than warships. After the great Armada, Spain mounted fresh attacks, and the privateering war continued: in the West Indies, Spanish defences and tactics were overhauled and improved, as Drake discovered on his unsuccessful last voyage (1595–6). He quarrelled with Hawkins, who participated in the venture, failed to capture San Juan de Puerto Rico, and failed again against Panama. On 20 January 1596, he contracted dysentery, which was ravaging his fleet, and died three days later. He was buried in Nombre de Dios Bay. In an age of great sea captains, Drake stands out both for the strength and power of his personality, and his supreme skill and daring as a seaman. His greatest exploit was undoubtedly the circumnavigation, in which his tiny ship, only seventy feet in length (the *Pelican* but better known by its later name *The Golden Hind*), fired the imagination of his own and succeeding generations. Yet he was inferior as a naval strategist to Hawkins. His most substantial contribution was in the creation of the ideal of English naval might, and, perhaps, in pioneering the notion of how naval supremacy could combine patriotism with profit.

Dreyfus, Alfred (1859–1935) French officer, central figure of the Dreyfus affair. Son of a Jewish textile manufacturer, Dreyfus had been educated at the Polytechnique and led an unexceptionable career in the artillery until, as a staff-learner at the ministry of war in 1894, he was accused of the treasonable transmission of documents to Germany and sentenced to be degraded and imprisoned for ten years on Devil's Island, French Guiana. His guilt was subsequently called into doubt, and the resulting efforts, some altruistic, some nakedly political, to clear his name, divided French society. Ultimately pardoned and reinstated, he retired as a lieutenant-colonel. Not until 1958 was France to undergo, over the recall of de Gaulle, an internal crisis comparable in severity to *l'Affaire*.

Driant, Emile August Cyprien (Capitaine Danrit; 1855–1916) French soldier, writer, anglophobe. A regular soldier of great promise, Driant made the dual mistake, in Third Republican France, of marrying the wrong wife – a daughter of Boulanger (q.v.) – and protesting against the wrong malpractice – the keeping of dossiers on 'clerical' officers. Retired, he became a deputy and used his parliamentary voice to advance the fortification of the frontier with Germany. He used his civilian freedom of expression to write – as Capitaine Danrit – a succession of imaginative works of the future, in some of which he merely indulged his anglophobia, but in others painted remarkably prescient pictures of coming battles. Returning to the colours in 1914, he was killed on 22 February 1916, while commanding a *chasseur* battalion in the Bois des Caures at Verdun, in the heart of the district whose lack of defences he had long deplored.

Dufour, Guillaume Henri (1787–1875) Swiss general. Educated at the Polytechnique, Dufour returned to Switzerland to become one of its army's few full-time officers. When in 1847 the Catholic central cantons attempted to form a special confederation (*Sonderbund*) of their own, it was he who was elected general by the Diet to put the rebellion down. (The general, of whom there can be only one at a time, in that of war, has virtually unlimited powers.) With skill and humanity he brought the rebellion almost bloodlessly to a close within two months: it was the last of Switzerland's wars. In 1864 he presided at the conference in Geneva which promulgated the first of the Geneva Conventions (*see* Dunant).

Dumouriez, Charles François (1739–1823) French general. Son of a military official of the *ancien régime*, Dumouriez fought in the Seven Years' War (1756–63) and as a volunteer for Paoli in Corsica, engaged in secret diplomacy for Louis XV in Hungary and was imprisoned in the Bastille. Ambitious and avaricious, he embraced the Revolution in a spirit of calculation, was appointed foreign minister in 1792 and made the declaration of war against the First Coalition. He was then in swift succession minister of war and commander-in-chief of the Army of the North in succession to Lafayette (q.v.). With Kellermann (q.v.) he won the battle of Valmy and reconquered Belgium from the Austrians. He then returned to Paris to intrigue, took up with Danton and, after his defeat at Neerwinden, refused to accept dismissal. He delivered the commissaries of the government into the hands of the Austrians, whom he then joined. He was never accepted as trustworthy by the royalist émigrés, however, and died after a bitter exile in England. Nevertheless, his name is inscribed on the Arc de Triomphe.

Dunant, Jean Henri (1828–1910) Swiss humanitarian, founder of the Red Cross movement. A Geneva businessman who had a proposition to put to Napoleon III, Dunant's pursuit of the emperor carried him unawares on to the battlefield of Solferino (24 June 1859). Appalled by the abandonment of the wounded, of whom about 30,000 were left on the field – the battle was bloody even by contemporary standards – he attempted to organize local relief and then, in the hope of averting such eventualities, wrote an eye-witness account called *Un Souvenir de Solferino*, in which he proposed the establishment in all countries of societies for the impartial relief of suffering caused by war, and the international agreement of rules for the treatment of wounded. The book had an enormous impact and led in 1864 to the promulgation of the first Geneva Convention. In later life he retired into complete obscurity. He was the recipient of the first Nobel Peace Prize in 1901.

Dundee, John Graham of Claverhouse, Earl of (1649–89) Scottish soldier. 'Bonnie Dundee', one of a constellation of romantic Scottish military heroes, combined soldierly skill with political and religious traditionalism. He served his military apprenticeship as a mercenary in France and the Low Countries, returning to Scotland in 1678, where he turned his tactical knowledge to the suppression of Protestant meetings (conventicles). To this work he brought a ruthless zeal which revealed a deep hatred both of the politics and religious views of the Presbyterians. But despite his experience he was outmanœuvred by the Covenanters, who knew the terrain, and beaten by them at Drumclog Moor in June 1679; a defeat somewhat redeemed by the victory at Bothwell Bridge, where an English army led by the Duke of Monmouth (q.v.) defeated the Covenanters decisively. It proved impossible, however, to enforce strict religious conformity on Scotland and despite the brutal suppression executed by Dundee's dragoons, the Presbyterian organization survived.

Dundee was much attracted by the personality of James, Duke of York, during his residence at Holyrood, and after 1679 was attached to his entourage in London. In 1682 he returned north with a renewed commission against the Covenanters, his ferocity now exceeding that of three years before. When James ascended the throne (1685), the Protestants in Scotland rose in renewed revolt, full of fear of a Catholic monarch; Dundee took this opportunity to use draconian methods to terrorize even non-militant Presbyterians. This repression brought many adherents to the rebel cause and helped to secure Scotland for William of Orange in the Glorious Revolution of 1688. After James's overthrow, Dundee immediately became the most influential of his Scottish adherents. In June 1689 he led a long-planned rising against the new regime. He ambushed the army of General Hugh Mackay (q.v.) in the narrow pass of Killiecrankie on 17 July 1689, a severe blow to the Williamite cause. But he was killed in the battle, and the rebel army, without his firm control, began to fragment. The most dangerous threat to the revolutionary settlement evaporated. Despite the romantic appeal of Dundee, heard in the songs and ballads embroidered around his career, he was in reality a merciless soldier, sparing neither his enemies nor his own men.

Dupleix, Joseph François, marquis de (1697–1763) French colonial administrator. The most notable of Clive's (q.v.) opponents in India, Dupleix first visited the sub-continent in 1720; by 1742 he had risen through various posts in the French administration to be governor-general, commanding all the French forces and ports in India. When the war of the Austrian Succession (1740–8) broke out between France and England in Europe, Dupleix sought to keep India at peace. But a British fleet arrived to buttress the position of the East India Company, and Dupleix took reciprocal action. With the aid of a strong fleet under La Bourdonnais and 1200 French soldiers, he captured the chief British town, Madras (1746), and defended it successfully against attacks by the Indian allies of the British. But he failed to capture the crucial Fort St George, and eventually, when Admiral Boscawen arrived with a strong fleet to reinforce the British, the French reluctantly withdrew. The eighteen-month siege had proved fruitless. Dupleix withdrew to his capital, Pondicherry, which the British made several vain attempts to capture.

After the peace of Aix la Chapelle (1748), Dupleix concentrated on extending French influence in the south, playing an active part in local Indian politics and establishing his supporters on the thrones of neighbouring states. By astute manœuvring he established his dominance over the Deccan, with a small but competent army under de Bussy. But his campaign of expansion met with a reverse at the hands of Robert Clive, and the elaborate system of clientage collapsed. In the autumn of 1751 Clive made a surprise attack on the capital of the leading francophile ruler, Chanda Sahib, who was at the time besieging a British outpost at Trichinopoly. Chanda managed to hold Arcot against determined attacks, but the whole strategy mapped out by Dupleix was thrown into confusion. The dominant position of the French was questioned and the delicate system of alliances, based as much on bluff as real French power, fell apart. In 1754 Dupleix was recalled to France in disgrace. Like his great opponent Clive he had recognized the realities of Indian politics, the unreliability of local rulers, the dominant need for European troops and a strong naval presence. But he was ill-served by the controlling interests of his *Compagnie des Indes* at home, and there was little substance behind his show of power.

Duquesne, Abraham, marquis de (1610–88) French admiral. A victim of Louis XIV's repressive attitude towards Protestants, Duquesne served France with undeviating loyalty and great competence. He sailed as a captain under de Sourdis, as well as Maillé-Brézé, and between 1644 and 1647 took service under the Swedish crown. He disagreed with Admiral d'Estrées after the failure at the battle of Sole Bay, when the Dutch fleet surprised the combined French and English

forces and defeated them. This criticism was not well received at court and he was removed from his command: rumours circulated of his doubtful loyalty, without justification. But after a period in disgrace he was recalled and gained his revenge over de Ruyter (q.v.), the Dutch victor at Sole Bay, when he drove off the combined Spanish and Dutch fleet from the port of Messina in Sicily (1676), which he had recently captured. He extended his territorial base with the capture of Agosta, and returned to France for more troops and supplies. The battle for Sicily continued: a French army under Marshal Vivonne beat the Spanish on land, and when de Ruyter attacked again with a stronger fleet Duquesne drove him off once more, in a battle (April 1676) which cost de Ruyter his life.

In 1678 the war with Spain was ended by the treaty of Nijmegen; three years later Duquesne was created a marquis, largely in gratitude for his services in the Dutch war. The superiority of the Dutch fleet, which had become almost legendary, was undermined in two battles where French seamanship and tactical skill had been shown to be equal or superior. Duquesne became something of a hero within the French navy, but his undisguised Huguenot convictions, in a France where Protestantism was being treated more and more harshly, made his further advance impossible. In 1685 Louis repealed the Edict of Nantes, the charter which allowed freedom of Protestant worship in France. Many were forced into exile, and many of those who stayed were oppressed. In all, France lost over 50,000 Protestants, a substantial proportion of the most skilled and best-educated members of the population. But Duquesne was not among them. Because of his reputation he was allowed to live in peace until his death. His achievement had been to enhance the status of the French navy.

E

Early, Jubal Anderson (1816–94) American (Confederate) general. A West Pointer and a Virginian, Early had resigned from the army in 1833 to make a successful career as a lawyer and politician, but was commissioned a colonel in his state militia at secession (1861) and a brigadier-general in the Confederate regular army after First Bull Run (at which he commanded the 6th Brigade). A divisional commander in the battles of Antietam, Fredericksburg, Chancellorsville, Gettysburg, the Wilderness, Spotsylvania and Cold Harbor, his most important individual contribution to Confederate strategy was his raid on Washington, 27 June–7 August 1864. His men reached the suburbs, caused panic in the city and compelled Grant to divert major forces to repel them. The counter-offensive by Sheridan (q.v.) in the Shenandoah Valley was, however, a decisive Union success and effectively eclipsed Early's career.

Egmont, Lamoraal, Graaf van (1522–68) Dutch patriot. A hero of the Dutch resistance to Philip II, Egmont was caught between his adherence to the lawful authority of the Habsburgs in the Low Countries, and his opposition to the ruthless policy of centralization adopted by Philip II, quite against the historic rights and privileges of the Netherlands. Born into one of the leading families in the northern Netherlands, Egmont was a staunch Catholic and a close confidant of the Emperor Charles V (q.v.). He was sent as part of a small delegation to England to secure the hand of Mary Tudor for Philip II of Spain, and was regularly entrusted with confidential missions. Created a Knight of the Golden Fleece, the leading noble order of the empire, his was a voice of moderation in the complex problems which stemmed from the growth of Protestant belief. He served Philip II well, playing a major part in the battle of Saint-Quentin, where the French were decisively defeated. In the following year (1558), he demolished a small army led by Marshal des Thermes in the sand dunes at Gravelines, a battle in which he was helped by the English fleet bombarding the French positions. In 1559, in recognition of his social position and his great services to the state, he was appointed *stadholder* of Flanders and Artois and a member of the Council of Regency under the regent, Margaret of Austria.

The point that was to be at issue between him and the Spanish crown was the liberty and independence of the towns of the Netherlands. The Spanish, in an effort both to increase their tax revenues, by extended application of Spanish taxes to the underburdened Netherlands, and to extirpate Protestant heresy, decided to abolish all the fiscal and political privileges of the provinces. This Egmont and other leading members of the Council – William of Orange and Count Hoorn – would not tolerate and they succeeded in persuading Philip to remove the hated Cardinal Granvelle, a symbol of the growing autocracy. But the moderate party were soon forced from the Council of Regency; Egmont withdrew to his estates and refused to become involved in the many plots being brewed. After Alva's (q.v.) appointment at the end of 1566, the situation began to deteriorate. Egmont was forced to take an oath of loyalty in spring 1567, but this did not save him from Alva's determination to destroy the natural leadership of the Netherlands. In a purge of the leadership of revolt, Egmont was swept into prison and illegally (for a Knight of the Golden Fleece could not be executed without an edict from the Order) condemned to death for treason, dying on the scaffold. With his death the last restraining influence was gone and prolonged and savage war became inevitable. Had he lived there seems little doubt that he would have been drawn into opposition, placing his military talents, which were substantial, at the service of the cause of resistance.

Eichelberger, Robert Lawrence (1886–1961) American general. Educated at West Point, of which he was later superintendent (1940–2), Eichelberger saw service in the American expeditionary force to Siberia, 1918–20. Appointed to command I Corps on America's entry into the Second World War, he directed the attack on Buna, New Guinea, which became one of America's first ground victories against the Japanese. Promoted to command the Eighth Army in September 1944, he led it throughout the rest of the Pacific campaign, including the amphibious assault on and capture of the Philippines. On 30 August 1945 he was at the head of a small party of soldiers which landed at Atsugi airfield on the Japanese mainland to begin the occupation.

Eisenhower, David Dwight (1890–1969) American soldier and president of the United States. Born the third son of seven to a Texas railway worker, Eisenhower was brought up in poverty but won a nomination to West Point and was commissioned in 1913. He saw no action in the First World War, gravi-

tated to the staff, served MacArthur (q.v.), 1933–9, both in Washington and the Philippines, and then attracted the attention of Marshall (q.v.). On the coming of war, and fresh from a successful spell as assistant chief of the war plans division, he was sent as liaison officer to London and shortly afterwards (25 June 1942) appointed commander of the European theatre of operations. In that capacity he commanded the American ground troops in North Africa, Sicily and Italy from November 1942 to November 1943, then returned to England to prepare the invasion of Europe (for which he had been named supreme Allied commander), in September 1944 following his armies to the Continent to direct the final advance into Germany.

The front line was then nearing Germany's western frontier and Eisenhower was called upon to make the most important operational decision of his career: whether to proceed, as the armies were, on a broad front, or to back one or other of his more thrusting commanders, Montgomery or Patton (qq.v.). Scarcity of resources would allow only one of these choices (Hitler's hold on the ports and the Allies' overefficient bombing of the railways having reduced the movement of supplies to a trickle), and Eisenhower eventually backed Montgomery, whose plan was for an air-borne descent on the Rhine bridges, followed by a swift armoured dash to the parachutists' relief. The plan misfired.

It is testimony to Eisenhower's evident lack of personal ambition, his sincerity and zeal for the common good and his remarkable warmth in personal relations with every manner of man – and Patton and Montgomery were extremely opposed types – that he was reproached neither at the time, nor seriously afterwards, for its failure. The failure does reveal, however, that Eisenhower was not really a general in the traditional sense but a chairman and conciliator, ideally suited to the management of an agreed programme between allies, and indeed to the presidency of the United States, but not to the making and changing of a personal strategy in the face of the enemy. But it is doubtful whether the alliance required or could have sustained generalship of that sort.

Elbée, Maurice Louis Joseph Gigost d' (1752–94) French (Vendéen) general. A former officer, d'Elbée initially accepted the Revolution with enthusiasm and was elected a member of the Third Estate but, objecting to the disestablishment of the Church, he retired to his estates in Brittany. Summoned in 1793 by the local Catholic and royalist peasantry to lead them to war against the atheist republic, after the death of Cathelineau he was proclaimed generalissimo of the *armée catholique et royale*. Victorious at Coron and Torfou, he was taken prisoner at Cholet on 17 October 1793 and executed (though so badly wounded that he had to face the firing squad sitting) at Noirmoutier early the following year.

Engels, Friedrich (1820–95) Socialist, philosopher and military commentator. It is little known that Engels was a prolific writer on military affairs, which interested him both in their own right and as a means of achieving the proletarian revolution. 'He was by nature a soldier and warrior ... proud of his early military experience as [a Prussian one-year volunteer] and as an active participant in the Baden insurrection ... of 1848.' Nicknamed 'the general' by his friends, he contributed articles on military subjects for many years to the *New York Tribune*, and wrote for two technical military journals, the *Darmstadter Allgemeine Militär Zeitung*, and the *Volunteer Journal of Lancashire and Cheshire*. The quality of his military writing, which exceeds in quantity all his political writing, was high enough to be attributed, when published anonymously, to

Prussian generals who wished to conceal their identity. His principal theme was the importance of putting armies on to a broad popular basis of recruitment, which would prevent their use by governments as an instrument of oppression at home and adventurism abroad. It has been of profound influence on Marxist military thinking, almost not at all on Marxist political practice.

Enver Pasha (1881–1922) Turkish general and revolutionary. The son of a member of Sultan Abdul Hamid II's court, Enver took up revolutionary politics almost as soon as he left the military academy by joining the Young Turk 'Union and Progress' cell in III Corps at Salonika, his first posting. But he was also a dedicated and skilful soldier, leading a band of Turkish irregulars in guerrilla fighting with Greek and Bulgarian partisans in Macedonia during 1903–7. He took a leading part in the deposition of the sultan in 1908 and was then sent as military attaché to Berlin, where he developed an abiding admiration for German military efficiency. He returned home to take part in the wars with Italy in 1911, when he was the last Turk to resist in Cyrenaica, and with Greece and Bulgaria, 1912–13, when he took part in the coup which established the Young Turks in power, and by his recapture of Edirne (Adrianople) from the Bulgarians became a national hero. He was by then chief of staff and in February 1914 was made minister of war. Thenceforward, he, Talat and Jemal Pasha ruled the empire.

Soon after the outbreak of the First World War they brought Turkey in on Germany's side and Enver, as effective commander-in-chief, embarked on an offensive strategy against Russia, which had the object of uniting the Turkic peoples of Russian Central Asia to Turkey. This Pan-Turanian scheme was overambitious and setbacks in the Caucasus diminished his prestige. It was partially restored by Turkish success against the British at Gallipoli in 1915, however, but too much of the credit for victory there belonged to Mustafa Kemal (q.v.) who became thenceforth his principal rival. Russia's collapse in 1917 allowed Enver to essay his Pan-Turanian offensive again, and his forces reached Baku on the Caspian, but Germany's collapse entailed Turkey's and he was forced to flee to Berlin. For the next three years he searched increasingly desperately for a road back to power, and tried to enlist Soviet help to overthrow Kemal. It was refused and he was ultimately killed at the head of anti-Soviet insurgents (*basmachis*) in Russian Turkestan, where the Soviet leaders had unwisely allowed him to go.

Erik XIV (*d.* 1577) King of Sweden, Erik XIV came to the throne of Sweden in 1561, and in many of his army reforms were to anticipate by thirty years those of Maurice of Nassau. He had delved into the classical writers on military tactics and, impressed by the flexibility and manœuvrability of the Roman legions, sought to emulate them in his reorganization of the Swedish army. This he divided into battalions each comprising 525 men, the battalions being subdivided into five *kvarters* of 105 men, four or five battalions making up a regiment, or, as Erik preferred to call it, a legion. In the field three of the five *kvarters* would be placed in the front line forming a single tactical unit, the other two acting either as a reserve or a skirmishing force behind the front line. The battalions would be placed side by side in two lines, and Erik can thus be credited with the first use of linear tactics since the invention of firearms. Moreover, he used the increased manœuvrability which the new formations brought to execute outflanking movements with his infantry. In addition to these changes in the deployment of troops, he reconsidered their functions

as fighting units. Having equipped them with pikes (the first time they had been issued in Sweden), he used the pikemen, supported by musketeers, as an attacking, rather than a merely defensive, force. Finally, he made use of the countermarch to provide a virtually continuous barrage of small-arms fire. The outcome of these reforms was the Swedish victory over the Danes at Axtorna in 1565.

Erik himself, however, must be denied the status of great commander, since owing to a strong trait of arrogance in his personality, he refused to be present on the field opposite Danish commanders who were his inferiors in rank. This habit of disappearing as soon as action was imminent caused much adverse reaction among his troops, with whom his brilliant experiments were not popular. He died in 1577, probably the victim of poison, and regretted by almost no one. After his death the army thankfully reverted to its old heavily defensive tactics and abandoned its heavy modern equipment, only to go into decline for the next half-century. Overbearing, testy, and given to temporary bouts of insanity, Erik XIV almost certainly had a touch of genius about him; he is now largely forgotten as an army reformer.

Espartero, Baldomero (1793–1879) Spanish general. A carter's son, whom his parents had intended for the priesthood, Espartero learnt the trade of arms in the popular rising (1808) against Napoleon's army of occupation. Like many fellow *guerrilleros* he subsequently gained entrance to the regular army, trained at the Colegio de Ingenieros at Cadiz but became an infantry officer. He returned from a tour of duty in the revolting American colonies a colonel and, when war broke out in Spain (First Carlist War), espoused the legitimist side and quickly rose to become commander-in-chief, winning a resounding victory at Luchana (1836) and, by raising the siege of Bilbao (1839), ending the civil war. Earning the popular nickname *el pacificador* and the title of *duque de la Victoria*, he subsequently adopted a wholly political career, was twice head of the government (1841–3, as regent, and 1854–6) but was obliged to spend the years 1843–9 in exile, his political touch, in an admittedly very difficult period of Spanish life, lacking deftness. Nevertheless, at the end of his life he was created *principe de Vergara* and awarded the title of royal highness.

Estaing, Jean Baptiste Charles Henri Hector, comte d' (1729–94) French admiral. His early career was spent as a soldier in the French armies in India, where he was taken prisoner at the siege of Madras (1759). Paroled on condition that he did not fight in India again, he became a sea officer and fought for a year around its coasts. During the American War of Independence he had created for him the title of 'Vice-admiral of the seas of Asia, Africa and America' and was given command of a fleet in the West Indies (where he had been governor of the Antilles, 1763–6). His knowledge of those waters gave him an advantage, which was partly cancelled however by his regarding sea warfare as an extension of that on land. Thus he was successful in blockading Admiral Richard Howe (q.v.) in Delaware Bay in 1778, but lacked the seamanship to cross the bar and destroy the British ships within. Transferring his fleet to the Antilles, he captured Grenada on 3 July 1779, but his battle with the inferior fleet of Admiral Byron was indecisive and at his unsuccessful attack on Savannah, Georgia, in October 1779, he was seriously wounded and retired to France. His liberal outlook led him to accept the Revolution with enthusiasm and he was appointed commander of the National Guard at Versailles (1789) and created Admiral of France in 1792.

During the Terror, however, he was arrested, tried and eventually guillotined.

Eugen, Prince of Savoy-Carignon (1663–1736) Imperial soldier, diplomat and military reformer. Prince Eugen was born in Paris on 18 October 1663, son of Eugène-Maurice, Prince of Savoy-Carignon, and Olympia Mancini, one of a bevy of nieces imported to France to further the ambitions of the detested Cardinal Mazarin. In 1673 his father died suddenly on active service, and Olympia, once a favourite of Louis XIV, made many enemies at court, including Madame de Montespan. She became involved in black magic and astrology, some said with the intention of winning back by magic her erstwhile place in the king's affections; in 1680 she was caught up in the '*affaire des poisons*', rumours were rife that she was involved in the death of her own husband, and she was banished from France. Eugen, with his brothers and sisters, was abandoned to the neglect of his grandmother (Olympia had made no financial provision for her children), and the king decided that he should enter the church. Already an unprepossessing child, he was tonsured and soutaned, and referred to in mocking tones as 'the little Abbé'. But Eugen was determined somehow to enter the army, and in 1683 engineered an audience with the king to request to join the colours; the answer was a peremptory 'no'. 'The request was modest, the applicant not,' the king later said of this audience, but whatever the reason, Eugen was henceforth determined to leave France and enter the service of some foreign army.

On 26 July of that same year he took his chance, fleeing from Paris disguised as a woman, and finally reaching Passau, where he encountered Emperor Leopold I and was received, as so many distinguished foreigners had been before him, into the multinational and polyglot imperial army. But he had transferred his allegiance to the empire at an unpropitious moment in its history: the emperor had fled to Passau to escape the Turkish army, which, for the first time in 150 years, was settling down to besiege Vienna with every prospect of success. Thus, Eugen's first encounter with the enemy was with the vast, fearsome and oriental army of the Porte. He was so to distinguish himself in the relief of Vienna, in which an imperial force under the Duke of Lorraine, and a Polish army under the dashing King John Sobieski (q.v.), fought their way down from the Kahlenburg Heights overlooking Vienna, that Leopold promised him the first regimental command to fall vacant, which was that of the Regiment of Dragoons of Kufstein. He covered himself in glory in the reconquest of Hungary, displaying great personal courage as well as brilliant qualities of leadership; his achievements did not go unnoticed, and he was rapidly promoted through major-general (1685) and lieutenant-general (1688) to, after the outbreak of the war of the Grand Alliance (1688–97), field-marshal, a remarkable achievement for a foreigner of only thirty with little in the way of money and background to expedite his progress. This meteoric rise culminated, in 1694, in his being appointed imperial commander-in-chief in Italy, though here he was to be severely handicapped by ill-equipped and inferior Spanish troops (recruited from the Spanish duchies in Italy), lack of money and support from Vienna, and the incompetence and excessive caution of the Italian generals, Carafa, and subsequently Caprara, in charge of 12,000 imperial reinforcements. He chafed, too, under the static conditions of siege-warfare, grasping, even at this early stage in his career, that only in movement and surprise lay the key to victory. The war of the Grand Alliance, however, gave him valuable experience of his other lifelong enemy, the French.

After the Hungarian campaign Leopold had refused to make peace with the Turks, setting his sights on Constantinople, with the result that Austria was now committed to a war on two fronts. In 1689 the Ottoman armies had retaken Belgrade, and were providing once again a serious threat in the east. In 1697 Eugen was despatched to the Turkish front as supreme commander and enjoyed the first major triumph of his solo career in the overwhelming victory of Zenta (1697). He had found the army in a deplorable state, unpaid, unclothed and desperately short of munitions and supplies, but in a matter of weeks he had succeeded, as usual with scant help from Vienna, in pulling them together into a tough fighting force. Having discovered that the sultan had thrown a bridge over the river Zenta to cross into Transylvania, and that much of the cavalry had already crossed, Eugen saw a chance he could not afford to throw away; despite the fact that his men had already done a ten-hour march, that they were still some distance from the river, and that there were only a few hours of daylight left, he reasoned that if he waited even a day the Turkish armies would slip across the river under cover of night. His inspired leadership spurred his soldiers on to greater effort, and with only two hours of daylight left he attacked the Turks in their encampment. They were taken completely by surprise as Eugen's pincer-movement forced them into an ever-decreasing space; the Austrians showed no quarter and 20,000 Turks were slaughtered, another 10,000 fleeing in panic to the river, only to be drowned by the crush of bodies; Eugen lost only 300 dead and 200 wounded. By the time darkness fell the Turkish army had been annihilated. It had been a bold and brilliantly audacious attack, the stakes made higher by the fact that Eugen had been instructed by Vienna to take no risks and engage with the enemy only if victory were certain. It being too late in the campaigning season to push on to Belgrade, Eugen turned south with a raiding force into Bosnia, retaking Sarajevo in October before returning to Vienna a hero, though not without the enemies which success brings.

On the outbreak of the war of the Spanish Succession (1701–14) Eugen took 30,000 Habsburg troops into northern Italy to fight the French under Catinat; discovering that the French army was sitting in the mouth of the pass, Eugen simulated a frontal attack while taking the main body of his army over the mountains towards Vicenza, a tremendous feat of organization and hardiness. The much larger French army was forced back over the Oglio river to defend Milan, and Catinat, disgraced, was replaced by Villeroi. Having been defeated by Eugen in a number of engagements, Villeroi retired for the winter of 1701–2 to Cremona, a strongly fortified city with unrivalled views of the Po and the plains of Lombardy; a siege or frontal attack being impossible in winter, Eugen conceived a plan to attack the city from within and without, infiltrating 4000 men through a disused canal into the heart of the town. Villeroi himself was taken prisoner, the French were in disarray, but the town remained untaken, for Austrian ammunition was running low. Disheartened by the failure of his plans due to lack of material assistance from Vienna, Eugen returned to Austria, and became president of the Imperial War Council (*Hofkriegsrat*); among the reforms he instituted were the abolition of the sale of commissions; the creation of a much stronger and more flexible cavalry – this was to have a lasting effect on Austria's subsequent military history – and the setting up of forward supply depots (hitherto it had been assumed that the army could not march more than five days away from its main magazine). He also did much to improve the lot of the common soldier.

Eugen returned to active service in 1703. Once again Austria was threatened from two sides: from the east, where Ferenc Rakoczy was leading a rebellion of Hungarian nobles and peasantry, and from the south, where a combined Franco-Bavarian army was pushing towards the Danube. He paid a brief visit to Hungary to pull together the disorganized Austrian forces, and then, as Marlborough (q.v.) marched eastwards from Holland into Germany, gathered all his available resources to join up with him to repulse the French and Bavarians. The battle of Blenheim (August 1704) was a resounding victory for Marlborough and Eugen, and removed the immediate threat to Austria. Eugen showed himself as much a master of the normal frontal assault as he had of the daring and ingenious plan, but the real triumph of the battle was the cementing of the brilliant partnership between the two great generals. So harmonious was their relationship, so unselfish their cooperation, that popular victory medals were struck depicting them as Castor and Pollux.

Eugen then turned once again to northern Italy, where he outflanked a French force besieging Turin, and having dealt the investing army a resounding rebuff in September 1706, proceeded over the next three months to sweep northern Italy clear of the French. In 1708 Eugen joined forces with Marlborough once again at Oudenarde (July 1708), another great allied victory which left the way open for the capture of Ghent and Bruges. On the fourth anniversary of Blenheim, 13 August 1708, the allied forces began their bombardment of Lille, a fortress constructed by Vauban (q.v.), and believed to be impregnable. On 9 December after a prolonged siege and heavy fighting, the citadel surrendered; it was the first time that any of Vauban's heavily defended fortresses had ever been breached. Malplaquet (September 1709) was the last battle that Eugen and Marlborough were to fight together; after a bloody and hard fight over difficult, heavily wooded terrain, the French, under Eugen's most redoubtable opponent Villars (q.v.), and, after he was wounded, Boufflers (q.v.), withdrew, but the allied victory was a Pyrrhic one; it brought them little strategic advantage, and they lost 24,000 dead or wounded against France's 12,000–15,000. It was also to induce a mood of war-weariness in England, which, skilfully exploited by the Tory opposition, led to Marlborough's downfall.

After the recall of Marlborough at the end of 1711, Eugen was left to fight on alone; deprived of support from England and with diminishing assistance from Vienna, he now faced the full weight of the French armies and the first major reverses of his career. But that his genius was not expended is amply demonstrated in the war against the Turks, which broke out in 1716. Having won a decisive victory at Peterwardein (August 1716) he proceeded to Belgrade, held by a garrison of 30,000 men, including the elite of the Janissaries. He invested the city with his 50,000 men, only to be besieged himself by a huge Turkish relief army of over 200,000 men. Although they seemed surely doomed, Eugen did not panic, nor did he allow his men to do so. Characteristically, he made the unexpected move, leading his men in a night attack against the Turkish lines, and despite heavy bombardment, instructed them to hold their fire until they were at close range, and then to lower their bayonets and charge. Within minutes the battery fell and the Turks were in full retreat; even now he would not let his men enter enemy lines, for he realized that a plundering army was especially susceptible to counter-attack. By the time daylight came victory was his, and Belgrade surrendered shortly afterwards. As active in peace as in war, he devoted the rest of his life to the reform and reconstruction of the Austrian army whose strengths and weaknesses he knew so well.

Classed by Napoleon as one of the seven great commanders of history, Eugen reintroduced a sense of enterprise into the static and formalized warfare of the late seventeenth and early eighteenth centuries. He was equally at home fighting the vast Ottoman hordes and the sophisticated French, equally the master of the conventional frontal attack and the ingenious and audacious plan. He used terrain brilliantly to his advantage, and made unprecedented use of cavalry, particularly of hussars and dragoons for reconnaissance work, a legacy which was to stay with the Habsburg army almost until its dissolution. Always willing to take risks, he never found himself incapable of taking the split-second decision which might win or lose the battle. Unselfish often to the point of self-effacement in his relationship with the great Marlborough, he never let any hint of rivalry or jealousy sully their partnership. Above all, he had the ability of the great commander to inspire both officers and men, and to extract every ounce of effort from often tired or disheartened troops.

Ewell, Richard Stoddert (1817–72) American (Confederate) general. A West Pointer, who had made a reputation in the Dragoons as a frontiersman and Indian fighter, Ewell chose the South in 1861, was at once commissioned colonel and quickly promoted brigadier. At First Bull Run he commanded the 2nd Brigade, was promoted major-general and given a division under Stonewall Jackson (q.v.) in the Shenandoah Valley campaign. Becoming one of Jackson's most trusted subordinates, he went with him to the Peninsula and fought in the Seven Days' battles. After his mentor's death he was promoted, but though showing bravery to the point of recklessness (he lost a leg at Groveton), he did not demonstrate the capacity for independent command. His command of a corps at Gettysburg, in the Wilderness and Spotsylvania was not really distinguished, and after he had been wounded again he was rightly retired to static duties at Richmond. He was much liked by his fellow officers and known as 'Old Bald Head' to his soldiers.

Exelmans, Remi Joseph Isidore (Baron; 1775–1852) Marshal of France. A volunteer of 1791, his exploits as an officer of cavalry attracted the attention of Murat (q.v.) who took him to Spain as chief of staff. Captured by the British, he escaped to become master of the horse to Murat, by then king of Naples, and to command a division in Russia. He rallied to Napoleon during the Hundred Days, took part in a charge at Ligny and directed the last action of the campaign at Rocquencourt near Versailles, 1 July 1815. Exiled, he was later pardoned and ultimately created a marshal by Napoleon III.

F

Faidherbe, Louis Léon Lesar (1818–89) French general and colonial governor. A Polytechnicien, he served first as a sapper in Algeria but in 1854 was sent as governor to the ancient West African colony of Senegal, which he found in a much decayed state. His boundless energy transformed its economy and equipped it with new hospitals, schools, roads, fortresses and harbours, including that of Dakar, while he added greatly to its extent by pushing expeditions into the neighbouring uncolonized territories. Detained by duties in North Africa during the opening stage of the Franco-Prussian war, he offered his services to Gambetta after the defeat of the field armies, organized a new Army of the North from untrained conscripts and won the victories of Pont-Noyelles (3 December 1870) and Bapaume (4 January 1871) against Manteuffel (q.v.) before being defeated at Le Mans (19 January). A soldier of 'luminous intellectual courage', he would, had the Republic not placed the marshalate in abeyance, surely have earned that dignity.

Fairfax, Thomas, Baron (1612–71) British soldier, 'Black Tom' Fairfax was the nearest approach on Parliament's side in the English Civil War to a military paragon. He excelled in battle, possessed outstanding physical courage, was honourable towards his enemies, trusted by his men, and stood outside the crude power politics which led to the death of Charles I and the establishment of a military dictatorship. In a war in which amateurs, perforce, played a large part, Fairfax had professional experience, having served with Sir Horace Vere in the Netherlands (1629–31) against the Spanish under Spinola (q.v.); it was a testing apprenticeship against some of the best troops in Europe. In the Bishops' War against the Scots (1639), Fairfax loyally answered Charles's summons to arms and raised a troop of dragoons; but in the Civil War he was firmly fixed on the Parliamentary side. Energetic in his native Yorkshire, raising troops and attacking the Royalists, he was surprised by Goring at Seacroft Moor (1643) and was forced to retreat in disorder. He lost again, to a much larger Royalist force, at Adwalton Moor later that summer, but he then put defeat entirely behind him.

In the autumn he joined Oliver Cromwell (q.v.) to meet the Royalist threat to Lincolnshire and the eastern counties. At the battle of Winceby, near Hagworthingham in Lincolnshire, the Royalist force was roundly beaten, and a sound partnership established between the two men. At Marston Moor (1644), where the battle was in the hands of Lord Leven (q.v.), Fairfax commanded 5000 men (infantry and cavalry) and Cromwell his troops of cavalry, the 'Ironsides'. It was Cromwell who delivered the decisive blow in the battle after all the other forces were committed. But Fairfax's role in the Civil War was as much in organization as on the field of battle. He argued hard for a professional army, independent of Parliament, trained and organized to the high standards which Cromwell had already established in his 'Ironsides'. Appointed captain-general of the New Model Army

(1645), he insisted on choosing his own officers and removing the army from the baleful political influence of Parliament. The New Model was his creation, not Cromwell's, and he remained the senior officer of the Parliamentary cause until 1650. The New Model was an army drilled and organized to the best European standards, 22,000 strong (although it was understrength at the outset), comprising 6600 cavalry, 14,400 infantry and 1000 dragoons. In its first major outing, the battle of Naseby (June 1645), it displayed discipline and courage, where the Royalists (particularly the cavalry of Prince Rupert, q.v.) showed courage but much less discipline. Again it was Cromwell who decided the battle; Fairfax's army had shown itself to have the makings of the fearsome 'godly army' it later became. In the western campaign later in the year Fairfax moved with ruthless efficiency, subduing towns and forcing the Royalists back into Cornwall.

In the Second Civil War (1648–9) Fairfax was occupied in the south-east of England, with a much reduced army, while Cromwell went north to face the Scottish army, who had now come out in support of Charles I. Capturing Colchester, which had declared for the king, Fairfax had a number of the senior officers defending the town shot, for they had broken the parole they had given in 1646. The mood of the army was grim, and Cromwell had determined on Charles's trial and death as the only sure solution to their problems. Fairfax could not agree, and a breach began to open between him and his former colleagues. He refused to have any hand in the king's death, and although he joined Cromwell in crushing Leveller agitation in the army, he refused entirely to take part in an aggressive war against the Scots. He laid down his command, leaving Cromwell to command in the Third Civil War (1650–1), and kept studiously out of politics, both during the period

of the English Republic and at the Restoration.

Fairfax was a tactician of great skill, supple in his responses to all circumstances. In two strokes, Naseby, and its sequel, the battle of Langport in Somerset, he applied a decisive strategy which resulted in the destruction of the two Royalist field armies of any strength. He had, it has been said, won the war in six weeks. At Colchester, and against the Levellers at Banbury, he behaved with strict justice but absolute firmness. Few, friend or enemy, had anything ill to say of him. He was a model soldier.

Falkenhayn, Erich von (1861–1922) German general. Born at Thorn, into one of the moneyless *junker* families which supplied the Prussian army with so many of its officers, Falkenhayn was commissioned into a line regiment. Selected for the *Kriegsakademie* and then posted to China where Germany had a large military mission as chief instructor at the Nankow Military School, his reports from Tientsin during the Boxer Rising attracted the attention of the kaiser. His favour propelled Falkenhayn up the ladder at exceptional speed, from the post of chief of staff of XVI Corps to command of the 4th Foot Guards – an almost unheard-of distinction for a line officer to receive – in 1911. In 1913 he was promoted general and made minister of war and, on the breakdown of the younger Moltke (q.v.) in November 1914, he combined that post with that of chief of the general staff. He proved a much more satisfactory commander than Moltke, but not the saviour of German strategy for whom the kaiser had hoped. His decision to transfer Germany's major military efforts to the east during 1915 was undoubtedly correct, and yielded the breakthrough victory of Gorlice-Tarnow. But Verdun (February 1916) was a mistake which in August cost him his appointment. During the rest of 1916 he commanded the Ninth Army against Romania, in 1917 the so-called Asiatic Corps in the Caucasus and in 1918–19 the Tenth Army in Lithuania.

Farragut, David Glasgow (1801–70) American (Union) admiral. A midshipman at eleven and prize-master of a captured British ship at twelve, Farragut's reputation dates from the Civil War, in which he first commanded the New Orleans expedition, opening the Mississippi as far as Vicksburg, 1862. In 1863 he was in the Gulf of Mexico operating against Port Hudson and in 1864 captured Mobile (5 August). He was promoted admiral in 1866, the first to hold the rank in the United States Navy.

Fayolle, Marie Emile (1852–1928) Marshal of France. Commander of the Sixth Army in the battle of the Somme, 1916, Fayolle was sent at the head of the French reinforcements to Italy after the disaster of Caporetto, November 1917. In 1918, as commander of the Reserve Army Group, he directed the counter-offensive of the Matz.

Ferdinand of Brunswick, Duke (1721–92) German soldier and statesman. Beset by enemies in the Seven Years' War (1756–63), Prussia possessed a military genius in Frederick the Great (q.v.); but the good fortune was doubled by the addition of a 'brilliant second' in Ferdinand of Brunswick. A soldier in the service of Prussia from his nineteenth year, he had proved his solid ability during the war of the Austrian Succession (1740–8). At the outset of the Seven Years' War George II of England requested that he should take command of the allied armies. After Frederick had crushed the French and Austrian troops at Rossbach (November 1757), the western campaign was left to Ferdinand and the allied army of 30,000 men.

When the winter was over therefore Ferdinand marched west and drove the

French back over the Rhine: at Crefeld (June 1758) the French commander Clermont decided to give battle, but was outfought by Ferdinand's smaller army and forced to retreat. But the following spring, the French attacked again, now under the more energetic Broglie (q.v.). At Bergen, near Frankfurt am Main, Ferdinand with 40,000 men met with a sharp defeat from Broglie's much larger army. Forced to fall back, with Broglie and Contades in hot pursuit, he decided to make a stand, much as Clermont had done at Crefeld the year before. But Ferdinand had better luck. At Minden (August 1759), he beat Broglie and Contades, despite the fact that they outnumbered him. But his troops were generally superior, and better handled. The British infantry, in an unheard-of manœuvre, advanced against the French cavalry, advancing and firing by volleys. This unhinged the French assault, and disaster for them was averted only by the failure of Lord George Germaine, Ferdinand's British subordinate commanding the British cavalry, to exploit the advantage despite clear orders to attack. Contades was able to retire in good order. The French had overstretched their lines of support and the bruising fight at Minden forced a withdrawal. The two armies sparred, and Ferdinand inflicted a further defeat on Broglie at Vellinghausen (1761). In the following year he drove the French out of Westphalia at the battle of Wilhelmstal and by the end of 1762 the French armies were, once again, beyond the Rhine. Prussia was safe in the west. But at the end of the war Ferdinand's relations with Frederick cooled and he left the Prussian army in 1766 to rule his duchy in tranquillity until his death, disturbed latterly by the tremors emanating from revolutionary France.

Ferdinand's greatest achievement was to weld a disparate allied army with some seven national elements into an effective fighting force. It required the talents of a consummate diplomat as well as those of a fighting general. He radiated confidence to all who came in contact with him, and he was fortunate in possessing in the Marquess of Granby, his British subordinate after the cowardly Germaine was withdrawn, an officer whose energy matched his own. Ferdinand had a clear grasp of the strategic needs of Prussia, and saw his aim to be that of protecting Frederick's back. He did not have his master's innate flair, but his unshakable steadiness fulfilled the need of the hour exactly.

Fisher, John Arbuthnot (1st Baron Fisher; 1841–1920) British admiral. The dominating figure of the Royal Navy in the late Victorian and Edwardian age, Fisher had been commissioned in 1854, seen service in the Crimea and distinguished himself at the bombardment of Alexandria, 1882. Appointed, after a series of senior commands, First Sea Lord in 1904, he embarked at once on a programme of reform and reconstruction which shook the navy to its topmasts. Fisher had enemies and few survived his first year of office. He also had ideas, of which the most startling (though it was not wholly his own) was that of the 'all big-gun ship', a battleship mounting guns of only one calibre, instead of several as hitherto, and thus capable of delivering a much heavier and more tightly bunched fall of shot.

To build such a ship meant making obsolete at a stroke the whole of the British battlefleet. But he overcame all opposition and the *Dreadnought*, armed with ten 12-inch guns and driven by high-speed turbines – also an innovation in a capital ship – was launched in 1906. Despite the cost, the Royal Navy was soon an all-Dreadnought fleet (while remaining larger than the German, its principal rival), with a scouting force of 'battlecruisers' (another, less successful, Fisher conception) to scout for them (*see* Beatty). Fisher retired in 1910 but

returned at the outbreak of war to replace Battenberg, who had been removed because of his German name and connections, and formed a close comradeship with Winston Churchill, then First Lord of the Admiralty. 'Yours till hell freezes over' was one characteristic farewell from Fisher to Churchill; but they fell out over the Dardanelles operation – for though he believed that 'the British army [ought to be] a projectile fired by the British navy' the target he favoured was the Baltic coast – and he retired in May 1915.

Foch, Ferdinand (1851–1929) Marshal of France. Foch was one of the genuinely great soldiers of the twentieth century, but rather in what he was – a man of warmth, humanity and fierce moral and physical courage – than in what he did (though his achievements were considerable). Born at Tarbes, near the shrine of Lourdes – his devout Catholicism was to retard his career during the anti-clerical reaction which followed the Dreyfus affair – he passed into the Polytechnique and was commissioned into the artillery in 1873. He had enlisted briefly as a private soldier in 1870, but had seen no fighting, and was to see none again until 1914, when he had command of a corps. In the intermission he made his name as a military teacher and thinker, returning to the Ecole de Guerre, where he had been a student in 1885 and professor of strategy and tactics, 1895–1900, as commandant in 1907. His teaching, epitomized in his book, *Principes de la Guerre* (1903), centred on the idea of 'the will to conquer', of the need for a general to cultivate a psychological superiority over his opponents and to imbue his soldiers with the same. It had a profound influence within the French army, so much so that by 1914 French tactics were based on the idea of the unrelenting offensive as a means of browbeating the enemy into subjection. But his mind was unusually flexible – having accepted as a result of the casualties suffered in his XX Corps' brave assault on Morhange in August 1914 that machine-guns defy browbeating, he sought more practical methods of overcoming the enemy.

Joffre (q.v.) had been impressed by Foch's handling of his corps in the battle of the Frontiers, and having sacked one-third of his generals by September, was able to offer him command of a force, soon to be called the Ninth Army, which is often credited with the decisive role in the battle of the Marne. Foch's signal during the battle has become famous: 'My centre is giving way, my right is falling back, situation excellent, I am attacking.' During the so-called Race to the Sea in October–November 1914, he co-ordinated, as Joffre's deputy, the operations of the British, French and Belgians on the northern wing and, as commander of the Northern Army Group, directed the spring offensive of 1915 in Artois. During 1916 he was titular commander of the French effort on the Somme but his reputation, with Joffre's, was failing.

Transferred to a meaningless advisory post in December 1916, it was not until early 1918 that power came his way again. In late 1917, as a means of co-ordinating Allied strategy after the Italian disaster at Caporetto (which Foch had a hand in repairing) a supreme war council, with a military committee of national representatives at Versailles, was set up. When the first German offensive broke in March 1918, Haig (q.v.), desperate for reserves, suddenly demanded that the military committee became an executive inter-Allied staff with power to direct troop movements. Lloyd George, anxious to curb Haig's power, and Clemenceau, delighted to strengthen a body that must have a French head, agreed and Foch was appointed generalissimo of the Allied armies, at first in the west, later everywhere. As such, he co-ordinated the Allied plans that first halted, then reversed the German offensives of April–July and led to their own war-winning offensive of August–September. In August Foch was created a marshal. He was also to be elected to the French Academy and to be made a Polish and British field-marshal. The piece of ground on which his statue stands opposite Victoria Station (from which the millions of British soldiers left for France, 1914–18) is French territory. On the plinth is written, 'I am conscious of serving Britain as I served my own country.'

Foix, Gaston de, duc de Nemours (1489–1512) French soldier. A military prodigy, Foix came from one of the most ancient families of France with an impeccable military pedigree. His military reputation however rests on one campaign, and two years of a short life. The French invasion of Italy had gone badly after the advent of the Spanish general Cordoba (q.v.) to head the Spanish–Neapolitan armies, but French fortunes had recovered after his recall in 1507. The French were decisively outnumbered, and their hold on their Italian conquests had become tenuous. It was therefore a major blow when their commander, the Duke of Nemours, was killed at the battle of Cerignola (1503). It was scarcely surprising that Louis XII (q.v.) made a frantic search for a new general after the death of Nemours's successor Amboise, but more unusual that he entrusted his fortunes to his young nephew, Gaston de Foix, Duke of Nemours in succession to his father.

Arriving in Italy at the end of 1511, Foix found a large force commanded by Raymond de Cardona besieging the French in Bologna (they had taken the city in May 1511). Travelling 'like a whirlwind', he spurred his men through day and night marches across the snow, to arrive completely unexpectedly in the rear of the Spanish and Papal forces.

The siege was hastily abandoned and Cardona retreated in disorder. A few weeks later, in February 1512, Foix appeared before Brescia, only nine days after he had left Bologna. He took the town by storm in an orgy of pillage which lasted for a week. Again displaying the same astonishing speed, he then hastened to invest Ravenna, which was strongly held by the Spanish, hoping to lure them from the town and tempt them into open battle. On 11 April Foix faced a somewhat smaller Spanish force commanded by Cardona and Pedro Navarro (Count of Alvetto). Both were good commanders, and they had the advantage of fighting on their own ground, their backs to a secure fortress. Foix on the other hand risked everything on the gamble of one battle. The superior Spanish artillery, under the command of Navarro, battered the French lines, but the French infantry, their ranks stiffened by 8500 *landesknechts* (German mercenary pikemen), held firm despite the large losses incurred in their exposed position facing the Spanish entrenchments. But the French artillery, causing less damage to the infantry and artillery than to the cavalry, raked the Spanish lines so that eventually Spanish discipline broke under the weight of fire and their cavalry charged prematurely. They broke against the French line, unable to provide any aid to the *tercios* (Spanish infantry) when the two masses of footsoldiers closed. The decisive moment came when a cannon, sent by Foix behind the Spanish position, opened fire on the demoralized Spanish. The bitter hand-to-hand fighting led to heavy casualties on each side: almost half the men engaged were either killed or wounded. But the victory was Pyrrhic for the French, for Foix was killed in an impetuous pursuit of the retreating Spanish. A career of enormous promise was thus brought to a premature close.

What Foix brought to the battlefield was energy and the fury of youth – he was only twenty-three at his death. He manœuvred his men at great speed, undertaking forced marches when his enemies had settled into their winter positions. He positively sought out battle, when his opponents were content to wage a war of position: he was prepared to take risks where others were not. Since he fought only one great battle it is hard to judge him as a tactician, but his skilled use of the element of surprise both before Bologna and at Ravenna, as well as his personal qualities of courage and daring, must indicate that had he survived he would have developed into a general of the highest calibre.

Fonck, René Paul (1894–1953) French fighter ace. Credited with seventy-five victories, Fonck was the Allied as well as the French Ace of Aces. He learnt to fly in 1915, survived the war untouched, remained in the service and retired as *inspecteur de l'aviation de chasse* in 1939.

Forrest, Nathan Bedford (1821–77) American (Confederate) general. A self-made and almost uneducated millionaire, Forrest joined the Confederate army as a private in 1861 but quickly raised, armed and mounted at his own expense a cavalry regiment, which he led in the Henry and Donelson campaign, later covering the retreat from Shiloh. Promoted brigadier-general in July 1862, he embarked on the series of cavalry raids into Union-held territory for which he was to become famous and feared. From December 1862 to January 1863 he devastated the railways in the rear of Grant's positions on the upper Mississippi. And during Sherman's Atlanta campaign, June–November 1864, he so harried the Union lines of communication that Sherman burst out, 'That devil Forrest ... must be hunted down and killed if it costs ten thousand lives and bankrupts the Federal treasury.' He took part with Hood (q.v.) in the Franklin and Nashville campaigns, his command by then having risen to the size of a corps. He was a man of immense personal toughness and ruthlessness. Attacked by one of his own officers over a grievance, he held his assailant's pistol hand, prized his penknife open with his teeth and fatally stabbed the man in his stomach. But he was also a soldier of near genius. Joseph E. Johnston (q.v.), asked to name the war's greatest soldier, answered, 'Forrest, who, had he had the advantages of a thorough military training and education, would have been the great central figure of the Civil War.' There is some evidence that he was first Grand Wizard of the Ku Klux Klan, the secret society raised by Southerners of Forrest's background to resist the consequences of defeat.

Franchet D'Esperey, Louis Felix Marie François (1856–1942) Marshal of France. 'Desperate Frankie' to the many British officers who knew him and welcomed his wholehearted co-operation during the First World War, this Saint-Cyrien, a veteran of the expeditions to China, 1900, and Morocco, 1912, was commanding I Corps in 1914. That splendid formation from the northern *départements* had actually to defend its home territory in August, doing so brilliantly under the direction of Franchet, who at Guise (29 August 1914) won a resounding minor victory, temporarily halted the German advance from Brussels to Paris and badly mauled the Imperial Guard Corps. Promoted to replace the vacillating Lanrezac (q.v.) at the head of the Fifth Army, he retook Reims in September and was later selected to command an army group: in 1915 that of the east, in 1917 that of the north. In 1918 he succeeded Guillaumat (q.v.) as Allied commander-in-chief in Macedonia and won the victory of the Vardar over the Bulgarians (15–29 September). Created a marshal in 1921, he was elected to the French Academy in 1934.

Francis I (1494–1547) King of France. Succeeding to the throne of France at the age of twenty-one, his life was dominated by the inner compulsion to continue the conflict with the Habsburgs, bequeathed to him by Louis XII (q.v.). He invaded Italy in 1515 with an army of 30,000, eager to capture Milan. At Marignano (1515), he experienced the power of the Swiss infantry, and only in desperate hand-to-hand fighting was their advance stemmed. But his objective was gained, and Milan was ceded to France. In 1521 war was resumed, and Francis's Italian army under the command of Lautrec smashed the Swiss at Bicocca (1522) by the use of fire-power against the solid mass of infantry. But Milan was lost and the tide of war turned against Francis. In 1524 the French renegade Charles de Bourbon (q.v.) marched into France, and Francis was forced to gather a large army to repel him. He then riposted by a new thrust into Italy, but at the battle of Pavia the superior tactical skill of the imperial general Pescara (q.v.) told against him, and although he led his cavalry with great bravery to regain the initiative, the battle was lost; Francis was taken prisoner and sent to Madrid, where he was forced to conclude a humiliating peace. Released in 1526, he renounced his pledges and renewed the war in Italy. But his luck had deserted him, and he was forced to unfavourable terms (1529) at the 'Ladies Peace' of Cambrai. He waged war on Charles V twice more (1535–8 and 1542–4), but without success. The later wars are most interesting for Francis's use of alliances with Protestant princes and the Turks against the Habsburgs, foreshadowing a technique to be widely used by French kings. Francis was a ruler of considerable talents and an able soldier, but like his great adversary Charles V he was not lucky in war.

Franco, Francisco (-Bahamonde; 1892–
1975) Spanish general and head of
state. The son of a naval paymaster,
Franco was himself intended for the
service until, a financial crisis interrupting the recruitment of naval cadets, he
entered the Toledo Infantry Academy
(the Alcazar, which was to figure
prominently in the Civil War of 1936–9)
in 1907. Commissioned into the 8th
Regiment in 1910, he was posted to
Morocco in 1913 and transferred to the
Regulares (native infantry) with whom
he showed himself to be an officer of
exceptional efficiency and courage. In
1918 the creator of the newly raised
Spanish Foreign Legion asked for him
as his second-in-command and in 1923
he became its commander, at thirty the
youngest lieutenant-colonel in the army.
He had been the youngest captain and
in 1926 was to become the youngest
general (perhaps in the whole of Europe)
for his part in the successful counter-
offensive against Abd el-Krim (q.v.). In
1928 he was appointed director of a
new General Military Academy at Saragossa, but for his loyalty to the king
during the abdication crisis of 1930 was
removed and stripped of seniority. His
outstanding talents eventually overcame
the republican government's mistrust of
him, however, and he was sent in 1933
to command in the Balearics, then to
suppress the Asturian rising of 1934,
and in 1935 as commander-in-chief to
Morocco. In early 1936, as fears of a
military rising took hold of the Popular
Front government, he was dispatched to
the distant Canary Islands, his Catholic
and monarchist loyalties, together with
his military reputation, making him a
prime object of suspicion. From that
post he nevertheless managed to keep in
touch with the officers' insurrectionary
movement and, on the outbreak of the
Civil War in July, flew to Tetuán, Spanish Morocco, to supervise the transport
of the Army of Africa to the mainland. He
was shortly, on the death of Sanjurjo,
to become commander of all 'Nationalist' forces in Spain, and political leader
of the anti-Republicans. His singlemindedness and strategic skills were
chiefly responsible for their victory in
1939, after which he became regent and
head of state.

Frederick II, 'The Great' (1713–
86) King of Prussia. A traveller who
visited the 'new Alexander', Frederick II
of Prussia, after his great victories,
would have been disappointed had he
expected to find a hero in the classic
mould. Frederick scarcely seemed a great
commander, with his shabby clothes and
unmilitary mien. He was not an 'intuitive' general; as Macaulay lucidly
phrased it: 'His proficiency in military
science was simply the proficiency which
a man of vigorous faculties makes in
any science to which he applies his mind
with industry and earnestness.' The hor-
rific circumstances of Frederick's childhood and adolescence, the son of the
militarist boor Frederick William I
(q.v.), made him a cynical, covert and
stoical personality, as free from deep
affection as from devouring hatreds.

Frederick's real inheritance from his
father was a fine army of 80,000 men
and a full war-chest, but more important
still, a centralized and perfectly subservi-
ent state. Frederick never had to worry,
even in the direst extremity, whether
taxes would continue to be collected,
recruits still arrive for their military service, and the whole apparatus of state
still function as his executive arm.
When, at the beginning of his reign, he
gave audience to the greatest of his
father's generals, Leopold I (q.v.) of
Anhalt Dessau, the 'Old Dessauer', he
told him: 'In this kingdom, I am the
only person to exercise authority.' He
spoke the exact truth, for he rapidly
centralized within his personal jurisdic-
tion even those few functions which his
father had delegated. His proficiency in
the military arts was quickly acquired,

and it was, indeed, an intellectual approach to war. Frederick took little notice of the established tactical and strategic conventions of war. He looked, instead, with a driving logic at the particular qualities of his troops and the restraints which the geographical situation of his territory imposed upon him. Prussia was a kingdom vulnerable to all his likely enemies: France, Russia, Austria. The Saxon border lay only some few miles from Berlin: there were no great natural defensive positions, such as the mountains surrounding Bohemia, which formed a line of defence. Prussia, therefore, depended on an active, mobile army to blunt the assaults of an enemy before they could gather strength. The essence of Frederican war was the offensive. As he acutely observed: 'Our wars must be short and active ... Those who lead the Prussian armies must be clever and careful, but must try to bring the issue to a decision.' In an age when generals still preferred the solid tempo of a siege to the myriad uncertainties of a battle, Frederick was prepared to take risks. As the sole master of Prussia he could afford to shrug off criticism of his methods, even from so professional and eminent a source as his brother Henry: most failed generals risked dismissal, while Frederick could accept the odd failure, though the stakes he played for were much higher.

Years of training by the 'Old Dessauer' had given Prussia the best infantry in Europe – the most flexible in manœuvre, the fastest-firing, the steadiest under attack. They also possessed something of the staunch Protestant spirit which had fired the armies of Gustavus Adolphus (q.v.). 'We fight for religion, for you, for the fatherland,' one veteran told Frederick after the battle of Liegnitz. The cavalry and the artillery were sadly deficient for the offensive campaigns which Frederick wished to wage, and he recast their structure and equipment for the Seven Years' War (1756–63). What

he lacked were the light 'auxiliary' troops – hussars and light infantry, which the Austrians possessed in such numbers. In his tactics Frederick tried always to match his methods to the terrain and particular situation, but the very qualities of speed and flexibility in attack which characterized his army at its best meant that he had to strike for a decisive advantage early in a battle, before it could develop into a bruising and costly fire-fight. He relied on the power and shock of his attack to break and disrupt an enemy: when the attack was weakened, as at Kunersdorf (1759), or the enemy stood their ground, as at Zorndorf (1758), Frederick risked disaster.

The first war of Frederick's reign was, despite all the excuses which have been made for him by his apologists, a naked aggression. Like the other powers of Europe, Prussia had accepted the Pragmatic Sanction, constructed by the Emperor Charles I so that his daughter Maria Theresa should be able to inherit his dominions unopposed; Frederick agreed to support her claims, provided Silesia was ceded to him. To make good his claim, he occupied the province. 'Frederick's first battle was fought at Mollwitz,' wrote Macaulay, 'and never did the career of a great commander open in a more inauspicious manner ... Not only did he not establish his title to the character of an able general; but he was so unfortunate as to make it doubtful whether he possessed the vulgar courage of a soldier.' Mollwitz was won by the steadiness of the Prussian infantry under von Schwerin: Frederick had followed advice to leave the battle when its outcome seemed in doubt. Never again did he leave the field of battle until the issue was clear, and thereafter behaved with an almost foolhardy bravery. The next major battle of the First Silesian War (1740–2) took place in the following year at Chotusitz (1742) where the cavalry, which had failed so lamentably in the attack at Mollwitz, carried the day. But neither of these battles displayed any great skill on Frederick's part, merely that he was served by excellent generals and well-trained troops. He succeeded in making a favourable peace at the treaty of Breslau (1742), leaving his French allies to fight on alone. But in 1744, alarmed at the great successes of the Austrians, and fearing that they would attempt to recover Silesia, he launched a Second Silesian War (1744–5).

In the two years of peace he had increased his armies to 140,000 and given his troops elaborate field training: he had learnt from the mistakes of the first war. But his plan was too ambitious, for he plunged deep into Bohemia, capturing towns and fortresses. Before long, however, he discovered that his intelligence was faulty, and he was in danger of being trapped by powerful Austrian armies in a hostile terrain. His retreat into Silesia almost turned into a disaster, and his Bohemian frolic cost him 17,000 men lost through desertion alone, so arduous were the conditions on the return. He was able to write from bitter experience in his *General Principles of War* (1748): 'On the whole, those wars are useless in which we move too far from our borders. All wars that others have led in this fashion we have seen end in disaster.' Fortunately for Frederick the assault which the Austrians now mounted into Silesia in the following spring (1745) was led not by the competent Marshal Traun, but by the much less effective Prince Charles of Lorraine (q.v.). Frederick 'baited the mousetrap' and drew the Austrians down on to the Silesian plain. At Hohenfriedburg (1745) Frederick wrong-footed the Austrian defence by a set of adroit feints, and then smashed home with infantry and cavalry.

In the few hours after dawn Frederick had established his reputation. The Austrians had lost over 13,000 dead and prisoner, the Prussians less than 1000. He advanced into Bohemia, but with no more success, ultimately, than in the previous year. On his return to Silesia his army was forced to fight against Charles of Lorraine in carefully prepared positions. He hoped to destroy the Prussians by massed artillery fire; but Frederick, contrary to all expectations, manœuvred his army with great rapidity and launched an all-out attack, uphill, on the Austrian left. Once again Charles had misjudged his enemy, and the result was a further 8000 Austrian casualties and free passage for the Prussians back into Silesia. Charles now tried yet another approach, attacking into Prussia itself through Saxony, but Frederick anticipated him and caught him unprepared, twice, at Hennersdorf and Görlitz (1745). The final blow to Prussia's enemies was the sharp defeat inflicted on the Saxon army under Rutowski. At Kesselsdorf (1745) the 'Old Dessauer', leading his beloved infantry across the snow, outfought his enemies and drove them from the field. This succession of hammer-blows brought the Austrians to the negotiating table and peace was signed at Dresden (1745).

Frederick had survived his apprenticeship and established himself as a new star in the military firmament. With Silesia firmly in his grasp, and as a result a 50 per cent increase in state revenues, as well as two and a half million new subjects, his main concern was to hold it. But considerable dangers confronted him. He had alienated his allies by abandoning obligations when it suited him; the Austrians under Kaunitz (who became chancellor in 1753) were working for an understanding with France; Russia was being drawn into his enemies' camp. Frederick's answer to these threats was to increase his army to 154,000 and extend his cavalry and artillery. But even with Silesia there was a limit to the revenue and manpower available for a prolonged struggle. He expected war and prepared for it: he wanted to amass a war-chest of twenty million thalers, enough for four campaigns, before attacking; in the event, in 1756, he had only thirteen million. In August 1756, believing his enemies would attack him in the next campaigning season, he struck first, occupying Saxony, a province he had always coveted. But Saxon resistance was stronger than he had expected, and although eventually he was in complete control, he was prevented from attacking into Bohemia by the onset of winter. At Lobositz (October 1756) he had beaten an Austrian army under von Browne, but casualties were about equal on both sides. Frederick could afford losses much less than his numerous enemies.

When Frederick invaded Bohemia after the winter, he found, as the foretaste of Lobositz had indicated, that the Austrians had learnt from their mistakes against him. He beat Charles of Lorraine outside Prague, but only because he exploited an Austrian error and split their army. But the victory cost him over 13,000 dead, many of them his elite Prussian troops. The Austrians sent up a relief army under Daun (q.v.), a much more dangerous adversary, and Frederick turned from the siege of Prague to attack this new enemy; but Daun was not to be tempted into an attack, and sat in a strong defensive location to await the Prussian assault. At Kolin (June 1757), he repulsed Frederick's assaults, for the loss of 8000 to the Prussian 12,000. 'My heart is broken,' Frederick wrote to Moritz of Dessau, 'yet I am not dejected ... and I shall try to make up for this defeat.' But disaster piled on disaster: Prussia, even Berlin itself was ravaged by his enemies' armies, and his mother, for whom he had some affection, died. But the year ended with a complete reversal of fate: he triumphed in two great battles, at Rossbach (November 1757) against the

French, and exactly a month later, at Leuthen, against the Austrians.

At Rossbach, Frederick faced a Franco-Imperial army of 64,000 with a third that number. He used the hilly contours to move his army, out of sight of the French, to a new position where he could trap the French between the anvil of his infantry and artillery and the hammer of his cavalry. The French, who had hoped to outflank Frederick's original position, were themselves outflanked; in a battle lasting little over an hour they lost 8000 men to Frederick's 165 dead. The decisive element in the battle had been speed: Frederick had used his greater flexibility to adopt new positions, and his cavalry under von Seydlitz (q.v.) attacked 'compact like a wall, and at an incredible speed', as an eyewitness reported. The French threat was shattered and Frederick turned east to face his more dangerous adversaries, the Austrians and Russians. Leuthen was Frederick's greatest battle and his final triumph against the ill-starred Charles of Lorraine. Once again Frederick took advantage of 'dead ground' to march his men secretly to a position where they could surprise the enemy in the flank. But the beauty of Leuthen was that both wings of the Prussian army worked in complete harmony: the cavalry provided the feint to the Austrian right, drawing in the Austrian reserves, while Frederick pounced on the Austrian left. Then, from left and right, they smashed through the Austrian defences. Once again Silesia had proved disastrous for Charles of Lorraine, who lost nearly 7000 dead, 20,000 prisoners, 116 guns and 51 colours. Prussian losses amounted to less than 7000. But this was to be the last victory where Frederick's casualties were so far outnumbered by those of his enemies. In 1758 he won smashing victories at Zorndorf and Hochkirk, but in both cases at great cost.

The strategy of blunting the enemy's

power to attack by forcing battle after battle was now more devastating for Prussia than her enemies: in the first two years of the war he had lost over 100,000 men, the veterans his father had trained and he himself had perfected. The new drafts had nothing like the quality of their predecessors, and although, numerically, his forces remained stable, he was no longer able to indulge in some of the wilder flights of tactical fancy, certain that his well-drilled troops could execute them. In 1759, as the Russian contribution to the allied war effort increased, Frederick was forced more and more on to the defensive, seeking to prevent the union of Austrian and Russian forces, which could be disastrous for him. At Kunersdorf (1759) he faced the combined armies of Laudon (q.v.) and Soltikov, who heavily outnumbered him. Frederick, desperate to snatch a victory where none was possible, continued his assaults long after it was clear they could not succeed. He lost more than 20,000 men, and entered a mood of black despair. But he recovered himself and again attacked. Aided by Daun's sensible strategy of avoiding battle except under the most favourable of circumstances, he regained Silesia; but he was now fighting for survival itself. At Liegnitz he skilfully avoided the converging Austrian and Russian armies and smashed through Laudon's Austrian forces, costing them 10,000 casualties. But at Torgau (November 1760) he beat Daun with the loss of 13,000 men, more than the Austrians suffered.

Although the war lasted for two more years, all the participants were exhausted. Frederick, in his strategy of aggressive attrition, had fought his enemies to a standstill, although no doubt it was the withdrawal of the Russians from the war in January 1762 after the death of the Empress Elizabeth, his most dedicated enemy, which allowed him to survive. He had fought for seven years, at enormous cost, to maintain what he

had held at the outset – Silesia. For years to come Prussians believed that 'Old Fritz' had discovered the ultimate secrets of the art of war, teaching the manœuvres he had used as if they were the stone tablets of the Law. They were wrong, as Napoleon's victories were to prove. But it was Napoleon himself, who as he stood before the tomb of Frederick in Potsdam remarked, 'Were he still alive, we should now not be here in Prussia', who appreciated the brilliance of Frederick's achievement. Frederick had demonstrated with utmost clarity that a state with an army in being could never be defeated until that army was finally destroyed. He was not hidebound in his tactics or methods, varying his techniques to match the occasion, but there was a limit to his scope for inventiveness as the quality of his troops declined. Ultimately his reputation is secured by his conduct of Rossbach and Leuthen, where the mind of the commander was reflected so clearly in the action on the ground. After the war Frederick, in the remaining twenty-three years of his life, set about the reconstruction and enrichment of his kingdom. As he remarked to his brother Henry: 'If I repair adequately the ravages of war, I shall have achieved something worthwhile, and that is now the limit of my ambitions.' But at the root of his greatness as a general lay a sense of audacity and boldness, which placed him alongside the other great captains of history who shared that simple but potent quality.

Frederick William, 'The Great Elector' (1620–88) Prussian monarch and statesman. At the start of the Thirty Years' War (1618–48) Brandenburg Prussia was a collection of states united only in the person or its ruler. By the death of the Great Elector it was a coherent state and the major power in northern Germany. The success of Frederick William, the 'Great Elector', was accomplished not so much on the battlefield as in the chancellery. He was successful in war, as his crushing victory over the Swedes at Fehrbellin (1675) clearly showed. But his real achievement was in reforming the finances of his estates to provide a regular revenue and thus to create a standing army financed from the profits of his fiscal reforms. Frederick William was a pragmatist, taking advantages where they could be gained from war or alliances, but never risking too much on the chance of war to the bitter end. He recognized that the greatest constraint on Prussia's policy was her poverty, which he attempted to remedy, and her lack of a proper army, which was really accomplished however only under his grandson, Frederick William I (q.v.).

Frederick William I (1688–1740) Prussian monarch and army reformer. It was Frederick William I who gave to the Prussian state its particular stamp of authoritarianism, which persisted until its final downfall. 'I must be served,' he wrote, 'with life and limb, with house and wealth, with honour and conscience, everything must be committed except eternal salvation – that belongs to God. But all else is mine.' Coming to the throne in 1713 he instantly disposed of the attempts at style and elegance which had distinguished the court of his father, and set about the construction of a court and state with total subordination to his will. He succeeded in creating in the lands which made up the kingdom of Prussia an economically productive secular state, with a total population of 2.5 million obedient subjects and an army of more than adequate size. He increased the inherited army of some 40,000 to 80,000, trained them to a peak of efficiency with the help of Leopold (q.v.) of Anhalt Dessau, the Old Dessauer, a stern soldier of the same cast of mind as Frederick William himself (Frederick William I always appeared in uniform, and thought of himself as a simple

soldier; he certainly displayed the callousness and boorishness which marked many soldiers), and brought their equipment and organization up to the best standards of the day. Some regiments, like his regiment of giant Grenadiers, for which he scoured Europe for recruits, were playthings, but the army as a whole was a fearsome instrument of war. It was the most professional army in Europe, well paid and armed, completely responsive to the ruler's command. But because Frederick William kept his kingdom at peace, Prussia was ignored by the great powers, his army dismissed as being fit only for the parade ground. To his son, he bequeathed an army; but, more important, he left him a state completely subordinated to the monarch's wishes, an aristocracy bent to the service of the state, and a war-chest of eight million thalers. No ambitious young man could have received a better inheritance.

Frémont, John Charles (1813–80) American (Union) general and explorer. 'A sincere and attractive person, but a giddy and fumbling general', Frémont had originally joined the army as a topographer, gaining the title 'The Pathfinder' for his exploration of the Rocky Mountains in 1838–45. Elected governor of California in 1846, having been instrumental in arranging its accession to the Union, he was court-martialled for disobedience to the orders of a presidential emissary, resigned his post and commission and was elected a US senator. In 1856 he stood against Buchanan for the presidency as the new Republican Party's candidate and in 1861 was offered major-general's rank and command of the Western Department. Conceiving his powers to be as much political as military, he emancipated the slaves of all who opposed the government, a measure which Lincoln at once revoked. On 10 August 1861 his troops were defeated by an invading

Confederate army at Wilson's Creek and he was removed. Appointed to the Mountain Department in March 1862, he was quite out-generalled by Jackson (q.v.) in the Shenandoah Valley campaign, but, when his force was placed under the orders of Pope (q.v.), he refused to accept his authority. He was relieved and spent the rest of the war in New York 'awaiting orders'.

French, John Denton Pinkstone (1st Earl of Ypres; 1852–1925) British field-marshal. A prototypal blimp in appearance, red-faced and white-moustached, French had begun service life in the navy (*Britannia* cadet, 1866–8, midshipman 1868–70), in which his father had served. A soldier at heart, however, he managed to transfer to the Suffolk Artillery Militia and thence to the 19th Hussars, which he rose to command at the early age of thirty-six, partly through professional application (a habit he later learnt to disguise), partly through the dash he showed in the Gordon Relief Expedition, 1884. Sponsored by Redvers Buller (q.v.), he passed to the staff, rewrote the *Cavalry Manual*, was promoted brigadier and in 1899 sailed to South Africa to command a brigade. The Boer War was the making of his career, his talents being exactly suited to the free-ranging cavalry tactics for which it called. As commander of the cavalry force he cleared Cape Province of rebels during 1899 and early the following year led the relief of Kimberley. For these and other achievements he was knighted and promoted substantive major-general.

Sent home to command at Aldershot, he took a major part in Haldane's (q.v.) reform of the army and, having served as inspector-general, was appointed chief of the Imperial General Staff in 1912 and promoted field-marshal in 1913. Although he was obliged to resign as CIGS for his ill-conceived efforts to palliate military hostility to Irish Home

Rule ('the Curragh Incident' of 1914) he nevertheless took command of the British Expeditionary Force in August and led it to France. Unfortunately the pressures to which he was to be subjected there were greater than he could bear. During the retreat from Mons (where his army had fought with effect and superb resolution), he became convinced that disaster was inevitable and that his duty was to save what he could of the BEF, even at the expense of abandoning the alliance; it took a visit by Kitchener (q.v.) to stiffen him. Once the Germans had entrenched, his mood reversed and he became overoptimistic, overestimating the possibilities of success in the first battle of Ypres (which city he must nevertheless be given the credit for saving) and in the minor trench offensives he launched during 1915 (Neuve Chapelle, Festubert, Aubers Ridge). By September, when he was called upon to co-operate with the French in a joint offensive, he had again to be pressured into action and threw away the opening success at Loos (25 September 1915). His growing incapacity had become a matter for comment in the army and at home and in December he was replaced by Haig (q.v.), his principal subordinate and critic. He was subsequently commander of home forces and lord-lieutenant of Ireland 1918–21, a period when no one of his temperament could have succeeded in the post. On his removal he was created Earl of Ypres. All efforts to rehabilitate his reputation have failed: he was not fit for high command.

Freyburg, Bernard Cyril (1st Baron Freyburg; 1889–1963) New Zealand soldier. Though British by birth, his parents took him, aged two, to New Zealand where he grew up, was educated and joined the army. In 1914 he took leave to serve on Pancho Villa's side in the Mexican civil war, but reached England in time to join the Royal Naval Division in the defence of Antwerp. In 1915 he took part in the Gallipoli landings, where he won the first of his DSOs for swimming two miles in the icy waters of the Hellespont to lay diversionary flares. In the following year he won the VC in France and was promoted brigadier-general, the youngest in the British army, and in the following year major-general as commander of the famous 29th Division. In the Second World War he was made general officer commanding the New Zealand forces, a post he held throughout the war. In 1941 he was obliged to defend Crete in very inauspicious circumstances and, after a heroic resistance, to abandon the island. After the war he became governor-general of New Zealand. A friend of poets – he was present at the burial of Rupert Brooke on Skyros – he seemed to his contemporaries a reincarnation of the classical ideal of manhood.

Friedrich Karl, Prinz (1828–85) Prussian field-marshal. Son of Prince Karl and grandson of King Frederick William III of Prussia, he had a military education (Roon, q.v., was his tutor), first saw action in the 1848–9 revolution, where he was wounded charging insurgents at Wiesenthal, and in 1860 was appointed to command III Corps. He was a disciplinarian and a zealot and his corps was soon second only to the Guard in standards of training. During the Danish war of 1864 he succeeded Wrangel (q.v.) as commander-in-chief, with Moltke as his chief of staff, and together they planned the capture of the island of Alsen which ended the war. In 1866 he commanded First Army and directed its operations up to and during the battle of Sadowa (Königgrätz), in which it played the decisive role. In 1870 he was less successful, his headstrong conduct of Second Army's operations seriously conflicting with Moltke's strategy in the opening stages. He recovered his mistakes, however, and contributed

greatly to the success at Vionville and Saint Privat, 16 and 18 August. He was then left to blockade Metz and took the surrender of Bazaine (q.v.), for which he was promoted field-marshal. In the war that followed in the French provinces he led First Army in the Loire campaign and won the victory of Le Mans on 12 January 1871 (against, it must be said. French forces inferior in quality). Called the Red Prince from his habit of wearing Guard Hussar uniform, he was the last of the Hohenzollerns to show the military skill by which the family had risen to pre-eminence.

Friedrich Wilhelm, Duke of Brunswick (1771–1815) Prussian soldier. He fought for Prussia against France in 1792 and 1806, when he was taken prisoner. Napoleon vetoed his succession to the duchy, so on his release he raised a free corps, fought the emperor in Bohemia in 1809 and made good his escape to England with his followers, whom he then took to fight in the Peninsula. In 1815 he brought his Black Hussars to fight in Belgium after Napoleon's escape from Elba and was killed at their head at Quatre Bras, 16 June. They fought with particular ferocity at Waterloo, two days later, to avenge his death.

Fritsch, Werner, Freiherr von (1880–1939) German general. An artillery officer, a horseman and a man of great personal charm, Fritsch was appointed chief of the general staff (*Heeresleitung*) in 1934 and thus head of the army; he was promoted colonel-general in 1936. In 1938 he and Blomberg (q.v.) were accused of improprieties (the latter rightly, he falsely), the Nazi leadership wishing to place its own nominees at the head of the armed forces. Paralysed by the shock of the accusation of homosexual behaviour, Fritsch accepted dismissal and retired. A military court of honour of senior officers subsequently established his innocence, but the only recompense he received from Hitler was the honorary colonelcy of the 12th Artillery Regiment. He insisted on accompanying it to war in 1939 and was killed by a stray bullet on reconnaissance outside Warsaw. The army's failure to oppose Hitler over the Fritsch affair is usually regarded as marking its capitulation to him.

Frunze, Mikhail Vasilievich (1885–1925) Russian general, commissar for war. A member of the lower middle-class – his father was a medical assistant – Frunze completed a technical education but, having become a Communist, embarked on the career of professional revolutionary. He found work in a textile mill, took part in the 1905 revolution in Moscow, was subsequently twice arrested and imprisoned and during the First World War organized anti-Tsarist groups among the soldiers on the western front. After the February revolution he was elected to various soviets, took part in suppressing the rebellion of Kornilov (q.v.) and in the October revolution in Moscow. An organizer of Red Army units against the Whites during 1918, in September he was appointed commander of the Fourth Army and fought with success against both Wrangel and Kolchak (qq.v.). After the civil war, he became chief spokesman of those who opposed the military methods of Trotsky (q.v.), particularly his belief in a workers' militia as the proper form of army for a socialist state. Frunze held that a standing army provided the only means of waging the kind of offensive warfare which the Soviet state must pursue if attacked. In 1924 he was appointed Trotsky's deputy, signifying that he had won the battle for control of the Red Army, and in January 1925 succeeded him as commissar for war. Shortly afterwards he died under surgery, the victim, it has been alleged, of a medical murder instigated by Stalin who feared his rising power. With Trotsky he

must be regarded as father of the Soviet army. Its staff college, of which he was briefly head, was named after him.

Fuller, John Frederick Charles (1878–1964) British general and military writer and thinker. Fuller entitled his autobiography *Memoirs of an Unconventional Soldier*, which indeed was what he became, but his beginnings were a period stereotype: Malvern, Sandhurst and the Oxford and Buckinghamshire Light Infantry. With the latter he fought in the Boer War (subject of his *Last of the Gentlemen's Wars*) where the Boers' skill awakened his interest in the training of amateur soldiers and led him, after studying at the Staff College, to take a post as adjutant of a Territorial battalion. Because of that appointment, he missed going to France in August 1914 and found himself on the staff, where he remained for most of the war. This did not mean that he dodged the front line – he was a fire-eater – but that he was saved from the great slaughter of young regular officers in 1914–15.

The gain was the British army's, for Fuller turned out a brilliant staff officer and, when posted to the new-born Tank Corps, a tactical innovator of genius. It was he who planned the battle of Cambrai (20 November 1917), the first great tank attack in history, and proposed 'Plan 1919' for a full-blown tank army. That idea was to mesmerize him throughout the postwar years, but the relentlessness, to say nothing of the intelligence and proselytizing skills with which he propounded it, increasingly irritated his superiors. A succession of important posts – chief instructor at the Staff College, 1922, military assistant to the chief of the Imperial General Staff, 1926, commander or the new experimental brigade, Aldershot, and GSO I of Ironside's 2nd Division – only brought him closer to those who most disfavoured his views. In 1930 he was placed on half-pay, firmly refused an appointment to command in Bombay, 'which he considered a waste of his talents', in 1932 published a book entitled *Generalship: Its Diseases and Their Cure* (he had been promoted major-general in 1930), and the following year was placed on the retired list. Thereafter his life took a very curious turn, when he became one or the principal ornaments of Mosley's British Union of Fascists, but he recovered from it to devote the rest of his life to what perhaps was his true vocation of authorship.

Fuller was a prophet, whose gospel failed to determine the future in every detail but whose message was in its central theme powerfully correct: that massed armoured forces were the key to victory in industrial warfare. It had been listened to with attention in Germany where Guderian (q.v.) acknowledged Fuller as his mentor and, through the hard lesson of defeat at German hands, was eventually heard in Britain and America. Fuller received no official recognition for the originality of his work and devoted his later years chiefly to historical writing. He was in all the author of some thirty books. Known as 'Boney' to his army contemporaries from his facial resemblance to Bonaparte and his Napoleonic impatience with failure to follow the quickness of his own military thinking, he might, given an opportune war, have achieved a British Austerlitz. But it seems unlikely, for his real talent was in making, not breaking, important enemies.

G

Galliéni, Joseph Simon (1849–1916) French general. Like so many of the outstanding soldiers of France of the First World War, his reputation had been made in the building of her empire. Commissioned from Saint-Cyr into the colonial infantry in 1870, he took part in the defence of Bazeilles (to the *Marsouins* what Camerone is to the Foreign Legion). In Africa after the Franco-Prussian war, he annexed Upper Niger, commanded in Senegal, and from 1896 to 1905 was governor-general of the new protectorate of Madagascar. He had retired on reaching the age limit in 1913, but on the outbreak of war was appointed military governor of Paris and, on the approach of von Kluck (q.v.), organized the sortie by the garrison which took his army in flank on the Ourcq and turned the decisive battle of the Marne in the Allies' favour. He was minister of war, October 1915–March 1916, and died from overwork. In 1921 the posthumous dignity of marshal was conferred upon him. Some attribute the conception of the Ourcq counter-stroke to Maunoury (q.v.), but Galliéni's reputation is nevertheless assured.

Galway, Henry de Massue, Earl of (1648–1720) French soldier in the service of England. A French Huguenot, Galway left France for England in 1688, after the revocation of the Edict of Nantes (1685); the Glorious Revolution (1688) provided opportunities for Protestants which no longer existed in France. In 1690 he entered the British army. He had gained his early military experience under Turenne, and his skilful use of cavalry after the battle of the Boyne (1690) broke the resistance of the remaining French units. In 1694 he was dispatched as the commander of the allied armies in Savoy against the victorious French army under Catinat.

After the treaty of Turin (1696) he returned to England and was created Earl of Galway in 1697. One of the close associates of William III, he was appointed to the sensitive position of the Lord Chief Justice of Ireland, still smarting after the defeat of the armies of James II. He felt uneasy in this complicated post and retired, only to be recalled in 1704 to take command of a combined English–Portuguese–Dutch army to combat the French army fighting for Philip (the French candidate for the Spanish throne). In 1706 his army took Madrid and proclaimed the allied candidate, the Archduke Charles, as king of Spain. But four months later (October) the new French commander forced Galway to abandon the city by a brilliant set of encircling moves. Galway's army, under the command of the Archduke Charles, retreated towards Valencia, while Galway himself left for Lisbon with his Portuguese and sailed from there to Valencia, where he rejoined the army. He led the army forward from the coast towards the capital, but was met by Berwick (q.v.) at the battle of Almanza (1707), and resoundingly defeated, losing 15,000 men killed or captured. The remnants of the army retreated along the coast towards Barcelona, under the protection of an allied fleet. Galway, relieved by Stanhope, then returned to England and retirement from military affairs. Although he was certainly outclassed by Berwick, he had shown himself a good soldier in his earlier campaigns.

Gamelin, Maurice Gustave (1872–1958) French general. He personified that type of 'pure staff officer' which the army of the Third Republic produced in greater numbers than was good for its health. On Joffre's staff in 1914, he worked as head of the operations section at general headquarters throughout the First World War. In the 1920s he was chief of staff to Sarrail (q.v.) in Syria, then commander-in-chief, and from 1935 was employed in the formation of national defence policy, first as vice-president of the war council, then as chief of the defence staff, finally commander of land forces. When the shock of the German assault came in 1940, he showed himself quite unfitted, by temperament as much as age, to the strain. He was replaced by Weygand (q.v.) on 19 May.

Garibaldi, Giuseppe (1807–82) Italian revolutionary and guerrilla general. An early member of the Italian unification movement, he was exiled from the kingdom of Piedmont for sedition in 1834 and took refuge in South America, where he fought first as a privateer for the secessionist province of Rio Grande del Sol against Brazil and then, as commander of an Italian Legion, for Uruguay against Argentina. On hearing news from Italy of the incipient 1848 revolution, he returned home, offered his services to King Charles Albert of Piedmont (q.v.) and raised an army of 3000 volunteers. After the defeat of Custozza, he took refuge in Switzerland but emerged to organize the defence of the Roman Republic, last outpost of the revolution, against a French expeditionary force. On the fall of the city he led his troops to safety, though pursued by French, Austrian, Spanish and Neapoli-

tan armies. He escaped to America but returned to Italy in 1854 and, in the Franco-Austrian war of 1859, commanded the Piedmontese Alpine troops which defeated the Austrians at Casale. He then embarked on the liberation of southern Italy from the Bourbon house of Naples, on 11 May 1860, landed, under British naval protection, in Marsala, Sicily, with his Redshirts and routed the Neapolitan army in a series of small battles – Calatafimi, Reggio and the Volturno. In September he entered Naples and in November welcomed King Victor Emmanuel into the city.

His subsequent career was less triumphant, for his efforts to liberate Rome from Papal rule for the new kingdom of Italy were judged impolitic and he was arrested when he tried. He commanded troops successfully in the war of 1866 with Austria and took a volunteer force to fight in France against Prussia in 1870. He eventually became deputy for Rome in 1874, after its surrender to the kingdom of Italy, an event which crowned his work of Italian unification but in which he had played no part. Garibaldi was the most remarkable and successful of all European nationalist revolutionaries of his century and an inspiration to all who have followed his road elsewhere.

Garnier, Marie Joseph François (1839–73) French admiral, explorer and colonial conqueror. A member of the early French expeditions to Indo-China and China, he took part in the circular ascent of the Mekong river to Yunnan and the descent of the Yangtse to Shanghai, 1866–8. At home in 1870, he helped in the defence of Paris (to which the navy contributed so much), but in 1872 was once more in Indo-China, whither he had been sent to explore a river route from China to Tibet, and to open the country to European trade. Negotiations with the emperor of Annam breaking down, he attacked Hanoi with 120 Frenchmen, took it, conquered the Red River delta and was eventually killed outside Hanoi by the Chinese 'Black Flags'. A prolific writer, Garnier perfectly incarnated the warrior-imperialist which France produced in such numbers in the nineteenth century.

Gates, Horatio (1727–93) American soldier. One of the few 'native' officers who had served in the British army. Gates was born in England and served in the French and Indian war (1754–63). He returned to England, as a major, but soon went back to settle in West Virginia. His military experience was valuable to the nascent Continental Army in 1775, and he was appointed adjutant-general. Succeeding General Schuyler in command of the retreat of the ill-starred Canadian expedition of 1775, he commanded during the campaign which led to Burgoyne's (q.v.) surrender at Saratoga (1777). His success led to his being made president of the Board of War by Congress, and considered by some senior officers as a replacement for Washington. It was because his star was in the ascendant that he was given the command of the Southern campaign in 1780, against the direct wishes of Washington. His ambitions were brought crashing down by the disasters of the campaign, beginning with the capture of Charleston (May 1780) and culminating with the battle of Camden, where Gates slightly outnumbered the British but was routed by them. He was recalled and an inquiry launched into his conduct; but he was acquitted of neglect of duty. He held no further command until 1782, and passed the rest of the war in comparative obscurity.

George II (1683–1760) British king. Usually remembered as the last English monarch to lead his troops in battle, his reign saw the Jacobite rebellion of 1745, the war of the Austrian Succession

(1740–8) and much of the Seven Years' War (1756–63). His moment of greatest glory came on 27 June 1743, while leading a mixed army, known as the Army of the Lower Rhine, composed of Hanoverian, Dutch and English troops. At Dettingen, thoroughly out-manœuvred and forced into a bad position for defence, George with 40,000 men met the French under the Duc de Noailles with 30,000. His battle formation was almost broken by the French cavalry, and George restored the situation only by the desperate expedient of leading his infantry on foot in a headlong assault on the French position.

George II showed great courage, as well as the hereditary stubbornness of the Hanoverians. Only once did he lose his nerve, during the rebellion of 1745, when he and the court panicked and left London in the face of the advancing Scottish army. George's passion was for military affairs, and he tried constantly to interfere in their conduct, to the horror of his ministers. He occupied the role of licensed critic of official policies, asking always for a sense of enterprise in operations and policies. The famous remark (if possibly apocryphal) he made about General Wolfe (q.v.) illustrates his character perfectly: told by one of his officers that General Wolfe, one of his few successful commanders, was mad, he snapped, 'Then I wish he would bite a few of my other generals.'

Georges, Joseph (1875–1951) French general. In 1940 he was directly subordinate to Gamelin (q.v.) as commander of the north-east front and therefore responsible for opposing the critical German onslaught in May. He had risen to that post through association with a succession of leading military figures, Foch, Pétain and Maginot (qq.v.), whom he had served respectively as director of operations in 1918, chief of staff in the Rif war and military assistant. Since 1935 he had been deputy to Gamelin.

He had had the bad luck to be wounded by the assassin of King Alexander of Yugoslavia in 1934 and his faltering conduct of the 1940 battle was attributed to the after-effects.

Georgey, Artur (1818–1912) Hungarian general. He took the leading military part in the Hungarian rebellion of 1848–9 against the Habsburgs in whose army he had formerly served. Appointed commander-in-chief of the national army, he surrendered the post after some early setbacks but resumed it in April 1849, recaptured Budapest, 21 May, and was only eventually defeated by much superior Russian forces at Komorn, 11 July. He succeeded Kossuth as national leader, signed the capitulation and fled into exile.

Giap, Vo Nguyen (1910–) Vietnamese general. A revolutionary from an early age, Giap originally earned his living as a schoolteacher but, after serving a term of imprisonment for sedition imposed by the French colonial government, left Vietnam for China; his wife, who remained behind, was later arrested and died in prison. After undergoing military training by the Chinese Communists (*see* Mao Tse-tung), he returned to Vietnam during the Japanese occupation and, on their surrender to the Allies in 1945 but before the return of the French, organized under the orders of Ho Chi Minh the nucleus of a national army. Its attempt to resist the disembarkation of the French at Haiphong in 1946 and their reoccupation of Hanoi was, however, unavailing and he led it in retreat into the mountains on the Chinese border (the Viet Bac). There, after a period of training and, in 1949, of re-equipment by the Chinese Communists whose victory in their civil war had brought them on to the border, he contrived the swift and total destruction of the French frontier garrisons. His victory provoked a panic in Hanoi, but his overestimation of its effects and of his own strength, coupled with the arrival from France of the dynamic de Lattre (q.v.) as commander-in-chief, led to his outright defeat when he attempted to invade the Red River delta region around Hanoi in early 1951. Recognizing that, as in 1946, he had acted prematurely – a breach of the Maoist doctrine of 'protracted warfare' – he returned to the Viet Bac and waited for the French to make a major false move. In 1954 at Dien Bien Phu (*see* Navarre, Castries and Bigeard) they did so and lost the war.

Giap became minister of defence in the People's Republic of (North) Vietnam created on the departure of the French and directed its strategy throughout its intervention in the war in South Vietnam against the nationalist government and their American allies. Clearly a general of the first class, he remains none the less a shadowy figure, whose philosophy of war, in so far as it differs from that of Mao, must be guessed at from what he has done rather than from anything he has uttered on the subject, which is very little.

Giraud, Henri (1879–1949) French general. A distinguished veteran of the First World War and the Rif campaign in Morocco, Giraud succeeded the unhappy Corap in command of the Ninth Army after its front had already been broken by the German panzer onslaught in May 1940. Taken prisoner, he escaped from Germany to Gibraltar in 1942 and was transported by British submarine to North Africa, the Allies at the time considering him a possible alternative to de Gaulle (q.v.) as leader of the Free French. He was backed particularly by the Americans, whom de Gaulle had affronted, and appointed to succeed Darlan (q.v.) as high commissioner, but when it became clear that he lacked political authority, he lost the Allies' backing and was obliged in November

1943 to resign his joint-presidency of the Committee of National Liberation.

Gneisenau, Augustus Wilhelm (Graf Neithardt von Gneisenau; 1760–1831) Prussian field-marshal and military reformer. The son of a Saxon officer, Gneisenau had served in the armies of Austria and of Bayreuth-Anspach (which took him as a British mercenary to America) before joining the Prussian army in 1786. He took part in the Polish campaign of 1793–4 but did not emerge as a soldier of promise until Napoleon's invasion of Prussia in 1806 when, by his maintenance of the defence of Colberg until after the signing of the peace treaty, he won promotion to lieutenant-colonel and the *Pour le mérite*. Adopted by Scharnhorst (q.v.) as a colleague in the clandestine reform of the army under the noses of the French, he helped to universalize conscription on the *Krümper* (swift rotation) method and to establish the officer-training system which would make the Prussian army pre-eminent later in the century. In 1813 he became quartermaster-general (chief of staff) to Blücher (q.v.) and was at his side throughout the war of liberation, the campaign of 1814 and that of Waterloo. He was ennobled after Leipzig. After the war he was for a time governor of Berlin. In 1831, on the outbreak of insurrection in Poland, he was appointed to command the army sent to suppress it, with Clausewitz (q.v.) as his chief of staff. Both died (at Posen) in the cholera epidemic then sweeping Europe. Gneisenau was a disappointed man, his plans for the constitutional and social reform of Prussia through military reform frustrated by the diehards of aristocratic privilege.

Godunov, Boris (1551–1605) Russian tsar and soldier. The effective successor of Ivan the Terrible, q.v. (for Ivan's son Fedor was incapable), Godunov was faced with a profusion of enemies, internal and external. By origin a member of a Tartar family which had migrated into Muscovy after Russian expansion against the Tartar hordes, he had established himself at the court of Ivan, gaining the confidence of that most suspicious of monarchs. His sister married Fedor, Ivan's heir, in 1580 and Godunov was raised to the status of a hereditary magnate (*boyar*). Godunov himself married the daughter of one of the tsar's close advisers, which further strengthened his position. The final stroke was his appointment as one of the guardians for Fedor, who was in no condition to take over so arduous a throne. Shortly afterwards, on Ivan's death in 1584, Boris quickly crushed his many enemies among the *boyars*, who regarded him as an upstart, and established a personal rule, albeit in the name of Fedor.

Against the external enemies, the Swedes and Tartars who were attacking along two frontiers, Godunov took equally resolute action. He won a decisive victory against the Tartars in 1591 and consolidated his gains by the construction of fortress and garrison towns, as at Samara, Saratov and Tsaritsyn. He pushed forward into Siberia, an expansion which had lapsed in the last years of Ivan the Terrible: territorially he achieved a considerable expansion of the Russian state, and his military success made his election as tsar after Fedor's death in 1598 a virtual certainty. Once he was tsar he attacked the power and privileges of the *boyar* families, a turbulent element in the state; in particular, he attacked the Romanovs, who had led the opposition to him. As a counterweight to the *boyars*, he extended the power and privileges of the service nobility, *dvorianin*, who thus became his staunch supporters. But his attacks on his enemies provided a natural party of rebellion. A pretender, the 'false Dimitri' (Dimitri was the younger brother of Fedor and had predeceased him), entered Russia and quickly acquired a large *boyar* army. The whole structure of Boris Godunov's achievement was threatened, and in particular, his desire to found a new dynasty. But he died, and because his son was not strong enough to crush all his enemies Russia entered the period of dynastic strife known as the 'Time of Troubles'.

Goltz, Colmar Freiherr, von der (1843–1916) German field-marshal and military writer. The author of a number of historical studies, he also wrote a work of prophecy, *Das Volk in Waffen* (The Nation in Arms), 1883, which emphasized that war was becoming a struggle between peoples instead of armies and forecast that its operations would become static and costly. In November 1914 he was sent as military adviser to the Turkish sultan and in December 1915, as commander of the Turkish First Army, laid siege to Townshend (q.v.) at Kut-el-Amara. He advocated an 'Oriental' solution to the war, exciting but impracticable, and died at Baghdad, perhaps of cholera, but perhaps poisoned by Young Turks.

Gonzaga, Giovanni Francesco II, marchese di Mantua (1466–1519) Italian mercenary. A main protagonist in the Italian resistance to the French eruption into Italy under Charles VIII in 1494, he led the combined army of Milan and Venice against the enemy. Charles, who had already captured Naples, marched north towards Piedmont. Gonzaga, who had a reputation as a successful mercenary leader, opposed him with nearly 15,000 men (mostly infantry) in the pass of Pontremoli. The French, with nearly 9000 men, and, crucially, an excellent field artillery train, met them in the battle of Fornovo (1495). Here the Italian cavalry attack and infantry advance was broken up by the French artillery, and a rapid assault by the French infantry: Gonzaga lost 3350 men to French losses of 400.

Fornovo clearly showed the superiority of the French infantry, tempered by excellent training and the contact with the Swiss, and their well-organized artillery and siege train, against the effete and formalized traditions of Italian warfare between mercenary armies.

Gorchakov, Mikhail (1793–1861) Russian general. A veteran of the Persian war and of the Polish Rebellion of 1831, he brought to an end the rebellion of the Hungarians, 1848–9 (*see* Georgey), and was commander-in-chief of the Russian army in the Crimea, 1854–5. His brother Piotr (1789–1868) played an important part in the conquest of eastern Siberia.

Gordon, Charles George ('Chinese'; 1833–85) British general, empire-builder and popular hero ('Gordon of Khartoum'). The son of a general, he was brought up on Corfu during the British administration of the island, educated at Taunton School and Woolwich, where he displayed talent as a cartographer, and commissioned into the Royal Engineers in 1852. In his first post he served with an officer of evangelical views, which became his own and deeply influenced his life. In the Crimea (1854–6) he served before Sebastopol and was later assigned to map the new Russo-Turkish frontier. In 1860 he went on the Peking expedition, took part in its capture (*see* Hope Grant), and during 1863–4 commanded a Chinese 'Ever Victorious' army raised by the Europeans of Shanghai to protect themselves against the Taiping rebels. Gordon's transformation of this rabble into a genuinely effective force, and his pacification of the region he conquered with it, made his name a household one. But he next took a humdrum engineering appointment in England, and it was a chance meeting with a courtier of the khedive of Egypt which took him there in 1873 on a mission to open the upper Nile to commerce. To that task he soon added his own of suppressing the slave trade, which was widespread on the equatorial Nile. By 1876 he had pushed his line of ports as far as Lake Albert, but finding that the slave traders had opened new routes through the Sudan, he then returned to Cairo to enlist Khedive Ismail's support for an extension of his activities into that region. Ismail, with whom he established a remarkable relationship, at once made him its governor-general. Gordon spent the next three years in its exploration but, his health and the khedive's support eventually failing, resigned and returned to England in 1879.

The next two years were of almost bewildering activity: he agreed with Leopold II to succeed Stanley when the latter gave up the administration of the Congo (because he intended to work against the slave trade there), accepted an appointment as private secretary to Ripon on his becoming viceroy of India, but resigned over a disagreement of principle as soon as he reached Bombay. He then visited Peking to dissuade the imperial government from war with Russia and next took up the post of chief engineer in Mauritius. Promoted major-general in 1882, he visited South Africa to mediate between the Cape government and the warring Basuto chiefs. Believing his mission undermined by a Cape official, he resigned again and spent 1883 in biblical study in Palestine. Meanwhile a rebellion had broken out in the Sudan and in January 1884 he accepted a request to resume the governor-general-ship and supervise the withdrawal of Egyptians and Europeans. Perhaps exceeding his instructions, which were ambiguous, he attempted to pacify the province, was besieged in Khartoum by the Mahdi (q.v.) and killed in his residence at the end of a long and heroic defence on 26 January 1885. A British relief force under Wolseley (q.v.) entered the city two days later. Gladstone's government was vilified over his death, which was seen – particularly by the evangelical middle class – as a martyr's. In technical terms Gordon was not a great soldier, but he possessed an almost mystical power to transform half-hearted Asians and Africans into efficient soldiers and adoring followers. For his own life he had no regard whatever.

Gorshkov, Sergei Georgievich (1910–88). Russian admiral. Put crudely, Gorshkov is the Russian equivalent of Germany's Admiral Tirpitz (q.v.); he forced through a new concept of the Russian navy on to a narrow, blinkered, political and military hierarchy. Born in the Ukrainian town of Kamenets Podolsky, the son of a teacher, Gorshkov moved up the career ladder of the small Soviet navy. He graduated from the Naval Academy in Leningrad in 1931 (despite the legend advanced by some enthusiastic biographer that he had fought with distinction in the Revolutionary navy in the Russian Civil War at the age of 11) and served most of his early career in the Black Sea Fleet. He commanded the Azov flotilla during the Second World War, as well as the Danube flotilla (1944), which was integrated with the land advance of the Russian forces. He won a reputation as a loyal, innovative officer, adept at handling political and interservice difficulties. Both qualities were of great value in his later career. By 1948, he was chief of staff of the Black Sea fleet until in 1955 he was promoted to be deputy commander in chief of the Soviet navy. In the following year, he was appointed to the command of the Soviet navy.

Gorshkov held supreme power in the navy for almost thirty years. He transformed it from being a port-bound navy into an instrument of international power politics. By doing so he increased both the strategic 'reach' of the Soviet Union, and its visibility in world affairs. When he took over, the Soviet Union had just tested its first submarine-launched missiles, to be followed shortly by surface-launched missiles. Gorshkov, although supporting the submarine strike force was also concerned to build a balanced, all-purpose fleet, such as (classically) the British navy had possessed in its heyday. He pressed for the construction of aircraft carriers, cruisers and destroyers, as well as a massive amphibious warfare capacity. This went contrary to previous Soviet practice, and indeed, to developing Western theories. Gorshkov believed that the nature of Russia's security needs, and the requirements of ideology, imposed a special kind of naval doctrine.

Analysts judged Gorshkov's intentions from the sort of navy which he built. Hints as to the theory emerged over the years, but he presented it *in extenso* in his famous book *The Sea Power of the State*, published in 1976. There he described 'The world ocean' and the claim of the Soviet Union to an equal share of its bounty and resources. Under Gorshkov, the Russian fleet actively patrolled the seas, in particular the Indian Ocean and the Mediterranean, in a way which seemed peculiarly offensive to the United States, which had hitherto sailed in solitary splendour. The navy became the overt evidence of 'Soviet expansionism', in American eyes. Gorshkov had staked out a claim for superpower parity in an unmistakable fashion.

It is often foolish to personalize military–professional issues in the Soviet Union, for policy is the consequence of a fiercely argued political process. But Gorshkov carried the political apparatus along with him for a whole generation, while at the same time avoiding many potential clashes with other elements in the military. It was this acute political sense which sustained him for so long. His replacement came when a new generation took over: he was dismissed in December 1985 by the new General Secretary Mikhail Gorbachov.

Gorshkov's legacy was what he called a 'balanced fleet'. This was, no doubt, a stage through which the Soviet navy needed to pass, to achieve world status. But it seems unlikely that it will be sustained in quite the same way by his successors. Like Tirpitz before him, Gorshkov has rewritten the rules of global politics by the creation of a navy, conjured more or less from the head of its creator. But he did not live to see the extinction of the Soviet Union and the end of his creation without its ever firing a shot in anger.

Gort, John Standish Surtees Prendergast Vereker, 6th Viscount Gort (1886–1946) British field-marshal. A Protestant Irish aristocrat and a Grenadier of legendary bravery – he had won the VC, the DSO and two bars and the MC with his battalion in the First World War – Gort had been promoted by Hore Belisha over the heads of hundreds of more senior officers in 1937 (*see* Liddell Hart) to be Chief of the Imperial General Staff. In 1939 he went to France with the British Expeditionary Force and commanded it from the onset of the German attack to the end of its evacuation from Dunkirk. His decision to disengage from the battle and fall back to the coast was both brave and right, for it saved Britain's only army, though at the expense of embittering relations with the French, who felt they had been abandoned. He was subsequently governor of Malta during the German air offensive on the island and then high commissioner in Palestine.

Gough, Sir Hubert de la Poer (1870–1963) British general and mutineer. The son of a VC winner, Gough commanded in 1914 the 3rd Cavalry Brigade at the Curragh Camp outside Dublin. Alerted for duty in the north, to impose the Irish Home Rule Act on resistant

Ulstermen, he conveyed to Asquith's government the unwillingness of himself and his officers to march. This 'Curragh Mutiny' procured the shelving of the Act. As commander of the Fifth Army on the Somme in 1916 and at Paschendaele in 1917, the slap-dash work of his staff contributed greatly to the casualties his units suffered and made him widely unpopular (where his arrogant manner had not already done so). In March 1918 his much understrength army was broken by the Germans on the Somme sector which it had recently taken over from the French and he was disgraced.

Gough, Hugh (1st Viscount Gough; 1779–1869) British field-marshal. After an exciting and varied career as a regimental officer, in which he served at the taking of Capetown, 1796, in the West Indies and in the Peninsula (his regiment, the 87th, captured the baton of Jourdan, q.v., at Vittoria), Gough saw no action until 1837. Posted in that year to India, he took part in the First China War, 1841–2, and in the Mahratta campaign of 1843. It is with the Sikh wars, however, that his name is chiefly connected. The Sikhs, last of the warrior peoples of India unsubdued by the British, broke out of the Punjab into British India in December 1845. Gough took the field against them and, after two hard-fought but strategically indecisive battles, Mudki and Ahival, drove them back into the Punjab by his victory at Sobraon on 10 February 1846. Two years later war broke out again and he was obliged to fight two further battles, Chillianwallah, 13 January 1849, and Gujrat, 18 February. Unknown to him. Charles Napier (q.v.) had been ordered to supersede him after the first battle because of the heavy casualties his army had suffered in it, but Napier did not arrive until he had won the second, a decisive victory which gave Britain the Punjab and brought Gough a viscounty. The Sikhs fielded the bravest, best-

equipped and most nearly equal of all the Indian armies the British fought during the conquest. By beating them, 'Old White Coat' made himself one of the greatest of the Sepoy generals.

Gouraud, Henri Joseph Eugène (1867–1946) French general. As a lieutenant of *Chasseurs à pied* fresh from Saint-Cyr, Gouraud had made a name for himself in the conquest of the French Sudan and was deputy to Lyautey (q.v.) in the occupation of Morocco. His great moment came in 1915 when he replaced d'Amade in command of the French troops at Gallipoli (where he lost an arm in the fighting). As commander of the Fourth Army he played a major role in the second battle of the Marne in 1918 and, after the war, was high commissioner in Syria, 1919–23, where he successfully suppressed a Moslem revolt (*see* Sarrail). A man of striking appearance, he was something of a popular hero during the First World War.

Gourko, Ossip Vladimirovich (Count; 1828–1901) Russian general. His invasion of Bulgaria, at the outbreak of the Russo-Turkish war of 1877, was a masterpiece of the indirect approach, although its success was negated by the slowness of the Russian main advance, which was blocked at Plevna. His action against the Turks' line of communications to Plevna eventually brought about its investment, and he went on to capture Sofia. He was made a count for his generalship, the best, on the Russian side, of the war.

Gouvion-St-Cyr, Laurent (marquis de; 1764–1830) Marshal of France. A painter by profession, Gouvion-St-Cyr rose through the ranks of the revolutionary army, which he joined as a private in Paris in 1792, to command of a brigade in 1793, and to the rank of general of division in 1794. Distinguished at the siege of Mainz, he briefly succeeded

Hoche (q.v.) in command of the Army of the Rhine and Moselle in 1797. He took part in the campaigns of Italy (1799 and 1805) and of the Rhine (1800), but did not achieve a properly independent command until he went to Spain in 1808, where he won the minor battles of Molins del Rey and Valls. In 1812 he was given command of the Bavarian Corps of the Grand Army and fought twice at Polotsk, winning the first battle, losing the second. For his victory he was promoted marshal. He commanded the French centre at Dresden, 25 August 1813, and then held the city until November. He was reconciled to the monarchy in 1814 and did not join Napoleon during the Hundred Days. Louis XVIII employed him as minister of war and of marine, and created him marquis. He retired in 1819.

Grant, (Sir) James Hope (1805–75) British general. A 9th Lancer, Grant spent the greater part of his military career in India and China. During the Indian Mutiny he played a major part in its suppression in the Central Provinces, and in the Second China War of 1860 he commanded the British contingent in the Anglo-French expedition to Peking (*see* Palikao). His troops took part in the burning of the Summer Palace (Yueng-ming-yueng), an aesthetic atrocity comparable to the burning of the Ptolemaic library at Alexandria by the Arabs in 646. To his credit, he had opposed the burning, which was ordered by Lord Elgin, and refused to share in the loot.

Grant, Ulysses Simpson (1822–85) American (Union) general and president of the United States. Grant's rise to supreme command of the Union armies in the Civil War was anticipated by nothing in his earlier career. He had passed out of West Point in the bottom half of his class and, though decorated for service in the Mexican war, had

later been obliged to resign his commission to avoid court-martial for the drunkenness into which the boredom of frontier duty had led him. As a civilian he failed in one minor enterprise after another and was destitute when the Civil War broke out. Not without difficulty he secured command of the 21st Illinois Volunteers (he was a mid-westerner by birth) and then, as a brigadier-general, of a district, with headquarters at Cairo, Illinois.

Union strategy required (*see* Scott) that the South be cut off from its western hinterland by the seizing of the whole length of the Mississippi, from Cairo southward to New Orleans (on which a seaborne attack was planned – *see* Farragut). Grant's first effort in that direction (battle of Belmont, 7 November 1861) was indecisive, but in the following February he caught the attention of the North (and the South) with his brilliant seizure of Forts Henry and Donelson on an upper tributary of the great river. In April he turned a surprise attack on his positions at Shiloh into a Confederate defeat and in the following year at Vicksburg, which he had reached by a brilliant series of manœuvres, inflicted a shattering defeat on the South, putting the whole line of the Mississippi in Northern hands. In November 1863 he was appointed by Lincoln commander of all Union forces in the west and quickly transformed a faltering Northern offensive in Tennessee (the Chattanooga campaign – *see* Rosecrans) into a victorious sweep of the territory, opening the way to an invasion of Georgia.

In March 1864, against the protests of more conventional soldiers, he was brought by Lincoln ('I need this man. He fights') to command in the east, with supreme authority over all Union armies. Abandoning the strategy of manœuvre, which the ratio of men to space made inappropriate in the Virginia theatre, he embarked on a campaign of naked attrition, and fought a succession of murderous battles: the Wilderness, Spotsylvania, Cold Harbor and the siege of Petersburg. He was present at the culminating episode at Appomattox to receive the surrender of Lee (q.v.) in person. After the war he was secretary of war in President Johnson's administration and in 1868, as a Republican, was himself elected president. He was re-elected in 1872 but, though his personal honour was never impugned, both his presidencies were disfigured by the mal-practices of his subordinates. In old age he once again lost his money in an unwise investment, recouped only by the publication of his remarkable autobiog-raphy, which he wrote while dying of cancer.

Whatever his defects as a businessman and politician, Grant was an undeniably great soldier. His talents were for the large strategic appreciation rather than for battlefield tactics, though he was a tenacious fighter. But his greatest gift was in the understanding of how indus-trialization had changed war and of the needs the new warfare laid on a general. 'He saw that the destruction of the enemy's economic resources was as effec-tive and legitimate a form of warfare as the destruction of his armies ... Lee was the last of the great old-fashioned gen-erals. Grant the first of the great mod-erns' (T. Harry Williams in *Lincoln and his Generals*).

Gravina, Don Carlos, duque de (1756–1806) Spanish admiral. A veteran of the second siege of Gibraltar (1779–83) and of the French expedition to Haiti (*see* Leclerc and Toussaint), Gravina commanded the Spanish fleet which, with the French under Villeneuve (q.v.), was destroyed by Nelson (q.v.) at Trafal-gar. He died at Cadiz the following year from wounds received in the battle.

Graziani, Rodolfo (1882–1955) Italian field-marshal. Having made his repu-tation in Italy's minor North African

wars, Graziani was in 1940 made gover-nor of Libya and commander-in-chief in North Africa. Under pressure from Mussolini he invaded Egypt in September but did not press the advance towards Cairo, and in December was decisively counter-attacked by O'Connor (q.v.). He was relieved of command in February 1941, his Tenth Army having ceased to exist, and court-martialled. Nevertheless he and Mussolini remained on terms and in September 1943 the dictator made him minister of war in his rump republic in northern Italy. After the war he was tried and sentenced for collaboration with the Germans.

Greene, Nathanael (1742–86) Ameri-can soldier. One of the more competent of Washington's subordinates, Greene had begun the American War of Inde-pendence as commander of the Rhode Island contingent. Later in 1775, Con-gress appointed him a brigadier-general in the Continental Army, and a major-general in the following year. He com-manded Fort Washington when it was captured by General Sir William Howe (q.v.) in 1776, and was criticized for his handling of the defence. Surviving the adverse comments on his performance with Washington's support, he com-manded the reserve at the battle of Brandywine (1777), and fought well at Germantown later in the same year.

Greene had not yet held an independ-ent command, and his opportunity came in 1780. Contrary to the advice of Wash-ington, Congress had appointed General Gates (q.v.) to command against a Brit-ish invasion of the south, but disaster after disaster had overtaken his troops. Greene was sent south with Washing-ton's blessing to recover the situation. His troops were in a parlous state, ill-equipped and in a low state of morale. His problem was the need to restore their spirits by a successful offensive at a time when he could not hope to defeat a substantial British force in open battle.

His strategy was to force the British to disperse their troops and energies in fruitless pursuit of his command. Cornwallis (q.v.) took the bait and also split his troops, following both Greene and his detached party under Morgan (q.v.), who managed a stinging defeat of the British at Cowpens (1781).

Although Greene was beaten at Guilford Courthouse (1781), he was the strategic victor, for the strain of the campaign on manpower and communications forced Cornwallis to break off the conquest of the Carolinas. Greene had defeated the most severe threat which the American cause had faced since the early days of the revolution and, moreover, with poor and exhausted troops. But his reputation was somewhat tarnished by constant allegations of corruption, some stemming from the time (1778) when he was quartermaster-general but mostly from the period of the southern campaign. But these trivial peccadilloes should not obscure the fact that he was an officer of great talent.

Grenville, Sir Richard (1542–91) English sailor. Remembered best for the manner of his death in battle with the Spanish fleet. Grenville's real significance was as a remarkable shipmaster and navigator (it was his plan which Drake used for his circumnavigation of the globe in 1577–80). Grenville was active and financially interested in the policy of 'plantation' (colonization), both in North America and in Ireland, and it was he who established the ill-fated colony on Roenoke Island. He took part in the Armada campaign of 1588, and in 1591 was second-in-command of a squadron of fifteen ships sent to intercept the Spanish treasure fleet off the Azores. Caught by some fifty-three Spanish vessels, and abandoned by his other ships, Grenville tried to run his ship through the Spanish line in an effort to escape. For fifteen hours his lone ship held off fifteen Spanish galleons; eventually, despite brilliant seamanship and gunhandling, the *Revenge* was disabled. On 10 September Grenville and the remaining crew surrendered. Grenville died a few days later. His best epitaph must be Tennyson's heroic tribute, in his poem 'The Revenge':

Sir Richard cried in his English pride,
'We have fought such a fight, for a day
 and a night,
As may never be fought again . . . !'

Gribeauval, Jean Baptiste Vaquette de (1715–89) French artillerist. Possibly the greatest innovator in artillery since Gustavus Adolphus (q.v.), Gribeauval entered the French army in 1732 and was promoted to officer rank in 1735. In the Seven Years' War (1756–63) he was attached to the Austrian army and served as a general of artillery. After the war he returned to the development of the French artillery service, and with the experience of the war as a background to all his work, in 1765 began his main task in the rationalization of the artillery equipment. He discarded the multitude of different calibres and patterns of gun and reclassified them all into 4-, 8- and 12-pounders, made to standard specifications. Guns were designed for their particular roles (as howitzers or field guns) and a new siege train was created.

Gribeauval extended the new system beyond the guns themselves to encompass the whole process of use and training. The technical changes – lighter weapons, horses harnessed for rapid movement, proper arrangements made for the carriage of powder and shot – made possible tactical changes. The field artillery acquired a capacity to manœuvre, to keep up with the other arms and, with improvements to sighting, to concentrate fire more accurately. In 1776 he was created inspector-general of artillery and thus was able to apply the results of his dedicated research in the previous decade. He concentrated on the training of competent specialist officers (one of whom was Napoleon) and on establishing a proper career within the service. In the lower ranks he established a new scale of pay and improved living conditions. He died on the eve of the Revolution. The result of his work was a century of French dominance of field artillery, and a crop of outstanding artillery officers and theorists.

Grierson, Benjamin Henry (1826–1911) American (Union) general. The counterpart, on a diminished scale, of the Confederate Forrest (q.v.); none of his cavalry raids into the South produced quite the effect of Forrest's great forays, but the so-called Grierson's Raid of 17 April–2 May 1863 did divert troops from the defence of Vicksburg. A music teacher by origin, Grierson volunteered in 1861 and remained in the army after the peace, to retire as a brigadier-general.

Groener, Wilhelm (1867–1939) German general. He had a distinguished military career, directing the railway section of the general staff during the mobilization of 1914, and acting as chief of staff of the army group commanded first by Linsingen, then by Eichhorn in the invasion of the Ukraine in 1918. But the real significance of his life was political and constitutional. Summoned by Hindenburg to replace Ludendorff in November 1918 (*see* Lossberg), he was chosen to present the army's ultimatum of abdication to the kaiser (cynics said because he was a Württemberg sergeant's son whose action would thus sully the Prussian officer corps only indirectly). In fact he was a realist, whose instinct told him that the kaiser must go if Germany and its army were to survive. It was he who arranged with Ebert the accommodation between army and republic which put an end to Germany's civil war of 1918–19 and gave the infant Weimar Republic, which he later served as minister of war, its start in life.

Grouchy, Emmanuel, marquis de (1766–1847) Marshal of France. A nobleman by birth, Grouchy served first in the artillery, then in the cavalry (*Royal-Etranger*), then in the *Gardes Ecossaises*. Despite, or perhaps because of, this association with the court, he embraced the Revolution, fought the Vendéen royalists and helped to repel the émigré landing at Quiberon Bay. In 1797 he took part in the misfired attempt to invade Ireland at Bantry Bay. A divisional commander at Novi (where he was severely wounded), Hohenlinden, Ulm, Eylau and Friedland, he was the officer responsible for repressing the Madrid revolt of 1808 – the Dos de Mayo commemorated in Goya's famous horror paintings. He was at Wagram and in the Russian campaign, when he commanded a cavalry corps, was wounded at Borodino and eventually took charge of the *bataillon sacré*, composed entirely of officers, which guarded Napoleon during the retreat. In 1814 he commanded the cavalry of the army in the defence of France and was again wounded. After Elba, Napoleon created him marshal (his last) and gave him command of the right wing of the Army of the North. It was this force which Grouchy failed to lead to the sound of the guns at Waterloo and whose arrival might – it is arguable – have turned the tide in Napoleon's favour. Disgraced after the Second Restoration, his rank of marshal was restored to him by Louis-Philippe. He bore the scars of nineteen wounds.

Guderian, Heinz (1888–1953) German general and theorist of tank warfare: 'the Father of the panzer divisions'. The son of a Prussian general, he was educated in cadet school and commissioned into the 10th (Hanoverian) *Jäger* in 1908 (*see* Balck). Selected for the *Kriegsakademie* in 1913, he was posted to command a cavalry division's wireless section at the outbreak of the First World War, and subsequently promoted operational staff officer of a division, a corps and an army on the western front. At the armistice he was sent to organize the volunteer armies in the Baltic states with which Germany was seeking illegally to retain the territories wrested from Russia at the treaty of Brest-Litovsk, and after the collapse of that enterprise was chosen as one of the 4000 (out of 32,000 surviving) officers allowed to Germany by the Allies for her peacetime army. He began to specialize in the military uses of mechanical transport and, in the teeth of official disapproval, had by the early 1930s got together the nucleus of a mechanized force. Hitler, on his seizure of power, recognized its potential and gave Guderian his backing. By 1935 three armoured (panzer) divisions had been brought into being along the lines advocated by Guderian and he was given command of the 2nd. He was thereafter swiftly promoted (major-general, 1936, lieutenant-general, 1938, general of panzer troops, November 1938), at the same time successfully propagating, through the publication of his book *Achtung! Panzer*, his ideas on armoured warfare. These were for the waging of war by very strong armoured forces on narrow fronts, aiming at breakthrough and rapid exploitation, a form later to be known as *blitzkrieg*. Almost at once, he was to be given the chance to put his ideas into practice and did so with great *élan* as commander of the XIX Corps in Poland and France. He was promoted colonel-general at the victory celebrations of July 1940. For the Russian campaign he was given one of the four panzer groups into which the expanded armoured force had been organized (it was subsequently retitled *Panzer-armee Guderian* and then 2nd Panzer Army) and subordinated directly to Bock's Army Group on the central front. Within six weeks he had won a series of extraordinary victories, encircling hundreds of thousands of Russians and carrying the battle to within 200 miles of

Moscow. Finding that Hitler then intended to transfer his armour to the more laggard Army Group South, he first attempted to thwart the Führer's wishes, finally bearded him in his headquarters and argued with him the error of his strategy, which he believed threatened to deprive Germany of the chance of total victory in 1941. Out-talked, he loyally acquiesced in Hitler's subsequent plans, but was dismissed, with scores of other generals, following the Russian winter counter-offensive. He was recalled to be inspector-general of panzer forces in February 1943 and, following the bomb plot of 20 July 1944, was appointed chief of the general staff (*see* Zeitzler). Hitler, however, would no longer heed the advice of any soldier, even of Guderian, whom he respected, and his tenure of the post was therefore frustrating. He was relieved of duty, after a disagreement on 21 March 1945, and taken prisoner by the Americans on 10 May.

Guderian, the quintessence of the German military intellectual, was also an inspiring leader. But he had a talent for falling out with equals and superiors and was too headstrong to be counted a really successful commander; though admired, he was not greatly liked in the German army. He found his real following among tank theorists in other armies.

Guevara, Ernesto ('Che'; 1928–67) Cuban guerrilla leader. Born an Argentinian, Guevara became a revolutionary as soon as he had qualified as a doctor, at first in Guatemala and then (having met Fidel Castro in Mexico) in Cuba, where from December 1956 until January 1959 he was a member of Castro's guerrilla army. Promoted to high rank after its victory, he left Cuba in 1965 to spread revolution elsewhere in Latin America and was killed by the Bolivian army. Guevara, though an orthodox Marxist and deeply influenced by the military ideas of Mao Tse-tung (q.v.), had come to believe that dedicated guerrilla fighters could create a revolutionary war even where the predisposing conditions did not exist; his belief, immensely attractive to intellectual left-wing youth in the 1960s, was disproved by the circumstances of his death, for his band was betrayed to its hunters by the peasants whom he sought to politicize.

Guillaumat, Marie Louis Adolphe (1863–1940) French general. He commanded the Second Army in the recapture of Côte 304 and the Mort-Homme at Verdun in 1916, from December 1917 to June 1918 was commander-in-chief of the Allied army at Salonika, and in October 1918 directed the Fifth Army in the final phase of the general offensive in France. After the war he commanded the French army of occupation on the Rhine, 1924–5, during the height of the reparation conflict, and was briefly minister of war during the same period.

Gustavus Adolphus (1594–1632) King of Sweden. When Gustavus Adolphus came to the throne in 1611 at the age of sixteen, Sweden was in the midst of a war. War, indeed, was to be the constant factor throughout his reign, and there was scarcely a time when he was not preparing for, fighting, or recovering from, a campaign. Popularly known as a great warrior king, '*il re d'oro*', 'the Lion of the North', his great victories were not the flashes of intermittent genius, but the culmination of years of administrative reform, and a hard apprenticeship fighting the Danes and the Muscovites for mastery of the Baltic, and the Poles for dynastic security. Gustavus Adolphus was confronted first with the inherent weaknesses of his troops. Although he believed them to be unsurpassed in the art of forest fighting, being almost entirely recruited from the woodsmen and peasantry, they were ill-equipped, undermanned, and generally unequal to the demands of modern war. At the same time he recognized that reorganized, properly equipped, and led by officers of high calibre, they could be shaped into a sturdy and self-reliant fighting force. This he resolved to do. His other alternative was to rely, as most of his forebears had done, on mercenary armies, but these were a constant drain on resources, prone to mutiny or to change sides at whim, and had the additional disadvantage that they were so attached to their status as fighting troops that they would refuse to engage in such mundane but necessary activities as digging (one important lesson Gustavus Adolphus was to draw from the first war of his reign was the significance of field fortifications).

A quarter of a century before, Maurice of Nassau (q.v.) had radically reformed the army of the Netherlands, creating a large standing army of highly professional native-born soldiers who earned a reputation higher than any except that of the crack Spanish units. Gustavus Adolphus was greatly influenced by the work of this great military reformer and thinker. But his reforms were to be even more radical and thorough-going than those effected in the United Provinces. Like Maurice of Nassau, however, the king believed in starting from basic principles, and the most basic of all was the problem of manpower; although Gustavus Adolphus was to use mercenaries, drawn for preference from England or Scotland, throughout his career, it was necessary, indeed essential, that the *Swedish* army should be kept up to strength. To this end he regularized the procedure of conscription which had evolved over the previous half-century to ensure that it was fairer, that it provided a regular supply of men, and, most important in many ways, that the standard of the new conscripts was higher; Gustavus himself was known to prefer property-owning conscripts since they would be at least adequately nourished, and he did not underrate the importance of a sound constitution when confronted with campaign conditions. A further side-effect of these reforms was that the conscripts, bound together by the Swedish language (often no doubt in its dialect forms), by a bond with the native soil of Sweden, and often even by family ties, were to provide the most homogeneous and closely knit infantry in Europe. And it was the bond with the soil which, strangely enough, was to be further exploited in Gustavus's reorganization of the army pay structure.

Maurice of Nassau had first laid down that the professional army should be indeed professional, that is, that it should be paid on a regular basis for its services. This was designed to dignify the status of the common soldier, and to prevent looting in time of war and large-scale desertion in time of peace. To these principles Gustavus adhered, but at the same time he was faced with the immense problem that he simply could not command the same resources as the wealthy mercantile Dutch. The system which was devised was ingenious and uniquely Swedish. His conscripts had to serve for twenty years, or until they reached the age of fifty, and therefore they deserved adequate recompense for what often amounted to half a lifetime spent under the colours. The answer was payment in kind, and the currency was land. In its simplest form this might mean that an officer would be given a farm, usually on crown land, and thus the right to collect rent from the crown tenant. In the case of a private the system was more involved. In addition to his yearly wage and his cloth allowance, a private would be allotted a share, usually an eighth, of a homestead, where he would actually be billeted; the farmer was entitled to deduct the equivalent amount from his rent or taxes, and would pay it over to the soldier, who

was equally bound to help with the farm work in exchange for his board and lodging. Thus, instead of being an outcast, as was the case in most other western countries, the ordinary soldier had his roots very firmly in society; on the reverse side of the coin, a large proportion of the common people were actively involved in the maintenance of the army. In these respects it was a truly national army. In time of war, however, Gustavus Adolphus took care to pay soldiers actively engaged against the enemy a monthly allowance of hard cash whenever possible. A large proportion of the credit for these administrative reforms must be given to Axel Oxenstierna, who gave form and substance to the king's often rather sketchy ideas.

In the other great sphere of army reform, that of tactics, Gustavus Adolphus was both progenitor and executor. His first major task was to rearm the soldiers with weapons more in accord with modern notions of war. Yet against the current of an age which was beginning to question the efficacy of the pike, he increased rather than reduced the proportion of pikemen in his ranks. Experiments with a greatly shortened pike came to nothing, but in 1616 he shortened the pikeshaft slightly, presumably to give greater manœuvrability, and, as a result of experience in the Polish wars, clad the top of the pikeshaft with iron so that the attacker could not simply sever it with his sword. His principal improvements in the field of small-arms included decreasing the weight of the musket, though the musketeer was still burdened with the fork-rest in addition to his cumbersome weapon; there was also considerable progress towards the standardization of powder, and attempts, again largely successful, to standardize calibre. But his most innovatory series of reforms concerned the artillery (dealt with under Torstensson, q.v.), for he recognized, just as Maurice of Nassau had done, that artillery had an increasingly important role in battle. Each of these changes was undertaken with a single aim in view: the creation of an army which was decisive in attack, unwavering in defence, and capable of great mobility. They were to be brilliantly justified in what was indubitably to be Gustavus's greatest battle, that of Breitenfeld in 1631.

The army which accompanied Gustavus Adolphus to Germany in 1630 differed radically from every other army engaged in the Thirty Years' War, with the possible exception of the Dutch. It was capable of more flexible battle formations, having been reorganized into tactical and administrative units of 408 men, plus officers and NCOs, as opposed to the unwieldy though formidable *tercios* of anything up to 1500 men favoured by the imperial side, and it must have been with some astonishment that the imperial cavalry perceived that its opposite number had reverted to the *arme blanche*, being equipped with both pistol and sword; but Gustavus Adolphus had learnt from fighting the Poles the effectiveness in cavalry operations of *élan* over the formalized and moribund *caracole*, where the cavalryman was, in effect, little more than a mounted pistoleer. Further, the Swedish army was much better disciplined; the reorganization and the re-equipment of the troops meant that training was a more vital part of the army's curriculum. Intensive drill was used to introduce a sense of corporate discipline, and this, along with troop exercises and large-scale manœuvres, meant that each man, and each section of the army, was thoroughly prepared for the part it would have to play in battle. This, too, was to pay brilliant dividends at Breitenfeld. Finally, it was somewhat better behaved than the other armies engaged in the war, for Gustavus's Articles of War, which were enforced, forbade swearing, blasphemy, drunkenness and fornication.

On the field of battle the extraordinary power of attack which the Swedes could command amazed Europe. While most armies relied on fire-power from musketeers to attack and maul the enemy, and the pikemen to act as a secure defensive wall to protect their musketeers from enemy horsemen, Gustavus used his pikemen and musketeers in complementary offensive roles. While an enemy infantry reeled under the fire from the musketeers (all the more effective since the Swedes fired by salvo, as one man), the pikes rushed forward and pressed into the gaps torn in the enemy line. In the case of the *tercio*, especially, with its huge body of men grouped in dense formation, any disruption of its solid front could prove fatal. To the shock tactics of his infantry, Gustavus could add the impact of his cavalry striking home *à la Polonaise*. At Breitenfeld it was the harmony between the various arms which brought the Swedes an unexpected victory. It enabled them, exposed by the collapse of their Saxon allies on their left wing to the full weight of the imperial advance under Tilly (q.v.), to reform a new line of defence facing the enemy. This new line, too weak to withstand the weight of an imperial attack, launched itself forward, using combined artillery and musket fire-power to break up the imperial formations, and the terrible Swedish pikemen to rend great holes in the ranks of the *tercios*. And it was Gustavus himself who captured the imperial artillery and turned it on the disordered enemy, then launched his horsemen to complete the rout of Tilly's fine army of experienced veterans.

At the passage of the Lech (1632), Gustavus managed to cross a river in spate over a bridge of boats, concealing his exact whereabouts by a dense pall of smoke given off by burning damp straw, and again smashed through the ranks of Tilly's men. The Swedish juggernáut seemed invincible. But at the battle of the Alte Veste (1632), Gustavus launched an attack on Wallenstein (q.v.), secure behind prepared fortifications, in a position which allowed neither the cavalry nor the artillery to play its wonted part. The attack was a failure and, more important, it was costly in men: 2400 precious infantry killed or wounded. Equally important, the benign myth of Swedish invincibility was shattered, and Wallenstein looked for an opportunity to defeat the Swedes in open battle. The armies met at Lützen (1632). Gustavus was now slightly weaker than his enemy, especially in cavalry. But his dispositions were excellent. He recognized Wallenstein's weak left wing, and attacked it with his best men, leading them himself. Delayed by mist and bad weather, he strove to smash the imperial army before reinforcements under Pappenheim (q.v.) could reach Wallenstein and turn the struggle in his favour. At a moment when victory seemed within his grasp, he led a charge against the enemy and was shot in the back. Falling from his horse, he lay immobile on the ground until an imperial pistol left him dead in the mud. His body was stripped by looters.

It has often been said that Gustavus Adolphus was the first great modern commander, and some indication of his influence may be drawn from the fact that no less a soldier than Marlborough (q.v.) was still using some of his infantry formations and offensive techniques some seventy years after his death at Lützen. Many of his innovations were not entirely original: he derived much of his inspiration from the Dutch, borrowed freely from the Poles in regard to cavalry, and the moral curbs he put on his soldiers were no less strait than those imposed on the Huguenot armies. But if the raw material of his reforms often, though not invariably, came from elsewhere, the use he made of them was the product of his own genius, and this was all-embracing. No detail was too small, no obstacle too insurmountable, no tactical reform too *outré* to attract his considered attention. The Swedish army of the Thirty Years' War was the product of his intense intellectual curiosity and enormous breadth of imagination, but based on solid foundations of practical experience, and it was his masterpiece. One of his officers said of him: 'He thought nothing well-done that he did not do himself,' but it is a tribute to the power of his reforms, and his willingness to delegate to the new school of officers which had grown up with them, that the army did not disintegrate after his death, but, though it lacked the vital spark of his genius, remained among the most powerful in Europe for many years to come.

Guynemer, Georges (1894–1917) French fighter ace. Second-ranking of French fighter aces of the First World War, Guynemer shot down fifty-four enemy aircraft. He disappeared after an aerial combat over Poelcapelle and is commemorated in the Pantheon.

H

Haig, Douglas (1st Earl Haig of Bemersyde; 1861–1928) British field-marshal and commander-in-chief of the British armies in France, 1915–18. Haig, the son of a Scottish distiller, was educated at Clifton and Brasenose College, Oxford, subsequently entering the Royal Military College, Sandhurst, and passing out first. He was commissioned into the 7th Hussars and served at home and in India. Failing to pass the Staff College examination, he secured admission by patronage and later left his regiment to command the 17th Lancers. He excelled at staff and junior command appointments during the Boer War, married after the shortest acquaintance one of Queen Alexandra's maids-in-waiting, became a minor member of the court circle and made his way by preferment and diligence up the ladder of the Edwardian War Office. He acted as Haldane's (q.v.) principal military adviser during the Liberal government's reforms of the army, 1906–8, became Director of Military Operations and in August 1914 was commanding the I Corps at Aldershot, earmarked to spearhead a British Expeditionary Force. His leadership of the corps during the battles of the Frontier and the Great Retreat was undistinguished, but he showed remarkable resolution in his defence of Ypres in the first battle for that city (October–November 1914) and was shortly promoted to command First Army. Encouraged by George V to correspond confidentially about the conduct of the war, he made clear his doubts about the suitability of Sir John French (q.v.) for the supreme command and on the field-marshal's removal in December 1915 was selected to replace him. His first test as commander-in-chief was in the handling of the battle of the Somme, for which Britain had assembled a volunteer citizen army of several million. Haig's hopes of a quick breakthrough were deceived but he persisted in keeping the battle going from July to November 1916, at a cost of over 400,000 casualties. These 'attritional' tactics were a foretaste of what was to prove his distinctive approach to the problems of the First World War. At the battle of Arras, April 1917, and above all Third Ypres (Paschendaele), June–October 1917, he enforced the pursuit of unattainable aims even at the price of the destruction of his own armies. Invoking the need to relieve the French of pressure, he nevertheless resisted Lloyd George's efforts, motivated by mistrust of his methods, to subordinate him to French command. Following the collapse of his front in March 1918, however, he was obliged to acquiesce in the appointment of a French supreme commander, Foch, and subsequently worked well with him. His final months of command were his most successful, bringing the victories of Amiens, a remarkable tank attack in August, and of the Hindenburg Line in September. Haig retired completely into private life at the war's end, devoting himself to the affairs of ex-servicemen through the British Legion.

He was no worse a general than many of the Great War to whom historical opinion has been kinder, and better than some of them, being comparatively open to new ideas and an efficient organizer.

But he was a cold, unimaginative and seemingly self-seeking man and is now irredeemably typecast as a flinthearted butcher of his own soldiers.

Haldane, Richard Burton, 1st Viscount Haldane (1856–1928) British military reformer. A liberal lawyer of great intellectual distinction, Haldane was appointed secretary of war by Campbell-Bannerman in 1905, and embarked on a series of reforms which were declared necessary by commissions of enquiry set up after the Boer War. Of these the most important were the creation of a true general staff, of the post of chief of the imperial general staff to co-ordinate the military efforts of the Empire (an unfulfilled ambition) and of an expeditionary force capable of immediately taking the field in an emergency (this became the BEF). He also brought about the integration of the Volunteers with the regular army as the Territorial Force.

Halder, Franz (1884–1971) German general and chief of staff. An artillery officer of the Bavarian army, Halder had been trained at the Bavarian Staff College and served on the staff of Prince Rupprecht (q.v.) during the First World War. Following the resignation of Beck in 1938, he became chief of staff of the army (the first Bavarian and first Catholic to do so), though he shared his predecessor's scepticism about the rightness and possibility of close co-operation between the army and Hitler. Almost at once he became the leader with Witzleben (q.v.) of a 'half-hearted conspiracy' to remove the Führer, but the weakness of Brauchitsch (q.v.) and his own indecision brought it to nothing. He attempted during the winter of 1939–40 to delay an invasion of France, which he feared would lead to Germany's defeat, by prevaricating over the production of plans, but when put on the spot transformed the ideas of Manstein (q.v.) into

the executive scheme which succeeded so brilliantly in May–June. He also planned the invasion of Russia, but disagreed with Hitler over its execution and was dismissed in September 1942. He was arrested after the bomb plot of July 1944, although not implicated, but escaped execution.

Halleck, Henry Wager (1815–72) American (Union) general. Known in the regular army before the war as 'Old Brains' because he had written a book (*Element of Military Art and Science*, 1846) and translated another, Jomini's *Vie de Napoléon*, Halleck acted for most of the war as Lincoln's military adviser, with the rank of general-in-chief (when Grant, q.v., became supreme commander in March 1864, he reverted to chief of staff). Between 1854 and 1861 he had practised successfully as a lawyer and was initially charged, after his reappointment to the army, to sort out the muddle left by Frémont (q.v.) in the Department of the Missouri. Good at that, he proved so inept at field operations (he took a month, though almost unopposed, to advance the twenty miles from Shiloh to Corinth) that Lincoln brought him to Washington to work on administrative affairs. His dabblings in strategy from on high were an irritant and sometimes a handicap to field commanders. 'A man completely lacking in physical attractiveness or charm – popeyed, flabby, surly and crafty – he had the reputation of being the most unpopular man in Washington.' But he possessed 'the happy faculty of being able to communicate civilian ideas to a soldier and military ideas to a civilian', and he acted as a vital medium between Grant and Lincoln during the months of their most fruitful co-operation.

Halsey, William Frederick ('Bull'; 1882–1959) American admiral. The son of a naval officer, a graduate of Annapolis and a naval aviator by training, Halsey was commanding the air arm of the Pacific fleet at the outbreak of war in 1941. Already an admiral, he was given command of the South Pacific force and in November 1942 directed the important and successful operations around Guadalcanal. In June 1944, as commander of the 3rd Fleet, he won (despite a faulty decision at the height of the action) the battle of Leyte Gulf, the largest sea battle of history, measured in numbers of ships engaged, and the decisive blow in the destruction of the Imperial Japanese Navy. He directed the final operations of the war, May–September 1944, around Okinawa. On 12 December 1945 he was promoted fleet admiral, one of the very few American sailors to have held that highest rank.

Hamilton, (Sir) Ian Standish Monteith (1853–1947) British general. Born on Corfu during the British occupation, Hamilton was educated at Wellington and commissioned in 1872 into the 92nd Highlanders. His early career, during which he became a protégé of Roberts (q.v.), was spent campaigning in the colonies (Second Afghan War, First Boer War, Nile Expedition 1884–5, Burma 1886–7, relief of Chitral). He commanded a division of mounted infantry in South Africa in 1900, and was deputy to Kitchener (q.v.) in the final stages of the campaign. He then held a succession of important posts at the War Office (military secretary and adjutant-general), interrupted by a spell in charge of Southern Command and a visit to Manchuria during the Russo-Japanese war. Out of his experience there he wrote what was to become a minor military classic, *A Staff Officer's Scrapbook* (two volumes, 1906–7). It still reveals both the charm and delicacy of character which made him so widely liked, as well as the intellectual detachment which proved so disastrous when he was appointed to direct the Gallipoli landings in 1915.

Hampton, Wade (1818–1902) American (Confederate) general. Not a professional soldier but a wealthy South Carolinan planter, Hampton raised at his own expense the Hampton Legion and led it at First Bull Run. In 1862 he was appointed deputy to Stuart (q.v.), commanding the cavalry of the Army of Northern Virginia, and fought at Antietam and Gettysburg, where he was wounded. After the Wilderness campaign he succeeded Stuart and in 1865 took his cavalry to cover J.E. Johnston's (q.v.) retreat through South Carolina. He attempted to carry on the war in Texas after the surrender at Appomattox, but eventually returned to his estates. In later life he was governor of South Carolina and US senator for the state. In his appearance and character he embodied the ideal type of Southern gentleman, and was a cavalry leader of talent.

Harris, (Sir) Arthur ('Bomber'; 1892–1984) British air marshal. His name is associated with the decision, controversial within government and the service at the time, and widely condemned in retrospect, to practise 'area' or indiscriminate bombing of German cities during the Second World War. Harris, who became head of Bomber Command in February 1942, had rightly concluded that the selective bombing of allegedly 'bottleneck' targets (e.g. railway marshalling yards) was ineffective. He therefore assembled the largest possible number of aircraft to attack large areas, arguing that this would heighten the probability of hitting targets of military value, besides certainly depressing civilian morale. Both premises remain unproved and Harris, who despite his long tenure of command received only a baronetcy in the victory honours, has attracted irremovable historical odium for his persistent belief in them. At the time, however, most British civilians regarded his bombing policy as fair retribution for what London and Coventry had suffered in the Blitz.

Havelock, (Sir) Henry (1795–1857) British general. One of four brothers, all of whom became soldiers, Havelock was commissioned into the Rifle Brigade in 1815, transferred to the 13th (Somerset Light Infantry) and in 1823 went to India, where he was to spend all but two years of the rest of his life. He was also to be twenty-three years a lieutenant (perhaps because, unfashionably, he had become a Baptist), but he then did outstandingly well in Afghanistan, 1839–42 (siege of Jellalabad) and began to rise. At the outbreak of the Mutiny in 1857 he was commanding a division in Persia but was hurried back to relieve Lucknow (of which his son was a defender). At his third attempt he broke through the sepoy lines and entered the Residency, the newspaper headlines and every Victorian schoolboy's book of heroes. He died, full of fight and of his austere faith, amid the ruins, of disease contracted on his remarkable fighting advance from the Persian frontier.

Haynau, Julius Jacob (Freiherr) von (1786–1853) Austrian general. An illegitimate son of the Elector of Hesse, Haynau entered Austrian service in 1801. He gained widespread notoriety for his actions during the revolutions of 1848–9, when he put down with great brutality a rising at Brescia in Italy, and then in Hungary where he defeated Georgey (q.v.) at Temesvar, 9 August 1849. On a visit to England in 1850 he was denounced as a tyrant and thrown into the Thames by draymen of the brewers Barclay and Perkins.

Henry IV (1553–1610) King of France and Navarre. The outstanding Protestant commander in the interminable French wars of religion (1562–98), Henry's skills were those of a battlefield commander rather than in the higher planning or organization of war. After the massacre of St Bartholomew (1572), the Protestant cause was decimated and the responsibilities of command devolved on Henry. In effective imprisonment at court when the massacre took place, Henry escaped dramatically early in 1576, and fled south to take up the Protestant cause. Thereafter, he remained in a perpetual state of readiness for war, fighting in all in some 200 battles and skirmishes during his military career; in his shabby, stained clothes, he looked, contemporaries said, more like a common cavalry captain than a great prince. Henry inspired his men to superhuman efforts: at the battle of Coutras (1587) he faced a Catholic army of 10,000 under Joyeuse, with 6500, in a position so disadvantageous that Henry, who preferred to wear down his enemy by lightning assaults and skirmishes, felt he had fallen into a trap. But his superior use of his artillery, and the weight and power of the experienced Protestant cavalry, battered through the royalist lines and destroyed the Catholic army. Over 3000 Catholics died to 500 of Henry's Huguenots. Much of the nobility of France lay dead on the battlefield.

After the assassination of Henry III in 1589, Henry succeeded to the French throne, an empty honour if he could not establish his authority over the powerful forces formed by the Catholic League, which was sworn to resist a Protestant monarch. In alliance with the league were the Spanish, whose troops were in the Netherlands under Parma (q.v.), and jointly they out-matched Henry both in numbers and quality of their troops. But Henry dealt them a devastating blow at the battle of Arques (1589). Henry, again faced by an army much larger than his own, created a strong position using both field fortification and the naturally marshy ground. His artillery was located so as to enfilade any attacking force.

Once again he was able to defeat a superior enemy, but this time in an essentially defensive battle. At Ivry in the following year he again faced Mayenne with the league army, who fielded 16,000 men to Henry's 11,000. As at Coutras, the battle was won by a determined cavalry charge, led by Henry himself against the pick of Mayenne's troops in the centre. But although it was the shock of the cavalry charge which decided the day, it was the mixture of fire-power and the *arme blanche* which distinguished Henry's tactical approach. His *arquebusiers* were massed to provide a far greater concentration of fire than was possible in the conventional arrangement, and his artillery was always carefully sited to give the most effective fire. The skill of his artillerymen was clearly seen at Coutras, where his few guns fired eighteen shots to the Catholic six. Although Henry was clearly successful in pitched battle, his preference was decidedly for irregular warfare; he never mastered the skills of strategy and his temperament was not suited to the slow pace of siegecraft. Against Parma in a war of manœuvre (1590-2) Henry showed his limitations as a commander; after Parma's death in 1592 he was never faced again by a general of real quality. In 1593 Henry abjured the Protestant faith, and Paris opened its gates to its lawful Catholic king. War continued for five more years, and at one pitched battle with the Spanish at Fontaine-Française (1595) Henry was nearly killed in the mêlée; he said afterwards that he had had to fight not only for victory, but for life itself. Peace was finally concluded at Vervins (1598), and Henry, now securely King of France, set about rebuilding a country ruined by over thirty years of war. It is for this process of reconstruction that he deserved his title 'the Great'. In battle he was an inspirational leader, and one of the first to realize the importance of shock and fire-power in the winning of battles, les-

sons to be reinforced by the Swedish successes in the Thirty Years' War. Like his predecessor, Henry III, he died at the hands of an assassin.

Herkimer, Nicholas (1728–77) American soldier. By birth a German, Herkimer led the New York militia at the outbreak of the War of Independence, his main concern being the preservation of New York from an attack by Indians and 'Tories' (American sympathizers of the British). In particular he had hoped to keep Chief Joseph Brant and the Mohawk tribe neutral in the conflict, but they allied with the British and besieged Fort Stanwix. Herkimer and his small force set out in relief, but he was ambushed some six miles from the fort at Oriskany (1777) and retreated in disorder. Wounded in the engagement, he was taken home to his family, where he made an edifying death after reciting the Thirty-Ninth psalm.

Hideyoshi, Toyotomi (1536–98) Japanese soldier. The principal soldier of the great Japanese *shogun* Oda Nobunaga, Hideyoshi conducted numerous campaigns in the west of Japan to extend his master's territories. After Nobunaga's suicide (1582) to avoid capture by rebels, Hideyoshi allied with another of his former master's principal soldiers, Tokugawa Ieyasu, to avenge his death. Together they gained control of the entirety of central Japan. In 1587 Hideyoshi defeated one of the remaining powerful clans, the Satsuma, at Kyushu, and in 1590 the consolidation of Japan under their control was completed by the victory at Odawara.

Hideyoshi now turned to the conquest of an empire on the mainland. In 1592 he invaded Korea, intending to strike into China. But the Koreans resisted, and his army had to fight its way slowly up the country. But in the battle of the Yellow Sea the Korean fleet under Yi

Sung Sin shattered a Japanese fleet, carrying troops and supplies. Fifty-nine Japanese ships were sunk, and the battle saw the introduction of two ironclad vessels, made to Yi's own requirements. The war teetered back and forward, and inconclusive peace negotiations were carried on. But in 1598 the Korean fleet sealed the fate of the Japanese force at the battle of Chinhae Bay, where some 200 Japanese ships, half the fleet, were sunk by Yi. Shortly before the disaster Hideyoshi had died in Japan, and peace negotiations were hurried to a conclusion. The reason for Hideyoshi's success in his various campaigns was his use of fire-power (small-arms had been recently introduced into Japan) and his departure from the stately formality of normal Samurai warfare. Hideyoshi, a commoner, had no time for the outworn practices of the chivalric code, and he thus brought the first elements of modern war into Japan.

Hindenburg, Paul Ludwig von (properly v. Beneckendorf und v. Hindenburg; 1847–1934) German field-marshal and president. A Prussian of Prussians (he was born at Posen, the son of an officer and of a family which traced its military tradition to the thirteenth century), Hindenburg was commissioned in 1866 into the 3rd Foot Guards (subsequently, and as a result of his connection with it, to be a nursery of generals, *see* Manstein). He won the Order of the Red Eagle at Königgrätz, 1866, and in 1870 the Iron Cross at Saint-Privat, the Guard Corps' *dies irae*. His subsequent career was, nevertheless, steady rather than exceptional. He passed the Staff College, but it was 'the ordinary process of promotion', not brilliance, which made him a general. He was patient and balanced in temperament, but lacked money and influence at court and in 1909, during the 'Kaiser manœuvres', made the mistake of allowing Wilhelm II to lose the sham battle. In 1911 he retired at his

own request, seeing no further chance of promotion. At the outbreak of war, however, a senior general being needed to command the isolated Eighth Army defending East Prussia against the invading Russians, he was recalled and sent thither, with Ludendorff (q.v.), the victor of Liège, as his chief of staff. Between them, with the assistance of Hoffmann (q.v.) and thanks to the ineptitude of Rennenkampf and Samsonov (qq.v.), commanding the Russian armies, they won the brilliant defensive battles of Tannenberg, 26–31 August, and the Masurian Lakes, 9–14 September. East Prussia was saved. In November Hindenburg was promoted field-marshal and commander of all German and Austrian forces on the eastern front; he had already become a popular idol.

The Austrians, despite the German victories, had failed against the Russians, and during 1915 Hindenburg, directly or indirectly, conducted operations to relieve pressure on them and maintain the advance on the German sector of the front. In February he won the Winter battle in Masuria and in May–June, through Mackensen (q.v.), achieved the great Gorlice–Tarnow breakthrough which pushed the Russian line 300 miles eastward by the end of the year. The next was less successful, because of the masterly counter-offensive by Brusilov (q.v.), but in September Hindenburg and Ludendorff left the east to succeed Falkenhayn in the west and in overall command. Their appointment revived flagging national morale and they instituted a rational strategy of defence in the west and offence in the east, reckoning the Russians the weaker and therefore the more beatable enemy. A new position (the *Siegfried-Stellung*; to the British, 'the Hindenburg Line') was constructed in France, against which both the British Arras and the French Nivelle offensives foundered. In the east the Riga offensive (September 1917) broke what was left of the Russian army's spirit and led directly to the armistice of Brest-Litovsk in December. But their appointment was, in the long term, disadvantageous to Germany, for they used it to political as well as military ends, insisting on the replacement of the 'defeatist' Hollweg by the more pliant Michaelis as chancellor, on the repudiation of an important Papal peace offer and on the initiation of unrestricted submarine warfare which brought America into the war. In 1918 their offensives, launched with the divisions released by Russia's capitulation, very nearly brought about, as Hindenburg intended, the defeat of France and Britain before American soldiers arrived *en masse*; but not quite. And their near-success was in effect total failure. In September the Hindenburg Line was breached. In November the old field-marshal was obliged not only to sue for terms but to call on the kaiser to abdicate, a hitherto unthinkable act of lèse-majesté to a Prussian officer.

From 1925 to 1934 Hindenburg acted as president of the republic; effectively and beneficially at first, but, as his health failed and social divisions widened, with decreasing power. He appointed two favourites, Papen and Schleicher, both ex-soldiers, to avoid sending for Hitler as chancellor, but was eventually left without an alternative. On his death the Führer succeeded him in office. It was an unworthy succession, for there was much nobility in Hindenburg's character.

Hipper, Franz (Ritter von; 1863–1932) German admiral. He commanded the battlecruisers of the High Seas Fleet from August 1914 to August 1918, when he succeeded Scheer (q.v.), and led them in the battles of the Dogger Bank, 24 January 1915 and Jutland, 31 May 1916; in the latter his ships sank two of the British battlecruisers led by Beatty (q.v.).

Hitler, Adolf (1889–1945) German dictator and war leader. Hitler served as a private soldier and junior NCO (*Gefreiter*) from August 1914 until after the armistice, for most of the time on the western front. These years as a *Frontkämpfer* (front-line soldier) equalled in importance in forming his outlook those he spent as a down-and-out in prewar Vienna; nothing surpassed them. He entered the war without military training (having first evaded and then been exempted for reasons of health from peacetime service in the Austro-Hungarian army) as a volunteer in the 16th Bavarian Reserve Infantry Regiment. With it he was sent in October to fight against the British in the first battle of Ypres, called by the Germans the *Kindermord* ('Massacre of the Innocents') *bei Ypern*, because the corps committed to it were formed of untrained volunteers, like Hitler, and suffered very high casualties in consequence. His job in the regiment was the dangerous one of *Meldegänger* (message-carrier or runner) which he held throughout the war; he was once wounded and once gassed and four times decorated, ultimately with the Iron Cross 1st Class (August 1918), an order given only for acts of exceptional courage.

A brief spell as a 'political education officer' followed the armistice, and after his clash with the *Reichsheer* in Munich in 1923, which ended his first attempt at a putsch, he had no further contact with the army until he came to power as chancellor of Germany in 1933. But the putsch and his trench experiences were to determine his attitude towards it throughout his dictatorship. Munich had taught him that to rule he must have power over the army: that he acquired by a steady erosion of its independence and self-confidence, which culminated in his management of the Blomberg–Fritsch (q.v.) crisis of 1938. The trenches had taught him, or so he thought, that he understood war in a way his generals did not. There was something in this. His first generation of military advisers, Brauchitsch, Bock, Leeb, Rundstedt (qq.v.), being Kriegsakademie graduates, had been kept out of the trenches during the First World War lest their valuable brains be blown out in some chance raid or bombardment. In strict terms, therefore, he knew war with an intimacy which they had been spared. At first, during the Polish and French campaigns, this conviction served only to help him intervene as an equal (that is, a fellow soldier) in arguments which he nevertheless let his military advisers decide. Proof that his judgement could be better than theirs, however, which the success of the Manstein (q.v.) plan – partly his own – awoke in him, led him increasingly to want to win his arguments, and eventually to expect no opposition to his views whatsoever. The turning point came in December 1941, over the Moscow counteroffensive. He and the generals – in particular, Guderian (q.v.) – had wasted six weeks of the campaign arguing how its initial success might best be exploited. Its imminent failure, as winter came down, could be averted, he decided, only if the army stood where it was. Proponents of manœuvre or retreat, which he judged disastrous, were dismissed and (when events bore out his judgement) so too were a host of commanders he thought unenterprising, self-willed or over-age: the purge matched in proportions the famous *limogeage* unleashed by Joffre (q.v.) on the French *Generalität* in August 1914. Thereafter he acted as his own commander-in-chief – he actually assumed the title on his dismissal of Brauchitsch, who had previously held it – dealing with the army through its chief of staff (*see* Halder, Zeitzler, Guderian) and with the other services through his own command organization, OKW (*Oberkommando der Wehrmacht*), set up in the aftermath of the Blomberg-

Fritsch (q.v.) crisis. He dictated, moreover, that while the army staff (OKH) should supervise ground operations in Russia, all other fronts were 'OKW theatres': thus he prevented any of his soldiers, except those of his immediate circle (*see* Keitel and Jodl), from grasping a picture in the round of Germany's strategic situation, and ensured that even the few, like Guderian, who were still prepared to stand up to him after 1941, lacked the ground on which to do so.

It became the custom among his personal staff during the last four years of his life, which were spent wholly in the direction of the war, to refer to him as the '*Grofaz*', an acronym of the German for 'the greatest commander (*Feldherr*) of all time'. And indeed he lived the part, so organizing his day that he could be awake for several hours both at noon and midnight in order to hold situation conferences – a routine which persisted from the outbreak of the Russian campaign until his suicide in Berlin and which did much in itself to bring on the appearance of old age which all visitors to his headquarters (the most used was at Rastenburg – the *Wolfsschanze* – but there were others in the Ukraine, on the Somme, and, in Germany, at Nauheim, Munich, Obersalzburg and Berlin) noticed from the middle of the war onwards. '*Grofaz*' he certainly was not. But, equally, he was not the strategic dunderhead which wartime Allied propaganda made him out to be. He had, during his years of idleness, read a great deal of military history and theory and he possessed, of course, many of the qualities essential to military success – self-confidence, boldness, intelligence, a hold over his immediate subordinates and a genuine indifference to human suffering. He had a nose for others' good ideas, among the many bad he was offered, was reasonably creative himself, and must be given the credit for conceiving or backing some of the best military judgements of the age – notably, the decision to create the panzer divisions, the Manstein plan, the outline (though not the execution) of the *Barbarossa*, and the 1941 invasion of the Balkans. But he suffered from a besetting and eventually fatal weakness of judgement – an inability to match his ambitions to his resources. While the impetus of his *blitzkrieg* victories lasted, the industrial and economic inferiority of Germany *vis-à-vis* the growing list of enemies he almost casually acquired (there was no diplomatic necessity for him to declare war on America in the aftermath of Pearl Harbor) was disguised. Once it ran out, as it did in the middle of 1943, he was left without initiative or room to manœuvre. He recognized that this was quite literally so – hence his insistence on holding ground everywhere, no matter what the cost, and his growing preference for generals, like Schörner (q.v.), who would stand fast long after there had ceased to be any point in so doing. At the very end – and he almost succeeded in carrying out his boast of fighting 'until five past midnight' – he clung obsessively to the single idea of staying put, surrendering his chance of escaping from Berlin when he still might have done, and ultimately dying by his own hand as enemy shells exploded on the ground over his head. The circumstances were a bizarre repetition of his youthful experience of war on the western front with which he had so often taunted his generals.

Hoche, Louis Lazare (1768–97) French general. The son of a groom, Hoche himself began work as an assistant groom in the royal stables. In 1784 he enlisted in the *Gardes françaises* and in 1789 was a corporal. Despite its royal associations, his regiment favoured the Revolution, and he himself prospered through it (though not materially, for he was of a puritanical temperament). By 1792 he was a captain and Carnot

(q.v.), impressed by a memorandum he had written to the Committee of Public Safety on the strategic situation brought about by the Austro-Prussian invasion of the north, made him a battalion commander. His part in the defence of Dunkirk was so successful that he was promoted general of brigade, then of division in quick succession, and then commander-in-chief of the Army of the Moselle. Initially unsuccessful at Kaiserlautern (28–30 November 1793), he recovered to beat the Prussians at Froeschwiller (22 December) and the Austrians at Geisberg (26 December). Through these victories he recaptured the lines of Wissemburg, relieved Landau and threw the invaders back across the Rhine.

His career was interrupted during 1794 by imprisonment, contrived by his rival Pichegru (q.v.), but he was released after the overthrow of Robespierre and conducted a successful pacification in Brittany, including the repulse of the émigré landing at Quiberon Bay, 27 June 1795. His own expedition to Ireland the following year (Bantry Bay) was, however, a fiasco, though not of his making. In 1797, in command of the Army of the Sambre-et-Meuse, he achieved the victories of Neuwied and Altenkirchen against the Austrians in northern Germany. It was there that he died of a disease of the chest, aged twenty-nine. 'One of the greatest and purest figures of the Revolution', Hoche's ruthlessness, even brutality, against the *Chouans* of Brittany make him difficult to like. But his generalship attracted even Napoleon's admiration.

Hodges, Courtney Hicks (1887–1966) American general. A Georgian, Hodges enlisted as a private soldier and served three years in the ranks. During the Second World War he commanded the US First Army throughout its advance from Normandy to Germany and during the German Ardennes offensive.

Hoepner, Erich (1886–1944) German panzer general and conspirator against Hitler. He commanded the Fourth Panzer Group with great success in the advance to Moscow in 1941 and came within sight of the city, but took the full brunt of Zhukov's (q.v.) December counter-offensive and was driven back. Hitler made him the principal target of his wrath; he was not only dismissed but stripped of his rank. He had been involved in the 1938 conspiracy and was now drawn into the Beck–Stauffenberg circle. At the critical moment on 20 July 1944, however, he hesitated in his role of supplanting the commander of the Home Army and was arrested that evening when the coup failed. He was hanged on 8 August.

Hoffmann, Max (1869–1927) German general. He was the most important subordinate of Hindenburg and Ludendorff (qq.v.) during their successful direction of operations on the eastern front, which brought them to the supreme command. In 1914 he was already in post as operations officer of the Eighth Army in East Prussia and advised General François during his brilliant defence against the invading Russians, for which, Hoffmann later alleged, Hindenburg and Ludendorff unfairly reaped the credit. After the duumvirate's departure to the west in September 1916, he remained as chief of staff in the east, negotiated the treaty of Brest-Litovsk with the Bolsheviks, and organized the annexation of the Ukraine. Perhaps the most brilliant German staff officer of his generation, the exact importance of his contribution to Hindenburg's and Ludendorff's success, though disputed by the latter, was certainly very great.

Hohenlohe-Ingelfingen, Prinz Friedrich Ludwig von (1746–1818) Prussian general. In 1806 he commanded the corps which defended the sector between the Saal and the Thuringian forests against Napoleon's invasion. Its leading elements were thrown back at the battle of Saalfeld, 10 October 1806, and the corps itself destroyed at Jena. The death of Brunswick (q.v.) at Auerstadt on the same day brought him the supreme command and, after directing the retreat of the army to the Oder, he capitulated.

A relative, **Karl Augustus von Hohenlohe-Ingelfingen** (1827–92), had a distinguished career in the reconstructed Prussian army and commanded the artillery at the siege of Paris, 1870–1. He was a prolific military writer and his *Letters on Artillery* were an influential text.

Holk, Heinrich (1599–1633) German soldier of fortune. Danish by birth, Holk first served Christian IV of Denmark before transferring to the imperial cause. He commanded in the heroic defence of Stralsund in 1628, when he held off Wallenstein (q.v.) for almost six months before the imperial army withdrew. But after the peace of Lübeck (1629), which took Denmark out of the Thirty Years' War, Holk joined his erstwhile opponent, Wallenstein. In 1632 he was given a cavalry command, and it was as a cavalry commander that he was to leave his mark.

'Holk's Horse' were notable for their zeal in battle, their enthusiasm in rape and pillage (his devastation of Saxony was notorious even in an age of atrocities), and their solidness under fire. At Lützen (1632) he commanded the cavalry facing Gustavus Adolphus (q.v.) and was hard pressed when the Swedish cavalry charged. But fortunately for Holk, Gustavus was killed and he managed to rally his troops in the confusion which ensued. After Lützen he was left in senior command but without an active role. He chafed under this enforced idleness, but his rising irritation was quenched by an attack of plague, from which he died. Holk's real talent was for irregular war, skirmishing and raiding.

Hood, John Bell (1831–79) American (Confederate) general. Not one of the South's great generals, he was one of its bravest fighters. A West Pointer (and only a lieutenant in 1861), he got command of a brigade, then of a division, in 1862 (he was promoted major-general on 10 October), and made it 'man for man perhaps the best ... in the Army'. He was badly wounded at Gettysburg and again at Chickamauga but retained spirit enough, when promoted to succeed Johnston (q.v.) as commander of the Army of Tennessee, to plan and lead a counter-offensive against Sherman (q.v.) after Atlanta. Neither he nor his soldiers could offer a match, however, and the Franklin–Nashville campaign was a failure. But he did not surrender until the following 31 May. For over two years he had commanded from the saddle with a crippled left arm and without a leg.

Hooker, Joseph ('Fightin' Joe'; 1814–79) American (Union) general. A West Pointer, Hooker had fought in the Mexican and Seminole wars but had retired in 1853. Moreover, having quarrelled with generals Scott and Halleck (qq.v.), he had difficulty in re-establishing himself in the army in 1861, but when he got command of a brigade showed himself a brilliant and brave tactical leader. At Second Bull Run he commanded a division, at Antietam, where he was wounded, a corps. At Fredericksburg he commanded the centre and, consequent on the poor handling of the battle by Burnside (q.v.), was himself appointed commander of the Army of the Potomac, a post he badly wanted and had intrigued to get. Lincoln wrote him a very remarkable letter of advice and warning, ending, 'Give us victories.' Unfortunately at Chancellorsville, 1–4 May 1863, he encountered Lee and Jackson (qq.v.) at the top of their joint form and was completely outmanœuvred. So perfect a (Confederate) victory was Chancel-

lorsville that some credit perhaps reflects on Hooker for helping to make it possible. Lincoln, understandably, did not take that view, and replaced him with Meade (q.v.). He spent the rest of the war a corps commander in Tennessee and Georgia. 'Fightin' Joe' was a pressman's nickname which stuck, and was partly deserved for it described his talent, which was 'limited to his field of vision ... he could not make war on the map'.

Hopton, Ralph, Lord (1598–1652) English soldier. Although initially a strong Parliament man, Hopton rallied to the flag of King Charles I in 1642 and was one of his most energetic and effective commanders. At the start of the war he galvanized Cornish resistance to Parliament, and defeated a Parliamentary army under Ruthven sent to secure the west. After beating Ruthven at Bradock Down and Lord Stamford at Stratton (1643), Hopton ravaged Devonshire. In July 1643 he attacked a larger force under Sir William Waller (q.v.) at Lansdown near Bath, but was wounded during the action and took refuge in Devizes. Recovered from his wound, he built on his earlier success and moved through Dorset into the south-eastern counties of England. But his advance was halted when he was beaten at Cheriton in Kent by Waller (March 1644). Hopton retreated in good order, however, and managed to save his precious artillery from capture. In 1646 he was less fortunate for he met his match in Fairfax (q.v.), who systematically reduced the centres of Royalist resistance in the west: at Torrington (1646) he was routed and retreated south-west into Cornwall. But at Truro he faced overwhelming odds and considerable doubts about the continuing loyalty of his own troops: he surrendered and was allowed to leave freely. He died, in exile, in the Netherlands.

Hopton's successes were those of

improvisation, transforming poor human material, training his troops and instilling a sense of duty and loyalty into them. His later campaigns were with men he did not know well and in whom he had little confidence. He was professional in his management of a campaign, benefiting from the experience he had gained serving with Mansfeld (q.v.) in the Palatinate in the early stages of the Thirty Years' War (1618–48). He was out-generalled by Fairfax, but he also lacked his strength both in men and support.

Howe, Richard, Earl (1726–99) English admiral. The most successful of the Howe brothers, Richard Howe joined the British navy in 1740, served under Anson (q.v.), and saw his first action against the French in 1746, when he was severely wounded. At the beginning of the Seven Years' War (1756–63) he held station in the Channel, and his career during the war amounted to a series of assaults, dashingly executed, on the French mainland, and the harassment of coastal shipping. In November 1759 however he commanded the lead ship in Hawke's victory at Quiberon Bay. Late in March 1776 he was appointed as overall commander in North America, to act in concert with his brother William (q.v.). But the naval part in the war was slight and, like his brother, he was accused of inaction and lack of zeal. He too resigned his command in 1778, to join William in the defeat of their political enemies.

In 1782, with a change of government, he accepted a new command and was responsible for the successful outcome of the relief expedition to Gibraltar, under attack by de Crillon and ably defended by Sir George Elliott. Howe's most lasting triumph came on 1 June 1794, The Glorious First of June, off Ushant, when as commander of the Channel fleet he defeated the French fleet of Joyeuse decisively. He was made a Knight of the Garter, and he and all his officers were lavishly rewarded. By now an officer of eminence, he held administrative posts, but it was his personal intervention which ended the dangerous Spithead mutiny of 1797. The sailors trusted 'Black Dick, as he was nicknamed (he shared his brother's dark features). He was an excellent and courageous seaman, and a naval officer of the traditional sort. He was, however, no great thinker or innovator.

Howe, William, Viscount (1729–1814) British soldier. The youngest of the three Howe brothers, his military reputation is a little less resplendent. Serving briefly under the Duke of Cumberland (q.v.) after the Culloden campaign, he later served with Wolfe (q.v.) at the siege of Louisburg (1758). In the following year Howe took a leading part in the capture of Quebec under Wolfe's command and completed his run of success with the capture of Montreal in 1760. He developed light infantry tactics, based on the general experience gained in North America, and was viewed as one of the most promising young officers. As such he was sent to stiffen the British command in the American colonies in 1775. At the battle of Bunker Hill, Howe followed his commander, Gage's, orders and launched a frontal assault against prepared positions: he lost over 1000 men.

In the campaigns of 1776 and 1777, Howe, now in overall command, was faced with the impossible task of imposing a scheme of united, co-ordinated action. But he had a good record of success, taking New York (1776), beating Washington at the battle of Brandywine (1777), and at Germantown in the following month (October). But his other generals reaped the rewards of their impetuosity, Burgoyne (q.v.) being forced to surrender to General Gates (q.v.) at Saratoga in October 1777. As the British position worsened, Howe tried to bring Washington into a position where he could inflict a decisive defeat. But he failed, and in 1778 he resigned his command, because he believed that the government in London had failed to support him properly. He returned to London to defend himself against a whispering campaign fostered by his enemies. He never held another command. Howe was a skilful field commander, an inspiring and imposing leader, a tall, saturnine figure, but he lacked the strategic grasp of a great general.

Huger, Isaac (1743–97) American soldier. One of no less than five brothers active in the American Revolution, Isaac Huger rose to the greatest military prominence in the war. Educated in Europe, he had experience both in Indian warfare and regular military service before the revolution broke out. Faced by regular troops, well handled, he had little success at the head of his South Carolina regiment. At the second battle of Charleston (1780) he was swept away by Tarleton's successful assault; at Hobkirk's Hill (1781) he was part of Nathanael Greene's (q.v.) force (which had already lost at Guilford Courthouse earlier in the year), and again went down to defeat. But despite this lack of success, Huger inspired his men with confidence, especially since he was always where the danger was fiercest in a battle. Wounded many times in action, he was not well served by his troops, who were never able to fulfil the demands he made on them. With better material, his undoubted energy should have had a more successful outcome.

Hughes, Sir Edward (1720–94) English admiral. Together with Eyre Coote, Hughes played a crucial role in the extension of British power in India. He provided control of the seas, always vital for a successful European campaign in India, while Eyre Coote had free rein on

land. Taking up command in the Indian Ocean in July 1778 for the second time, since he had served there from 1773 to 1777, his first act was to raid the French coastal possessions, in 1782 capturing the important fort of Trincomalee. But he had very rapidly to defend his new conquest as a superior French fleet arrived to challenge his dominance of the coast.

Hughes and the French admiral, Suffren (q.v.), fought four fleet actions in seven months. Suffren recaptured Trincomalee and generally had the best of the encounters, but Hughes, by excellent seamanship, never allowed the advantage to pass decisively to the French. By keeping his fleet in being, and at sea, he posed a constant threat to the French, who could never concentrate on using their fleet to support their forces on land. The running battles were ended by the treaty of Versailles (1783). Hughes returned to England with a massive fortune, acquired in India by means which were never disclosed. He never held a command again. The interest of the campaign lies in its duration: both fleets were at sea for nearly a year. Suffren's was the greater achievement, however, for he had no secure base which he could use to refit and repair his ships. But both admirals anticipated some of the techniques used in the blockade during the Napoleonic wars.

Huntly, George Gordon, Earl of (1514–62) Scottish soldier. In the tumultuous Scottish politics of the mid-sixteenth century, Huntly was an arch-conniver, and in a generation devoid of military skill in Scotland he passed for a leading soldier. In 1542 he repulsed an invading English force in a skirmish at Hadden Rig, and, more important, kept the powerful army of the Duke of Norfolk from moving much beyond the Tweed. (The English army of 30,000 smashed the main Scottish army at Solway Moss, however, a battle at which Huntly was not present.) Two years later he turned his attention to the Highlands, crushing rebellious clans with great firmness. But at the battle of Pinkie (1547), his career received a reverse, for in the general panic which followed the rout of the Scots, Huntly fled and was taken prisoner.

But nothing served to reduce the great power, based on lands and wealth, which he held in the north of Scotland. After his release by the English, on payment of a substantial ransom, he again assumed a leading role in Scottish politics, in the tumult over religious change adopting a Catholic or Protestant stance as the situation and his own advantage demanded. Trusted by none, Huntly was, nevertheless, too powerful to be disregarded. But his many enemies at the court of Mary, Queen of Scots, united against him. Driven finally into rebellion, he died in a pathetic mêlée between his few remaining supporters and the royalist party. His death was caused, it was said, by being crushed in the throng, 'being a corpulent man'. Heart failure, the most probable reason, saved him from the executioner's axe. In few respects an attractive character, he was the least unsuccessful Scottish soldier of his era.

I

Ironside, Edmund (1st Baron; 1880–1959) British field-marshal. Six feet four inches in height and muscular in proportion, 'Tiny' Ironside played rugby for Scotland, spoke seven languages, and, through his escapades as an intelligence officer in the Boer War, provided John Buchan with the model for his famous character Richard Hannay (of *The Thirty-nine Steps* and other novels). After a distinguished regimental and staff career, 1914–18, he was appointed to command the allied forces in North Russia (see his *Archangel, 1918–19*), an episode which Buchan might have hesitated to write as fiction, was subsequently commandant of the Staff College and, after his career had faltered in the 1930s, was chosen by Belisha, who had found difficulty in working with Gort (q.v.), to be Chief of the Imperial General Staff on 3 September 1939. A commander at heart, who would have preferred to go to France in Gort's place, was not happy in the post and was relieved after Dunkirk.

Ivan the Terrible (1530–84) Tsar of Russia. Although the main activity of Ivan's reign was the construction of a strong centralized state, involving the bloody destruction of *boyar* (noble) families and privileges, he was active in foreign conquest. In 1547–8 and 1549–50 he sent expeditions against the Tartar khanate of Kazan. The expeditions failed and the generals suffered execution, the usual consequence of Ivan's displeasure. In 1552 he himself led a much stronger force, and the city succumbed. But in 1555 the country was invaded from the south by the Crimean Tartars, who ravaged the land and took Moscow, although the Kremlin of Moscow held out against them.

In general, Ivan's campaigns in the east and south were successful, but his attempts to conquer territory in Livonia, on the Baltic, brought him into direct conflict with Poland. By 1582 all Russia's gains in Livonia had been lost, despite the rigours of a long war. In 1570 Ivan destroyed the city of Novgorod the Great, believing they were treating with the Poles; and as the years went on, looming insanity clouded his mind. He built up a private army, the *oprichniki*, and terrorized his more eminent subjects. His rages were devastating: in one of his passions he killed his son, and guilt for the deed soured his life. The achievement of Ivan's reign was to subordinate all considerations to the building of military power and an unassailable royal autocracy. The first ruler of Russia to take the title 'tsar', he is still revered as a great patriot.

J

Jackson, Andrew (1767–1845) Seventh president of the United States; victor of the battle of New Orleans. A lawyer turned politician, Jackson had gained some experience of fighting as a major-general of Tennessee militia and in 1814 conducted a campaign in Alabama against the Creek Indians, allies of the British with whom America was then at war. In May he was commissioned major-general in the regular army and on 8 January 1815, with a rag-tag army, defeated General Pakenham at New Orleans (a victory to which a line in 'The Star-spangled Banner' refers). He became overnight a national hero. He later campaigned successfully against the Seminole Indians (1818).

Jackson, Thomas Jonathan ('Stonewall'; 1824–63) American (Confederate) general. Jackson won his nickname, now inseparable, at First Bull Run, his undying reputation for will-o'-the-wisp generalship in his Shenandoah Valley campaign, May–June 1862. Originally a regular officer (West Point, class of 1846), he had left the army in 1851 to teach at the Virginia Military Institute, a private academy. Appointed a brigadier in the Confederate army in June 1861, he raised the brigade which he commanded with such tenacity in the first battle of the war ('There is Jackson, standing like a stone wall,' said General Barnard E. Bee, who fell on the field). In the following year he was given an independent command and the mission of detaining Federal troops in the Shenandoah Valley so that they might not assist the advance of McClellan (q.v.) on Rich-

mond. Initially unsuccessful at Kernstown, 23 March 1862, he then proceeded to defeat in detail a superior Union force in a succession of minor but brilliantly contrived victories – Winchester, Cross Keys and Port Republic. These two months of campaigning have been a subject of study at American and British staff colleges ever since.

Jackson's next passage of command, in support of Lee (q.v.) during the Seven Days' battles, was curiously inept. But he recovered his form at Second Bull Run, took a prominent part at Fredericksburg and, with Lee, achieved one of the masterpieces of battlefield strategy at Chancellorsville. Reconnoitring after the battle, he was accidentally shot by his own men and died eight days later of pneumonia. His last words, typically elegant and enigmatic, were, 'Let us cross over the river and rest under the shade of the trees.' Lee in particular and the Confederacy in general were stricken by his loss. Austere in manner and habits, passionately religious and obsessively secretive, he set a style of generalship which influenced many English-speaking soldiers, chiefly through the remarkable *Life* by G.F.R. Henderson.

James II (1633–1701) King of England and British admiral. The second son of Charles I, and known as the Duke of York until his accession, James II showed himself to be the most competent, in military terms, of the House of Stuart. When his brother Charles II was restored to the English throne in 1660, James was appointed Lord High Admiral, a post of considerable responsibility in view of the strength of the Dutch navy, England's most persistent maritime rival.

While in exile, James had served in both the French and Spanish army, and good opinions were held of his capacities as an officer (he fought with great courage at the head of an English Royalist force at the battle of the Dunes, 1658). But in high command he lacked that power of firm and immediate decision which was necessary in a senior officer. In the naval battle of Lowestoft, in the Second Dutch War (1665–7), he was relieved of his command for failing to follow up a badly battered Dutch fleet. At the battle of Sole Bay (1672), in the Third Dutch War (1672–4), he fought with tremendous physical courage, but lost the battle to the greater skill of de Ruyter (q.v.). His real achievement for the navy, however, was in the sphere of administration and organization. Some of the credit usually loaded on Samuel Pepys belongs by right to James, who had a keen interest in ship design and military organization.

He became a covert Catholic in 1669 and loosed on his head the fury of a political outcry that he should be excluded from the throne; in 1672 he was forced to retire as Lord High Admiral. When he acceded to the throne in 1685 he began a programme of reform in the army, which had, indeed, the motive of purging it of his enemies, but also of introducing needed reforms. Ousted in the Glorious Revolution of 1688 by William of Orange and many of the leading English families, he displayed the same vacillation which had handicapped his earlier career. All attempts, in Ireland and Scotland, to restore him to the throne failed, and he died in exile in Saint-Germain, passing on the Jacobite cause to his eldest son James Edward (the Old Pretender). A brusque, tactless man, he was capable of deep affection within his own family. He had none of the subtlety of his brother, or of his enemies.

Jaurès, Jean-Léon (1859–1914) French socialist. Founder of the French Socialist Party (PSI) and the journal *L'Humanité*, his *Armée nouvelle*, published in 1914, which argued for the transformation of the French army into a classless national militia, has influenced socialist military thinking ever since.

Jellicoe, John Rushworth (1st Earl Jellicoe; 1859–1935) British admiral. The son of an officer of the merchant marine, on which the Royal Navy traditionally looked down, Jellicoe's great abilities carried him quickly up the ladder of promotion in the gunnery branch, which then enjoyed primacy in the service. Unlike many contemporaries, he saw little foreign adventure (though he was aboard *Victoria* in her never-to-be-forgotten collision with the *Camperdown* in 1893, and at the relief of Peking). Picked by Fisher (q.v.) as early as 1908 as the officer most suitable to command the Grand Fleet in war, he was nominated to that post before war broke out in 1914. From August 1914 to May 1916 he kept watch from Scapa Flow for a sortie by the German High Seas Fleet and when it occurred on 30 May he led his ships to a costly strategic victory at Jutland, his conduct of which battle has been ever after debated. Replaced by Beatty (q.v.), he was First Sea Lord, 1916–17, but was removed by Lloyd George for his supposed resistance to the introduction of the convoy system. He was promoted admiral of the fleet in 1919 and created earl in 1925, and from 1920 to 1924 was governor-general of New Zealand. A man of flawless character and cool brain, he lacked the hold on his subordinates which made Beatty, though a worse admiral, a more effective commander.

Jodl, Alfred (1890–1946) German general. An artillery officer of the Bavarian army by origin, Jodl was chosen in 1938 to become chief of operations section of OKW, the tri-service staff set up to replace the War Ministry in 1938 by Hitler, and so his chief military adviser, which he remained throughout the war. A brilliant staff officer and tireless worker, he gave executive form to all the military decisions which the Führer made at his twice-daily situation conferences, while in those theatres designated as OKW instead of army spheres of operations (roughly everywhere except Russia) he acted as immediate chief of staff. He was arraigned as a major war criminal at Nuremberg and hanged.

Joffre, Joseph Jacques Césaire (1852–1931) Marshal of France. A Polytechnicien, Joffre took part, as a junior engineer officer, in the defence of Paris, 1870–1. In 1885 he embarked, like so many officers of his generation, on a colonial career, first in the Pacific and Indo-China, where he organized the defence of Hanoi, then in the French Sudan, where he established French power at Timbuctoo, finally in Madagascar. Appointed director of engineers at the War Ministry in 1905, he became in 1911 vice-president of the Higher War Council and therefore responsible for framing war plans. Plan XVII, with which his name is associated, rejected as its basis the supposition that Germany might violate Belgian neutrality and put the main French weight opposite the common Franco-German frontier, across which it was intended to launch a major offensive if war broke out. When, in August 1914, the Germans appeared in strength out of Belgium, Joffre was slow to reapportion his forces. He nevertheless kept his nerve during the long retreat into which his faulty dispositions forced him and was eventually able, through his subordinates, to launch the counter-offensive which made the battle of the Marne a decisive victory.

His strategy during the subsequent 'Race to the Sea' established a strong defensive line in north-east France, while his purge in September of one-third of the French *Generalität* – the most ruthless ever carried out in time of war, exceeding in scale even Hitler's mass *limogeage* of December 1941 – immensely improved the quality of operational leadership.

During the following year a series of 'nibbling operations' ('*Je les grignote*') led on to two major offensives, in Artois in May and in Champagne in September, both of which failed for lack of material. In 1916 he conducted the defence of Verdun and the attack on the Somme but in December, his influence with the government having been overtaken by that of others, notably Nivelle (q.v.), he was elevated to an honorific position (and created marshal, the first since 1870, in compensation). Joffre was not a great general and certainly not an inspired one. But he possessed certain qualities, 'an imperturbable calm and a rough good sense', which were of perhaps greater use to France, in the face of problems which no general anywhere proved capable of solving, than the technical excellence of a weaker character might have been. During the worst months of 1914 his enormous bulk, expressionless face and stated determination to let nothing interrupt his regular mealtimes were in themselves a vital reassurance to French national morale.

John III (Jan Sobieski; 1629–96) King of Poland. Jan Sobieski was not of royal birth, but the son of the castellan of Cracow. Having made the 'grand tour', spending two years in France, England and the Netherlands, he returned to Poland in 1648 and was present at the battle of Beresteczko (1651), in which 34,000 Poles defeated 200,000 Cossacks and Tartars. When the Swedes invaded Poland (1656) and King John Casimir left the country in exile, Sobieski, along with many other Polish leaders, defected to the invaders, taking a large part of the army with him. In the following year, however, he changed sides again and was instrumental in driving the Swedes out of the central Polish provinces. For this, and for further services to John Casimir, especially in the Ukraine against the Tartars and Cossacks, he was created grand marshal and field commander of the Polish armies.

In 1672, when Sobieski was in the midst of a particularly sordid episode involving his accepting bribes from the French in return for supporting their candidate in the election of John Casimir's successor, a 200,000-strong army of Turks invaded Poland. They marched into the south-eastern provinces and the new, but weak, king concluded the disgraceful treaty of Buczacz, which ceded large territories to them. Sobieski hastened to meet them with every available man and mitigated the effects of the treaty by winning four victories in ten days. The Polish people rallied to his flag, and in November 1673, with an army of 40,000 men, he destroyed an army of 30,000 Turks at the second battle of Chocim. On the eve of the battle the king died, so Sobieski, having driven the Turks from Polish territory, abandoned the frontier to its fate and hurried to Warsaw to present himself as a candidate for election. He was duly elected at the diet of 1674, although the army of 6000 veterans which he took with him must have impressed the electors more than his inherent suitability. He ascended the throne as King John III. In 1675 the Turks invaded the Ukraine, retaking Chocim, and threatening Lvov. Sobieski went to meet them, but the Polish generals refused to support him, and he had difficulty in raising a large army. Nevertheless in the subsequent campaign he gradually drove their invading army, reinforced with 100,000 Tartars, out of Poland, except for Kamieniec, and recovered two-thirds of the Ukraine.

It had been Sobieski's ambition to secure Louis XIV's help to regain ducal Prussia from the Hohenzollerns and thus weaken the opposition of the powerful Polish magnates who had always resented him. His plans came to nothing, however, and Franco-Polish relations became strained. In 1683 he signed the treaty of Warsaw with the Holy Roman empire, now itself threatened by a huge invading army of Turks. The emperor had been forced to flee Vienna, which, defended by Rudiger von Starhemburg and 15,000 men, was under siege by 150,000 Turks. After a remarkable march of 220 miles in fifteen days Jan Sobieski arrived with his army to join up with German and Austrian forces on the Kahlenburg Heights west of the city. He was to be in overall command. On 12 September 1683, the allied armies and the besieged garrison made a simultaneous attack on the Turks. The decisive factor of the battle was a Polish cavalry attack, led by the king himself, on the headquarters of Kara Mustapha. Having thus driven the Turks back from Vienna, Sobieski spent the rest of the year beating them back across northwest Hungary. But Poland profited little from this triumph, being left to fight on alone against the Turks in the Ukraine. The last twelve years of Jan Sobieski's life brought him nothing but disillusion; his allies were ungrateful, the diet mutinous, and the Polish nobles constantly involved in intrigues against him. His last campaign, in 1691, was a failure and he died at Wilanow on 17 June 1696, a bitter and broken-hearted man.

John, Archduke of Austria (1782–1859) Austrian general. Son of Leopold II, who was Grand Duke of Tuscany at his son's birth, John commanded in 1800, at the age of eighteen, the army of Bavaria in the battle of Hohenlinden (3 December). The

French under Moreau (q.v.) completely defeated him. In 1809, however, he successfully invaded Venetia and defeated Eugène de Beauharnais at Sacile: later he conducted the army safely into Hungary.

Johnston, Joseph Eggleston (1807–91) American (Confederate) general. An engineer who had been at West Point with Lee (q.v.), Johnston was the most senior American officer to declare for the South in 1861, but he nurtured a grievance for much of the war over the Confederacy's failure to recognize his seniority. He was in overall command at First Bull Run, was severely wounded at Four Oaks (31 May 1862) and failed, through want of numbers, to relieve Pemberton (q.v.) during the Vicksburg campaign. In 1864 he conducted an efficient withdrawal through Georgia before the advance of Sherman (q.v.), opposing his invasion into the Carolinas with determination before being obliged to surrender. An able strategist and tactician, he had a high reputation among Southern leaders, who did not, however, always take his advice. He died of pneumonia contracted by standing hatless in the rain at Sherman's funeral.

He was no relation to **Albert Sidney Johnston** (1803–62), also a West Pointer, who was regarded during his short tenure of command as the most brilliant officer to come over to the South. He had commanded the army of independent Texas, the Mormon expedition of 1857 (for the conduct of which he was promoted brigadier) and the 2nd US Cavalry, with Lee as his deputy. He was killed at Shiloh, commanding the Confederate army there.

Jomini, Antoine Henri (Baron; 1779–1869) Swiss military theorist and general. A citizen of Switzerland (Vaud), he began his life as a bank clerk but was drawn to a military career, and on the outbreak of the Swiss revolution was given military rank in the French-sponsored Swiss army. From 1801 to 1804 he was writing the first of his great treatises, *Traité des grandes opérations militaires*, but in 1805 he found a place on the staff of Ney (q.v.) for the Austerlitz campaign. His forecast in 1806 of the outcome of the impending war with Prussia led Napoleon to attach him to his own staff, and he was therefore present at Jena and Eylau. In 1807 he was promoted chief of staff to Ney and created baron, besides being given a commission in the Russian service, which Napoleon allowed him to hold jointly with his French rank. With Ney he campaigned in Spain, but declined to serve on the Russian expedition, rejoining his chief only for Lützen and Bautzen after it had ended. Falling foul of Berthier (q.v.), who, long jealous of his talents, had him arrested on a technicality, Jomini took up his Russian commission and, though refusing to assist in the invasion of Switzerland and France in 1814, remained in the tsar's service for the rest of his life.

From 1823 to 1829 he was military tutor to the tsarevich (later Nicholas I) and busy in establishing the Russian Staff College (opened 1832); in 1828 he served against the Turks at the siege of Varna; and from 1853 to 1856 he lived at St Petersburg, advising Nicholas I during the Crimean War. From 1829, however, his chief abode was Brussels, where he wrote his *Précis de l'art de guerre* (1836), one of the most influential books of military theory ever published: it was used, for example, as a textbook at the United States Military Academy (*see* D. Mahan) and formed the thinking of many generals of both sides in the American Civil War. They believed, as did Jomini himself, that he had isolated 'the secret of Napoleon' and that it consisted in the correct choice of a 'line of operations' which would allow a campaigning general to dominate the theatre of war. He also believed in the importance of the strategic initiative, surprise and the concentration of force against a single weak point. In many respects his ideas resemble those of Clausewitz (q.v.). But, brilliant though his analysis of Napoleon was, Jomini failed, where Clausewitz did not, to perceive the true object of Napoleon's style of warfare: the destruction of the enemy's field army. The importance of Clausewitz's ideas, hidden until the 1870s, then cast into shade all Jomini's writings.

Jones, John Paul (1747–92) American sailor. An outstanding naval captain in the American War of Independence, Jones was born in Scotland. After a slightly chequered early career, he was commissioned as senior lieutenant in the Continental navy in 1775. His audacity quickly made him a naval legend, for with a single ship, the *Ranger*, he carried the war into British home waters, raiding English shipping in the Irish Sea, landing at Whitehaven and spiking the guns of the fort. To cap this remarkable cruise he fought and captured HMS *Drake* and took her into Brest as a prize (spring 1778). In the following year a more ambitious project was launched, with a small squadron comprising Jones's new ship *Bonhomme Richard*, the US frigate *Alliance* and three French ships. This small fleet scoured the sea lanes around Scotland and Ireland and ended their cruise with a classic sea battle, attacking the Baltic merchant convoy with a strong escort.

Off Flamborough Head, Jones fought the much stronger and better-armed British frigate *Serapis* to a standstill, refusing to surrender his crippled vessel with the words, 'I have not yet begun to fight.' In the end it was the British captain who surrendered, and Jones abandoned his sinking ship, transferring his command to the *Serapis*. The effect that this news had on the morale of the revolutionaries in America, as well as on the government and opposition in London was substantial. Jones was a hero of the United States. But he craved action rather than reward, and he entered Russian service against the Turks in 1788. He shattered two Turkish attacks on the Russian Black Sea fleet (June 1788), but nothing in his later career could match the epic fight with the *Serapis* on 23 September 1779. He returned to revolutionary France, but found no openings for his talents and died, a rather embittered man, in Paris.

Joseph, Chief (Heinmot Tooyalaket; 1831–1904) American Indian war leader. Chief of the Nez Percés, in 1877 Joseph conducted a brilliant campaign along the Snake river in Oregon to frustrate a government plan to remove the tribe to a reservation. Encumbered by their women and children, the tribe was eventually surrounded and its resistance overcome. Joseph is sometimes called 'the Napoleon of the Indians'.

Joseph-Ferdinand, Archduke (1872–1942) Austrian general. A member of the Tuscan branch of the Habsburg family, Joseph-Ferdinand commanded in 1914 the Fourth Army, with which in December he won the battle of Limanova-Lapanov, the concluding phase of the battle of Lodz and one of Austria's few singlehanded victories of the war. In June 1916 his army was beaten at Lutsk, during the Brusilov (q.v.) offensive, and he was removed.

Joubert, Pietrus Jacobus (1831–1900) South African general. A veteran of the Boers' Kaffir wars, Joubert was elected general in 1881 on the outbreak of war with Britain (First Boer War) and defeated Methuen (q.v.) at Majuba. In 1896 he suppressed the Jameson raid, taking its leader prisoner. Reappointed commandant-general of the Orange Free State and Transvaal armies in 1899, he was in nominal command during their early success (siege of Ladysmith,

Kimberley and Mafeking), but was already dying. Roberts sent Kruger (q.v.) a message of condolence on his death.

Jourdan, Jean Baptiste (comte; 1762–1833) Marshal of France. A former private soldier of the royal army and subsequently in the drapery business, Jourdan's career as a soldier of the revolution began in the National Guard. He commanded a battalion and then a brigade at Jemappes and Neerwinden and in September 1793 was given the Army of the North, with which he won the battle of Wattignies. In the following year, with the Army of the Moselle, he won the victory of Fleurus. During the Peninsular war he acted as chief of staff to Joseph Bonaparte and was at Talavera and Vittoria. He was president of the court which condemned Ney (q.v.) in 1815 (though he himself had rallied to Napoleon after Elba). Jourdan ranked with Kléber, Hoche and Carnot (qq.v.) among the military saviours of the young republic.

Juan of Austria, Don (1545–78) Spanish sailor and soldier. The illegitimate outcome of a brief union between Charles V and the daughter of a Regensburg merchant, Don Juan was born on an auspicious day, the anniversary both of his father's birth and coronation, and of the battle of Pavia (1525), so crucial to the Habsburgs. He was taken to Spain as a child and brought up near Valladolid. On his accession in 1556, Philip II recognized his half-brother and brought him into the royal circle. Don Juan's great desire was to become a soldier and in 1568 he was given command of a galley squadron operating against the pirates of Algiers: later in the same year the oppressed Moors (Moriscos) of the kingdom of Granada rose in rebellion. Don Juan was given command in the bitter war which followed, conducting an accomplished campaign against the isolated mountain villages, although the revolt took two years to quell. His experience thus gained was in small-scale irregular warfare, but in 1571 he was given command of a fleet of 300 ships which gathered at Messina to confront the Turkish fleet under Ali Monzinande. The advantage of numbers and skill lay with the Christians, and the battle consisted of a series of mêlées and close combat between some 20,000 Christian soldiers and 16,000 Turks carried on the ships. The victory went to the Christians and the Turkish fleet was annihilated, with only 47 of its 270 galleys escaping capture or destruction. Lepanto marked the high point of the Turkish naval dominance of the Mediterranean. Never again would so powerful a Turkish fleet threaten the west, and Lepanto, the last great battle fought by galleys, was a new stage reached in the containment of Ottoman power.

After the battle Don Juan's ambition and confidence were boundless, but his aspirations found an outlet only in the capture of Tunis (1572). In 1576 he was appointed governor of the Netherlands, where it was hoped that his amiable nature and military reputation would help to calm the political and religious troubles. Although he succeeded in occupying Brussels and Ghent, he was no match in politics for the Protestant leader, William of Orange (q.v.). His troops ran amok in Antwerp and sacked the city (1576), and town after town rose in renewed revolt against the Spanish. In the complicated negotiations which followed, Don Juan made many concessions, but did little to improve his position. The States-General raised an army of 20,000 under de Coignies, while Don Juan was reinforced by a new army under his cousin Alexander Farnese (Parma, q.v.) and subdued the Protestant stronghold at Namur. At Gembloux, in January 1578, the two armies faced each other, each with 20,000 men. The battle was a dramatic victory for the Spanish, largely a result of Parma's dashing cavalry attack, which drove the Dutch from the field in ruins. Don Juan moved quickly and consolidated his hold on the south: the Dutch, who had lost 6000 men at Gembloux for Spanish casualties of about 20, were in no state to resist. But Don Juan was starved of the money and supplies necessary for an extended campaign, and the opportunity was lost. He was forced to remain inactive throughout the campaigning season, while the Dutch rebuilt their forces. In October 1578 he sickened and died, aged thirty-three.

Don Juan suffered from Philip's deeply suspicious nature, fuelling the king's doubts about him by his transparent ambition. His victories were the product of great energy (and good fortune) rather than military genius, although in the difficult conditions of the Morisco campaign his plan was excellently conceived and executed.

Juarez, Benito (Pablo; 1806–72) Mexican revolutionary, guerrilla leader and head of state. Of Indian descent, Juarez led the struggle against clerical and military influence in the young republic and conducted three years of civil war, 1858–61, to establish his power. When the country was invaded by Napoleon III in 1862 (*see* Bazaine), allegedly to enforce payment of debts, actually to aggrandize his power, Juarez declared war on France and fought the puppet Emperor Maximilian's army until the United States insisted on its withdrawal (1867). Then almost at his last gasp, Juarez advanced from the Texan border to re-enter the capital. He had Maximilian executed, but was unable to restore the country to stability and, though elected president, was threatened by revolt on all sides. He died of apoplexy

in Mexico City. Power eventually passed to his foremost rival Diaz, but Juarez is remembered as the nation's principal hero.

Juin, Alphonse Pierre (1888–1967) Marshal of France. The son of a gendarme and a classmate of de Gaulle (q.v.) at Saint-Cyr, from which he passed out head of the list, Juin fought in Morocco and the First World War, was captured commanding a division in 1940 and subsequently, under Vichy, became military governor of Morocco. Joining Free France after the Allied invasion of North Africa, he commanded the French forces in Italy, 1943–4. Appointed chief of staff of the army after the liberation, he was later resident-general in Morocco and a senior NATO commander. He was posthumously created marshal.

Juno, Andoche (duc d'Abrantès; 1771–1813) French general. As a sergeant of volunteers Junot became secretary during the siege of Toulon to Napoleon, who was much attracted by his flamboyant temperament, took him to Italy and Egypt and assisted his promotion (colonel, 1796, general of brigade, 1798). Since he later fought at Marengo and was made fortress commander of Paris, Junot was bitterly disappointed not to be created marshal in the 'great promotion' of 1804. An independent mission to Portugal was initially successful (hence his dukedom of 1807), but after his defeat by Wellington at Vimeiro, 21 August 1808, he retreated to France in disgrace, fell into a depression and committed suicide by jumping from a window of his father's house. Junot is often erroneously included in the list of marshals of the Empire, where perhaps he rightly belonged.

K

Kalb Johann (1721–80) French soldier in American service. One of the most competent foreign professionals in the army of the nascent United States, Kalb joined the French army in 1743 and rapidly showed himself an officer of great accomplishment, both in the war of the Austrian Succession (1740–8) and the Seven Years' War (1756–63). He paid his first visit to North America as a French agent, making confidential reports on the growing rift that was becoming apparent between the colonies and Britain. With the outbreak of the American War of Independence (1775–83), anxious to serve in North America with the rebel cause, he arrived in America in 1777, with a letter of recommendation from the American agent in Paris, and was given a commission by Congress as a major-general. He served under Washington, whom he respected, and in 1780 was sent south by him to the relief of Charleston with a force of 900 men. Under the command of General Horatio Gates (q.v.), Kalb took part in the battle of Camden (August 1780), which was badly conceived by Gates. In the battle Kalb's infantry were surprised and cut to pieces by the British cavalry, and Kalb himself was mortally wounded while trying to rally his men. He was a considerable loss to the American revolutionary cause.

Kearny, Stephen Watts (1794–1848) American general. A brigadier-general at the outbreak of the war with Mexico, Kearny conquered New Mexico, invaded California and, after his defeat at San Pascual, 6 December 1846, occupied Los Angeles.

His nephew **Philip Kearny** (1814–62) was one of the most dashing cavalry leaders of the Union army in the Civil War. He had lost his arm in the Mexican war, served with the French cavalry at Solferino and Magenta in 1859, being awarded the Legion of Honour, and was killed with the Army of the Potomac at Chantilly, when he entered the enemy's lines by mistake and tried to fight his way out.

Keitel, Wilhelm (1892–1946) German field-marshal. In 1938, deciding to replace the Ministry of War with an interservice command organization (OKW – *Oberkommando der Wehrmacht*) which he would run, Hitler asked Blomberg (q.v.), the war minister whom he had just disgraced, for the name of a soldier to act as its professional head. Blomberg said his own assistant, Keitel, was unsuitable, being 'merely the man who runs my office'. 'That's exactly the person I want,' was Hitler's answer and for the rest of the war Keitel acted in name as the Führer's foremost general, in practice as his yes-man and mouthpiece. *Lakeitel* (*Lakai* – lackey) to the rest of the high command, he presided over the court of honour which condemned to death the military conspirators of July 1944. He himself was condemned to death at Nuremberg for 'planning and waging a war of aggression, war crimes and crimes against humanity' and hanged in 1946.

Keith, George Keith Elphinstone (1st

Viscount Keith; 1746–1823) British admiral. A veteran of the naval side of the American War of Independence, Keith served at the siege of Toulon, 1793, and was sent to capture the Cape of Good Hope in 1795, making his fortune from the prize money won in the operation. He helped to suppress the great mutinies of 1797, was second-in-command in the Mediterranean in 1798 at the time of the French Egyptian expedition's breakout (*see* Brueys), for which he was unfairly blamed, and in 1801, with Abercromby (q.v.), restored British power in Egypt. From 1803 to 1807 he commanded in the North Sea and from 1812 to 1815 in the Channel. Napoleon surrendered after Waterloo to a ship under his command (HMS *Bellerophon*).

Kellermann, François Christophe (duc de Valmy; 1735–1820) Marshal of France. The oldest of Napoleon's marshals, he was one of the few to have made a reputation independent of him (he had won the battle of Valmy before the emperor was a general). An Alsatian, he had begun life as a regular officer of the royal army, served in the Seven Years' War and was promoted to high rank at the onset of the Revolution. After Valmy he won other successes against the Prussians and against the Austrians in Italy, was imprisoned during the Terror, commanded again in Italy, 1795–7, and thereafter generally held titular posts. A simple patriot and a good general, he was loaded with honours both by Napoleon and by Louis XVIII.

His son **François Etienne Kellermann** (1770–1835) was a general of cavalry and led the decisive charge at Marengo.

Kemal Ataturk, Mustafa (1881–1938) Turkish soldier and statesman. Educated in the military schools of the Ottoman empire, Kemal was arrested and banished for sedition on the day of his commissioning as lieutenant in 1904,

but, forgotten by the Ottoman bureaucracy, he pursued his political and military life in the province of Syria. After the revolution of 1908, with the aims of which he was in sympathy, he fell out with its leaders (*see* Enver) and devoted himself wholly to the army. He took part in the war of 1911–12 against Italy in Libya, whither he had gone without permission, became during the Second Balkan War of 1913 chief of staff of a corps on the Gallipoli peninsula, for which he prepared a detailed defensive plan, and in 1915 returned there as commander of the garrison just in time to oppose the Anglo-French landings. His spirit inspired the defence and led eventually to victory. During the rest of the war he commanded formations in the Caucasus (where he recovered Bitlis and Mush from the Russians) and in Palestine. On the Turkish surrender in 1918 he secured command of IX Corps in north-Eastern Anatolia where, determined to resist Allied efforts to partition his country, he organized from the deliquescent corpse of the wartime army the nucleus of a new army of national resistance. Disowned by the Ottoman government, he led the fight against the invading Greeks, who had calculated on annexing large parts of Anatolia while their fellow Allies were distracted by other postwar problems, and brought about the total defeat of their army. At the end of the decisive twenty-one-day battle of the Sakaria, he was promoted field-marshal and granted the traditional title of *Ghazi* (Victorious) by the anti-Ottoman government. Thereafter his life was taken up wholly with his rebuilding of Turkey as a state and nation. His achievements as a soldier, however, equal those as a statesman, besides having been the precondition for the country's modern renaissance.

Kesselring, Albert (1885–1960) German field-marshal. By origin a Bavarian gunner officer, Kesselring served during the First World War on the staff of Prince Rupprecht (q.v.) and was embodied in the *Reichswehr* in 1920. In 1933 he transferred to the fledgling *Luftwaffe* and in 1939–40 commanded the air fleets in the campaigns of Poland and France and in the Battle of Britain. In 1941 he was appointed commander-in-chief south, shared with Rommel (q.v.) the direction of the North African campaign and eventually took over from him, directing the withdrawal from Tunisia. In 1943 he assumed command of land and air forces in Italy as commander-in-chief. His control of the battle in the peninsula has been recognized by friends and enemies alike as a brilliant passage of defensive strategy, all the more so since the Allies enjoyed complete air superiority. In March 1945 Hitler, whose confidence he had retained without compromising his own independence, an achievement unparalleled in the German high command, appointed him commander-in-chief west in succession to Rundstedt (q.v.) and it was he who negotiated the surrender with the Americans. Condemned to death for ordering the execution of Italian hostages, he was eventually reprieved.

Keyes, Roger John Brownlow (1st Baron Keyes; 1872–1945) British admiral. In 1915, as chief of staff in the eastern Mediterranean, Keyes planned the naval side of the Gallipoli operation and in 1918, as commander of the Dover Patrol, led the Zeebrugge Raid. In 1940 Churchill appointed him first director of amphibious warfare (later combined operations).

His son, **Geoffrey Keyes** (1917–41) won the Victoria Cross for leading the raid on Rommel's headquarters in 1941, in which he was killed.

Khair-ed-Din *see* Barbarossa

King, Ernest Joseph (1878–1956) American admiral. Chief of staff to the com-

mander of the Atlantic fleet during the First World War and a pioneer naval aviator, King was appointed commander-in-chief of the fleet immediately after Pearl Harbor and in March 1942 chief of naval operations, thus becoming the only officer to hold both appointments simultaneously. He was also a member of the Joint Chiefs of Staff Committee throughout the war and *ex-officio* of the Allied Combined Chiefs of Staff Committee. His influence on Roosevelt and on Allied strategy was of immense but controversial importance, for he placed success in the Pacific campaign first among America's priorities and warred with his American and Allied rivals to secure resources for its prosecution even at the expense of honouring the 'Germany first' strategy. A British observer described him as 'rude, chauvinistic and conscious of only half the facts', but all testified to the brilliance of his logistic arrangements and strategic direction in the war against Japan.

Kirbysmith, Edmund (1824–93) American (Confederate) general. His name is associated with the Confederate effort along the Mississippi (though he commanded a brigade at First Bull Run). He organized an invasion of Kentucky in 1862, frustrated Banks's (q.v.) Red River campaign in 1864 and was the last Confederate commander to surrender, 2 June 1865, at Galveston, Texas.

Kitchener, Horatio Herbert (1st Earl Kitchener of Khartoum; 1850–1916) British field-marshal. On the outbreak of war in 1914, Kitchener, then on leave from his post as British agent (governor) in Egypt, was appointed secretary of state for war. His military experience was unrivalled. As a young man in 1870 he had fought as a volunteer for the French against the Prussians. As a junior Royal Engineer officer he had taken part in the Gordon (q.v.) relief expedition and had later acted as sirdar (commander) of the Anglo-Egyptian army, 1892–1900, his command culminating in the triumphant recovery of Khartoum from the Mahdists and the victory of Omdurman, 2 September 1898, which restored the Sudan to Egypt. In 1900 he had been sent as chief of staff with Roberts (q.v.) to South Africa, to impose order on an ill-directed campaign, had eventually succeeded him in command and, through methods thought by many then as now too rigorous, eventually broken the power of the Boer guerrillas. He had next proceeded to India as commander-in-chief where he reorganized the three presidency armies into a single force and brought about the resignation of Curzon, the viceroy, with whom he had come into conflict over the extent of his authority. In 1909–10 he had inspected the forces of the colonies and dominions and submitted much-praised plans for improving their efficiency and in 1911 he had returned to Egypt as agent.

It was thought highly fortuitous, therefore, that in August 1914 he should have been on home leave, and he was actually plucked off the Channel packet to take up his seals as war minister. But in practice he was a failure at the War Office. His judgement about the length of the war – at least three years – was unfortunately correct, his success in raising volunteers and forming them into fighting divisions (outside the planned Territorial scheme) astonishing, and his insistence on total support for France (hence his firmness with French, q.v., before the Marne) admirable. But he was a prima donna, unable to delegate to his subordinates, secretly contemptuous of his political colleagues, and he progressively isolated himself from them all, not least by overwork. The most regrettable consequence was that GHQ in France became almost autonomous and it took Lloyd George

nearly two years of his premiership to re-establish civilian control of strategy. By then Kitchener was dead, drowned in the accidental sinking of HMS *Hampshire* while *en route* to Russia. His loss, popularly regarded as a national tragedy, was not much regretted in government and by no friends, for he had never had any.

Kléber, Jean Baptiste (1753–1800) French general. Kléber began his career as an architect but was drawn to the military life and briefly took a commission in the Austrian army. At the outbreak of the Revolution he enlisted in the volunteers of the Haut-Rhin, his native department, and was quickly promoted. A general of brigade after the siege of Mainz, 1793, he went on to win victories over the Royalist Vendéens at Cholet (*see* d'Elbée) and Le Mans, and in 1794 played a decisive role against the Austrians at Charleroi and Fleurus. As commander of the left wing of the Army of the Sambre-et-Meuse he defeated them again at Altenkirchen and Friedberg in 1796 and might then have had the chief command on the Rhine but declined. In 1798 Bonaparte took him to Egypt, where he was the real victor of Mount Tabor, and left him in command in 1799, when he was obliged to sign with the British and Turks the humiliating convention of El Arish. Outraged at their refusal to ratify it, he took up arms again, defeated the Turks at Heliopolis and recaptured Cairo, where he was shortly afterwards assassinated. A brilliantly gifted general, and one of the military heroes of the Revolution, he doubted, Hamletlike, his real abilities. Nevertheless, and although they had been political opponents, Napoleon babbled on his deathbed of meeting him 'in the Elysian fields'.

Kleist, Paul Ewald von (1881–1954) German field-marshal. It was his panzer group that broke the Ardennes front in May 1940 and drove the 'panzer corridor' through the Allied lines to the sea. In June 1941 his Panzer Group I led the advance of Army Group South to Kiev, less quickly than Hitler would have wished (but as fast as circumstances permitted). In September 1942 he was given command of the newly created Army Group A and directed its advance into the Caucasus, an operation which suffered badly from 'overstretch' and had to be called off as soon as the Russians counter-attacked at Stalingrad. During the slow retreat from Russia he directed defensive operations in South Ukraine (to which name that of his army group was changed). He died in Russian captivity.

Kluck, Alexander von (1846–1934) German general. A veteran of 1866 and 1870 – he suffered a double wound at Colombey during the siege of Paris – it was Kluck who in 1914 found himself on the right wing of the German invasion of France. His First Army was supposed to envelop the French army from the west, having arrived in the vicinity of Paris by way of Brussels and Amiens. But the Schlieffen (q.v.) plan which dictated this had not prescribed whether it should leave the city on its left or right flank, a matter of some considerable importance, as Kluck better understood the nearer he approached. Choosing initially to pass it to his left, he opened a gap with his neighbour into which the BEF strayed. Changing direction to close the gap, he was struck in flank by the Paris garrison (*see* Galliéni and Maunoury) – the decisive act of the battle of the Marne. In 1915 Kluck was wounded on a tour of the trenches and invalided.

Kluge, Gunther von (1882–1944) German field-marshal. An outstandingly successful Fourth Army commander in Poland and France 1939–40, Kluge was the superior of Guderian (q.v.)

during the 1941 battle in Russia, and constantly at cross-purposes with him. Promoted to command Army Group Centre in December 1941, following Hitler's wholesale dismissal of generals, he successfully directed its defensive battle during the Russian counter-offensive which followed Kursk in 1943. Summoned to replace Rundstedt (q.v.) as commander-in-chief west on 1 July 1944, he organized the Avranches counter-attack on 6–10 August, during which he briefly lost contact with his headquarters and Berlin. Hitler, choosing to believe that he had been seeking terms from the Allies and that he was a 'July conspirator', recalled him, but he committed suicide on his way back to Germany.

Koenig, Marie Pierre Joseph François (1898–1970). French general. A veteran of the First World War, the Rif campaign and the 1940 expedition to Norway, Koenig joined de Gaulle (q.v.) in Britain. At Bir Hakeim, during the Gazala battles of 1941, he conducted a heroic defence of the southern end of the British line, which frustrated Rommel's (q.v.) strategy. After the liberation he was appointed commander of the forces of the interior (resistance) and then of the army of occupation in Germany.

Kolchak, Alexander Vasilievich (1875–1920) Russian admiral and White leader. Commander of the tsarist Black Sea fleet, he assumed a leading role in the White campaign against the Bolsheviks in Siberia in 1917. In November 1918 the White government at Omsk named him supreme ruler of Russia and during the first half of 1919 his army, with ample western aid, had considerable success. In the summer, however, it began to disintegrate and in November 1919 Omsk fell to the Reds. In January 1920, under pressure from the White leadership, he resigned in favour of

Denikin (q.v.), shortly afterwards fell into Bolshevik hands and was executed.

Konev, Ivan Stepanovich (1897–1973) Marshal of the Soviet Union. Principal rival to Zhukov (q.v.) for primacy among Russian field commanders of the Second World War, Konev was, like him, originally a private soldier in the tsar's army. As a front (army group) commander, he took part in the defence of Moscow, 1941, the Kursk–Orel battle, 1943, the conquest of Romania and south Poland, 1944, and the capture of Berlin, 1945. His troops (First Ukrainian Front) were the first to make contact with the advancing Americans on the Elbe in April 1945.

Koprulu, Fazil Ahmed (1635–76) Ottoman grand vizier, soldier and statesman. The eldest son of Mehmed Koprulu (q.v.), Fazil Ahmed became grand vizier on his father's death in 1661, following very much on the lines already established by Mehmed. He exterminated all those who challenged his authority, even including long-standing friends and supporters of his father on his death-list. His youth told against him, and he was compelled to act more firmly than would normally have been necessary to consolidate his position. He pressed forward at once with the campaigns begun in the previous decade, pushing onwards into Hungary, and carrying all before him. He took Neuhausen (1663) and razed Zerinvar: the momentum was halted only by an imperial army led by Montecuccoli (q.v.) at the battle of the Raab (1664), where his small but well-organized forces threw back the Turks. There, as in Suleiman the Great's (q.v.) campaigns, the distance from a secure home base began to tell. But the Habsburgs were in no position to take advantage of the Turkish reverse, and the peace of Vasvar (1664) confirmed the Turkish hold on Transylvania.

A much more successful operation was the capture of the town of Candia on Crete (1669), which Koprulu conducted in person. The siege and capture of the city from the Venetians was an epic: the city, gallantly defended by the garrison under Francisco Morosini (q.v.), was under siege for three years. But eventually the newly won command of the seas enjoyed by the Ottomans, and the weight and power of the besieging armies, brought the city to the point of surrender. This was a major reverse for the Venetians, and in a sense for France, for a French contingent had been present for most of the siege. By this victory Koprulu had recovered virtually the whole of Crete for the sultan, and cemented his relationship with Mohammed IV.

In 1672 Koprulu launched a new attack, with a vast army, on the northern frontier: this time he attacked Poland, taking advantage of the disunity of the country. His huge force of 200,000 gained the province of Podolia, but it also roused a section of Polish society, galvanized by the leadership of Jan Sobieski (John III, q.v.), to unite against the Turkish menace. In November 1673 Sobieski routed a section of the Turkish army at Chocim, and they withdrew. But in 1675 a new Turkish force returned, with some 60,000 Turks and 100,000 Tartars, only to be repulsed by Sobieski at the battle of Lvov; and in the following year at the battle of Zurawno (1676) he threw back a Turkish army of some 200,000, under Ibrahim Pasha, with only 16,000 men of his own. Once again the great distances involved in a Turkish campaign in the north, coupled with the extraordinary difficulty of supplying so vast a force, meant that an invasion had lost its impetus by the time it had reached its destination.

Despite these problems Fazil Ahmed continued to press forward in the north, and it was at the start of the 1676 campaign that he died, leaving the conduct of the war to Ibrahim Pasha. He was worn out, it was said, by the strain of constant campaigning, inordinate drinking and eighty wives. He had perhaps greater military talent than his father, his policy of constant warfare providing him with ample opportunity to display his abilities, and certainly the energy of youth to sustain him on campaign. His policy of unceasing campaigns year after year, however, had valuable internal repercussions. It drained the capacities of the Janissaries to foment treason, and kept the administration of the state fully occupied. He left the empire stronger than it had been since the days of Suleiman, with its frontiers more secure and its armies further advanced in Europe than ever before in living memory. Yet he also brought about, in his campaigns in the north, the genesis of a conflict with Russia, which was to have dire consequences for the Ottoman state in the long term.

Koprulu, Mehmed Pasha (1583–1661) Ottoman grand vizier, soldier and statesman. The founder of a virtual dynasty of warrior–statesmen who dominated the Ottoman empire in the seventeenth century, Koprulu is believed to have been of Albanian origin, as were many of the most successful Ottoman officials. Born at Adrianople, in European Turkey, he entered imperial service as a court page, but as was common in the Ottoman court rose quickly to become court marshal to the grand vizier. Subsequently he followed the normal round of administrative appointments in the provinces, but always managed to survive the devious intrigues which permeated Ottoman government. Eventually, through a carefully fostered friendship with the sultan's mother, and the backing of a small clique of supporters at court, he was appointed grand vizier. He at once consolidated his position by buying the support of the Janissaries, the elite corps of Turkish troops,

and then by purging all his enemies, as well as any possible sources of opposition. In all, some 50,000 were killed by Koprulu in his struggle to secure his position, a large total even by the sanguine standards of Turkey.

His first priority in the state was to deal with Turkey's external enemies. The Venetians, who had been steadily gaining ground in the eastern Mediterranean, were halted at the naval battle of the Dardanelles (1657), and he quickly recovered the islands of Tenedos and Lemnos. Soon he had swept the Venetians out of the whole of the Aegean, taking island after island in a swift advance. On land he took the offensive in the north, mounting an attack on Hungary against George Rakoczy II; although Rakoczy managed to defeat the Turks at the battle of Lippa (1658), he was driven out of Transylvania. The war surged backwards and forwards, but the outcome was that the Turks were confirmed in their possession of Transylvania, and brought, once again, face to face with the Habsburgs. Renewed war on a large scale between the two main powers was virtually inevitable. However, Koprulu did not live to see the beginning of this new, and wider, war. Already an old man when he came to power, his furious energy belied his age.

In the military sphere Koprulu's achievement was largely organizational. After a period in which strong central control had lapsed, Koprulu purged the administration of corrupt and incompetent officials. He embarked on an elaborate programme of ship-building, and on land strengthened the fortifications of the Dardanelles (to protect Constantinople from naval assault), and those of the northern border. He hardened the discipline of the largely irregular Turkish levies, which made them a more effective force, and he even tackled the central question of Ottoman warfare: the discipline of the Janissaries. Although highly trained and splendid shock troops, they were a constant danger – like the Praetorian guard in the Roman empire – to the stability of the state. Despite his reliance on the Janissaries for his support, he tried to tame them, by savage repression of the potentially disloyal, by rewards lavishly distributed among the rank and file, and by giving them new commanders, whom he felt he could trust. His attitude towards internal enemies was invariably savage: he treated a number of rebellious provincial governors in Syria and Anatolia with an iron hand. Koprulu's aim was to concentrate power at the centre, to revivify the traditional methods of the Ottoman state. His achievement was therefore to give to his successors a well-tuned administrative and military machine. But it did need a strong central hand: without a firm and successful leader, the latent centrifugal tendencies would emerge again. The empire had to go forward. On his deathbed he recommended his young son Fazil Ahmed (q.v.), aged only twenty-six, as the new grand vizier. Such was the sultan's confidence in his advice, that a stripling was given the supreme administrative power in the empire.

Kornilov, Lavrenti Georgievich (1870–1918) Russian general. A Cossack, Kornilov was trained as an artillery officer, took part in the Russo-Japanese war and distinguished himself from the outset of the First World War as a divisional commander under Brusilov (q.v.) and then at the head of the Eighth Army. After the February revolution he replaced Brusilov as commander-in-chief (August 1917) but fell out with Kerensky and led a counter-revolutionary march on Petrograd, where he was captured by the Bolsheviks. Escaping, he joined Denikin (q.v.) on the Don and in March 1918 led a makeshift army in an assault on Ekaterinodar. He was killed and his body burnt by the Bolsheviks.

Korsakov, Aleksander Mikhailovich (Rimski; 1753–1840) Russian general. During the Allied 1799 campaign against France, Korsakov's army was intended to support Suvorov's (q.v.) advance from Switzerland into Italy. Surprised by Massena (q.v.) he was overwhelmed in the third battle of Zurich, 25 September. He had fought previously in Holland and Persia (1796).

Kosciuszko, Tadeusz Andrzej Bonaventura (1746–1817) Polish soldier in the service of the United States. Educated in both Poland and France, Kosciuszko was forced to leave Poland under a cloud when a love affair brought him into conflict with the girl's powerful father. In 1776 he went as a soldier of fortune to the Americas, volunteering for service in the revolutionary cause. Although he had no active experience of war, his knowledge of fortification and military engineering was impressive, and by late 1776 he had been promoted to colonel of engineers for his effective work in fortifying Philadelphia. After playing an active part in the Saratoga campaign, he constructed the elaborate fortifications for West Point (1778–9). In 1780 he was chief engineer in the southern theatre of war, and late in the war was a prime organizer of the siege of Charleston (1782).

After the war, Congress rewarded him lavishly, promoted him brigadier-general and gave him citizenship. But he returned home to Poland, where he entered the Polish army as a major-general (1789). He defeated a Russian invading army at Dubienka (1792), and when a patriotic rising broke out in 1794, Kosciuszko, now living in exile, returned to lead it. In the field he was heavily outnumbered by a joint Russian and Prussian offensive and suffered several defeats. But at the defence of Warsaw his genius for positional warfare came into its own. He conducted a brilliant defence and forced the large enemy armies to withdraw. But in the open he was less successful, and was wounded and taken prisoner at Maciejowice (1794). Imprisoned for two years in St Petersburg, he was released on the accession of Paul I and left for America. But he decided to settle in Paris, where he lived throughout the Napoleonic wars; with the Bourbon restoration, he decided to move to Switzerland, where he died. Like many of the other foreign soldiers in the American War of Independence, he brought to the conflict higher standards of military skill than most of the American officers possessed.

Kruger, Stephanus Johannes Paulus ('Oom Paul'; 1825–1904) South African (Boer) statesman and war leader. Though chiefly remembered for his leadership of the Transvaal (and effectively of all Boer resistance to the British) during the war of 1899–1902, Kruger had had long experience of war, both against the Matabele and Zulu tribes and against the British in the First Boer War, where, with Joubert (q.v.) and Pretorius he negotiated the successful peace terms. Too old to go 'on commando' again, he fled after the fall of Pretoria in 1900 to Holland.

Kuribayashi, Tadamichi (1885–1945) Japanese general. The defender of Iwo Jima, coveted by the Americans as a forward base for their air offensive against Japan. Kuribayashi held out to the end, dying with his soldiers. Its capture cost 6800 American lives, and those of all but 1000 of the 23,000 Japanese.

Kuroki, Baron Jamemoto (1844–1923) Japanese general. He commanded the First Army in Manchuria in the Russo-Japanese war of 1904–5, winning the battle of the Yalu and taking an important part in those of the Liao-Yang and Mukden. A Samurai, his first military experience had been in the re-

pression in 1877 of the revolt of the reactionary Satsuma, the clan to which he himself belonged.

Kuropatkin, Alexei Nikolaievich (1848–1925) Russian general. His brilliance as a junior commander and staff officer, in particular as chief of staff to Skobolev (q.v.) during the Russo-Turkish war of 1877–8, earned him promotion to general at the age of thirty-four. In 1903, on the approach of war with Japan, he was given command of the Manchurian army but, plagued by the interference of the viceroy, Alexeiev, and the disloyalty of subordinates, he failed to make his strategy work. After his defeat at Mukden, February–March 1905, he exchanged places with one of his subordinates and passed into deepening obscurity.

Kutusov, Mikhail Larionovich Golenishchev (Prince of Smolensk; 1745–1813) Russian field-marshal. Though remembered chiefly for his campaigns against Napoleon, most of Kutusov's soldiering was done in the eighteenth century. The son of a distinguished military engineer, he was one of the first members of the new Jäger corps, of which he rose to be chief, fought in Poland, 1764–9, against the Turks, 1770–4, when he lost an eye (he was later to be shot again through the head), and also from 1788 to 1791, where he was present at the sieges of Ochakov, Odessa, Benda and Ismail and the battles of Rimnik and Mashin. In 1805 he resisted Napoleon's advance into Austria, where he won the action of Dürrenstein, and opposed the decision to fight at Austerlitz, where he was nevertheless wounded. In 1812, by popular demand but against the tsar's wishes, he was appointed commander-in-chief of the western armies to oppose Napoleon's invasion of Russia (he had just concluded a successful Danubian campaign against the Turks). After falling back before it, he gave battle at Borodino, one of the bloodiest of the Napoleonic wars, and, though beaten, inflicted such damage on the Grand Army that he thereby frustrated the enemy's chance of victory. Moreover he kept his army together and, when Napoleon was obliged to begin his retreat, followed, harried him and saw him off Russian soil; less than 50,000 foreign-ers escaped. But, already feeble at the beginning of the campaign, he did not long survive to enjoy the laurels of victory. After his death, historians chose to portray him as a simple *muzhik*; the British general Wilson, however, found him 'polished, courteous, shrewd as a Greek, naturally intelligent as an Asiatic, and well-instructed as a European'.

L

Lacy, Franz Moritz, Graf von (1725–1801) Imperial soldier. With Laudon (q.v.), the leading Austrian subordinate commander in the Seven Years' War (1756–63). Like his great rival Laudon, Lacy came from outside the Habsburg domains: born in Russia, the son of an army officer, educated in Germany, he entered the Austrian army in 1743. During the war, he served under Daun (q.v.) in the campaigns of manœuvre against Frederick the Great (q.v.). At the end of the war, with Laudon's retirement, the senior commands of the army began to descend on him. A field-marshal by 1765, he acted as president of the imperial war council (*Hofskriegsrat*), the senior office in the army. In that position he actively fostered reform of the army, with the positive support of Joseph II when he ruled jointly with his mother Maria Theresa after 1765. In the Turkish war of 1787–92, although he began successfully, he failed to make much headway against the Turks; however, he was a sick man and not fit for field command. He was replaced by Laudon, recalled from retirement, who reaped the benefit of his careful planning. His career illustrates the greatly improved quality of Austrian leadership, to a considerable extent the result of the new ethos and institutions that Eugen (q.v.) gave to the army.

Lafayette, Marie Joseph Paul Roch Yves Gilbert Motier, marquis de (1757–1834) French general. This aristocratic officer of the royal army was a passionate devotee of the ideas of the *Philosophes*, and on the outbreak of the American revolution made his way thither. Returning to France to solicit official help, he arranged the Rochambeau (q.v.) expedition, took part in its operations (1781) around Yorktown and led Cornwallis (q.v.) to surrender. In 1798 he was elected to the Estates-General, took a leading part in the proclamation of the Rights of Man and was the organizer and first chief of the National Guard. He commanded the Army of the Centre and then of the North during the early stages of the Austrian–Prussian attack on France, 1792, but isolated himself by his desire to protect the royal family from personal harm and had to flee abroad, where he was imprisoned. His subsequent career was unfruitful. But Pershing (q.v.), disembarking in France in 1917 at the head of the American Expeditionary Force, proclaimed as he stepped ashore, 'Lafayette, I am here.'

Lake, Gerard (1st Viscount Lake; 1744–1808) British general. One of the leading 'Sepoy' generals. Lake became commander-in-chief in Bengal in 1800 and, during the war against the Mahratta confederacy, won the decisive victories of Laswari, 1 November 1803, and Farrukhabad, 17 November 1804. The former put paid to Sindhia, greatest of the Mahratta leaders, the latter forced his confederate Holkar to flee into the Punjab where at Amritsar in December 1805 Lake compelled his surrender. Before his Indian career, he had commanded under the Duke of York (q.v.) in Flanders, 1793–4, and during the 1798 rising in Ireland, where he defeated the rebels at Vinegar Hill, 2 June, and their French supporters at Ballinamuck, 8 September.

Lally, Thomas Arthur, comte de (1702–66) French soldier. Like the British Admiral Byng (q.v.), Lally was executed for a military misfortune, in Voltaire's immortal phrase, '*Pour encourager les autres.*' The son of an Irish Jacobite, Lally accompanied the Young Pretender in his rebellion of 1745. In 1758 he was sent with an expeditionary force to India to counteract the menace of Clive (q.v.), a task in which he was entirely unsuccessful. In January 1761, despairing of relief from France, he surrendered the chief French town of Pondicherry to the British. He returned to France to face charges of treason, was convicted and, after a long imprisonment, beheaded. Such severity if exacted for military failings far more serious than that committed by Lally – who had, after all, defended the city for many months against huge odds – would have kept the public executioners of England and France in regular employment. Lally, like Byng, was simply unlucky.

La Marmora, Alfonso Ferrero, Marchese (1804–78) Italian general and statesman. An officer of the Piedmontese army, La Marmora played as a junior leader so spectacular a part in the war of 1848 against Austria that he was made major-general and minister of war, in which post he embarked on a successful reform of the army. He was twice premier, in 1859 and 1864–6, when he left to command a corps against the Austrians in the penultimate round of the war of independence. But he was defeated at Custozza (*see* Archduke Albrecht), frivolously accused of treason and obliged to retire.

His brother **Alberto La Marmora** (1789–1863) served in the French army; another brother **Allessandro La Marmora** (1799–1855) died on campaign with

the Piedmontese army in the Crimea and is remembered for his creation of the *bersaglieri*, the Italian army's light infantry; both were also generals.

Lamoricière, Louis Christophe Léon Juchault de (1806–65) French general. As an officer of the newly raised Zouaves (local infantry), Lamoricière played a major role in the French conquest of Algeria, contributed greatly to the victory of the Isly in 1844 and took the surrender of Abd el-Kader (q.v.) in 1847. He then entered politics, was minister of war under Cavaignac (q.v.), opposed the policies of Louis-Napoleon and was exiled after the latter seized power. In 1860 he accepted command of the army of Pope Pius IX, whose territories were threatened by the Piedmontese army, and was defeated at its head at the battle of Castelfidardo. His name ranks with that of his chief Bugeaud (q.v.) in the annals of the Army of Africa and was for a century commemorated in a celebrated feature of the Zouave uniform, the '*trou Lamoricière*' (cf. the Sam Browne belt), conceived by him to allow the quick drainage of the voluminous Zouave trousers after the river fordings that were so frequent a feature of the conquest.

Langle de Cary, Fernand Louis Armand Marie de (1849–1927) French general. Commissioned from Saint-Cyr before the Franco-Prussian war, in which he was wounded, in 1914 Langle de Cary commanded the Fourth Army, whose operations he directed in the battle of the Ardennes and at the Marne, where it occupied the line between those of Foch and Sarrail (qq.v.). He was promoted to command the Group of Armies of the Centre in December 1915, but was relieved, probably because of his advanced age, in the following March.

Lannes, Jean (duc de Montebello; 1769–1809) Marshal of France. A dyer's apprentice, Lannes enlisted as a volunteer in the army of the Revolution and, by reason of his remarkable bravery and drive, rose quickly through the regimental ranks. Bonaparte, to whose Army of Italy he was transferred in 1796, made him a general of brigade and took him on the Egyptian expedition, where he was twice wounded. He served Bonaparte well during the coup of 18 Brumaire (1799) and was promoted to command the vanguard of the reserve army in the Marengo campaign (1800), in which he won the independent victory of Montebello. Created marshal in 1804, he took a foremost part in the campaigns of 1805–7, commanding the centre at Jena and Friedland. But at Essling, 21 May 1809, he was again wounded and died after an amputation. He was greatly regretted by Napoleon (whom he alone was permitted to address with the familiar '*tu*'), his tenacity and disregard of danger making him a perfect subordinate in the types of battle the emperor chose to fight.

Lanrezac, Charles Louis Marie (1852–1925) French general. In 1914 Lanrezac commanded the Fifth Army. Convinced that it was wrongly located and that it risked envelopment by a German movement through Belgium, for which the French war plan made no provision, he prevailed on Joffre (q.v.) to allow him to transfer it to the line of the Sambre on which, with the British Expeditionary Force, he fought the battle of Charleroi–Mons, 21–3 August. His handling of the army in combat was weak, however, and his retreat overprecipitate in the view of Joffre, who had ordered it. Moreover he did not conceal his (unjustified) contempt for the British. Despite his better showing at Guise, 29 August, he was removed from command on 3 September and *limogé*. Lanrezac is an interesting example of a general whose strategic perception far outstripped his tactical nerve.

Larrey, Dominique Jean (baron; 1766–1842) French military surgeon. Chief surgeon to Napoleon, with whom he campaigned from Egypt to Waterloo, where he was wounded, he was not only a remarkable practitioner but a brilliant organizer of medical services and an improviser of succour in the field: his most famous improvisation was to boil soup for the wounded in the breastplates of unhorsed *cuirassiers* from the flesh of their mounts. He was also a prolific author of memoirs, histories and clinical treatises. Called *Providence du soldat* by the French army, his was the most beneficial influence on the treatment of the wounded between Ambroise Paré and Florence Nightingale.

Lasalle, Antoine Charles Louis (comte de; 1775–1809) French general. A junior officer of the royal army (and the great-great-nephew of a marshal), Lasalle enlisted in the cavalry of the army of the Revolution and at once demonstrated his extraordinary *élan* and disregard for danger. His bravery in Italy in 1796 at Rivoli prompted Bonaparte to take him to Egypt, where he played a dashing part in the battle of the Pyramids. In 1806 he forced the Prussian general Hohenlohe (q.v.) to capitulate at Prenzlow, and at Medellin in 1808 he saved the army by leading his cavalry into a square of 6000 Spaniards. He was killed the following year at the head of a charge at Wagram. Lasalle was the *beau idéal* of the hussar general.

Lattre de Tassigny, Jean Marie Gabriel de (1889–1952) Marshal of France. His career embraced two widely separated military epochs: severely wounded by a sword-thrust in mounted single combat in 1914, he inflicted in 1951 a rare defeat on the forces of the Vietnamese general Giap (q.v.), foremost exponent of people's war. During 1940–2 he served the Vichy regime, but was imprisoned for protesting at the German invasion of the unoccupied zone, escaped and made his way to England. Appointed to command the First (Free) French Army in Algeria, he led it in the campaign of Italy, southern France, Lorraine and south Germany. In 1950 he went to Indo-China as high commissioner and commander-in-chief, instructed to save the *Corps expéditionnaire* from impending defeat and won three crucial victories in the Red River delta in early 1951, which deferred the collapse for three years. But by then he was already fatally ill and his death, hastened by that of his beloved only son Bernard in action, occurred in Paris a year later.

Laudon, Gideon Ernst, Freiherr von (1717–90) Imperial soldier. Like so many of the Habsburgs' most successful generals, Laudon had no natural ties with Austria. The son of a Swedish officer of Irish origins, he had first entered the Russian army in 1732, and then sought to transfer into Prussian service; rejected, he turned to Austria as the last resort. He entered the army of Austria in 1741, and fought all through the war of the Austrian Succession (1740–8), attracting favourable attention for his courage and efficiency (he was still in his twenties). So high was his reputation that by the Seven Years' War (1756–63) he held a general command. It was at Laudon's hands, leading Austrian troops who had joined forces with a Russian army under Soltikov, that Frederick the Great (q.v.) met his most costly and shattering defeat. At Kunersdorf (1759) the Austro-Russian army outnumbered him substantially, but that was no novelty. This time, however, the coordination of the Prussian attack went awry; in the ensuing disaster the Prussians lost 20,000 men, 178 guns and 28 colours in the space of six hours.

But Laudon's real quality was as a subordinate commander of genius. His relationship with the senior Austrian commander, Daun (q.v.), was excellent, and it was their capacity to act so effectively in concert that posed the greatest threat to Prussia. Laudon achieved no other smashing victory over Frederick: indeed Kunersdorf had been so costly to both sides that he became inhibited in the risks he could take. Frederick escaped envelopment by the united armies of Laudon, Lacy (q.v.) and Daun, and caught Laudon in the flank at Liegnitz (1760). It was the last substantial encounter between them. In 1763, at the war's close, Laudon retired, to be called back, firstly to face the Prussians in the inconclusive war of the Bavarian Succession (1777–9), and, in old age, to repel a Turkish invasion of Bosnia (1789), in a campaign which led to the storming of Belgrade. He died in the following year.

Lawrence, (Sir) Henry Montgomery (1806–57) British general. A product of the East India Company's Military Seminary at Addiscombe, Lawrence joined the Bengal Artillery in 1823, took part in the First Burmese, First Afghan and Sikh wars and was commanding at Lucknow in 1857 on the outbreak of the Great Mutiny, on the imminence of which he had given warnings. Through his foresight the British garrison was able to defend the Residency until relief came four months later – one of the epic episodes of Victorian imperial history. He was killed at an early stage.

His brother, **John Lawrence** (1st Baron Lawrence; 1811–79), also served in India, but on the civilian side. The crisis of 1857 blurred such distinctions and John, lieutenant-governor of the Punjab, showed that he possessed the elements of generalship. He disarmed the local mutineers, raised an army of 59,000 (mostly Sikhs) and with it captured Delhi, seat of the mutiny. He was later governor-general of India.

Lawrence, Stringer (1697–1775) British soldier and drillmaster extraordinary.

Like so many army officers, Lawrence devoted a lifetime's service for a derisory reward; the only factor which distinguishes him from the myriad soldiers now forgotten was his extraordinary capacity to train unpromising material into effective troops. A life of service in the British army, ending with the Culloden campaign of 1745 and its bloody aftermath, decided Lawrence to seek his fortune in India. In 1748 he was placed in charge of the forces of the East India Company at Madras. In a few months he had constructed from a heterogeneous mob of Indians and men of mixed blood a force capable of standing up to French regulars and troops trained by the French. Fostering an intense loyalty to himself among all his soldiers, officers and men, his methods involved the selection and training of under-officers to share the burden of command. His military exploits were executed with his much better-known colleague and friend Robert Clive (q.v.), but he independently played a decisive part in loosening the French grasp on India. In 1761 he was made commander of all the Company's forces in India and given a royal commission in the rank of major-general; in 1766 he left India for retirement in England. Lawrence laid the foundations of the native (sepoy) army which was to create the British empire in India; but handled with none of the care which Lawrence lavished on it, it was to break out in mutiny in 1857.

Lawrence, Thomas Edward ('Lawrence of Arabia'; 1888–1935) British adventurer. The illegitimate son of an Anglo-Irish gentleman, who had left his wife to raise a family elsewhere, Lawrence had worked as an archaeologist in the Middle East from 1911 to 1914 and on the outbreak of war secured an appointment there as a staff officer. In 1916 he was sent with a mission to Jidda (in modern Saudi Arabia) to foster an Arab revolt against the Turks. He quickly established a remarkable relationship with Abdulla, Sharif of Mecca, and Husein, his brother, embarking with the latter on a guerrilla campaign against the Turkish-held towns and their connecting railway. In 1918 they brought a so-called Arab Army to the assistance of Allenby (q.v.) in the conquest of Palestine and Syria. At the peace conference, Lawrence pleaded the Arab cause, with considerable success, but subsequently retired from public life into ostentatious obscurity, serving (under the name of J.H. Ross and later T.E. Shaw) as an aircraftman in the Royal Air Force from 1922 to 1935. During those years, he wrote a number of books, of which the most famous is *Seven Pillars of Wisdom*, an account of his adventures with the Arabs hailed on its (posthumous) publication as a masterpiece but now thought interesting chiefly as a period piece of elaborate prose. Lawrence himself was hailed in his own lifetime, particularly by Liddell Hart (q.v.), as a master of guerrilla tactics, and even as the true architect of victory in Palestine, but his military renown has worn even less well than his literary reputation.

Lebœuf, Edmond (1809–88) Marshal of France. A Polytechnicien, Lebœuf's achievements in the field of gunnery attracted the attention of Napoleon III, who made him minister of war in succession to Niel (q.v.) and created him marshal on the eve of the Franco-Prussian war. Lebœuf was not a bad minister nor an incompetent chief of staff to Napoleon in the field, but he has never been forgiven his unwise assurance to the French parliament on the declaration of hostilities that the army was 'ready down to the last gaiter button'.

Leclerc, Charles Victor Emmanuel (1722–1802) French general. A brother-in-law of Napoleon, Leclerc was the captor of Toussaint L'Ouverture (q.v.). He died of yellow fever on Haiti.

Leclerc, Philippe François Marie, Vicomte de Hauteclocque (1902–47) Marshal of France. Wounded in 1940, Leclerc escaped from captivity to join de Gaulle, one of whose most devoted and successful military lieutenants he was to become. Sent to West Africa under the pseudonym Leclerc, he led the garrison across the Sahara from Chad to Tripolitania and commanded it in the Desert campaign. In 1943 this *Division Leclerc* was transferred to England and re-equipped to become the 2nd Armoured Division in order to take part in the invasion and liberation of France. At its head, Leclerc entered Paris on 25 August 1944. After the war he organized and commanded the expeditionary force which restored French rule in southern Indo-China. He was killed in an air accident and in 1952 was posthumously created marshal.

Lee, Henry (1756–1818) American soldier. 'Lighthorse Harry', the father of a more illustrious soldier, Robert E. Lee (q.v.), first served as a soldier at the start of the American War of Independence (1775–83); by 1778 he commanded three troops of cavalry and three companies, showing his expertise in the highly mobile warfare by raiding British outposts and harrying weak points. In 1779 his men stormed the British position at Paulus Hook, winning strong approval from Washington (q.v.) for the skill and daring of his attack. In the Southern campaign, part guerrilla, part regular warfare, his dragoons were some of the most successful raiders against the British lines of communication. After the war he took a lead both in local Virginian politics and in the affairs of the nation.

Lee, Robert Edward (1807–70) American (Confederate) general. The son of a foremost family of Virginia – his father, once leader of Washington's (q.v.) Light Cavalry in the War of Independence, had been governor – Lee passed second out of his class at West Point (as its superintendent, 1852–5, he was to expel James McNeill Whistler for stating in an examination that silicon was a gas, thus benefiting both the US army and the cause of art). He won an outstanding reputation in the Mexican war and, at the moment of secession, was offered command of the Federal armies. Though opposed both to secession and slavery, he felt bound nevertheless to 'go with his state' and it was as commander of the Confederate Army of Northern Virginia that he entered history (he did not, contrary to general belief, become generalissimo until February 1865). Between April 1861 and May 1862 he held local command in Virginia and acted as adviser to President Davis. But from June 1862, with the Army of Northern Virginia, he campaigned continually in the eastern theatre, frustrating to the end every Federal effort to capture Richmond and twice undertaking invasions of the north. His greatest tactical achievement was at Chancellorsville, 1–4 May 1863, where, with Jackson (q.v.), he achieved the envelopment and humiliation of the Army of the Potomac under Hooker (q.v.). His principal setback was at Gettysburg, 1–3 July 1863, when his daring invasion of Pennsylvania was halted and repulsed by Meade (q.v.), its failure in some measure being due to the dilatoriness of his principal subordinate, Longstreet (q.v.).

If Lee had a fault as a commander, and faults in either his character or capacity are difficult to find, it was a lack of firmness with headstrong or sceptical juniors. It was compensated by his ability to achieve creative partnerships with most others, notably Jackson, whose actions at Chancellorsville were a perfect and intuitive accompaniment to his own. After the failure of Gettysburg, the war in the east ceased to offer Lee those opportunities for manœuvre and quick decision which suited his talents. He nevertheless conducted the battles of 1863 – the Wilderness, Spotsylvania, Cold Harbor – with great defensive skill and during the protracted siege of Petersburg (June 1864–March 1865) frustrated all Grant's (q.v.) efforts to turn the position and strike at Richmond. It was only after his last railway supply line had been cut that he was forced into the retreat which culminated in Appomattox, where he and Grant met face to face to sign the surrender. Lee's greatness – which was universally recognized then as now – lay as much in his character as his abilities and achievements. He combined in his person 'profound thought, indomitable will and decision' together with 'humanity, loyalty and a complete lack of [personal] ambition'. His last words were, 'Strike the Tent.'

Leeb, Wilhelm Ritter von (1876–1956) German field-marshal. A gunner officer of the army of Bavaria and a member of one of its noble families, Leeb was selected to join the 100,000-man army after the peace of Versailles. During the 1930s he and Rundstedt (q.v.) held the two highest command appointments in the army, but neither was pro-Nazi and after the Blomberg–Fritsch (qq.v.) crisis both retired, only to be recalled for the Polish campaign. In that and the French campaign Leeb commanded Army Group C (which was deployed opposite the Maginot Line in 1940), and in Russia Army Group North, which made the advance to Leningrad. He was relieved of command in January 1942, one of a host of generals to suffer for the failure of Hitler's short-war strategy. Leeb was a considerable strategist in his own right, an advocate of the power of the 'active defence' and had explained his ideas in an important book, *Die Abwehr* (Defence), published in 1938.

Lefebvre, François Joseph (duc de Danzig; 1755–1820) Marshal of France. A sergeant of the *Gardes françaises*, Lefebvre was unlike many of his regiment in showing a personal loyalty to the royal family during its time of troubles. But he was quite prepared to accept the Revolution and was promoted by its leaders in spectacular fashion: by 1793 he was a general of brigade, and as such contributed significantly to the victory of Fleurus, and actually commanded the immortal Sambre-et-Meuse for a few weeks in 1797. In the coup of 18 Brumaire (1799) he did Bonaparte signal service, dispersing the Five Hundred (parliamentarians) with twenty-five grenadiers. He took Danzig for the emperor in 1808, hence his dukedom, and commanded the Old Guard during the Russian campaign. He was a simple, brave, loyal soldier, and his wife Catherine, the regimental laundrywoman he had married in 1780, retained her forthright style in the bosom of the Napoleonic court.

Leigh-Mallory, (Sir) Trafford (1892–1944) British air marshal. A successful Battle of Britain fighter group commander, and later head of Fighter Command, Leigh-Mallory was appointed in 1943 commander-in-chief of the Allied air forces for the coming invasion of Europe. His conduct of air operations during the campaign (albeit that the Allies enjoyed, through the deployment of 9000 aircraft, almost total air supremacy) was highly successful. He was killed in an air crash on his way to take up a similar post in South-East Asia.

Leman, Gerard Mathieu (comte; 1851–1920) Belgian general. A native of Liège, Leman was commanding the 3rd Division in the city at the time of the German assault on it, led by Ludendorff (q.v.) in August 1914. Its forts proving unexpectedly vulnerable to the fire of the attackers' super-heavy artillery, they were taken or forced one by one to surrender. Leman stifled all thoughts of capitulation and held out for ten days, eventually blowing up the fort of Loncin, with himself inside, as a last gesture of defiance. He was found unconscious in the ruins, offered honourable captivity and returned after the war to die in his native city.

Le Marchant, John Gaspard (1766–1812) British general. A cavalry officer, Le Marchant conceived the idea, while his regiment was stationed at Windsor in 1798, of improving the standard of education and training of the younger officers. Out of this scheme grew his plan for the foundation of the Royal Military College (Sandhurst), of which he became lieutenant-governor, 1801–10. He then went to command a cavalry brigade in Spain and was killed at its head at Salamanca.

Leopold I, Prince of Anhalt Dessau (1676–1747) Prussian soldier. One of the prime architects of Prussia's military greatness, the 'Old Dessauer' spanned the military worlds of the seventeenth and mid-eighteenth centuries. He served in the war of the Grand Alliance (1688–97), and was present at the siege of Namur (1692). In the war of the Spanish Succession (1701–14) he served under Prince Eugen (q.v.) at Blenheim (1704) as commander of a Prussian corps; he fought with great courage and distinction at Turin, Tournai and Malplaquet, to the extent that he was made commander of all the Prussian forces at the front in 1710. In 1712 he showed his mastery of tactics when he surprised the garrison of the fortress of Mörs and captured it without a shot being fired. He was promoted to the rank of field-marshal, and in 1715 he led an army of 40,000 against Sweden, with considerable success at the siege of Stralsund

and the investment of the island of Rugen.

After the participation in the Great Northern War was ended, Leopold was given the task of building a large army for Prussia. He enjoyed the full confidence of his master, Frederick William I (q.v.), and their views on the structure and quality of the army coincided exactly. Leopold built a force of infantry more skilful than any other in Europe. While outsiders might scoff that the Prussians were fit only for the parade grounds of Potsdam, in fact their training made them the most flexible and adaptable force on the field of battle. Practicality was the prime watch-word for Leopold. He demanded 'quick shooting, quick loading, intrepidity and vigorous attack'. If his infantry was an automaton, it was an ideal instrument for advanced tactical manœuvre. He pushed forward relentlessly in pursuit of perfection. Wooden ramrods were replaced with iron, a major technical advance for it enabled a much brisker loading procedure and a faster rate of fire. He altered uniforms, cutting off the old full-skirted coats so that the files of men could stand closer together. The ranks were reduced from three deep to two, a reduction allowing a longer front: faster firing made up the loss in fire-power. By the time he had trained the infantry it was capable of three to four shots per minute; this coupled with the sheer speed of a Prussian advance made them a uniquely effective offensive weapon. He also oversaw the introduction of an effective system of conscription in Prussia, to provide the steady supply of recruits for his training mill. With the accession of Frederick the Great (q.v.) in 1740, Leopold was a little piqued to be excluded from much of the planning for war, for he considered himself the country's leading soldier, a position Frederick intended to arrogate to himself. But he did have one last triumph on the battlefield – at Kesselsdorf his immaculate infantry swept the Saxons from the snow-covered field (1745). By then in his seventy-first year, he retired to Dessau; his three sons, Leopold II (the Young Dessauer), Dietrich and Moritz, all served as generals under Frederick the Great.

Lettow-Vorbeck, Paul Emil von (1870–1964) German general and colonial guerrilla leader. Few of the kaiser's officers had the chance to live the life of soldiering and empire-building so freely available to the British and French; Lettow was one of them. He was also an irregular soldier of genius. Son of a Prussian general, he had taken part in suppressing the Boxer Rising, fought against the Hereros and Hottentots in German South-West Africa in 1904, and in 1914 was posted to command the garrison in German East Africa (Tanganyika). It never numbered more than 20,000, but he nevertheless repulsed a major British landing (Tanga, November 1914) and kept an international force, which at its peak numbered 130,000, in play until after the European armistice.

Leven, Alexander Leslie, 1st Earl of (1580–1661) Scottish soldier. The epitome of the 'godly soldier', Leven began his career in the service of the United Provinces, although it was in the army of Gustavus Adolphus (q.v.) that he made his reputation. He defended Stralsund in an epic siege against the armies of Wallenstein (q.v.), 1628, and fought bravely at Lützen. He venerated Gustavus Adolphus and continued to serve Sweden after his death, reaching the rank of field-marshal in 1636. On his return to Scotland, as an ardent Protestant and signatory of the Covenant, he helped to build up the Covenanter army into a formidable force. Under his command the Covenanters seized Edinburgh, as well as most of the Royalist strongholds in Scotland.

Charles I was forced to agree to their demands, and the First Bishops' War ended (1639). But the peace was merely a truce and Charles intended to impose an episcopacy by force. In the Second Bishops' War (1640–1) Leven's army of 20,000 men, with many officers fresh from the European war, marched into England and took Newcastle; the Scots were eventually bought off. Charles, in an effort to conciliate the Scots, in 1641 raised a number of the leaders to the peerage, among them Leven (formerly Leslie).

Leven's next task, a congenial one, was to attack the rebellious Catholics in Ireland, a duty which he exercised with great vigour and cruelty (1642–4), until he was recalled to take command of the Covenanter army which was to intervene on the Parliamentary side in the English Civil War. The intervention of his army had a crucial influence on the successful outcome of Marston Moor (1644), but thereafter, although they were a powerful force in the North, they operated with one eye on Montrose's victories in Scotland. After the threat of Montrose declined they moved south, and it was to Leven, at Newark, that Charles surrendered in 1646. The end of the First Civil War marked the end of Leven's command. His offers of help in the Second Civil War (1648–9) were brushed aside, and although he was present at Dunbar (1650), it was left to his kinsman David Leslie to take command. He was captured at Alyth by the English, trying to raise troops for the defence of Dundee. He was imprisoned in the Tower until 1654, when he retired to his estate.

Liddell Hart, (Sir) Basil Henry (1895–1970) British military theorist, historian and biographer. Born in Paris, son of the pastor of the English Congregation church there, Liddell Hart was educated at St Paul's and Corpus Christi College, Cambridge, and commissioned as a temporary officer in the King's Own Yorkshire Light Infantry in 1915. Badly wounded on the Somme, he occupied his convalescence by writing a pamphlet on platoon tactics, which was issued to the army in France in 1917, and later, at official request, he rewrote the official *Infantry Training*. Between 1922 and 1924 he served in the newly created Army Educational Corps, but his individualism made him an unsuitable regular officer and he retired from the army to become a journalist and author. He was successively military correspondent of the *Morning Post*, the *Daily Telegraph* and *The Times*, 1924–39, and unofficial (but highly influential) adviser to the war minister, Hore Belisha, 1935–7. His success in unseating numbers of over-age or under-talented senior officers and initiating new policies (*see* Gort) won him the intense dislike of the army establishment and, though he continued to proffer excellent advice both privately and in published form to the end of his long and productive life, he never again acceded to a position of power.

But his achievement was already secure: in a stream of books issued during 1925–40 he had, with Fuller (q.v.), set out the principles on which modern mobile warfare, combining the action of tanks, mechanized infantry and aircraft, would be fought, and had converted to his way of thinking forward-looking soldiers everywhere, but above all in Germany (*see* Guderian). President Kennedy superscribed his presentation photograph, 'To the Captain who teaches Generals', and the inscriptions on its companion portraits in the sage's study – a gallery of modern victors – echo his salutation. He was knighted in 1966.

Liman von Sanders, Otto (1855–1929) German general. A cavalry officer, Liman von Sanders was sent as head of Germany's military mission to her ally Turkey in 1913, assuming command of the Turkish troops on the frontier with Russia in the Caucasus on the outbreak of war. In 1915, as commander of the Turkish Fifth Army, he successfully opposed the British and French landings at Gallipoli and in 1916 followed von der Goltz (q.v.) in higher command. In 1918 he directed the Turkish opposition to the advance of Allenby (q.v.) into Palestine and Syria. Sanders's Levantine involvement invests his reputation with a romantic allure attaching to that of few German generals.

Lincoln, Benjamin (1733–1810) American soldier. An amateur soldier, Lincoln had the misfortune to be responsible, if not entirely to blame, for the greatest rebel disaster in the American War of Independence. In 1777 he was appointed a major-general in the Continental army, after competent service with the Massachusetts militia, and in the following year he was given a general command in the South. He was unlucky from the outset. An attack on Savannah, Georgia, October 1779, was repulsed by the British, his command (together with 4000 French troops under d'Estaing, q.v.) losing 800 casualties for the loss of 150 British. In the following year the British forces of General Clinton (q.v.) besieged Charleston. Clinton had a total of 14,000 men at the siege, while Lincoln, defending, possessed only 5400. A naval squadron under Arbuthnot entered Charleston harbour and bombarded the town. After a month of siege Lincoln surrendered the town, together with the huge stocks of war material it contained. Exchanged in 1781, he was immediately subject to savage criticism from all sides. The argument that he had sold the town too lightly had some force: little pretence of a determined defence had been made. On the other hand he had been faced with overwhelming odds, with no prospect of relief, and capture had been inevitable. With the highly ambiguous state of affairs which had existed at Charleston, and the fact that tempers had cooled during his imprisonment, no action was taken against him. But he held no further military position during the war, although he served Congress as secretary of war.

Lin Piao (1908–71(?)) Marshal of the People's Republic of China. A graduate of the Whampoa Military Academy (*see* Chiang Kai-shek and Blyukher), Lin Piao was taken up by Chu Teh (q.v.) before the Long March of the Communist armies from south to north China, in which he commanded units of the advance guard. He was wounded fighting the Japanese in 1937 and sent for treatment to Russia where, after recovery, he took part in the defence of Leningrad. After the Japanese surrender in the Far East, he organized the occupation of Manchuria by Communist troops so that, when Chiang Kai-shek's armies returned, they found him largely in control of the territory. When the civil war broke out, it was his troops which won most of the battles which gave the Communists the victory. He successively occupied Kirin, Changchun and Mukden, and by November 1948 had taken complete control of Manchuria. He emerged from the war as the new state's most honoured soldier and one of Mao Tse-tung's closest advisers, and in 1959 became minister of defence. In the late 1960s, however, he and Mao fell out, apparently over his refusal to further the aims of the Cultural Revolution within the army; Lin Piao disappeared and was eventually reported to have died in an aeroplane accident.

List, Wilhelm (1880–1971) German field-marshal. A Bavarian engineer officer by origin, List commanded the Fourteenth Army during the Polish campaign and in France in 1940 the Twelfth, which made the crucial crossings of the Meuse between Namur and Dinant.

Made field-marshal in the mass promotion of 19 July 1940 (to celebrate victory), he was commander-in-chief of the German forces in the invasion of Greece, and of Army Group A in Russia, July–October 1942, during its advance into the Caucasus.

Longstreet, James (1821–1904) American (Confederate) general. A South Carolinan and West Pointer, he was commissioned brigadier-general by the Confederacy in time to command the 4th Brigade at Bull Run and thereafter held divisional or corps command in the Army of Northern Virginia so consistently that the soldiers called him 'Lee's Old Work Horse'. His record is mixed. His mistakes at the battles of Fair Oaks, Seven Pines and Second Bull Run contributed to Confederate failure. But he did well during the Seven Days' battles, at Fredericksburg and in the Wilderness, where he was gravely wounded by a Confederate bullet. The South remembered him best, however, for his dilatoriness at Gettysburg, both on the second and third days (he had disapproved of the Gettysburg campaign, which he thought foolhardy) and reproached him so harshly for it that his postwar life was made a misery.

Lossberg, Fritz von (1868–1943) German general. A Guards officer and a former instructor at the *Kriegsakademie*, Lossberg was appointed in January 1915 deputy chief of the operations section of OHL (*Oberste Heeresleitung*), German general headquarters on the western front. But his immense energy and tactical flair prompted Falkenhayn (q.v.) to employ him as a roving chief of staff to subordinate armies at moments of crisis. Thus it was that he served as chief of staff to Third Army during the French offensive in Champagne of September 1915, to Second Army on the Somme during the British offensive of July 1916, to Sixth

Army in Artois during the British spring offensive of 1917 and to Fourth Army at Ypres during the British offensive (Paschendaele) of that autumn. His experiences led him to conceive of a new method of meeting these great offensives, prepared by enormous artillery bombardments and delivered by infantry *en masse*; his authority as chief of staff – by German army practice almost greater than that of the commander he served – gave him the power to implement it. For the 'rigid defence of a single line', which regulations stipulated, he substituted the preparation of a position laid out in great depth on a reverse slope, behind which counter-attack (*Eingreif*) divisions were placed to come to the aid of those garrisons hardest pressed. The Hindenburg Line, backbone of the German defence in France from 1917 to 1918, was largely laid out on these principles and if any one soldier, therefore, can be held responsible for the frustration of the Allies' offensives of those years and for the millions of casualties they suffered, Lossberg is he. On the retirement of Ludendorff (q.v.) as chief of staff at OHL (26 October 1918), Lossberg was nominated to succeed him but, for political reasons, he was swiftly replaced by Groener (q.v.). The days of the pure technical expert were by then over for the German army.

Louis XII (1462–1515)   King of France. Passionate in his commitment to French involvement in Italy, Louis succeeded Charles VII on the throne of France in 1498. He was faced by Cordoba (q.v.), when France and Spain were unable to divide the spoils of the Italian campaigns, as agreed by the treaty of Granada (1500). Until the eruption on to the scene of Gaston de Foix (q.v.) as French commander (1511), Louis had no general able to overcome his enemies: after Foix's death in his first campaign, he found no competent re-

placement. The Italian war, which became Louis's obsession, dominated his reign and drained French power and resources. As the conflict in Italy developed into a more general conflict of fundamental interests between France and the Habsburgs, a cast was given to French diplomacy and military affairs which persisted for two centuries.

Louis XIV (1638–1715)   King of France. Until the battle of Blenheim in 1704, the reign of Louis XIV, one filled with war, had seen no major reverse: in the second half of the seventeenth century, French arms acquired the reputation for an absolute superiority which the Spanish had held before them. Although Louis never commanded an army in the field, in a practical sense his influence was crucial both in the successes and ultimate failure of French armies. His first experience of war came when he watched the rival armies of Turenne and Condé (qq.v.) battle for the control of Paris in 1652; in 1657–8 he joined the army in Flanders, inspected fortifications, was fired at, and acquired a passionate interest in siege warfare.

At the heart of his military system was a strong central control, vested in the king, and his small cabinet: in the whole of his reign he used only seventeen ministers. Two families – le Tellier and Colbert – came to dominate military and naval administration. Of the former, a father and son, Michel le Tellier and his son Louvois (q.v.), built the army that Turenne, Condé and their successors used to great effect. Colbert virtually recreated the French navy, as well as the sound taxation-base which enabled France to field large and well-equipped armies. Louis himself insisted that the army and navy were careers open to talent, and that no officer, however well born, could command without training and military discipline; he himself served briefly as a cadet under

Turenne. He supported one great military genius – Vauban (q.v.) – against the bitter criticism of his comparatively low birth, and he was quite willing to accept officers from any source who would serve him well: the privateer Jean Bart (q.v.) is a good example.

Despite the sound logical principles on which France's military structure was founded, the bitter experiences of Louis's youth impeded the full development of the system. He was intensely suspicious after the experience of the Frondes; he was bitterly jealous of the military talents of his brother, the duc d'Orleans, and prevented him from continuing in active military command in the main theatres of war. In later life he was dubious of soldiers' prodigality with men's lives and equipment, and his generals in the war of the Spanish Succession (1701–14) went into battle hedged about by so many prohibitions against risky and impetuous actions that they were virtually hamstrung; initiative was stifled, commanders feared to take decisions on their own account, and operated in the sure knowledge that the king observed their every move and counted every *louis* expended.

Louis fought the war of Devolution against Spain (1667–8) and two wars against the Dutch (1672–8, 1688–97), certainly with glory and national expansion in mind, but also with a firm resolve to give France secure and defensible frontiers. The final war, the conflict over the Spanish Succession, was not of his making and ended with virtual bankruptcy and starvation for France. But the military machine continued to function, provided streams of new recruits and new equipment. The overall quality of both junior and senior officers was high, the product of Louis's encouragement of military education and training. French military superiority was the product of a system, rather than brilliant individualism: that system was the creation of Louis and his ministers.

L'Ouverture, Pierre Dominique called **Toussaint** (1743–1803) Haitian revolutionary and general. He took part in a black slave rising in 1791 to preserve royal authority in the island, then took service with the Spanish, who controlled the other half of the island, then abandoned them on the French revolutionary government's proclamation of the abolition of slavery. Made a general of division, he fought off a British invasion, but then decided he wanted to rule independently, expelled the French representative and later the Spaniards. In 1801 Napoleon sent an expedition to restore French rule but, failing to overcome Toussaint's guerrilla resistance, it offered to negotiate. Its leader (*see* Leclerc) treacherously seized Toussaint and transported him to France where he died in captivity. The black struggle was carried on successfully by Jean-Jacques Dessalines who ultimately proclaimed himself Emperor Jacques I and built the Haitian Versailles of Sans Souci.

Louvois, François le Tellier, marquis de (1641–91) French administrator. With his father, Michel le Tellier (1603–85), Louvois was responsible for the creation of a French army which reigned supreme in Europe for almost forty years. He was, in Saint-Simon's phrase, 'A haughty man, brutal in all his ways.' Louvois was trained by his father to succeed him as the controlling force behind the development of the French military machine. His passion was for central control, as the only means to destroy fragmentation into many independent and often conflicting entities. Under Louvois, all matters concerning military affairs were recovered from independent control into the hands of the war minister and his bureaucrats. Regulations were laid down – and, for the first time, enforced – governing almost every aspect of military life. The training of officers was regulated, the special privileges enjoyed by the nobility within the army were abolished and a proper career structure established. The basic organization of the army was reformed root and branch, and in 1663 Louvois created a new regiment, the *Régiment du Roi*, to act as a model for the new army: its commander, Colonel Martinet, has become a synonym for harsh and effective discipline. The same process of reform was applied to the artillery and engineers, culminating in 1673 with the establishment of the *Royal-Artillerie*.

Until 1677, when his father became chancellor of France, Louvois worked under him; thereafter he was sole secretary of state for war. A thoroughly autocratic man, he quarrelled violently with Turenne (q.v.) and with his collegue Colbert; but after 1675, when Turenne died and Condé retired, he had no direct competitors in the military field. Both le Tellier, who pressured Louis to withdraw the Edict of Nantes, which had granted toleration to Protestants, and Louvois were stern Catholics, and the use of troops in 'dragonnades' to pressure Protestants into conversion was actively fostered by Louvois after 1685. Louvois created a system, which if it did not function to its full efficiency without his driving personality, survived him, and the extraordinary resilience of the French army in the war of the Spanish Succession (1701–14) is a tribute to him.

Lucan, George Charles Bingham, 3rd Earl of (1800–85) British field-marshal. Though slightly less quarrelsome than his brother-in-law, Cardigan (q.v.), he was also the imperious and overbearing nobleman, besides being professionally inferior to many officers over whom he was preferred for command of the cavalry in the expedition to the Crimea in 1854. Once arrived, he and Cardigan quickly put a private quarrel on to an official basis, their staffs ceased to co-operate and his orders to the light bri-

gade at Balaclava, contemptuously transmitted by Nolan, his ADC, and misconstrued by Cardigan, brought about its destruction. Lucan was nevertheless subsequently promoted to the rank of field-marshal, almost the last British soldier to owe his rise wholly to worldly position.

Luckner, Nicolas (1722–94) Marshal of France. A Rhinelander who had entered French service, Luckner was created marshal in 1791 – last but one of the *ancien régime* – and appointed in June 1792 to command the Army of the North with orders to invade the Austrian Netherlands. After capturing Menin and Courtrai he lost heart and retreated. Accused of treason, he was arrested, tried and guillotined.

Ludendorff, Erich (von; 1865–1937) German general. In many superficial respects the archetypal Prussian officer, Ludendorff stands in essentials apart from the breed: its ethos of personal self-effacement, political moderation and strategic orthodoxy was not his. As a result he became one of the very few German generals to wield real political power and to be instrumental in losing a major war. His origins were modest and he was commissioned accordingly into one of the dowdier regiments, but his brilliant intelligence and immense mental and physical energy carried him effortlessly into and through the *Kriegsakademie* and on to the general staff. Patronized by Schlieffen and the younger Moltke (qq.v.), he quickly reached its summit and was head of the key mobilization section from 1908 to 1913. But in that year, and as a punishment for improper parliamentary lobbying to increase the size of the army, he was posted to an unimportant regimental command. On the outbreak of war, however, he was temporarily assigned as chief of staff to the task force detailed to capture the vital Liège forts (*see*

Leman), for which operation he had made the plan; its success, to which his courageous personal intervention greatly contributed, retrieved his career. He was then sent as chief of staff to Hindenburg (q.v.) to direct the defence of East Prussia in late August and, with the assistance of Hoffmann (q.v.), transformed the campaign into a brilliant victory (Tannenberg and the Masurian Lakes).

The Hindenburg–Ludendorff team continued to win victories in the east and, on the dismissal of Falkenhayn (q.v.) in 1916, was brought to the west to assume supreme command of the war effort. Ludendorff was to interpret his commission so liberally that within a year he was effectively wartime dictator of Germany. He contrived the dismissal of the 'defeatist' Bethmann-Hollweg, insisted on the institution of unrestricted submarine warfare (which brought America into the war) and negated plans for a separate peace with Russia by refusing to accommodate Polish national aspirations. He felt justified in taking these extreme decisions because he believed the defeat of Russia, which impended throughout 1917, would allow him, with the troops released from that front, to win outright victory in the west before American troops arrived or the German economy, which he had mobilized totally for war, collapsed. His timings were wrong. His great spring offensive of 1918 (on the Somme in March, on the Lys in April, on the Aisne in May) all failed and he was then unable to stem the Allied counter-offensives of July–September (to which the Americans made a significant contribution). On 26 October he was dismissed, after he had vacillated for several weeks between making peace and seeking *Gotterdämmerung*. In later years he took up extreme nationalistic politics, marched with Hitler in the Munich putsch of November 1923 and was tried (and acquitted) for treason. During the war Ludendorff had been ennobled (granted the

'von') but few found nobility in his character.

Luxembourg, François Henri de Montmorency-Bouteville, duc de (1628–95) French soldier. The wars of conquest begun by Louis XIV depended on a superb army, well supplied, and generals of talent to command it. In the galaxy of fine soldiers Turenne and Condé (qq.v.) shine brightest; but next in significance must come Luxembourg. Born a hunchback and feeble in physique, he had the good luck to be brought up with his cousin Condé: he fought with outstanding courage with him at the battle of Lens (1648), where the Imperial army under Archduke Leopold Wilhelm launched the last assault of the Thirty Years' War: he followed him into the revolt of the second Fronde against the rule of Cardinal Mazarin, and went into exile with him to Spain and thence into the army of Spain. When Condé effected his return to favour, Luxembourg followed in his footsteps. Condé supported his protégé procuring a commission for him as a lieutenant-general in 1668.

In the Dutch war (1672–8) Luxembourg showed his real talent for war. His army pushed deep into Holland, threatening both Leyden and the Hague; but he had undertaken a winter campaign (against the normal practice of the times) and when a sudden thaw threatened to turn the terrain into a quagmire, Luxembourg carried out a brilliantly executed withdrawal to his base at Utrecht. Much of his army melted away, however, when the contingents supplied by France's German allies left him, as their governments made peace with Holland. There were no smashing victories in the campaign, but Luxembourg had shown his ability to handle an army in the field, to be enterprising when the occasion demanded, but not reckless: these were all qualities which recommended him to Louis XIV.

In July 1675 he was made a marshal of France and given command over the Rhine army after the death of Turenne. Although Philippsburg was lost to Charles of Lorraine, Luxembourg was left in the stronger position strategically, and he was to end the war with another victory, over William of Orange at St Denis, initiated by William who was unaware that peace had been signed at Nijmegen (1678). But Luxembourg, who should have been high in Louis's favour, now fell into disgrace through his supposed involvement in a court scandal involving witchcraft, poisons and black magic. Thrown into prison for some months, then acquitted, he was nevertheless banished from the court. But the royal displeasure did not last and he was recalled, this time in the coveted position of captain of the king's personal guard (1681).

When the war of the Grand Alliance (1688–97) broke out Luxembourg was the obvious choice for the overall command of the French armies, given that Louis always kept his generals on a tight leash. After the French defeat at Walcourt by George Frederick of Waldeck (1689), the command was quickly given to Luxembourg, who restored French prestige with a fine victory over George Frederick at Fleurus (1690), although Louis's caution prevented him from exploiting it. Luxembourg followed Fleurus with an uninterrupted run of victories, as important for French morale as Marlborough's record of success in the following war of the Spanish Succession (1701–14). William of Orange, now William III of England, revealed that he was no match for the skills of Luxembourg. The French took Mons and Hal, followed by Namur (1692), and at Steenkirk (1692) William repeated his failure at St Denis fourteen years before by attacking Luxembourg and losing the battle. The French riposte was the battle of Neerwinden (1693) where, in a hard-fought engagement, the French routed the smaller Dutch and English army. But again the attitudes of caution instilled by Louis prevailed, and Luxembourg did not move in for the kill. It was his last great victory, for he returned to France a hero, but also a man worn out by his campaigning. He died at Versailles early in January 1695. With his death the tide turned back in favour of William III: he at last found that he could beat the French. Luxembourg was no great innovator or philosopher about the nature and practice of war; like his patron, Condé, he was a fine, practical general.

Lyautey, Louis Hubert Gonzalve (1854–1934) Marshal of France. Lyautey's enormous reputation, comparable to that of Kitchener (q.v.) in Britain (though the Frenchman was incomparably more agreeable in character), was won exclusively in the empire. A subordinate of Galliéni (q.v.) during the pacification of northern Indo-China, he was taken by him to Madagascar after its annexation by France in 1897. Faced again by problems of pacification, he devised the system of *quadrillage* – the division of disaffected regions into zones for progressive subjection – which became a model for colonial campaigns everywhere. He applied it so successfully in the border regions of Algeria, 1903–10, that on France's decision to annex Morocco (1912) he was appointed high commissioner in the protectorate. His achievement in that country, where he remained until 1925, was to bring about not only its pacification but its apparent reconciliation to French rule – an achievement latterly somewhat compromised by the revolt of Abd el-Krim (q.v.). A writer of great perception and elegant style, his book, *Le Rôle social de l'officier* (1891), is one of the most important documents in the intellectual history of the modern French army. He was created marshal in 1921.

M

MacArthur, Douglas (1880–1964) American general. Commander of the all-state 42nd Rainbow Division in France at the age of thirty-seven, MacArthur returned to West Point as superintendent in 1919, was chief of staff of the army, 1930–5 (in which capacity he dispersed the Washington Bonus March), and, 1935–7, organized the army of the Philippines, where he held the rank of field-marshal, the only United States citizen to do so. He retired in 1937, but was recalled in July 1941 and appointed commander of US (and Philippines) troops in the Far East. He and his main body were in the Philippines when it was attacked by the Japanese in December and he conducted a dogged and costly defence of the Bataan peninsula and Corregidor island until ordered by Roosevelt on 11 March to leave for Australia. He did so, but promised, 'I shall return.' After Midway, which crippled Japanese naval striking power (see Spruance), he began the reconquest of the Pacific territories with a brilliantly conceived and directed strategy of 'island hopping'. Its nub was to seize as bases for his advance small, weakly held islands, leaving 'to wither on the vine' the larger islands which Japan had strongly garrisoned in expectation of attack. During 1943 he secured northern New Guinea and the Solomons and in October 1944 made good his promise to return by landing on Leyte in the Philippines. In March and June 1945 (by which time he was supreme commander of all Allied land forces in the Pacific) he captured Iwo Jima and Okinawa and in September took the surrender of Japan aboard USS *Missouri* in Tokyo Bay.

Between 1945 and 1950, as chief of occupation forces in Japan (and 'uncrowned emperor') he oversaw the introduction of constitutional government to the country, but on the outbreak of war in Korea reverted to active command as head of United Nations forces there. The Inchon operation, 15–25 September 1950, by which he rolled back the North Korean invasion of the South, remains the last great exercise in modern amphibious warfare, of which he was the undoubted master. However, his subsequent advance to the Chinese border, provoking Chinese intervention and a dispute with Washington over the aims of the war, led to his dismissal by Truman in April 1951. Some expected him to carry his disagreements with civilian authority into the domestic politics of the United States. But before a session of both houses of Congress on his return he asked only to be allowed like an old soldier 'to fade away'. His name undoubtedly will not: in Liddell Hart's view he was 'supreme ... His combination of strong personality, strategic grasp, tactical skill, operative mobility and vision put him in a class above Allied commanders in any theatre.'

His father, **Arthur MacArthur** (1845–1912), won the Congressional Medal of Honour at Missionary Ridge in the Civil War and was military governor of the Philippines, 1900–1. He was less handsome than his son, one of the most physically striking of all Great Captains.

McClellan, George Brinton (1826–85) American (Union) general. A regular officer (West Point, class of 1846), McClellan had resigned from the army before the Civil War, like many others, and made a successful career as vice-president of the Illinois Central Railroad (to which Abraham Lincoln was attorney). Appointed major-general of Ohio Volunteers at the outbreak, and in the regular army shortly after, word of his little victory of Rich Mountain, 11 July 1861, arrived in Washington just in time to offset, very slightly, the bad news from Bull Run (*see* McDowell) and to recommend him as a promising senior commander. He was appointed first to the Army of the Potomac, then as general in chief to succeed Winfield Scott (q.v.). His success in organizing the raggle-taggle armies of the Union during 1861–2 was genuinely remarkable. But the soubriquet 'The Young Napoleon', which Northern newspapers bestowed on him and he accepted with satisfaction, was proved the exaggeration it was by his utterly indecisive conduct of the Peninsula campaign, March–July 1862.. His initial amphibious landing took the Confederates by surprise, and, had he pushed ahead rapidly towards Richmond, his success might have been considerable, for he greatly outnumbered them. Instead, sensing danger everywhere and calling always for reinforcements, he crawled forward, thus allowing Lee (q.v.) to summon sufficient troops to block his advance and Jackson (q.v.), in the Shenandoah Valley to put Washington under apparent threat. Only when forced to fight under a disadvantage he himself had created during the Seven Days' battles (25 June–1 July) did he show the talent that might have given him victory while it was his for the taking. Pope (q.v.) was accordingly given charge of the next major campaign (Second Bull Run). On his failure, however, McClellan resumed command, only again to throw away the chance of

success in the Antietam campaign, September 1862. Lincoln then relieved him (for having what he called 'the slows'). In a more considered explanation, which might stand as a final judgement, he said, 'He is an admirable engineer, but he seems to have a special talent for a stationary engine.' McClellan was outraged by his dismissal and stood, unsuccessfully, as Democratic candidate against Lincoln in 1864.

McClernand, John Alexander (1812–1900) American (Union) general. A state militia, not regular, officer, McClernand took part in the Henry and Donelson and the Vicksburg campaigns, briefly commanding a small army which bore his name and with which he captured Fort Hindman in January 1863. His understanding of press relations was excellent and he thereby acquired much credit to which he was not due. Grant (q.v.), under whom he served, rightly doubted his real ability and tried to be rid of him. He retired sick in November 1864. He personified in an extreme form the type of ambitious political general, 'resenting dictation, disliking West Pointers and ever mindful of opinions in his home state', who infested the Union army throughout the war.

McCreery, (Sir) Richard (1898–1967) British general. A 12th Lancer, McCreery was appointed in August 1942 chief of staff to Alexander (q.v.) in Egypt. Two months later he produced the plan which Montgomery (q.v.) adopted during the latter stages of the battle of Alamein, his own scheme having miscarried. Alexander wrote later, 'His was the key decision of the Alamein battle', and described him as 'one of those rare soldiers who are both exceptionally fine staff officers and fine commanding officers in the field'. He commanded X Corps in the Salerno landings, September 1943, and, on Montgomery's departure to lead the D-Day armies in November 1943, moved into his place at Eighth Army, which he directed for the rest of the Italian campaign.

Macdonald, Jacques Etienne Joseph Alexandre (duc de Tarente; 1765–1840) Marshal of France. The son of a family of Scottish Jacobite exiles, Macdonald was born at Sedan, and had served as an officer in the Dutch army, the *Légion irlandaise* and the *régiment de Dillon* before the Revolution. He was quickly promoted during it (general of brigade 1795, of division 1796), in 1798 became governor of Rome and in 1799 commander of the French Army of Naples. He then fell into obscurity because of his loyalty to Moreau (q.v.), and did not re-emerge until 1809, when, for breaking the Austrian centre at Wagram, he was created marshal by Napoleon on the field of battle – a unique distinction at the emperor's hand. He commanded a corps in Russia, in the 1813 campaign and in the defence of France, negotiated Napoleon's abdication and held discreetly aloof during the Hundred Days.

McDowell, Irvin (1818–85) American (Union) general. Principally notable for being in command of the North's troops at First Bull Run, where he was 'the first general in American history to command ... 30,000 men', McDowell was trusted only with lesser commands thereafter and did consistently badly. He was relieved of command (III Corps) after Second Bull Run, and, though exonerated by court-martial, not re-employed in the field.

Mack, Karl Freiherr von Leiberich (1752–1828) Austrian general. Chief of staff of the Austrian army of the First Coalition against France, Mack proposed the 'plan of annihilation', which was brought to nought by Jourdan and Kléber (qq.v.) in 1794. Appointed

commander-in-chief of the Neapolitan army in 1797, he captured Rome in November 1798, only to be beaten and captured by Championnet. He escaped from captivity in 1800, was given command of the main body of the Austrian army in the 1805 campaign, was encircled by Napoleon at Ulm and forced to capitulate (14 October). He was condemned to death, a sentence later commuted to imprisonment, but was not pardoned until 1819.

Mackay of Scourie, Hugh (1640–92) Scottish soldier. Mackay was a major-general in the service of William of Orange and accompanied him on his invasion of England in 1688. Appointed by William commander-in-chief in Scotland, Mackay was ambushed in the Pass of Killiecrankie by the Jacobite forces under Dundee (q.v.), 1689, but with Dundee's death in the battle, was able to recapture the initiative and subdue Scotland. He afterwards took part in William's last war with France and was killed at the battle of Steenkirk (1692).

Mackensen, August von (1849–1944) German field-marshal. Mackensen served as a volunteer in the Franco-Prussian war and subsequently as a regular in the 1st (Death's Head) Hussars, of which he later became colonel and whose uniform he then always wore. It was the German–Austrian force under his command (*see* Seeckt) which in Galicia, on 2 May 1915, achieved the great breakthrough of the Russian front between Gorlice and Tarnow. In 1916 he directed the invasion of Romania. He was one of the few German soldiers to be promoted field-marshal during the war and, in his dotage, was much paraded by Hitler at national festivals. 'Before 1914 he boasted of Scottish descent ... after 1939 his name was said to derive from a German village called Mackenhausen.'

His son **Eberhard von Mackensen**

(born 1889), also a 1st Hussar, became colonel-general and commanded the Fourteenth Army which contained the Anzio landing.

MacMahon, Marie Edmé Patrice Maurice, comte (duc de Magenta; 1808–93) Marshal of France and President. Son of a family of Irish exiles and of a peer of France, MacMahon was educated at Saint-Cyr, took part in the invasion and conquest of Algeria, and in 1855 as commander of the 1st Division captured the Malakov tower ('*J'y suis, j'y reste*'), a principal strongpoint in the defences of Sebastopol. In 1859 it was he who was chiefly responsible for the victory over the Austrians at Magenta (hence his dukedom) and from 1864 to 1870 he was governor-general of Algeria. In 1870 he was appointed to command the 1st Corps in the war with Prussia. His advance guard was destroyed at Wissembourg on 4 August and his main body at Froeschwiller on 6 August. Falling back on Châlons, he was given the Army of Châlons to command, and, after the defeat of Bazaine (q.v.) at Metz moved to engage the enemy at Sedan, where he and his army were overwhelmed on 1 September. He was wounded and taken prisoner. After his release he organized the Army of Versailles, which retook Paris from the Commune, though he was not responsible for the brutality of the repression. He was called to replace Thiers as president of the republic in 1873, but his conservatism brought him into continual conflict with the radical republicans and he resigned in 1879.

Maginot, André (1877–1932) French minister of war. Elected member of the National Assembly for Bar-le-Duc in 1910, Maginot held the post of undersecretary for war when hostilities broke out in 1914. Mobilized in his reservist rank of sergeant, he was seriously wounded in the trenches and returned

to political life. In 1924 he became minister of war in the cabinet of Poincaré and retained the post under Briand and Tardieu until 1931. During his ministry he raised the funds for and directed the construction of the great line of forts in his native Lorraine to which his name became attached. Designed to check a German invasion (to which in 1940 it offered in fact considerable resistance), its building was a symptom of that national unwillingness to wage war that brought about defeat in the Battle of France.

Magruder, John Bankhead (1810–71) American (Confederate) general. A regular infantry officer (West Point, class of 1830), Magruder resigned to join the Confederate army in April 1861 and at Big Bethel, 10 June, won the first, if very small, battle of the war. During the Peninsula campaign he did well at Mechanicsville and Gain's Bluff, less so during the Seven Days' battles, and was sent to command in Texas, where his principal achievement was to capture Galveston on 1 January 1863. After the war he went to Mexico to serve in Maximilian's army. His nickname was 'Prince John', and he indeed looked more of a military figure than he was.

Mahan, Alfred Thayer (1840–1914) American admiral, naval historian and theorist. Mahan's influence upon the use of sea power is well known; what is not is that he himself had an active naval career behind him when he turned to writing. After graduating from Annapolis in 1859, he served afloat during the Civil War and commanded a sloop on the South American Station, 1883–4. He was by then a noted naval writer and in 1885 was invited to lecture at the recently founded Naval War College, where he was to serve (twice as president) for most of the rest of his career. His lectures formed the basis of his first and best-remembered book, *The Influence of Sea Power upon History, 1660–1783* (1890), which he followed with studies of sea power in the wars of the French Revolution and Empire (1902) and the war of 1812 (1905), and of naval strategy (1911). He also wrote biographies of Nelson, Farragut (qq.v.) and other naval officers.

Mahan was the Clausewitz (q.v.) of naval strategy: he advocated nothing less than 'command of the sea' as the proper object of naval power, which was to be gained by the 'offensive action' of a 'preponderating fleet'. Commerce raiding, coastal defence and the 'strategy of the fleet in being' (the possession of a fleet merely to threaten, rather than to exercise power) he rejected as ultimately fruitless and wasteful half-measures. His ideas, to which the impressive scholarship, style and organization of his books lent great weight, had a strong and immediate influence on naval policy in America, Germany and Britain, encouraging the first two to proceed with the construction of fleets able to challenge the Royal Navy's and the latter to bear the cost of maintaining her existing preponderance ('the two-power standard'). Mahan's geopolitical ideas – on the importance of geographical position and the relative strengths and weaknesses of land-locked and maritime states – also fertilized the thinking of writers like Haushofer and Mackinder on which Hitler (q.v.) was to draw for much of his *Weltanschauung*.

His father, **Dennis Hart Mahan** (1802–71), was not without importance as a thinker: while professor (1832–71) at West Point, he propagated the ideas of Jomini (q.v.) among those who would fight the Civil War. He was appointed to West Point by Sylvanus Thayer, whose name he gave to his son.

Mahdi, The (properly Mohammed Ahmed; 1843–85) Moslem religious leader and conqueror of the Sudan. Born in Dongola province, he was for a time in the Egyptian civil service, then a slave-trader, finally an inspired religious revivalist and successful rebel. He defeated an Egyptian army under Hicks Pasha on 5 November 1883 at El Obeid and in January 1885 took Khartoum, the capital, after a long siege (*see* Gordon). After his death, war and government in the Sudan were carried on by his subordinate, known as the Khalifa Abdullah el Taashi, whose army was eventually defeated at Omdurman in 1899 (*see* Kitchener).

Makarov, Stepan Osipovich (1848–1904) Russian admiral. A noted naval inventor, Makarov was appointed on the outbreak of the Russo-Japanese war to command the Pacific fleet at Port Arthur. He was killed when his flagship *Petropavlovsk* struck a stray Japanese mine while returning from a sortie on 13 April. Thereafter the Russian fleet stayed in harbour, eventually to be destroyed by land artillery.

Manchester, Edward Montagu, Earl of (1602–71) British soldier. Born into a Northamptonshire aristocratic family, Manchester was one of the few peers to support Parliament (he was one of the five members whom Charles I attempted to arrest in January 1642) and at the outbreak of the Civil War he commanded a regiment of foot under Essex. Present with Cromwell and Fairfax (qq.v.) at the battle of Winceby (1643), it was under his command that the siege of Lincoln was brought successfully to a close, an attack which he handled efficiently but without great enterprise. Recognizing his lack of energy, Cromwell took over two of his brigades at the battle of Marston Moor (1644), although Manchester was notionally the senior officer present; the bulk of the men under his direct command were swept away in the general confusion of the battle. Moving south to counteract the king's manœuvres, his part in the second battle of Newbury was inglorious. Once again, lack of energy on his part frustrated attempts at co-ordination on the Parliamentary side, and the Royalist armies escaped under cover of darkness.

Manchester's failure at Newbury, and his general lack of success, allowed Cromwell to lay charges of neglect against him before Parliament; he resigned his commission before the charges were heard. He later opposed the trial and execution of King Charles in 1649, which stood him in good stead in 1660 at the Restoration. His last military enterprise was to raise a regiment of foot during the panic fear of Dutch invasion in 1667. As a general he lacked any deep grasp of tactics or strategy, and remained essentially an amateur where many of his contemporaries went on to become successful professionals. His relations with his troops were always good, and their loyalty to him constant.

Mangin, Charles Marie Emmanuel (1866–1925) French general. An officer of colonial infantry, Mangin first attracted attention as commander of the troops on the Marchand (q.v.) expedition to Fashoda (1898) and later for his part in the annexation of Morocco under Lyautey (q.v.). During the French counter-offensive at Verdun, October–November 1916, he planned and directed the recapture of forts Douaumont and Vaux, the loss of which had gravely disheartened France at the start of the battle, and for that achievement was given command of an army in the ill-fated Nivelle (q.v.) offensive. Retired after its failure, he was not re-employed until 1918 when, with the Tenth Army, he brought off the counter-attack in the second battle of the Marne, 18 July, which put paid to German hopes of winning the war. A fighter to his finger-tips, he was an ardent imperialist and his book (one of several), *La force noire*, argued that France should create a great army of colonial subjects to offset her inferiority in numbers *vis-à-vis* her European neighbours.

Mannerheim, Carl Gustaf Emil, Baron von (1867–1951) Finnish field-marshal, statesman and national hero. A member of a Finno-Swedish noble family, born a subject of the tsar, Mannerheim rose to the rank of major-general in his army but, on the outbreak of the Bolshevik revolution, returned to Finland to command the local White forces against the Red, which he defeated after a bloody civil war in April 1918. Recalled to active service in 1939, he directed first the Winter War against the Russian invaders, November 1939–March 1940, so skilfully that Finland, though defeated, was granted reasonable terms, and later the so-called Continuation War of 1941–4, in concert with the Germans against the Russians. As president, 1944–6, he secured terms from Russia which again left Finland independent.

Mannock, Edward (1887–1918) British fighter ace. Britain's leading fighter ace of the First World War, Mannock shot down seventy-three enemy aircraft and was awarded the Victoria Cross, Distinguished Service Order and two bars and Military Cross and bar. The son of a private soldier, he was working as a telegraph engineer in Turkey in 1914 and did not learn to fly until November 1916. He seems to have been shot down by a bullet from a German infantryman's rifle.

Mansfeld, Ernst, Graf von (1580–1626) German soldier of fortune. A leading mercenary leader at the outset of the Thirty Years' War (1618–48), Mansfeld, although a Catholic, served exclusively on the Protestant side. An illegitimate son of the Prince of Mansfeld, he entered the Austrian army and fought throughout Europe; but because of his inauspicious birth, and the taunts it brought, he gradually estranged himself from imperial service. At the outbreak of the Bohemian rising of 1618, the opening moves of what was to develop into the Thirty Years' War, he was in the service of the Protestant Evangelical Union. In October 1618, leading an army of 20,000 provided by Charles Emmanuel of Savoy and the Elector Palatine, he attacked the fortress town of Pilsen and sacked it with great brutality. He wintered in Pilsen, and in the following spring moved south-east to Budweis, hoping to repeat his success. But his army was attacked and routed by an imperial force led by de Bucquoi at Sablat (June 1619). Mansfeld withdrew to lusher pastures in Germany, and his failure to support the Protestant armies led to the defeat at the battle of the White Mountain (1620), a disaster for the Protestant cause. For two years his armies lived off the rich pickings of the Rhineland provinces.

In his first encounter with the general of the Catholic League, Tilly (q.v.), at Mingolsheim (1622), Mansfeld was successful, but he lost to Tilly at Wiesloch later in the year. At the battle of Wimpfen (May 1622), he prudently withdrew when he saw that the combined forces of Spain and the Catholic League had beaten the Protestant troops of George Frederick of Baden. As the cause of the Elector Palatine worsened and his purse emptied, Mansfeld was forced to transfer to Dutch service, for his army had to be paid. His condition was parlous, and only an English subsidy staved off mutiny. He remained a force in Germany, with a fair record of success, but his main aim was to preserve his army rather than to achieve any decisive result. In 1626 he came up against the new imperial mercenary general, Wallenstein (q.v.). The two armies met at Dessau. Underestimating his opponent,

Mansfeld launched a frontal assault on Wallenstein's carefully located guns and infantry. He lost heavily (leaving 4000 men – a third of his force – dead on the battlefield) and moved east into Silesia, and then turned abruptly south, intending to take service with the Venetians. But he died *en route* and his army melted away. Scarcely an admirable character, nor a great commander, he lacked the organizational genius of Wallenstein, or the brilliance of Tilly. Yet he was one of the better Protestant commanders, a sad commentary on the level of generalship in the Protestant interest before the eruption of Gustavus Adolphus (q.v.) into Germany.

Manstein, Erich von Lewinski gennant von (1887–1973) German fieldmarshal. Commissioned into the 3rd Foot Guards (Hindenburg's, q.v., regiment and a nursery of generals) in 1907, Manstein first achieved prominence by advocating, while chief of staff of Army Group A in 1940, a plan to break through the Franco-British line in the west. It came to the ears of Hitler and formed the basis of the plan the German army executed with such startling success in May. By his presumption he had, however, incurred the hostility of his seniors and he was posted to an unimportant appointment during the campaign. In September 1941, however, he achieved command of the Eleventh Army with which he captured the Crimea and after the winter went on to clear the Kerch peninsula and advance into the Caucasus. Appointed to Army Group Don (later South) in November 1942, he conceived Operation Winter Storm, which might, but for the timidity of Paulus (q.v.), have resulted in the relief of Stalingrad. In February–March 1943, his counter-offensive at Kharkov briefly recaptured the initiative. It was lost at Kursk, an operation of which he was an advocate but which was delayed beyond the date when he thought it safe to launch. He was relieved in March 1944, his advocacy of 'fluid defence', which Hitler interpreted to mean retreat, having exhausted his credit with the Führer. Manstein was regarded by friend and foe as the most expert practitioner of mobile tactics in the war.

Manteuffel, Edwin Hans Karl Freiherr von (1809–85) Prussian field-marshal. Head of the military cabinet to William I, Manteuffel was a diehard opponent of the dilution of the Prussian officer corps with 'bourgeois elements'. He commanded a corps in the Danish war, led the Army of the Main against Austria's south German allies in 1866 and the First Army in 1870, with which he took part in the battle of Metz. Subsequently he was engaged against Faidherbe and Bourbaki (qq.v.) in the provinces, and commanded the army of occupation after the capitulation, 1871–3.

A descendant, **Hasso Eccard von Manteuffel** (1897–1978), commanded the Fifth Panzer Army in the Ardennes offensive of December 1944.

Mao Tse-tung (1893–1976) Chinese statesman, soldier and military theorist. Born the son of a prosperous peasant of Hunan, Mao served as a soldier in the army of the first Chinese revolution of 1911–12, but later returned to his studies, was converted to Marxism while working as a librarian at Peking University and in 1921 took part in the founding congress of the Chinese Communist Party at Shanghai. After the open break between the nationalist Kuomintang and the Communists in 1927, he organized, with Chu Teh (q.v.) a Red Army – one of several – in Kiangsi. Although it was not at the outset the army of politicized peasants with whom alone (he had come to believe) a true revolution could be made, he worked to make it one, meanwhile fighting off a succession of attacks, first by local forces, then by the full weight of the army of Chiang Kai-

shek (q.v.). The fifth of these 'annihilation campaigns' so nearly succeeded that he decided in 1934 to leave south for north China and set off, with 100,000 men, on the anabasis now known as the Long March.

At the end of it, a year later, his army had shrunk to 20,000, but he had left Communist cells along his 6000-mile route and found at the end of it a secure sanctuary in the hills of Yenan in Shansi. There he made his peace with Chiang, both agreeing to turn their arms against the Japanese who, since the 'Manchuria incident' of 1931, had overtaken the warlords as the principal threat to the integrity of China. In practice it was Chiang who fought the Japanese; Mao, in his fastness far from the centre of operations, built up an army of a million and extended his territory until, by 1945, he ruled 95 million people. The two sides then reverted to open war, despite American efforts to mediate between them, and in an all-out campaign, beginning in mid-1948, Mao's armies swept southward, winning or buying over many of Chiang's men, until by October 1949 he had expelled the Nationalists from the mainland.

Mao thereby established himself as one of the great military leaders of history, a reputation not diminished by the only partially successful intervention of his 'volunteers' in the Korean war in November 1950. More important, the intellectual foundations of his strategy, published in a flood of writing on military affairs, inspired and guided Communist guerrilla leaders in a score of other countries, notably Vietnam (*see* Giap). His ideas defy brief summary but they centre on the concept of 'protracted war' – one fought without hope of victory within measurable time – and that of the unity of army and people. It is the duty of the army, in Mao's view, so to politicize the population among which it fights that it not only draws from it the men, supplies and information that it needs for combat, but transforms the cultural and political structure of society step by step with the military successes it wins. Revolution thus comes about not after and as a result of victory but through the process of war itself. Hence his best-known slogan, 'Power flows out of the barrel of a gun', and the remarkable resilience of the Communist guerrilla movements both in China and Vietnam. Attempts to apply his ideas in South America and Africa have been less successful (*see* Guevara), suggesting that they may be of less universal application than apostles of Mao claim.

Marceau (-Desgraviers), François Séverin (1769–96) French general. A sergeant of the *régiment d'Angoulême*, Marceau was a member of the crowd which stormed the Bastille and rose quickly through the ranks of the National Guard to command of a division in the war against the Vendéens, in which he defeated Rochejacquelein (q.v.) at Le Mans. After a short but brilliant passage of command in the Army of the Sambre-et-Meuse under Jourdan (q.v.), 1795–6, he was fatally wounded near Altenkirchen; Kray (q.v.), his chief opponent, shed tears at his deathbed.

Marchand, Jean Baptiste (1863–1934) French general and explorer. A private soldier of the colonial infantry, Marchand rose through the ranks to take part as an officer in the French conquest of West Africa and in 1897 was given command of an expedition charged to extend French possessions to the Nile. News of his arrival at Fashoda, 10 July 1898, provoked concern in Britain, and his expulsion by Kitchener (q.v.) outrage in France; this 'Fashoda incident' strained relations between the two countries for some time. Marchand became through it a national idol. During the First World War he commanded the 10th Colonial Division, at whose head – for he led it in person – he was severely wounded in the assault on the Main de Massiges, 25 September 1915, the French army's last attempt at *l'offensive à outrance*.

Marion, Francis (1732–95) American soldier. Known as the 'Swamp Fox', Marion's hit-and-run tactics against the British during Cornwallis's (q.v.) advance into the South proved effective. Marion had, like many Southerners, fought in the Cherokee war of 1759, but it was not until the surrender of General Benjamin Lincoln (q.v.) at Charleston (1780) that he used his small body of troops to harry the British, while living rough in the swamps of South Carolina. In August 1781 his marauders rescued the Americans trapped by the British at Parker's Ferry. In the same year he was created a brigadier-general, and, with the retreat of the British, resumed more traditional military duties. His attacks showed how a tiny band of skirmishers, who had the advantage of terrain on their side, could unhinge the operations of a much larger body of traditionally deployed troops, even troops who had been led to expect this type of attack.

Marlborough, John Churchill, 1st Duke of (1650–1722) British soldier. Writing 'On War', Clausewitz (q.v.) stressed the daunting risks which a general faced when he chanced to fight a battle: 'If an army was completely destroyed it was impossible to make another; and behind the army there was nothing. This called for great prudence. Only when some decisive advantage was likely to be gained, could the risk be undertaken. It was in the creation of such chances that the art of the commander lay.' In an age, after Vauban's (q.v.) decisive improvements to the art of fortification, where the power of the defence had acquired an unshakable dominance, attacking, offensive generalship was a scarce commodity. The simplest distinction which cut off Marlborough from almost all his contemporaries was his passion for the decisive action, the stunning blow delivered to an enemy's army in the field. And because of the tendency for his enemies to avoid battle if possible, he had to use all his art to persuade them that, for once, the chance was there. How he had arrived at his attitudes to war is perhaps hard to establish, for he left no statement of his theories of war or of his practice. His early experience was broad. His elder sister Arabella had established herself in public as the maid of honour to the Duchess of York, and in private as the accomplished mistress of James, Duke of York, and later James II; she organized a position for her brother as page to the Duke of York.

In 1668 Marlborough joined the military garrison of Tangier, and thus had his first experience of war against the Moors and Barbary pirates of North Africa. Returning to court he made a more valuable conquest in the form of Barbara Villiers, Duchess of Cleveland, one of the mistresses of Charles II. The king, once interrupting them in close combat, overlooked Marlborough's poaching of royal game, remarking, 'You do it to get your bread.' It so proved, for the duchess rewarded her ardent young lover with £4500, which provided him with a settled income for life.

He served aboard ship with the Duke of York at the battle of Sole Bay, and in 1673 joined a detachment under the Duke of Monmouth (q.v.) which fought against the Dutch during the Third Dutch War (1672–4). He went on to fight under Turenne (q.v.), for Louis XIV, and fought with great courage and effect at the battles of Sinzheim and Entzheim (1674): Turenne himself prophesied a rosy future for the 'handsome Englishman'.

Returning to the English service, Marlborough moved slowly upwards, until the accession of his mentor, as James II,

gave a fillip to his career. Soon after James's arrival on the throne, the young Marlborough received the colonelcy of the King's Dragoons; shortly afterwards he was sent with a commission against his former commander, the Duke of Monmouth, who had invaded the west of England. Although the command of the expedition eventually went, to Marlborough's fury, to Lord Feversham, he fulfilled his part, as the official dispatch had it, 'with all the courage and gallantry imaginable'. The reward was a colonelcy in the Life Guards. When the opposition to James II rose to a crescendo in 1687 and 1688, Marlborough temporized, but when the opposition developed into a full-blown rebellion, with the landing of a powerful Dutch force under William of Orange to claim the throne, Marlborough's highly developed sense of self-interest caused him to desert James at the crucial moment. Like Lord Stanley at the battle of Bosworth, he was determined to be on the winning side, and no scruples of honour or debt to James, who had fostered his career, stood in his way. But he maintained his contact with the exiled James II, and his ambivalence made William, and, moreover, Queen Mary, distrustful of him. He was created Earl of Marlborough (1688), and in the next year given command of the English in Flanders. Although the campaign was largely uneventful, Marlborough won glowing tributes from his commander, Waldeck, who said that he had displayed in a single campaign more military aptitude than most generals displayed in a lifetime. What he referred to was a hard-fought encounter at Walcourt, where Marlborough delivered a shattering blow to the French, charging at the head of his men. Later in the year he took a small force to Ireland and captured the fortresses of Cork and Kinsale in short order. Still, however, he yearned for a major command and failed to achieve one.

In 1692 his career was brought to a juddering halt, when he was sent to the Tower, a victim of royal irritation and of his devious correspondence and connections with James II. Although released, and after the death of his most implacable enemy Queen Mary in 1695, allowed to return to court, Marlborough was barred from military command. But in 1698 he and William III were reconciled in the great objective of securing a firm set of allies for the war William believed might come over the vexed question of the succession to the throne of Spain, the great issue in international politics. By the end of 1700, after Louis XIV had torn up all agreements he had reached over the Spanish question, war was inevitable. Marlborough was to have the command of the English troops in Flanders and over the army at home. But the plans were upset by the death of William III, after his horse tripped on a mole hill ('the little gentleman in black velvet', as the Jacobites toasted the instrument of their enemy's demise). Anne, the loyal friend of the Marlboroughs, both the earl and his wife, Sarah, now gave to him both the supreme role in the army and a decisive voice in policy at home. He was at last in a position of real power.

For nine years Marlborough was to control the destiny of the nation, to determine its alliances and foreign policy, to administer its armies on the battlefield, and to act in a capacity as 'supreme commander' unparalleled in English history until recent times. It was Marlborough's unique talent to be capable of operating, with almost equal success, at all levels of activity, from mighty considerations of international relations, down to infinitesimal detail as to the size of a soldier's rations and equipment. In the war of the Spanish Succession (1701–14), which has immortalized him, his first maxim was, 'Attack!' But his second was, 'Leave nothing to chance.' The results were, as his admirer, Cap-

tain Parker, wrote with strict accuracy: 'Upon all occasions he concerted matters with so much judgement ... that he never fought a battle he did not gain, nor laid siege to a town which he did not take.' In real terms, in the nine years of war there were: four great battles won, with another four encounters gained, and twenty-six sieges which ended in the capture of the objective. Of his great battles – Blenheim (1704), Ramillies (1706), Oudenarde (1708) and Malplaquet (1709) – Blenheim is the most astonishing. For the first time in forty years a French army had suffered a major defeat at the hands of a polyglot allied army, under the command of a general with virtually no experience. To win at Blenheim, Marlborough had to march for 250 miles across Germany, with all the dangers of leaving his base in Holland unprotected. He arrived on the Danube with his troops comparatively fresh and eager for battle. This unique achievement was the result of plans and preparations of an unparalleled complexity. Marlborough had designed special carts for carrying all the army's supplies. He laid out at various points advance depots, so that at Heidelberg, for example, every man found a new pair of boots waiting for him. On each day's march the camp was prepared in advance of the main body's arrival so that 'the soldiers had nothing to do but pitch their tents, boil their kettles and lie down to rest'. The army rose at 3 am and marched to 9 am, making it hard for an enemy following to judge their progress in the half-light. By contrast with the British army in its progress across Germany, the French shadowing force under Tallard lost almost a third of its strength on the march, as well as many horses. When Marlborough met the imperial army under Prince Eugen on the Danube, his difficulty was in bringing the French and their allies, the Bavarians, to battle. When he did so, on 13 August 1704, the enemy was confident of victory. Marlborough's tactic in the battle was to push hard on the enemy flank, draw him into thinking that the main assault was to come there and to commit his reserves, and then to deliver a smashing blow in the centre. In the victory which followed, Marlborough and Eugen lost 13,000 and the French 34,000 killed or wounded, including Marshal Tallard himself.

None of Marlborough's later triumphs were on this scale. Although Blenheim established him as one of the great commanders in history, his problems increased rather than diminished. As the years passed, the French became more wary about giving battle, and on many occasions withdrew from encounters which he had planned. Although he waged a most successful war, France itself was untouched, and with the advantage of the interior lines of communication found it easier to plan concerted strategy than the allies. And at home, as political strife became more embittered, Marlborough, who had attempted to stand above party, was drawn increasingly into the political arena. Finally relations with his allies (except the loyal Eugen, who shared his view of war) demanded more and more of his energies. The Dutch in particular proved a constant restraint on his plans. All his attempts at an embracing strategy, which would batter France from all sides, by land and sea, were frustrated. Thus the decisive victory at Ramillies (23 May 1706) led only to the failed Toulon expedition under Eugen and stalemate in Flanders. Despite all his abilities Marlborough could not prevent the natural lethargy of eighteenth-century warfare from overtaking his campaigns. At Oudenarde (11 July 1708) he showed that in a battle where the enemy was met unexpectedly his good eye for terrain and his capacity to improvise could bring, again, a splendid victory. But by his final great field battle at Malplaquet (11 September 1709)

the French commander Villars (q.v.) had clearly learnt how to counter a Marlburian battle plan, and the victory, although it went to Marlborough because of the quality of his troops, was costly in men's lives. The opportunities for a 'decisive advantage', in Clausewitz's phrase, were becoming slimmer. In 1711 the great general was brought down by the collapse of his political support at home and the loss of royal favour. He never fought another battle.

There are good reasons for considering Marlborough Britain's greatest soldier, for there was no talent for war which he did not possess. He had the imagination and the command of detail to plan a grand strategy; he was an able generalissimo of allied armies, always ready to flatter a foreign ruler for some political advantage. His capacity for innovation really lay off the battlefield, in his immense gifts as an organizer and administrator (his battle plans were not as original as those of some other commanders of equal genius). But his greatest strength lay in his attention to the economic underpinning of the war, and in his concern for morale and the welfare of his men. He ensured that he always possessed proper resources for the campaign he had in mind; his friend, Godolphin, ensured that the English Treasury always kept him in funds. He was thus able to pay his troops regularly and ensure proper channels of supply. This concern for supply was directly connected with his deep concern for his men's welfare. 'Corporal John', as the soldiers called him, never wasted lives unnecessarily, or asked them to perform tasks that were not necessary. As a result he could call for feats of courage and pertinacity greater than those given to any other general. In this combination of military virtues Marlborough's greatness nestled, but most of all in his understanding that the army was precious and that its value resided in the officers and men who made it up. Of what other general would his men sing on his supersession?

Grenadiers now change your song
And talk no more of battles won
No victory shall grace us now
Since we have lost our Marlborough.
You who have fought on Blenheim's field
And forced the strongest towns to yield
Break all your arms and turn to plough
Since we have lost our Marlborough.

Marmont, August Frederic Louis Viesse de (duc de Raguse; 1774–1852) Marshal of France. Gently born and well educated, Marmont was commissioned into the army of the *ancien régime* and rose swiftly after accepting the Revolution. He was a clever gunner, was promoted captain at nineteen for services at the siege of Toulon, attracted the attention of Bonaparte and at twenty-two found himself *chef de brigade* (though not general, a rank for which he had to wait until he was twenty-three). Bonaparte took him to Italy, Malta and Egypt and back to France for the coup of 18 Brumaire in which his handling of the artillery put Bonaparte in his debt – a debt whose size Marmont overestimated and could not forget. He therefore conceived a grudge when not included among those created marshal in 1804. Nevertheless he was given a corps in the 1805 campaign and created duke for his achievements as governor of Dalmatia, 1806–8. He won several small battles in the 1809 campaign, was defeated at Salamanca in 1812 (a victory reckoned Wellington's, q.v., masterpiece) and wounded, but recovered to command a corps in the campaigns of 1813 and 1814. In the latter he took his corps over to the enemy outside Paris, thus bringing about Napoleon's first exile. Neither Bonaparte nor any Bonapartist ever forgave him and the word *raguser* was coined to mean 'to betray'. Perhaps by way of compensation, he stuck to Charles X in 1830 and followed him into an exile which lasted until his own death.

Maroto, Rafael (1785–1847) Spanish (Carlist) general. Given command of the army of Biscaya by Don Carlos at the outbreak of the civil war, in 1835 Maroto defeated Espartero (q.v.) at Avrigoria. Promoted commander-in-chief in 1838 he recognized that the Carlist cause was hopeless and negotiated the treaty of Vergara.

Marshall, George Catlett (1880–1959) American general. Educated at the Virginian Military Institute, foremost of America's private military academies, Marshall fought in the First World War, was ADC to Pershing (q.v.), 1919–24, served in China, 1924–7, and in 1935 was appointed chief of staff, a post he held until the end of the Second World War. Although anxious to exercise a field command, and expected to act as Allied supreme commander in the invasion of Europe, he was ultimately retained in Washington as principal adviser to Roosevelt, his services at the centre of strategic decision being judged indispensable. Marshall's achievements were many: he was instrumental in expanding the army before the outbreak of war, in reorganizing it into three components (army ground forces, army air forces, and army service forces, the latter servicing the first two), in establishing the Joint Chiefs of Staff Committee, of which he was first chairman, but above all in fostering unity of decisions and action between the Allies, particularly the Americans and British, by whom he was deeply liked and respected. After the war he was ambassador to China, 1945–7, secretary of defence, 1950–1, and as secretary of state, 1947–9, sponsored the Marshall Aid programme, which allowed the ruined economies of western Europe to ride out the early years of the Cold War with Russia.

Marwitz, Georg von der (1856–1929) German general. Having commanded a cavalry corps in the invasion of Belgium in 1914, it was Marwitz's Second Army which held the Cambrai sector against which the British directed the first great tank attack of history on 20 November 1917. His counter-attack of 30 November recovered most of the ground lost. On 8 August 1918 his army again suffered a major tank assault by the French, on what Ludendorff (q.v.) called 'the black day of the German army'.

Masséna, André (duc de Rivoli, prince d'Essling; 1756–1817) Marshal of France. Born at Nice (he was distinctly Italian in appearance and manner), Masséna was orphaned young, went to sea as a cabin-boy, and became a sergeant in the army at nineteen (*régiment Royal-Italien*). He retired in 1789, apparently to set up as a smuggler at Antibes, but re-enlisted in 1791. Self-confidence and quick wits ensured his rapid rise. Appointed general of division in the Army of Italy in 1794, he became one of Bonaparte's most trusted subordinates. and, for his part in the battles of Arcola, Rivoli and La Favorita, won from him the title of '*enfant chéri de la Victoire*'. In 1797 he saved France from a major disaster by his defeat of Suvorov (q.v.) at Zurich and in 1800 directed a heroic defence of Genoa, which made possible Napoleon's great victory at Marengo. He was created marshal in 1804 ('one of eighteen' was his only comment) and, for his successful command of the Grand Army's right in 1807, Duke of Rivoli; he was made prince for his tenacity at Essling and his successful command of the left at Wagram in 1809. Translated to the Peninsula, he lost his touch. Repulsed by Wellington at Busaco, 27 September 1810, he followed him towards Lisbon only to discover that the newly built lines of Torres Vedras barred his route. Starvation drove his army away and Napoleon did not employ him

again in a major command – curiously, for he was among the ablest of the marshals.

Maunoury, Michel Joseph (1847–1923) Marshal of France. On the approach of the German armies towards Paris in August 1914, following their victories in the battle of the Frontiers, Maunoury, who had commanded the *ad hoc* Army of Lorraine, 19–27 August, was given command of the new Sixth Army which Joffre had formed northeast of Paris from troops brought from eastern France. With it, and under the orders of Galliéni (q.v.), he organized the counter-stroke into the flank of the German First Army (von Kluck, q.v.), which halted the German advance, recovered the initiative for the French and led on to the victory of the Marne. During the subsequent battle of the Aisne he was blinded while touring the trenches. He was posthumously created marshal (1923).

Maurice of Nassau, Prince of Orange (1567–1625) Dutch soldier, stadtholder and military innovator. Maurice succeeded his father William the Silent (q.v.) in 1584 with little practical experience, and the pressing demands of war upon him. Together with his cousins, William Louis of Nassau and John of Nassau, he secured the effective independence of the Netherlands from Spain, but also created a uniquely efficient army. Until 1589 the remorseless pressure from Parma (q.v.) had been forcing the Dutch from their strongholds in the south, and back into the northern provinces of Holland and Zealand. But in 1589 Parma was directed by Philip II (q.v.) to move south into France against the armies of Henry IV (q.v.), and the Dutch had time to reorganize their resistance. The mainspring of the Mauritian reforms was an intellectual approach to the art of war. Intense interest had already been shown in the military practice of the Romans, and it was a Dutchman, Justus Lipsius, who produced the definitive treatise on the topic in 1595: Maurice learnt much from him. But whereas earlier attempts to employ 'Roman' methods had been largely impractical, antiquarian exercises, Maurice attacked the problem of tactical reform with a unique thoroughness. He reorganized the system of pay so as to ensure that troops were paid with complete regularity, and he concentrated with passionate energy on the training of infantry. Unlike the Spanish *tercios*, Maurice's pikemen stood only five deep, in an oblong formation, flanked by solid platoons of musketeers. Each unit could manœuvre independently, or as a mass. While the *tercio* was limited in the evolutions it could perform, Maurice hammered into the Dutch army the entire gamut of manœuvre, drawn from the Romans, in particular from Aelian. Whereas the *tercio*, and similar units which depended on their mass and weight to achieve their results, once committed, were hard to withdraw, the Dutch system allowed a commander great latitude in the handling of his forces during an encounter. The effect of the Mauritian reforms was to allow more men to be used effectively in a battle, for the men in the centre of a *tercio* never came even within a pike's thrust of the enemy, passing a battle by simply leaning on the man in front. In the smaller Dutch formation every man came into direct contact with the enemy, and each man knew exactly the part he had to play in a manœuvre. To this highly successful infantry, Maurice added a vastly superior artillery, scrapping many of the old arms and standardizing by calibre on a new set of weapons. It was in the realm of artillery and siege warfare that his imagination had full play. In his passion for system and order, he developed a style of war which eschewed pitched battles: it was said that he waged war as though he was

playing chess. The attraction of siege warfare was that it could be processed according to a simple logical pattern, and in his techniques, particularly in his use of mass artillery for concentrated fire during bombardments, he anticipated the reforms of Vauban (q.v.). Because of his passionate intellectual interest in the art of war, Maurice advanced the technological services – engineers, artillery – by sending his better officers to study at university, especially at Leiden, where he had himself been a student. It was John of Nassau who established a highly successful military academy at Siegen, and princes from all over Protestant Europe were sent to study the art of war under Maurice and his cousins – including the young Turenne (q.v.). Although Maurice improved the quality of the Dutch cavalry, mostly by vigorous training, he was not a cavalry leader and their quality was definitely inferior to the new infantry.

The effect of these developments could be seen in the campaign of 1591–2, where although the reforms had not been completed, the Dutch army now showed itself superior to the Spaniards, and the capture of Zutphen in seven days, and the fall of Deventer in eleven, showed the effectiveness of his new siege tactics. Wisely, he never allowed Parma to bring him to battle, and after Parma's death he was faced, until the advent of Spinola (q.v.) in 1603, by inferior Spanish commanders. The battle of Tournhout (1597) showed the professionalism of Maurice's army, as his cavalry and infantry acted in unison to demolish a slightly smaller Spanish force under Varas, with Spanish losses of 2500 for only 100 Dutch. But Maurice avoided battle, and his field reputation rests on his triumphs at Tournhout and at Nieuwpoort (1600). There he beat the Spanish in a close battle, where once again it was the co-operation between arms, with the artillery playing a crucial role, which won the day. But it was a pointless victory, for Maurice made no strategic gain. In his battles, or more properly, encounters, with Spinola, Maurice was much less successful, and most of the gains made after Parma's death were lost. Maurice took a different view of the likely outcome of the war from the States-General which insisted on concluding a twelve-year truce in 1609; the period of peace was spent in conflict with the 'peace party', although the issue became centred on a religious controversy. Maurice was eventually successful, and the leader of his enemies, Johan van Oldenbarnveldt, was executed in 1619. Maurice refused to allow a renewal of the truce in 1621, and engineered the Dutch entry into the early stages of the Thirty Years' War (1618–48). But Spinola had expected the resumption of hostilities, and kept his army of mercenaries in being throughout the truce. Maurice had no more success against him than he had had twenty years before and he died with Breda under siege by Spinola's army.

But if he achieved no smashing successes in battle, his work as an organizer and reformer provided the United Provinces with a professional army of high capacity, and under his brother, Frederick Henry of Nassau, who was stadtholder throughout the battles of the Thirty Years' War, independence from Spain was finally ensured: the eighty-years' war for Dutch liberty ended at the treaty of Munster (1648). But Maurice's contribution extends far beyond the confines of the Netherlands, for his reforms revolutionized the whole face of war. In the Swedish army of Gustavus Adolphus (q.v.), the Mauritian reforms found their best exemplar, but all over Protestant Europe armies were remodelled along the Dutch lines. His most farsighted innovations, however, were not in tactics or equipment, but in the fields of logistics, training and economics. In the well-paid, well-drilled and well-disciplined Dutch army lay the pointer to the professional forces of the future.

Maximilian I (1459–1519) Holy Roman emperor. It was one of Maximilian's many opponents, Matthias Corvinus, who is reputed to have coined the phrase that what other states gained by war Austria gained by marriage. Maximilian did indeed follow a pattern of marriages as a form of foreign policy, but they brought war and not peace. From his first marriage, to the daughter of Charles the Bold, Duke of Burgundy, he was forced to fight to sustain his claims. The Burgundian match sowed the seeds of permanent hostility with France, an effect redoubled when another marriage gave Maximilian a claim to Brittany, and still another, a close personal involvement in the affairs of Milan. On the eastern front Maximilian tried a similar process of consolidation, uniting his enemies to him by ties of marriage. He was elected emperor in 1493, and became involved in battles to maintain his possessions in the Netherlands (1494), in an unsuccessful struggle with the Swiss (1499), and an intermittent conflict with the French in Italy until his death. Maximilian was not an inspired military leader, although a field commander of great courage. He created a force of German infantry modelled on Swiss lines, *Landesknechte*, which were never quite as good as their prototype. He bequeathed to his son, Charles V, a set of unresolved problems, including the nascent Protestantism, and few means, either financial or military, to apply to them.

Meade, George Gordon (1815–72) American (Union) general. Born in Spain of American parents, it was this disqualification by foreign birth for presidential candidature which led Lincoln to choose Meade as commander of the Army of the Potomac in place of Hooker (q.v.) after Chancellorsville. He certainly had no outstanding talents. But he was by no means an incompetent and held doggedly to his position at Gettysburg, a battle he had to fight only two days after assuming command, 28 June 1863. From March 1864 he ceased to exercise independent command, without relinquishing his appointment, since Grant (q.v.), though then general-in-chief, stationed himself at the Army of the Potomac's headquarters and directed its operations. In the early stages of the war he had commanded a brigade (Peninsula campaign), division (Antietam and Fredericksburg) and corps (Chancellorsville). He became customarily so bad-tempered under the strain of command in battle that his subordinates feared 'to approach him even with information'.

Mehemet (commonly Mohammed) **Ali** (1769–1849) Ottoman soldier and viceroy of Egypt. Mehemet was sent to Egypt originally in 1798, with a contingent of troops from his native Albania, to fight Bonaparte. In the troubles following the expulsion of the French he was named viceroy (1804) and in 1811 used his Albanians to overthrow and massacre the Mamelukes who had made themselves dominant in the country. He also won the gratitude of the Ottoman sultan by sending soldiers to Mecca to expel Wahabite fanatics from the city, and his army and fleet to assist in the suppression of the Greek independence movement (the latter formed part of the Turkish fleet destroyed at the battle of Navarino in 1828 – *see* Codrington). He then, through his adopted son Ibrahim, embarked on the conquest of Syria, over the government of which he had fallen into dispute with his Ottoman overlord, and in which he was confirmed by the treaty of Koutaieh, 1833. Determined to establish himself as sovereign ruler of Egypt, he renewed war with Turkey and in 1839 won so total a victory at Nezib (*see* Moltke) that he might, but for the opposition of the great powers, have

acceded to the Ottoman throne itself. He died insane.

Melas, Michael Friedrich Benedikt Freiherr von (1729–1806) Austrian general. A veteran of the Seven Years' War, Melas was in command of the army in Italy in 1799. With Suvorov (q.v.) he shared in the victories of Cassano, the Trebbia and Novi against Moreau, Macdonald (qq.v.) and Joubert, and was singly responsible for the victory of Grenolo, 4 November, against Championnet. At Marengo, 14 June 1800, he believed at the end of the morning that he had beaten Napoleon, but was counter-attacked while leaving the field in the afternoon, lost over half his army and subsequently capitulated.

Melo, Francisco Manuel de (1608–66) Portuguese scholar, writer and soldier in the service of Spain. Commanding in Flanders in 1639, and later in the same year defending Corunna against a French fleet and driving them off with great losses, Melo did not achieve substantial success as a soldier. But he returned to the northern front and in 1643 invaded France at the head of 27,000 men. Besieging the town of Rocroi, he was met by the twenty-two-year-old Condé (then duc d'Enghien, q.v.) with a force of 23,000. The French cavalry charges failing to shake the main Spanish force of infantry, Enghien determined on the demolition of the solid but unwieldy Spanish *tercios* by artillery fire. The Spaniards asked for quarter, but mistaking Enghien's intentions when he advanced to accept their surrender, fired on him. The French, infuriated by this treachery, poured fire into the *tercios* and moved forward to finish the task at close quarters: 8000 Spaniards were killed and 7000 captured, Melo among them. The disaster to Spanish arms was scarcely his fault, since the difficulty lay with the slow-moving, clumsy *tercios*. Melo returned to Portugal, having entered the service of the new king of Portugal, John IV, founder of the house of Braganza, and for obscure reasons was imprisoned. It was during this period that his literary output was at its peak.

Menshekov, Prince Alexander Sergeivich (1787–1869) Russian general. By his lack of diplomacy while special ambassador to Turkey in 1853, Menshekov helped to bring on the Crimean War, during which he commanded, and was beaten, at the Alma and Inkerman (*see* Raglan).

Mercy, Claudius Florimund, Graf von (1666–1734) Imperial soldier. A protégé of Eugen (q.v.), Mercy entered the Austrian cavalry in 1682 and fought in the campaign following the retreat of the Turks from Vienna (1683), and in that in support of the Duke of Savoy during the war of the Grand Alliance (1688–97). He quickly caught Eugen's eye as an enterprising officer, and he led his horsemen into Cremona in the surprise dash that captured the commander of the French army, Villeroi (1702). He accompanied Eugen in his campaigns in the Low Countries; he also served in the Rhineland and Bavarian campaigns with considerable distinction. But he made his name fighting, not against the French and their allies, but against the Turks. He had fought in the campaign waged with some bitterness against the Hungarians under Ferenc II Rakoczy. After his defeat Rakoczy went to Constantinople to enlist Ottoman aid and the rebellion merged into a wider war with the Turks. In 1716 the Turks advanced against the Habsburgs with an army over 100,000 strong. Eugen met them at the fortress of Peterwardein, with his cavalry under the command of Mercy. In the ensuing battle it was the headlong charge of Mercy's hussars and cuirassiers which drove the Turkish cavalry from the field and harried the routed Turkish infantry.

Thereafter, Mercy was invaluable in the mobile war which followed, with the Austrian army pushing deeper into territory long held by the Turks: Belgrade surrendered and Eugen's troops occupied Serbia, Wallachia and the Banat of Temesvar. These gains were consolidated by the treaty of Passarowitz (1718), and Mercy was given command over the new military frontier. He created, with Eugen's active support, a network of strategic settlements to provide defence in depth against any further Turkish advance. Apart from a short campaign in Sicily (1719–20), the construction of the military frontier became Mercy's life work, and the means by which the security of Austria from the east was secured. Mercy was killed when he was recalled to repel the French and Italian invasion of Lombardy and the kingdom of Naples during the war of the Polish Succession (1733–8): his last battle, Parma (1734), was also his last victory. Unlike so many able field commanders of cavalry, Mercy had enormous administrative and organizational gifts. Under his aegis a new society developed on the borders of the Austrian empire, a region which was to provide her best regiments, and many of her best officers, in future wars.

Mercy, ·Franz, Freiherr von (1590–1645) Imperial soldier. A dogged and redoubtable imperial general in the Thirty Years' War (1618–48), Mercy entered the Austrian army in 1606. He was wounded at Breitenfeld (1631), and thereafter faced Bernhard of Saxe-Weimar (q.v.) in the campaigns on the French frontier. In 1638 he left the imperial army to join Maximilian I of Bavaria (1638); it was Mercy's planning which frustrated the French advance into Bavaria in 1643; in 1644 the battle of Tuttlingen consolidated his success. In the same year he faced the duc d'Enghien (Condé) and

Turenne (qq.v.); in the first battle of Freiburg the hard-fought encounter was effectively a draw, for the Bavarians under Mercy were able to construct a new position and were ready to fight the exhausted French troops again. At the second battle two days later, 5 August 1644, Mercy repulsed the French assault with heavy casualties on both sides. At the third battle, avoiding a pincer movement devised by Enghien and Turenne, he abandoned the field to them, but left with his army intact. In the following year he administered a sharp defeat to Turenne at the battle of Mergentheim, surprising the French army: only Turenne's great skill averted a catastrophe for France. But later in the same year (1645) the combined armies of Turenne and Enghien caught Mercy at Allerheim, and he was killed leading his men in battle. A skilful, courageous commander, Turenne's tribute is his best epitaph. On the spot where he fell, Turenne had a stone erected with the inscription, 'Sta viator, heroem calcas (Wait, traveller, for you trample on a hero).'

Methuen, Paul Sandford, 3rd Baron Methuen (1845–1932) British field-marshal. A Scots Guardsman and a protégé of Wolseley (q.v.), Methuen had a successful career in the minor Victorian colonial campaigns, but when sent to South Africa in November 1899 to command the 1st Division he embarked on a passage of disaster so unrelenting that hindsight makes it comic. Checked at the Modder river, 28 November, he was humiliatingly outgeneralled at Magersfontein, 11 December, when many of his soldiers ran away. Finally, having spent over a year chasing the elusive de Wet (q.v.), Methuen was captured by de la Rey (q.v.) in the last month of an almost extinct war.

Mihailovic, Draza (1893–1946) Yugoslav guerrilla leader. After the defeat of

the regular army by the Germans in April 1941, Mihailovic took to the hills and organized a guerrilla force which came to be called Chetniks. Royalist, Orthodox and Serb nationalist in character, the Chetniks soon fell out with the Communist partisans and eventually into conflict with them. The British, who made contact with Mihailovic in September 1941 and with Tito (q.v.) in June 1943, discovered from the latter that Mihailovic had made tacit peace with the Germans the better to wage internecine war, on which they withdrew their support from him. He was eventually rejected by his own government-in-exile, captured by Tito and executed in 1946. He was a genuinely tragic figure, whose life is best summed up by the words he used at his trial, 'I wanted much, I began much, but the gale of the world blew away me and my work.'

Miles, Nelson Appleton (1839–1925) American general. Regarded with Crook (q.v.), as the greatest of the US Army's Indian fighters, Miles in 1877 overcame both Crazy Horse and Sitting Bull (qq.v.). He had enlisted originally as a Civil War volunteer and ultimately rose to be general-in-chief (the last before the post was abolished in 1902).

Mina, Francisco Espozy (1784–1836) Spanish general. Made famous by his leadership of guerrilla bands during the Napoleonic occupation, 1808–13, Mina opposed King Ferdinand on his restoration and had to flee into exile. After his return he rejoined the army to oppose the French intervention of 1823, and defended Barcelona against Moncey (q.v.). After another period of exile he returned to fight against the Carlists and was fatally wounded in 1836.

Miranda, Francisco (1750–1816) South American revolutionary; *'el precursor'* ('the forerunner'). Miranda's nickname sums up his achievement: to have been the prophet and instigator of the independence of Spain's American colonies, which Bolivar (q.v.) consummated. A Venezuelan, he emigrated in 1771 to join the Spanish army, but was cashiered, fled to the United States and became inflamed with the ideals of the North American revolutionaries. He went to France in 1792 to fight for the Revolution there, received a command in the Army of the North, captured Antwerp but was dismissed for his failures at Maastricht and Neerwinden. Lucky to escape with his life from the Terror, he attempted to win English support for an invasion of Spanish America, twice led (unsuccessful) invasions of his own and in 1810 was brought by Bolivar from London to Caracas, where he was made a general. In 1811, on Venezuela proclaiming its independence, he became dictator, but, rather than see the country suffer a Spanish reconquest, then made terms. Bolivar delivered him to Spain and he died in prison in Cadiz. A man of words and postures rather than of real achievements, he bears comparison none the less with Garibaldi (q.v.) as a revolutionary type.

Mitchell, William ('Billy'; 1879–1936) American airman. Originally a signal corps officer, he transferred in 1917 to the air service and by the end of the First World War was in charge of its operations on the western front. He then toured Europe visiting foreign air forces and on his return home in 1921 was promoted, as brigadier-general, assistant chief of the air service. A tireless protagonist of the strategic and tactical importance of air power, he encouraged his airmen to venture on intercontinental flights and fostered experiments to prove the ability of aircraft to sink armoured ships. He also ceaselessly advocated the creation of a separate air force, independent of the army and navy, while waging

bureaucratic war with their staffs, a campaign which culminated in his accusing the navy and war departments of 'incompetence, criminal negligence and almost treasonable administration of the national defence'. For that he was court-martialled and sentenced to suspension of his rank for five years. He resigned in 1926 and devoted the rest of his life to propaganda in the cause of independent air power. Though not a truly original thinker like Douhet (q.v.) nor a successful bureaucratic in-fighter like Trenchard (q.v.), he is rightly regarded by the modern US Air Force as its John the Baptist.

Mitscher, Marc Andrew (1887–1947) American admiral. Mitscher's record of success in command of aircraft carriers is without parallel: it was from his *Hornet* that Doolittle (q.v.) took off to bomb Tokyo on 18 April 1942, and later the air groups which shared in the great strategic triumph of Midway. In 1944 he commanded Task Force 58, principal air striking force of the US Navy in the Pacific, which in the battles of Truk, the Philippine Sea, Leyte Gulf, Iwo Jima and Okinawa destroyed 795 Japanese ships and 4425 planes.

Model, Walther (1891–1945) German field-marshal. Becoming known during the second half of the Second World War as the 'Führer's fireman' for his success in stemming enemy irruptions and stabilizing the front anew, Model's greatest success was in sealing off the Russian breakthrough after the action known as the Destruction of Army Group Centre (22 June–1 July, 1944). He was then brought west to replace Kluge (q.v.) in an attempt to check, with Army Group B, the Anglo-American advance from Normandy, in which he again had considerable success. He was responsible army group commander during the Arnhem and Ardennes battles, but after the Allies' crossing of the Rhine was encircled in the Ruhr pocket. Holding that 'a field-marshal does not become a prisoner' (an oblique and contemptuous reference to Paulus, q.v.), he shot himself on 21 April.

Mola, Emilio (1887–1937) Spanish general. On the outbreak of the Civil War in 1936 Mola concentrated the garrisons of Burgos, Saragossa and Huesca, hostile to the government, and led them in four columns against Madrid, while warning in blood-curdling daily radio broadcasts that he had a 'fifth column' in the city. It is from these broadcasts that the term 'fifth columnist' derives. He was killed in an aeroplane crash before the fall of the city.

Moltke, Helmuth Karl Bernhard (Graf) von (1800–91) Prussian field-marshal, architect of victory in 1866 and 1870, father of modern staff systems. Though German by birth, Moltke served first in the army of Denmark, where his family had settled, but, seeking wider horizons, transferred in 1821 to Prussian service. Having thereby lost seniority, being already poor but possessing a literary gift, he combined soldiering with writing during his first years of duty. In 1834 he got leave to visit the Turkish empire, publishing in 1839 what is now regarded as a German classic, an account of his travels in Albania, Anatolia, Mesopotamia and Syria, during which he took service in Sultan Mahmud's army in the war against Mehemet Ali (q.v.) and commanded the artillery in its disgraceful defeat at Nezib (24 June 1839) (the artillery was the last portion of the Turkish army to run away). Such picaresque experiences, though familiar to thousands of British and French officers of the period, set Moltke apart from his Prussian contemporaries, whose lives are in the main stories of monumental dullness. It may also, by exposing him to the conse-

quences of thorough-going military incompetence, have encouraged his devotion to the pursuit of that excellence in staff duties through which he was to make the Prussian army a military wonder of the world. He had, however, already shown by his performance at the *Kriegsakademie* (1823–6) that he was a born staff officer. What subsequent events were to reveal was that he was also a commander of genius.

After two decades spent on staff duty, during which he had written much, particularly on railways, of whose military importance he had an early appreciation, married an English lady, been appointed in 1857 chief of the Great General Staff (not at the time a post of influence) and acted during the Danish war of 1864 as chief of staff of the Austro-Prussian forces, he took the field in 1866 against Austria as effective commander-in-chief. It was the sureness of his touch against the Danes which had prompted Wilhelm I (long his patron) to entrust the armies to him and, though he meddled in details, he generally left Moltke a free hand. His trust was repaid within six weeks by the decisive victory of Königgrätz (Sadowa), which left Prussia the master of Germany. Four years later, by methods very similar to those by which he had brought about Sadowa – rapid mobilization of reserves, surprise concentration of overwhelming strength by the choice of convergent lines of march, and the brilliant use of railways for movement and supply – Moltke completely outgeneralled the French field army in the Sedan campaign and then fought a bitter irregular war in the provinces while holding Paris under siege. For his achievements he was created count and promoted field-marshal. The completeness of his victory ensured that, though he remained chief of staff until 1888, his services as a commander were not again required during his lifetime.

In the hope of perpetuating his

mastery, Kaiser Wilhelm II, grandson of his patron, appointed Moltke's nephew, **Helmuth Johann Ludwig von Moltke** (1848–1916), to be chief of the Great General Staff in 1906, in succession to Schlieffen (q.v.). His hope was quite misplaced. 'The lesser thinker' (as the nephew self-deprecatingly referred to himself) collapsed under the strain of defeat after the Marne and was replaced by Falkenhayn (q.v.). He had admittedly inherited an unworkable plan (*see* Schlieffen), but, ignoring his uncle's most famous aphorism ('No plan survives the first five minutes' encounter with the enemy'), had persisted in trying to realize it after it had palpably broken down. A great-great-nephew, Helmuth (1907–44), was a principal conspirator against Hitler and executed for his complicity in the July plot.

Moncey, BonAdrien Jeannot de (duc de Conegliano; 1754–1842) Marshal of France. A junior officer of the royal army, Moncey rose quickly under the Revolution and commanded the Army of the Pyrenees, which occupied Navarre and forced the Spaniards to sign peace in 1795. Denounced as a royalist, he did not regain an appointment until 1800, when he fought in the Marengo campaign and commanded the Army of Italy in succession to Brune (q.v.). Napoleon made him inspector-general of gendarmerie and created him marshal in 1804. He had a successful passage in the invasion of Spain in 1808, for which he received his dukedom. In 1814, as commander of the National Guard of Paris, he bravely defended the city against the Allies. Though his refusal to sit in judgement on Ney (q.v.) temporarily lost him the favour of the restored Bourbons after the Hundred Days, he eventually regained all his honours; during the French intervention in Spain in 1823 he conquered Catalonia (*see* Mina).

Monck, George, Duke of Albemarle (1608–70) English soldier and sailor. Perhaps the most successful 'political' general in the English Civil War and its aftermath, Monck stood apart, both geographically and intellectually, from the intellectual ferment of the age. He had served with the Dutch and fought against Spain from 1629 to 1638, and his main activity during the Civil War was concerned with the periphery of the conflict – Scotland and Ireland. At the start of the war he was fighting for the king, but, taken prisoner at Nantwich, he was persuaded to join the Parliamentary army after a stay of two years in the Tower of London. As a general he could not compare with the best of the Parliamentary commanders, as his campaign in Ireland (1646–9) served to indicate, but he had a genius for naval warfare. In 1652 he was appointed one of the commanders of the English fleet in the First Dutch War (1652–4). With Blake (q.v.) he had considerable success, especially in the battle of the Gabbard Bank (1653); he had a strong influence in the formulation of the fighting instructions, which established the line-ahead formation for warships in battle, increasing their effective fire-power by bringing more of their guns to bear, a process analogous to the growth of linear formations in land warfare.

In 1654 Monck returned to Scotland, which he had ruled most effectively since the battle of Dunbar (1650). He was successful in winning the allegiance of many of the more prosperous and economically active Scots for the English connection, so uprisings against English rule by dissidents were easily crushed by him. In Scotland he was outside the squabbles which followed the death of Cromwell (1658), although with a powerful army his would inevitably be a decisive voice. But on New Year's Day, 1660, he marched south, brushing Lambert's opposing forces aside. In London he summoned Parliament and began secret negotiations with Charles II for his restoration to the throne. A grateful king created him Duke of Albemarle, and he occupied all the leading military offices in the state. With the outbreak of the Second Dutch War (1665–7), Monck was in command of the English fleet, which achieved notable success against a strong Dutch fleet brilliantly led by de Ruyter (q.v.). The Four Days' battle and the battle of the North Foreland (1666) were tributes to his skilful leadership; he had no responsibility for the disaster when the English fleet was destroyed at anchor in the Medway, a possibility he had foreseen and counselled against.

By the time of his death Monck had thus served Charles I, Parliament and Charles II; but he was not a plotter or conniver. His government of Scotland showed a brilliant understanding of the political needs of the situation. He flattered the Scots and took great pains to conceal the naked use of English power. He encouraged trade and commercial development, and gently showed the ben-efit of the English connection. In Ireland he was less successful, and he left mass-acres and burnt towns in the wake of his army. In essence Monck was the reverse of the fanatic, and his pursuit of a sen-sible middle course at last achieved the political stability both in England and Scotland, which represented the popular will.

Monmouth, James Scott, Duke of (1649–85) Royal bastard, and pretender to the English throne. The illegitimate son of Charles II, Monmouth was viewed as a possible successor to the English throne, given the overt Catholicism of his uncle James, Duke of York, later James II. Charles acknowledged his bastard, found him an heiress and gave him the title Duke of Monmouth. In 1668 Monmouth was made captain of the king's bodyguard, and he commanded the English contingent on the Continent in the Third Dutch War

(1672–4); in 1678 he was made captain-general of the army in England and beat the rebellious Scottish Covenanters at Bothwell Bridge (1679). But after this success he became involved in the various political manœuvres designed to exclude his uncle James from the throne on the grounds that he was a Catholic, thus making himself the prime candidate. After the death of Charles II, Monmouth landed in open revolt against James II; but he was only able to gather an army of villagers and a few local gentry, in total some 8000 infantry and 1000 horsemen; they faced a royal army of some 3000 under the Earl of Feversham and Marlborough. The result was a rout of Monmouth's force at Sedgemoor (1685); it was then scattered and subjected to savage reprisals by both the army and the civil authorities. The unfortunate Monmouth was found in a ditch, taken to London and executed, although it took five strokes of the executioner's axe to sever his head. It was a wild, foolish adventure, a perfect reflection of its instigator.

Montalambert, Marc René, marquis de (1714–1800) French military engineer. Although Montalambert had considerable practical experience of war, in the service of Sweden and Russia as well as of France, his greatest military achievement was intellectual: to have proposed a system of fortification different from and, given the changed circumstances of warfare, superior to that of the prince of military engineers, Vauban (q.v.). It was known as the polygonal system and consisted in protecting the main body of a fortress by smaller detached forts (*caponnières*). Though rejected by the engineers of his own army, it was widely adopted abroad, notably by the Prussians, and inspired the thinking of the great nineteenth-century engineers Todleben and Brialmont (qq.v.). He also conceived a special sort of coastal fort, high and heavily armed, which was built in numbers on the shores of Europe and America and of which Fort Sumter was an example. His most important publication was *La Fortification perpendiculaire* (1776–86).

Montcalm, Louis Joseph, marquis de (1712–59) French soldier. Montcalm, a soldier trained in the rigorous formal disciplines of eighteenth-century warfare, transferred to the New World, took root and virtually invented a new form of warfare. He never had many men under his command, nor the sophisticated devices of European warfare. What he used to achieve what amounted to a minor revolution was the wilderness of North America as an active strategic principle. Earlier commanders had looked upon the vast forests as hostile wastes, barriers to the proper exercise of war, refuge for Indians and social outcasts. Montcalm recognized that they could guarantee to his operations the quality so often lacking in European war – total surprise. His background was entirely conventional: he entered the army at twelve, fought under Broglie (q.v.) in the war of the Austrian Succession (1740–8), then in northern Italy where he was wounded and captured at Piacenza (1746). In 1747, after his exchange, he was raised to the rank of brigadier in command of a cavalry regiment. In 1756 he was promoted to major-general and sent to Canada with a limited commission.

The British and American settlers were mounting a series of attacks on the French forts and commercial interests – Montcalm's task was to recover the position. His approach was to concentrate, with all his available force, on a single point with as much secrecy as possible. He used Indians and scouts to prepare for his advance, and to lay false tales of his intentions. Late in August 1756 he descended on Fort Oswego, destroyed the garrison and settlement, and gave France, once again, complete control of

Lake Ontario. He wintered at Fort Ticonderoga, and in the autumn of 1757 appeared before Fort William Henry on Lake George with a siege train of thirty cannon, which he had transported by river and hauled over land. The post fell quickly, and the massacre which ensued at the hands of Montcalm's Indian allies horrified him. He made great efforts to stop the slaughter of helpless prisoners, but the news of the massacre served only to increase the awe and horror with which he was beginning to be regarded by British and Americans alike. In reply the British forces were substantially reinforced, and a major effort was made to destroy the French threat. In the spring of 1758 an expedition was successfully mounted against the French outpost at Louisburg, an important strategic loss for the French. In July 1758 an expedition sent against Fort Ticonderoga was rebuffed by Montcalm himself, whose 3000 troops drove off Abercrombie's 12,000 men. But later in the same year another strategic base was lost to the French with the destruction of Fort Duquesne, which was resettled as Fort Pitt, a British forward post; Fort Frontenac fell in the same autumn (1758).

With the loss of these bases Montcalm was forced back on the city of Quebec itself, where possibly the worst of his enemies, the provincial governor Vaudreuil, opposed him in every decision. In the summer of 1759 the British captured Fort Niagara; a day later (26 July) General Amherst (q.v.) with 11,000 men captured Ticonderoga: the French were now firmly pinned back into Quebec. The final expedition against the virtually impregnable fortress city was undertaken by Wolfe (q.v.). The famous ascent of the Heights of Abraham, led by Colonel William Howe (q.v.), was a last-ditch attempt to assault the city before the onset of winter forced the expeditionary force to withdraw. In the event Wolfe managed to locate his 4800 men in front of the walls of Quebec. Montcalm attacked with 4500 men, but without the artillery which would certainly have swung the battle in his favour: Vaudreuil refused him permission to use the fortress guns. In the battle both Wolfe and Montcalm met noble and heroic deaths. France lost a soldier still in his prime, with an open mind and an active intelligence, great tactical skill and a real understanding of the new strategy he had advanced so effectively. The French and Indian war had a profound effect on the British army, which learnt for the first time the new dimensions of war in an empty continent.

Montecuccoli, Raimundo (1609–80) Italian soldier in the imperial service. The eldest son of a noble Italian family, Montecuccoli began his career in 1625, in the midst of the Thirty Years' War, serving under his uncle, Ernest of Montecuccoli. He fought well at Breitenfeld (1631) against Gustavus Adolphus (q.v.) and at Lützen (1634). He distinguished himself at Nordlingen and at the storming of the town of Kaiserlauten, where he led his heavy cavalry through a breach in a wall, a heroic dash which earned him his colonelcy. But at Wittstock (1636) he was captured and held prisoner by the Swedes in Stettin and Weimar; his release in 1642 cost them a heavy defeat, for he trounced a Swedish corps at Troppau. When his native state of Modena went to war, he involved himself on its behalf (1642–4), but afterwards rejoined the Austrian army, fighting with the Archduke Leopold in his campaign against the Hungarian Protestants under George Rakoczy I (q.v.). But it was against the Swedes that he was to achieve consistent success. In 1647 he beat a well-led Swedish force at Triebel and was created a general; the following year he fought a masterly rearguard action which covered the retreat of the shattered imperial army under Peter Melander, beaten by Turenne (q.v.) at the battle of Zusmarshausen and pursued by the eager French and Swedish armies.

When the peace of Westphalia brought an end to a generation of war, Montecuccoli travelled and went to Sweden, where he formed a close friendship with Queen Christina. By now a field-marshal for his success in the Thirty Years' War, Montecuccoli was recalled to face the invading Swedes in the First Northern War (1655–60), and dispatched to aid King John Casimir of Poland. His old enemy, George Rakoczy, entered the war against him, but Montecuccoli resoundingly beat him, before moving swiftly to northern Germany (1657) to join the Great Elector (q.v.) against Charles X of Sweden. They battered the Swedes in a series of rapid victories, and by 1660 the Swedes were ready for peace. The immediate call on Montecuccoli was for defence against the Turks, who were moving forward into Hungary (1657–62). When a great Turkish host advanced in 1663 under Grand Vizier Fazil Ahmed Koprulu (q.v.), Montecuccoli met and defeated it at the battle of the Raab (1664). Here, his brilliant management of his much smaller army routed the much larger Turkish force.

Honours were now heaped upon him as the saviour of Europe: so complete was his victory that the Turks remained at peace for two decades. Montecuccoli was created president of the Imperial War Council, the supreme military body of the Habsburg state, as well as director of artillery. In these positions he was able to indulge his passion for military experiment and reform. Montecuccoli was remarkable by virtue of his success as an 'intellectual' soldier as well as a brilliant battlefield general. His reforms had been long considered. During his captivity he had studied military science, read Euclid and Tacitus, and discovered the architectural writings of Vitruvius.

Convinced of the primacy of fire-power, he introduced, against much opposition, a new and lighter musket, substantially increased the proportion of musketeers to pikemen, and created the grenadiers as an elite infantry group. But he matched the increase in fire-power with a much tighter fire discipline, and greater capacity for the units to manœuvre, so that their offensive quality was improved. He also systematized the whole range of military organization, from the method of pay and provisioning, to the detailed construction and manufacture of artillery.

In 1673 Montecuccoli was called on to lead the imperial armies against the French under Turenne. If anything, his skill had increased during the period of peace. The two men, Montecuccoli and Turenne, were a match for each other; if Turenne was the better tactician, Montecuccoli displayed an impressive capacity for manœuvre. The campaign was one of position, each commander feinting against the other in a series of moves across southern Germany. At the battle of Turckheim the honours went to Turenne, who surprised the imperial army and pursued it across the Rhine. But only once was he able to manœuvre the wily Montecuccoli into a position of real danger, at Sasbach near the Swiss border (1675). But Turenne was killed by a chance cannon ball, and Montecuccoli was able to seize the initiative, driving the French back across the Rhine and pursuing them into Alsace. Here he met another worthy opponent, Condé (q.v.), who had left the command of the Dutch theatre of the war to meet this new threat. Condé advanced in force, and the imperial armies drew back across the Rhine. The final military act of Montecuccoli's career was the siege of the great fortress of Philippsburg, executed with all his usual skill.

In retirement, Montecuccoli found ready acceptance among the intellectual circles of Vienna, and even founded, at the emperor's request, an academy of sciences. In 1679 Leopold I created him, undoubtedly the premier soldier of the Empire, a prince; he died, as the result of an accident, on a visit to Linz in the following year. His great text on war, *Dell'arte militare* is an outstanding work of military science, and his shorter *Memorie della guerra ed instruzione d'un generale* (Venice 1703) was widely read by contemporaries. He was one of the major architects of war in the later seventeenth century, creating the army which Prince Eugen (q.v.) was to use to good effect in the war of the Spanish Succession (1701–14). Montecuccoli had a clear view of the economic factors involved in the great wars in which he participated, expressed clearly in his best-known saying: 'For war you need three things, 1. Money, 2. Money, 3. Money.'

Montgomery, Bernard Law (1st Viscount Montgomery of Alamein; 1887–1976). British field-marshal. A bishop's son, educated at St Paul's (where, in 1943, he was to establish his headquarters for the Overlord operation), Montgomery joined the Royal Warwickshire Regiment from Sandhurst, having failed to pass out high enough for the better-paid Indian army on which, like most unmoneyed cadets, he had set his sights. He had nearly failed to pass out altogether, his conduct at the RMC having been excessively violent, and he persisted in such behaviour as a young officer, his part in smashing up the Bombay Yacht Club on his first posting to India being viewed more gravely than his fellow vandals' because, unlike them, he did not have the excuse of being drunk (he was a life-long teetotaller). The war redeemed his reputation: he was gravely wounded at the head of his platoon in France in 1914, doing so well in the succession of staff jobs he held thereafter that he was a lieutenant-colonel and battalion commander by the armistice. In

1939 he was commanding the 3rd Division, which he took to France and evacuated efficiently from Dunkirk, and he next commanded first V then XII Corps in England. On the death by accident of General Gott, who should have succeeded Auchinleck (q.v.) in command of Eighth Army in the Western Desert, Montgomery was chosen in his place and arrived there in August 1942.

He found a dispirited and under-equipped army waiting to be attacked by an apparently invincible enemy, Rommel (q.v.). With generous reinforcements of men and material, and by his own skills at self-propaganda, he transformed its physical and mental state, blunted Rommel's drive to Cairo in the battle of Alam Halfa, 31 August–7 September (by a plan he probably inherited from Auchinleck), and on 23 October launched his own counter-offensive at El Alamein. After twelve days of heavy fighting, of a highly methodical and orthodox kind, and at the cost of 13,000 casualties, the Eighth Army at last broke through (see McCreery) and drove the Germans and Italians westwards, towards the Anglo-American First Army which had just landed in Algeria. Montgomery's conduct of the battle has been criticized, as has his lack of speed in the pursuit. But it was Britain's first victory of the war and he may rightly not have wished by rashness to put it in jeopardy.

In July 1943, the war in North Africa being over, he led the army to Sicily and then in September to Italy. After he had reached the river Sangro, he returned home to help plan the invasion of Europe (Overlord), for which he had been named land commander under Eisenhower (q.v.). On D-Day he was perhaps unlucky not to capture Caen, which then became the chief focus of fighting, but the rightness of his strategy of attracting German armour to that flank, while the Americans on the other built up their strength for a break-out, was confirmed by its success at the end

of July. However, his overestimation of the completeness of the Allied victory and his insistence on advancing into Germany at the highest speed on a narrow front culminated in the tactical and strategic reverse of Arnhem in September. In December he played a major part in stemming the German counter-offensive in the Ardennes. After the war he was chief of the Imperial General Staff and deputy commander of NATO. It is difficult to isolate in what Montgomery's greatness as a soldier lay: he got on badly with colleagues and allies who often found him rude; he was original neither in thought nor action – though distinctly an original in manner; but his belief in himself and in his relationship with the divine power and his total dedication to efficiency at every level in the formations he commanded made him one of the most successful practical generals of the century.

Montmorency, Anne, duc de (1493–1567) French soldier. One of the leading soldiers of sixteenth-century France, whose long career spanned the Italian wars to the French wars of religion (1562–98), Montmorency served three French monarchs. Brought up with Francis I, he became marshal of France in 1522, after successful campaigning in northern Italy. In 1524 he helped to repulse the imperial assault on the south of France, and in the following year was captured with Francis I at the disastrous battle of Pavia: he was released, and from this point became Francis's chief adviser and main architect of French policy. In 1536 he again crossed swords with Charles V: the emperor advanced from north Italy into France and penetrated as far as Aix-en-Provence, before Montmorency pushed him back across the frontier. In 1538, after peace terms were agreed, he was created constable of France, the highest military office in the state. For a time out of favour, he was recalled to court on the accession of

Henry II (1547), with his influence fully restored.

The first real test of his capacities came in 1557 at the battle of Saint Quentin, when he was forced hurriedly to raise an army to meet a Spanish invasion of northern France. His army was caught, literally, mid-stream while crossing the Somme in an effort to outflank the Spaniards besieging the city; almost half his army of 26,000 were killed or made prisoner, among them Montmorency himself. By the outbreak of the French wars of religion (1562), Montmorency was already an old man and uncertain as to which cause he should support. But he rallied to the Catholic cause, and at the battle of Dreux (1562), at which a Protestant and a Catholic army fought each other virtually to a standstill, he was captured – for the second time in his career. So too was Condé, the Protestant commander; Montmorency was released in 1563. Perhaps the most interesting aspect of Dreux was that here, for the first time, the cavalry used the *caracole*, turning themselves into mounted pistoleers. In 1567, in the second war of religion, Montmorency attacked Condé, who had only 3500 men with him, with a force of 16,000. Condé, with amazing skill and luck, held off the constable's army, and in the course of the battle Montmorency was killed. He died just in time, for new styles were developing in war, for which he had no aptitude.

Montrose, James Graham, Marquis of (1612–50) Scottish soldier. Never commanding more than a handful of men, fighting invariably against superior odds, Montrose's career is, rightly, the material from which heroic legends are created. After an education which developed his substantial artistic and intellectual abilities, he rapidly revealed himself as one of the leaders of Scottish resistance to Charles I's aim to impose episcopacy on Scotland. He was instrumental in the creation of the National Covenant (1638), which provided a united body of opposition to the king, and, eventually, an army to resist him. When the First Bishops' War came (1639), Montrose held a senior command under Leven (q.v.); he struck quickly to frustrate the gathering of Scottish support for Charles and captured Aberdeen. When the town was recaptured, he took it again; and a third time, after he had been forced to withdraw to gather reinforcements in the face of a superior enemy. In the Second Bishops' War in the following year, Montrose commanded the cavalry under Leven, but saw no action, for the English collapsed at the approach of the skilled and effective Scottish army. But while he was clearly a gifted soldier, he was no match for his political enemies among the Covenanters, led by the infamous Argyll (q.v.), who feared his attractive personality and moderate political and religious views. Imprisoned briefly as a result of Argyll's conniving, Montrose after his release became a natural leader of the Royalist cause in Scotland. But Charles did not trust him, and only in 1644, after all his other ploys had failed, and the Scots had entered the English Civil War (1642–6) on the Parliamentary side, did the king accept him. Created captain-general in Scotland (February 1644), but given only 100 men, he soon recruited a small army of 2000 and invaded Galloway, catching the Covenanting forces entirely off guard. The recurrent scenario of the Scottish campaign soon emerged: a brilliant lightning stroke from Montrose, frustrated by lack of resources to maintain his gains. He took the town of Dumfries, but could not hold it against a large force under Argyll. After the Royalist disaster at Marston Moor, he decided to chance everything, including his life, for he had been proclaimed a traitor to the Covenant, in an attempt to slip through enemy lines in disguise to reach a small force of Macdonalds, who had come over from Ireland in support of the royal cause. The gamble succeeded, and he placed himself at the head of a force of 1100 men. With this tiny band of ill-disciplined Highlanders, he routed a Covenanter army six times his size at Tippermuir (1644), using the tremendous attacking force of his wild clansmen to overcome the superior organization and equipment of his enemy. He captured Perth, but the essence of his strategy was to use the Highlands as his base, and to strike at his enemies where they least expected it. Aberdeen fell to him for the fourth time in his career, and he led Argyll's pursuing army in a wearying chase, turning and beating him at Fyvie, before slipping into the mountains. During the winter, he taunted Argyll by attacking him in his stronghold at Inverary, and ravaging his enemy's lands. But the Covenanters believed that he had overreached himself, and set to trap him deep in enemy territory. Again, Montrose, by an epic march through the mountains in the depths of winter, avoided the trap. At Inverlochy (February 1645), he attacked the Campbells and slaughtered them, once again the attacking power of Montrose overcoming vastly superior opponents.

His victories had unhinged the whole strategy of the Covenanters. The Scottish army in England now looked fearfully at Montrose's depredations in their homeland; in Scotland all efforts were concentrated on defeating him. Montrose responded with even greater audacity. With 700 men he snatched the stronghold of Dundee from the Covenanters, and then escaped with all his men. At Auldearn (1645), he outflanked their army under Hurry, snatching a victory from a likely defeat; Alestair Macdonald, in a defence reminiscent of Horatio in his epic 'holding of the bridge', held back the whole weight of the enemy infantry, severing their pikes with his broadsword. At Alford, two months later (July 1645), he outfought Baillie

and the best army to face him so far; marching west, he met Argyll again at Kilsyth, and again the Campbell was forced ignominiously to flee from the battlefield. Glasgow fell to Montrose, and Edinburgh hurried to submit: he was now the master of Scotland.

The king now demanded that he should abandon his tried strategy, and move south to face an army advancing from England under David Leslie, a kinsman of Leven. In unfamiliar terrain, betrayed by his supposed allies, Montrose's forces were surrounded at Philiphaugh (1645) and forced to surrender; they were all put to the sword or saved for later execution. Montrose, who had stayed with his cavalry, escaped to reform his shattered forces. But Charles, for reasons of dubious propriety, now repudiated Montrose in an effort to bring the Scots to his aid in the English Civil War. Montrose, left to fend for himself, without legal sanction, made peace and went into exile. Betrayed by one monarch, he received the same treatment from his son. Returning to Scotland to raise an army for Charles II, Montrose was repudiated by his new master who like his father sought an alliance with the Covenanters. Defeated at Carbiesdale (1650), he escaped the battle, only to be betrayed afterwards into the hands of his enemies. Thereafter, as an acknowledged traitor, his fate was certain, and after unnecessary indignities, he was hanged at the Market Cross in Edinburgh from a gibbet thirty feet high. He had fulfilled his own prophetic hopes for himself, expressed in a poem he had written at the age of seventeen:

So great attempts, heroic ventures shall
Advance my fortune, or renown my fall.

Montrose was a superb natural soldier, one of the finest leaders to emerge during the English Civil War. Although he never commanded a great army in the field, each of his small battles revealed a military talent of the highest order. He enjoyed above all a unique inventiveness, an ability to react to circumstances and to take advantage of opportunities which terrain or natural features could give to him. He worked always with inferior, ill-equipped and frequently disunited forces; yet he managed to mould them, in the heat of battle or in headlong forced marches, to his own will.

Moore, Sir John (1761–1809) British general and military reformer. A Glasgow doctor's son, Moore had made the grand tour in the entourage of the Duke of Hamilton before joining the army, in which he served as a junior officer in America and as a commander at Toulon and Corsica, 1793–4; in the West Indies, 1796; Ireland (where he helped to put down the 1798 rising); Holland, 1799; Egypt, 1801; and Sicily and Sweden, 1802. In 1808 he was sent with an expeditionary force to Spain and in August was promoted to command all British troops there. Napoleon had just undertaken its conquest and his armies much outnumbered Moore's, who was forced into a terrible winter retreat through the northern mountains to Corunna. In the successful action he fought to cover its evacuation from the port, he was killed, his death prompting Thomas Wolfe to write one of the most famous poems in the English language. Although not a great general, his experiments with light infantry tactics and his success in training soldiers in them ensured his abiding influence on the British army, in which he was much loved and whose light infantry and rifle regiments rightly regard him as their founder.

Moreau, Jean Victor (1763–1813) French general. The son of a barrister, for which career he was training at the outbreak of the Revolution, Moreau rose through the ranks of the National Guard to become in 1794 general of division in the Army of the North and, after the arrest of Pichegru (q.v.), its commander. Successively commander of the armies of the Rhine and Moselle, Sambre-et-Meuse and Italy, 1796–9, he assisted Napoleon in the coup of 18 Brumaire and, returning to command of the Army of the Rhine, inflicted on the Austrians the major defeat of Hohenlinden (3 December 1800). Subsequently his immensely ambitious wife, a member of Josephine Bonaparte's circle, persuaded him to intrigue against Napoleon and he was banished. After the Russian campaign he returned to Europe from America and became an adviser to Tsar Alexander I, at whose side he was killed at the battle of Dresden. Moreau rivalled Napoleon in his military talents, which were very great indeed, but not in political canniness.

Morgan, Daniel (1736–1802) American soldier. An outstandingly able commander in the American War of Independence (1775–83), Morgan was commissioned as captain in the Virginian riflemen at the outbreak of the revolution. He took part in the abortive expedition led by Benedict Arnold (q.v.) to Quebec: in the attack at the end of December 1775 Morgan's men penetrated well into the city until forced to surrender to the garrison of Governor Carleton. Morgan was exchanged in 1776 and was able to take part in the campaign that led to Burgoyne's (q.v.) surrender at Saratoga (October 1777). In 1779, stricken with ill health, he resigned his commission and retired to Virginia. But after the success of Cornwallis's (q.v.) Southern campaign (1780) and the extreme danger of the rebel cause in the South, he rejoined Gates (q.v.) under whom he had served at Saratoga, as a brigadier-general commanding a corps. Gates was decisively beaten at Camden by Cornwallis (1780), a defeat which Morgan did something to redeem when, pursued by the troops of Colonel Banastre Tarleton, he rounded on his pursuers at Cowpens (1781) and completely destroyed them. Of 1100 men under Tarleton's command, only 160 escaped from the battle. Morgan's judgement of when and where to fight, his timing and control in the battle were of the highest order. Although the forces engaged on both sides were tiny, it was a considerable achievement.

Morosini, Francisco (1618–94) Venetian admiral. One of the most distinguished families of Venice, the Morosini had a long tradition of service as admirals of the Venetian republic. Francisco Morosini was the most successful of his illustrious dynasty. He served as commander of the Venetian fleet from 1657 and ravaged the Turkish possessions in the eastern Mediterranean, rousing the Turks to fury and an immediate response. In 1667 he was sent to organize and stiffen the defence of Candia in Crete, which was under siege by a large Turkish army. The city held out until September 1669, but a French contingent which formed a vital part of the defence was withdrawn by Louis XIV and Morosini had no option but to surrender. It was an epic defence, but the loss of Candia meant the end of Venetian domination of the Aegean and Crete itself.

Morosini could not be blamed for the loss, despite efforts by his enemies to do so. In 1684 he redeemed the defeat of Candia by an immensely successful expedition into the Peloponnese. His forces were victorious throughout southern Greece and recovered Venetian possessions lost in Dalmatia. The Peloponnesus was captured in 1686; Morosini then advanced through the isthmus of Corinth and captured Athens in the following year. (It was in this campaign that a Venetian shell destroyed the Acropolis, used as a Turkish powder store, and left the ruins known today.) He returned to Venice with a greater record of suc-

cess than any Venetian admiral of the epoch. He was elected doge of Venice on the wave of popular acclaim. At the age of seventy-five he mounted his last campaign in the year of his death, cruising into the Turkish-held Aegean. Such were his power and reputation that the Turks withdrew rather than risk battle. Morosini was a fine tactician, economical in his use of both men and ships.

Mortier, Edouard Adolphe Casimir Joseph (duc de Trevise; 1768–1835) Marshal of France. Of bourgeois origin and the son of an English mother, Mortier's career began in the National Guard. He quickly showed himself a fine fighting officer, was promoted general of brigade in 1799 and, for his conquest of Hanover in 1803, marshal in the great creation of 1804. A corps commander in 1805, where he fought valiantly at Dürrenstein in 1806–7, and in Spain 1808–11, he commanded the Young Guard in Russia and was the last to leave Moscow. He defended Paris in 1814 and would have commanded the Old Guard in 1815 had he not fallen ill with sciatica. He made his peace with the Bourbons after Waterloo, and later transferred his loyalty to Louis-Philippe, at whose side he was killed by Fieschi's infernal machine in the boulevard du Temple.

Moultrie, William (1730–1805) American soldier. Like so many senior officers of the American War of Independence, Moultrie had fought in the Indian wars; when the revolt against the British developed, he joined the rebellion in his home state of South Carolina. In March 1776 he took command of a small post on Sullivan's Island, which commanded the approaches to Charleston, the capital of South Carolina and the only substantial port available in the South. Building a wooden blockhouse and stockade, and field fortifications of sand, Moultrie emplaced his artillery to command the sea lanes. From this tiny redoubt he drove off the full squadron of Admiral Parker (q.v.), after inflicting substantial damage on the British ships (June 1776). In recognition of this extraordinary feat, the tiny post was renamed Fort Moultrie, he received the official thanks of Congress and a post as a brigadier-general in the Continental army. He continued to command in the South, repelling General Prevost's attempt to take Port Royal and himself capturing the town of Beaufort, South Carolina, in the following month (February 1779). But he was forced to surrender when Charleston was captured by Clinton's (q.v.) army (May 1780), and he was a prisoner on parole until early in 1782, when he was exchanged. He participated in the final campaigns of the war, and after its close served as a distinguished governor of South Carolina. His epic defence of Sullivan's Island was an 'amateur' action, for no seasoned artilleryman believed it was possible to hold such a position against a full naval bombardment. He defiantly proved them wrong.

Mountbatten, Louis Francis Albert Victor Nicholas, Earl (1900–79) Some may be born with a silver spoon in their mouths; few are christened in a golden font with names of the Tsar of Russia and the Queen of England. Prince Louis (of Battenberg) had a glittering pedigree, and a driving ambition to succeed by the standards of other men in his chosen career, as a naval officer. The two qualities were often at odds with each other. In a sense, his passion for the British navy was also an inheritance. His father and namesake was First Sea Lord until in the First World War a campaign of abuse about his *German* origins forced him into retirement. Transforming the German Battenberg into its English equivalent, Mountbatten, could not save him. Lord Louis Mountbatten bore a deep sense of

resentment at the unjust treatment meted out to his father; it was the greatest triumph of his life when he too became First Sea Lord in 1955.

Mountbatten lived in two worlds, the more so after his marriage to Edwina Ashley in 1922. Her huge wealth, a great London house, and eventually the Broadlands estate in Hampshire, provided a style of life to which no naval officer could aspire. Mountbatten was a talented and hardworking officer, but he inspired great and often justified suspicion among his superiors. He was never trusted. His equals and inferiors, by contrast, tended to idolize him. He passed up the navy at a slightly accelerated pace, serving much of his time in the glamorous and highly visible Mediterranean fleet. Lord Louis had a very 'modern' approach to naval matters. He became expert in communications, and did much to improve fleet wireless telegraphy, until in 1933 he was given his first command, a destroyer, HMS *Daring*. There and in a succession of other ships, the Mountbatten technique was always the same. His ship had to be the best in the fleet: in 1935, HMS *Wishart* under Mountbatten's command was 'Cock of the Fleet'. He drove his crews hard, but equally lavished care on them that a poor captain could never have afforded.

Mountbatten's great passion was fast cars, driven furiously. He approached his naval career with the same obvious, and unBritish, desire to *win* at all costs. War in 1939 proved him to be outstanding in public relations and 'man management', but a poor sea captain under wartime conditions. His ship HMS *Kelly* spent an excessive time in port undergoing repairs to minor damage which resulted from poor ship handling. More serious damage – and twenty-seven dead from the crew – came when Mountbatten recklessly exposed the *Kelly* to submarine attack. After a major refit, the *Kelly* was transferred to the

Mediterranean fleet, and again under Mountbatten's command, was sunk by German bombers off Crete in May 1941. Characteristically, Mountbatten behaved with great bravery, staying on the bridge of the doomed ship until it sank. This episode was the core of the Mountbatten legend: the happy ship under the command of a great and courageous sailor. It was the plot of Noel Coward's film *In Which We Serve* (1942) a patriotic drama which was received with some cynicism by sailors but thrilled the wartime public at home, and stimulated warm responses in the United States.

Off-screen, Mountbatten's wartime career posed more of a problem. He was not a great seaman, nor a notable strategist. He had won no victories, but had won admiration for his courage in defeat. Most of all he had a lively and creative intelligence which sought out the unconventional, indirect solutions to problems. Moreover, he had the social and political connections essential for success. He went to the United States to oversee the refit of his new command, the carrier HMS *Illustrious*, and instantly became a Press and Radio celebrity. He was summoned back to London by Churchill himself, to work in that essentially Churchillian conception, Combined Operations. This was dedicated to 'hitting back' at the Germans by launching small-scale raids on the European mainland. The task involved liaison between the services, and creating a working unit in an area riven by inter-departmental rivalry.

Combined Operations revealed Mountbatten's great talent. He was a fixer, using diplomacy, flattery, threats and cajolery to achieve his ends. He was also unstoppable, as all those who stood against him were to find. He rarely had angry scenes with those who opposed him: he outmanoeuvred or outsmarted them. Combined Operations did not, in fact, achieve very much, and one operation – at Dieppe in 1942 – proved a disaster. The qualities which Mountbatten had revealed both in success and failure showed him well equipped for the problems of supreme command rather than the day to day issues which occurred at lower levels. Like Eisenhower, the other great success of the war in this role, Mountbatten revelled in a game where there were no rules save those he created. In October 1943, he left England to take up his new post as Supreme Commander in Asia.

The reality of the tasks was less grandiloquent than the title. The Supreme Commander had a difficult relationship with General Stilwell (q.v.), the United States plenipotentiary in China, and many problems with his own, British, subordinates. But Mountbatten ground them down. Over time, Stilwell was recalled, and Lord Louis engineered the replacement of his more difficult British commanders. He also took to the grandeur of life as Supreme Commander. In 1944 he moved his quarters from Delhi to Kandy in Sri Lanka, to be closer to the area of operations in Burma, Malaya and Indo-China. But the vast staff created to sustain this new enterprise was almost 10,000 men and women, and there were many complaints about the opulence and luxury of the lifestyle. It was also suggested that Mountbatten surrounded himself with a travelling group of like-minded cronies, who went with him from command to command. That too was true.

Mountbatten performed best in unconventional circumstances. His armies drove the Japanese from Burma and the other former colonies, French and British, but this owed little to the Supreme Commander. After the end of the war, however, the decisions were essentially political rather than military, and Mountbatten showed that he, unlike the other commanders, recognized the problems posed by dealing with local armies of liberation, unwilling to return to colonial rule. He produced solutions which worked, except in one case – in Indo-China – where the commander on the ground disobeyed his direct orders. In Indonesia, similarly, his instincts were to have the Dutch 'negotiate' with the Indonesians.

At the end of the war, he wished to return to being a simple sailor. In fact, he became the last Viceroy of India, accomplishing the first act of de-colonization. His role in India is being increasingly criticized, with the benefit of hindsight. The reality is that he acted decisively, pursuing a course that he alone determined, under enormous pres-sure both from the British government and the factions in India. His role was not military, but he displayed all the quali-ties of a great commander, in a way which he had never done during war-time. It was the zenith of his achieve-ment. He was still only in his forty-eighth year.

After India, he returned to the navy. There he proceeded upwards towards the summits of his profession, handi-capped still by the deep suspicion that he was a 'champagne sailor'. By 1950, he had a seat on the Board of Admiralty; in 1952 he was appointed to command the Mediterranean fleet. In 1955, he became First Sea Lord, where he insisted in moving his office back to the room which his father had used more than forty years before. As a sailor he could go no higher. But his final appointment harked back to the days at Combined Operations, where he had fumed at senseless inter-service rivalries.

In 1958 he became the second holder of the new post as Chief of the Defence Staff; the first Chief had foundered on the rocks of military and naval vested interests. Over six years Mountbatten accomplished a root-and-branch recon-struction of British defence, adapting it to the political, military and economic conditions of the day. Even he could not overcome the entrenched conservatism of his most senior colleagues (as so often

before in his career, his ideas struck home with the less senior officers); but he gained the high ground. The course of reform has followed more or less along the lines laid down by Mountbatten.

In 1965, he retired, to indulge his hobbies. With Mountbatten, this in-cluded planning his grand State Funeral, rewriting (and even recreating) history to set himself at the centre of the picture, and to enjoy his new appoint-ment as Colonel in Chief of the Life Guards. He died by violence at sea, blown up not by a shell or torpedo from an enemy ship, but by a terrorist bomb. It was an unexpected end to an improbable life.

It is hard to pin down Mountbatten's significance as a military leader. In retrospect, his weaknesses and petty qualities seem to dominate. But what he possessed were the classic military virtues: courage, implacable determin-ation, energy and enthusiasm, and good luck allied with charm. He created roles for himself and filled almost all of them with success. The art of being a Supreme Commander is an aspect of invisibility: working and manipulating behind the scenes, massaging egos, re-buking without hurting or offending, and taking brutal, unpleasant decisions without inner doubts. In all these arts, Mountbatten excelled, and in conse-quence, he was a great Supreme Com-mander, in war, and even more so, in peace.

Mountjoy, Charles Blount, Baron (1562–1606) English soldier. A politi-cal and military rival of the Earl of Essex, Mountjoy succeeded where Essex failed. He served first against the Span-ish in the Netherlands, and he accompa-nied Essex and Raleigh on an expedition to the Azores, hoping to catch the annual Spanish treasure fleet. His eyes, however, had been on an appointment in Ireland, which had been in a state of rebellion since 1594. In August 1598 the Irish leader Hugh O'Neill, Earl of Tyrone (q.v.), defeated the English army under Sir Henry Bagnal at Yellow Ford, and a sustained offensive became essential. The appointment went to Essex, however, and relations between the two men reached a low ebb. But Essex failed disastrously and was recalled: Mountjoy took over his command. In 1601 a Spanish force of 4000 men under Juan d'Aquila arrived at Kinsale, and it was there that Mountjoy met the combined Spanish and Irish army (Tyrone had brought all his forces south from Ulster and attempted to relieve the Spanish whom Mountjoy had besieged in the city). In open battle the Spanish–Irish army was completely outmanœuvred by Mountjoy's cavalry, and the Irish fled. O'Neill returned to his strongholds, but the backbone of the rebellion was broken. He surrendered to Mountjoy six days after Queen Elizabeth's death in 1603 and was given clemency by James I on Mountjoy's urgent appeal. In 1603 a grateful monarch created Mountjoy Earl of Devonshire.

Mukhtar, Ahmed (1839–99) Turkish general. During the Russo-Turkish war of 1877–8 Mukhtar defended Erzerum and Kars, for which he received the title *ghazi* (victor), a trifle surprisingly, for the honours in that theatre of war went to the Russians.

Muley Hacen (Abul Hassan; *d.* 1484). Granadine sultan and warrior. The last ruler of a truly independent kingdom of Granada, in the most fertile region of southern Spain, Muley Hacen came to the throne in 1466 and was faced immediately with extreme danger from many external enemies, Moslem rulers as well as the Christian kingdoms to the north. He attacked along his western borders with Cordoba (1470), moved against Malaga (1474) and launched attacks to the east against Murcia three years later.

Much of this warfare was in the tradition of the border warfare endemic on the frontier for centuries, but by means of his campaigns Muley Hacen was able to protect his frontiers more successfully than his predecessors.

His first major enterprise was to launch an attack on a strong fort at Zahara near Ronda (1481), the first move in a massive attack on the Catholic monarchs Ferdinand and Isabella. It was a dangerous move to make, for the inherent strength of the kingdoms of Castile and Aragon was much greater than that of Granada. But he believed (correctly) that they would soon be in a position to attack his kingdom and thus dispose of the last independent Moslem state in the peninsula. However, his own position was complicated by an involved dynastic struggle with his brother and his son, Boabadil; it was a situation which the Christians soon used for their advantage. But meanwhile Muley Hacen had beaten Ferdinand at Loja (1482) and the Christians had retired to prepare a stronger attack.

A delicate peace was arrived at, whereby Boabadil (who had been captured in 1483 and sworn fealty to the Catholic kings) was to occupy the throne of Almeria while his father continued in Granada itself. In reality the Christians held the balance as soon as they were strong enough to press ahead with the conquest. They were soon able to raid the kingdom with impunity, for Muley Hacen, old and almost blind, could no longer undertake the defence of the kingdom: he abdicated in favour of his brother Abdullah el Zagal, who promptly murdered him. He was buried on the peak of the highest mountain of his kingdom, which now bears his name. Under his rule Granada had a final flowering, both in military and cultural terms, before its final humiliation at the hands of the Christians. His son's reign after Abdullah was brief and entirely ignominious.

Münnich, Burkhard Christoph, Graf von
(1683–1767) German soldier in the service of Russia. A leading exponent of Russia's expansion in the East, Münnich came to Russia in 1721, after service in the French and Polish armies. In 1728 he was appointed commander-in-chief of the Russian army by Peter II and promoted yet again by the Empress Anna to field-marshal and president of the war council in 1732. In 1733 he commanded the force of 30,000 Russians which entered Poland in the war of the Polish Succession (1733–8), and captured Danzig in the following year. But his main interest lay in Russia's expansion against the Turks.

In 1736 he led an army of 58,000 into the Crimea. The campaign was not a success. His army was riddled with disease, and no proper lines of supply could be developed: Münnich lost 30,000 men before he retreated. In the following year, when he raided deep into the Turkish-held Ukraine, he was again struck by epidemics and was forced to withdraw. At the battle of Bendery (1738) he was forced by firm Turkish opposition to abandon an attempt to cross the Dniester river, and he withdrew again, leaving half his army sick, dead or dying, together with much of his artillery. Only in the following year did he succeed in bringing the Turks to battle, and achieved a decisive victory. At Khotin (1739) his army of 68,000 beat 90,000 Turks, advanced through Moldavia, scattering the Turks as they went, and prepared to launch an offensive on Constantinople. But the Austrians, Russia's allies in the war, now made a separate peace with the Turks, and Russia was forced to open hurried negotiations for a settlement if they were not to face the Turks alone. The Russians retained the crucial port of Azov, and Münnich's reputation (despite the early reverses) was high in St Petersburg. He had paved the way for Russia's further expansion in the south-east.

On his return to St Petersburg Münnich became involved in the complicated dynastic manœuvring which followed the death of the Empress Anna, and he ended in exile in Siberia (1741). He was released from constraint nineteen years later to spend his last years in the service of Catherine the Great. His problems in the war with Turkey were a result not so much of faulty generalship, but the inevitable consequence of campaigning so far from his base; but he was lucky not to have been attacked by the Turks when at his weakest. His reputation thus owes as much to the inertia and indolence of his enemies as to his own abilities.

Murad (1750–1801) Egyptian Mameluke chief. Murad's army was defeated by Napoleon at the battle of the Pyramids but after a dispute with his Ottoman overlords he held aloof from the fighting at Heliopolis and later allied himself with Desaix (q.v.) against them. He died of plague while marching to relief of the French in Cairo.

Murat, (Prince) Joachim (grand-duc de Berg et de Clèves, roi de Naples; 1767–1815) Marshal of France. The son of an innkeeper, Murat was educated for the church, though a less likely candidate for the priesthood is difficult to imagine. On his expulsion from the seminary of Toulouse he joined the cavalry and, after five years in the ranks, was commissioned in 1792. In 1795 he brought the guns to the Tuileries with which Bonaparte fired the 'whiff of grapeshot' on 13 Vendémiaire, ended the royalist counter-revolution and established himself as a major political figure. He was to enjoy the young general's bountiful favour thereafter, becoming a general of brigade in the Army of Italy in 1796 and of division during the Egyptian expedition (on which he was severely wounded). In 1800 he also became Napoleon's brother-in-law, by his marriage to Caroline Bonaparte. But it was on the field of battle, and at the head of light cavalry, that he continued to justify Napoleon's esteem for him.

Murat commanded a major cavalry formation in each of the great campaigns from 1800 to 1807 and, though his contempt for staffwork and for most of his fellow marshals (he had been promoted in 1804) made him dangerous to employ in independent operations, his superb courage and tactical sense in action always cancelled out his strategic mistakes: at Essling, in 1807, he led a mass cavalry charge which transformed the battle from a certain disaster for the French into a semi-victory. He had been created a sovereign grand duke after Austerlitz and, after a short sojourn in Spain (during which he suppressed the *Dos de Mayo* rising), he became king of Naples (1 August 1808). He was thus spared the necessity of fighting Wellington and was provided with enlarged opportunities for designing the extravagant uniforms in which he always paraded. He commanded the cavalry on the Russian expedition and the whole of the Grand Army after Napoleon's departure ('*A vous, roi de Naples*'), but thereafter devoted himself chiefly to his kingdom. He changed sides in 1814 in order to keep it and back again in 1815 for the same reason. He lost it to the Bourbons after Waterloo none the less and, attempting his own Hundred Days, was captured and executed. Vain to the last, he ordered the firing-squad, 'Spare my face, aim at the heart.' Although by no definition a great general, or even a particularly good soldier, Murat was the supreme personification of the *beau sabreur* who magnetizes his men's loyalty by excelling all in bravery and who (sometimes) wins a kingdom with his sword. He had many imitators in what remained of the era of cavalry warfare.

Muraviev, (Prince) Nicholas Nikolaievich (1794–1867) Russian general. As a young officer Muraviev led an expedition to Khiva (later to be annexed to the Russian empire), fought in the 1828 war with Turkey, took part in the repression of the Polish insurrection of 1830–1, and in 1832 successfully undertook a mission to Mehemet Ali (q.v.) of Egypt to urge him to war against Turkey, during which he commanded the soldiers aboard the fleet sent to Constantinople. In the Crimean War he led the expedition to Kars, which, after a heroic defence, fell to him on 26 November 1855. He was consequently authorized to append *Karski* to his name.

His brother **Mikhail Muraviev** (1795–1866) acquired notoriety for his harshness in helping to repress the Polish insurrection of 1831.

A cousin, **Nicholas Muraviev** (1810–81), was in 1857 the conqueror of the Amur region of Siberia from China, for which he was authorized to append *Amurski* to his name.

Murray, Lord George (1694–1760) Jacobite soldier. An able commander, certainly the best leader possessed by the Jacobites in the rebellion of 1745, Murray's skills could not overcome their enormous organizational deficiencies. Murray began his career as an officer in the British army in 1712, but his obvious Jacobite sympathies and his barely concealed support for them during the 1715 rising made him a marked man. He fled to the Continent and remained in exile for nine years, returning to Scotland in 1724 and gaining a pardon in the following year. But in 1745 he revealed himself in his true colours, this time as a commanding general of the Jacobite army. Edinburgh was captured, and Murray routed an English army under Sir John Cope at Prestonpans (September 1745). The Scots moved south, spreading panic, until indecision paralysed them at Derby. There was great uncertainty as to whether they should march on

London, given that there had been no popular uprising in their favour (as they had expected), or whether they should return to Scotland. The latter course was followed, and Murray organized the withdrawal.

Much of the spirit and fighting zeal had left the clansmen and an atmosphere of gloom persisted. This partially lifted when, again under Murray's able direction, they trounced another Hanoverian army, under General Hawley, who had taken Edinburgh in their absence. But Falkirk (January 1746) was the last Jacobite victory. Cumberland's (q.v.) army caught up with them at Culloden, near Inverness, destroying the army and the Jacobite cause. Murray had been against the decision to fight at Culloden, believing that the Highlands, territory they knew well, would give them natural advantages over their enemy, in particular reducing the advantage his artillery gave to him. But Culloden (April 1746) spelt the beginning of the end for traditional Scotland; Murray, who had retreated into the interior, took ship for the Continent and died in exile. Had the army been securely his to command, the outcome both of the English campaign and the Scottish sequel might have been entirely different.

Murray, James (1721–94) British soldier. Born a Scot, Murray entered the British army in 1740 and made his reputation serving in Canada. He was sent to North America in 1757 as a lieutenant-colonel and commanded a brigade at the capture of Louisburg by Abercrombie in the following year; Wolfe (q.v.), one of his fellow officers in this outstandingly successful campaign, arranged for his appointment to the Quebec expedition, and again Murray showed great competence during the assault. Once the city had been taken he was made military governor of the area around Quebec; after the treaty of Paris (1763) ceded Canada to Britain, he was appointed governor of the province. Having adopted a sensible policy of reconciliation with the French Canadians, whom he had hoped to turn into loyal supporters of the British crown rather than a constant threat in any future war, he left this post in 1768, his enemies having accused him of mismanagement of the province's affairs. He took up the less important post of governor of Minorca in 1774. There he was attacked by a strong French and Spanish force in 1782 and forced to surrender. His position was not nearly so defensible as that of Gibraltar, which Sir George Elliott had been successfully defending for three years against a large army under de Crillon, but he was court-martialled (unjustly); he was acquitted, however, and promoted to general. An able subordinate of Wolfe, he achieved less prominence than some of his colleagues in the Quebec campaign.

N

Nadir Shah (1688–1747) Shah, tyrant and conqueror. From humble origins as a simple Turcoman tribesman, Nadir rose to become shah of Persia and to recreate a Persian empire stretching from the heart of India to the borders of Turkey. In seventeen years, from 1730 to 1747, he waged a series of wars which expanded the somewhat elastic boundaries of Persia in every direction. Defeating the Turks at the battle of Hamadan (1730), he smashed the Turkish army sent against him and occupied Iraq and Azerbaijan. Next he marched east and destroyed a threat to his eastern frontier. He flirted with Russia against Turkey, beat the Turks again at Baghavand (1735) – after some earlier reverses – and secured a favourable peace (1736) in return for remaining neutral in any new conflict between Russia and Turkey.

Elected shah in 1736, Nadir conquered Afghanistan in the following year, taking Kandahar after a nine-month siege (1738). After the conquest of Afghanistan he moved into India, avoiding a defending Mogul army in the Khyber Pass and attacking them from the rear. He then moved south, seizing Peshawar and Lahore, and securing the key points in northern India. He enticed the Mogul emperor Mohammed II into battle at Karnal, defeated him and occupied Delhi. Returning to Persia with a huge fortune and dominion over all of India west and north of the Indus, Nadir next attacked the khanates to the north of Persia (1740), incorporating them in his empire, but he failed to subdue the mountain tribes of Georgia (1741), one of his few failures. In 1743 war with Turkey was resumed with a Turkish invasion: Nadir defeated them at the battle of Kars (1745) and occupied Armenia. But in 1747, after concluding a most satisfactory peace with the Turks, he was murdered by his own bodyguard. His death was greeted with rejoicing by his subjects, for he was a man given to the most abominable cruelty as a ruler. His conquests soon collapsed – the empire he had established had no lasting qualities, and much of his power was illusory.

Nagumo, Chuichi (1886–1944) Japanese admiral. Having commanded the carrier force since before the war, it was Nagumo's First Air Fleet which carried out the attack on Pearl Harbor, 7 December 1941. In 1942 he supplied air cover for the capture of the Dutch East Indies, raided Ceylon in March and in June fought the American carrier fleet at the battle of Midway (*see* Spruance). His superiority ought to have given him the victory, but a tactical misjudgement at the height of the battle put his ships at the mercy of American dive-bombers, which destroyed three out of his six carriers in a few minutes. This disaster reversed the balance of naval power in the Pacific and initiated Japan's decline. Nagumo committed suicide in June 1944 when Saipan, of which he was ground commander, fell to the American marines.

Nana Sahib (properly Dandu Panth; 1825–59?) Indian general. Adopted son of the last peshwa of the Mahrattas,

Baji Rao, Nana Sahib was denied the succession and its attached pension by the British on his foster father's death. The outbreak of the Mutiny of 1857 gave him the opportunity to avenge his grievance in a particularly terrible form: persuading the Cawnpore mutineers not to join the main body at Delhi, he laid siege to the entrenchment that the British commander Wheeler had improvised and, when its garrison was induced to surrender by promises of safe conduct, massacred men, women and children alike. His army was subsequently defeated by Havelock at Fatehpur, Aong and Cawnpore itself (12–16 July 1857) and he fled to Nepal: the date of his death is not known. British revulsion at news of the massacre principally motivated the counter-atrocities of the campaign of suppression.

Napier, (Sir) Charles James (1782–1853) British general. He had a distinguished career as a junior officer in the Peninsula, was British military resident in Cephalonia, 1822–30, where he met Byron and was offered but declined command of the Greek forces in the War of Independence, and commanded in the North of England during the Chartist disturbances of 1839. But he made his name in India after 1841, principally for his conquest of the province of Scinde where, on 17 February 1843, 2800 soldiers under his command defeated 30,000 Baluchis at Miani. He subsequently pacified and administered the province, in the process managing to quarrel with everyone of importance in India and at home, while retaining nevertheless his reputation as the greatest Indian general of his day.

His brother, General (**Sir**) **William Francis Patrick Napier** (1785–1860), served very bravely in the Peninsula, commanding the 43rd Light Infantry at Salamanca, but derives his reputation from his great *History* of the war (six

volumes, 1828–40). He was also his brother's biographer.

A first cousin, (**Sir**) **Charles Napier** (1786–1860), led a career in the Royal Navy not incomparable to that of Cochrane (q.v.): as captain of a frigate in the Azores in 1833, he accepted command of the Portuguese constitutionalists' fleet and with it destroyed that of the Miguelite party; during the civil war on land he directed the defence of Lisbon in 1834, for which he was created Count Cape St Vincent, but was struck off the (British) Navy List. He was subsequently restored but during the Crimean War, as admiral commanding the Baltic fleet, declined to attack Cronstadt, despite his success at Bomarsund (*see* Baraguay d'Hilliers), and fell into disgrace.

Napier, Robert Cornelis (1st Baron Napier of Magdala; 1810–90) British field-marshal. Educated at Addiscombe, Napier joined the East India Company's army as an engineer officer and took an active part in almost all its campaigns between 1845 and 1859: in the Sikh wars he fought at Mudki, Ferozeshah (wounded), Sobraon, Multan (wounded) and Gujrat; during the Mutiny he took part in the first relief of Lucknow, directed the defence until the second relief and then the capture of the town from the mutineers, in the final stages defeating and capturing Tantia Topi (q.v.). He went on the 1860 expedition to China and in 1867, having been commander of the Bombay army since 1865, was ordered to raise the Abyssinian expeditionary force to free British subjects who were being held captive by the Emperor Theodore. The expedition, culminating in their release at Magdala, 13 April 1868, was a brilliant success, a model among Victorian minor colonial campaigns. For it he was ennobled and promoted commander-in-chief in India.

Napoleon (Bonaparte) (1769–1821) Emperor of the French. Born at

Ajaccio, Corsica, into a family of the island's minor nobility, he was sent to France for his education at the age of ten on a government bursary given as a reward for his father's adherence to the newly imposed French regime. The schools he attended, at Brienne and Paris, though military in name, offered a gentleman's rather than a soldier's training. His military education, for which he had prepared himself by his voracious private reading, did not really begin until, as a young artillery officer, he came under the influence of the Baron du Teil, brother of the well-known writer on tactics, at Auxonne. Moreover, he was not, despite the outbreak of the Revolution and the declaration of war upon it by the dynastic powers, to acquire any direct military experience until its fourth year when, on his family's expulsion from Corsica by the anti-republican Paoli, he was found by patrons the post of artillery commander in the siege of Toulon, then also in rebellion against the republic. For his part in bringing the siege (September–December 1793) successfully to an end, he was promoted general of brigade and given command of the artillery of the Army of Italy. Because of an association with Robespierre, however, his career suffered a setback during the Thermidorean reaction and then by his refusal to fight during the Vendée war. It did not revive until October 1795, when Barras, who had known him at Toulon, used him to put down the royalist rising of 13 Vendémiaire in Paris. As a reward he was given command of the Army of Italy, which he joined in March 1796.

He found it ragged, hungry and dispirited, and its veteran generals (*see* Augereau, Masséna, Sérurier) by no means ready to accept his unproved leadership. Yet he almost at once inspired the imagination of them all and within eighteen months had led them to victory against the Austrians and the Piedmontese and made the whole of northern

Italy French. Setting out first to separate and then to defeat in detail his two enemies, he beat the Austrians under Beaulieu (q.v.) at Montenotte, 12 April, and the Piedmontese at Mondovi, 21 April. On 10 May he beat Beaulieu again at Lodi (from which word of his bravery in leading a column across a bridge over the river Adda spread through Europe) and advanced to make the Piedmontese surrender and conclude peace at Milan on 21 May. The Austrians remained at war; but his victory over the newly arrived Würmser (q.v.) at Castiglione, 5 August 1796 (*see* Augereau), kept them on the defensive and he inflicted another severe defeat on them at Arcola, 15–17 November. On 14 January 1797 he defeated Alvinczy (q.v.), who had replaced Würmser, at Rivoli, one of the greatest victories of the twenty years of war, and went on to invade Austria, despite the efforts of the Archduke Charles (q.v.) to stop him. When he was within 25 miles of Vienna (6 April), the Austrian emperor sued for peace.

He was now a substantial enough figure in national circles to choose for himself his next strategic scheme. Hence the Egyptian expedition (1 July 1798) by which, through the menace it would offer in the direction of India, he hoped to bring Britain also to make peace. But it was a project which French naval inferiority made over-rash; he was lucky to get his army to Egypt without interception (*see* Nelson) and its marooning, as a result of the battle of the Nile (*see* Brueys), was not offset by the brilliance of his victories over the Mameluke rulers of the country (battle of the Pyramids, 21 July 1798) or their Turkish overlords (Mount Tabor, 17 April 1799 and Aboukir, 25 July). Conscious of the campaign's growing pointlessness, and dispirited by his failure to capture Acre (*see* Sidney Smith), he left the army to Kléber (q.v.) and escaped home.

He arrived just in time to provide Sièyes, the increasingly distracted leader of the Directory, with the political 'sword' for which he had been searching to restore the authority of the republic. Through his organization of the coup of 18 Brumaire (9 November 1799) against the renascent royalists, he rose to the position of first consul and achieved that effective control of France which he was to hold until 1814. His wish now was for peace and though in pursuit of it he and his subordinates were to win great victories over the Russians (Zurich, 25 September 1799 – see Masséna) and the Austrians (Marengo, 14 June, and Hohenlinden, 3 December 1800 – for the latter, see Moreau), these were battles of diplomatic calculation rather than aggression, fought to regain or protect territory, not to conquer it. His strategy was rewarded by the Russians' withdrawal from the anti-French coalition and the conclusion of peace with the Austrians (February 1801) and the British (March 1802).

The peace was shortlived. In May 1803 he resumed against Britain the hostilities which were to last until 1814 and in which she was to be joined (or rejoined) passim by the Austrians, Russians, Prussians, Spanish and Portuguese. Within a year of the resumption, Napoleon (the Bonaparte was now dropped) was to proclaim himself emperor and within two years to embark on the most spectacular of his campaigns: against Austria in 1805 (victories of Ulm, 17 October, and Austerlitz, 2 December), against Prussia in 1806 (victories of Jena and Auerstadt, 14 October) and against the Russians, who had also fought at Austerlitz, in 1807 (drawn battle of Eylau, 8 February, victory of Friedland, 14 June). After a two-year peace, instituted by the treaty of Tilsit with Russia, he again went to war with Austria, suffered the first serious defeat of his career at Aspern-Essling, 21–2 May 1809 (see Archduke Charles), but redressed it by the shattering victory of Wagram, 5–6 July.

Yet, despite the vast scale of these wars, and the military lustre which they added to his name, Napoleon the Emperor was in many respects less the soldier than had been General Bonaparte. He took a diminishing share in the direction of the battles themselves, which he left increasingly to his subordinates, interesting himself more in the strategy which made his victories possible, but looking chiefly to the political results which they would yield. Given his responsibilities as absolute ruler of the most powerful state in Europe, it is only natural that that should have been so. But from 1809 onwards, his anxieties or ambitions led him to persist in military endeavours or undertake adventures which his soldier's judgement should have warned him were fruitless or dangerous.

The long drawn-out campaign in Portugal and Spain (November 1807–April 1814) typifies the first; the invasion of Russia in 1812 the second. Napoleon visited Spain only once, for long enough to send packing the army of Moore (q.v.); thereafter he left command in the country to his marshals, none of whom could bring to an end either the guerrilla war waged by the Spaniards or the semi-amphibious campaign conducted by the British under Wellington (q.v.). He went to Moscow himself, though he had not intended to go so far, but his arrival in the capital did not bring the peace he had expected, nor did his presence on the Russian battlefields (Smolensk, 7 August, Borodino, 7 September) bring decisive victory. As a result of these military mismanagements, he lost two armies, one slowly in Spain, the other almost overnight in the eastern snows. With what remained to him, he was able to play out the war on foreign territory for another year (victories of Lützen, 2 May 1813, battle of Bautzen, 20–1 May, victory of Dresden, 26–7 August) but his Austrian, Russian and Prussian enemies eventually so outnumbered him that at Leipzig (the 'Battle of the Nations', 16–19 October) his inexperienced troops were overwhelmed and he was forced to fall back on France.

The return of adversity rekindled Napoleon's tactical flair. At Hanau, 30–1 October, his defeat of Wrede (q.v.) won him the time to make an ordered retreat to the Rhine. And through a series of small but brilliantly timed blows against his pursuers on the soil of France itself (against Schwarzenberg, q.v., at Brienne, 29 January 1814, and La Rothière, 30 January; against Blücher, q.v., at Champaubert, Montmirail, Château-Thierry and Vauchamps, 10–14 February; again against Schwarzenberg at Montereau, 18 February, and finally against Blücher at Craonne, 7 March, Laon, 9–10 March and Rheims, 13 March), he seemed set, if not to regain the initiative, at least to stave off defeat indefinitely. By now, however, his enemies had learnt to see through the fog of his strategic wizardry to the lack of substance beyond and pressed forward undeterred. He and his lieutenants were defeated outside Paris (Arcis-sur-Aube, La Fère-Champenoise, 20 and 25 March) and one of them, Marmont (q.v.), was persuaded to allow the allies entrance. Abdication and exile to Elba followed.

The Hundred Days – encompassing his return from exile, resumption of power and hostilities against the allies, attack on and defeat by the British and Prussians in Belgium and final flight into captivity – began on 1 March 1815. The army, the loyalty of whose officers and veterans he had never lost, rallied to him as soon as he landed at Fréjus from Elba (but see Ney), and his initial deployment of it into Belgium caught the allies separated and off guard. On 16 June he defeated both the Prussians and the British, at Ligny and Quatre Bras, and, expecting the Prussians, as prudence dictated, to fall back into Germany, moved to destroy the British, whom he cornered at Waterloo on 18 June. He had, how-

ever, miscalculated, for Wellington's stout resistance and Blücher's loyalty in marching to his aid resulted in an envelopment – one of his own favourite manœuvres – from which he could not extricate his army. It and his career were destroyed together. He placed himself in the hands of the British, who sent him under guard to the loneliest island of the Atlantic, St Helena.

It was impossible, none the less, for Napoleon to be forgotten, as man, emperor or soldier. Indeed as a soldier, his influence was to persist, in only slowly diminishing strength, into the twentieth century. Much of what is called the 'Napoleonic military innovation' can be shown to have roots in the work or thoughts of others: to Guibert, Bourcet and du Teil, for example, he owed most of his ideas on mobility and on the combination of all arms in a single formation. He was also the beneficiary of certain economic and industrial developments which would have eased the path of anyone wishing to make war on a 'Napoleonic' scale at that particular time – notably the recent improvement in the European road network and the increased productive capacity of the French arms industry, while his ability to raise armies depended upon the rigorous registration and administration of the population introduced by the Revolution. But it is true of any innovator that he is in the debt of his predecessors. Napoleon was a genuine original in his ability to see what was new and important in his own world, and to adapt and integrate his discoveries, discarding at the same time what was no longer of any value. His supreme synthetic achievement was the *bataillon carré*, the corps of all arms (*corps d'armée*), so disposed on the march that it might instantaneously deploy into battle formation no matter in which direction it encountered the enemy. His supreme operational achievement was to integrate, once his *corps d'armée* were on the march, the prodrome, action and follow-up of a battle, so that it was fought exactly when and where he chose, and yielded exactly the results he wanted from it. His failure was in creating no machinery through which the 'Napoleonic secret' could be transmitted to future, less talented commanders than he. It would take Jomini, Clausewitz (qq.v.) and many others years of work to isolate in what exactly his secret lay and the genius of a Prussian (see Moltke) to create a body – the Great General Staff – which could translate it into dependable battlefield routines. By the time it learnt to do so, the force of the secret had been dissipated by its overwide dissemination, through catchphrases about 'seizing the initiative' and 'maintaining the offensive', and 'Napoleonic' battles – which is what the Marne and the Aisne (see Joffre and Moltke the Younger) were intended to be – which resolved themselves into pointless stalemates. A twentieth-century Napoleon, one surmises, would have grasped at some other method than warmaking to achieve his objects.

Narvaez, Ramon Maria (1800–68) Spanish general. Springing to prominence for his bravery as a young officer under Mina (q.v.) in the resistance to the French invasion of 1823, Narvaez inflicted a crushing defeat on the Carlist forces at Majaceite, 1838, in the First Carlist War. He was later drawn wholly into politics, becoming the chief rival of Espartero (q.v.).

Navarre, Henri Eugène (1898–1993) French general. Succeeding Salan (later to lead the 'revolt of the generals' against de Gaulle) in command in Vietnam, Navarre conceived and implemented the Dien Bien Phu operation. Its failure, marked by the fall of the 'aero-terrestrial base' on 7 May 1954, effectively ended the first Indo-China war, 1946–54, and French rule in the area.

Negrier, François Oscar de (1839–1913) French general. After escaping from Metz in 1870, Negrier commanded a battalion under Faidherbe (q.v.), later campaigned against dissident tribes in Algeria and in 1884 led the offensive to expel the Chinese 'Black Flags' from upper Tonkin (Vietnam). His success was compromised by the loss of his major prize, the citadel of Langson, after he had been wounded. News of the citadel's fall brought down the government of the imperialist Ferry, but the offensive nevertheless greatly contributed to the French conquest of Indo-China.

Nelson, Horatio (1st Viscount Nelson, Duke of Bronté; 1758–1805) British admiral. A Norfolk parson's son, Nelson entered the navy in 1770, served much in the West Indies until 1787 (when he married a widow), was on half-pay, 1787–93, and then appointed to command the *Agamemnon* (sixty-four guns) in the Mediterranean. The next twelve years were to bring him greater glory than any other sailor has ever won. During the campaign in Corsica, 1794, he was blinded in the right eye at the siege of Calvi, but recovered to act as commodore of an independent squadron, 1795–7. Under Jervis (see St Vincent) he played a major part in the great victory of Cape St Vincent, 13 February 1797, for which he was knighted and promoted rear-admiral. Later in the year, at Santa Cruz, Tenerife, he lost his right arm in a rash attempt to capture the port by *coup de main* but, healed and reappointed the following April, he went in May to command the blockading squadron off Toulon. The French fleet therein escaped, while he was making good storm damage to his ship *Vanguard*, and got Bonaparte's army safe to Egypt, but, after a nerve-racking and brilliantly conducted pursuit, Nelson caught it in Aboukir Bay (see Brueys) and destroyed it (battle of the Nile, 1 August 1798). His success was due to his recognition that the French had discounted the possibility of an attack from inshore because of its risks, which he nevertheless was prepared to take: for his victory he was created Baron Nelson of the Nile. He was next ordered to Naples, which had fallen into French hands, recovered the city, for which he was made Duke of Bronté in Sicily by the Neapolitan king, and then took up residence at his court in Palermo, from which he directed the naval blockade of Egypt and Malta and began a famous romance with the British ambassador's wife Lady Hamilton.

Home to England in 1800, Nelson led an expedition which destroyed the immobilized Danish fleet in Copenhagen harbour on 2 April 1801; it was during this battle that he raised his telescope to his blind eye to avoid seeing his superior's signal to break off the uncompleted action (*see* Parker). It was for this battle also that he was created viscount, having just before it been promoted vice-admiral, the highest rank he was to hold. He had now separated from his wife and was established in a *ménage à trois* with the Hamiltons. On the collapse of the peace of Amiens in 1803, he left them to command the blockade of the French fleet in Toulon, from which Villeneuve (q.v.) successfully broke out – a necessary preliminary to Napoleon's plan for the invasion of England – and escaped to the West Indies in April 1805. Nelson failed to intercept him, both turned back and Villeneuve made a junction with the Spanish fleet and took shelter in Cadiz. Fearing supersession, Villeneuve then led his and the Spanish fleet to sea, where they were intercepted by the British and overwhelmed in the battle of Trafalgar, 21 October 1805. Nelson himself received a fatal musket shot from the mizzen top of the *Redoutable* and died at the moment of victory. Its completeness was due to his carefully prepared and highly unorthodox plan of 'breaking the enemy line from the windward' in two columns, led by himself and Collingwood (q.v.), which then laid themselves along the Franco-Spanish ships but upwind of them so that their escape was impossible. Nelson was not only a great tactical innovator and naval strategist of genius; he was an extraordinary human being, whose effect on his close subordinates was mesmeric and on the sailors in his ships almost as intense: 'The power to arouse affection and the glow indicating the fire within are noted by all who ever looked Nelson in the face.' Moreover, just as Napoleon's achievement supplied Clausewitz (q.v.) with the raw material for his theory of war, Nelson's intuitive understanding of the nature of naval strategy expressed in his campaigns provided the foundation for the theories of Mahan (q.v.).

Ney, Michel (duc d'Elchingen, prince de la Moscowa; 1769–1815) Marshal of France; 'the bravest of the brave'. The best-loved and remembered of Napoleon's marshals, Ney was an Alsatian ('the son of the barrel cooper of Sarrelouis') who had enlisted as a trooper of hussars in 1787. Being able and brave – how brave he would shortly demonstrate – he was commissioned soon after the outbreak of the Revolution, but his climb to the heights was slower than that of some others, e.g. Brune and Soult (qq.v.) who were both generals by 1794. He was not promoted general until August 1796, after much service as a cavalry leader on the Sambre, Meuse and Rhine, and was still only a general of division in 1799. His part in the victory of Hohenlinden (*see* Moreau) decisively elevated him, however, from the ruck of the merely competent and, having briefly and provisionally commanded the Army of the Rhine in 1799, in 1802 he was given the Army of Switzerland, with which he induced peace between Switzerland and France. He was created marshal in the great promotion of 1804. In 1805 he commanded 6th

Corps, employed Jomini (q.v.) as his ADC, lending him the money to publish his *Traité des grandes opérations*, and blocked the escape of Mack (q.v.) from Ulm to Elchingen (hence his first title). In 1807 the fighting of his corps at Eylau and Friedland in each case greatly contributed to the victory.

He was next in Spain where, like all Napoleon's marshals, he did badly, fell out irretrievably with Masséna (q.v.) and was sent home early in 1811. In 1812 he commanded 3rd Corps in the invasion of Russia and the rearguard in the retreat; it was his conduct then that won him from Napoleon the title '*le brave des braves*' (the soldiers called him '*le rougeaud*' – 'ginger' – for his red hair and redhead's temper). He was the last Frenchman to leave Russian soil. In 1813 and 1814 he served the emperor well in the campaigns of Leipzig and France (he was wounded for the sixth time at Lützen), but at the first restoration he rallied to the Bourbons. Sent to recapture Napoleon on his return from Elba, and promising to 'bring him back in an iron cage', he changed sides as soon as he felt Napoleon's spell and was given command by him of the left wing in the invasion of Belgium. He led it at Quatre Bras; at Waterloo he effectively commanded the whole army, which he led in person, to no detectable plan. He had four horses shot under him and left the field only after he had failed in every effort to get himself killed. Arrested by the Bourbons for treason, he was tried by his peers, who included five fellow marshals, and shot in the Luxembourg gardens on 7 December. He himself gave the firing party its orders. Three of his four sons became generals of the Second Empire, a grandson a general of the Third Republic.

Nicholas Nicholaievich, Grand Duke (1856–1929) Russian general. Son of Grand Duke Nicholas Nicholaievich (1831–91), who commanded during the Russo-Turkish war of 1877–8, grandson of Tsar Nicholas I, nephew of Alexander II and uncle of the last tsar, Nicholas II, he was very widely experienced in the administration and command of the Russian army, though up to 1914 he had seen action only during 1877 and then briefly. Nicholas II appointed him commander-in-chief on 1 August 1914 at the entreaty of his advisers, appalled by the tsar's expressed intention of exercising command in person, and he held the post throughout the period from Tannenberg to Gorlice-Tarnow. When in August 1915 Nicholas II made good his threat to exercise supreme command, Grand Duke Nicholas was sent to the Caucasus where, against his showing in Poland, he proved very successful, capturing from the Turks the whole of Armenia. At the outbreak of the February revolution, the tsar reappointed him commander-in-chief, an immensely popular move, but the provisional government cancelled it at once. He took no part in the Civil War, left Russia in 1919 and died in exile.

Nicholson, John (1822–57) British general. The son of an Irish doctor, Nicholson was appointed originally to the Bengal army, with which he fought in the First Afghan War, but subsequently transferred to political service under Lawrence (q.v.) in the Punjab. His manner of administration of the Bannu district – personal, impartial, direct and when necessary absolutely ruthless – became legendary both with the British and the Indians, some of whom later deified him as Nikalsain (the sect is said to survive to this day). On the outbreak of the Mutiny in 1857, he disarmed the sepoy regiments in the Punjab without hesitation and persuaded his superiors to let him form a 'Movable Column' to put down mutiny wherever it arose; it was at its head that he destroyed at Trimmu Ghat and the river Ravi large parties of sepoys hastening towards

Delhi. He himself then went there to reinforce the beleaguered besiegers on the ridge and led the main assault on the city, 14 September 1857, in which he was killed. Nicholson was not God but he believed that God and he were in communion, which made him the most effective anti-mutineer of 1857.

Niel, Adolphe (1802–69) Marshal of France. A Polytechnicien, Niel led one of the assaulting columns in the capture of Constantine in 1833, and in 1854 helped to capture Bomarsund (*see* Admiral Napier) from the Russians (in the little-known Baltic campaign of the Crimean War). He commanded the 4th Corps at Solferino and Magenta in 1859, and in 1867 became a reforming minister or war, introducing the successful *Chassepot* rifle to the French army and setting up the *gardes mobiles* reserve.

Nimitz, Chester Williams (1885–1966) American admiral. An Annapolis graduate, Nimitz served as chief of staff of submarines during the First World War. In the Second World War he was appointed to command the Pacific fleet shortly after Pearl Harbor, and it was he who accepted battle at Coral Sea and Midway (May and June 1942). The Americans' crushing victory in the latter battle, besides dooming Japanese naval power in the long run, led immediately to his success in winning back the Solomons and in the following year the Gilberts and then (February 1944) the Marianas. The battles of the Philippines (Leyte Gulf), Iwo Jima and Okinawa crowned his success. Nimitz was a skilful inter-service diplomatist, as he needed to be with MacArthur (q.v.) as a principal collaborator.

Nivelle, Robert Georges (1856–1924) French general. Promoted very quickly from command of an artillery regiment to that of a corps between 1914 and 1916, Nivelle then recaptured Fort Douaumont, whose loss in the opening phase of the battle of Verdun had greatly depressed the French, by a clever and novel tactical combination of infantry and artillery. Claiming that his method was of wider application ('I have the secret'), he was chosen in December 1916 to replace Joffre (q.v.) as commander-in-chief on the western front and at once undertook the planning of an offensive (generally known by his own name) which was to achieve, on his word, '*rupture*' (breakthrough). So convincing were his arguments, delivered as fluently in English (his mother's nationality) as in French, that Lloyd George, whose confidence in Haig (q.v.) was less than total, agreed to subordinate the British armies to his operational authority, thereby provoking one of the most spectacular civil–military rows of the war. The Nivelle offensive, delivered on the Chemin des Dames ridge above the river Aisne on 16 April 1917, proved a bloody fiasco and was the precipitatory cause of the refusal of fifty-six French divisions to undertake further attacks (the '1917 mutinies'). He was relieved within the month and replaced by Pétain (q.v.).

Nogi, Maresuke (1849–1912) Japanese general. A Samurai, Nogi was one of the first officers of the Europeanized army, fought in the suppression of the revolts of the Samurai clans of the Aisuki and Satsuma, took part in the capture of Port Arthur in the Sino-Japanese war of 1894–5 and became governor of Formosa, which he pacified. In 1904 he was appointed to command the Third Army and directed the siege and capture of Port Arthur. He then took part in the battle of Mukden. On the death of Emperor Mutsuhito, he and his wife committed ritual suicide.

Nungesser, Charles Eugène Jules Marie (1892–1927) French fighter ace. Third-ranking of French fighter aces of the First World War, Nungesser was credited with forty-five victories. He had learnt to fly before the war, was seriously wounded several times in combat but survived to the armistice, only to disappear in the Atlantic, trying to fly it from east to west.

O

O'Connor, (Sir) Richard Nugent (1889–1981) British general. Commissioned into the Cameronians (Scottish Rifles), he was serving in 1940 as commander of the 7th Division in Palestine. At the behest of Wavell (q.v.), he was promoted to command Western Desert Force (later the Eighth Army) and with it launched, in December 1940, against the Italian invaders of Egypt under Graziani (q.v.), one of the most successful surprise counter-offensives of the war, driving them back into Libya and taking 130,000 prisoners. He was later himself taken prisoner while reconnoitring too far forward and held until the capitulation of Italy in 1943. He then commanded VIII Corps in the liberation of north-west Europe.

O'Donnell, Josef (conde de La Bisbal; 1769–1834) Spanish general. A descendant of Irish émigrés, he was one of the few Spanish soldiers to win a victory against Napoleon's invaders (La Bisbal, 1810). In 1822 he defended Madrid against Bessières (q.v.) in the second French invasion, but was accused of treason by his officers and fled to France.

His son **Leopold O'Donnell** (1809–67) was a political opponent of Espartero (q.v.), minister of war 1854–6, and successful soldier. He captured Tetuan (Morocco) for Spain in 1859, for which he received a dukedom. He had already corruptly made himself a fortune as captain-general in Cuba, 1844–8.

O'Higgins, Bernard (1778–1842) Chilean soldier and liberator. Son of an Irish–Spanish governor of Chile, he was educated in England and on his return took up the cause of independence. Initially defeated by the Spanish at Rancagua, 7 October 1814, he and San Martin (q.v.) together won in February 1817 the victory of Chacabuco, which confirmed Chile's independence. Its security was assured by the naval victories of Cochrane (q.v.), sailing his flagship *O'Higgins*, whose namesake was proclaimed dictator. He was overthrown in 1823.

Oku, Yasukata (Count; 1846–1930) Japanese field-marshal. He commanded a division in the war with China, 1894–5, and, in 1904–5, the Second Army against the Russians, whose right flank he turned at the battle of Liaoyang.

Omar Pasha (formerly Michael Lattas; 1806–71) Turkish general. A Croat, he deserted the Austrian army to enter Ottoman service, becoming a Moslem to do so. He found quick promotion and was widely employed to suppress revolts within the empire – Albania 1843; Kurdistan 1846; Bosnia 1850–2. At the outbreak of war with Russia, October 1853, he defeated the Russians at Oltenitza, helped to raise the siege of Silistria the following year, but was disgraced for his failure to relieve Kars in 1855 (*see* Muraviev). Nevertheless he was re-employed in the invasion of Montenegro, 1861, and in the repression of the Cretan revolt, 1866–8. In 1867 he was promoted commander-in-chief.

Orléans, Ferdinand Philippe Louis Henri, duc d' (1810–42) French general.

Eldest son of Louis-Philippe (king of the French, 1830–48). Educated at the Polytechnique, he took a considerable part in the conquest of Algeria. He is best remembered fo re-raising the light infantry battalions of the French army, originally known (1842) as the Chasseurs d'Orléans.

Orlov, Aleksey Grigoryvich, Count (1737–1808)　Russian soldier. The younger of the two Orlov brothers (his elder brother Grigory was a lover of Catherine the Great), he was instrumental in organizing the military coup which replaced Peter III with his wife Catherine on the Russian throne, and in arranging for the murder of Peter after his deposition. Immediately after the coup, a grateful empress raised Orlov to the rank of major-general, and he was given command of the Baltic fleet. He sailed with it into the Mediterranean and defeated the Turks at the naval battle of Chesme (1770), off the island of Chios. Much of the credit belonged to Samuel Greig, a Scottish naval officer in Orlov's command who controlled the action, but Orlov was welcomed in St Petersburg as a hero and further honours were showered upon him. A more congenial employment was the seduction aboard his ship, at Livorno in Italy, of a potential female pretender to the throne, after which she was carried away to imprisonment in Russia. After this dramatic finale to a career full of action, Orlov retired to breed racehorses.

Ormonde, James Butler, Duke of (1665–1745)　British soldier. A High Tory who ended his life as an avowed Jacobite, Ormonde served in the wars of William III as a soldier, and in Ireland as lord-lieutenant under Queen Anne. In 1711, after the change of administration which resulted in Marlborough's dismissal, Ormonde took command of the English troops serving in the Netherlands, with orders to engage only in

defensive operations; no inkling was given to England's allies of this change of plan. The direct result was Eugen's (q.v.) defeat by Villars (q.v.) at Denain (1712). In 1714 Ormonde was removed from his command on the accession of George I, for his avowed support of the Stuarts made it impossible to leave him in so sensitive a position. In 1715 he was impeached by his Whig enemies and he fled to France, thereafter meddling in Jacobite conspiracies. With the failure of his schemes he retired from active sedition and settled in Spain.

Osman, Pasha (1837–1900)　Turkish general. He commanded an army in the war with Serbia in 1876 and subsequently against the Russians at Plevna, from which he so menaced their advance into Bulgaria that they were forced to halt and attack the city. His engineer Tewfik had so fortified it that all their assaults failed and it eventually fell only after a long siege conducted by Todleben (q.v.), the foremost military engineer of the day. Osman attempted to break out, was wounded and captured. After the war he reformed the Ottoman army, of which in 1897 he became commander-in-chief.

Ott, Peter Karl, Freiherr von (1738–1809)　Austrian general. In the Italian campaign of 1800 he caught Masséna (q.v.) off guard, drove him into Genoa and forced his capitulation after a long siege (4 June). On 9 June, however, his army was defeated by Lannes (q.v.) at Montebello.

Oudinot, Nicolas Charles (duc de Reggio; 1767–1847)　Marshal of France. The son of a brewer of Bar-le-Duc, he was a private soldier of the royal army until the Revolution, when he advanced rapidly to command of a brigade in 1794. He served as chief of staff to the Army of Switzerland in 1799 and of Italy in 1800; under the Empire he was promoted marshal (1809) and reached command of a corps (2nd, in Russia). But it is as a fighting soldier that he is remembered: Napoleon in 1807 introduced him to the tsar as the 'Bayard' of his army. He was wounded twenty-two times in action.

His son, **Charles Victor Oudinot** (1791–1863), captured Rome from Garibaldi (q.v.) in 1849.

Outram, (Sir) James (1803–63) British general. The son of a naval surgeon, he joined the Indian army in 1819, served widely on the frontiers of Bengal, pacifying unsubdued territory, raising troops from the tribes and carrying on a variety of warlike operations: in 1842 C.J. Napier (q.v.) called him the 'Bayard of India' (though they were later to quarrel). In 1854 it was he who, as resident at Lucknow, organized the annexation of Oudh, an act which led directly to the Mutiny of 1857. In that year he was directing operations in Persia (battle of Khushab), but was recalled to take command of the two divisions in Lower Bengal. Joining forces with Havelock (q.v.), to whom he subordinated himself, they together effected the first relief of Lucknow. He commanded the garrison until the second relief by Campbell (q.v.) and then held the city in check until the third relief and final recapture, in which he took a major share. For his part he was promoted lieutenant-general and created baronet.

Oyama, Iwao (marquis; 1843–1916) Japanese field-marshal. A Samurai, he took an active part in the restoration of the emperor in 1868 and in the suppression of the reactionary Satsuma revolt of 1877. In the interim he had observed the Franco-Prussian war, and as minister of war (1880) and chief of staff (1882) did much to advance the Europeanization of the Japanese army. In 1894 he commanded the Second Army against the Chinese and captured Port Arthur from them (for which he was promoted 'marshal of the empire'). In 1904–5, as commander-in-chief, he directed the battles of Liaoyang, the Sha-Ho, Sandepu and Mukden.

P

Palafox y Melzi, José de (duque de Sara-gossa; 1780–1847) Spanish general. In the uprising of May 1808 against the French invaders he was proclaimed captain-general of Aragon by the people of Saragossa, which he defended in two long sieges: 15 June–15 August 1808, and 20 December 1808–20 February 1809. At the end of the second he was forced to capitulate to Lannes (q.v.). He was subsequently a prominent anti-Carlist.

Palikao, Charles Guillaume Marie Apol-linaire Antoine Cousin-Montauban, comte de (1796–1878) French general and politician, Palikao bore simply the name Cousin-Montauban until 1860, when he was put at the head of the French military expedition to China (the British was led by Sir James Hope Grant, q.v.) and there earned the title by which he was afterwards known. On the outbreak of the Franco-Prussian war (1870) he became prime minister, formed the Army of Châlons after the initial defeats and put Paris in a state of defence. He was swept from power by the capitulation of Napoleon III.

Pappenheim, Gottfried Heinrich, Graf zu (1594–1632) German mercenary in the imperial service. Pappenheim was born a Lutheran, but became a Catholic, and, by profession, a mercenary cavalry commander of considerable talent. His early experience as a soldier was gained in Poland, where he learnt the tra-ditional tactics of the Polish cavalry, using sword, lance and a mad gallop at the enemy, rather than the more fashionable *caracole* where the cavalryman became merely a mounted pistoleer. Pappenheim served the Catholic League, led by Maxi-milian I of Bavaria, and soon gained a reputation of being a ruthless pillager. He was a difficult subordinate, as Wal-lenstein (q.v.) discovered, since he was always pursuing his own ends rather than the objectives laid down by his commander. In 1623 he was promoted colonel of his own regiment, the Pappen-heim Cuirassiers; his men worshipped him, partly for his tremendous courage as a leader, partly because they lived well on the pickings of his conquests. He fought through the Bohemian cam-paign at the start of the Thirty Years' War (1618–48) and in northern Italy. In 1626 he was summoned back from Italy to crush a peasant uprising in Upper Austria, which he achieved with sum-mary brutality. He captured the town of Wolfenbüttel in 1627, and went on to even greater success when he stormed and sacked Magdeburg (which Tilly, q.v., his commander, did not believe could be taken): 25,000 of the inhabit-ants were slaughtered.

At Breitenfeld (1631), however, Pap-penheim discovered that the Swedes of Gustavus Adolphus (q.v.), and in particu-lar his splendid Finnish cavalry, were much tougher enemies than any he had met before. His horsemen charged re-peatedly, only to be driven back by musket salvoes and cavalry charges. Pap-penheim's men broke under the pressure and fled, although they regrouped later under his furious orders and covered the retreat of Tilly's army, which had done little better. In April 1632 Tilly was killed, and Pappenheim, who had become an imperial general, came under the orders of Wallenstein. Despite pursuing his own ends and resisting attempts at co-ordinated action with Wallenstein's army, he was summoned to join Wallenstein at Lützen, arriving on 27 September 1632. He was then dispatched to Halle, some way off, with a substantial body of cavalry. When it became clear that the Swedes intended to attack Wallenstein in his positions at Lützen, an urgent message was sent to Pappenheim to rejoin the main camp. Arriving at a crucial moment after battle was joined, the power of the attack by his fresh troops began to turn the battle against the Swedes. But a stray cannonball mortally wounded him and he was carried off the battlefield in a cart. His cavalry, without their charismatic leader, panicked and then withdrew. The advantage swung back to the Swedes. At that moment Gustavus himself was killed leading his horse, and Pappenheim heard, before he died, the news that his greatest opponent had preceded him.

Parker, (Sir) Hyde (1st Baronet; 1739–1807) British admiral. Son of another admiral of the same name, he distinguished himself in American waters during the War of Independence (*see* Moultrie), but is chiefly remembered for hoisting at Copenhagen, 2 April 1801, the signal to 'discontinue action' to which Nelson (q.v.) turned his blind eye.

Parma, Alessandro Farnese, duque di (1545–92) Spanish soldier and administrator. The son of Charles V's illegitimate daughter Margaret of Austria, Parma, like his cousin Don Juan (q.v.), was educated for a high position by Philip II, in honour of his father's wishes. Similar in character, impatient with external restraints, the two cousins also shared the experience of the battle

of Lepanto (1571), where Parma fought with great skill and daring in the bitter hand-to-hand struggles which dominated the battle. After Lepanto he reluctantly returned to the boredom and idleness of married life in Parma. In 1577 Don Juan, who was governor of the Netherlands, asked Philip II to send Parma to serve under him, and it was Parma's timely arrival with reinforcements and his zest in battle which produced a decisive victory for the Spanish over the Dutch rebels at Gembloux. It was Parma who led the cavalry charge, headed by lancers, which smashed the Dutch infantry and harried them in their headlong retreat. His appointment to the Netherlands was a masterstroke. He knew the country well, for he had spent much of his youth and childhood there (his mother was the regent for some twenty years). Many of his friends and acquaintances were now the leaders of the rebel camp, and he had great insight into the attitudes and motives behind the rebel cause.

After Don Juan's death in 1578, Parma stepped up to take his place. Because of his special knowledge of the country, he tried a new approach. By personality he had none of Alva's (q.v.) stern hatred of rebels or savage enmity for heretics, attitudes which had done so much to harden the spirit of revolt between 1567 and 1573. He knew that much of the opposition to Spain was disunited and that many loyal subjects had been forced into opposition by the excesses of Alva's Council of Blood. Thus, on the one hand, he waged a military campaign of consummate skill; on the other, wooed the natural leaders of Flemish society, hoping to detach them from the hardline opposition in the north. In May 1579 he signed a peace agreement with the southern Catholic nobles at Arras; he made many concessions, and hindered his capacity to make war in the short term. But he had neutralized the opposition in the south and was able to concentrate his assaults on the core of Protestant opposition, which had counteracted his peace of Arras with a union of Utrecht among themselves. He had a small army, only 27,000 men, but he deployed it skilfully, concentrating on reducing the cities still in rebel hands, and waging war with traditional brutality against his avowed enemies. Maastricht fell after a siege of four months (which cost him 4000 men) and 8000 of its inhabitants were massacred. Tournai fell in 1581 and Parma established his headquarters there. Bruges, Ghent and Ypres surrendered in 1584, and finally, late in the same year, the great siege of Antwerp was begun.

Throughout these years of campaigning Parma followed a deliberate strategy: to undertake only those operations for which he had adequate strength and to isolate each centre of enemy resistance. Thus, it was only in 1583, after the arrival of reinforcements from Spain and a careful policy of re-equipment, that he moved decisively on to the offensive. He cut communications between Brussels and Antwerp and secured the small ports through which the Protestant towns had been supplied. His aim was to strangle Antwerp, by cutting it off from its hinterland and from the sea. The inhabitants, led by Philip de Marnix, had created a series of elaborate fortifications designed by an expert engineer, Gianibelli. Parma constructed a barrage of boats to sever the city from the sea, and invested it with all his available forces. Finally, in August 1585, starvation forced the city's surrender: citizens with fearful memories of the Spanish fury and the massacres of 1576 found the terms moderate. Parma's aim was the strictly limited one of bringing the south back to obedience, not of waging a crusade against heretics. His campaign had been helped by the murder of William of Orange (q.v.), the Protestant leader, in May 1584, which dealt a temporary body blow to the rebel cause.

However, the opportunity to carry the campaign into the north was lost, to Parma's fury, for Philip's preoccupation with the conquest of England, and his insistence on Parma's intervention in the French wars of religion, turned his armies south. This proved the salvation of the Protestant cause, allowing Maurice of Nassau (q.v.), Orange's son and successor, to consolidate his position and retrain and regroup his men. Maurice was a great organizer, and the success of his methods was seen in the campaign which he launched in 1589 while Parma was occupied in France. He took Breda in a surprise assault, and in the following year, 1591, Zutphen and Deventer, after sieges of amazing brevity. Although Parma turned back to meet him, he was ordered south again, and Maurice, in a brilliant campaign, took Hulst and Nijmegen (1591). Parma, seeing all his successes squandered by Philip's policy, lost heart. He was wounded in the arm during a skirmish at Caudebec, and soon after fell ill and died. His plans for the conquest of the Netherlands died with him.

Philip II was never willing to allow his soldiers free rein, and it was his interference and suspicions which frustrated Parma's campaigns. Like his cousin, Don Juan, Parma fell under Philip's disfavour. He was blamed for the failure of Philip's pet scheme, the invasion of England, in 1588. Support from Spain dwindled, and he was forced to pay his army from his own pocket when threatened with mutiny. He never faced Maurice of Nassau in a major battle, and it is difficult to know who would have had the best of such an encounter. In many ways they were alike: a strong grasp of strategy when the difficulties of early modern warfare made such planning almost impossible, an offensive spirit (stronger in Parma's case), and immense skill in the predominant warfare or siegecraft. But Parma's claim to be the greater soldier is strong.

He lacked Maurice's genius for training men, and his grasp of logistics, but he compensated for it by a subtlety in his approach, which enabled him to succeed with inferior forces, both in numbers and equipment. He also brought to the war an Italian cunning in his diplomacy, dividing his enemies by political manœuvre, using the results of military intelligence to undermine the opposition. But most of all he brought a love of battle into a war dominated by the stately progress of siege and manœuvre. If anything characterized him, it was the headlong charge at Gembloux, which was his first contribution to the war for the Netherlands.

Paskievich, Ivan Fedorovich (count of Erivan, Prince of Warsaw; 1782–1856) Russian general. A Ukrainian, he entered the army in 1800 through the Imperial Corps of Pages and was promoted lieutenant-general for his conduct at Leipzig, 1813. In the Persian war of 1825–8 he won the battle of Ganja (Kirovabad), captured Erivan (for which he was allowed to append 'Erivanski' to his name) and obliged Persia to sign the treaty of Turkomanchi. He took a major part, after the death of Diebitsch (q.v.), in the suppression of the Polish rebellion (1831) and of the Hungarian insurrection of 1848–9. In 1854, after war with Turkey had broken out again, he invaded Bulgaria and laid siege to Silistria, but was obliged to raise it by threat of Austrian intervention (9 June). He was, from 1825 to 1850, the 'dominating influence in the Russian army'.

Patch, Alexander McCarrell (1889–1945) American general. Appointed to command American troops on Guadalcanal in the Solomon Islands, South Pacific, 9 December 1942, Patch achieved the distinction of winning the first American land victory of the Second World War. On 15 August 1944 the Seventh Army, of which he had been given command, landed in the south of France and advanced, more or less unopposed, up the Rhone valley to Alsace (Operation Anvil-Dragoon), and subsequently defeated the German Army Group G in the battle of the Saar, 15–26 March 1945.

Patton, George (1885–1945) American general and tank commander. Educated at West Point and commissioned into the cavalry, Patton first made his name in the fighting on the western front by the American Expeditionary Force in 1918. He instantly recognized the promise of the tank, was promoted to command a tank regiment and highly decorated for his exploits. Between the wars, when the American army showed itself even more hostile to the concept of armoured warfare than the British or French, he continued to believe in the tank as the weapon of future land warfare. His first chance to experiment with armoured forces on a large scale came with the invasion of North Africa in November 1942, in which he acted as Eisenhower's (q.v.) deputy. He commanded the US II Corps in the Tunisian campaign and was promoted to lead the Seventh Army in the invasion of Sicily. Once landed on the island, he became impatient with the subordinate role he had been allotted and embarked on a self-declared race with Montgomery (q.v.) for the capture of Palermo. Shortly afterwards, an overpublicized incident, in which he accused a shell-shocked soldier of cowardice, led to his suppression. His talent and dynamism ensured, however, that he was restored to command the Third Army during the invasion of north-west Europe and he proved an excellent choice. No other American – or indeed British – commander of the Liberation Army had his flair for seizing an opportunity and when in July 1944 he was offered the chance of breaking out of the Normandy bridgehead and encircling the German defenders, he embraced it enthusiastically. The advance which followed carried him to the Seine and, almost without securing permission, he crossed it to harry the remainder of the German army to the West Wall, not scrupling to acquire the necessary supplies by subterfuge. He argued at the time, and latterly, that had he been given the administrative priority granted to Montgomery, advancing on the northern front, he would have reached the frontier of the Reich before the winter broke, and perhaps ended the war. Rationed for supplies, his advance halted and he was forced to fight a stalemate battle throughout the autumn. His quick reactions nevertheless were crucial in reversing the ill-effects of the German Ardennes offensive of December 1944 and in the spring counter-offensive he rediscovered his secret of lightning advance to reach Czechoslovakia, covering a greater distance than that of any other Allied army commander. He was killed in a road accident in Germany in December 1945.

Patton was not a great thinker, and does not stand beside Fuller, Liddell Hart or Guderian (qq.v.) in the history of the development of tank warfare. But he was one of its greatest practitioners and kept the idea of armoured attack alive in the American army during one of its most defensive-minded periods.

Pau, Paul Marie César Gérald (1848–1932) French general. Passing out of Saint-Cyr in 1869, he lost a hand in the battle of Froeschwiller against the Prussians in the following year. On 10 August 1914 Joffre (q.v.) recalled him from retirement to command the newly created Army of Alsace, with which he recovered part of the province lost to Germany in 1871 – the only French general to capture territory from the enemy in 1914.

Paulus, Friedrich (1890–1957) German field-marshal. As the son of a minor civil servant, Paulus belonged to that 'aristocracy of character' that Wilhelm II called on in the 1890s to supplement the aristocracy of birth with which hitherto his army had been officered. An efficient regimental (111th Infantry) and staff (Alpenkorps) officer during the First World War, he fought with the Freikorps on the eastern border during the postwar troubles, was accepted by the 100,000-man army, received general staff training, transferred to the panzer arm at its formation and in 1939 was appointed chief of staff to the Tenth (later Sixth) Army under General Reichenau (q.v.). In May 1940 he was appointed *Oberquartiermeister I* (deputy chief of the general staff) under Halder (q.v.) and in January 1942 replaced Reichenau (promoted to replace Rundstedt, q.v., at Army Group South) at the head of Sixth Army in Russia. During the summer campaign he directed its advance to Stalingrad and the battle for that city and maintained its defence after it was encircled by the Russian counter-offensive. However, when called upon by Manstein (q.v.) in early December to organize a break-out to meet his rescue column, he failed to do so, claiming that he had inflexible orders from Hitler not to leave the Volga. Opinion differs as to what latitude he had been left by Hitler, who made him a field-marshal on 30 January 1943 and declared his name 'infamous' when he abandoned his hopeless resistance the following day. In captivity he joined the Russian-sponsored Free Germany Committee, later broadcast appeals to the German armies to cease fighting and after the war settled in the Soviet zone of Germany. Hitler's judgement on his surrender was that it proved Germany paid 'too much attention to the development of the intellect and too little to the development of character', in which, as applied to Paulus, there may well have been some truth.

Pélissier, Aimable Jean Jacques (duc de Malakof; 1794–1864) Marshal of France. One of the bravest spirits of the conquest of Algeria, Pélissier actually managed to see action in the last days of the First Empire, as well as in the invasions of the Morea and Spain. A strong supporter of Napoleon III's *coup d'état*, he went to the Crimea as commander of the 1st Corps, then replaced Canrobert (q.v.) as commander-in-chief. It was due to his energy that the Malakov, strongpoint of the Russian defences of Sebastopol, was eventually taken (8 September 1855). He was created marshal and duke for the achievement.

Pellew, Edward (1st Viscount Exmouth; 1757–1833) British admiral. He was the first frigate captain of the French revolutionary war to capture (1793) a French frigate (for which he was knighted), and in 1797 he won a celebrated fight, with another frigate captain, over the French battleship *Droits de l'Homme*. In 1804 he went as admiral to command the fleet in the East Indies where, in 1807, he destroyed the local Dutch fleet. He was appointed commander-in-chief in the Mediterranean in 1811 and in 1816 won international renown and a viscountcy for his bombardment of Algiers, on the ruler's refusal to abolish the enslavement of Christians.

Pemberton, John Clifford (1814–81) American (Confederate) general. Although a Pennsylvanian, he went south in 1861 and was promoted lieutenant-general in command of the central Mississippi in October 1862. Thus it was he who had to face Grant (q.v.) during the Vicksburg campaign, in which he was completely outgeneralled, though his subsequent defence of the fortress during a starvation-siege was brave and well conducted. Its surrender on 4 July 1863, the day following Gettysburg, was almost as severe a blow to Southern morale as that defeat, and militarily more injurious, for it put the North in command of the Mississippi and cut the Confederacy in half.

Penn, Sir William (1621–70) British admiral. A leading British admiral, first in the service of Parliament and then of Charles II, Penn was responsible for codifying British naval tactics. He served Parliament at sea throughout the Civil War (despite a brief period of imprisonment for suspected Royalist sympathies). In 1654 he offered to deliver the fleet to Charles II for use in a restoration attempt, but the plan came to nothing, and in the following year he led the expedition which captured Jamaica. At the Restoration he was knighted and appointed a commissioner for the navy: his secret diplomacy with Charles II had reaped its due reward. Working closely with James, Duke of York (q.v.), later James II, he aided him in his attempts to reform the fleet and naval administration and was the creator of the code of naval tactics which formed the basis of the 'Duke of York's Sailing and Fighting Instructions'. As a sailor and tactician, he was not the equal of his colleagues Blake and Monck (qq.v.).

His son **William Penn** (1644–1718) was responsible for the foundation of the state of Pennsylvania.

Percival, Arthur Ernest (1887–1966) British general. Appointed to command in Malaya in April 1941, he was obliged to order the retreat to Singapore Island from the mainland on 27 January 1942, under pressure from Japanese attackers (*see* Yamashita) whom his own troops outnumbered, and to surrender on 15 February, the greatest humiliation suffered by the British army in the Second World War.

Pérignon, Catherine Dominique, marquis de (1754–1818) Marshal of France. A nobleman and an officer of the royal army. Pérignon passed via the National Guard into the service of the Revolution. He saw some fighting in the Pyrenees, 1793–5, and in Italy, where he was wounded and taken prisoner at Novi, 15 August 1799. Released the next year, he held a variety of civil offices under the Empire. Napoleon created him marshal in 1804, but he rallied so promptly to the Bourbons that his name was struck off during the Hundred Days (and restored afterwards). He was one of the peers who voted for the execution of Ney (q.v.).

Perry, Matthew Calbraith (1794–1858) American admiral. A pioneer advocate of the usefulness of steam power to navies, he captained (1837) the *Fulton*, one of the first steam warships. In the Mexican war he commanded a squadron and in 1852 was sent to Japan to negotiate the treaty which opened the country to commerce.

His brother **Oliver Hazard Perry** (1785–1819) built the flotilla on the Great Lakes with which he contested their control with the British during the war of 1812 and won the victory of Lake Erie, 10 September, 1813.

Pershing, John Joseph ('Black Jack'; 1860–1948) American general. A poor boy, he worked as an assistant teacher to raise money for his own education and eventually won a nomination to West Point. He showed outstanding bravery in the Cuban campaign of 1898 and, in the Philippines, 1901–3, a remarkable tactical and political flair by his pacification of the ferocious Moros of Mindanao. For that achievement he was promoted by President Theodore Roosevelt from captain to brigadier-general and appointed governor of Mindanao (1906–13). In 1916 he was sent to command the expedition which the American government, invoking the legal justification of 'hot pursuit', dispatched into Mexico to track down the

anti-American bandit Pancho Villa. It was for his success in that mission that he was chosen in 1917 to command the US Expeditionary Force in Europe. Very early on he surprised the War Department by announcing that he would need a million men, an estimate he later advanced to three million. Meanwhile he alarmed his French and British allies by his insistence that US units should be held out of battle until sufficient had been assembled for a whole American army to intervene decisively. The Allies' extreme plight in the face of the German offensive of July 1918 forced him to compromise fractionally (hence the American battle honour of Belleau Wood), but he held so firm to his principle that the first major American offensive of the war was not launched until September (Saint-Mihiel). The next and last was the bloody Meuse–Argonne battle. It was characterized by great bravery, tactical rigidity and limited military (but great moral) achievement, attributes equally those of Pershing and of the inexperienced but courageous soldiers under his command. After the war he was promoted 'General of the Armies', a unique rank, superior to that of 'General of the Army' created for Marshall (q.v.) in the Second World War.

Pescara, Fernando Francesco de Avalos, marchese di (1490–1525) Imperial soldier. A leading imperial commander in the Italian wars between Charles V (q.v.) and Francis I (q.v.), Pescara learnt the craft of war under Prospero Colonna, one of the more successful *condottieri* in the imperial service, and eventually took over the command of the armies in Italy after Colonna's death in 1523. Pescara was taken prisoner at Ravenna in 1512, when Gaston de Foix (q.v.) overwhelmed the Spanish army of Cardona. Released, he broke his agreement never to fight against France again and rejoined Colonna. He beat the Venetians at Vicenza, captured Padua (1514) and Milan (1521); Genoa fell to him in 1522. After Colonna's death, the nominal command of the imperial armies went to Lannoy, the viceroy of Naples, but Pescara exercised effective control of the troops. It was Pescara rather than Lannoy who should be credited with the smashing victory of the imperial forces over the French at Pavia (February 1525), a battle in which the French king Francis I was captured. Apart from the king, the French lost 8000 men, to casualties on the imperial side of 1000. Pescara died later in the year, after he had foiled a plot by the Milanese to lure him over to the French side. A competent and imaginative general, his greatest advantage over his enemies was the quality of the Spanish troops under his command, and the greater concentration of firepower in his forces (a benign legacy of Cordoba, q.v.). It was this factor which determined the outcome of Pavia, as much as the excellent plan he produced for the conduct of the battle.

Pétain, Henri Philippe Omer (1856–1951) Marshal of France. Son of a prosperous peasant family of the Pas-de-Calais, Pétain gained admission to Saint-Cyr and was commissioned into the infantry. His ability ensured his appointment to influential positions, such as the professorship of tactics at the Ecole de guerre, but the unfashionableness of his views – he opposed the doctrine of *offensive à outrance* – slowed his promotion. He was only a colonel in 1914 (of the 33rd Regiment, in which de Gaulle, q.v., was serving as a lieutenant) and, on the outbreak of war, was given command of a brigade without being promoted. His success at its head, however, rapidly brought him command of the XXXIII Corps in the second battle of Artois, May 1915, when his leading troops reached the crest of Vimy Ridge, and then (*vice* Castlenau, q.v.) of the Second Army during the

Champagne offensive of 25 September 1915. In February 1916, when the decision was made to contest the German attack on Verdun, he was sent to direct the defence; his brilliant organization of the lines of supply to the fortress and his iron nerve in maintaining resistance ('they shall not pass') made him a national figure. In May he was promoted to command Army Group Centre and in May 1917 he replaced Nivelle (q.v.) as commander-in-chief on the western front. His first task was to quell the mutinies which Nivelle's miscarried offensive had precipitated and then to rebuild the army's fighting spirit through a series of carefully engineered and limited attacks (e.g., the Malmaison, November 1917). In the following spring, however, he failed to offer wholehearted co-operation to the British during the first of the German 'war-winning' offensives and, at their request, was subordinated to an international commander-in-chief, Foch (q.v.), though remaining in supreme command of the French. He was created marshal in November 1918.

Between the wars Pétain held every major post at the head of the army, besides directing the campaign which crushed Abd el-Krim (q.v.). He was acting as an ambassador to Spain when recalled, in May 1940, to become deputy prime minister, and then head of the government (16 June) with the task of seeking terms from the victorious Germans. He then interpreted it as his duty to establish a new regime (*Etat français*) to replace the Third Republic, thus presenting all French officers with a crisis of loyalty which only a few solved by choosing to follow de Gaulle (q.v.) into exile. At the end of the war he gave himself up to stand trial, was condemned to death, reprieved and imprisoned alone on the Ile d'Yeu, where he died. Petain's military abilities remain unquestioned: he understood the nature of mass warfare as practised between

1914 and 1918 and had grasped the importance of preponderating fire-power before it broke out. He also understood the common soldier. But he was sceptical and pessimistic by nature and therefore in practice a less inspiring and resilient leader than the ebullient Foch.

Peter the Great (1672–1725) Tsar of Russia. The effect of the reign of Peter the Great in Russia was to create a new 'European' state, and nowhere was this effort of modernization more obvious than in the military sphere. Coming to the throne as a minor, and excluded from all power and influence, Peter spent his early years in simple surroundings; slighted and ostracized by many Russians, he found his friends among the 'foreign' colony near his house at Preobrazenskoye. From childhood, Peter was possessed of a monumental energy: he walked at six months, talked volubly as a child and practised the most complicated games involving model forts and using his companions as well-drilled soldiers. In 1687 these informal regiments became the Preobrazensky and the Semyonevsky Guards. In 1689 a revolt by the *streltsy* (professional musketeers) allowed Peter to engineer a coup and seize effective power. In the reign which followed, only one year saw undisturbed peace. During the first eleven years of his reign comparatively little progress was made, save for a campaign against the Turks which resulted in the capture of Azov (1696) and the birth of Russian naval power (*see* Apraxin). From 1697 to 1698 Peter travelled abroad, mainly to Holland and England, where he applied his voracious appetite for learning to the problems he would engender in the modernization of Russian society, and in particular the creation of her military power. In 1698 the *streltsy* rebelled again, and Peter on his return from Europe crushed them with a savagery reminiscent of the bloodbaths of Ivan the Terrible (q.v.).

The path to the creation of a western style of army, created by western specialists, was open. In 1699 he conscripted 32,000 commoners into the army, and in 1705 extended this *ad hoc* arrangement into a regular system of recruitment; every twenty households were to provide one recruit. By the end of his reign, Russia possessed a regular army of 210,000 plus over 100,000 irregulars and supplementary troops. The financial burden of this huge force, almost three times what contemporaries regarded as 'normal' for a state with Russia's population, was enormous: it occupied almost 85 per cent of Russian revenues. To support it, Peter revised the whole of the tax system to increase his revenues. Russian plants were established to manufacture small-arms and artillery: foreign experts were introduced to teach the Russians drill and military arts. as well as shipbuilding and the skills of military technology. Russian designs, some of them by Peter himself, were adopted for flintlock muskets for the infantry, field artillery and fortifications. In 1716 a set of army regulations was introduced embodying the best of western practice, stating that the objective of an officer was 'to know the soldier's business from first principles and not to rely on rules ...'. The whole service class was reorganized to provide officer material for the administration and armed forces (1718).

The effects of all this activity are harder to gauge. In the Great Northern War (1700–21) the Russians were successful against the Swedes, but Peter's great victory over Charles XII at Poltava (1709) was won by overwhelming superiority of numbers over a Swedish army on the verge of starvation, deep in enemy territory, and with their commander wounded and in great pain. Against a much larger Turkish army in Moldavia in 1711, at the battle of the Pruth, Peter allowed himself to be trapped and brought to the verge of disaster. Only the ineptitude of Turkish

Grand Vizier Baltaji Mehmet, and the cunning of Peter's negotiator Shafirov, allowed him to extricate himself. Peter was no great military commander, although some of his subordinates were exceptionally able. His military achievement was, as in the Russian state, to make the giant stride which brought Russia from eastern backwardness to the beginnings of a modern, European, army. If such a development was revolutionary within Russia's army, it was doubly so within her navy: by the end of Peter's reign, the Russian navy had displaced the Swedes as the masters of the Baltic and could be reckoned as one of the major European forces. Peter threw himself body and soul into the creation of the military might of Russia: he greeted the birth of a son with delight as 'another recruit!'. Yet he was not a militarist boor, like Frederick William I of Prussia; his passion was the childish enthusiasm he had shown at Preobrazenskoye. He could often be found marching alongside common soldiers, serving guns with his seamen, leaping into a ditch to use his enormous strength (he was over 6½ feet tall and massively built) in freeing an artillery piece. He died as the result of a chill gained after plunging into an icy Finnish river to rescue some drowning soldiers; a characteristic end.

Philip II (1527–98) King of Spain. 'I do not propose, nor desire', Philip wrote to the Pope in 1566, 'to be the ruler of heretics.' On that cardinal principle his life and his work were based, and it provided the inspiration behind the military activity of his reign. From 1543, when he acted as regent in Spain for his father, Charles V, Philip was at the heart of government and politics. In a long life he spent only three years (1548–51) outside Spain; and speaking only Spanish fluently, he seemed to subjects and foreigners alike the most straitlaced and Castilian of monarchs. His father had advised him early in life never to trust his advisers, and this precept vitiated many of the most successful enterprises of his reign. His best generals – Alva, Parma (qq.v.), and many others – were always constrained in their operations by the detailed scrutiny which Philip gave to the voluminous reports he required them to submit. He confided in no one, and kept all his servants on a short rein. Generals were starved of money and reinforcements, confidence was suddenly withdrawn without reason: Philip saw in every successful general a potential rebel. All the military enterprises of importance in his reign had a religious tinge to them. In the case of the Netherlands, he was determined to blot out heresy; with the Ottomans, a desire to further the crusade against Islam; and as far as England was concerned, a wish to return an erring sheep to the fold of the True Faith. And yet religion masked political and economic, as well as personal, motives. With the Dutch he longed to gather for the state some of the immense wealth of a prosperous mercantile province; the battle with the Turks was war for the economic domination of the Mediterranean. In the case of England, the issue was more personal. Once the husband of Queen Mary, Philip felt that he had prior rights, which Elizabeth spurned; it was the English who financed and stiffened Dutch resistance, raided his colonies and shipping, and acted generally as a gadfly. But in this, as in all his military enterprises, he failed. The Dutch had by his death acquired effective independence in the northern provinces. The expeditions against England, from the great Armada of 1588, foundered; his interventions in the French wars of religion were ineffectual. Even the Turks, who had been decisively beaten at Lepanto (1571), were, by Philip's death, once more in a commanding position on land and sea.

The reasons for the failures of Philip's enterprises are complex, but at root lay the quality of his own personality. From his office in the palace monastery of the Escurial, in his later years, he continued the habits of a lifetime. He ruled and decided everything, from the frankly trivial to matters of supreme urgency. His soldiers depended on his instructions, and his understanding of the situation gleaned from their reports. Yet he was no soldier: he had experience of one battle (Saint-Quentin, 1557), and acquired a distaste for war. 'He fears war as a burned child dreads the fire', wrote a Catholic contemporary. He had no sense of the exigencies and needs of war, and acted always as his dutiful generals' arch-critic rather than their aid and support. Thus some, though not all, of the explanations for the failures of the reign can be found buried in the dark recesses of Philip's nature.

Piccolomini, Ottavio, principe (1599–1656). Italian soldier in the imperial service. Scion of one of the most ancient families of Italy, Piccolomini served the Habsburgs, in one capacity or another, throughout his military career. He served against the Protestants in Bohemia at the outbreak of the Thirty Years' War (1618–48), and in the assault on Gabor Bethlen, Prince of Transylvania, who laid siege to Vienna in 1619; in 1623, however, he returned to Italy in the service of the Spanish Habsburgs. His stay south of the Alps was short-lived, for in 1627 he was recruited by Wallenstein (q.v.) and soon became captain of his elite bodyguard.

Piccolomini had already revealed himself, both in the marauding campaign against the Hungarians and in Italy, as a cavalry commander of skill and daring. His knowledge and experience of Italian politics (for the Piccolomini retained great influence in the affairs of Tuscany) made him a natural choice for a command in Italy. This meant that he was absent when Wallenstein was dismissed as imperial commander, but on his return in 1631 he made use of his privileged position with Ferdinand II to press for Wallenstein's reinstatement as the only answer to the menacing dominance of the Swedes under Gustavus Adolphus (q.v.). At Lützen (1632) Piccolomini also turned the battle into an imperial victory, after the death of Gustavus had unhinged the Swedish advance. Wallenstein sent Piccolomini with his cavalry to batter the Swedes. His cuirassiers charged again and again, seven times in all; not with the ambling *caracole*, still common practice, but full-blooded sabre charges, at the gallop. Piccolomini had five horses shot under him and six musket wounds in his body; but he fought on. Only the grim determination of the Swedes to avenge their king's death, and Wallenstein's mental and physical exhaustion allowed them to snatch their army from seemingly certain ruin. After Lützen, Piccolomini became disillusioned by Wallenstein's blatant self-interest and his determination to carve out a kingdom for himself. He took a leading part in the group of officers who refused to support his bid to move against Ferdinand II, and was active in the plot which caused Wallenstein's murder in 1634. But the supreme command which Piccolomini had hoped for went to Matthias Gallas.

In a spirit of some disillusion Piccolomini re-entered Spanish service and triumphed over the French at Thionville (1639), where he smashed the army besieging the town; a grateful Philip IV created him Duke of Amalfi for this signal service. Once again he was lured back, with large inducements, to serve the Emperor Ferdinand III; at the second battle of Breitenfeld (1642) he met with one of his few reverses. Although his cavalry was successful against the Swedish army of Torstensson (q.v.), his infantry failed under the repeated Swedish assaults and many of his men were captured. Now less favoured in Vienna he returned to the Netherlands, to be summoned for the last time in the imperial cause in May 1648, when Ferdinand III appointed him commander-in-chief to save the imperial armies, shattered by repeated French victories. Piccolomini had some success, but the odds against him were extreme, as enemy armies pressed forward from both north and south on the Habsburg domains. Peace resolved the problems, however, and Piccolomini, a skilled negotiator, played an important role as the head of the imperial delegation at the congress of Nuremberg, which settled the final points outstanding between France and the empire. Raised to the dignity of an imperial prince in 1650, he spent the remainder of his life in Vienna. Piccolomini was a field commander of cavalry rather than a great commander of armies, a courageous, indomitable soldier, but no great thinker or innovator.

Pichegru, Charles (1761–1804) French general. Of humble birth but some education, Pichegru was first an usher at the military school of Brienne, then served in the ranks of the artillery until the Revolution opened the road of promotion to him through the National Guard. Having soldiered in America and acted as president of a revolutionary 'club' in Besançon, he was fluent in the language of revolution, attracted the attention of Saint-Just and Robespierre and with their support quickly became a general of division (4 October 1793). In December he was appointed to command the armies of the Rhine and the Moselle in succession to Hoche (q.v.) and in February 1794 the Army of the North in succession to Jourdan (q.v.). He fought three brilliant campaigns in that year, first against the Austrian Clerfayt (q.v.) in Belgium, then on the Rhine, lastly in Holland, where his cavalry charged across the ice to capture the imprisoned Dutch fleet. The Convention, which had overthrown his patrons, named him *Sauveur de la patrie* and in

its name he put down the sansculotte insurrection in Paris of 12 Germinal (1 April 1795). He was now commander of almost all the armies of the republic – Nord, Sambre-et-Meuse, Rhine. His ambition next led him, however, to enter an anti-republican conspiracy with the émigrés; he was uncovered, tried and deported to Cayenne in 1797. He escaped, served as chief of staff to Korsakov (q.v.) during the 1799 campaign in Holland, but foolishly returned to Paris in 1803 to join Cadoudal, the Vendéen leader, in an anti-Bonapartist coup, was rearrested and found strangled in prison in unexplained circumstances.

Pickett, George Edward (1825–75) American (Confederate) general. His name is indissolubly linked with the disastrous 'Pickett's Charge', the high moment of the battle of Gettysburg, although he did not command the attack, nor his troops form a majority of those taking part in it. He was a close personal friend of Longstreet (q.v.) and his favourite divisional commander (though he had passed bottom out of West Point in 1846). He commanded at the battle of Five Forks in the last days of the Confederacy.

Picton, (Sir) Thomas (1785–1815) British general. He commanded the 3rd Division in Portugal, 1810–13, pursued Masséna after the latter had abandoned his watch outside the lines of Torres Vedras, did well at Fuentes d'Onoro, 5 May 1811, conducted the siege of Badajoz, March 1812, was severely wounded in the storming, which he led, and was chiefly responsible for the success at the battle of Vittoria. In the 1815 campaign he commanded the 5th Division, was wounded at Quatre Bras, but nevertheless stayed at duty during the retreat (though a junior officer overheard him groaning with pain in the night) and was shot through the head in the early afternoon of Waterloo. A quick-fingered grenadier relieved him of his gold spectacles as he fell, a gesture by which this iron-hearted old disciplinarian of the Peninsula might well have been amused.

Pilsudski, Joseph (1867–1935) Polish marshal, founder and head of the modern Polish state. Born a subject of the tsar and the son of an ancient Polish noble family, he took up nationalist politics from his earliest youth and was twice imprisoned. After 1905, when he had failed to interest Japan in supporting a Polish rebellion, he transferred his activities to Austrian Galicia, where he began to organize an army-in-exile. On the outbreak of war in 1914 he put it under Austrian orders to fight the Russians, but refused to operate outside 'Polish' territory. After the overthrow of the tsar, he and the Central Powers fell out and he was imprisoned by the Germans, July 1917–November 1918. Released, and recognized by the German puppet government in Warsaw as head of state, he gathered the various patriot armies and organized a large, strong national army, later (1919) to be armed by the French. Its first battles were with Czech, Ukrainian and German forces over border disputes, but in 1920, following an extension of Polish boundaries to the line of the 1772 frontier with Russia, it entered into serious fighting with the Red Army. Pilsudski's advance to Kiev (7 May 1920) was repulsed by Tukhachevsky and Budenny (qq.v.) and he was forced back to the outskirts of Warsaw, where with French aid (*see* Weygand) he won a decisive victory (16–25 August). In his subsequent advance (battles of the Niemen and the Szczara) he recovered all the territory under claim. He resigned as head of state in 1923, but in 1926, impatient with the pettiness of the parties, he organized a coup and thereafter personally administered power almost until his death.

Pizarro, Francisco (1474–1541) Spanish conquistador. The success of the Spanish conquerors of South America was in large measure due to an extraordinary audacity, a quality most conspicuously displayed by Pizarro. After early service with Balboa on his voyages of discovery, Pizarro determined to strike out on his own. In 1522 he established a syndicate with Hernando de Luque and Diego de Almagro, a soldier, for the exploration of the unknown west coast of South America. Their small party pushed south, but were stricken by illness and by disasters which left Pizarro quite isolated with only sixteen companions. The main result of this exploration was that firm reports of a fabulous empire far to the south seemed to be confirmed. Pizarro's scheme was to mount an expedition into this unknown region under his command, but his plans were thwarted by the total opposition of the governor of Panama. Pizarro was determined to pursue his plan, however, and in 1528 sailed to Spain to appeal to the Emperor Charles V in person. His plans were sanctioned and he was given wide powers over any conquests on the west coast. But it proved difficult to find the support for an expedition, and he was forced to set out with only 3 ships, 180 men and 27 horses (1531). Although his partners were angry at the power granted to him personally, the force made a united assault over the mountains (a major feat in itself) into the Inca empire. They were faced by a well-trained army of 30,000 under Atahualpa (q.v.), the victors in a bitter civil war against their leader's brother, Huascar. Atahualpa disregarded the threat from so small a force and was lured into a meeting with Pizarro at Cajamarca (1532). The Spanish seized him, rendering the Inca army leaderless; once his uses were exhausted, and his huge ransom paid, Atahualpa was murdered.

Pizarro, like Cortes, was adept at exploiting factional strife among his enemies for his own advantage. A brother, and rival, of Atahualpa, Manco Capac, was appointed Inca, and potential opposition neutralized. The capital, Cuzco, was occupied peacefully in 1533, and two years later Pizarro built his own city at Lima. A rebellion by Manco Capac was brutally crushed in 1536, and the last pretence of Inca independence suppressed. But the Spaniards fell out among themselves: Almagro declared war on Pizarro and succeeded in taking Cuzco. But in 1538 Pizarro defeated him in battle and had him executed. Almagro's son and his other supporters had their revenge, however, when they arranged for his assassination. The effect of all these squabbles was state intervention from Spain, and although Pizarro's faction continued to resist royal authority, they were beaten and royal supremacy finally established in 1569. In Pizarro bravery and brutality were found in equal measure; his skill as a soldier had no great subtlety, either in tactics or planning.

Plumer, Herbert Charles (1st Viscount Plumer of Messines; 1857–1932) British field-marshal. An officer of the York and Lancaster Regiment, Plumer first made his name as a commander of mounted infantry in South Africa. He became quartermaster-general after the Boer War and in December 1914 was appointed to command II Corps (from May 1915, Second Army) in the Ypres salient. That, until 1917, was a quiet sector, the main British offensives of 1915–16 being fought in Artois and on the Somme, but in June 1917, as a preliminary to the coming offensive at Ypres itself (Third Battle, or Paschendaele) he organized the efficient and cheap capture of Messines ridge by a limited advance following the explosion of several enormous mines. The victory typified his approach to the problems of trench warfare, which he thoroughly understood and, after the failure by the

slapdash Gough (q.v.) to make headway in the Third Battle itself, the main effort was transferred to his Second Army (such success as the battle achieved was won by it). In the following April he succeeded in holding Ypres against the second of Germany's great 'war-winning' offensives. As much as Gough was disliked by his soldiers, Plumer was liked and trusted. He was arguably the best British general of the First World War, though his white moustache, red face and dumpy figure provided the model for the cartoonist David Low's famous Colonel Blimp.

Polk, Leonidas (1806–64) American (Confederate) general. Three months after graduating from West Point, Polk left the army to take episcopal orders and was bishop of Louisiana when war between North and South broke out. Commissioned a major-general, 'more as a symbol than a military leader', he nevertheless defeated Grant (q.v.) at Belmont, Missouri, on 7 November 1861. He commanded the Confederate right at Shiloh, leading four charges in person, and was killed by a shell at Pine Mountain in the Atlanta campaign. 'There died a gentleman and a high church dignitary,' a fellow general wrote, adding a little unfairly: 'As a soldier he was more theoretical than practical.'

Poniatowski, Prince Josef Anton (1763–1813) Marshal of France. Although his father was a general in Austrian service, his own birthplace Vienna, and he himself served first in Austrian regiments (he was wounded by the Turks on the river Save in 1788), he both was and felt himself to be Polish and went home at once when called to defend his country in 1789. He commanded a division against the Russians in 1792 and again, under Kosciuszko (q.v.), in 1794. He lived then in inactivity until 1807 when Napoleon offered him rank and office in the Grand Duchy of Warsaw, which had been taken under French protection. He campaigned against the Archduke Ferdinand (q.v.) in 1809, commanded the 5th (Polish) Corps in the Russian campaign and the right of the army at Leipzig the following year (16–18 October). Napoleon created him marshal on the eve of that battle; the day after, he was wounded in a skirmish and, plunging mounted into the river Elster to escape his pursuers, was drowned (while his companion Macdonald, q.v., got to safety).

Pontiac (1720–69) Chief of the Ottawa Indians and war leader. Creator of the great Indian confederation against the British at the end of the Seven Years' War (1756–63), Pontiac became the chief of his tribe by 1755. After contact with British and American settlers, he came to hate and distrust them, seeing in their steady penetration eastwards the beginnings of real control and colonization, quite unlike the loose alliance system which the French had operated. With French backing he united the forest tribes – an enormous feat in itself – in a joint plan against the British: each tribe would rise against the British, attack and destroy their commerce, forts and trading posts, massacring all the inhabitants. In May 1763 this elaborate strategy was accomplished. Of twelve fortified posts attacked by the tribes, all but four fell to them, and the line of defence for the colonies vanished. Pontiac's own surprise attack on Detroit was betrayed, and despite settling down to besiege the fortress in approved fashion, he had neither the men nor the equipment to capture it. But he won a definite victory at the battle of Bloody Run (July 1763), although he was worsted in an engagement with the Royal Americans under Bouquet (q.v.) at Bushy Run a week later. He resorted to the more normal guerrilla warfare with very great success: the frontier reeled under the repeated Indian attacks.

With his acute understanding of the possible, however, Pontiac realized that in a long-drawn-out war the inherent disunity among the tribes would surface once more and his forces would melt away. Bargaining from a strong position with Sir William Johnson, the leading expert in Indian affairs, at Oswego in 1766, he reached an acceptable treaty of peace for the Indian federation. By this agreement the Indians were given guarantees that a firm frontier would be established, beyond which the white men would not pass. It could not be policed, however, and renewed conflict eventually became inevitable.

Pontiac had achieved a remarkable success, only to be murdered by an Indian at St Louis, Missouri, three years later. His grasp of the strategic situation, and his immensely powerful personality, made possible the synchronized attacks over a vast area, and even in defeat he managed to maintain a unified front against the enemy. After his death the confederation which he created fell apart for lack of any strong personality at its centre, a fact which the white men on the frontier were quick to exploit. But his strategy – of separate but coordinated attacks spread over a vast distance – was a genuine innovation for the period, a brilliant exploitation of the advantages which the vast wilderness of North America could give to the Indian tribes.

Pope, John (1822–92) American (Union) general. A West Point graduate, commissioned into the Topographical Engineers, Pope was promoted from captain to brigadier-general (of volunteers, not the regular army) at the outbreak of the Civil War. He led the Army of the Missouri in the advance to Corinth (see Halleck), April–June 1862, and was then chosen by Lincoln to command the new Army of Virginia. Asked by a reporter where his headquarters would be, he answered, 'in the saddle'. This promise of dynamic generalship was belied in practice, for he was shortly and soundly beaten by Lee and Jackson (qq.v.) in the second battle of Bull Run. He was at once relieved, the reward, his army (whom he had annoyed) said, for 'keeping his headquarters where his hindquarters should have been'.

Portal, Charles (1st Viscount Portal of Hungerford; 1893–1971) British air marshal. Former head of Bomber Command, Portal was appointed chief of the air staff in 1940 and held the post to the end of the war. His principal contribution to its winning was in proffering advice to Churchill, who greatly respected his judgement, and in arguing the British case at inter-Allied conferences with the Americans, by whom he was much liked and trusted. He had a rapport with Arnold (q.v.) similar in closeness to that between Marshall and Dill (qq.v.).

Porter, David Dixon (1813–91) American (union) admiral. A halfbrother of Farragut (q.v.), Porter commanded the river fleet under Grant (q.v.) in the Vicksburg campaign, in which his brother William David (1809–64) also served. Their father David (1780–1843) had commanded the frigate *Essex* with panache in the war of 1812 and, after dismissal for unauthorized action against Spanish ships while on antipiracy patrol in the Caribbean, had transferred, together with David Dixon, to the Mexican navy (1826–9).

Potemkin, Grigori Alexandrovich, Prince (1731–91) Russian statesman and soldier. Potemkin, a dominating figure, began his career as a soldier in a Guards regiment, but his real triumphs occurred in the boudoir of Catherine the Great, first as her lover and then as her main adviser for some seventeen years. In the military sphere his career was closely bound up with Russia's wars

with Turkey and her expansion in the east, around the Black Sea, into the Crimea and the Caucasus. Potemkin served in the Turkish war of 1768–74 and achieved considerable success; he also attracted attention at court. In 1774 he became Catherine's fifth lover, and when this relationship ended after a passionate three years he continued as her confidant and chief adviser. Potemkin's vision was of a Russian empire stretching towards India, and he set about creating the basis for this advance. He constructed an arsenal at Kherson, in 1778, which increased Russia's offensive potential, and fortified Sebastopol, after Russia's peaceful annexation of the Crimea in 1783. He rebuilt Apraxin's (q.v.) Black Sea flotilla, and sought by a process of 'plantation' to colonize the Ukraine. Most of this activity was only partly successful, the product of a furious energy which characterized all his activities. But he lacked real, sustained, administrative talent. In 1784 Catherine raised him to the rank of field-marshal; in 1787 he took her on a splendid tour of her newly won possessions. Where the policy of settlement had failed, he simply built fake villages and communities and filled them with peasants, only to serve the purpose of letting her see the progress that had been made (the phrase 'a Potemkin village' has entered literary currency).

With the outbreak of the second Russo-Turkish war (1787–92), Potemkin took command. The war was not a great success and failed to produce the dramatic gains in Georgia and Bessarabia for which he had hoped. As the French Revolution began to affect international politics and alliances, the focus of attention turned to the west and a hurried peace was made with Turkey. Potemkin died while travelling to the peace conference at Jassy (in Romania). His great achievement, with the sustained support of Catherine the Great, was to give Russian policy its strong southern and eastern bent. The lure of Constantinople, which figured so strongly in Russian eyes in the next century, was virtually his creation. A gigantic, Promethean character, his ambitions were on a similar scale.

Pound, (Sir) Alfred Dudley Pickman Rogers (1877–1943) British admiral. Executive head of the Royal Navy during the first years of the Second World War, Pound had sailed as flag captain in the battleship *Colossus* at Jutland in 1916, was postwar head of the plans division, and commanded the Mediterranean fleet between 1936 and 1939, when he was promoted admiral of the fleet and First Sea Lord. In that post he 'virtually worked himself to death', attending to administrative duties in the Admiralty by day and sleeping there in a camp-bed by night, during which he often rose to intervene directly in the conduct of operations in progress. This habit, as his senior subordinates had warned, eventually contributed to a disaster, in the handling of the defence of the ill-fated convoy PQ 17 in July 1942. He was, moreover, acting as chairman of the Chiefs of Staff Committee until March 1942 (when he was succeeded by Alanbrooke, q.v.), although his sleepiness and the slow growth of a brain tumour, of which he was aware, made him increasingly ineffective in that role. He nevertheless died in harness.

Powell, Colin Luther (1937–) American general and Chairman of the Joint Chiefs of Staff during the Persian Gulf War of 1991. The first black American to reach the United States' highest military appointment, Powell was also the youngest Chairman of the JCS, the most famous since Omar Bradley (q.v.), and the only one never to attend either West Point or Annapolis. He represents the embodiment of the military version of the American dream, and will always be seen as much as a

political symbol as a military commander.

Powell's father and mother were native Jamaicans who emigrated in the mid-1920s to the Harlem district of New York City where they married, later settling in the South Bronx where both worked for garment firms, his father eventually rising to foreman. This multicultural upbringing left Powell with an ease at all levels of society, and a habit of peppering his speech with Yiddish words when necessary. The pronunciation of his name, originally KAH-lin in Caribbean fashion, changed to KOAH-lun after 1941 in imitation of Captain Colin P. Kelly Jr, a famous American fighter pilot of the Second World War.

Ability and achievement showed strongly in Powell's wider family, which believed in education as a means of betterment. Later in life, he would count among his cousins two senior judges, an ambassador and a television station owner. Powell himself showed a mechanical aptitude which led to a lifelong hobby of repairing old cars, but was academically undistinguished. His parents put him through City College, New York, where he scraped a degree majoring in geology. He joined the university Army Reserve Officers Training Corps (ROTC) in 1956 for no better reason than that he liked the uniform. On graduation his parents allowed him to volunteer as an infantry officer rather than wait to be drafted, before finding a proper job. But like many young men before him, Powell had found his vocation. He remained in the army, opting for the elite airborne forces. In 1962, shortly after his marriage, he began the first of two tours in Vietnam which earned him the rank of major and eleven medals and decorations.

With the US Army desegregated only in 1948, and the emerging Civil Rights movement in America, race would always be an important factor in Powell's career. In 1969 he returned to college to earn a master's degree in business administration from George Washington University. His first major break came in 1972 when against fierce competition he was made a White House Fellow in the Office of Management and Budget under Casper Weinberger, followed by a rapid rise through army staff and command appointments. In the murky bureaucratic world of official Washington, Powell established a remarkable reputation not only for competence, but for the almost impossible combination of both loyalty and probity, keeping himself carefully neutral between the two main political parties. From 1976 he served in the office of the Secretary of Defense under Democrat President Jimmy Carter, but in 1983 Weinberger, now Secretary of Defense under Republican President Ronald Reagan, made Powell his Military Assistant. Powell's military philosophy matched that of Weinberger; both believed that America should avoid the use of force, but that if used it should be as strong and decisive as possible. The beginnings of this approach were seen in the American intervention in Grenada in 1983 (Operation Urgent Fury) and the punitive bombing raid on Tripoli in 1986, in both of which Powell played a small role.

Even in Reagan's scandal-prone but indestructible 'Teflon Presidency', Powell's ability to walk between the raindrops was highly prized. Despite his minor involvement in the bizarre 'Iran-Contra Scandal' of 1986, in which the Reagan government illegally sold arms to its arch-enemy Iran in order to fund a further illegal war in Nicaragua, Powell was able to show that he had acted under direct orders, managed to be out of the country commanding troops when the scandal broke, and was never called to account for his actions in public. In 1987 he was appointed as National Security Adviser to the President, and a year later promoted to full general.

By this time Powell was both a celebrity and a symbol, who worked hard to promote awareness of race issues, including the neglected role of black soldiers in American military history. He had also established a formidable reputation as a political soldier. When Reagan's vice-president George Bush ran for the presidency in 1988 there was some early speculation that Powell might be his vice-president. Instead, Powell returned to active service with the army. In October 1989 President Bush appointed him to a two-year term as Chairman of the JCS, a position which had been strengthened in 1986 to make its holder the principal presidential military adviser. In December 1989 the American intervention in Panama (Operation Just Cause) showed to the full Powell's military philosophy of using overwhelming force to achieve a quick and decisive victory.

The culmination of Powell's military career came with the Iraqi invasion of Kuwait in August 1990, which led to the American decision to commit combat forces first in defence of Saudi Arabia and then in January–March 1991 to expel the Iraqis from Kuwait in Operation Desert Storm. Powell functioned as the critical link between President Bush and the American armed forces in holding together a coalition of almost thirty countries and managing the direction of the war, including an often fraught relationship with the American commander in the Persian Gulf, the flamboyant and sometimes prickly General Norman Schwarzkopf (q.v.). The Persian Gulf War was an overwhelming American victory, and a testimony to Powell's skill. This was reinforced by a carefully crafted media image for which Powell always denied direct responsibility, which portrayed him as advising caution after the Iraqi invasion of Kuwait, and as a man of peace reluctant to go to war. In the euphoric aftermath of the victory President Bush, to quell rumours of disagreement between himself and

Powell, appointed him to a second term as Chairman of the JCS four months early in May 1991.

Powell completed his appointment as Chairman of the JCS under the new Democrat President Bill Clinton, and retired from the army in 1993, still carefully neutral in his political allegiances, but amid great speculation that he might return to politics once more. The boy from the South Bronx who made it to the top, Powell remains a role-model for black Americans, and the epitome of a successful political general.

Price, David (1790–1854) British admiral. Appointed commander-in-chief in the Pacific at the outbreak of the Crimean War, though he had never before captained more than a single ship, he arranged with the accompanying French squadron to attack Petropavlovsk on the Kamchatka peninsula, but shot himself with his pistol at the opening of the action. It is surmised that this bizarre suicide was committed in recognition of how wholly unfitted he was to exercise a major command.

Prim y Prats, Juan (conde de Reus, marques de Los Castillejos; 1814–70) Spanish general and politician. Rapidly promoted during the Carlist wars, he won great success in Spain's Moroccan war, 1856–60, and led the Spanish troops in the joint Franco-Spanish expedition to Mexico, 1861–2. On his return, his career became wholly political and chiefly dedicated to finding a ruler suitable to the establishment of a true constitutional monarchy in the kingdom. His offer of the throne to Leopold of Hohenzollern-Sigmaringen in 1870 precipitated the Franco-Prussian war. He himself was shortly afterwards assassinated.

Primo de Rivera, Juan, marques d'Estella (1870–1930) Spanish general and dictator. A politician rather than a soldier, for his early military career coincided with one of Spain's rare passages of internal and external peace, he seized the opportunity presented by the humiliating defeat of the army in Morocco at Anual, 21 July 1921 (*see* Abd el-Krim) to take dictatorial powers. His principal aim was to suppress internal disorders, both anarchist and separatist, but depressed by his failure to establish secure government he resigned in 1930, after taking the unusual step of polling the officers of the army as to whether or not they wished him to continue in power.

His son **José Primo de Rivera** (1903–36), was the founder of the Falange, the Spanish fascist movement, and was shot by republicans at the outbreak of the Civil War.

Putnik, Radomir (1847–1917) Serbian *voivod* (commander-in-chief). He took part in the wars of 1876–7 with Turkey, by which Serbian independence was definitively established, and of 1885–6 with Bulgaria. Appointed *voivod* at the approach of the Balkan wars of 1912–13, he commanded the Serbian army in the fighting. At the outbreak of war with Austria in July 1914, he again took the field and won the victory of the Jadar, a brilliant success for a commander so outnumbered. After being forced to surrender Belgrade in November, he counter-attacked (battle of Kolubra, 3–9 December), recaptured the capital and expelled the Austrians from the national territory. In October–November 1915, however, the Serbian army was overwhelmed by vastly superior German–Austrian forces (*see* Mackensen) and its survivors, carrying the desperately sick *voivod* on their shoulders, made a terrible retreat through the mountains to the Adriatic, whence they were evacuated to Corfu. Among the Serbs' many national heroes, he stands with the foremost.

R

Radetzky von Radetz, Joseph Wenzel, Graf (1766–1858) Austrian field-marshal. His career in a remarkable manner embraced two worlds, beginning in one of Austria's familiar frontier campaigns against the Turks in the Balkans and ending with the suppression of nationalist insurrection within the Habsburg empire, a prodrome of the conflicts which would lead to its break-up in 1918. As a young cavalry officer, he distinguished himself in the French revolutionary wars, was wounded at Marengo, acted as chief of the general staff (a less influential post then than later), 1809–12, was chief of staff to Schwarzenberg (q.v.) in 1813, when he helped to plan the Leipzig campaign, and campaigned successfully in the 1814 invasion of France. Between 1815 and 1829 he was again chief of the general staff and persisted in attempts to reform the army which merely won him enemies. Afterwards he served chiefly in Italy, and was commander-in-chief there when the 1848 rebellion in Milan erupted. He withdrew from the city into the 'Quadrilateral' (Mantua, Verona, Peschiera, Legnano) and when King Charles Albert (q.v.) of Sardinia took the field at the head of the united Italian patriot armies, he first conducted a brilliant delaying manœuvre, then at Custozza (24–5 June) and Novara (23 March 1849) completely crushed him. He next starved Venice into surrender and in the following year prevented a resumption of revolt in Milan. He was eighty-four and was not to retire until he reached ninety-one. Adored by his soldiers, who called him 'Vater Radetzky', and idolized by Habsburg loyalists, he stands among the very greatest of Austrian generals.

Raeder, Erich (1876–1960) German admiral. During the First World War he served as chief of staff to Hipper (q.v.) and was present at the battles of the Dogger Bank and Jutland. Promoted admiral in 1928 as commander-in-chief of Germany's tiny post-Versailles navy (allowed no submarines or ships larger than cruisers), he built the 'pocket' battleships and, after Hitler's seizure of power, the first of a new generation of U-boats. He was promoted grand admiral in 1939. Raeder's aim was to create a new High Seas Fleet (*see* Tirpitz), but the coming of war found it not yet built and he was obliged to make his main effort with his U-boats. Their success, and the failure of his surface ships in their rare sorties, lost Raeder Hitler's support and he was replaced by Dönitz (q.v.), commander of the submarine force, in January 1943.

Raglan, Fitzroy James Henry Somerset (1st Baron Raglan; 1788–1855) British field-marshal. Younger son of the 5th Duke of Beaufort, he acted as aide-de-camp to Wellington in the Peninsula, was on his staff at Waterloo, where he lost an arm, and served as secretary at the Horse Guards (army headquarters), 1827–52, when he succeeded the Duke as commander-in-chief and was ennobled. Promoted field-marshal in 1854, he was sent to the Crimea to take charge of the British army there, won the battles of the Alma and Inkerman, but became the scapegoat for the terrible sufferings of the army on the heights of Sebastopol during the winter of 1854–5. He died ten days after the failure of the attack on the Redan and the Malakov (18 June). His self-reproaches were more severe than those of his critics.

Rakoczy, George I (1593–1648) Hungarian soldier and monarch. As Prince of Transylvania, Rakoczy existed in an uneasy no-man's-land between the Ottomans, his theoretical overlord, and the Habsburgs. He came to the throne in 1630, succeeding Gabor Bethlen, who had taken over the throne from Rakoczy's father, Zsigmund. Rakoczy had taken an active part in Gabor's wars with Ferdinand II and participated in the Thirty Years' War (1618–48) on the Protestant side. By the treaty of Nikolsburg (1621) much of Habsburg Hungary was ceded to Transylvania. As what amounted to a minor Protestant power, Rakoczy allied himself with the Swedes after their entry into the war and continued his campaign against the Habsburgs. His power as an irritant was considerable, and in 1645 he was bought off by the treaty of Linz, which exacted further recognition of Transylvanian independence and imposed freedom of religion for Protestants in Habsburg Hungary.

Ramsay, (Sir) Bertram Home (1883–1945) British admiral. As flag officer at Dover in 1940, he was in charge of the Dunkirk evacuation. From April 1942 he worked on amphibious landings, of which he was to be Britain's chief practitioner during the Second World War. He planned the North African, Sicily, D-Day and Walcheren landings, and was naval commander-in-chief for the cross-channel invasion. He was killed in an air crash on his way to confer with Montgomery (q.v.) during the Ardennes battle.

Rapp, Jean (comte; 1772–1821) French general. Intended by his family for the Protestant ministry, Rapp enlisted instead in the cavalry in 1788, was commissioned in 1794, was taken by Desaix (q.v.) to Egypt and became aide-de-camp to Napoleon in 1805. Rapp was a simple fighting soldier but one of extraordinary bravery: he was wounded at least twelve times in action between 1793 and 1812 and in 1813 sustained a year-long defence of Danzig against the Russians.

Rawlinson, Henry Seymour (1st Baron Rawlinson; 1864–1925) British general. He commanded the Fourth Army on 1 July 1916, the first day of the battle of the Somme, when 57,000 of its largely volunteer soldiers were killed or wounded. On 8 August 1918, the Fourth Army, by then a veteran formation and equipped with nearly 500 tanks, won the remarkable victory of Amiens against the Germans.

Reichenau, Walter von (1884–1942) German field-marshal. A Guards artillery officer of the imperial army, Reichenau's early and fervent conversion to National Socialism made him notorious among his fellow generals before Hitler's seizure of power. The latter twice tried to appoint him commander-in-chief, first in succession to Hammerstein-Equord in 1934, then to Fritsch (q.v.) after the Blomberg–Fritsch crisis of 1938; on both occasions he deferred to the objections of Reichenau's enemies (who included, in 1934, Hindenburg). By the time the next opportunity arose (*see* Brauchitsch), he had decided to fill the post himself. Reichenau was a man of overbearing personality and ruthless disposition: as commander of the Sixth Army in Russia (June–December 1941) he issued a 'Severity Order' which encouraged acts of 'vengeance' against Russians in general. Previously he had commanded the Tenth Army in Poland and captured Warsaw, and the Sixth in Belgium, where he received the capitulation of King Leopold. He replaced Rundstedt (q.v.) at the head of Army Group South in Hitler's great purge of senior commanders in December 1941 and commanded it in the advance to Stalingrad (*see* Paulus). He died in an aeroplane crash while on his way to hospital for treatment of a heart attack, it not being established which of these calamities was the cause of his death.

Rennenkampf, Paul Karlovich von (1853–1918) Russian general. Of Baltic-German descent, he had fought in the Russo-Japanese war, when he and Samsonov (q.v.) had quarrelled so violently on Mukden railway station that they had come to blows. It was unfortunate therefore that in 1914 they should have been given command respectively of the First and Second armies, between which perfect co-operation was necessary if the planned invasion of East Prussia were to succeed. Separated by the Masurian lakes, and communicating *en clair* by wireless (which was intercepted by the Germans), the two generals allowed themselves to be defeated in turn, Samsonov at Tannenberg (26–31 August), Rennenkampf at the Masurian lakes (9–14 September). These great victories made Hindenburg (q.v.) a German national hero and led on to those of the Masurian Winter Battle and Gorlice-Tarnow (*see also* Ludendorff, Hoffmann, Mackensen). Rennenkampf was removed from active command and was eventually shot by the Bolsheviks.

Requesens, Luis de Zuniga y (1528–76) Spanish soldier. The unfortunate successor of the Duke of Alva (q.v.) in the Netherlands, he inherited the full measure of the hatred created by Alva's savage rule. Like Alva, he could do little to control the ravages of the Sea Beggars, who routed yet another Spanish fleet off Walcheren (1574). Requesens

did not have Alva's military skill, and the Spanish were forced back, losing town after town to the Dutch. The only success was the capture of the island of Zierikzee, when a strong Spanish force landed at low tide and stormed the defenders; the leader of the Sea Beggars was killed in the encounter. But this did little to stem the Dutch advance, and when Requesens died the Spanish cause was in a state of crisis. The new governor, Don Juan (q.v.), was something in the nature of a vain hope. But the hope was fulfilled, for Don Juan and his cousin Alexander Farnese (Parma, q.v.) began to rebuild the fortunes of Spain.

Richard III (1452–85) English king and soldier. Whatever the black legend created by the Tudors may say of the character of Richard III, it does nothing to conceal his skill as a soldier. One of the foremost practitioners of arms in his day (the 'deformed' shoulder was, in fact, the overdeveloped arm and shoulder of an expert swordsman), with his brother, Edward IV, Richard was in control of the Yorkist cause; in 1470 they were forced into exile when the Earl of Warwick, 'The Kingmaker', switched his support to the Lancastrian cause and placed Henry VI once again on the English throne. In 1471 Richard and Edward returned; in the ensuing battles of Barnet, where Warwick was killed, and Tewkesbury, in April and May, Richard commanded the Yorkist right with great success and ruthlessness. The Lancastrian cause was in ruins. It seems likely that after Tewkesbury Richard was instrumental in arranging the murder of Henry VI, now both a danger and an inconvenience. Edward, now king, relied heavily on his brother, heaping riches and offices upon him. In 1480 he was created lieutenant-general of the North and was successful in achieving the pacification of what had been largely Lancastrian territory. When Edward IV died prematurely in 1483 Richard was created protector to the young Edward V. He immediately executed his rivals, the Woodville faction centred on the queen dowager, Elizabeth Woodville, and had the young king declared a bastard. He now took the throne as Richard III, crushing a revolt by the Duke of Buckingham and executing all its leaders.

A more serious danger was posed by Henry Tudor, an associate of Buckingham who had fled abroad. In August 1485 Henry landed with 3000 French mercenaries in Wales, the base of his power. The two opposing forces met at Bosworth in Leicestershire, Richard with 10,000 men, Henry with half that number. But Richard's army dwindled as first the troops of the Duke of Northumberland, and then those of Lord Stanley, revealed that they had sold out to Henry Tudor. In the fight which followed Richard was cut down in a 'death or glory' bid to reach Henry and kill him. Had Richard had the chance to display his military talents on a wider, European field, his military reputation would stand much higher.

Richthofen, Manfred Freiherr von (1892–1918) German fighter ace; 'the Red Knight'. Germany's leading fighter ace of the First World War, Richthofen was credited with eighty victories, more than claimed by any other pilot of any nationality. A regular cavalry officer, he learnt to fly in 1916, eventually rose to command a group of fighter squadrons, *Jagdgruppe* I, brought together by the high command as an intervention force intended to secure air superiority over a chosen section of the front, and, after a charmed career of destruction, was shot down by small-arms fire from an Australian artillery battery.

His brother **Lothar von Richthofen** (1894–1922) also became an ace, credited with forty victories, and died in an accident after the war.

Rickenbacker, Edward Veron (1890–1973) American fighter ace. The leading American ace of the First World War, credited with twenty-six victories, Rickenbacker had made a reputation for himself before 1914 as a racing driver and it was as chauffeur to General Pershing (q.v.) that he first served in France. He did not make an operational flight until March 1918. In later life he became chairman of a major American airline and during the Second World War, when he returned to the service, survived twenty-one days on a raft in the Pacific Ocean.

Roberts, Frederick Sleigh (1st Earl Roberts of Kandahar, Pretoria and Waterford; 1832–1913) British field-marshal. Born at Cawnpore, the son of a general, he was educated at Eton and Sandhurst and then, in order to enter Indian service, Addiscombe, from which he was gazetted to the Bengal Artillery in 1851. He won the Victoria Cross in 1858 saving the life of a loyal Indian trooper from mutineers, served on the staff of Robert Napier (q.v.) in Abyssinia, commanded the illustrious Punjab Frontier Force 1878–80 and with it, and later other troops, fought the Second Afghan War virtually singlehanded. His march from the capital of Afghanistan, Kabul, to relieve a beleaguered British garrison at Kandahar made him famous throughout the Empire and he was appointed to command the Madras army. Promoted field-marshal in 1895 (though now known everywhere by his soldier nickname 'Bobs') he was sent in 1900 to assume command in South Africa after the disasters of Black Week, with Kitchener (q.v.) as his chief of staff. He remained there until the Boers' main forces were beaten in October (though much of the credit for that must go to the unlikable but efficient Kitchener), returning home to become commander-in-chief – the last, as it turned out, for in 1904 the post was abolished. Roberts devoted his declining years to advocating conscription. A tiny man of great charm, he was the most popular of Victorian generals and, in a small colonial campaign, by no means a bad one.

Robertson, (Sir) William Robert (1st Baronet; 1860–1933) British field-marshal. His autobiography, *From Private to Field-Marshal*, relates the story of his remarkable life. Born the son of a village tailor and employed first as a domestic servant, he enlisted as a trooper in the 16th Lancers, by superhuman hard work passed the examination to become an officer and eventually secured entry to the Staff College – the first ranker to do so. Thereafter his immense energy and ability carried him to the top of the army. As chief of the Imperial General Staff, 1915–18, he zealously propagated the 'Western' strategy of attacking in France (instead of Gallipoli or Salonika) and was ultimately dismissed by Lloyd George, the leading 'Easterner'. He was universally known as 'Wully' and dropped his aitches to the end of his life.

Rochambeau, Jean Baptiste Donatien de Vimeur, comte de (1725–1807) Marshal of France. As a junior officer he took part in the capture of Minorca in 1756 (*see* Byng) and the battle of Minden. Sent by Louis XVI with an expeditionary force to assist the American colonists in the War of Independence, he helped bring about the capitulation of Cornwallis (q.v.) at Yorktown on 19 October 1781. In 1790 he accepted the Revolution, was appointed to command the army of the North, created marshal (last of the *ancien régime*), but fell out with Dumouriez (q.v.) and resigned in 1792. Arrested in 1793, he survived the Terror.

His son, **Donatien Marie Joseph de Rochambeau** (1750–1813) replaced Leclerc (q.v.) as governor of Haiti and was killed at Leipzig.

Rochejacquelein, Henri du Vergier, comte de (1772–94) French (Vendéen) general. A former royal cavalry officer, he put himself (at the outbreak of the royalist Vendée uprising in 1793) at the head of his peasants, commanding them, 'If I advance, follow me; if I retreat, kill me; if I fall, avenge me.' After the disablement of d'Elbée (q.v.) at Cholet he was named generalissimo and was killed in the course of a successful guerrilla campaign he had organized.

His brother **Louis de Rochejacquelein** (1777–1815) was killed in the Vendée rising he led during the Hundred Days. His brother August (1784–1868), wounded in the skirmish in which Louis died, had formerly served Napoleon, had been wounded also in Russia, and later served in the Spanish (1823) and Turkish (1828) expeditions.

Rodney, George Brydges, Baron (1718–92) British admiral. In a naval career marked by conspicuous success, Rodney helped to maintain British maritime superiority through the wars of the mid-eighteenth century, at a time when it was under strong threat from France. He served under Hawke in the war of the Austrian Succession (1740–8) and took part in the fierce engagement against the French under de l'Entenduere off Finisterre (1747). Two years later he was appointed governor of Newfoundland, leaving his post to go to sea again in the Seven Years' War (1756–63). Most of his naval career was now to be associated with the Americas. He took part in the successful expedition against Louisburg under Boscowan (1758). In 1762 he took his squadron on a dramatically successful cruise in the West Indies. He captured Martinique, France's last outpost in the West Indies and a rich sugar island, followed by Grenada, St Lucia and St Vincent. On his return to England after one of the most economically rewarding expeditions of the war (for Havana had also been taken, with extensive booty), he was created a baronet, and in 1771 a rear-admiral.

In the American War of Independence (1775–83), Rodney dealt hammer blows against the French and Spanish fleets that threatened Britain's long lines of communication with her troops in North America. He brought desperately needed troops and supplies to Gibraltar (1780), where Sir George Elliott, with 7000 men, was resisting a prolonged Franco-Spanish investment. On the way he managed to defeat a smaller Spanish squadron under Langara in a night action off Cape St Vincent; he captured six ships, a fortune in prize money for Rodney and his crews. After the relief of Gibraltar, he sailed for the West Indies. He fought a set of battles without any decisive result with the French force under de Guichen, and, after the French retired, captured the rich Dutch island of St Eustatius, which was one of the sources by which the United States received supplies and revenue through contraband. Rodney's share of the prizes on this expedition, added to his earlier rewards, meant a substantial fortune. In 1782, in the final great battle of his career, he fought the substantial French fleet under de Grasse off Domenica. Diverging, quite without authority, from the accepted manual of naval tactics, he burst through the French line, breaking it into small disunited segments. Seven ships were captured, including the French flagship; his fellow commander Hood captured two more in pursuit of the remnants of the French fleet. It was an equal battle: the British had thirty-four ships; the French twenty-nine. The result was the establishment of complete British naval superiority off the American coast. Rodney was the model of the successful admiral. His exploits were profitable, through prize money; he was popular with his crews as a result. But he was a clear naval thinker, ready to improvise tactics as needed.

Rogers, Robert (1731–95) American soldier. Founder of a group of some 600 backwoodsmen, who used the Indian techniques of ambush and woodcraft, known as Rogers' Rangers. Born the son of a farmer, Rogers soon took to the less restrictive life of a trapper. In 1755 he was commissioned by the governor of Massachusetts to form a small force to attack the French in Nova Scotia. Although the expedition was a success, Rogers had been forced to flee across the state boundary for one of his numerous peccadilloes, in this case, counterfeiting. But in the following year he was back in Massachusetts; he now formed the company of Rangers which bears his name.

The basic aim of the Rangers was to fight fire with fire; thus they terrorized the French posts and the Indian villages as the French and their allies did the American settlements. Rogers' men were mercenaries, selected for their known skill as woodsmen and Indian killers. They took scalps, tortured their prisoners, and emulated their enemies in every respect. They were also remarkably successful in military terms. Many British officers were seconded to the Rangers to learn the secrets of irregular warfare: Rogers therefore had an influence on British tactical practice.

He was active throughout the war with the French and Indians (1756–60), and raided deep into French territory. In 1758 he was promoted to major and given command over nine independent Ranger companies. Peace did not suit Rogers and his career assumed a downward path, involving imprisonment for debt and innumerable minor frauds; when the American War of Independence broke out, he attempted to woo both the British and the American rebels. Washington imprisoned him as an enemy spy (1776) and when he escaped he therefore threw in his lot with the British. Once again he set about raising a Ranger company, and under Major

French it fought well against the Americans. Rogers, finally undone by his dishonesty and general shiftiness, was forced to leave North America and died in poverty in London. For all his many vices, he was an excellent mercenary organizer and an expert in forest warfare. He developed the technique of the lightly armed, rapidly moving, raiding party to a high degree, and was an innovator in the tactics of skirmishing.

Rokossovski, Konstantin Konstantinovich (1896–1968) Marshal of the Soviet Union. A Pole, the son of a stone mason, he fought both in the tsarist army and the Red Army, 1915–20. He was arrested during the great purge in 1938 but survived to command an army in Zhukov's (q.v.) Moscow counter-offensive of December 1941. Promoted to command Don Front (army group), he helped to encircle the German Sixth Army (see Paulus) at Stalingrad and to bring about its surrender. He next commanded the Central Front at Kursk, the battle which in July 1943 destroyed the German army's striking power in Russia, and then directed the advance of his front (renamed Belorussian) into Poland, where it played a major part in the battle called the Destruction of Army Group Centre, June–July 1944. In early 1945 he invaded and occupied East Prussia. He was subsequently installed as commander of the army of postwar Poland, where he was widely detested for his failure to come to the aid of the Polish Home Army in its death-struggle with the Germans in the Warsaw uprising of August 1944.

Rommel, Erwin (1891–1944) German field-marshal. The most widely celebrated battlefield general of the Second World War, a brilliant and daring tactician and an inspiring leader of men, Rommel, the son of a schoolmaster, was born in Württemberg, and so, on both those counts, far from the traditional

centre of influence in the German army. He showed himself from the first moment of the First World War, however, a natural fighter, transferred, after trench warfare had set in, from the 124th Infantry Regiment to the wider-ranging Württemberg Mountain Battalion and, as one of its company commanders, won the *Pour le mérite*, the highest imperial award for bravery, in the battle of Caporetto, October 1917. His success against the Italians, of whom he captured 9000 with 200 men of his own, seems to have formed his attitude to leadership, for it was by placing himself at the front and penetrating without regard for security into the Italian position that he achieved the triumph that was his.

Rommel's outlook was perfectly attuned to *blitzkrieg* and when promoted (partly through a lucky association with Hitler as commander of his headquarters escort in 1939) to lead 7th Panzer Division in the attack into France across the Meuse in May 1940, he required no period of preparation to work himself in. Though he betrayed an uncharacteristic flash of panic when counter-attacked by the British at Arras on 21 May, his race to the sea was overall as headlong and successfully dramatic as, on a smaller scale, had been his adventure in the mountains of Caporetto twenty years before. On Hitler taking the decision in 1941 to send help to his stricken Italian allies in North Africa (see O'Connor), Rommel was chosen to lead the expeditionary force – the *Afrika Korps* – and in a typically ferocious counter-offensive reversed the tide soon after his arrival. During the next year he generally retained the initiative, though British strength increased throughout, and in the summer of 1942 was poised to strike at Cairo. But, checked at Alam Halfa, 31 August–7 September, he suffered a major defeat in October at Alamein by the greatly reinforced Eighth Army under Montgomery (q.v.). He conducted a skilful withdrawal to Tunisia, where an Anglo-American army had landed in his rear, and, by his stalwart defence of the Mareth Line, delayed the inevitable surrender of the Axis forces in North Africa until May 1943.

By that time he had been summoned to Berlin, allegedly to recover his health but probably to prevent his capture, and was next appointed, after a limbo period, to command Army Group B under Rundstedt (q.v.) in France. His task was to repel the coming Allied cross-Channel invasion, but he quickly fell out with his superior, who underestimated the effect of Allied tactical air-power, as to how best that might be done – Rundstedt wishing to reserve the armour for a counter-stroke, Rommel to deploy it at the water's edge. The compromise imposed by Hitler was satisfactory to neither, but the argument was probably irrelevant, for Allied air-power proved irresistible. At the height of the struggle to contain the Allied bridgehead, 17 July 1944, his own car was strafed by a British fighter and he was gravely wounded. Before he had fully recovered Hitler had come to suspect his implication in the bomb plot of 20 July (though he was no more than a silent accomplice) and offered him the alternative of suicide or public disgrace. He chose the former, was said to have succumbed to his wounds and accorded a hero's funeral. Rommel possessed neither the innovative imagination of Guderian (q.v.) nor the large-scale operational mastery of Manstein (q.v.), but was nevertheless regarded at home and abroad as one of Germany's greatest generals and deserves his reputation.

Roon, Albrecht Theodore Emil von (1803–79) Prussian field-marshal. After the Napoleonic wars the Prussian army underwent a serious decline, its regular element dwindling to an ineffective size, while its citizen *Landwehr* reserve became politically unreliable. In 1859 Prince (later Kaiser) Wilhelm appointed Roon, former military tutor to Friedrich Karl (q.v.) to succeed the liberally inclined General von Bonin as minister of war. An 'intelligent conservative', he brought about that integration of the *Landwehr* with the regular army which was to make the Prussian army the first which could quickly mobilize large numbers of trained, disciplined, effective reserves, as it did with such shattering success in 1866 and 1870. These administrative achievements of his complemented those of the elder Moltke (q.v.) on the staff and operational side.

Root, Elihu (1845–1937) American military reformer. As secretary for war, 1899–1904, he established the post of chief of staff and created a general staff for the army, reforms similar to those achieved by Haldane (q.v.) slightly later in Britain. Competition for control between the secretary, the general-in-chief (a post he abolished – *see* Miles) and the headquarters bureaux was thereby eliminated. He subsequently became prominent in the field of disarmament and was awarded the Nobel Peace Prize (1912).

Rose, Hugh Henry (1st Baron Strathnairn; 1801–85) British fieldmarshal. Born and educated in Berlin, son of a diplomat, Rose joined the army in 1820 but served in semi-diplomatic posts for much of his career: in 1840 he was attached to the Ottoman army during its campaign against Mehemet Ali (q.v.) in Syria (*see* Moltke); he was consul-general in Syria, 1841–8, and in 1853 temporarily replaced Stratford Canning as ambassador to Constantinople, where his action in sending for the British fleet on the arrival of Menshikov (q.v.) precipitated the crisis which led to the Crimean War (in which he served). On the outbreak of the Indian Mutiny he volunteered for duty there and, at the head of a contingent of the Bombay army, virtually extinguished the uprising in central India, defeating both the rani of Jhansi and Tantia Topi (q.v.). He succeeded Colin Campbell (q.v.) as commander-in-chief.

Rosecrans, William Starkey (1818–98) American (Union) general. A West Pointer, he had, like so many fellow graduates, left the army before the war and was in business when it broke out. In October 1862 he was appointed to succeed Buell (q.v.) in command of the Army of Cumberland, led it during the Stones River and Tullahoma campaigns, and by his conduct of the latter forced Bragg (q.v.) out of Chattanooga, Tennessee, long an object of Union strategy. In his pursuit of Bragg, however, he neglected security, was forced to fight against his will and lost the ensuing battle (Chickamauga, 19–20 September 1863) by an error of judgement. He was then besieged within Chattanooga by Bragg until dismissed in October.

Ross, Robert (1766–1814) British general. He is remembered for his leadership of the military expedition (the naval side was commanded by Cochrane, q.v.) to Washington during the war of 1812. His victory (24 August 1814) at Bladensburg (which name his descendants were authorized to add to the family's) gave him possession of the American capital, to which, in retaliation for the burning of York in Canada, he set fire. The gutted presidential mansion was subsequently painted white to disguise the soot marks, whence its modern everyday name. Ross was mortally wounded at the battle of Baltimore, 12–14 September, where the resistance of the local militia inspired Francis Scott Key to compose 'The Star-Spangled Banner'.

Rozhdestvenski, Zinovy Petrovich (1848–1909) Russian admiral. A former chief of the naval staff and squadron commander, he was selected in 1904 to take the Baltic fleet to the Far East after the blockading by the Japanese of the Russian Pacific fleet in Port Arthur (*see* Makarov). It was composed of ships of very unequal quality and its voyage (begun 15 October 1904) of 20,000 miles was a nightmare of bad seamanship. At the start the Russians mistook some British trawlers in the North Sea for Japanese torpedo-boats and sank several, an incident which almost brought Russia to war with Britain and denied the admiral coaling facilities in Africa and Asia, except at the widely separated French colonial stations. Arriving off the Japanese home islands in May 1905, by which time Port Arthur had fallen (*see* Nogi and Stössel), he chose to make for the haven of Vladivostok by passing between them and Korea. Intercepted by Togo (q.v.) in the straits of Tsushima, 27 May 1905, his fleet, whose speed was that of its slowest battleship (14 knots), was headed off by the Japanese steaming at 21 knots, encircled and destroyed. Of his eight battleships and eight cruisers, all but one cruiser were sunk or captured; Rozhdestvenski himself was made prisoner. Tsushima ranks with Trafalgar, Midway and Leyte Gulf among the most crushing naval defeats of history, but as a battle it was hopelessly one-sided. In some sense it was to Rozhdestvenski's credit that he shepherded his fleet as far as he did.

Rundstedt, Karl Rudolf Gerd von (1875–1953) German field-marshal. After service on the staff during the First World War, Rundstedt rose steadily up the narrow ladder of promotion in the 100,000-man army to reach its very top as one of the two army group commanders. He retired in 1938 on reaching the age limit, though also because he had differed with Hitler in his treatment of Blomberg and Fritsch (qq.v.), but was recalled in 1939 to help plan the Polish campaign, in which he commanded Army Group A. He commanded it again during the attack on

France in 1940 and it was on his advice that Hitler issued the controversial 'stop order' to the panzers outside Dunkirk on 26 May. His army group operated on the southern sector of the Russian front during Operation Barbarossa, making slow progress because of its sparse allocation of armour, and he was relieved in the great purge of commanders in December 1941. Recalled from retirement in March 1942, he acted as Commander-in-Chief West until 2 July 1944, when he was removed again (for suggesting that the only sensible strategy against the Allied invasion of Normandy was to make peace) but again reappointed (*vice* Model, q.v.) in September to the same post, which he held until March 1945. Hitler then 'very politely' requested his resignation. The secret of Rundstedt's relationship with the Führer lay in his relationship with his fellow regular officers, by whom he was admired as the 'last Prussian' and the 'Black Knight of the German Army'. Hitler perceived and, in his case, respected his nobility of character – hence his unparalleled reappointment of him on three occasions. As a general, Rundstedt was competent but quite unoriginal: in his dispute with Rommel (q.v.) before D-Day on how best to repel the coming Allied invasion, his orthodox views were almost certainly the wrong ones.

Rupert of the Rhine, Prince (1619–82) German soldier, in British service. Nephew of King Charles I of England and the son of the ill-fated Elector Palatine (expelled from his territory after the battle of the White Mountain in 1620), Rupert acquired an enviable reputation first as a commander of cavalry, and latterly as an admiral. He gained his military training under Frederick Henry of Orange, and served in his bodyguard. In 1636 he visited England with his brother, and much impressed the king: the English ambassador at the Hague also saw his early promise: 'His

spirit is too active to be wasted in the softness and entangling of pleasure ... he will prove a sword to all his friends if his edge be set right.' From the age of fifteen he had been engaged in the practice and organization of war: in 1637 he took part in the epic siege and capture of Breda, and until his capture at the battle of Vlotho (1638) he was one of the most promising officers in the Dutch army. During his three years of imprisonment at Linz, he studied military theory, charmed his captors, and developed his considerable talents as an artist. His release was secured primarily through the good offices of Charles (1641). When Charles issued his call to arms at Nottingham, Rupert was present and was given command of the Royalist horse, by far the most impressive part of his army. The raw material he had to work with was excellent, men of quality who were well mounted, and, if they had little experience of war, were natural riders. Much of the strength of the Dutch army lay in its high standards of training, and Rupert attempted to instil discipline and co-ordination among his troops; however, as subsequent events proved, he was not entirely successful.

In his first action, at Powick Bridge, he roundly beat an equal force of Parliamentarian horse: it 'rendered the name of Prince Rupert very terrible indeed ... [all] talked loud of the incredible and irresistible courage of Prince Rupert and the King's horse'. At the battle of Edgehill (October 1642) the plan of battle was devised by Rupert, and its execution was generally satisfactory. But although his cavalry carried all before them, once launched, they proved impossible to restrain. Thus they were a decisive weapon, but one which could be used only once in a battle: this was to prove almost fatal at Edgehill and disastrous in subsequent encounters. After the battle Rupert urged an immediate advance on London to finish the war at a stroke; Charles, fatally, preferred a more cautious strategy. In the war of manœuvre he conducted his small forces brilliantly and, as at the capture of Bristol (1643), with a relentless attacking spirit. In early 1644 he began a march north into Lancashire, and across the Pennines into Yorkshire, creating devastation in his wake, and by a sudden feint relieved the Royalist garrison of York. At Marston Moor (1644) Rupert devised the plan of battle. In the ensuing action the Royalist horse, although shaken by the Parliamentarian attack, were successful and the battle seemed to have swung in their favour. But Cromwell's Ironsides remained intact while the Royalist horse had dispersed itself in pursuit. At the crucial moment in the battle they were launched against the unshielded Royalist infantry. It was a massive Parliamentary victory, and Rupert's rapid advance in the north was frustrated.

In November 1644 Rupert was appointed lieutenant-general of all the king's armies, a belated recognition that he was, beyond doubt, the most able leader on the Royalist side; if he had failed at Marston Moor, he had been successful almost everywhere else. But his promotion brought to a head the deep personal antagonisms in the Royalist camp, and his enemies struggled to undermine his position. The Royalist Council of War began to fall apart. It was the king's own insistence, egged on by his civilian advisers who disliked Rupert, that forced the army to give battle at Naseby (1645) to the much larger Parliamentary army under Fairfax (q.v.). Rupert produced a well coordinated plan for the joint action of infantry and cavalry, but despite his best efforts he could not regroup his horse after their initial success, until with much delay he led them back to the battle. In the space of an hour the battle had been lost, the product not so much of bad planning by Rupert, as a divided command and spiteful petty jealousies.

On its first outing at Naseby the Parliamentarian New Model Army had shown it was more than a match for the best Royalist forces; the Royalist cause was doomed. Rupert fell back on Bristol, but despite his attempts to organize a defence, he was forced to surrender to Fairfax (September 1645), a reverse which Charles, prompted by Rupert's many enemies at court, could not forgive. He was dismissed from his command, with bitter words: 'seek your subsistence beyond the seas, to which end I send you a pass.' He left England, to return with Charles II at the Restoration; in the Second Dutch War (1665–7) he commanded the fleet with Monck (q.v.) with considerable success; in the Third Dutch War (1672–4) he took over command from James, Duke of York, in 1673, and manœuvred his ships as skilfully as he had done his cavalry thirty years before.

As a commander, Rupert was one of the outstanding generals of the English Civil War: where he failed, it was due less to his planning than to the execution by his subordinates, a constant problem on the Royalist side. Had he possessed the bevy of able subordinate commanders on whom Fairfax or Cromwell could latterly rely, the war might have had a different conclusion.

Rupprecht, Crown Prince of Bavaria (1869–1955) German soldier. Because Bavaria retained a semi-autonomy within the German empire after 1871, its army, amounting in 1914 to three corps, remained separately organized from the Prussian and formed, for the invasion of France, the sixth of the seven German armies deployed in the west. Rupprecht commanded it, but unlike the German Crown Prince and the Duke of Württemberg, his fellow princely army commanders, he not merely understood but excelled at his duties and by 1917 had risen to command an army group.

Jacobites recognized his father as legitimate king of England.

Ruyter, Michiel Adriaanzoon de (1607–76) Dutch admiral. In the golden age of the Dutch navy, de Ruyter stands as one of her greatest admirals. First going to sea at the age of nine, he gained valuable early experience in the Dutch merchant service, then embarking on its most expansive phase; by 1635 he was a merchant captain, but in 1641 he served briefly as rear-admiral of a fleet assisting Portugal against Spain before rejoining the merchant service. The next ten years were spent fighting the Barbary pirates on the North African coast. In 1652 the First Dutch War (1652–4) against England broke out and de Ruyter accepted a regular naval command, serving under the great Maarten Tromp (q.v.); in 1653, after the battle of Texel in which Tromp was killed, he attained the rank of vice-admiral. After the conclusion of peace, de Ruyter took a Dutch fleet to the Baltic in 1659 to support the Danes against Sweden in the First Northern War (1655–60), and in 1664–5 patrolled the Guinean coast of Africa, skirmishing constantly with the English who had seized the West African slave ports from the Dutch West India Company in the previous year.

In 1665 this prolonged harrying came to a head when the Dutch recaptured the slave trade ports, de Ruyter attacked Barbados, and the Second Dutch War (1665–7) was declared. De Ruyter, now lieutenant-admiral of Holland, and close associate of de Witt (q.v.) in his plans for strengthening the Dutch navy, played a leading part in the war. In the Four Days' battle (June 1666) he beat back Monck and Prince Rupert (qq.v.), the leading British admirals, into the mouth of the Thames, an engagement which cost Monck a quarter of his eighty ships. De Ruyter threw a blockade across the Thames, but Monck broke the blockade and defeated de Ruyter at the battle of North Foreland (28 July 1666) before proceeding to the coast of Holland and destroying 160 anchored merchantmen. Peace negotiations were set in motion, but in June 1667, in a brilliantly effective and audacious coup, de Ruyter led a surprise raid into the Thames estuary, advancing up the Medway to within twenty miles of London and destroying much of the English fleet; Anglo-Dutch peace negotiations begun at Breda the previous April were brought to a speedy conclusion.

The crowning achievements of de Ruyter's career, however, were in the Third Dutch War (1672–4), which England and France engineered against Holland. In May 1672, at the battle of Sole Bay, de Ruyter, with seventy-five ships, surprised a French and English fleet; the withdrawal of the thirty-five French ships enabled de Ruyter to engage the English fleet, and although the arrival of English reinforcements forced the Dutch to retire, it was not before they had inflicted heavy damage. In 1672 Prince Rupert attacked de Ruyter's fleet in its coastal anchorage at Schoonveldt Channel, but de Ruyter was ready and drove off the English, again with heavy loss. Later that year he forced the English fleet, by a series of minor engagements, to retire to the Thames, but he was unable to impose a blockade because of an outbreak of plague on board his ships. In August 1673, while the allied fleets were blockading the Dutch coast, William of Orange ordered de Ruyter to the protection of an East Indies convoy. After a closely fought engagement the French retired, leaving the English to fight a more sustained defensive action; this having proved effective, the French returned and the Dutch were forced to retreat, but not before de Ruyter had brought the convoy in, thus breaking the blockade and frustrating as he did so the allied plan for a seaborne invasion of the United Provinces: this is usually known as the battle of Texel (August

1673). De Ruyter's long career ended in 1676 when fighting, yet again, against the French, he received a mortal wound at the naval battle of Messina. With the Tromps, de Ruyter had raised the power of the Dutch navy to supreme heights.

S

Saint-Arnaud, Armand Jacques Leroy de (1801–54) Marshal of France. Son of a prefect of the First Empire, Saint-Arnaud enlisted in the *gardes du corps* of Louis XVIII (1817) but left the army to fight in the Greek War of Independence, 1827–31. In 1836 debts obliged him to join the Foreign Legion in Algiers, where he attracted the attention of Bugeaud (q.v.) and made a reputation as a man of blood and iron in the taking of Constantine (1837) and the fighting against Abd el-Krim (q.v.). As minister of war in 1852 he crushed the resistance to the *coup d'état* which made prince-president Louis-Napoleon emperor and for it received his baton. In 1854 he was given charge of the Army of the Orient, commanded (with Raglan, q.v.) at the Alma but, stricken with cholera, handed over to Canrobert (q.v.) and was soon dead.

St Vincent, John Jervis, 1st Earl of (1735–1823) British admiral. A staunch Whig, St Vincent owed at least some of his progress in the navy to his politics. He entered the navy in 1749, and four years after he entered Parliament in 1783 he rose to flag rank. But he was also a highly competent officer and a stern disciplinarian. Appointed to take command of the Mediterranean fleet in 1795, after a successful cruise in the West Indies, he improved the performance of the fleet and sealed the French into Toulon. Forced to leave the Mediterranean as a result of Napoleon's conquests in Italy, which removed his bases, he shadowed the Spanish fleet at Cadiz. In February 1797, the Spanish fleet sailed to join the French at Brest: St Vincent, with fifteen ships of the line, intercepted the twenty-seven Spaniards. His aggressive tactics, and the energy of his subordinate Nelson (q.v.), brought a complete victory. A grateful king created him Earl of St Vincent; Parliament voted him a pension of £3000. Thereafter, although his harshness prevented mutiny in his fleet (1797), and when he took command of the Channel fleet (1800), his ferocious energy raised it to a peak of efficiency, he won no more stunning victories. He held no command after 1807, but was given the title of Admiral of the Fleet by George IV at his coronation in 1820.

Samsonov, Alexander Vasilievich (1859–1914). Russian general. Having commanded a cavalry division in Manchuria, where he had quarrelled with Rennenkampf (q.v.), between 1909 and 1914 Samsonov was military governor of Turkestan. Summoned in August to command the Second Army and to co-operate with Rennenkampf in an invasion of East Prussia, he revealed the position of his units to the Germans by broadcasting orders *en clair* and was defeated in the shattering battle of Tannenberg (26–31 August) by Hindenburg and Ludendorff (qq.v.). He himself hid and committed suicide on 29 August.

San Martin, José de (1778–1850) South American soldier and statesman. Although born in Argentina, his upbringing and early career were spent in Spain, which he served as a regular artillery officer for twenty-two years. On the outbreak of revolt in Buenos Aires, however, he returned home and embarked on a plan to liberate the southern half of the subcontinent, as Bolivar (q.v.) was doing in the northern. His scheme was methodical: he took two years to raise and train a small army with which he intended to clear the Spaniards first out of Chile and then Peru. Early in 1817 he crossed the Andes, defeated the Spaniards at Chacabuco, 12–15 February, entered Santiago, where he installed O'Higgins (q.v.) as ruler, and went on to win the battle of the Maipo (5 April), which confirmed Chile's independence. His invasion of Peru was less decisive. The defeat of the Spanish fleet by Cochrane (q.v.) allowed him to transport his army thither by sea and in July 1821 to capture Lima, but the Spanish withdrew into the mountains and he was unable to secure Bolivar's co-operation in crushing them. Disappointed in his relations with the Liberator and resentful of being thought a potential tyrant, he retired permanently to France.

Santa Anna, Antonio Lopez de (1794–1876) Mexican soldier and politician. His extravagant and erratic political career defies summary. As a soldier, he began life in the Spanish colonial army, after independence defeated a Spanish invasion at Tampico in 1829, fought against the Texans in 1836, lost a leg resisting the French at Vera Cruz in 1838, and on the outbreak of war with the United States, by then president, led his army in a disastrous march across the northern desert to be defeated by Zachary Taylor (q.v.) at Buena Vista, 22–3 February 1847. Retreating south, he was brought to battle by Scott (q.v.) outside Mexico City, defeated in the battle of Churubusco, 20 August, obliged to seek terms, and banished by his fellow countrymen.

Santa Cruz, Alvaro de Bazán, marques de (1526–88) Spanish admiral. The greatest of Spain's sailors in the six-

teenth century, Santa Cruz was the son of a Spanish naval officer. Although he gained his first experience in the galley warfare of the Mediterranean, he is best known as an exponent of the quite different techniques of sailing ships in the Atlantic. He commanded the reserve at Lepanto (1571), and entering the battle at a critical moment, played an important part in the great victory. His first major participation in an Atlantic campaign was in support of the Duke of Alva's conquest of Portugal in 1580, and in 1582 he defeated a French fleet under Filippo Strozzi at the battle of Terceira off the Azores; in the following year another French fleet under Aymard de Chaste went down in battle with Santa Cruz.

After the Portuguese conquest had been assured, Santa Cruz turned his entire attention to the conquest of England, which became an obsession with him. In 1583 he proposed the invasion of England, and Philip II, despite his essential caution, was fired by the idea. Santa Cruz began the slow business of assembling a huge fleet, hampered by lack of supplies and manpower. In 1587 Drake 'singed the King of Spain's beard' by sacking the port of Cadiz, which disrupted the preparation of the great Armada for the invasion of England. But the fleet was painstakingly repaired, although some items, such as water casks for the many troops to be carried on the ships, could not be made up. Santa Cruz's sudden death was a further setback to the fleet, for he was replaced by the Duke of Medina Sidonia, who was no sailor. It has been suggested that if Santa Cruz, a great seaman, had been in command, the outcome of the Armada of 1588 might have been different.

Sarrail, Maurice Paul Emmanuel (1856–1929) French general. In a republican army which, though Catholic and conservative at heart, prided itself on its political silence ('*La grande muette*), Sarrail, the radical and anti-clerical, naturally stood out. Moreover his politics advanced his career and increased his prominence. Assistant to General André, minister of war during the Dreyfusard reaction (*see* Dreyfus), he replaced the incompetent Ruffey at the head of Third Army in August 1914 and commanded it at the Marne and in the fighting (1914–15) in the Argonne. Relieved for squandering lives by Joffre (q.v.), whose power at the time outweighed that of his political protectors, he was, as a sop to them, given command of the expedition to Salonika where, in 1916, he recaptured Monastir from the Bulgarians and, in 1917, dethroned the neutralist King Constantine of Greece. He was removed again in 1918 and, after a postwar spell as high commissioner in Syria, which culminated in a revolt of the Druses, finally retired. His name remains a synonym for a 'political' general.

Saxe, Hermann Maurice, comte de (1696–1750) German soldier, in French service. The natural son of Frederick Augustus I of Saxony and Aurora von Königsmark, Saxe gained his first experience of war under Prince Eugen (q.v.) in the Malplaquet campaign (1709); in 1711 he was given the title Graf von Sachsen by his father, although he is usually known in the French form, for it was in the service of Louis XV that he made his reputation. In 1719 Frederick Augustus, having settled on a military career for him, purchased the colonelcy of a German regiment in the French army. Saxe's handling of his regiment, and in particular his development of a high degree of proficiency in musketry, and the inculcation of a strong offensive spirit in officers and men, soon attracted the favourable attention of the court. While France was at peace, Saxe devoted himself to the study of war, a process of research and analysis which culminated in the writing of *Mes Rêveries* in 1732,

although it was not published until after his death. But he found that the French army was not capable of the necessary mechanical precision, in fire and manœuvre, which was to become the hallmark of the Prussians. As he himself wrote: 'Our infantry, though the bravest in Europe, is not fit to stand a charge where infantry less brave, but better drilled and in a better formation, can close with it ...'

Saxe's standing in the French army was high, and at the end of the war of the Polish Succession (1734–8) he was a lieutenant-general. At the beginning of the war of the Austrian Succession (1740–8) Saxe was attached to the army of French 'volunteers' sent to the aid of the Bavarians: it was Saxe who devised and executed the successful attack which led to the capture of Prague (1741). But the Austrian riposte forced the French to withdraw (1742). Saxe was closely involved in the plan to send a French force to the aid of Prince Charles Edward's (q.v.) rising in Scotland. But a series of violent storms wrecked the French fleet off Dunkirk and the attempt was abandoned. In 1744 France declared war, and he was given command of one of the subsidiary armies in Flanders, together with the rank of marshal of France. When the main French armies moved off into the Rhineland, the Flanders campaign was left to Saxe. With his relatively small army he out-manœuvred the combined forces of Britain, Austria and the Netherlands, to the extent that he was at once given the main command. In 1745, now controlling an army of 70,000, he marched to besiege Tournai; the allied army under Cumberland (q.v.), 50,000 strong, marched to meet him. At Fontenoy (1745) Saxe selected a strong natural position, strengthened it with field fortifications, and made every effort to steady his wayward and somewhat unreliable troops. The opposing forces were now nearly equal. But it required Saxe himself, stricken with dropsy, to rise from his bed and to rally his men into a counter-attack, before the battle turned in the French favour. The turning point came when Saxe began to batter the English square with concentrated artillery fire (the French infantry showed themselves inferior to the British). But the strategic effect of Fontenoy was that all the great cities of Flanders – Ghent, Brussels, Antwerp, Mons, Namur – fell to the French. Saxe's later victories, at Rocourt (1746), where the English army was largely absent, having returned home to face the Scottish invasion, and Lauffeld (1747), after they had returned, were monuments to his superior skill as a general, working with poor raw material.

In recognition of his supreme talents, Saxe was created marshal-general of France, an honour held only by Turenne and Villars before him. The last major campaign of the war by him resulted in the capture of Maastricht (1748), and after the war ended he spent his remaining years in great state at Chambord, amused by his sequence of mistresses, troops of entertainers and a curious menagerie; his regiment was kept in the park of the château. In fact Saxe's greatest influence came after his death, with the publication of his military writings. He understood perfectly the strengths and weaknesses of the French army, and he devised his battles to suit them. In his use of field fortification and the development of the columnar form of infantry attack, both designed to sustain inferior, or poorly trained soldiers, he was a great innovator and pioneer.

Scharnhorst, Gerhard Johann David (von; 1755–1813) Prussian general and military reformer. A Hanoverian, Scharnhorst distinguished himself as an artillery officer in his own army under the Duke of York (q.v.) at Hondschoote on 6 September 1793, but finding promotion eluding him for his want of the

aristocratic 'von', transferred (1801) to the Prussian service, in which he was granted it and appointed to the military school in Berlin. During Napoleon's invasion of 1806 he was wounded at Auerstadt, but recovered to fight at Eylau the following year. Promoted general, he, with Gneisenau (q.v.), Stein and Hardenberg, began work under the noses of the French conquerors of Prussia to rebuild the spirit of the army, to accumulate a secret reserve of trained soldiers, larger than the treaty with France allowed, and to awaken the national feeling of the Prussian people for an eventual war of liberation. He was obliged at French insistence to quit the Prussian service in 1810, but reappeared as chief of staff to Blücher (q.v.) in 1812, served in the awaited war of liberation and was fatally wounded fighting the French at Lützen. His military achievements, including his scheme for universal military service, survived him, his liberal *tentatives* did not.

Scheer, Reinhard Karl Friedrich (1863–1929) German admiral. A former chief of staff of the High Seas Fleet, Scheer was chosen to succeed the dying Pohl as its commander in January 1916. Always an advocate of an offensive strategy *vis-à-vis* the British Grand Fleet, he provoked an encounter between the two on 31 May 1916. The battle of Jutland, though a German success in the ratio of major ships sunk (one German battlecruiser: three British) left Jellicoe (q.v.) strategically the master as before. Though continuing to argue for, and occasionally to risk, major fleet sorties, Scheer therefore sought to strike at Britain through a campaign of unrestricted U-boat attack, for which he secured governmental permission in February 1917. The British defeated it by the adoption – too long delayed – of convoy. Scheer, who was promoted to command the naval general staff in August 1918, was planning a final fleet sortie when the naval mutinies, which were the precursor of internal political collapse, broke out.

Schlieffen, Alfred, Graf von (1833–1913) German field-marshal. Chief of the Great General Staff, author of the Schlieffen Plan. A Guard Cavalry officer – he commanded the 1st Guard Uhlans, 1876–83 – Schlieffen epitomized that peculiar nineteenth-century phenomenon, the 'pure staff officer'. He attended the *Kriegsakademie* in 1858–61, served on the staff in the wars of 1866 and 1870 and from 1883 until his retirement in 1906 was continuously with the Great General Staff in Berlin, first as head of various sections, after 1891 (when he succeeded Waldersee, q.v.) as chief. 'Continuously' is moreover almost exact, for the early death of his wife left him free to devote himself entirely to his work, which occupied the whole of every day of his year. On Christmas Eve for instance he set his subordinates tactical problems which he expected to receive completed on Boxing Day.

The problem with which Schlieffen became obsessed after 1891, however, was that of achieving victory on both eastern and western fronts in the event of simultaneous war with France and Russia, an eventuality made almost unavoidable by the young kaiser's non-renewal of Bismarck's reinsurance treaties with the tsar. The scheme on which he eventually hit was one of extreme but calculated risk: estimating that Russia would take six weeks longer than France or Germany to mobilize, he decided to leave only a single army in the east (*see* Hindenburg, Ludendorff and Hoffmann), to cover the common Franco-German frontier with three more, and to use the remaining and strongest four to envelop the left flank of the French army (which he rightly guessed would attack into Germany) by a great wheeling movement through Belgium. He expected to fight a decisive battle east of

Paris within his six-week margin and be able to transfer his victorious armies eastwards in time to meet and beat the Russians before they had invaded East Prussia. The plan, which he bequeathed to his successor Moltke the younger (q.v.) in a Military Testament, acquired after his retirement the force of holy writ and, only slightly amended, was put into operation in August 1914. Unfortunately it contained a flaw, which Schlieffen recognized but could neither solve nor admit – it provided no formula for neutralizing the powerful garrison of Paris – and on that flaw it came to grief in September (*see* Kluck, Galliéni and Maunoury). Despite the catastrophe his plan brought about, his name remained revered among German general staff officers, whose professional association was named the *Schlieffenverein* in his memory.

Schomberg, Friedrich, Graf von (1615–90) German mercenary. A German soldier of fortune, Schomberg fought for France, England and Portugal, and died in the service of William III. In 1637 he fought for the French in the Thirty Years' War (1618–48), commanding an army against the Spanish in the south of France. He smashed a Spanish army besieging the fortress of Leucate, and drove it back beyond the border. This began a long-standing connection with the Iberian peninsula. He entered Portugal, beat the Spanish at Villaviciosa (1665) and executed a palace revolution against the feeble Afonso VI, placing Pedro II on the throne. Under Pedro, he carried out a thorough reorganization of the Portuguese army. He re-entered the French army and again defended the south against Spain. In 1674 his army repelled a Spanish attack on Roussillon, and then moved to the Flanders front. He held Maastricht against William of Orange (1676). But the repeal of the Edict of Nantes (1685) made French service less attractive, and in 1688 he took command of a force for William of Orange, now William III, against the Jacobite army of James II in Ireland. He was killed during the battle of the Boyne (1690).

Schörner, Ferdinand (1892–1973) German field-marshal. A Bavarian, who served in the *Leib-Regiment* (Bodyguard) during the First World War, Schörner achieved a quicker promotion than perhaps any other German soldier of the Second World War, chiefly through his ostentatious Nazism and sycophancy to Hitler, manifested in his meticulous execution of pointless orders. He remained unprotestingly in command of the surrounded Army Group North on the Baltic coast for six months, July 1944–January 1945, was then transferred to Army Group Centre in Czechoslovakia, where he so fed the Führer's groundless optimism by his promises of victory that he was promoted field-marshal in April. Despite his failure to relieve Berlin in the last days of the war, he was named by Hitler in his will his successor as commander-in-chief, a post he held nominally for eight days.

Schwarzenberg, Karl Philip, Fürst zu (1771–1820) Austrian field-marshal. First noted for his powers of decision at Hohenlinden, December 1800, where he saved the right wing of the army from destruction (*see* Moreau), Schwarzenberg repeated the feat during the Ulm campaign, when he led a division through the encircling French lines. He fought at Wagram, was sent to Paris to arrange the marriage between Marie-Louise and Napoleon, who formed a warm impression of him and insisted on his commanding the Austrian corps which took part in the invasion of Russia in 1812. In 1813, having been promoted field-marshal, he was put in command of the allied army which brought Napoleon to battle in Bohemia, was defeated at Dresden, 27 August, but

contributed largely to the victory of Leipzig, 16–19 October, and followed the emperor relentlessly into France the following year. His victories of Arcis-sur-Aube and La Fère-Champenoise in late March brought about Napoleon's first abdication.

His son **Friedrich Karl Schwarzenberg** (1800–70) was a remarkable military adventurer who served with the French in the invasion of Algeria, 1830, with the Carlists in Spain, 1832, in Switzerland during the Sonderbund war of 1846 (*see* Dufour) and in his own army against the Poles, 1846, the Italians, 1848, and the Hungarians, 1849.

Schwarzkopf, H. Norman (1934–) American general and theatre commander in the Persian Gulf War of 1991. This charismatic and articulate giant of a man was both born and named to be a warrior. Descended from German immigrants, his father, also H. Norman Schwarzkopf, chose a military career only to find that West Point required him to be known by his disliked first name of Herbert. Schwarzkopf senior saw active service in the First World War before leaving the army in 1919 for the superintendentship of the New Jersey state police. He gained fame for his handling of the Lindburg kidnapping in 1932, and after 1936 as a radio personality presenting the *Gangbusters* show. Returning to active service in 1941, he spent most of the Second World War in Persia, retiring in 1947 with the rank of brigadier-general. Left to raise two daughters and a son alone his wife became an alcoholic, a fate all too common in the military. Schwarzkopf's own account of his career before and during the Persian Gulf War, *It Doesn't Take A Hero*, deals with this and other intimate matters in a disarmingly folksy way. But despite his professed admiration for the memoirs of the great commanders of the past, it has disappointingly little to say regarding his military philosophy and the serious issues of command.

The youngest child of the family, Herbert Norman Schwarzkopf Jr was born in New Jersey, and educated at a nearby military school. After the Second World War the family was reunited with their father, first in Tehran and then on army duty in Europe. Schwarzkopf completed his education at Valley Forge Military Academy, showing remarkable ability as a scholar. Just before entering West Point in 1952, he legally changed his name to 'H. Norman', so dropping the hated 'Herbert' and 'Jr' and confounding army regulations. But as a relentless and painfully earnest over-achiever – who was also over-weight and over-clever – he continued throughout his life to be afflicted with a variety of insulting nicknames, of which 'the Bear' was the most common, replaced after the Persian Gulf War by the more affectionate 'Stormin' Norman'.

In 1957 Schwarzkopf was commissioned into the infantry, choosing that great forcing-house of American military talent, the airborne forces. His career prospered, and in 1962 the army sent him to gain a master's degree in mechanical engineering at the University of Southern California, with a view to becoming a West Point instructor. In 1965 Schwarzkopf volunteered from West Point for his first tour in Vietnam, as a military adviser. He married in 1968, followed by a second tour in Vietnam a year later including experience with headquarters staff and command of a battalion.

Schwarzkopf emerged from Vietnam with a determination that next time the army would do better. He persevered with his career in the United States and Europe, rising through brigadier-general in 1978 to full general ten years later, one of a generation of officers trying to turn the army around from the humiliation of Vietnam and the corruption which had accompanied it. In 1983 as a major-general he was appointed ground forces commander for the American intervention in Grenada (Operation Urgent Fury). In 1988 he received his final posting, to Central Command (CENTCOM) in the United States. Including army, air force and marines forces, CENTCOM had been formed in 1982 with the improbable mission of defending the Middle East from a Soviet invasion, despite the absence of any formal treaties or agreements between the United States and the Persian Gulf countries, and was seen as something of a retirement posting. Schwarzkopf took CENTCOM seriously, looking with his staff at the new threat posed by Iraq under its dictator Saddam Hussein to the oil fields of the Gulf. When in August 1990 Iraqi troops occupied Kuwait and threatened Saudi Arabia, Schwarzkopf could offer President George Bush a viable plan to defend the region. With Saudi agreement, Schwarzkopf and his CENTCOM forces left for the Middle East to begin Operation Desert Shield.

From August 1990 to the end of the Persian Gulf War Schwarzkopf remained in Saudi Arabia as the senior American commander. Arab political sensibilities required that a Saudi officer of the royal house, General Prince Khalid bin Sultan, should be overall commander, while American needs for wider political support led to almost thirty countries contributing in some way to Desert Shield. Against this, the United States provided the vast majority of forces used and dominated the coalition. As the commander in fact if not in name, Schwarzkopf had to walk a tightrope between American requirements and those of his Arab and coalition partners. Inevitably his relations with Prince Khalid and with Washington (in the person of General Colin Powell q.v., Chairman of the Joint Chiefs of Staff) were often tense. Complaints were heard of Schwarzkopf's temper and ego, or insenstitivity to Arab problems which, given the political stakes, were a counsel of perfection against which no real commander could ever measure up.

By October 1990 Desert Shield was complete and Saudi Arabia safe from an invasion that had never looked likely. According to Schwarzkopf's memoirs, he successfully resisted calls from Washington for an early offensive to liberate Kuwait, demanding extra reinforcements which would mostly arrive in the new year. Schwarzkopf's plan for Operation Desert Storm, the liberation of Kuwait, was one of the most remarkable pieces of military science in recent history, seeking to reconcile Arab requirements that Kuwait should be liberated, and Iraq humbled but not completely destroyed, with American requirements for a crushing victory at minimum human cost to themselves. The plan drew self-consciously on the lessons of the great attacking victories of the past, but was based heavily on fire-power and treated the Iraqi enemy with a respect that, in the event, they scarcely deserved. Starting in January 1991 with a devastating initial air attack, the plan culminated in a four-day ground offensive at the end of February which expelled the Iraqis from Kuwait. Saddam Hussein survived in charge of Iraq, but with both his army and his political power severely weakened. American casualties in the war were negligible, with fewer than two hundred killed in action.

Schwarzkopf had masterminded the single largest military operation since the Second World War. By winning one battle in one campaign he found himself lifted by American gratitude into the pantheon of the great military commanders of history that he so much admired. Entrusted with restoring American pride after Vietnam, he had not failed. He retired from the army a few months after the war to earn a personal fortune from his memoirs and lecture tours, a genuine American hero.

Scott, Winfield (1786–1866) American (Union) general. Scott was the most important military figure produced by the United States between Washington and Lee (qq.v.); though too old to take the field in 1861, he proposed the strategy which eventually won the war (the 'Anaconda Plan' of seizing the line of the Mississippi and crushing the South by concentric advances). He had been commanding general of the US Army since 1841 and was a national hero for his victories in the Mexican war (battles of Molino del Rey and Chapultepec, capture of Vera Cruz and Mexico City), 1846–7. He had been nominated for president by the Whig Party in 1852 and as a young officer had won a gold medal from Congress for his bravery in battle in the war of 1812. Though known as 'Old Fuss and Feathers' to impatient Civil War officers, who usually found him asleep at his desk, he was still a wiser strategist and might even have proved a better battlefield commander than McClellan (q.v.), who succeeded him in November 1861.

Seeckt, Hans von (1866–1936) German general. A Guards officer (*Kaiser Alexander Garde-Grenadiere*), he served as chief of staff to Mackensen (q.v.), 1915–18, being responsible for the planning of the Gorlice-Tarnow breakthrough and the second invasion of Serbia. After the collapse of the monarchy he became *Chef des Truppenamts* (i.e. commander-in-chief) and oversaw the reduction of the army to 100,000 men, as dictated at Versailles. He succeeded none the less in rebuilding its spirit by making each regiment the 'tradition-bearer' of several of the old, which he intended would be reborn in better times, and by teaching the officers that they were the guardians of Germany's past and future greatness. However, his political message to the army – that it must remain 'above party' – unintentionally prepared the way for its acceptance of Hitler by deprecating the process of party politics itself.

Selim I (1470–1520) Turkish sultan, tyrant and soldier. Although he reigned for only eight years, Selim (nicknamed 'the Grim') extended the frontiers of the Ottoman empire and virtually destroyed the power of Persia. His interests lay in the east rather than the west, partly the product of a political decision to restore the erosion of territory by Turkey's Moslem neighbours, and partly the result of an extreme religiosity which set him against the 'heretical' Shiite sect predominant in Persia. The first act of his reign, after his father Bayezid had abdicated in his favour, was to murder all his relatives who could challenge his accession to the sultanate. Thereafter he turned to the problem of Persia. The Persians had supported his brother Ahmed in the contest for the throne, and Selim was implacable in his hatred of them. He first annihilated the Shiite sect in his own domains, to safeguard his rear, and then concluded a set of agreements with the western powers to secure his other borders.

In 1515 Selim marched east with some 60,000 men; a proportion of these were skilled Janissaries, certainly the best infantry in Asia, and the *sipahis*, equally well-trained and disciplined cavalry. The remainder were the levies and irregular troops which made up the bulk of any Ottoman army. As the army marched east, the Janissaries complained about the likely length of the campaign and the rigours of the march: Selim immediately executed the grumblers and their officers. With this stern warning before them the resolve of the army hardened, and when in August 1515 the Turkish forces met the Persian army, morale was high. The Persian army, under Shah Ismail, was almost entirely composed of Turcoman tribal levies, a courageous but ill-disciplined cavalry army. Slightly inferior in numbers to the Turks, their charges broke against the Janissaries, who had taken up fixed positions behind rudimentary field works. The battle of

Chaldiran was a complete Turkish victory; the Persian capital was taken and the land ravaged. But the Turks had no means to maintain themselves in hostile territory, and they were forced to retreat.

The experience of the campaign affected Selim considerably, and on his return to Istanbul he instituted a thorough overhaul of the Janissary command and training. But he was prevented from renewing his Persian war by troubles in Iraq and Egypt. In 1516 he moved against the Mameluke sultan of Egypt, Kansu al Gauri, who had entered into an alliance with the Persians. The Turks were once again strong in infantry and artillery, whilst the Mameluke army, like the Persian, was composed largely of cavalry. Despite the high quality of the Mameluke horsemen, the Turkish infantry and artillery resisted their attack. Kansu al Gauri was killed and his troops fled from the battlefield. The battle of Merj-Dabik, like that of Chaldiran, revealed the value of firepower and the elaborate training of the Janissaries. The Mamelukes hastily elected Kansu's nephew, Touman Bey, as their new leader. He recognized the crucial role artillery had played and bought ships' guns from Venetian vessels to create a strong field fortification which might offset the Turks' advantages in skill and equipment. But at the battle of Ridanieh (1517) the Turkish armies outflanked the fixed fortifications and used their own guns, better located, to harry the Mameluke cavalry, which charged but swiftly met the same fate as their forces at Merj-Dabik: 7000 Mamelukes were killed, but the Turks lost almost as many, some 6000, many of whom were virtually irreplaceable infantry. Cairo was occupied, and the inhabitants who resisted, massacred. The last vestiges of Mameluke opposition were brutally crushed.

Taking the titles of sultan of Egypt and caliph of Islam, the latter acquired from the last of the Abbasid rulers of Baghdad, Selim moved on into Arabia and visited the Holy Places of Mecca and Medina. On his return he crushed revolts by religious sectarians in Syria and Anatolia with little difficulty. He was now unchallenged throughout Asia Minor, and his thoughts turned to the Mediterranean. In 1520 he accepted the homage of the dey of Algiers, the noted pirate Khair-ed-din (Barbarossa, q.v.), an act which was to have far-reaching consequences under his son Suleiman (q.v.). Later in the same year he made plans to attack the island of Rhodes, assembling a great fleet and large army for the purpose. But death overtook him and the campaign was left to Suleiman. Selim was an outstandingly successful soldier and ruler. He brought the Ottoman empire a huge increase of rich territory, great prestige (with the title of caliph), and unification by the draconian suppression of the slightest opposition. But equally significant were his reforms of the Janissary system and his purges of their higher ranks, while the enlargement of the navy spelt eventual doom for Venetian power in the eastern Mediterranean. Of the great succession of Ottoman rulers who succeeded Mehmed the Conqueror, Selim was the most consistently successful. He used the great strength in infantry and fire-power which his father Bayezid II had left him to shatter the traditional cavalry armies of the Persians and Mamelukes. It was .left to his son to turn the great army against the west.

Sérurier, Jean Mathieu Phibilert (comte; 1742–1819) Marshal of France. An officer of the *ancien régime* and a veteran of the Seven Years' War (1756–63), Sérurier accepted the Revolution and rose, under the sponsorship of Barras, to become general of division in 1795. He held commands in the Army of Italy, 1793–9, under Bonaparte and helped him in the *coup d'état* of 18 Brumaire.

He was created marshal in 1804 (reckoned as one of the four – with Kellermann, Lefebvre and Pérignon, qq.v. – honorary marshals), and thenceforward held the entirely honorary post of governor of Les Invalides until 1815.

Seydlitz, Friedrich Wilhelm, Freiherr von (1721–83) Prussian soldier. Embodying the very essence of the bold cavalryman, Seydlitz was born to his profession. The son of a cavalry officer, who died when he was seven, Seydlitz had to find his own way in the world. Becoming a page at the court of Margrave Frederick William of Brandenburg-Schwedt, a small Prussian territory, in 1740 he entered the margrave's cuirassier regiment and fought in the war of the Austrian Succession (1740–8), until his capture at the battle of Chotusitz (1742), a bitter encounter with the Austrians under Charles of Lorraine. At this battle the quality of the Prussian cavalry had been of crucial importance, and when Seydlitz was exchanged he was given a superior post. At the battle of Soor (1745), again against Charles of Lorraine, Seydlitz's mastery of his men and their effectiveness in the battle brought him to the notice of Frederick the Great, who in 1753 gave him command of the 8th Cuirassiers, which by a process of constant drilling Seydlitz turned into a model regiment.

His methods, albeit very conventional in their content, were used in other regiments and the results were excellent: by the outbreak of the Seven Years' War he had been instrumental in increasing the effectiveness of the Prussian cavalry, in particular fostering a uniquely aggressive spirit in battle. In the Seven Years' War (1756–63), with Prussia beset by many enemies, speed of transit and manoeuvre was at a premium. At the battle of Prague (1757) it was the cavalry which enabled Frederick to exploit a fault in the Austrian position, by pressing on the flank while his infantry pushed forward into a gap in the centre. At Kolin a month later (June 1757) it was the cavalry on both sides which decided the day: the Austrians broke the back of the exhausted Prussian infantry, and Seydlitz's cavalry fought a magnificent rearguard action which prevented the Prussian retreat becoming a rout. Frederick, in gratitude, created him a major-general. At Rossbach (November 1757) it was Seydlitz's intervention, charging full-tilt with his thirty-eight cavalry squadrons into the right flank of the Austro-French army under Hildburghausen and Soubise (as Prussian infantry pressed heavily on the left) which gained a smashing victory (21,000 Prussians beating 64,000). But in the charge Seydlitz was wounded and was out of action until the following year: he was one of only 500 Prussian casualties in a battle which had cost the enemy 8000.

Seydlitz returned to service at the battle of Zorndorf (1758), where Frederick faced the Russian army of 45,000 under Fermor, and again played a decisive part. The Russian infantry held against the Prussian assault until Seydlitz charged to disrupt their formation; it was a costly struggle for both sides, but a Prussian defeat had been averted. At Hochkirk (1758), as at Kolin, the cavalry protected the Prussian retreat after a wasting fight which caused 9500 Prussian casualties. These successive battles, involving heavy Prussian losses, bled the army of its best men, particularly in the cavalry where men were difficult to train. At Kunersdorf (1759), a battle which Frederick mishandled, the Austrians and Russians held against Prussian attacks (delivered piecemeal, for the formations had broken up in the marshy terrain), the Austrian hussars harrying the struggling Prussian infantry. Once again the cavalry were thrown in to cover the retreat, but on this occasion they could not stem the strength of the enemy attack. Seydlitz was again severely wounded in the bitter hand-to-hand struggle, and was absent from duty until 1761. He returned to serve, not with Frederick, but on the western front. He joined Prince Henry of Prussia and beat the Austrian army of Serbelloni at Freiburg (1762), almost the last major engagement of the war. Here he commanded both infantry and cavalry, and showed that his talents were not at all one-sided.

When peace came Seydlitz was promoted general of cavalry (1767), as well as inspector-general of the Silesian cavalry, a force he had done so much to train to a peak of efficiency. Seydlitz had the qualities inherent in all great cavalrymen: a simple, up-and-at-them approach, untempered by any great theory of the art of war. Like all great cavalry officers, he was a superb horseman, and much of the extraordinary loyalty owed him by his men came simply from the fact that he led from the front, was the first in any charge, the first to tackle the enemy. But his rigid training gave them a control and discipline which made them much more valuable than horsemen who were spent at the first charge. Certainly much of the success achieved by the Prussian armies must be to his credit and lasting glory.

Shaka Zulu (1787–1828) The by-blow of a Zulu chief, who came upon his mother bathing in a stream, Shaka was an outcast both from his father's people, and from his mother's, the Langeni. Even his name (*Shaka* was an intestinal beetle) was a mark of shame and contempt. But this rootlessness allowed him to develop his military ideas outside the rigid conventions of traditional warfare in southern Africa, as well as a ruthlessness quite alien to normal custom. As a military and political innovator, he had no equal in his own time. Even the great leader of the Mthethwa confederation, Dingiswayo, who had had the vision to see Shaka's talents and allowed him to remould his army, could not compare with his protégé.

Shaka gave system and order to the often haphazard conditions of traditional warfare. This consisted of little more than hurling insults and a few spears at an enemy: wars were won by guile and ambush rather than set-piece battles. Indeed, Shaka's developments were so original that for decades they were thought to have been inspired by western models. This was not so, for all his changes came from a clear understanding of the potentials in Zulu society. It was well ordered, with a rigid system of age groups organized on military lines. Zulus were used to discipline. Shaka's first change was to turn his few soldiers (at first numbered in the hundreds rather than the thousands) into a force for fighting at close quarters: he abandoned the throwing spear as a principal weapon, for a short handled, broad-bladed spear intended for stabbing. To this he gave the name *iKlwa*, which sounded (it was said) like a blade being withdrawn from a body. The new weapon was accompanied by a savage hardening programme: his soldiers were not allowed to wear sandals, and were forced to march over sharp thorns to prove their imperviousness to pain; the penalty for failure was death. With his small force he conquered local clans on behalf of Dingiswayo, who in 1816 provided him with men and resources to capture the chieftaincy of his father's people, the Zulu.

Dingiswayo was assassinated in 1817, and over the next ten years, Shaka made himself supreme in the former Mthethwa territories, and over a much larger area of southern Africa. With an army of some 40,000 Shaka simply absorbed surrounding peoples, exterminating all who attempted to resist. He took revenge on his mother's clan, slaughtering all those who had once slighted him; at his first major battle, at Gqokli Hill

in 1817, he showed the fate which would befall all who opposed him. The powerful Ndwandwe army (much larger than his own forces at that time) was devastated by his tactic of outflanking their main force with fast moving skirmishers while the main body of his army smashed through their centre. This was the tactic of the 'horns' and the 'chest': Shaka likened his army to the buffalo, the most dangerous animal of the veldt. The 'horns' enveloped an enemy, while the chest 'ate him up'. This was the phrase which Shaka used of his enemies. By 1824, all the surrounding peoples had been 'eaten up', or fled to the north or south.

Shaka's ruthlessness was at first deliberate, but it eventually became uncontrolled. When his mother Nandi died, over 7000 people were killed for failing to display adequate grief. He decreed that no crops should be planted as a sign of mourning, which meant starvation in the following year, and any woman found pregnant should be killed (and her husband with her). In the year between his mother's death in the summer of 1827 and his own in September 1828, Shaka began the long-expected attack on his last remaining enemy, the European settlers in Cape Colony. This last plan was foiled only by his murder at the hands of his half-brothers, who feared that they would shortly suffer from his vengefulness. On the day before he died, Shaka ordered the massacre of some 400 women, on the grounds that they were engaged in witchcraft. His murderers, led by his brother Dingane, rightly feared they might be next.

Shaka created the Zulu empire over some eleven years. The process is believed to have cost two million lives. For much of the eleven years, his ruthlessness was a matter of policy. It was the only plausible means to enforce discipline over a huge area with very limited communications: fear replaced administration. In his last years, the terror was sustained by his increasingly wild fears and hatreds. His legacy to his people was a military machine unique in Africa, and one capable of defeating even well-armed European troops. Fanciful commentators called him The Black Napoleon, and allowing for different societies and customs, the comparison is apt. Shaka was without doubt the greatest commander to come out of Africa.

Shaposhnikov, Boris Mikhailovich (1882–1945) Marshal of the Soviet Union. A tsarist general staff officer, Shaposhnikov volunteered for the Red Army in 1918, joined the operations section of the Supreme Military Soviet and planned the strategy of the campaigns against Denikin (q.v.) and the Poles. He was later head of the Frunze (q.v.) Military Academy and three times chief of staff, 1928–31, 1937–40, 1941–November 1942. He was removed on the first occasion for having written praise of Trotsky (q.v.); on the second and third because of ill-health. His intellectual influence on the Red Army and, allegedly, on Stalin, was very great, through his writing, his lectures and his associations.

Sheridan, Philip Henry (1831–88) American (Union) general. Too young to have climbed far in the army at the outbreak of the Civil War, Sheridan got command of a cavalry regiment in May 1862 and thereafter his achievements carried him rapidly upwards. A divisional commander at Perryville and Stones River, his leadership in the Chattanooga campaign, when his division captured Missionary Ridge and nearly made Bragg (q.v.) and his staff prisoners, prompted Grant (q.v.) to appoint him commander of the cavalry corps of the Army of the Potomac. Leading it in a raid in May 1864, he clashed with the corps of Jeb Stuart (q.v.) at Yellow Tavern, where the latter was fatally wounded.

Later in the year he embarked on a campaign in the Shenandoah Valley, which rivalled that of Jackson (q.v.) for its brilliance and brought about the destruction of the army of Early (q.v.). On 1 April 1865 he defeated Pickett (q.v.) at Five Forks and a week later prevented Lee (q.v.) from withdrawing beyond Appomattox, thus determining that the Civil War should, effectively, be ended there and then. In later years he succeeded Sherman (q.v.) as general-in-chief (1884–8). Sheridan was a cavalry leader and tactician of the first class.

Sherman, William Tecumseh (1820–91) American (Union) general. Named after a famous fighting chief of the Shawnee, Tecumseh (q.v.), Sherman was unusual among Northern generals in having lived long in the South and in coming from an established family: his foster-father was a member of the cabinet and ex-senator, his wife the daughter of a secretary of the interior, his brother a successful politician and secretary of state-to-be. But his rise, unlike that of so many Union 'political' generals, owed nothing to influence. After twelve years in civilian life (as head of Louisiana State University), he was out of touch with the army, which he had entered from West Point in 1840, but he commanded a division with distinction at Shiloh, took a major part in the Vicksburg and Chattanooga campaigns under Grant (q.v.), and, on Grant leaving the west in March 1864, succeeded him in command there. It was in the subsequent Atlanta campaign, March to the Sea and campaign in the Carolinas that he made his name and his reputation for a ruthless and (in modern terms) original style of warmaking.

Sherman took the view that it is in resources rather than soldiers that a state's power to make war resides and he accordingly set out to deprive the South of as much material as he could. Having seized the rail centre of Atlanta, thus again bisecting the territory of the South (*see* Scott and his Anaconda Plan), he cut a swathe of devastation 60 miles wide and 400 miles deep to the sea at Savannah, where he arrived on 10 December 1864. He then turned north to repeat the treatment in North and South Carolina. J.E.Johnston (q.v.) tried ineffectively to oppose him and was eventually forced to surrender at Goldsboro, 13 April 1865. Sherman's best-known dictum, 'War is hell', accurately encapsulates his strategic outlook, and unfortunately prefigures that of a multitude of generals in the twentieth century. His army's speed of advance on its marches (450 miles in fifty days through the Carolinas) bears comparison, even though it was little resisted, with that of later mechanized forces. After Grant's election to the presidency (1868), Sherman succeeded him as general-in-chief, a post he held for fifteen years. Modern scholarship has come to regard him as one of the greatest generals of the industrial world.

Shun Chih (1638–61) Manchu emperor. The ninth son of Abahai, leader of the Manchu tribes, Shun Chih succeeded to the throne in 1643 at the age of five. In 1644 his paternal uncle, Dorgon, captured Peking: the Ming dynasty was ended and the young king was proclaimed emperor. Under Dorgon, Manchu power was extended further and further into the south, and by his death in 1650 the whole of northern China was firmly ruled by Manchu Peking. The generals of Shun Chih continued the conquests, and by 1659 the rest of the Ming supporters were driven out to the island of Formosa. But Shun Chih himself was a peaceable man, and he ended his life as a Buddhist priest.

Sigismund III Vasa (1566–1632) King of Poland. Under his rule the crowns of Sweden and Poland were temporarily united, from 1592 to 1599. A Catholic,

Sigismund was forced to promise to uphold freedom of worship for Swedish Lutherans, but it was impossible to control both kingdoms, and Sigismund's regent in Sweden, his uncle Charles, rose in rebellion against him. Charles defeated an invading army from Poland at Stängebro (1598) and the Swedish parliament declared Sigismund deposed. An intermittent war continued until Charles's death in 1611. Sigismund was no soldier himself, but he was lucky in his commanders, notably the great cavalry commander Chodkiewicz (q.v.). The Poles had some success in Russia during the chaos within that country, the Time of Troubles, 1604–13, but the early victories against Charles were reversed when Gustavus Adolphus (q.v.) (Charles's son) invaded Polish Livonia and recaptured the areas his father had sought, although the Poles under Koniecpolski resisted strongly. Only gradually were the Swedes able to match the power and dash of the Poles, and the war was concluded by the treaty of Altmark (1629), which freed Gustavus for action in Germany and secured the Baltic coast. By Sigismund's death the initiative had passed decisively to Sweden. The perennial problem of Poland was the number of enemies she faced – Russia, Turkey, Prussia, Sweden. But by embroiling Poland in what was essentially a private, dynastic squabble Sigismund drained his country of wealth and men.

Sitting Bull (1834–90) American Indian (Sioux) chief. Head of the Sioux war council in 1875, when war broke out afresh between the tribe and the US Army, he and Crazy Horse (q.v.) were the leaders at the battle of the Little Big Horn in which Custer (q.v.) and his 7th Cavalry were destroyed.

Sivaji (1627–80) Indian soldier and statesman, founder of the Maratha state. One of the greatest exponents of the skills of guerrilla warfare, Sivaji began his career as the head of a small rebel band, fighting against the sultan of Bijapur. His successes rallied widespread Hindu support, and in 1659 the sultan sent an army of 20,000 men against him, under the command of his best general, Afzal Khan. Sivaji retreated into the mountains and sent emissaries to the general for a parley. He then murdered him and destroyed his leaderless army. With the arms of the 20,000 defeated Bijapuris, and many new recruits to the rebel cause, Sivaji was now a major force. The Mogul emperor Aurengazeb sent several detachments against him, all of which Sivaji managed to destroy piecemeal. Infuriated, Aurengazeb sent a substantial army against him under Jai Singh, after he had taken the main Mogul port of Surat. With 100,000 men against him, Sivaji was forced to surrender, and was sent into house arrest at Agra. He pretended sickness and great remorse at his disloyalty; he succeeded in escaping (1666) most dramatically, concealed in a huge bowl of sweets he had sent out for distribution to the poor. Returning to the Deccan, he reverted to guerrilla war, raising the flag of revolt against the Moguls.

By 1668, Sivaji had recaptured all the territory he had lost and extended his dominions into a unitary Maratha state. He started to extend the navy he had begun in 1659, and in 1674 he proclaimed an independent Hindu kingdom. In doing so, and in the careful diplomacy and alliance system he created with his small Moslem neighbours, he set a barrier to the southward extension of the Mogul empire. The strength of the Maratha state lay in its arid and mountainous terrain, which was impossible for an enemy to dominate, and in the superb army of light cavalry he created. For over a century the warlike Marathas were to dominate central India, and posed a dangerous enemy for the Europeans in their advance.

Sixt von Armin, Friedrich (1851–1936) German general. A survivor of the massacre of the Guard Corps at Saint-Privat in 1870 (*see* Hindenburg), he rose to command Fourth Army, which on 25 April 1918 achieved the remarkable surprise capture of Kemmel Hill, south of Ypres, in the second of the great German 'war-winning' offensives of that year.

A descendant, **Hans-Heinrich Sixt von Armin** (1890–1952), was captured at Stalingrad commanding the 113th Division and died in captivity.

Skobolev, Mikhail Dimitrievich (1843–82) Russian general. Son of a distinguished general, Dimitri Ivanovich Skobolev (1821–80), he was promoted major-general at thirty-four for his leadership of the expedition to Khokand in Turkestan, to which region he returned, after playing a leading part in the Turkish war of 1877–8 (siege of Plevna, battle of Senova), to complete the conquest (1881). Apparently destined to rise to the first place in the army, he died of a heart attack in the midst of an orgy in Moscow, aged thirty-eight.

Slim, William Joseph (1st Viscount Slim; 1891–1970) British field-marshal. Of humble origins, Slim was commissioned from the ranks during the First World War, after which he transferred, with a regular commission, to the Indian army (6th Gurkhas). A brigade commander at the outbreak of the Second World War, he rose quickly to command a division and in 1942 was sent to Burma to take command of I Corps at the very outset of the Japanese attack. Between March and May he conducted its retreat of 900 miles from Rangoon to Imphal in India. There the British remained on the defensive until, in December 1943, he was given command of the Fourteenth Army and at once undertook an attack into the Arakan (February 1944).

war he was retired from the army and became court chamberlain at a small Prussian court of Hohenzollern Hechingen. In 1777 he left the court abruptly under a cloud and failed to obtain a military post with any of the great powers, or even with the East India Company. He was therefore not much of a catch for the American agents, Benjamin Franklin and Silas Deane, who sent him off to Washington at his camp in Valley Forge with fulsome recommendations.

Their instincts were correct, however, for Steuben turned out to be a superb instrutor for the colonial troops and turned an army of civilians into soldiers. He formed a model drill company and trained them, if not to the standard of a Potsdam parade ground, at least able to fulfil normal military evolutions. He took an intense interest and pride in the growth of his pupils' understanding of military skills; appointed inspector-general of the army, with the rank of major-general, his tactical manual (*Regulations for the Order and Discipline of the Troops of the United States*) became the training guide for the entire army. It was thanks to Steuben's tireless efforts that American troops were able to match the professional skills of British regulars in the later battles of the war. In 1780 he was given, as he fervently desired, a field command; but his skills, it was revealed, lay on the drill ground rather than the battlefield. A raucous, larger-than-life character, he recognized both the weaknesses and the potential of his raw recruits; after the war, loaded with honour and rewards by Congress and the state of New York, he succeeded in dissipating his resources, but eventually contrived a life pension.

Stilwell, Joseph (1883–1946) American general. Having spent thirteen years of his inter-war service in China, Stilwell was the obvious general to send in 1941 as American representative to Chiang Kai-shek (q.v.), who made him his chief of staff. Stilwell was also given command of all US forces in China, though these consisted initially only of airmen under the dynamic Chennault (q.v.). During the British retreat from Burma he brought two Chinese armies, Fifth and Sixth (equivalent to two western corps), to their aid and tried to keep open the Burma road along which supplies from India went to Chiang Kai-shek. He was, however, defeated and forced to take refuge in India. In 1944 he returned to the offensive with Chinese and American troops (Merrill's Marauders) and took part in the second Chindit operation (*see* Wingate) but, following a difference of opinion between himself and Chiang as to how best to counter a renewed Japanese offensive in China itself, he was relieved on 18 October 1944. This was the last of a series of quarrels he had had with almost everyone of note in South-East Asia, including Wavell, Slim, Wingate (qq.v.), Mountbatten and Chennault. Not for nothing was he universally known as Vinegar Joe – though his victories were also ready witness to his ability and integrity.

Stössel, Anatoli Mikhailovich (1848–1915) Russian general. His direction of the defence of Port Arthur, May 1904–January 1905, in the Russo-Japanese war (*see* Nogi) was so uninspired that he was tried by court-martial after the war and sentenced to death (later commuted).

Strachan, Sir Richard John, 4th Baronet (1760–1828) British admiral. His squadron captured four of the French ships which had escaped from Trafalgar off Cape Ortegal, where he was lying in wait for them, on 3 November 1805. In 1809 he was naval commander of the disastrous expedition to Walcheren.

Straussenberg, Artur Freiherr Arz von (1857–1935) Austrian general. Commander of VI Corps against the Russians in 1915, he led the First Army in the invasion of Romania, August 1916, and in May 1917 succeeded Conrad (q.v.) as chief of staff. It was he who planned the great breakthrough of the Italian front at Caporetto in November and the abortive offensive on the Piave in June 1918.

Stuart, Charles Edward, Prince (1720–88) The Young Pretender. For all the romance of 'Bonnie Prince Charlie', Charles Edward was a foolish young man, who brought the disaster of Culloden (1746) upon his own head. The rebellion of 1745, despite the fact that the Scots reached Derby, was doomed from the outset; Lord George Murray (q.v.), the only commander of ability on the Jacobite side, argued in vain for a rapid descent on England before the Hanoverian forces could recover from the shock of a rising in the North. The victories – Prestonpans and Falkirk – were the work of Murray. It was Charles himself who insisted on attacking the army of the Duke of Cumberland (q.v.) at Culloden, when saner voices argued for a retreat into the Highlands and a war of attrition. On 16 April 1746 the English guns raked the Jacobite ranks, and after a charge, easily repulsed, the battle was lost. Charles began his heroic journey of escape, finally arriving in France in September 1746. Thereafter, his progress was rapidly downhill as disappointment engulfed him. He lived the rest of his life a shabby figure, first in France and then in Italy, falling repeatedly into bouts of drunkenness. Undoubtedly the '45 was a vain hope, but with more support both in Scotland and England, effective French support, and a more modest submission by Charles to military minds more expert than his, the chance of success was there.

Stuart, James Ewell Brown ('Jeb'; 1833–64) American (Confederate) general. The outstanding cavalry leader of the Civil War, whose raids seriously alarmed and discommoded the Union armies and brought valuable information to the Confederates on several occasions: in August 1862 he captured papers from Pope (q.v.), which allowed Lee (q.v.) to begin the manœuvre of Second Bull Run with confidence; in the following December he destroyed much Federal property in the Fredericksburg district. He also commanded cavalry and other formations in battle, e.g. Jackson's corps at Chancellorsville, and with his own cavalry corps fought the battle of Brandy Station, 9 June 1863. But his operations were not always successful or useful; he failed to keep Lee informed during the Gettysburg manœuvre, with grave consequences. He was mortally wounded in the Wilderness campaign, 11 May 1864. His panache and his magnificent appearance – like Murat (q.v.) he liked velvet and feathers – ensured the survival of his reputation.

Student, Kurt (1890–1978) German general; pioneer of parachute warfare. A *Jäger* officer, Student was seconded to the air corps in 1913 and saw service over the battlefields of Tannenberg, Champagne and Verdun. Under the Weimar republic he was for ten years aviation adviser at the defence ministry, then assisted in the formation of the *Luftwaffe* and finally turned to the creation of a force of military parachutists. He led it in the invasion of Holland in 1940, which his troops' bold descents did much to expedite, and in which he was badly wounded. In May 1941 he planned and executed the airbone invasion of Crete, an operation ultimately successful (*see* Freyburg) but so costly in the lives of his highly trained soldiers that Hitler embargoed further parachute offensives. The parachute divisions (officially part of the *Luftwaffe*) remained in being, their number eventually rising to ten, but were used henceforward – with the single exception of a battalion-sized drop during the Ardennes offensive of 1944 – in a ground role. They retained none the less their elite reputation and won particular renown for the stoutness of their resistance in Italy, 1943–4, and for repelling, as part of Student's own First Parachute Army, the British armoured-air-borne offensive of Arnhem in September 1944. It was particularly unfortunate for the British that Student should have been on the spot, for it was his expert appreciation of the situation which did much to negate the value of the surprise they had won. In recognition of his success, he was subsequently promoted commander of Army Group G in the Low Countries, a post he held to the end of the war.

Sturdee, (Sir) Frederick Charles Doveton (1st Baronet; 1859–1925) British admiral. At the outbreak in 1914 Sturdee was serving as chief of the naval war staff, but was selected in November to take a squadron into the South Seas and to find and destroy the von Spee (q.v.) squadron (*see also* Cradock). His battle cruisers annihilated the German ships at the battle of the Falkland Islands, 7 December. He was created baronet for the victory. He commanded the 4th Battle Squadron at Jutland and, after the war, was the moving spirit in restoring Nelson's *Victory* to its Trafalgar condition.

Suchet, Louis Gabriel (due d'Albufera; 1770–1826) Marshal of France. Born at Lyons, son of one of the city's silk manufacturers, Suchet joined the army through the revolutionary National Guard, served as a soldier and junior officer at the siege of Toulon, 1794, and in the Army of Italy, 1796–1801, in which he was promoted general of brigade, 1798, and acted as chief of staff, July 1799–January 1800. In the 1805

campaign he commanded a division at Ulm and Austerlitz, in that of 1806–7 at Saalfield, Jena, Pultusk and Ostralenka. From 1808 to 1814 he was in Spain, where he gained his marshal's baton and title, testimony to his unique achievements as a soldier and administrator (of Catalonia). Most of the small battles he fought against the Spanish armies were victories. He rallied to Napoleon during the Hundred Days but was not usefully employed.

Sucre, Antonia José de (1795–1830) South American soldier. A Venezuelan by birth, Sucre had enlisted in the republican army at the outbreak of war with Spain and in 1821 was lieutenant to Bolivar (q.v.) in the campaign in Quito province. In 1824 he led the army of Peru, which the Spanish were attempting to subdue, to victory at Junin (6 August) and Ayacucho (9 December) and dictated the treaty under which Spain withdrew. He was subsequently elected president of upper Peru (Bolivia), but resigned and later was assassinated.

Suffren de Saint-Tropez, Pierre André de (1729–88) French admiral. An admiral of enterprise, Suffren was one of the most redoubtable enemies of Britain in the American War of Independence, first in Admiral d'Estaing's fleet, which arrived off New York in 1778, and later in India, where he displayed a tactical imagination far in excess of most of his contemporaries. Early in 1781 he was sent to support French ambitions in India; in April he attacked a British flotilla under Commodore Johnstone on the way to the Cape of Good Hope. He damaged the British ships and Johnstone was forced to withdraw. Early in 1782 he arrived off India and provided support for Hyder Ali, the sultan of Mysore, who was a bitter enemy of the British. He began an epic series of battles with Sir Edward Hughes (q.v.), which marked a new epoch in naval warfare, and managed to keep his fleet in fighting trim, despite the lack of proper port facilities. By keeping the fleet at sea, he posed a constant, mobile threat to the British, who were likewise kept at sea and therefore unable to provide useful support to their land forces. Suffren tried a new tactic, which was applied with some success by his captains: an enemy fleet was scattered and each section 'marked' by French vessels, which by concentrated fire-power were thus able to destroy the enemy fleet piecemeal. These actions caused a strain on Hughes's superior forces and the honours of the battles should go to Suffren. In August 1782 he captured the important port of Trincomalee. The conflict was ended with the signature of the treaty of Paris (1783).

Suleiman I (1495–1566) Turkish sultan and soldier. The tenth Ottoman sultan and undoubtedly the greatest, Suleiman, 'The Magnificent' as he was admiringly known in the west, has been compared with Charlemagne as a great leader in war and peace: in his long reign he fought thirteen great campaigns, leading his troops in person. Building on the work of his father and grandfather, Suleiman established the Ottoman empire, territorially and legislatively, on the firmest foundations. He reformed and codified military organization and administration, improved the quality of his officers and provincial rulers by more elaborate training and stricter discipline, and made his court a centre of culture renowned throughout Europe and Asia. In Turkey he was known as Suleiman the Lawgiver for the quality of his justice and his reforms to the legal system. But it is as a soldier that he is generally remembered.

Unlike his father Selim I (q.v.) Suleiman's preoccupations were with the Christian west. His grandfather Bayazid and Selim I had created an army that was larger than any the west could create, and also, in its professional infantry, artillery and cavalry, of the highest quality. In 1521 Europe experienced the first of Suleiman's invasions. Angered by the insolent treatment of his envoys in Hungary, Suleiman declared war on the Christian princes of Transylvania who did not accept his rule. Belgrade fell in August 1521, and there the armies waited. In 1522 Suleiman turned his attention to the siege of Rhodes, the great stronghold of the Knights of St John, and supervised the final six months of the siege himself. Almost 200,000 Turks invested the fortress and its tiny garrison, but in December 1522 terms were agreed and the island passed into Turkish hands. The capture of Rhodes meant that the last great Christian stronghold in the eastern Mediterranean was gone, and the advantage at sea passed to the Turks. For four years Suleiman with his new admiral Barbarossa (q.v.) built up the Turkish fleet, extending its ambit ever further into the western Mediterranean. Meanwhile border warfare in Hungary was increasing and Suleiman prepared for an advance in the north. He reached an agreement with the Poles, thus removing the danger of their intervention, and in April 1526 an army of almost 80,000 moved north from Constantinople. By July they were past Belgrade, and although they were delayed for two weeks by the gallant, if hopeless, defence of the fortress of Peterwardein, by the end of August the Turkish host faced the army of Hungary, under King Louis, on the plain of Mohacs. In a hard-fought battle (29 August 1526) the Hungarian cavalry shattered the Turkish feudal levies (*timariots*), but themselves broke against the steady lines of the Janissaries and reeled under the co-ordinated attack of the Turkish cavalry. A defeat soon became a rout, and the Hungarians left 15,000 dead on the field, including their king and much of his nobility. Early in September, Buda, the Hungarian capital, was taken without resistance, but, as it was late in the year, the Turks then withdrew leaving a puppet king on the Hungarian throne.

The Turks now faced the Habsburgs directly in the conflict for Hungary; in 1529 Suleiman mounted a new expedition, this time with more than 80,000 men at his disposal, aiming to take Vienna. The great army set off in May, recaptured Buda early in September and arrived at the gates of Vienna before the end of the month. The garrison of 17,000, ably led by Count Salm and Wilhelm von Roggendorf, had strengthened the city's defences and prepared to resist (their resolve having been stiffened by the fate of the Buda garrison, which was massacred). But the Turks had arrived too late in the year, and no Turkish army was capable of sustaining a long campaign far from home. A slow retreat began in mid-October and the Austrians harried them across Hungary inflicting heavy losses, the Turks losing much of their baggage and a number of guns. Suleiman was determined to redeem the débâcle. But his next expedition, in 1532, although it ravaged southern Austria, achieved little positive result, and the same uneasy balance of power continued in Hungary, neither side willing to abandon its position. Once again, a heroic defence, that of Güns, held up the Turkish advance, so that the impetus of their assault was lost.

After the failure of this attempt to win all of Hungary, Suleiman and the ruler of Austria, Ferdinand, reached an agreement to divide the country. Suleiman was now anxious to secure his western frontier, for he faced dangers in the east. The Persians, despite the shattering blows dealt to them by Selim I, were fomenting religious strife in Anatolia, and the Persian Shah Thamasp was able to capture many of the towns lost by his predecessor. Suleiman also faced revolts in Iraq and an uprising in

Egypt. The pattern of the war with Persia was unsatisfactory for the Turks: Suleiman advanced, but the Persians retreated without giving battle. Although much of the territory lost during the European wars was retaken, in ten years of campaigning in Persia Suleiman was never able to meet and destroy the Persian army. On each occasion, as he retreated, the local populations rose and expelled any Turkish garrison. Soon after Suleiman's final assault on Persia in 1553, agreement was reached to provide a stabilization of the frontier, fixed by the treaty of Amasia (1555).

But neither on the east nor the west was a stable frontier possible. The treaty of peace signed with Ferdinand had not lasted, and in 1541, after years of intermittent strife, Suleiman mounted a new expedition which annexed Hungary to the Ottoman empire. The pattern – of peace settlement, border strife and renewed conflict on a major scale – persisted until Suleiman's death. After the great expedition of 1529, Suleiman had never been able to concentrate his attention either on the eastern or the northern frontier. Once again, in 1566, he had to mount a new campaign against the Austrians, although he was by now an old man crippled with gout; he died during the siege of Szigetvar, on 6 September. After his death the war was ended by the treaty of Adrianople (1568), but there could be no real solution to the problem of a turbulent and uncertain military frontier. If Suleiman was unable to resolve these problems, he did, however, find solutions to many of the traditional problems of the Ottoman state. He was plagued, as all sultans were, by Janissary revolts, but he suppressed them with comparative ease. His pattern of constant campaigning, although it created discontent among the Janissaries, also drained off much of their disruptive energy. At sea, the state of constant war, ably waged first under Barbarossa, and then under his successor Torghoud, gave Turkey supremacy over almost all her enemies; only when they united, as at Lepanto (1571), after Suleiman's death, could the Turks be decisively defeated. Despite this plethora of military activity, it would be wrong to see him as an exclusively belligerent figure. Unlike those of his father, most of Suleiman's wars were defensive in purpose, seeking to maintain and consolidate what was already in his possession.

Sullivan, John (1740–95) American soldier. Appointed in June 1775 as a brigadier-general in the Continental army of Washington, Sullivan participated in the siege of Boston (1775), but was then sent to Canada to control the American army under Arnold which had failed at Quebec. Faced with much superior British forces, Sullivan speedily extracted his men and rejoined Washington to concentrate the American forces. He was captured at the battle of Long Island, where Howe (q.v.) took over 1000 American prisoners; fortunately he was exchanged and commanded the right wing of Washington's army at Trenton (1776), where Washington, having crossed the Delaware in a snowstorm, took the Hessian garrison by surprise. At the battle of Staten Island (1777) a night attack launched by Sullivan was failure. His best-known exploit, however, was an expedition which finally destroyed the power of Chief Joseph Brant and his British allies at Newtown (1779). The Mohawks had terrorized the north of New York and rendered life impossible for civilians: Sullivan, by destroying their villages as well as burning their crops, earned the gratitude of Congress for this swiftly executed reprisal. He was forced by ill-health to retire in 1779.

Sumter, Thomas (1734–1832) American soldier. Known as the 'Carolina Gamecock', Sumter served as a skilled guerrilla commander against the British regulars and 'Tories' (American sympathizers) in the American War of Independence. He had considerable experience in wars with the French and Indians, and later settled in South Carolina. Escaping from the siege of Charleston (1780), when Clinton captured 5400 American troops, Sumter went to North Carolina, where he was made a brigadier-general in the state militia. He harried the British, winning encounters at Catawba and Hanging Rock, but failed in another skirmish at Fishing Creek. He beat stronger British formations under Wemyss and Tarleton in November 1780. None of these were great battles, but he used the traditional skills of woodcraft and ambush to keep the enemy in a constant state of suspense. After the war he entered politics, and he survived to be the last remaining general of the War of Independence.

Suvorov, Alexander Vasilievich (Count Suvorov Rimniksy, Prince Itolsky; 1729–1800) Russian field-marshal. Although his reputation in the west derives from his victories against the armies of the French Revolution in 1799, Suvorov's campaigning days were by that date nearly over. A veteran of the Seven Years' War (1756–63), he was promoted general during the war with Poland in 1768 and won the important victory of Kosludscki against the Turks in the Balkans, 1773. In Catherine the Great's Second Turkish War, 1787–92, he won two further important victories, Focsani, 1 August 1789, and the Rimnik (22 September) for which he was created count. In the following year (22 December) he stormed Ismail in Bessarabia, which he allowed to be sacked with great cruelty, as he did Warsaw during the Third Partition of Poland, 1794–5. Catherine's death in 1796 led to his eclipse, but in 1799 he was recalled to take command of the Russian armies campaigning in Italy, where he won three victories in quick succession: against Moreau (q.v.)

at Carsano, 27 April, against Macdonald (q.v.) on the Trebbia, 17–19 June and against Joubert at Novi on 15 August. As a result he recovered from the French all the territory won by Bonaparte in his fabled campaign of 1796–7. However, on 25 September his subordinate Korsakov (q.v.) was defeated by Masséna at Zurich, and he had to abandon Italy and make a punishing retreat through the Alps to Austria. He fell into disgrace and died shortly afterwards. But he was almost instantly rehabilitated and is regarded today as an incarnation of the Russian military spirit – brave, shrewd and tenacious (see Dragomirov). He was also coarse and brutal but (perhaps because of that) was immensely popular with his soldiers.

T

Tantia Topi (1819–59) Indian soldier. A Mahratta – which nation still smarted from their recent subjugation by the British – and a subordinate of Nana Sahib, who had his own grievance against them, Tantia Topi instigated the massacre at Cawnpore, 27 June 1857, formed an army of the local mutineers, was defeated by Havelock (q.v.) at Bithur but raised fresh troops. He defeated Windham at Cawnpore, 27–8 November, and then marched on Jhansi, whose rani, subsequently to be made a heroine of Indian nationalism, was besieged in her castle by Sir Hugh Rose (q.v.). He succeeded in defeating Tantia without raising the siege. Tantia lived to fight another day at Gwalior, 19 June 1858, but was then decisively defeated, captured and executed. He was the only leader of the mutineers of 1857 to show real military talent.

Taylor, Zachary (1784–1850) American general, twelfth president of the United States. A regular soldier since 1808, Taylor took command of the army in Texas in 1845 and, on the outbreak of war with Mexico, won the battle of Palo Alto (8 May 1846), captured Monterey (24 September) and defeated Santa Anna (q.v.) at Buena Vista (22–3 February 1847), thus ending the war in the northern half of the country. He was elected president in 1848 but died after only a year in office.

His son **Richard Taylor** (1826–79) rose to the rank of lieutenant-general in the Confederate army, and defeated Banks (q.v.) in the Red River campaign of 1864.

Tecumseh (1768–1813) American Indian leader. A Shawnee, he, with his brother Teuskwatawa, attempted to unite the western Indians against the expansion of the white settlers, but during his absence his brother was manœuvred into battle by an American army under Harrison and completely defeated (Tippecanoe, 7 November 1811). Tecumseh threw in his lot with the British during the war of 1812 and was killed in action at the battle of the Thames, 5 October 1813.

Tedder, Arthur (1st Baron Tedder; 1890–1967) British air marshal. Commander of the Desert Air Force during the Eighth Army's battles with Rommel (q.v.), Tedder designed a scheme of 'pattern bombing', which greatly assisted the victory of Montgomery (q.v.) at Alamein. In 1943 he became Allied air commander in the Mediterranean and in 1944 deputy supreme commander for the invasion of Europe to Eisenhower (q.v.), who called him 'one of the few great military leaders of our time' – perhaps an exaggerated expression of inter-Allied regard, but justified apparently by Tedder's remarkable grasp of strategic essentials. The two worked perfectly in harness throughout the campaign to liberate the Continent.

Terauchi, Count Seiki (1879–1946) Japanese general. A former war minister, Terauchi was commander-in-chief in North China, 1938–42, and then in the South-West Pacific, with headquarters in Manila. He had overall command of the Japanese troops fighting the Americans in the Pacific islands, the Chinese in South China and the British in Burma. Tanaka, the commander of the Imphal–Kohima offensive of 1944, and Kimura, Slim's (q.v.) opponent in central Burma, were his subordinates.

Thomas, George Henry (1816–70) American (Union) general; 'the Rock of Chickamauga'. A regular officer (West Point, class of 1840), Thomas was a Southerner by birth and a former comrade of Lee (q.v.), but remained loyal none the less to the Union in 1861. He commanded a division at Shiloh and was second-in-command of the Army of the Ohio at Perryville, but his reputation and nickname derive from his leadership at Chickamauga, 19–20 September 1863, where he commanded the left and held the line after Rosecrans (q.v.) had fled from the field. Promoted to command the Army of the Cumberland, he remained with it throughout the battles and campaigns of Lookout Mountain, Missionary Ridge, Atlanta, Franklin and Nashville.

Tilly, Johann Tserclaes, Graf von (1559–1632) Flemish mercenary, in the service of the Catholic League. With Albrecht von Wallenstein (q.v.) Tilly was the main support of the Catholic cause, a thoroughgoing professional soldier brought up in the campaigning atmosphere of the Low Countries, possibly the equal of Parma (q.v.) and Spinola (q.v.) in his adept use of the *tercio*. Born in Brabant, he was educated in Germany because his father had been forced to flee from Alva's (q.v.) Council of Blood. But after Alva left the Netherlands, the policy of repression relaxed and the Tserclaes family, which was entirely loyal to the Habsburg regime, was allowed to return. Entering a Walloon regiment, Tilly served under Parma in the brilliant campaign which led to the capture of Antwerp in 1585, learning from him the

need for a methodical approach to campaigning, to leave nothing to chance, and Parma's own brand of tactical magic in the management of infantry. He served Parma until the latter's death in 1592; thereafter the army in Flanders fell back steadily under pressure from Maurice of Nassau (q.v.). Tilly next took service in the imperial army organized to fight the Turkish threat under the grand vizier, Sinan Pasha. He fought through the campaign and was present at the battle of Kerestes (1596), a disastrous defeat for the Austrians. Tilly continued in the service of Rudolf II until 1610, when he was invited by Maximilian I, Duke of Bavaria, to head the army of the Catholic League which had been founded in February 1610. The Bavarian army, which formed the basis of the army of the League, had already been partially reformed by Maximilian; for ten years Tilly worked to make it the most powerful force in southern Germany. In 1618 the Bohemian revolt against imperial authority broke out, and in 1620 Maximilian reached an agreement to intervene, in return for the estates and territories of Frederick, the Elector Palatine, who had accepted the crown of Bohemia from the rebels. Tilly invaded with his army of 25,000 well-trained and well-armed men: the Protestants had nothing to equal him. At the battle of the White Mountain (1620) Tilly and an imperial army under de Bucquoi routed the Bohemians. Next, Tilly turned back into Germany and methodically began to conquer the Protestant states which supported Frederick. Although he lost to the Palatinate army under Mansfeld (q.v.) at Mingolsheim (1622), he went on to shatter the Protestant forces at Wimpfen and Höchst (1622) to gain control of the Palatinate; in September 1622 he took Heidelberg and ravaged the city after a siege of eleven weeks; and in the autumn of the following year he smashed the last substantial German army, under Christian of Brunswick, at the battle of Stadtlohn where he reduced a Protestant army of 12,000 to a shattered remnant of 2000. In every case the quality of Tilly's troops told against the less experienced opponents who faced him. Only Mansfeld remained as a potential threat, but Tilly had beaten him at Wiesloch (a satisfactory revenge for Mingolsheim) and he was not inclined to take the field.

In the summer of 1625 the Danes entered the war and the Emperor Ferdinand II recruited Albrecht von Wallenstein (q.v.) to fight for him with an army of 20,000. The relationship between the two men was ambiguous: Tilly, a loyal servant of Maximilian, Wallenstein, an adventurer happy to serve the emperor only so long as it advanced his own ends. Although the two men co-operated, they worked with a wary eye on each other as well as on the enemy. Christian of Denmark, after some initial success, met the same fate as the German Protestants. At Lutter (1626), Tilly routed the Danes, who lost almost half their army; they were no match for Tilly's expert veterans. In the following year the Danes were forced back beyond their own borders by the steady advance of Tilly and Wallenstein. In the summer of 1630 the much more powerful Swedish army intervened, freed from a long involvement in a war with Poland. Tilly had now, reluctantly, assumed command of the combined imperial and league armies – the princes of Germany had become alarmed at Wallenstein's ambitions and forced his dismissal as their price for co-operation with the emperor. Tilly had not wanted to assume command of the force, not out of affection or respect for Wallenstein, but because the joint command was hedged about with innumerable political constraints and complications. He was also now seventy-one years old and many questions were raised as to his competence to assume so large a command. Tilly besieged the strategic town

of Magdeburg, hoping to make it a strongpoint in his defensive scheme against the Swedes. But when the city fell, the troops of his subordinate Pappenheim (q.v.) ran amok and sacked the city. Tilly, who had not believed that the city would fall, could not control the carnage (May 1631). All but 5000 of the citizens and defenders of Magdeburg – of a total of 30,000 – were slaughtered. Deprived of his base, Tilly was ordered into Saxony by his new master the emperor. The attack served no purpose, save to unite the Swedish and Saxon armies against the common enemy. The Swedish and imperial armies met at Breitenfeld, near Leipzig, on 17 September 1631. Pappenheim, who had overcome Tilly's caution and encouraged him to give battle, tried to outflank the Swedes, only to discover that it was difficult to overcome the curious linear formation which the Swedes favoured. Tilly was successful with the smooth attack by his *tercios* on the Saxon army, and drove them off; he now attacked the exposed Swedish left flank with his 20,000 infantry and 2000 horse. Conventionally, the Swedes should now have been annihilated by the overwhelming power of this attack – cries of 'Victoria' were even heard from the imperial ranks. But the Swedes, again using the flexibility of their formation, formed a new, if thin, front against the massive imperial assault. The *tercios* aligned themselves for a new, and it was believed the final, advance of the battle. As they were making ready, the small Swedish force comprising musketeers, pikemen, cavalry and field artillery attacked them, thrusting forward into the gaps in the imperial ranks created by artillery and small-arms. The imperial army was thrown into confusion, and the main body of Swedish cavalry attacked it in the flank, delivering a body-blow. The imperial guns were captured and poured a withering fire into Tilly's ranks. It was a catastrophe for the imperial cause, a total reversal of the expected result.

It was now that Tilly revealed his indomitable courage and professionalism. He rallied his shattered forces, regrouped them and sought replacements of the men and material which had been lost. By the beginning of October he was in the field with a new army, wiser perhaps and much more wary of the Swedish power. But he had no means with which to counter the new tactics of the Swedes. More important, he had lost many of his hardened regulars at Breitenfeld (7000 dead and 6000 prisoner), and the new drafts did not have the quality of the troops he had trained himself. In any event one burden was taken from him, for the emperor had re-employed Wallenstein and Tilly was able to play his part once more as the defender of the Catholic League. He sat with his army just inside the borders of Bavaria on the river Lech, ready to face Gustavus Adolphus (q.v.) as he moved slowly through southern Germany. The position which Tilly had chosen was a strong one, protected by the terrain and in particular the fast-flowing river. He had stripped the countryside of every tree and every boat, and believed that the Swedes would not cross to attack his entrenched position. But Gustavus did attack, across a thin bridge of boats and covered by artillery fire, the smoke from burning damp straw misleading Tilly as to the exact point of attack. The Catholic camp, pitched too close to the river, now became an impediment rather than a bastion for Tilly's men, and they were forced back into Bavaria. Tilly himself, mortally wounded in the fighting, was carried off to Ingolstadt, where he died on 20 April 1632; Gustavus had sent him a famous surgeon, at Tilly's request, but to no avail. It was recorded that in Wallenstein's camp at the news of Tilly's death there was 'more joy than sorrow'. Tilly was a hard-bitten soldier, of a traditional cast

of mind, unable to accustom himself to the new tactics and devices the Swedes had introduced. In his seventy-fourth year when he died, he had outlived the style of war to which he was accustomed. An honourable and moral man, there was a professional integrity and honesty about him which made him stand out from his murky contemporaries, both for his real excellence as a commander and his devotion to the cause that paid him.

Timoshenko, Semën Konstantinovich (1895–1970) Marshal of the Soviet Union. Of peasant birth, Timoshenko served in the ranks of the cavalry, 1915–16, joined the Red Army in 1917, rose to command a cavalry division against Denikin (q.v.) in Poland and against Wrangel (q.v.) in south Russia. A front (army group) commander in the war with Finland, 1939–40, he became deputy commissar for defence at its close and instituted a regime of strict discipline and restraining to repair the deficiencies in the Red Army which the war had disclosed. At the outset of the German invasion he commanded Western Front (Voroshilov and Budenny, qq.v., commanding respectively the North-Western and South-Western) and had therefore to resist the enemy's advance along the central axis which led to Moscow. After giving much ground, he was transferred to replace Budenny, failed to prevent the German advance in 1942 into the Crimea and to Stalingrad, and was eventually transferred to Stalin's staff and then to the dormant north-western sector. He was the only one of the prewar marshals to retain his standing throughout the war, chiefly through his achievements as an iron disciplinarian of demoralized troops.

Tippu Sultan (1749–99) Indian sultan and soldier. The son of Hyder Ali of Mysore, Tippu was trained by the French officers who had organized and equipped his father's army. In 1767 he commanded a corps of cavalry in his father's first war with the Marathas, and continued in almost constant action. He had been beaten with rods by his father for failure at the battle of Chinkurali (1771), and was estranged from him. But in the Second Mysore War (1780–3) the breach was repaired and Tippu defeated a British force under Braithwaite at the Coleroon river (1782), succeeding his father on the throne of Mysore later in the same year. He immediately made peace with the British and his other enemies, for the French had now withdrawn with the general conclusion of peace in Europe by the treaty of Paris (1783). In 1784 Tippu made an agreement with the British and assumed the title of sultan. In 1787 he tried again for a French alliance, but failing to receive it, entered on a new war with the British, alone. He attacked the client British state of Travancore, and waged an effective campaign against the British under Cornwallis (q.v.), who, a good general himself, took two years to defeat Tippu. But at the treaty of Seringapatam (1792), he lost heavily, both in money and territory. He still sought allies against the British, however, and in 1799, after hearing of his negotiations with revolutionary France, Lord Mornington, the governor-general, was ordered to exterminate this persistent enemy. He sent two armies, one under General Harris, the other under Arthur Wellesley (the future Duke of Wellington, q.v.). In May 1799 Seringapatam was stormed and Tippu died bravely in the attack, cut down in the bitter fighting. Known as the 'Tiger of Mysore', he had an outstanding military talent, but a savage trait in his character, which gained his subjects' respect if not their affection.

Tirpitz, Alfred (von; 1849–1930) German admiral. One of the earliest entrants (1865) to the Prussian navy, Tirpitz was largely responsible for its transformation from a coastwatching squadron into a High Seas Fleet capable of challenging the British. He successfully communicated to Kaiser Wilhelm II his own enthusiasm for direct naval competition with Britain, secured, as naval secretary from 1898, the necessary funds to build new ships and, from 1906, commissioned large classes of excellent dreadnoughts and battlecruisers. He was granted the 'von' in 1900 – a dignity much appreciated by a service which felt itself to be the army's social inferior – and in 1911 was promoted grand admiral (*Grossadmiral*), the first to hold the rank. During the First World War, however, he failed to persuade the kaiser to risk a 'blue water' strategy and resigned in March 1916.

Tito, Josip Broz (1892–1980) Yugoslav guerrilla leader and head of state. Born Broz, son of a Croatian peasant, he was captured by the Russians in 1915 while serving in the Austro-Hungarian army, but after the October revolution joined the Red Army. His life for the next twenty-five years was that of an international Communist agent: in 1920 he returned to his native country, the former Yugoslavia, suffering imprisonment for subversion between 1928 and 1933; he then went to Moscow to work in the Comintern's Balkan secretariat; in 1936 he organized recruiting in Paris for the International Brigades in Spain, and then until the German invasion of Russia worked secretly at home again – after August 1939 towards the aim of keeping Yugoslavia out of the western camp.

With the change of the Soviet line in June 1941, he raised and led Communist partisans and between August and September, with the co-operation of Mihailovic (q.v.), cleared Serbia of Germans. The two then fell out, however, the Germans returned, and Tito led his partisans into hiding in Montenegro and Bosnia. He was for the next two years constantly on the move, while sustaining a major guerrilla war, but from November 1943 he enjoyed recognition by the western Allies as well as Russia as the legitimate leader of Yugoslav national resistance. From August 1944 he was able to go over to the offensive and in October, with Tolbukhin (q.v.), he entered Belgrade. His achievement, unique among those of partisan leaders of the Second World War, in liberating his country virtually singlehanded, ensured his inheritance of power in postwar Yugoslavia and eventually permitted him, alone among East European Communist politicians, to establish his independence from Soviet influence. He ranks among the very greatest guerrilla generals of history.

Todleben, Franz Eduard Ivanovich (Graf; 1814–84) Russian military engineer. A Balt, Todleben was educated at the school of military engineering in St Petersburg and commissioned in 1836. Posted on the outbreak of war with Turkey in 1853 first to Silistria and then to the Crimea, he became, though a junior officer, the 'animating genius' of the defence of Sebastopol. The city, strongly protected to seaward, was quite undefended on its landward side, from which the British and French would attack. Taking advantage of the slowness of their advance, Totleben (the alternative spelling is common) designed and constructed a line of massive earthworks four miles long, of which the most important strongpoints were the Redan and the Malakov (*see* MacMahon). He himself directed the defence until wounded on 20 June 1855; his account of the siege became a nineteenth-century military textbook. In essence, his idea was that fortification need not be, as hitherto thought, rigid and permanent, but could be elastic and temporary, adapted to an army's manœuvres and allowing it to advance or retreat as necessary. At Plevna (*see* Osman) in 1877 he himself

used earthworks to bring about the collapse of the Turkish defence. His theories were to exert a powerful influence on tactics until the moment when the development of the tank robbed entrenchments of their usefulness.

Togo, Heihachiro (Count; 1849–1934) Japanese admiral. A Samurai, Togo joined the infant Imperial Japanese Navy in 1863 and studied in England, 1871–8. In 1894, as captain of a cruiser, he sank a Chinese troopship *en route* to Korea, thus precipitating the Sino-Japanese war. In the Russo-Japanese war he was first responsible for the blockade of Port Arthur, then, on the approach of the Russian Second Pacific Squadron (*see* Rozhdestvenski), for its interception, which he achieved in the straits of Tsushima, May 1905. The extent of the Russian loss in the battle made his victory one of the most tactically crushing of all time. It was also strategically decisive, giving Japan command of the whole north-eastern Pacific. His flagship *Mikasa* is, like Nelson's *Victory*, preserved in drydock, while the 'z' attack flag he flew on it at Tsushima was hoisted by Nagumo (q.v.) on the carrier *Akagi* as the signal to start the attack on Pearl Harbor in December 1941.

Tojo, Hideki (1884–1948) Japanese general and politician. One of the most aggressive of the Japanese imperialists, Tojo succeeded the more cautious Konoye as prime minister in October 1941 and at once embarked on the policy which culminated in the attack on Pearl Harbor. As the course of the war progressively turned against Japan, he made himself minister of war and chief of staff, but after the fall of Saipan in July 1944, which brought the home islands within range of the advancing Americans' bombers, he resigned. At the surrender in August 1945 he shot himself, but was nursed back to health and, after trial and conviction as a war criminal, hanged by the Americans.

Torrington, Arthur Herbert, Earl of (1647–1716) British admiral. An English admiral under William III, Torrington lost to the French admiral Château-Renault (q.v.) at Bantry Bay (1689) and lost control of the sea lanes with Ireland. He failed again against Tourville (q.v.) at the battle of Beachy Head (1690), in which his fifty-nine ships faced seventy-five French vessels. He had wished to avoid a fight against a superior enemy to preserve his 'fleet in being' as a continuing threat, but he was ordered to fight by the Admiralty. He lost twelve ships, and was subsequently court-martialled. Although acquitted, his career suffered.

Torstensson, Lennart (1603–51) Swedish artillerist. Torstensson, at the age of fifteen, became page to Gustavus Adolphus (q.v.), and accompanied him on the campaigns in Livonia in 1621–3; possibly as a result of some early promise shown at this time he was sent, in 1624, to study under the great Maurice of Nassau (q.v.) in the Netherlands. Maurice was one of the first great commanders to realize the full potential of artillery, using it to great effect in siege warfare, and doing much to standardize calibres and train officers in its specialized uses. Upon his return to Sweden in 1626, Torstensson served for three years in the Prussian campaigns. His peculiar talent as an artillery-man coincided with Gustavus Adolphus's large-scale reform of the army; previous innovations in the field of artillery had proved so dramatically successful that the six companies which had made up the artillery section of the Swedish army were being amalgamated to form the First Artillery Regiment, the first, indeed, in Europe. The new position of command was given to Torstensson, aged only twenty-seven.

Although Gustavus Adolphus's reforms were not yet complete, Torstensson took over the most thoroughly modern artillery of the day. A revolution had been effected in both the concept and the effectiveness of artillery, hitherto unreliable, inaccurate and unwieldy in the field. Maurice of Nassau had first classified guns by the weight of their projectile, and by 1630 Gustavus Adolphus had reduced the sixteen assorted types of cannon in commission at the beginning of his reign to three main types: the 24-pounder, the 12-pounder and the 3-pounder, each designed for a specific role in the field. Above all, Gustavus Adolphus strove for mobility, envisaging an artillery which could be brought into action wherever it was needed and form part of a unified fighting force with other branches of the army. Greater mobility meant, above all, decreased weight; the massive 48-pounder siege guns requiring from thirty-three to thirty-nine horses were abandoned, the army's heaviest weapon now being the 24-pounder. Improvements in the quality of gunpowder meant that both the thickness and the length of the barrel could be reduced without detriment to performance, range or safety. Above all, vast natural resources of copper, then the principal component of gunmetal, in Sweden made the creation of a large artillery force and experiment in pioneering techniques an economic possibility; this was not the case elsewhere.

By the time Torstensson took over the management of the artillery, the famous 'leather gun' (a thin copper barrel bound with rope and covered in leather) had largely been withdrawn; although representing a technological breakthrough, it had sacrificed too much to mobility. Its brilliant successor was the regimental gun, a 3-pounder which could be moved by a single horse, or, if necessary, two to three men. It was, moreover, capable of rapid fire, since it was designed to take the newly developed artillery cartridge, the charge being wired to the shot for ease and speed of loading. It remains to say that artillery pieces were plentiful in the Swedish army, the guns to men ratio at the beginning of the German campaign being an impressive 9.4 per 1000.

At the battle of Breitenfeld (September 1631) Torstensson showed what his well-trained and disciplined field artillery could do. The Swedish gunners proved themselves a superior and formidable force, firing three rounds to the imperialists' one; Pappenheim (q.v.) believed them to be a major factor in deciding the issue of the battle. Increased mobility paid off brilliantly when the regimental guns were able to accompany their infantry forward in the final counter-attack. As a result of his direction of the field artillery at Breitenfeld, Torstensson was promoted to general in 1632. At the battle of the Lech in April 1632 Swedish batteries under the command of Torstensson provided a massive barrage and show of force which forced the enemy to take cover and misled him as to the point of attack: powder-smoke, reinforced with the burning of damp straw, concealed the real preparations and the army was able to make a successful crossing of the river, which brought them into Bavaria. At the end of August 1632 the Swedish army attacked Wallenstein's (q.v.) camp at the Alte Veste; because of the nature of the terrain the artillery was rendered impotent, and it was Torstensson's further misfortune to be captured as he fought 'within a paternoster' of the king. Thus he was not present at Lützen, at which Gustavus Adolphus was killed, though his artillery showed their wonted mobility in moving to give support to other arms at crucial moments. The following year he returned to Sweden after an exchange of prisoners.

In 1635 Torstensson became chief-of-staff to Baner during his successful campaign in eastern Germany; in 1641 Baner

died and Torstensson was persuaded to take command of the Swedish army in Germany; his health was poor, and he took the new post only with extreme reluctance. He was promoted to field-marshal and did much to restore discipline in the now rather unruly army. In the spring of 1642 he was victorious at the battle of Leipzig, and his armies overran most of Saxony and, the following year, Bohemia and Moravia. That same year Oxenstierna ordered him to attack Jutland, and in 1644 Torstensson outgeneralled Gallas, with a combined Danish and imperial army, forcing him to retreat into Bohemia. As he advanced on Prague, however, he was intercepted by an imperial and Bavarian army under Werth. They met at Jankau on 15 March 1645 and Torstensson gained a brilliant victory, his artillery achieving unparalleled feats of mobility; its readiness to move from one sector to another during the course of the battle was ultimately the decisive factor. This was his last battle, however, as the following year he resigned on the grounds of ill-health. His genius as an artillery general, advances in the technology of warfare, and the flowering of Sweden as a major power under the great Gustavus Adolphus, combined to elevate him into the select band of great Swedish field commanders during the Thirty Years' War. He has been called the father of field artillery.

Totleben *see* Todleben.

Tourville, Anne Hilarion de Cotentin, comte de (1642–1701) French admiral. A Norman by birth, from a family with an ancient and established maritime connection, Tourville learnt his seamanship on a Maltese frigate of the Knights of St John in the near-piracy of Mediterranean warfare. Entering the French navy in 1666, he took an active part in the wars with the Dutch and developed a great respect for Dutch seamanship, which he investigated in detail. He was created a lieutenant-general in 1682 and expanded the French fleet, building new dockyards and shore establishments, and ensuring a steady flow of recruits for the navy by founding naval schools. One of the continuing difficulties of the French navy was a chronic shortage of manpower, since only the traditional maritime districts provided any real quantity of sailors. Tourville extended the sweep of recruitment inland, but made up for their deficiencies in practical experience by an (albeit rudimentary) scheme of training.

In the war of the Grand Alliance (1688–97) Tourville cracked the English blockade of Brittany, and was promoted to be vice-admiral of the Mediterranean fleet and commander-in-chief. Beating the combined English and Dutch fleet at the battle of Beachy Head (1690), he seized command of the Channel, but no use of this temporary dominance was made, much to the irritation of Tourville and his commanders; in 1692, however, his fleet of forty-four men-of-war engaged ninety-nine English and Dutch warships at the battle of La Hogue. Terribly outnumbered and heavily outgunned, the French fleet was smashed despite all Tourville's skill. But Louis XIV, uncharacteristically, did not hold the defeat against him, and he was created a marshal of France. He retired from the navy in 1697. Tourville was a naval commander of outstanding ability, both in battle and in the realization that a fleet could survive only with a proper infrastructure of supplies and manpower. In this respect he continued the great work of Colbert in the creation of an outstanding French navy.

Toussaint *see* L'Ouverture.

Tovey, John Cronyn (1st Baron Tovey; 1885–1971) British admiral. Commander of the Home Fleet, 1940–3, Tovey was responsible in May 1941 for

the pursuit and destruction of the *Bismarck*, pride of Hitler's navy, whose escape into the north Atlantic threatened all British commerce on the North American routes. The sinking was the most important surface battle fought by the Royal Navy in home waters during the Second World War.

Townshend, (Sir) Charles Vere Ferrers (1861–1924) British general. As a young officer of the Indian army, Townshend sprang to fame by his defence of the romantic frontier fortress of Chitral in 1895. His career prospered, he transferred to the British army and as a general he added to his reputation in 1915 by his remarkably speedy pursuit of the Turks up the Tigris in Mesopotamia. The advance overreached, however, and in December he and his army were besieged in Kut-el-Amara. The siege lasted until April 1916, when starvation and cholera (of which von der Goltz, q.v., also possibly died) obliged him to surrender. While he retired to comfortable captivity in a villa on the shore of the Black Sea, from which he returned in 1918 to a hero's welcome and a seat in Parliament, his men entered on an even more bitter privation in Turkish prison camps, which very few survived. Justly, his reputation is now quite demolished. He was a dashing and lucky captain, but a bad general and no gentleman.

Trenchard, Hugh Montague (1st Viscount Trenchard; 1873–1956) British airman; 'the Father of the Royal Air Force'. Trenchard's life demonstrates how on rare occasions a revolution – in this case a technical one – may elevate a man of humdrum career to the heights of power almost overnight. At the age of thirty-nine, Trenchard was a major without prospects. He had failed in youth to get into the navy, had failed to get into Woolwich (for the artillery or engineers), had apparently not even tried to get into Sandhurst and had passed the militia examination, last hope of a candidate for an army commission, only at the third attempt. After twenty years of routine soldiering in the colonies, and seeing no prospect of promotion, Trenchard was contemplating resignation when a friend, who had recently taken up flying, suggested he should do the same. Glimpsing in the idea the last chance of distinguishing himself from a thousand similarly qualified (or unqualified) soldiers, he took it up, graduated easily and found himself, by virtue of his age alone, one of the most senior officers of the fledgling Royal Flying Corps. In August 1915 he succeeded to command of its units in France and began at once, by force of character rather than persuasion or inspiration, to imbue it with his own aggressive spirit. He strove to create ever larger units and to give them more intrusive and offensive roles over the German front, which, by the end of the war, the RFC dominated. By then it had combined (1 April 1918) with the Royal Naval Air Service to form the Royal Air Force, of which Trenchard was made first chief of staff. But he had also, before the armistice, resigned the post over differences with the first air minister, Lord Rothermere, and returned to France to command the inter-Allied Independent Air Force, which was subordinate to Foch (q.v.) and had as its role an entirely original one, that of the strategic bombing of Germany.

After the war Trenchard again became chief of the air staff and fought hard in committee (his nickname was 'Boom') to preserve its independence from the navy and army alike. In that he was perhaps oversuccessful, the subordinate role he forced on the Fleet Air Arm severely stunting the growth of British naval aviation almost until the outbreak of the Second World War. He retired in 1929, having been named the first marshal of the Royal Air Force, a rank equivalent to field-marshal or admiral of the fleet, in 1927. Perhaps his most important legacy to the service he had largely created was the doctrine (not his own – he apparently drew no profound conclusions from his early experience with the Independent Air Force – but one which he espoused and fostered) that air power was a war-winning weapon in its own right (see Douhet).

Trochu, Louis Jules (1815–96) French general. Aide-de-camp to Bugeaud and Lamoricière (qq.v.), Trochu opposed Louis-Napoleon's seizure of power, though he had also been his military assistant, but continued nevertheless to be promoted by him, commanded a brigade in the Crimea and led a division at Solferino and Magenta during the Franco-Austrian war of 1859. His publication of a secret and over-frank official report as a sensational book, *L'Armée française en 1867*, led to his supersession but was proved justified when in 1870 the field army collapsed before the Prussians for exactly the reasons of which in it he had given warning. Summoned to lead the Government of National Defence on 4 September, he directed the defence of Paris under the Prussian siege, stifling internal unrest, organizing sorties (Champigny, Villiers, Bourget, Buzenval) and promising throughout that a secret scheme of his own (*'le plan Trochu'*) would eventually secure relief. But, on the Prussians opening a bombardment of the city (5 January 1871), he was obliged to resign and his colleagues to sue for terms.

Tromp, Sir Cornelis van (1629–91) Dutch admiral. Growing up in the shadow of his father's reputation (see Tromp, Sir Maarten), but less successful than he had been, Tromp's career is notable for the feud which developed between him and the greatest Dutch admiral of the day, de Ruyter (q.v.). Beginning his career on his father's ship, his rise was rapid: he was a captain by 1649 and a rear-admiral after a successful encounter with the English off Leghorn, during the First Dutch War (1652–4). In 1654 he crowned his fruitful Mediterranean cruise with an attack on the Algerian pirates. During the First Northern War (1655–60), he was sent with de Ruyter to the aid of the Danes (1659), and together they succeeded in releasing Copenhagen from the grip of a Swedish blockade. Even at this stage, however, relations between the two men were not easy.

In 1663 Tromp returned to the Mediterranean in command of a fleet, but achieved only small success. Largely inactive until 1665, with the outbreak of the Second Anglo-Dutch War (1665–7) he was immediately appointed vice-admiral; and in the following year commanded the whole Dutch home fleet. But when de Ruyter returned from his attack on the West Indies, Tromp was forced to relinquish command to him as the senior and more experienced admiral: their latent hostility became overt. After the battle of the North Foreland (1666), where he lost twenty ships in an assault by Monck (q.v.), de Ruyter blamed the defeat on Tromp for failing to support him adequately. Tromp resigned his command in pique, refusing a tempting offer from the French to enter their service. The feud smouldered until, in the midst of the Third Dutch War (1672–4), William of Orange managed to effect a reconciliation. The two admirals now fought together with considerable success at the battle of Schoonveldt (1673), where the fleet under Prince Rupert (q.v.) was repulsed with heavy losses to the English.

After the treaty of Westminster (1674), which ended the conflict (although the war between France and Holland continued), Tromp harried the French coast. He then sailed on, quite against orders, on an independent mission into the Mediterranean, hoping for glory and success. The voyage achieved little, and on his return home his con-

duct was investigated and he was severely rebuked. But he was sent north to assist the Danes, once again fighting the Swedes, who had taken up the French alliance offered to them. With the Danish admiral Niels Juel he beat the Swedes at Jasmund (1676); thereafter he took service with the Elector of Brandenburg, returning to Holland as the leading Dutch commander, for de Ruyter had been killed in 1676. In 1691 he was created lieutenant-admiral-general of the Dutch republic, but was a sick man, unable to take up his command. A proud and sometimes irresponsible man, he inherited his father's seamanship, if in a lesser degree.

Tromp, Sir Maarten van (1598–1653) Dutch admiral. In de Ruyter (q.v.) and the two van Tromps, the Netherlands possessed a trio of outstanding naval commanders. Maarten van Tromp, the son of a naval officer, at the age of twelve had been captured by pirates, who held him prisoner for two years after killing his father. In 1617 he joined the Dutch navy and one of his first acts was to take part in a punitive expedition against the Barbary pirates, who threatened Dutch trading vessels in the Mediterranean. The pattern of his life now repeated itself. He joined the Dutch merchant service in 1619, and in 1621 again fell into the hands of pirates; he was not able to rejoin the navy for over a year, by which time Holland was at war, and the opportunities for an ambitious naval officer correspondingly improved. In 1624 he was promoted captain, attracting such favourable attention that by 1629 he commanded the admiral's flagship. But a new admiral, van Dorp, whom van Tromp found uncongenial, was appointed and he resigned his command in 1634. After a period of unemployment ashore, he was appointed director of equipment in the admiralty of the Maas. But his talents had been noted, and on van Dorp's resignation he was created lieutenant-admiral of Holland.

Early in 1639 Tromp executed a successful punitive raid on the privateers of Dunkirk, but it was in October that he achieved a complete command of the sea over the Spanish. Arriving off Beachy Head with eighteen ships, to face a Spanish fleet of forty-five warships and thirty merchantmen, which were carrying over 13,000 infantry for an assault on the Netherlands, Tromp completely outsailed the Spanish under Oquendo in a six-hour battle and forced them to take refuge in Calais Roads. He summoned reinforcements, and in the ensuing battle of the Downs the Spanish were utterly defeated. For his service he was ennobled by Louis XIII of France, and two years later (1642) knighted by Charles I (q.v.) on the occasion of the marriage of his daughter to William II of Orange.

Much of Tromp's activity was in support of Dutch commercial interests, hence the ceaseless war against pirates and privateers. In 1646 he assisted the French in the assault on Dunkirk; but the navy was being steadily run down, a process accelerated after the peace of Westphalia (1648). However, by 1651 the threat to trade had become so great that a substantial programme of new building and revitalization was undertaken, with Tromp's active encouragement. In the First Dutch War (1652–4), Tromp met his match in Admiral Blake (q.v.), although he succeeded at the battle of Dungeness (1652) with a fleet of eighty ships, twice that of Blake. When odds were more equal, at the battle of Beachy Head (1653), Tromp was badly beaten. He had no more luck off the Gabbard Bank, when he lost twenty ships in a battle with Blake and Monck (q.v.). The English blockaded Holland, but Tromp slipped through. The direct result of this skilful evasion was the battle of Texel, where in a hard twelve-hour battle Monck defeated the Dutch, leaving over 1600 Dutch dead, including Tromp himself. His greatest talent was as a brilliant shipmaster, and a master of infighting. But the English tactics and equipment were superior and Tromp's skill could not overcome the advantage this gave them.

Trotsky, Lev Davidovich (1879–1940) Russian revolutionary, military leader and creator of the Red Army. A Jew, born Bronstein, Trotsky was educated at Odessa, arrested for revolutionary activity in 1898 and imprisoned, but he escaped and fled to England, where he lived from 1902 to 1905. He returned to Russia during the 1905 revolution, was again arrested and again escaped and thereafter lived abroad until 1917, making his living chiefly as a journalist. He was then able to re-enter Russia and played a part almost as important as Lenin's in the October coup which brought the Bolsheviks to power. His policy of 'No peace, no war' *vis-à-vis* the Germans, however, resulted not in the demoralization of their armies and an easy peace, as he had predicted, but in their imposition of the cruelly extortionate treaty of Brest-Litovsk. Trotsky was in consequence ousted from his post of commissar for foreign affairs and made commissar for defence. Civil war had just broken out (*see* Denikin and Kornilov) and it became his task to create, arm and train the Red Army which would save the Bolshevik revolution from defeat. After its victory he retained the direction of defence until 1923, when he was ousted by Frunze (q.v.) at the end of a long and bitter ideological struggle between proponents of the regular army concept and those who favoured, like him, a militia system. He was propelled by Stalin into increasing obscurity and eventually to exile and death, but despite every effort by the dictator to deprive him of the title, Trotsky remains acknowledged as the Carnot (q.v.) of Soviet Russia.

Tukhachevsky, Mikhail Nicolaevich (1893–1937) Marshal of the Soviet Union. Born into an impoverished but aristocratic family, Tukhachevsky was educated in the Corps of Pages and at the Alexandrovski Military Academy, commissioned in 1914, but taken prisoner early in 1915. Despite many attempts to escape, he did not succeed in returning to Russia until October 1917, when he put himself at the disposal of the Bolsheviks and was taken up by Trotsky (q.v.). His motives in siding with the revolution were patriotic rather than ideological: he yearned for the re-establishment of Russian greatness and saw in Bolshevism the best chance of achieving it. After successfully filling junior commands against Kolchak (q.v.), he was appointed in April 1920 to supreme command in the west and undertook the great drive on Warsaw (*see* Pilsudski); he thus accomplished his ambition of achieving by the age of thirty either fame or death. Despite defeat in the war with Poland, he remained among the leaders of the Red Army of which he became chief of staff in 1926.. His influence upon its development into a modern, regular, mechanized force was very great, but his cultivation of an independent 'professional' outlook made him suspect to Stalin and in 1937 the NKVD, acting partly on evidence fabricated by the German *Sicherheitsdienst* (which suspected Tukhachevsky of friendship for France), arrested and executed him. He was the first important victim of the great purge.

Turenne, Henri de la Tour d'Auvergne, vicomte de (1611–75) Marshal of France. Although generally acknowledged to be one of the great French commanders, Turenne is often denied the unique glory which his achievements deserve; the effulgence of his reputation is inevitably diffused by constant comparison with his slightly younger contemporary Condé (q.v.). The careers of these two great generals are inextricably linked – because of the political turmoil of their age they fought against each other as well as side by side – and although it is Condé, premier Prince of the Blood, notoriously supercilious and with a distinct *penchant* for self-publicity, who was accorded the accolade of '*le grand*', an examination of the exploits of the rather more self-effacing Turenne reveals him to be the subtler and more consistently successful soldier.

Turenne was the son of the duc de Bouillon, a minor princeling who had his seat in the small but strategically placed city of Sedan; his mother was Elizabeth of Nassau, sister of the great Maurice of Nassau (q.v.), and Turenne was born, and remained for the greater part of his career, a Protestant, a rare phenomenon among the high-ranking servants of Louis XIV. The young Turenne was sent to the Netherlands to study the military arts under the tutelage of his uncle and after his return to France was given command of an infantry regiment in 1630. France's involvement in the Thirty Years' War (1618–48) provided great opportunity for rapid advancement, and having served his apprenticeship on the Rhine and been wounded in the assault on Saverne (1636), Turenne found himself in 1638 at the head of a force sent to reinforce Bernhard of Saxe-Weimar (q.v.) in the investment of Breisach. The surrender of the city gave the French the key to the Rhine, and Turenne's reputation was further confirmed in the two subsequent campaigns he fought against the imperial-Savoyard army, which culminated in the capture of Turin (1640).

In 1642 Turenne faced a potential setback to his career when it came to light that certain leading members of his family had been involved in the Cinq Mars conspiracy against Louis XIII. Nevertheless in 1643 he was created a marshal of France and given the command of France's Weimar army after its defeat by Franz von Mercy (q.v.) at Tuttlingen (1643). Turenne had succeeded to the command after the capture of von Rantzau, and the army he took over was a broken force of only 10,000 men. He was joined at Breisach by a small army under the duc d'Enghien (later Condé), who had enjoyed a meteoric rise since his brilliant defeat of the Spanish at Rocroi earlier in the year. Despite the fact that he brought an army of only 7000 and that he was only twenty-two, Enghien's princely rank entitled him to overall command, a situation apparently resented not at all by Turenne.

In the campaign the two generals fought against the Bavarian army under Mercy, Turenne revealed himself the master of the unlikely manœuvre, which was later to stamp him as the most original and daring commander of his age; at the first battle of Freiburg (1644) he undertook a long march to hit the entrenched Bavarians in the rear, and, similarly, at the third battle of Freiburg later in the same month took most of the army by mountain paths to attack the Bavarian entrenchments from behind. Despite heavy French losses the Bavarian retreat left most of the Rhine valley in French hands, and Enghien was able to depart for a series of mopping-up operations, capturing the fortresses of the middle Rhine Valley. In 1645 Turenne was surprised and defeated by Mercy at the battle of Mergentheim, but later in the year, and once again reinforced by Enghien, the French inflicted a crushing, though costly, defeat on Mercy, who was killed in the intense and desperate struggle; Turenne later erected a generously worded monument on the spot where his great adversary fell in battle. In 1646 Turenne undertook a secret forced march down the Rhine to Wesel, then turning south-east to join a Swedish army under Wrangel (q.v.) near Giessen; he had been alarmed by the heavy losses sustained by the French in their successful campaigns against

the Bavarians, and henceforth determined to wage a war of manœuvre. At the battle of Zusmarshausen (1648) Turenne's army caught up with and virtually annihilated the imperial rearguard and the Franco-Swedish forces reached the Inn, the nearest the French had come to Austria. Maximilian fled from Bavaria, and Turenne's success was a crucial factor in the emperor's decision to sue for peace, which was concluded in the peace of Westphalia (1648).

After the end of the Thirty Years' War the widespread resentment in France against the increased burdens of taxation and the accumulation of royal power under Richelieu, and subsequently Mazarin, broke into the open revolt known as the Fronde (1648–53). Turenne, largely prompted by his passion for Condé's sister, the Duchess of Longueville, who was heavily involved like all her family (except for Condé himself) in the rebel cause, prepared to intervene with his army. But Mazarin anticipated the threat, sent a new general and paid off the troops. Turenne fled to Holland, but returned to Paris in 1649. In 1650 Mazarin imprisoned Condé, whom he distrusted, along with his brother Conti and his brother-in-law, the duc de Longueville; Turenne, feeling himself threatened, fled to join the duchess in Champagne, where he assumed military leadership of the Second Fronde. Plans to invade France from the Spanish Netherlands with a combined Spanish–Frondeur army fell through, largely due to the mutual suspicions of Turenne and the Spanish leaders, and Turenne waged ineffectual war in Champagne until he was soundly defeated by a much larger and better-trained royalist force at Rethel (1650). Turenne himself narrowly escaped capture. In 1651 public pressure forced the princes' release under a general amnesty and Mazarin fled to Germany. Turenne was recalled to Paris at Condé's instigation; later in the year civil war broke out again, Condé this time led the rebels, signing an alliance with Spain: the hated Mazarin was recalled from exile by the queen regent. Turenne, conscious of the cardinal's malevolent scrutiny, was careful to remain aloof and to dissociate himself from this third rebellion and from Condé's faction; in addition, the young Louis XIV had now been declared legally of age, and Turenne was genuinely loyal enough to balk at the prospect of taking up arms against the king's person, rather than against government in the hands of an Italian cardinal and a Spanish queen regent. Moreover, in the same year, his brother, the duc de Bouillon, heavily embroiled, needless to say, in the rebel cause, came to terms with the court, and Anne of Austria was free to affirm her faith, once again, in Turenne's loyalty by putting him in command of one of the two divisions of the royal army, each 4000 strong, which had been assembled in the Loire to oppose Condé. In the campaign of 1652–3 Turenne used his meagre resources with great skill; unable to defeat Condé and his Spanish backers outright, he out-thought and out-manœuvred his enemies; he was able to save the young king from capture by blocking the bridge at Bléneau, and also to ensure that the court did not have to take refuge far from Paris, an achievement which was to prove important when Louis was at last able to re-enter his capital.

In July 1652 Turenne, with a strongly reinforced royalist army, caught up with Condé outside the walls of Paris, which had declared itself neutral. Under the anxious surveillance of the king and Mazarin, who watched from a nearby hill, the bitter struggle for the capital took place outside the gate of St Antoine, after which the battle was to be named. From the outset the fight went in favour of Turenne and the royalist army, but just as decisive victory seemed within their grasp, the cannon of the eight-towered Bastille fortress began to fire

into their ranks; casualties were heavy, and in the resulting disarray, Paris opened her gates and allowed Condé and the rebel army to enter in triumph. The treachery had come from within the royal family itself; the king's cousin, Anne-Marie-Louise (*Mademoiselle*), had obtained written permission from her father, the intriguing and treacherous Gaston d'Orléans, to enter the Bastille and order the training and firing of the cannon as she thought fit. But although Condé had evaded capture, the rebel cause began to fragment: he himself fled to join the Spanish who, with the imperial troops of the Duke of Lorraine, were preparing to invade France's north-eastern frontier. Turenne hurried north and, although heavily outnumbered, fought a brilliant campaign across northern and eastern France, preventing the junction of the armies of Condé and Lorraine and gaining precious time for negotiations between *parlement* and court in Paris. In October 1652 Louis was able to re-enter his capital, and the Fronde came to an end, although war with Spain continued.

Turenne was the hero of the hour, and never lost the gratitude and respect of the king for being the saviour of the royal cause. Meanwhile Condé had defected to the Spanish camp, and was put in command of a Spanish army in north-eastern France. Despite having superior forces he found that once again Turenne's adroit dispositions foiled any plans to draw the French into direct combat under unfavourable conditions. In 1657 Mazarin and Cromwell agreed to combine their separate wars against Spain, and concluded a strategy whereby a joint force, aided by the English fleet, would attack the coastal towns of Mardyk, Dunkirk and Gravelines. Mardyk quickly succumbed to Turenne's army, and he proceeded straight to Dunkirk, despite the Spanish attempts to halt him by opening the dykes. His investment of the city was threatened, however, by the arrival of a Spanish Netherlands relief force under Don John of Austria and Condé himself. Turenne's victory at the ensuing battle of the Dunes was decisive; he used the change of the tide on the beach, where the right flank of the Spanish infantry was drawn up, to carry out a cavalry envelopment of the Spanish left flank, on the inland side. Knowing that he had little to fear from the Spanish on the beach, whose sole anxiety was to escape fire from the offshore English fleet and to avoid the suddenly encroaching tide, he was able, at a crucial moment, to concentrate the main weight of his cavalry on the Spanish left. The battle, which lasted only four hours, resulted in casualties of only 400 men for Turenne and 6000 for the Spanish, who had fought against Condé's advice and without the bulk of their artillery. It was a brilliant manifestation of Turenne's ability to use and incorporate in his battle plan local or natural phenomena. It allowed him to go on to capture Ypres and to threaten the great Flemish cities of Brussels and Ghent and it secured advantageous peace terms for France (in the treaty of the Pyrenees, 1659) just as his threat to Austria had done at the end of the Thirty Years' War. In 1660 Turenne was appointed 'marshal-general of the camps and armies of the king', an extraordinary honour which implied that, had it not been for his Protestant faith, he might have been made constable of France. In 1668, after the death of his wife, he abjured his religion, but by now Louvois's reforms had incorporated the coveted title into the fold of royal privilege, and Louis took command of his armies himself.

The Dutch war of 1672–8 saw Turenne at the height of his powers. Although constantly undermined by Louvois (q.v.) with whom he had a long-standing feud, holding only a secondary command, and invariably outnumbered, often by two to one, Turenne, in the invasion of Holland (1672) and the subsequent Rhineland campaign, revealed himself a commander and tactician of consummate genius. Although his forces in Holland never exceeded 20,000 men he was so successful in using his slender resources that by 1673 he broke the German coalition of the Emperor Leopold I and the Elector of Brandenburg for a time and could have reached Bohemia had not Louvois refused him reinforcements; instead, Turenne was called back to cover Alsace, and the imperial forces were able to break the French control of the Lower Rhine.

Many German princes rallied to the imperial flag, and although by seizing the initiative, at Sinzheim (1674), and by skilful manœuvre throughout the summer, Turenne managed to prevent a concentration of allied forces, it seemed after the inconclusive battle of Entzheim that the sheer weight of numbers must gain Alsace for the allies. In October 1674 their forces were swollen to 57,000 by the arrival of the armies of the Great Elector (q.v.), and they were quartered for the winter in all the towns from Belfort to Strasbourg. They were apparently secure in their possession of Alsace. But Louvois's reform of the French supply system meant that Turenne was able to maintain active operations throughout the winter, and, having placed the fortresses of Middle Alsace in a state of defence in order to deceive the enemy, he led his 28,000 men in an epic march of secrecy and feint. He turned southwards behind the mountains of the Vosges into Lorraine, and then split his forces into many smaller bodies further to deceive enemy spies; they then crossed the mountains, thick with snow, reassembled near Belfort, and marched speedily into Alsace from the south. At the battle of Turckheim (1675) Turenne, despite the exhaustion of his troops, was able to deliver so heavy and vigorous a blow on the flank of the main allied army, that they could offer only perfunctory resistance. The enemy recrossed the Rhine and Alsace was saved. In the summer of the same year Turenne prevented Montecuccoli (q.v.) from retaking Strasbourg, but on 27 July, while preparing to attack the retreating German army in a defensive position, he was killed by a cannonball.

Turenne's unique genius was as a field commander; unlike other great commanders – Gustavus Adolphus (q.v.) or Cromwell (q.v.) – he did not possess, in his army, a force moulded for the exercise of his own brand of military genius. Often placed in command of inferior fighting troops, and usually outnumbered, he lived on his wits, and the result was spectacularly successful. Although the only Frenchman to figure in Napoleon's list of the seven great commanders of history, Turenne's real military heir was not a Frenchman but an Englishman, the Duke of Malborough (q.v.), who served under him in his campaign in Holland and who admired him intensely. The great campaigns of his maturity were remarkably low in casualties, and he inspired great loyalty in his troops; when, in 1647 his German cavalry mutinied after having been ordered away from a successful campaign in Bavaria, Turenne rode with them far into Germany and brought them back to French service by the sheer force of his personality. And few generals could have split their forces up secure in the knowledge that they would later regroup, as he did in the Belfort march. All these qualities combine to make him the greatest field commander and tactician of his age.

Tyrconnell, Richard Talbot, Earl of (1630–91) Irish Jacobite soldier. Tyrconnell held Ireland for James II in the Jacobite uprising against William III and the Glorious Revolution of 1688. He had fought with the Royalists in Ireland during the English Civil War and had been imprisoned by Cromwell as a conspirator against the state. As a leading Catholic, he gravitated towards the group around the brother of King Charles II, and when James ascended the throne as James II, Tyrconnell was created lieutenant-general of the army in Ireland (1686) and lord deputy of Ireland. He was active in encouraging the 'Catholicization' of the army and navy, replacing ardent Protestants with Catholics pliable to the king's will. As a result, and because of his powerful position in Ireland, he was considered by the supporters of William III one of the most dangerous of their adversaries. He died before the final doom of the Jacobite cause in Ireland was accomplished, but it was already clear that he had lost the campaign.

Tyrone, Hugh O'Neill, Earl of (1540–1616) Irish soldier and rebel. Leader by talent and family connection (the O'Neills were the greatest family in Ulster) of the Irish opposition to Elizabeth I. Appointed by Elizabeth to a variety of influential posts in the island after he succeeded his uncle as Earl of Tyrone in 1568, he soon established himself as the most powerful man in the murky world of Irish politics. In 1593 he inherited the chieftainship of the O'Neills and the cornerstone of his power was secured. Thereafter his relations with England deteriorated, and in 1598 he came out in open revolt. He defeated an English army at the battle of the Blackwater River, and all Ireland rose in rebellion. He outwitted the Earl of Essex, sent with a substantial army to subdue him, leading him in an aimless pursuit through the marshy, inhospitable Irish landscape. But late in 1601 the Irish army, reinforced by 4000 Spanish troops, was routed at Kinsale by Mountjoy (q.v.), a much more competent commander than Essex. O'Neill retired to regroup his forces, but the rebellion was doomed as many of his lukewarm supporters left him. In 1603 he submitted to

Mountjoy, and received good treatment from James I, being allowed to retain his extensive estates despite his treason. But he engaged in constant intrigues to recover his former power, and in 1607 he sailed with some one hundred northern chieftains for Spain; blown ashore in the Netherlands, the party ended up in Rome. Tyrone lived there until his death, outlawed by the English.

U

Udet, Ernst (1896–1941) German fighter ace. Second-ranking of German aces of the First World War, credited with sixty-two victories, Udet had learnt to fly before 1914. He rejoined the *Luftwaffe* after its reformation in 1934, but though he rose to become head of its technical office, he also came to believe himself a failure and committed suicide. Ironically his life had been spared early in his fighting career by Guynemer (q.v.), who had chivalrously withdrawn from a single-combat when the German's gun jammed.

V

Vasilevsky, Aleksander Mikhailovich
(1895–1977) Marshal of the Soviet
Union. A veteran of the Civil War,
Vasilevsky replaced Shaposhnikov (q.v.)
as chief of staff of the Red Army in
1942, directed operations at Stalingrad,
1942–3, and commanded the Third Belorussian Front in its advance into East
Prussia in 1945. In August he directed
Russia's belated military effort against
Japan in the Far East.

Vauban, Sebastien le Prestre de (1633–
1707) French military engineer and
theorist; Marshal of France. In a century
in which siege warfare was the most
common form of encounter with the
enemy, France was indeed fortunate in
possessing the engineering and innovat-
ing genius of Vauban. In 1651 the third
War of the Fronde (1651–3) broke out,
and the young Vauban threw in his lot
with the Frondeurs, accepting a cadet-
ship from their military leader, Louis II
of Bourbon, Prince of Condé (q.v.). In
1653 he was taken prisoner, and perhaps
because he had already shown great aptitude in the throwing up of field fortifications, his royalist captor, Marshal
Henri de la Ferte-Senneterre, induced
him to change sides, promptly granting
him a commission in his own regiment.
In 1655 Vauban became a 'king's ordinary engineer', being drafted to a corps
specializing in fortification and siegecraft, and fought in Turenne's (q.v.) war
of siege and manœuvre against the Spanish, now led by Condé, temporarily in
Spanish service. In 1658, Vauban was
chief engineer at the siege of Gravelines,
and won recognition for the importance

of military engineering when the king
awarded him a company of the Picardy
regiment.

After the War of Devolution (1667–8)
in which he played a leading role in the
siege and capture of Douai, Tournai
and Lille, he was presented with a great
opportunity to air his theories on the
role of fortifications when he assisted
and advised Louvois (q.v.) in his reform
of the army. A chain of fortresses was
conceived which would be fully equipped
as bases for an army on the march, and
which could not be taken except by the
immensely time-consuming business of
full-scale siege. Vauban was largely responsible for their construction, and
spent the next years building thirty-three
new fortresses and remodelling three
thousand others; in addition he created
the great fortified naval bases of Brest,
Dunkirk, Le Havre, Rochefort and
Toulon in response to Colbert's plans
for the creation of a strong French navy.
He engaged in minute correspondence
with the king on the subject of fortification, and his long series of essays written
at this time became standard texts on
the subject for the next hundred years.

Vauban's successful career as an
active soldier also continued without apparent let or hindrance. In the Dutch
war of 1672–8 he evolved and used for
the first time (at Maastricht in 1673) his
system for dealing with the sophisticated
Dutch scheme of defensive fortification
which had been developed by their great
engineer Simon Stevin and perfected
over a generation. The technique was
almost invariably successful, and over
the years such apparently successful

bulwarks as Philippsburg (1688), Mons (1691), Namur (1692) and Charleroi (1693) fell to Vauban. At Philippsburg he introduced ricochet gunfire, whereby cannonshot was made to bounce forward over parapets, thus possibly hitting several targets before its energy was spent. At about this time, too, he pioneered the use of the socket bayonet, which, unlike its predecessor, the plug bayonet, made it possible for the musket to be fired while the bayonet was fixed; this latter development had the supplementary effect of rendering large contingents of pikemen obsolete. In 1702, after a long, distinguished and successful military career, Vauban retired from the army owing to ill-health; on 14 January 1703 he was created, fittingly, a marshal of France. Not only had he revolutionized the role of the military engineer and been a great innovator from the use of artillery to the wider education of junior officers; he was a prolific writer and left behind him a vast body of literature, providing food for military thought for succeeding generations. He died in retirement on 30 March 1707.

Vendôme, Louis Joseph, duc de (1654–1712)   French soldier. A great-grandson of Henry IV of France (q.v.), Vendôme was possibly the ablest of Louis XIV's latter 'crop' of generals, although he was not of the quality of Turenne or Condé (qq.v.). He served with distinction in the early wars of Louis XIV, especially in Flanders, fought with great effectiveness under Luxembourg (q.v.) at Steenkirk (1692), and took command in Catalonia in 1695, capturing Barcelona in 1697. In the war of the Spanish Succession (1701–14), he replaced the senescent Villeroi (who had been captured by Eugen, q.v., in the battle of Cremona, 1702) on the Italian front. Vendôme had a powerful army and he fought Eugen to a costly drawn battle at Luzzara (1702), but could not snatch the initiative from him.

In the succeeding campaigns Vendôme used his forces with great enterprise: he took Vercelli in 1704, and again held Eugen in the battle of Cassano (1705). In May 1706 he was transferred to the northern front, the graveyard of many French military reputations, where he now faced Marlborough (q.v.), who had just beaten Villeroi at Ramillies. Vendôme met his match at Oudenarde (July 1708) where Marlborough and Eugen had joined forces, when he was held back from fulfilling his battle plan by the doubts of his joint-commander, the duc de Bourgogne. He recovered with great speed from the long wasting battle, and the failure was not entirely his. None the less he was in disfavour at court as a result, and his temporary disgrace was completed when he failed to outsmart Eugen and Marlborough and relieve Boufflers (q.v.) besieged in Lille. But in 1710 he was recalled to take command in Spain, where the French cause had languished after Berwick (q.v.) had been summoned north in the panic after Ramillies. Vendôme took firm charge of the situation, recaptured Madrid, beat the British under Stanhope at Brihuega (admittedly he substantially outnumbered the British forces), and the next day beat the other part of the allied army under Guido von Starhemburg at the battle of Villaviciosa. Dying before he could complete the conquest of Spain for Philip V, his work was completed by Berwick.

Verdy du Vernois, Julius von (1832–1910)   Prussian general. One of the many officers of Huguenot descent in the Prussian army, he and Bronsart von Schellendorf were the principal agents (known as the 'Demigods') of Moltke (q.v.) in the direction of strategy in the war of 1870, Verdy du Vernois being particularly responsible for the intelligence department. He became in later life one of the most prolific and influential of Prussian military authors and was minister of war in succession to Schellendorf, Waldersee (q.v.) procuring in turn their appointments.

Victor Amadeus II, Duke of Savoy (1666–1732) Italian ruler and politician. In Victor Amadeus the dukedom of Savoy possessed a skilled opportunist, who began a tradition of cunning perfidy which served the house of Savoy well in its struggle to become supreme in northern Italy (and eventually to unite the whole peninsula). He juggled neatly between the two power blocs, the Bourbons of France and the Habsburgs of Austria and Spain. In the war of the Grand Alliance (1688–97) he supported the Habsburgs and allowed his allies to fight his battles for him, but in 1696 welched on them by making a separate peace with Louis XIV at Turin. In the war of the Spanish Succession (1701–14) Victor Amadeus began on the French side, but transferred his support to the Habsburgs in 1703, and enjoyed the comfort of his cousin Eugen's (q.v.) army in support of his territory. In the treaty made at Utrecht (1713) he received Sicily, the title of king and some of the Spanish territories in Italy. In 1720, after the war of the Quadruple Alliance (1718–20) in which he played a suitably inglorious part, he was rewarded for the loss of Sicily (which was allocated to Austria) by being given the kingdom of Sardinia and the title of king of Sardinia. The house of Savoy-Piedmont was thereby established, a monument to political turpitude; however, the last laugh did not lie with Victor Amadeus II. In 1730 he abdicated in favour of his son Charles Emmanuel, thought better of it and tried to regain his throne. His son imprisoned him for the remainder of his life.

Victor, Claude-Victor Perrin (called Victor; duc de Bellune; 1766–1841) Marshal of France. A private soldier of the royal army, Victor became an officer of the National Guard during the Revolution and was promoted general of brigade in 1793. He served on the Spanish frontier and in the Army of Italy, 1795–1800, was promoted general of division by Bonaparte and took a notable part in the battle of Marengo. Chief of staff to Lannes (q.v.) during the 1806 campaign, he got command of the 1st Corps in 1807, led it at Friedland and was created marshal. Posted to Spain, he defeated a number of Spanish generals, including Don Gregorio de la Cuesta ('arguably the worst general of all time') at Albacon on 26 July 1809. Against the British he was less lucky: he was beaten by Wellington (q.v.) at Talavera and by Graham at Barossa. In Russia he retrieved his reputation by his brave defence of the crossing of the Beresina. He fought at Dresden and Leipzig in 1813, took part in the defence of France, 1814, remained faithful to the Bourbons during the Hundred Days and acted as minister of war, 1821–3.

Villars, Claude Louis Hector, duc de (1653–1734) French soldier. Arguably the most competent of the generals to serve under both Louis XIV and Louis XV. Villars, the son of a soldier-diplomat, had a touch of genius in the management of cavalry. Entering the army in 1669, he quickly established a reputation as an enterprising officer (although promotion was slow, for he did not have the ear of the war minister Louvois). As commissary-general of cavalry in the Low Countries, Villars led the French cavalry with considerable success against the enemy at Walcourt (1689) early in the war of the Grand Alliance (1688–97). In 1693 he was appointed lieutenant-general, and after the war, his star more in the ascendant, was appointed as ambassador to Vienna. At the outset of the war of the Spanish Succession (1701–14) Villars was at the peak of his powers. Ordered to protect Alsace from attack, he immediately took the offensive, crossed the Rhine and attacked Louis of Baden, who had taken the fortress of Landau and was preparing to descend on Strasbourg. At Friedlingen (October 1702) his adventurous use of his cavalry outflanked Louis of Baden and gave victory to the French. He was created marshal of France and given command of the army in Germany. Forced to serve with the Elector of Bavaria, whom he could stomach neither personally nor militarily, he won the battle of Höchstadt (1703), beating the Austrians under Styrum despite his antipathy for his allies, who vetoed his plan for an advance on Vienna. He left his command and turned to harrying the rebel Camisards in the south of France. But after Marlborough's victory at Blenheim (1704) he was recalled, given a dukedom and sent to face the marauding allied armies. Again he chose to attack, across the Rhine and deep into southern Germany, the equivalent of his thrust the previous year (1705) into Alsace, which had also unhinged allied plans for an advance. But he was unable to follow up the results of these enterprising strokes because he was transferred to face Eugen in northern Italy. His daring advances in the north had not helped to avert the disastrous battle of Ramillies (1706), and he was not in high favour at the court of Louis XIV.

However, after Vendôme (q.v.) failed to beat the allies at Oudenarde and Lille (1708), Villars was sent for as the only man who might retrieve the situation. In 1709 he was appointed commander in Flanders (where he had experienced his first taste of victory at Senef, 1674), with a badly shaken army. He was instructed by Paris to avoid a major combat, but after he was ordered to relieve Mons, a major battle became inevitable. At the battle of Malplaquet, Villars was wounded severely (as was Eugen on the opposing side) and it was owing to the calm good sense of Bouf-

flers (q.v.), who was serving as Villars's second-in-command, that the French were able to retire in good order. After Malplaquet, a punishing battle for both sides, although the allied armies of Marlborough and Eugen had had much heavier losses than the French, Marlborough was under pressure not to fight so costly an action again and Villars felt likewise. They fenced delicately with each other, Marlborough taking a few fortresses and undermining Villars's supposedly impassable 'Ne Plus Ultra' line of fortifications by some deft manœuvres. But in 1712 Marlborough was recalled, and Villars defeated Eugen's army at Denain (1712), Eugen arriving too late for the battle. Now on the offensive, his natural stance, Villars recaptured the fortresses of Douai, Quesnoy and Bouchain; and moving down the Rhine, Landau and Freiburg (1713). Eugen and Villars met for peace talks, which were concluded with the treaty of Rastatt (1714).

By his energy at the end of the war, Villars had eased France's position at the treaty settlement, and after the death of Louis XIV (1715), he became a leading member of the Council of Regency for Louis XV, but he was never popular at court. In the war of the Polish Succession (1733–8) the septuagenarian Villars was trundled out from retirement, given the extraordinary title of marshal-general and sent to outwit the Austrian army in northern Italy. Here he displayed his wonted skill, but age had not improved his temper: finding it no more possible to work with the unscrupulous Charles Emmanuel of Sardinia than he had with the Elector of Bavaria, he demanded his recall. He died at Turin on his way home. By temperament an offensive general, he fought in an age where caution was considered more virtuous. Freed from the restraint which, in common with many of the best French generals who were his contemporaries, he suffered under – the critical eye of

Louis XIV – his achievement might have been still greater.

Villeneuve, Pierre Charles Jean Baptiste de (1763–1806) French admiral. Present at the battle of the Nile (1798), where he commanded the rear division, Villeneuve was in 1805 admiral of the Toulon fleet. In order to draw the British away from home waters, which Napoleon (q.v.) had to cross to invade England, he broke through the blockade, sailed to the West Indies with Nelson (q.v.) in pursuit, recrossed the Atlantic, fought off a minor British fleet under Calder and entered Cadiz. There he was joined by the Spanish fleet under Gravina (q.v.) and blockaded again by Nelson. Warned that he was to be replaced, Napoleon's invasion plans having been frustrated by Nelson's return from American waters, he determined to fight before his successor could arrive. He took his and the Spanish fleet to sea and was utterly defeated at Trafalgar, 21 October 1805. Taken prisoner, but released, he committed suicide at Rennes while on his way to an audience with the emperor.

Vorontsov, Mikhail Semenovich (1782–1856) Russian field-marshal. Born and brought up in London, where his father was ambassador, Vorontsov fought against both the Turks and the French, 1803–13, and actually commanded against Napoleon (q.v.) at Craonne in 1814. After Waterloo, he commanded the Russian army of occupation in France, 1815–18. Appointed governor in 1823 of New Russia, as its southern provinces were then called, he captured Varna during the war with Turkey, 1828–9, and as governor of the Caucasus, 1844–8 subdued two-thirds of Daghestan.

Voroshilov, Kliment Efremovich (1881–1969) Marshal of the Soviet Union. An experienced party worker, Voroshilov had helped to organize the Cheka (Bolshevik political police) before going to command the Fifth Red Army in the Ukraine in 1918. He was an early collaborator of Stalin in the First Cavalry Army, fought against Denikin and Wrangel (qq.v.) and in the Polish campaign was a main opponent of Trotsky (q.v.) and succeeded that other enemy of Trotsky, Frunze (q.v.), as commissar for war in 1925. In 1934 his title was changed to commissar for defence, but he remained effective political head of the Soviet services until May 1940, when Timoshenko (q.v.) took over the task of reorganizing the Red Army after its failure in the Finnish war. At the outbreak of war with Germany he directed the North-Eastern Front, but was not a success in operational command and was relieved. He continued nevertheless to enjoy Stalin's favour and was president of the USSR, 1953–60. A political, not a professional, soldier, his achievement was to sustain the subjection of the army to the party throughout the first twenty years of the Communist state's existence.

W

Waldersee, Alfred Graf von (1832–1904) German field-marshal. For a brief interval (1888–91) between the reigns of Moltke and Schlieffen (qq.v.), Waldersee held the post of chief of the Great General Staff, which he had long intrigued to get. He had been Moltke's principal assistant and his opposition to the policies of Bismarck and enthusiasm for preventive war against Russia (which terrified Bismarck and Moltke alike) had established him as the favourite general of Wilhelm II, while the latter was still heir-apparent. In office, their ambitions clashed and he was quickly dismissed. In 1900 the kaiser nevertheless procured for him the command of the Allied relief expedition to Peking, urging on him the role of 'another Attila', but the Boxers had abandoned the siege before he arrived. He consoled himself with a Madame Butterfly romance.

Wallenstein, Albrecht Eusebius Wenzel von, Duke of Friedland and Mecklenburg (1583–1634) Czech adventurer. Like some mighty personification of Ambition in a morality play, Wallenstein over-reached himself and came crashing down, the vast territories he had briefly united under his rule quickly falling asunder. His ambition for power is evident throughout his life. Born and educated a Bohemian Protestant, he abjured his faith for the sake of advancement in the Habsburg service, his apostasy also bringing him a rich wife in 1609, who conveniently died five years later leaving him the sole possessor of huge estates in Moravia, and one of the richest men in the kingdom of Bohemia. He continued

to serve the emperor, raising a cavalry regiment at his own expense to serve in a war against Venice (1618). When the Bohemian revolt broke out Wallenstein remained loyal to Ferdinand II, only to see his estates confiscated by the rebels. But revenge came quickly. He raised a regiment of horse and served with great courage in the campaign for the recovery of Bohemia. After the battle of the White Mountain (1620), his estates were restored to him and he was appointed governor of Bohemia by a grateful emperor. In this new position he bought up the lands of his vanquished enemies at knock-down prices, and within three years held virtually the whole of northeast Bohemia as his private estate. The emperor created him first prince, and then duke, of Friedland (1625), and he exercised within his lands many of the privileges of an independent monarch. He was by the outbreak of the war with Denmark, which marked a new stage in the Thirty Years' War, the richest man in the empire, and was able to make the penurious emperor an enormously attractive offer: that he should equip at his own expense a huge mercenary army of 24,000 men for the service of the empire: he was to recover his outlay from the profits of the war. Ferdinand accepted his offer, since he had no other means of creating so large a force. Wallenstein chose his own officers and bound them to him in close financial ties. He showed his practical administrative genius by using the technical and agrarian resources of his duchy as the commissariat for his army, creating workshops and small 'factories' to manufacture almost all his needs. Wallenstein thus differed from the normal mercenary leader, not only in the scale of his operations, but in the thoroughness of his preparations. He had, of course, ambitions beyond those of the normal soldier of fortune.

After his first success, a decisive victory over Mansfeld (q.v.) at Dessau (1626), Wallenstein took the opportunity to harden his terms for service. He demanded an army of 70,000, and full powers to recruit officers in his own name rather than that of the emperor. Ferdinand reluctantly agreed, and Wallenstein dutifully rid him of the Hungarian menace on his doorstep. Forcing Gabor Bethlen to peace at Pressburg and leaving Vienna secure, he turned west and drove the Danes back into their own borders, for which Ferdinand awarded him the duchies of Mecklenburg and Pomerania (1629). Wallenstein was now one of the leading powers in northern Germany, his aim to carve out a kingdom from the debris of the war. He became less tractable, less willing to take the field save in his own interest. Thus the siege of Stralsund (1628) was dictated by his own needs rather than those of his master. His power alarmed the princes of Germany, Catholic and Protestant alike, and they put pressure on the emperor to dismiss him. Shortly after the Swedes arrived in northern Germany (1630), Ferdinand was forced to dismiss his general and reluctantly to place his troops under Tilly (q.v.). Wallenstein vowed vengeance on his enemies and negotiated with the Swedes for a joint attack on the emperor and the princes of Germany. Arrangements moved ahead for the armies to act together; the emperor received news of these discussions, however, and hurriedly reappointed Wallenstein, on the terms dictated by his over-mighty general.

A double-edged sword for the empire, almost as dangerous as the Swedes, Wallenstein was now virtually a privateer operating under the imperial flag: all he could capture was his. After the death of Gustavus Adolphus (q.v.) at Lützen in 1632, he virtually disregarded his duty to Ferdinand. Having demanded as a prior condition for his return the right to make alliances and treaties, he now exercised this power on his own account. He negotiated with the Saxons and Swedes, with Brandenburg and France, in a complicated and oversubtle diplomacy that left him trusted by none. Ferdinand was well informed by a loyal group of Wallenstein's generals – Piccolomini (q.v.), Gallas, Aldringen, Hatzfeldt – of his conniving and encouraged a counter-plot against him. In January 1634 the 'loyalists' struck and informed Wallenstein that they would serve him only so long as he was in imperial service; only a few weeks later Ferdinand signed orders for his dismissal and apprehension – dead or alive. Gallas was appointed in his stead. Still manœuvring to save his position, Wallenstein professed his loyalty – at the same time that he sought French and Saxon assistance against the empire. He left Prague for Eger, to be closer to the Swedes with whom he hoped to ally. But a group of officers, headed by two of his Scottish colonels, Walter Leslie and John Gordon, murdered all his few remaining adherents; Wallenstein himself was run through with a pike, crying for quarter.

His cupidity, treachery and general moral turpitude have long obscured his qualities of genius. His ambitions were reasonable, for many of the ruling families of Europe had started out with a pedigree no longer than his, and often much less ability. He saw war more clearly than most in terms of its economic realities. He equated money with power, and his capacity as a mercenary commander to pay his men was his sole call on their loyalty. His methods of war finance and the administration of his duchy as his powerhouse were remarkable; in his financial agent, Hans de Witte, he found an assistant of great capacity. His political skills did not match his talent for organization, and it was this failing which brought him down. As a general, he was a clever tactician and a cunning improviser: his attempts at Lützen to disguise the weakness of his left wing were intelligent, and he tried to leave nothing to chance. But the generals facing him after Gustavus's death were of inferior quality, and his real ability as a field commander is something of an enigma.

Waller, Sir William (1597–1668) British soldier. Like so many of the more effective commanders in the English Civil War (1642–6), Waller had fought with Mansfeld (q.v.) for the Elector Palatine at the start of the Thirty Years' War (1618–48). A staunch Parliament man, he became a colonel in the Parliamentary forces at the outbreak of civil war and moved against the Royalists in the south-west. *En route* he took Portsmouth and several other towns, but his advance was stopped by Hopton (q.v.) and his Royalist army at Roundway Down (1643). The men were well matched (both had served with Mansfeld). Taking his revenge when he beat Hopton's force at Cheriton in Kent (1644), Waller joined with Essex for a campaign in the Midlands, but was beaten by Charles I at Cropredy Bridge near Banbury (June 1644). Waller supported the demands for a more professional army and actively advanced the formation of the New Model Army. He resigned his commission under the Self Denying Ordinance, which debarred MPs from holding military posts. Always a moderate, he was active in his opposition to the creation of a military dictatorship under Cromwell, and languished in prison for his outspoken attitudes. He supported the Restoration of Charles II in 1660.

Washington, George (1732–99) Amer-ican soldier and first president of the United States. As the 'father of his country' Washington's reputation is secure regardless of his military talents; indeed, it has become fashionable to see him as an inferior commander, with little flair and originality. But the very qualities for which his enemies at the time criticized him so bitterly – an unwillingness to fight unless he was confident of success and an active support for foreign adventurers and soldiers within the Continental army – are aspects of his considerable qualities as a military leader, if not as a field commander. The officers of the Continental army 'quarreled like cats and dogs', according to John Adams, and Washington was responsible to a Congress composed of self-interested, warring factions. He was thus faced with a campaign both in front and behind him, against the British and against his rivals and enemies in the revolutionary camp. In the British he faced a professional army of considerable competence, officered to a high standard and well equipped. The problems of control and co-ordination which were to bedevil British efforts were not obvious at the time. Even the costly battle of Bunker Hill (1775), although it provided a great propaganda buttress for the rebel cause, was a clear demonstration of the British steadiness under fire; the Continental army, which Washington commanded, although large in size, was a poorly organized militia and in no way equalled their opponents. The initial successes gave way to a British recovery.

At the battle of Long Island (1776) a British army under Howe (q.v.) outmanœuvred half Washington's army under Putnam and pushed on to New York, which Washington defended with the remainder of his force. Washington began a long retreat, and the encounters as he moved south through New Jersey usually ended in British victories. But Washington had good judgement as to when he should give battle: thus, he crossed the Delaware and won the battle of Trenton (1776), but skilfully retreated when confronted by a much larger force under Cornwallis (q.v.). But while he was retreating, he met and defeated a British force hurrying to join Cornwallis at Princeton (1777), capturing a large quantity of equipment in the town. Cornwallis ruefully referred to him as the 'old fox', while Frederick the Great considered these snap attacks and skilful retreats to be military masterpieces. Washington was at his best when all the tactical and strategic options were open to him; forced to a battle on the enemy's terms, he had less success. In the campaign for the defence of Philadelphia (1777) he lost to Howe at Brandywine, and after the fall of the city failed at Germantown. The Continental army was forced to take up winter quarters in conditions of acute distress at Valley Forge.

The year 1778 marked a turning point of the war. The Americans acquired a powerful ally, France, which would act as a counterweight to British naval power; since the battle for Philadelphia, Washington had been acutely aware of the dangers which the lack of naval power posed. The British could use the sea as a refuge, as well as the means by which they could shift troops and supplies rapidly from one theatre of war to another. The winter in Valley Forge had also been used to transform the Continental army into a disciplined fighting force, the work of Steuben (q.v.), who operated with Washington's complete support. The results of this training were seen at the battle of Monmouth (1778), where for the first time the army stood up to a prolonged battle against a good British general (Clinton). Late in the year the focus shifted to the south, where the British waged a successful campaign resulting in the capture of Savannah (1778) and Charleston (1780). Washington had been excluded by Con-

gress from control over appointments to the Southern command, but the disasters forced them to call for his assistance. He sent one of his most competent subordinates, Nathanael Greene (q.v.), to take control. His strategy – of forcing Cornwallis, now commanding the British in the south, to pursue his force and dissipate his strength – was successful, and in 1781 Cornwallis withdrew into Virginia. In August, Cornwallis was ordered to occupy Yorktown on the Virginia Peninsula, an isolated position unless it could be reinforced from the sea. Washington, encamped near New York against a large force under the British commander-in-chief, Clinton, planned a joint operation against the British at Yorktown, involving the French fleet under de Grasse, which was cruising in the West Indies, as well as his army and French troops under Rochambeau (q.v.). The trap was sprung. Control of the sea was snatched from the British at the battle of the Capes (1781), and Cornwallis's position became untenable as Washington's armies invested the town from the landward side. Hopelessly outnumbered, and with no sign of relief from Clinton, Cornwallis surrendered (19 October 1781). Five days later Clinton arrived from New York with a powerful force. After Yorktown the war dragged on, with steady American gains from the demoralized British: peace was made at the treaty of Paris (1783).

Washington, who had served without pay for the whole of the war, returned like Cincinnatus to his farm. His military achievement was considerable. He had welcomed foreign soldiers, however dubious their origins, who could provide professional backbone to his amateur army: the American representatives in Paris, Benjamin Franklin and Silas Dean, became active recruiting sergeants. He had sustained them against Congressional criticism, and supported them against less able American officers.

Washington fought and defeated his critics in Congress and the army, who railed against his inactivity and lack of success: he insisted on the slow building of an army capable of defeating the British, and of an officer corps combining both courage and professional skill. He was loyal to his supporters, and had a good eye for a talented officer: most of those who failed were forced on him by political pressure. In the military arts he was no great tactician and lacked the experience to detect and counter obvious manœuvres in battle by his enemies. But he did have a head for the main strategic implications of the war: that it would be of long duration, that the terrain and the great distances to be covered must be used to wear down the British resolve and co-ordination. The Yorktown campaign is a classic example of Washington's strategic capacity: first, the recognition of the opportunity to achieve a decisive result; second, the speed and energy with which the complicated plan was put into effect. Washington, as Jefferson said, 'often failed in the field'; but by a combination of luck and skill he persevered and nurtured his army from its rough origins until it was capable of winning the war. He was a great commander.

Wavell, Archibald Percival (1st Earl Wavell; 1883–1950) British field-marshal. Appointed to command in the Middle East in 1939, it was his troops (see O'Connor) which counter-attacked, defeated and eventually utterly humiliated the Italian army under Graziani (q.v.), which had invaded Egypt from Libya in September 1940. The victory – until Alamein, Britain's only victory of the war – became known as Wavell's offensive. Under Churchill's orders he was obliged to break it off to send troops on the ill-fated expedition to Greece, and he shortly after had to deal with the arrival of Rommel (q.v.) in the desert. Transferred by Churchill (whose

regard for him was qualified) to the Far East in July 1941, he again had to preside over a worsening situation and then over a disaster. He ceased to exercise command in June 1943, when he was made viceroy of India. Wavell was an aloof and unnervingly silent man – hence Churchill's suspicion of his powers of decision – but a highly intelligent soldier and a sensitive soul, who wrote poetry and compiled one of the best-known of modern anthologies, *Other Men's Flowers*. Had he had any real enthusiasm for making war, which, despite a great deal of prewar writing on the subject, he admitted he had not, he might have been a general of the first class.

Weichs, Maximilian Freiherr von (1881–1954) German field-marshal. Commander of the Second Army in the invasion of France, May 1940, and of Yugoslavia, April 1941, Weichs succeeded Bock (q.v.) at the head of Army Group B in Russia in July 1942. He was sent back to the Balkans as commander-in-chief south-west in August 1943 and remained there until the end of the war.

Wellington, Arthur Wellesley, 1st Duke of (1769–1851) British field-marshal, commander-in-chief and prime minister. The fourth son of an impoverished Irish peer, Lord Mornington, Arthur Wellesley (the family had recently changed the form from Wesley) was educated at Eton and, at his own insistence, at a French military school in Angers. Obtaining a commission by purchase, his promotion from the age of sixteen to twenty-four was rapid: ensign, 73rd Regiment, 7 March 1787; lieutenant, 76th, 25 December 1787; exchanged next to the 41st, then to the 21st Light Dragoons, then to the 58th Regiment; captain, 1791; exchanged to the 18th Light Dragoons, 31 October 1792; major, 33rd Regiment, 30 April 1793; lieutenant-colonel commanding the 33rd, 30 September 1793.

So rapid a series of exchanges, between such a variety of regiments, though not irregular, was unusual; so too was his election as a member of the Irish Parliament while he was a lieutenant. Both testify to strong personal and family ambition, and to the importance of influence in promoting a contemporary military career.

The Wellesleys were not however an important enough family to push Arthur much beyond the point he had now reached. He commanded his regiment successfully in the Netherlands in 1793; but it was not until his brother Lord Mornington obtained in 1798 the governor-generalship of Bengal, whither the 33rd had been ordered, that his career gained real impetus. India was, for neither brother, the posting he would have desired, being a military and political backwater. But through the spread of French ambition it was now about to become important. Arthur was to be immensely successful in defeating the Indian allies of the French and defeating other enemies of the British administration: first Tippu (q.v.) at Seringapatam (1799) in the south, then the Mahrattas at Assaye and Argaum (1803) in the west. He was promoted major-general in 1802 and returned home in 1805 established as the leading 'Sepoy General'.

Elected to the Westminster Parliament, he served as Irish chief secretary, 1807–8, interrupting his political progress to campaign against the Danes (victory of Kioge, 19 August 1807). But his real military career was now about to begin. It had a false start in the Portuguese campaign of 1808, in which he beat a French army at Vimiero, but from 1809, following Moore's (q.v.) abortive Corunna campaign, he led the British army, and its Portuguese allies, into five years of campaigning against the French in the Peninsula which were to become a personal and national epic. Always outnumbered, his ability to sur-

vive and to win stemmed from his skilful and prudent use of seaward communications. The French, who lived off the land, were obliged to keep their large army dispersed so as to forage. Wellington could keep his small army concentrated because the navy supplied him either with victuals or the cash to purchase produce from the peasantry. As a result he never fought at a disadvantage; and when threatened by an overwhelming force could retire into a strong coastal position and wait while the enemy starved, as he did in the Torres Vedras campaign of 1810–11. Before the construction of those famous lines outside Lisbon, he had fought and won a succession of battles: Talavera, 28 July 1809, and Busaco, 26 September 1809; after the French withdrawal from them, he followed to win at Albuera (16 May 1811) and to conduct successful sieges against the French-held fortresses of Ciudad Rodrigo (8–19 January 1812) and Badajoz (16 March–6 April 1812). Entering Spain through the strategic passage these successes opened, he brought the retreating French army to battle at Salamanca (23 July 1812), defeated it and captured Madrid on 12 August. His campaign, starved of funds, then lost impetus; but in the following year he defeated the French again at Vittoria (21 June) and on 3 August won a battle called 'The Pyrenees', which signalled the arrival of the British army on the border of France. A series of actions, San Sebastian (8 September 1813), the Bidassoa (7 October), the Nivelle (10 November) and the Nive (9–13 December) carried him into France. On French soil he was to win the victories of Orthez (27 February 1814) and Toulouse (10 April) before Napoleon departed for Elba.

His greatest victory was, of course, to come. Appointed to command the British force assembled to join the allies converging on the escaped emperor in March 1815, Wellington (he had been created duke in 1814) positioned it between Brussels and the sea. On Napoleon's approach, he marched to meet him, intervened in the French–Prussian battle of Ligny on 16 June at Quatre Bras but did not encounter the full force of the enemy until 18 June, when Napoleon came forward to attack him in the Waterloo position. Napoleon thought the British abandoned by the Prussians and therefore easy prey. Wellington in fact had a warm understanding with Blücher (q.v.) and was never a general to trifle with. He had disposed his army in his favourite 'reverse slope' position, just behind the crest of the long ridge which crosses the Waterloo field, holding two fortified places, Hougoumont and La Haye Sainte in extra strength. Napoleon tried five major attacks on his line and was unsuccessful in all. After the last, Wellington ordered a general advance and drove the French from the field. He followed up the retreat of the French army to Paris where, after Napoleon's exile, he was appointed generalissimo of the allied armies of occupation.

At the close of the occupation in 1818, Wellington was made master-general of the ordnance, with a seat in Lord Liverpool's cabinet. Promoted commander-in-chief in 1827, he resigned both offices on Canning's succession to the premiership. In January 1828, however, he was himself prevailed upon to take office as prime minister, and survived two unhappy years in power. A High Tory, he nevertheless introduced Catholic emancipation, but was beaten over parliamentary reform. He thereafter withdrew slowly from politics. In 1842 he was reappointed commander-in-chief, for life, but his influence over the army at the end of his career is generally considered unfortunate, he having become unshakably conservative. He died in 1852 in Walmer Castle, which he occupied as lord warden of the Cinque Ports.

Wellington's military reputation has waxed and waned. He was a brilliant defensive tactician and a master of profit-ing by his enemy's mistakes; that is universally conceded. The facts of his career demand recognition also of his remarkably sure and long-sighted strategic judgement, his superbly economic management of his armies, his personal charisma, and the perfect timing of his offensive strokes. He is Britain's greatest general.

Westmoreland, William C. (1914–) American commander in Vietnam, 1964 to 1968. Westmoreland, who was educated at The Citadel and West Point, was commissioned into the field artillery in 1936, commanded the artillery of the Ninth Division in N.W. Europe (1944 to 1945) and was commanding general of the 101st Airborne Division in the post-war years. Appointed commander of the US Military Assistance Command, Vietnam, in 1964, he was responsible for the victories that secured the frontiers of South Vietnam from open invasion in 1964–5, and thus for the aggressive counter-strategy of 'Search and Destroy'. His command was, however, compromised by the Communist 'Tet' offensive of 1968 and he was relieved. An honourable and conscientious soldier, he lacked the touch of grand and good fortune which distinguished the plodder from the victor. Appointed Army Chief of Staff in 1969, he did much to rebuild the US Army after Vietnam. His later years have been spent in defending his own reputation and achieving recognition for his men.

Weygand, Maxime (1867– 1965) French general. His parentage remains a matter of intriguing speculation: he was certainly illegitimate and born at Brussels, the son, some say, of King Leopold II, others, of Emperor Maximilian of Mexico. Despite his foreign birth, Weygand was accepted into the French army, commissioned from Saint-Cyr into the cavalry and, in September 1914, plucked by Foch (q.v.) from command of a hussar regiment to be his chief of staff. Promoted general in 1916, he remained Foch's chief collaborator throughout the war, acting in 1918 as French representative on the inter-Allied committee at Versailles of which Foch was the generalissimo. Sent to Warsaw in 1920, he did much to train and equip the young Polish army for its war against Russia (*see* Pilsudski). He subsequently held a succession of senior military posts until 1935, when he retired.

Recalled to service (he used those words as the title of his memoirs) in 1939, Weygand was brought home from an appointment in the Lebanon by Reynaud on 19 May 1940 to fight the battle which Gamelin (q.v.) had failed to do. In many respects the two were versions of the same military type, Gamelin having been factotum to Joffre (q.v.), with the difference that Weygand, like his old warrior chief, had preserved his fire into old age. Hopeless though the situation he inherited was, he tried to organize a 'Weygand line' south of the Somme to bar the German advance into the interior, fought the Battle of France, 5–13 June, and only when resistance was revealed to be hopeless advised Pétain (q.v.) to sue for an armistice. He was subsequently Vichy minister of war, June–September 1940, and then delegate-general in North Africa, where he so strongly opposed German interests that at Hitler's insistence he was dismissed (18 November 1941). Arrested by the Gestapo in 1942, he was imprisoned by the French after the liberation, but exonerated and released in 1948. A patriot and a fighter, he might, given better luck and different times, have died a hero of his adopted country.

William the Silent (1533–84) Soldier, statesman and stadtholder of the Netherlands. Burdened with the nickname 'the Silent' in English, a misreading of the Dutch *schluwe*, meaning prudent or cunning, William was in fact a passionate leader and the virtual creator of an independent Netherlands. A trusted friend of Charles V (q.v.), he roused the dislike and suspicion of Charles's son Philip from their first meeting, an antipathy which was to have profound effects on his attitude towards the Dutch. William was forced reluctantly towards rebellion, knowing the strength and power of Spain, but unlike Count Egmont (q.v.) was realist enough to recognize that revolt might be necessary. Against the tumultuous Dutch, Philip II in 1567 sent the Duke of Alva (q.v.) to root out nationalism, rebellion and the Protestant heresy with fire and sword. He arrested the bulk of the active Dutch nobles, confiscated estates and purged the administration, and establishing the infamous Council of Blood, dispatched a torrent of victims to the executioner's block.

William was not among them, for he had, prudent as ever, left the country with the intention of raising an army of revolt. The first opportunity was missed when William failed to attack before Alva had tightened his hold on the country. The war began well for the Dutch, with William's brother, Louis of Nassau, an able soldier, beating a small German–Spanish force under Aremberg at Heiligerlees (1568). But at Jemmingen two months later (July 1568), against Alva, Louis's army was shattered, losing almost 7000 men out of 15,000, and Louis himself escaping only by swimming the river Ems to the safety of the far bank. William himself now invaded the Netherlands with 25,000 men; but the country was by now effectively terrorized by Alva and there was no great popular uprising, on which he had depended. He sparred with Alva, who had the best of the encounters, and was forced eventually to retreat, the great gamble having failed. Alva wrote confidently to Philip: 'We may regard the Prince of Orange as a dead man'; however, he reckoned without William's extraordinary determination and spirit. For three years resistance was largely in the hands of the Sea Beggars, privateers sailing under William's commission; they raided Spanish shipping and harried the coastal regions. Within the Netherlands, opposition to Alva was increasing; terror had become counter-productive, and the huge cost of the Spanish occupying army, paid for by the Netherlands, caused enormous discontent. Alva's attempt to impose a rigid Spanish system of taxation created, firstly, a campaign of passive resistance and then outright rebellion. As one contemporary wrote: 'If the Prince of Orange had kept his army in reserve until this time, he would have succeeded in what he undertook.'

The spark came with the surprise capture of Brill by the Sea Beggars (April 1572), followed by Louis of Nassau who immediately seized the initiative and took Flushing. One by one the towns of the Netherlands rose in revolt and murdered or expelled the Spanish garrison. Louis, firm in the attack where William was cautious, thrust into the southern Netherlands with an army of French Huguenots and mercenaries. But William consolidated his position in the north, where the bulk of his real support lay. His strategic judgement was impeccable, for in a long war the advantage lay with the Spanish unless he could make 'Holland his fortress'. Alva responded with his traditional weapon, terror, and sent his armies north under the command of his son Don Fadrique and Julian Romero (William's adjutant in former times) with orders to crush the revolt in blood. They burnt Naarden and slaughtered every living thing within it; at Zutphen they killed the population and hung the soldiers of the garrison by their feet over the smouldering ruins. Finally, in the following year, Haarlem fell, with similar butchery. But the Spanish advance was checked at Alkmaar, where the enraged

citizens repulsed the Spanish and then opened the dykes, flooding the Spanish camp. At sea the Sea Beggars destroyed the Spanish fleet off Enckhuysen, and took its admiral, Bossu, prisoner. Most important of all, Alva had failed to defeat the revolt and was recalled, to be replaced by Requesens, who had none of his savage determination and military skill. But the pattern of the war settled down: the south difficult for the Dutch, the north a trap for the Spanish. An invading army under Louis (1574) was beaten at Mookerheyde and Louis was killed. But in the autumn of the same year the long Spanish siege of Leyden ended in failure, when the dykes were opened and after agonizing delays the Sea Beggars under Boisot (q.v.) relieved the starving city. The lack of success weakened the discipline of the Spanish armies, and a regular series of mutinies broke out, the most notorious resulting in the sack and massacre at Antwerp (1576): William used these divisions to recruit waverers to his cause. But the military situation was always precarious, and when in 1577 Philip II sent fresh troops and a fine young commander, Alexander Farnese, to join Don Juan (Requesens's successor), the delicate balance was upset.

Farnese (later Duke of Parma, q.v.) routed the Dutch army at Gembloux, and the southern allies of William now began to turn against him, spurred by Parma's adroit diplomacy. Once again the rebel cause looked bleak, and increasingly, to William's distaste, a split developed between Calvinists and Catholic Netherlanders. Parma systematically reduced the rebel strongholds in the south and was diverted from moving into the northern provinces only by orders to intervene in the French wars of religion. In 1580 Philip II declared William an outlaw and put a price of 25,000 écus on his head: two years later Jean Jáureguy almost earned the reward, with a close-range pistol shot that nearly killed

William. There were several subsequent attempts on his life, but no one could come near him. In May 1584, however, a certain Balthasar Gérard arrived penniless at William's court with some information; William took pity on his poverty and gave him twelve crowns. With these Gérard purchased a pair of pistols, and with a single shot dispatched his benefactor – as he had long planned to do.

The loss of William was not that of a great field commander, for his son and successor Maurice (q.v.) or even his brother Louis were superior to him, but of a leader who saw the real nature of the war and its likely duration and consequences. His was a rebellion on a financial and military shoestring, against the most formidable army in Europe. William improvised strategy, armies, policy, as the situation demanded. But although the war went from disaster to disaster, first against Alva, and latterly, against Parma, he never lost his self-possession and capacity to sustain the flagging spirits of his supporters. He recognized the crucial importance of propaganda and flooded the Netherlands with pamphlets arguing his case and taking advantage of the mistakes of his enemies. Only a man of his unique personal and moral qualities could have forged the instrument of Dutch resistance which finally, after a war of eighty years, established a secure and independent Dutch nation.

Wilson, (Sir) Henry Hughes (1st Baronet; 1864–1922) British field-marshal. A successful military intriguer rather than a commander (it was said of him during the First World War that 'he got into a state of sexual excitement whenever he saw a politician'), Wilson's rise dated from his appointment as commandant of the Staff College in 1906. An early and enthusiastic advocate of military co-operation with France, he formed a warm friendship and collaboration with his opposite number Foch (q.v.), and on assuming the directorate of military operations in 1910, drew up the plans for the deployment of a British Expeditionary Force on the left wing of the French army in the event of war with Germany. On its outbreak, he became deputy chief of the general staff of the BEF, but was consistently denied transfer to an active command by his fellows, who rightly suspected both his competence and integrity, and, appropriately enough, was eventually shunted into the post of chief liaison officer at French headquarters.

Adopted by Lloyd George as an ally in his campaign against Haig (q.v.) in 1917, he was in November made by him British representative on the Supreme War Council, the body the prime minister had contrived to help stalemate Haig's strategic excesses, and then, on Lloyd George's successful removal of Haig's principal ally Robertson (q.v.), succeeded him as chief of the Imperial General Staff. Wilson had the ultimate satisfaction of seeing Foch made generalissimo, a move he had worked long and hard to bring about, but was denied to the end the supreme direction of British strategy which he had always craved for himself. After the armistice he prosecuted the anti-Sinn Fein campaign in Ireland with great enthusiasm and, on retirement from the army, entered Parliament as a member for Ulster, his home province. He was shot by Sinn Fein gunmen on the steps of his house in Eaton Square and died sword in hand (he was returning from an investiture), undoubtedly the last, if indeed not the only, British field-marshal to do so.

His namesake, Field-Marshal **(Sir) Henry Maitland** ('Jumbo') **Wilson** (1881–1964), British commander-in-chief, Greece, 1941, Persia, 1942, and the Middle East, 1942–3, and Allied supreme commander, Middle East, 1944, though often confused with him –

understandably, for 'Jumbo' stood out only in silhouette – was no relation.

Windisch-Graetz, Alfred Candidus Ferdinand Fürst zu (1787–1862) Austrian field-marshal. Chiefly notable for the firmness of his repression of the 1848 revolution in Austria: he put down the uprising in Prague, 17 June, after subjecting the city to bombardment, in Vienna, 31 October, and in Budapest, 5 January 1849. Then faced by a rebel Hungarian army under Dembinski, he defeated it at Kapolna, 26–7 February, but was himself defeated by Georgey (q.v.) at Gödöllö and removed from command.

Wingate, Orde Charles (1903–44) British general. The most controversial British soldier of the Second World War, Wingate established himself as an eccentric early on by his enthusiasm for the training of Zionist settlement guards ('Special Night Squads') during the Arab revolt in Palestine in 1936; in consequence, his name is reverenced in the modern state of Israel and he is regarded as one of the founders of its army. Posted to Burma in 1942, after leading a guerrilla force ('Gideon') against the Italians in Abyssinia, he conceived the idea of reactivating the offensive in that torpid and dispirited theatre of war not by leading frontal assaults (which consistently failed) but by the creation of air-supplied bases deep within Japanese-held territory. The forces he raised, which came to be called Chindits, undertook two 'deep penetrations', in February 1943 and March 1944. Both, but particularly the second and larger, were extremely harrowing and costly in lives, and their military value has been debated ever since in a spirit of bitterness attaching to no other British operation of the war. It is explained by Wingate's extraordinary character, which appeared to his admirers (who included Churchill) a blend of the mystical and the magnetic, to many others a combi-nation of charlatanry and obscurantism. He did himself no good with senior officers of conventional outlook by eating onions as if they were fruit and wearing an Old Testament beard. But then he is perhaps best seen as a prophet of doom: his strategic ideas supplied the French (*see* Navarre and Castries) with the germ of the plan for the Dien Bien Phu operation.

Witt, Johan de (1625–72) Dutch politician and statesman. The architect of Dutch policy during the period of war with England, Spain and France, de Witt was largely responsible for the creation of the successful Dutch fleet. The head of the party opposed to the house of Orange, his every action had to be tempered by the knowledge that a bitter opposition could be mounted against him. Appointed grand pensionary of the Netherlands, the leading political figure, he ended the unsuccessful war with England, which was disliked by many Dutchmen, who favoured a Protestant alliance. He used the ensuing period of peace to rebuild the Dutch navy, building ships capable of supporting the burgeoning Dutch empire, rather than simply being designed for Channel and Atlantic use.

Trade was always at the forefront of de Witt's policies: he intervened in the First Northern War (1655–60) on the Danish side to safeguard Dutch shipping to the Baltic, and entered into a war with England (1665–7) for commercial dominance of shipping and the herring trade. Under de Ruyter (q.v.) the Dutch fleet showed its superiority, burning the English dockyards at Chatham (1667) and establishing mastery at sea (he did however lose to Monck, q.v., at North Foreland, 1666). After the close of the war de Witt entered into an alliance with England against France. But this brought invasion by France and cavalry raids into central Holland, the fall of Utrecht, and even a threat to Amsterdam. A popular demand was raised for the Prince of Orange once again to take command in Holland's time of need; the de Witts (Johan and his brother Cornelis) were arrested, expelled from office and torn to pieces by an enraged Orangist mob who believed them to be traitors. In fact the policy of the de Witts exactly reflected Holland's needs, their rule laying the real basis of Dutch maritime and colonial power.

Wittgenstein, Ludwig Adolf Peter, Prinz von Sayn-Wittgenstein-Ludwigsburg (1769–1843) Russian field-marshal. Son of a Prussian general in Russian service, Wittgenstein fought at Austerlitz, commanded a corps in 1812, which burnt (too late) the Beresina bridges, was defeated in 1813 by Napoleon at Lützen, 2 May, and Bautzen, 20–1 May, and took a major part in the battle of Leipzig. He also campaigned in France in 1814. In 1828 he opened the war against Turkey, but was replaced by Paskievich (q.v.).

Witzleben, Erwin von (1881– 1944) German field-marshal. Commander, 1939–40, of the First Army, which broke the Maginot Line in the Battle of France, Witzleben was among the twelve generals promoted field-marshal by Hitler at the victory celebrations in Berlin on 18 July 1940. He acted as commander of Army Group D and commander-in-chief West, 1940–2, when he retired through ill-health. Long an anti-Nazi, he joined the military conspiracy against Hitler and was hanged for his part in the bomb plot of 20 July 1944. Had it succeeded, he would have been proclaimed commander-in-chief of the army. Whether it would have accepted his by then fumbling leadership is debatable.

Wolfe, James (1727–59) British soldier. Promise as much as performance was the salient feature of Wolfe's short career. The son of a soldier, he joined the army in 1741. Thrown into the thick of the war of the Austrian Succession (1740–8), he served as adjutant of his regiment at Dettingen (1743) although only sixteen at the time, and such was the reputation he gained in a brief period, in Europe and in the Culloden campaign, that he was a major by 1748 and a colonel by 1750. His keenness as a regimental commander became legendary, and his soldiers were renowned as some of the best trained in the army. In 1757 he took part in the failed expedition to Rochefort on the French coast. Other reputations suffered from the reverse, but Wolfe had carried out his role with such energy that he was appointed to the much more important Louisburg expedition in North America (1758), under the command of Amherst (q.v.). Here, success was complete, and Wolfe, now a brigadier, gathered most of the laurels for the expedition, leading his men in romantic and gallant assaults on the French positions. Promoted to acting major-general on his return to London, Pitt decided to give him command of the expedition which was to be mounted against Quebec (1759). This was to be Wolfe's first and only independent campaign. His conduct of the siege was not encouraging and it was on the point of failure when the last desperate throw, an assault by a force led by Howe (q.v.), one of Wolfe's long-standing friends, up the precipitous Heights of Abraham, established him with 4800 men on the plain in front of Quebec. Montcalm (q.v.), lured out at last from his stronghold, lost the brief encounter with the British, and both Wolfe and Montcalm died as a result of the exchange of fire.

Wolfe was a safely dead hero, and many of the less attractive features of his personality were forgotten. Had he lived, he might have been the brilliant general which the British so desperately needed in the American War of Independence; but perhaps (more likely) he would have been yet another of the insubordinate generals whose wild schemes were to ruin the British cause. But such questions are academic, for even if Quebec had not killed him, the raging consumption from which he suffered most certainly would have.

Wolseley, Garnet Joseph (1st Viscount Wolseley; 1833–1913) British field-marshal. A shopkeeper's son – a more unpromising start in life for a Victorian soldier with a career to make could not have been wished upon him by the harshest of bad fairies – he was commissioned into the 12th Foot in 1852. A great deal of foreign service – Second Burma War, Crimea, Indian Mutiny, Second China War – came his way early on, allowing him the opportunity to display exceptional abilities which offset his social origins; after a long spell of staff duty in Canada, 1861–70, he had established himself as one of the most efficient and forward-looking officers in the army. A collaborator of Cardwell (q.v.) in the reform of the army, 1871–3, a cause very much his own as well, he got command of the expedition to Ashanti,. 1873–4, for which he gathered round himself a group of the cleverest young officers in the army (to become known as 'the Ring' and to be bitterly resented by non-members) and returned home a triumphant victor, hailed as 'the very model of a modern major-general' (W.S. Gilbert) and as 'our only general'. With that reputation he was sent to South Africa to repair the disaster of Isandhlwana, 1879, and to Egypt in 1882 to relieve Gordon (q.v.). It was as a reformer, however, that the rest of his service was chiefly spent, locked in combat with the reactionary commander-in-chief, HRH the Duke of Cambridge ('There is time for everything. There is even a time for change. And that is when change can no longer be resisted.'). To the disgust of the duke's cousin (Queen Victoria) he eventually succeeded him in 1895 as penulti-

mate commander-in-chief (the post was abolished in 1904, *see* Roberts), seal of his success in dragging the army into the twentieth century.

Wrangel, Friedrich Heinrich Ernst (Graf von; 1784–1877) Prussian field-marshal. He commanded the federal German troops in Schleswig-Holstein in 1848, crushed the revolution in Berlin in the same year and in 1864 was supreme commander of the Austro-Prussian army in the war with Denmark.

Wrangel, Petr Nikolaevich, Baron (1878–1928) Russian (White) general. Of noble Swedish descent, Wrangel served in a Cossack regiment in the Russo-Japanese war, transferred to the Horse Guards and during the First World War rose to command a division, again of Cossacks. He was one of the first to take the field against the Bolsheviks, allied himself with Alekseev and Denikin (qq.v.) and took a leading part in the defence of Tsaritsyn (Stalingrad) against Voroshilov (q.v.). After the retreat of Denikin in April 1920, he was appointed commander of the White volunteer army, then in the Crimea, reorganized it and went over to the offensive. However, the signing of the Russo-Polish peace (*see* Pilsudski) set free Bolshevik troops, who overwhelmed his army and obliged him to evacuate it, with western help, from the Black Sea. He then returned to his civilian profession of mining engineer.

Wrede, Karl Phillip (Prinz von; 1767–1838) Bavarian field-marshal. After Hohenlinden (*see* Moreau), Wrede covered the retreat of the Austrian army, but, through a diplomatic reversal, fought for France against it in 1805 and 1809. He led the Bavarian contingent on the Russian campaign and commanded the Army of the Inn in 1813, but then changed sides, attempted to bar Napoleon's line of retreat after Leipzig and was defeated at Hanau, 30–1 October 1813. In the invasion of France he took part in the battles of La Rothière, Rosny, Bar-sur-Aube and Arcis-sur-Aube. He was created prince and promoted field-marshal in 1815, represented Bavaria at the congress of Vienna and became commander-in-chief of the Bavarian army in 1822. Contemporaries regarded him as one of the vainest men alive.

Würmser, Dagobert Sigismund (Graf von; 1724–97) Austrian general. An Alsatian, Würmser originally joined the French army but transferred to the Austrian in 1747, took part in the siege of Mainz, 1793, recaptured Mannheim in 1795 and, at the head of the Austrian army in Italy in 1796, was beaten by Bonaparte at Castiglione, 5 August (*see* Augereau), besieged in Mantua and obliged to capitulate, 2 February 1797.

Wu San-kuei (1612–78) Chinese general and warlord. Allowing the Manchus to enter China, and thus becoming directly responsible for overthrowing his masters, the Ming emperors, Wu took service with them and for nearly three decades devoted himself to exterminating the last remains of Ming resistance. In 1659 he was given command in the south of China, never susceptible to the rule of Peking, and established what amounted to an independent kingdom in Yunnan. In 1673 he came out in open revolt against the Manchu Ching dynasty and proclaimed a new dynasty, the Chou, led by himself. He advanced into central China, defeating the armies sent to oppose him; but he did not press his campaign because his son was held a hostage by the Manchu. The war turned against him and he died of dysentery. The rebellion he had started, known to history as the Revolt of the Three Feudatories, lasted until 1681: with its suppression Manchu power was firmly established in China.

Y

Yamagata, (Prince) Aritomo (1838–1922) Japanese general, creator of the modern Japanese army. One of the earliest Japanese visitors to Europe, where he went as a young officer in 1869, he returned impressed by the Prussian military system and alarmed by the dangers of liberalism. He was responsible for introducing both conscription and a general staff on the Prussian model, and for keeping control of the new army and navy safe from civilian hands by making their chiefs directly responsible to the emperor and by prescribing that the ministers of war and marine be chosen only from the list of serving generals and admirals. He himself held all the most important ministries at one time or another, including the premiership, 1890 and 1898, and commanded the First Army in the war with China, 1894–5.

Yamamoto, Isoruku (1884–1943) Japanese admiral. A seaman of the stature of Togo (q.v.), some would say of Nelson (q.v.), he had been educated in America, later served there as naval attaché and before 1941 was strongly opposed to Japan going to war with her. Obliged nevertheless to plan for and instigate hostilities, he prepared for the only campaign he thought might bring Japan victory: one designed to give Japan possession of the whole of the western Pacific and to destroy American land, sea and air power within it, all in the space of twelve months. Should the war last longer, he warned, Japan would lose it. Success required that the war should begin with a surprise attack, which he launched against Pearl Harbor on 7 December 1941. Overriding the objections of the naval general staff, he then went on to bring what remained of the US Pacific fleet – principally its aircraft carriers – to battle, but the second engagement to which this strategy led, Midway, 4–5 June 1942, ended in crushing defeat and thereafter the train of events he had feared – a transfer of the initiative to the Americans and a rapid outbuilding of Japanese strength was set in motion. He persisted nonetheless in the struggle, launching the Guadalcanal offensive in August 1942, but shortly after it had ended in failure he was trapped in flight by a specially trained and briefed American fighter unit (acting on wireless intercepts) and shot down. This was the only instance of a direct attempt on an enemy leader's life (except on that of Rommel – see Keyes) undertaken by the Allies during the war and testimony of the awe in which the Americans held Yamamoto. They continued to respect his reputation as the first great practitioner of air–sea warfare.

Yamashita, Tomokjuki (1888–1946) Japanese general. His lightning conquest of British Malaya, December 1941–February 1942, won for him the title 'the Tiger of Malaya'. In 1944 he was put in command of Japanese forces in the Philippines only a week before the Americans landed, conducted a tenacious defence and, when defeated, took to the mountains and held out to the end of the war. He was afterwards hanged as a war criminal.

Yeremenko, Andrei Ivanovich (1893–

1970) Marshal of the Soviet Union. A veteran of the First Cavalry Army of Budenny (q.v.), Yeremenko commanded armies under Zhukov (q.v.), both in the Moscow counter-offensive of December 1941 and in the Stalingrad encirclement of November 1942. He subsequently commanded the Second Baltic Front (army group), the Maritime Territory Army, which reoccupied much of the Crimea in 1944, and the Fourth Ukrainian Front, which fought its way into Czechoslovakia at the end of the war.

Yorck von Wartenburg, Hans David Ludwig (1759–1830) Prussian field-marshal. Something of a soldier of fortune – he had fought for the Dutch in the East Indies after being cashiered from his own army for disobedience – he regained his Prussian commission in 1794, fought in the Jena campaign (1806), but, as second-in-command of the corps requisitioned by Napoleon for his invasion of Russia, took it over to the tsar by the convention of Taurrogen (30 December 1812). This was the effec-tive beginning of the Prussian War of Liberation, in which he led his corps at Bautzen and Leipzig. In the invasion of France in 1814 he fought in the battles of Montmirail and Laon.

York and Albany, Prince Frederick, Duke of (1763–1827) British field-marshal and commander-in-chief. George III's second son, he was trained for the army and in 1793 took the British contingent to the allied army of the First Coalition in Flanders. Neither there ('The Grand Old Duke of York, he had ten thousand men . . .') nor at the Helder in 1799 did he prove any sort of general. As commander-in-chief, however, from 1798 until his death, he proved an efficient administrator and, despite a scandal over the dabbling of his mistress in the commissions trade, which obliged him to surrender office between 1809 and 1811, not apparently a corrupt one. He was called 'the soldiers' friend', though probably not by the soldiers themselves.

Z

Zeitzler, Kurt (1895–1963) German general. Appointed chief of the general staff of the army (OKH), from the staff of Army Group D, in September 1942 (*see* Halder) he was the strongest advocate of Operation Citadel, and, at a time when Hitler's powers of decision had been shaken by his mistakes over Stalingrad, was able to carry opinion for its execution. The battle it precipitated (Kursk, July 1943), though not as long or harrowing as Stalingrad, proved an even greater disaster, for it destroyed Germany's strategic armoured reserve and transferred the power of the initiative to the Russians. He was replaced in July 1944 by Guderian (q.v.).

Zhukov, Georgi Konstantinovich (1895–1974) Marshal of the Soviet Union. Russia's leading soldier of the Second World War, he had joined the imperial army in 1916, distinguished himself in the ranks of the cavalry (10th Novgorod Dragoons), fought in the Civil War in the First Cavalry Army, risen steadily upward in the Red Army and delivered the counter-offensive against the Japanese in Manchuria, July–August 1939 (battle of Khalkin-Gol). Appointed chief of staff of the Red Army, January 1941, he was transferred at the start of the German invasion to assist Voroshilov (q.v.) in the defence of Leningrad, then to organize the Moscow counter-offensive, December 1941, which halted and turned back the advance of Army Group Centre on the capital. From then until 1944, as first deputy commander-in-chief of Soviet armed forces, he planned and directed most of Russia's major military operations, including the Stalingrad counter-offensive and the Kursk–Orel battles.

In 1944 Zhukov returned to a field command at the head of the First Ukrainian and First Belorussian fronts with which he conducted the crossing of the Vistula and the advance to Berlin where, in May 1945, he supervised the signing of the German army's capitulation. Soon displaced from high command by Stalin, for whom he had become an overmighty subject, he was reinstated after the dictator's death and was minister of defence, 1955–7, when he was again removed by Krushchev. Zhukov appeared to combine in his person all the qualities of great generalship – strategic decision, tactical judgement, political persuasiveness, physical and moral courage, a magnetic influence over others and – that most needed during Russia's war with Hitler – an apparent insensitivity to the frightful cost of the operations which he instituted. In many ways, he was the complete twentieth-century soldier.

Glossary

Army: A major military formation (q.v.), in modern war comprising at least two corps (q.v.) and commanded by a full general.

Army group: The largest military command, first formed during the First World War comprising at least two Armies.

Arquebus; Arquebusier: An early form of musket; the soldier who fired it.

Battalion: The principal unit (q.v.) of infantry 600–1000 strong, commanded by a lieutenant-colonel, often loosely called a regiment (q.v.).

Battery: The basic unit of artillery, comprising 4–8 guns; in a fort, the place from which guns were fired.

Battlecruiser: A large cruiser, carrying guns but not armour of a battleship's weight, developed before the First World War to scout for the battleship (q.v.); see also Capital Ship.

Battleship: The largest gun-firing warship; see Capital Ship.

Brigade: A group of 2–4 regiments of cavalry or 3–8 battalions of infantry; the smallest formation (q.v.), in that it also contained troops of other arms besides those forming its principal bulk (e.g. a cavalry brigade usually included a complement of horse artillery).

Capital ship: A late nineteenth- and twentieth-century term, meaning Battleship or Battlecruiser.

Chasseur: See Jäger.

Column: A military or naval formation (q.v.), greater in depth than breadth.

Company: A sub-unit (q.v.) of infantry traditionally commanded by a captain, 100–250 strong; as few as four and as many as twelve form a battalion (q.v.).

Corvette: A minor naval vessel, smaller than a frigate (q.v.).

Cruiser: The gun-firing warship next in size after a battleship (q.v.), developed for reconnaissance, commerce protection and raiding; see also Battlecruiser.

Cuirassier: A heavy cavalryman who wore a cuirass (breast- and backplate).

Destroyer: A fast warship, smaller than a cruiser (q.v.), developed to fight torpedo boats, c. 1890, and later submarines.

Division: The principal army formation (q.v.), comprising infantry or cavalry (or more recently tanks, or a mixture of infantry and tanks) with such supporting troops as artillery, engineers, signals; it is traditionally commanded by a major-general and numbers 12,000 to 20,000.

Dragoons: Originally (c. 1700) mounted infantry, later (1750 onwards) heavy cavalry.

Dreadnought: The name given to the Royal Navy's first 'all big gun' battleship, launched 1906, and later attaching to all battleships of the type.

Enfilade: Fire which hits a formation (q.v.) in flank (q.v.); hence 'to enfilade'.

Flag officer: An admiral, but usually only when in command; the flag lieutenant is his personal staff officer.

Flank: The side of a military formation (q.v.); a column (q.v.) has longer flanks than a line (q.v.).

Fleet: The largest naval formation (q.v.), commanded by an admiral.

Flotilla: A naval formation (q.v.) of small ships.

Formation: (1) a body of units (q.v.) of several arms – infantry or cavalry, with artillery, engineers or others in support – and thus capable of operating independently of the main army; brigades, divisions and corps are formations, (2) a pattern or method of drawing up naval or military or air units for battle, e.g. column or line (qq.v.).

Frigate: A naval ship; in sailing days, smaller than a ship of the line (q.v.) but larger than a corvette (q.v.), nowadays next in size and speed after a destroyer (q.v.).

Galley, Galleas: Oared fighting ships, with auxiliary sails; the galleas was more of a sailing-ship than the galley and carried more guns. The term galleon, now loosely applied to almost any sort of sailing or oared warship, was properly applied in the sixteenth century to the larger sailing warship.

Gendarme: Originally a mounted man-at-arms, later a (mounted) policeman, under state rather than municipal control.

Grenadier: An infantryman equipped and trained to throw grenades; the grenadier company (q.v.) of a battalion (q.v.) was usually composed of the tallest men and used as a shock force when required.

Group of Armies: See Army Group.

Howitzer: An artillery piece, firing explosive shells at a high angle.

Hussar: A light cavalryman, originally (*c.* 1700) recruited into Western Europe from Hungary.

Jäger: Literally 'hunter' (German); the name was given to the soldiers of the light infantry regiments of the German and Austrian armies, on which were modelled the French Chasseurs (C. *à pied* = light infantry, C. *alpins* = mountain infantry, C. *à cheval* and C. *d'Afrique* = light cavalry; in imitation of the latter, Kaiser Wilhelm II formed regiments of *Jäger zu Pferd*).

Janissary: The regular soldiers of the Ottoman empire. They were disbanded in 1826.

Kriegsakademie: The staff college of the Prussian army, founded at Berlin in 1810; model for all other staff colleges.

Landesknecht: German (mounted) mercenary soldier of the sixteenth–seventeenth century.

Light troops: Infantry or cavalry equipped and trained to operate as skirmishers or scouts; see Jäger and Rifleman; the light infantry company of a battalion (q.v.) was formed from the nimblest and most intelligent men and, with the grenadier (q.v.) company, stood on the flank – hence 'flank companies', i.e. the best of the battalion.

Limoge: 'Relieved of command' (French slang); French generals of the First World War dismissed in the field for incompetence were sent, so popular belief had it, to command at Limoges, headquarters of the military district furthest from the zone of operations.

Line: (1) A military or naval formation (q.v.), greater in breadth than depth, (2) the ordinary infantry and cavalry, as opposed to that of the guard or the light troops (q.v.).

Mameluke: Member of a military body, originally of Caucasian slaves, which seized power in Egypt in the thirteenth century and ruled under Ottoman suzerainty.

Maria Theresa Akademie: The principal Austrian military cadet school, founded at Wiener Neustadt.

Monitor: A coastal warship, armed with guns of battleship (q.v.) size for shore bombardment; a United States Ship so named fought the first (1862) ship-to-ship action (with the Confederate *Merrimac*) of modern naval warfare.

Mortar: A smooth-bore artillery piece, firing explosive bombs at an even higher angle than does a howitzer (q.v.); formerly much used in siege warfare, it is now an infantry support weapon.

Oblique order: A method of moving troops on the battlefield so as to mass on an enemy's flank (q.v.), allegedly invented by Frederick the Great.

Panzer: 'Armour' (German); today applied to formations of tanks and, loosely, to tanks themselves.

Platoon: A sub-unit (q.v.) of infantry, commanded by a lieutenant; usually three form a company (q.v.).

Polytechnique: The Ecole Polytechnique founded in Paris in 1794 was until the twentieth century the French army's principal source of artillery and engineer officers.

Regiment: The principal unit (q.v.) of cavalry, about 500 strong, commanded by a lieutenant-colonel; a unit of infantry, comprising 2–4 battalions (q.v.), commanded by a colonel, but an administrative rather than a tactical body.

Rifleman: Originally (*c.* 1800) a soldier equipped with a rifle instead of a smooth-bore musket; the rifle regiments were used as skirmishers – see Light Troops.

St-Cyr: The French cadet school for the infantry and cavalry (and today for all arms), founded at St-Cyr, near Paris, as the *Ecole spéciale militaire* in 1802; now at Coëtquidan in Brittany.

Samurai: The feudal warrior class of Japan.

Sandhurst: The British cadet school for the infantry and cavalry (Royal Military College), founded in 1798, established in its present buildings in 1810 and amalgamated with Woolwich (q.v.) in 1947 to form the Royal Military Academy Sandhurst for cadets of all arms.

Saumur: The training centre of the French cavalry (*Ecole d'application de cavalerie*); *not* a cadet school.

Sepoy, Spahi: From the Persian word for a soldier (*sipahi*); sepoys were the native infantry of the British Indian Army, spahis the native cavalry of the *Armée d'Afrique* of French North Africa.

Ship: In sailing days, the principal vessel of war, of 64, 74, 80, 90, 98, 100 and eventually even 120 guns, arranged in broadside batteries. Ships were classified fourth- to first-rate (terms often used) and were also known as ships of the line, being 'fit to lie in the line of battle'. HMS *Victory* is a first-rate.

Sloop: A naval vessel smaller than a corvette.

Squadron: A sub-unit (q.v.) of cavalry, commanded by a captain, about 100 strong; or a group of ships, detached from, or forming a division within, a fleet (q.v.) (e.g. the Battlecruiser Squadron of the Grand Fleet at Jutland).

Staff: The general's or admiral's assistants. In the British army, their duties are usually organized into operations and intelligence (G), administrative and personnel (A) and supply (Q) categories, G standing for general staff, A for adjutant-general and Q for quartermaster-general; in the American army, the staff is divided into G-1, 2, 3, 4 and 5 categories, G-3 being the equivalent of the British operations and intelligence section. Most armies have a triple division: in the German army the key officer was the 2a, in the French army the *Deuxième bureau* was the intelligence section.

Staff College: A school for training officers, usually of the rank of captain or major, in the duties of the staff (see *Kriegsakademie*); in particular, the Staff College, Camberley, principal source of staff officers for the British army, opened 1861.

Sub-unit: A division of a unit (q.v.), such as a squadron or a company (qq.v.).

Tercio: A regular regiment of Spanish infantry, sixteenth century; the

Spanish Foreign Legion is still so organized.

Tirailleur: A French sharpshooter; see Light Troops.

Troop: A sub-unit (q.v.) of cavalry or artillery.

Uhlan: German or Austrian lancer, recruited originally in Poland.

Unit: A body of soldiers all of the same arm (e.g. artillery or infantry), divided into sub-units (q.v.) and directly subordinate to a formation (q.v.); battalions, batteries and regiments (qq.v.) are the principal units.

Van: The head of a column (q.v.) of troops or ships.

Voltigeur: A French light infantryman.

West Point: Principal cadet school of the United States Army, founded in 1802.

Woolwich: The British cadet school (Royal Military Academy) for the artillery and engineers, founded 1746 (see Sandhurst).

A Note on Titles and Ranks

Titles: These have been left, except where inappropriate, in the original language, but the following key gives the English equivalents:

Knight: Ritter (G.), Chevalier (F.)

Baron: Freiherr (G.)

Viscount: Vicomte (F.)

Earl, Count: Graf (G.), Comte (F.), Conte (I.), Conde (S.)

Marquis: Markgraf (G.), Marchese (I.), Marques (S.)

Duke: Duc (F.), Herzog (G.), Duce (I.), Duque (S.)

Archduke: Erzherzog (G.)

Prince: Prinz, Fürst (G.), Principe (S. and I.)

Electoral Prince, Elector: Kurfürst (G.)

The Ottoman titles Pasha, Dey and Bey, suffixed to the name, were territorial but, strictly, not hereditary.

Ranks: Modern military ranks derive from the titles of the three officers of the late mediaeval mercenary company: the headman, *hauptmann* or captain, his deputy or lieutenant (cf. locum tenens) and the sergeants. When formed, as the companies were in the sixteenth century, into a larger group or column (colonne), they were put under the authority or 'regiment' of a colonel (*colonnello*). When a number of regiments were grouped to form an army, its superior officers assumed 'general' instead of 'regimental' rank. Combinations of these titles, with the use of the suffix 'major', yield most of the ranks of modern armies; it should be explained that the 'major-general' was originally 'sergeant-major-general', hence his juniority to the lieutenant-general. An exception to these rules are Austrian ranks, which include oddities like '*Feldzeugmeister*' = campaignmaster (general), in effect, a general of artillery or infantry, and '*Feldmarschalleutnant*' = field-marshal lieutenant (major-general). 'Marshal' was originally a state rather than a military rank and remains so in France, where it is regarded as a '*dignité d'état*', separate from as well as superior to the military hierarchy.

The rank structure is thus more logical than it might appear. It usually runs: lieutenant (first and second), captain, major, lieutenant-colonel, colonel, brigadier(-general) – a fairly modern innovation, major-general, lieutenant-general, general, marshal or field-marshal. The Germans, Austrians and Russians also have or had a 'colonel-general', who was superior to a general, and the Spaniards a captain-general, which was their highest rank.

Naval ranks derive from the title of the headman of the soldiers embarked on a ship – captain – and his lieutenant, but 'admiral' comes from the Arabic *amir* (commander) *al* (of the) *bahr* (sea), the head of the great fleets with which the Muslims established their power in the Eastern

Mediterranean. 'Commander' and 'Commodore' were added later (they have the same etymological derivation) to fill out the hierarchy. The 'vice-admiral' was deputy to a commanding admiral, the 'rear-admiral', junior to both, commanded the rear of a fleet when it was the practice to divide it into three. Thus was established the conventional order: lieutenant (usually junior and senior), lieutenant-commander, commander, captain, commodore (strictly an appointment rather than a rank), rear-admiral, vice-admiral, admiral, admiral of the fleet. The French, and later the Germans, had a slightly different system in which *capitaine de corvette* or *Korvettenkapitän* was equivalent to lieutenant-commander, *capitaine de frégate* or *Fregattenkapitän* to commander and *capitaine de vaisseau* or *Kapitän zur See* to captain; *lieutenant de vaisseau* or *Leutnant zur See* was equivalent to lieutenant.

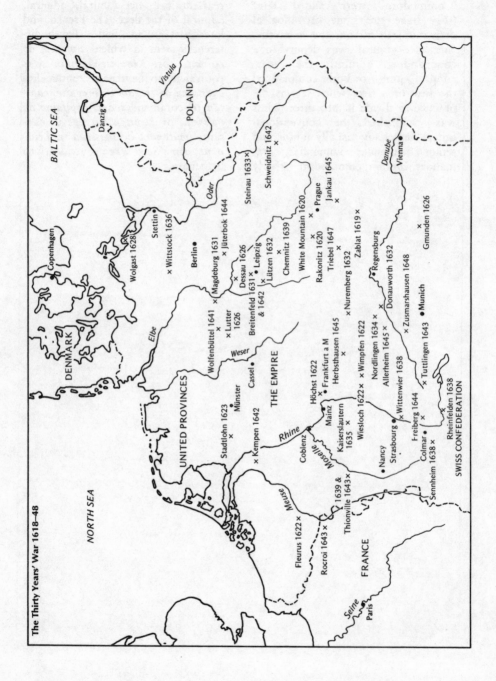

The Thirty Years' War 1618–48

BALTIC SEA

NORTH SEA

DENMARK

Copenhagen

POLAND

Vistula

Oder

Danzig

Stettin ×
Wolgast 1628 ×
Wittstock 1636 ×
Berlin ●
Magdeburg 1631 ×
Jüterbok 1644 ×
Dessau 1626 ×
Leipzig ×
Breitenfeld 1631 & 1642 ×
Lützen 1632 ×
Chemnitz 1639 ×
Steinau 1633 ×
Schweidnitz 1642 ×
White Mountain 1620 ×
Prague ●
Rakonitz 1620 ×
Triebel 1647 ×
Zablat 1619 ×
Jankau 1645 ×
Vienna ●
Gmunden 1626 ×
Regensburg ●
Donauworth 1632 ×
Zusmarshausen 1648 ×
Munich ●

Elbe

Weser

Rhine

Moselle

Meuse

Seine

THE EMPIRE

UNITED PROVINCES

Wolfenbüttel 1641 ×
Lutter 1626 ×
Münster ●
Cassel ●
Stadtlohn 1623 ×
Kempen 1642 ×
Coblenz ●
Höchst 1622 ×
Frankfurt a M ●
Mainz ●
Herbsthausen 1645 ×
Wimpfen 1622 ×
Nordlingen 1634 ×
Allerheim 1645 ×
Wittenwier 1638 ×
Tuttlingen 1643 ×
Kaiserslautern 1635 ×
Wiesloch 1622 ×
Nancy ●
Strasbourg ●
Freiberg 1644 ×
Colmar ●
Sennheim 1638 ×
Rheinfelden 1638 ×

SWISS CONFEDERATION

FRANCE

Paris ●

Fleurus 1622 ×
Rocroi 1643 ×
1639 & 1643 ×
Thionville 1643 ×

Mediterranean. 'Commander' and 'Commodore' were added later (they have the same etymological derivation) to fill out the hierarchy. The 'vice-admiral' was deputy to a commanding admiral, the 'rear-admiral', junior to both, commanded the rear of a fleet when it was the practice to divide it into three. Thus was established the conventional order: lieutenant (usually junior and senior), lieutenant-commander, commander, captain, commodore (strictly an appointment rather than a rank), rear-admiral, vice-admiral, admiral, admiral of the fleet. The French, and later the Germans, had a slightly different system in which *capitaine de corvette* or *Korvettenkapitän* was equivalent to lieutenant-commander, *capitaine de frégate* or *Fregattenkapitän* to commander and *capitaine de vaisseau* or *Kapitän zur See* to captain; *lieutenant de vaisseau* or *Leutnant zur See* was equivalent to lieutenant.

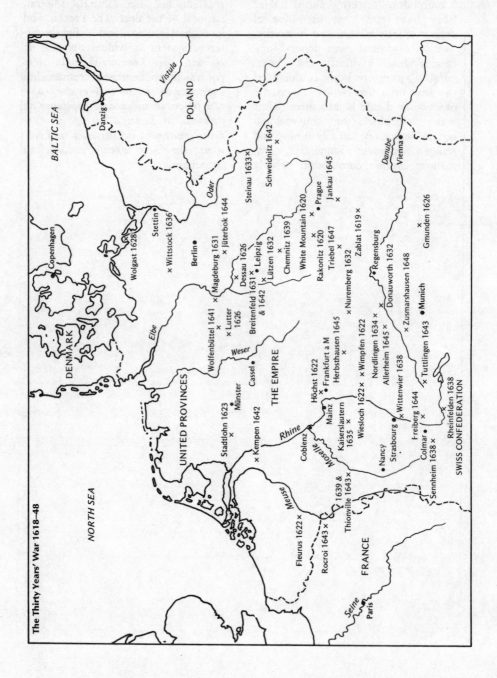

The Thirty Years' War 1618–48

NORTH SEA

BALTIC SEA

Copenhagen ●

DENMARK

POLAND

Vistula

Danzig ●

Stettin ●
× Wittstock 1636

Wolgast 1628 ×

Berlin ●

Oder

× Magdeburg 1631
× Jüterbok 1644

Steinau 1633 ×

Schweidnitz 1642 ×

Chemnitz 1639
White Mountain 1620

Prague ●
Jankau 1645 ×

Rakonitz 1620 ×
Triebel 1647

Zablat 1619 ×

Vienna ●

Danube

Gmunden 1626 ×

Elbe

Dessau 1626
× Leipzig
Lützen 1632

Breitenfeld 1631 ×
& 1642

Wolfenbüttel 1641 ×
× Lutter
1626

Weser

Nuremberg 1632 ×

Regensburg ●

Donauworth 1632

Zusmarshausen 1648 ×

Munich ●

THE EMPIRE

Cassel ●

Münster ●

UNITED PROVINCES

Stadtlohn 1623 ×

× Kempen 1642

Höchst 1622 ×
× Frankfurt a M
Herbsthausen 1645 ×

Wimpfen 1622 ×

Nordlingen 1634 ×
Allerheim 1645 ×
Wittenwier 1638 ×

Tuttlingen 1643 ×

Coblenz ●

Mainz ●

Kaiserslautern
1635 ×

Wiesloch 1622 ×

Freiberg 1644 ×

Colmar ×

Moselle

Rhine

Nancy ●

Strasbourg ●

Sennheim 1638 ×

Rheinfelden 1638 ×

SWISS CONFEDERATION

Meuse

Fleurus 1622 ×

Rocroi 1643 ×

Thionville 1643 ×
1639 &

FRANCE

Seine

Paris ●

332

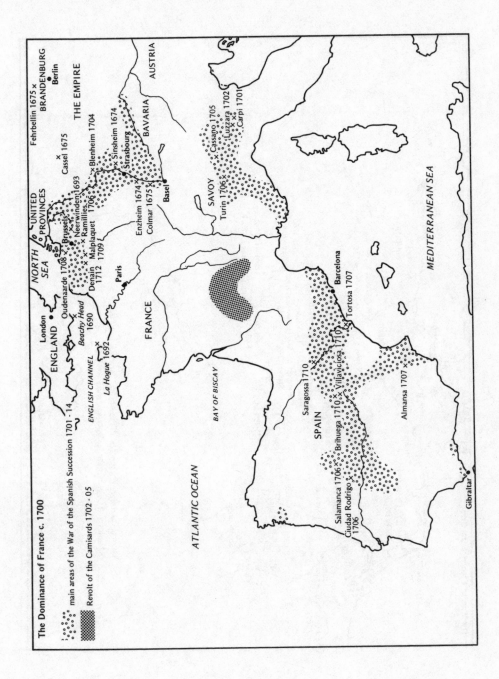

The Dominance of France c. 1700

· · · main areas of the War of the Spanish Succession 1701 - 14

▓▓ Revolt of the Camisards 1702 - 05

Fehrbellin 1675 x
BRANDENBURG
Berlin ●

THE EMPIRE

Cassel 1675 x

BAVARIA

AUSTRIA

× Blenheim 1704
Newinden 1693 × × Sinsheim 1674
× Ramillies Strasbourg
1706

UNITED
PROVINCES
Brussels

Enzheim 1674 × Colmar 1675 ×
Basel ●

SAVOY
Cassano 1705
× Luzzara 1702
Turin 1706 × × Carpi 1701

Oudenaarde 1708 ×
Demain × × Malplaquet
1712   1709
Paris ●

NORTH
SEA

London ●
ENGLAND
Beachy Head
1690

La Hogue 1692 ×

ENGLISH CHANNEL

FRANCE

MEDITERRANEAN SEA

Barcelona ●
Tortosa 1707 ×

BAY OF BISCAY

Saragossa 1710
Brihuega 1710 × × Villaviciosa 1710

Almansa 1707 ×

SPAIN

ATLANTIC OCEAN

Salamanca 1706 ×
Ciudad Rodrigo
1706

Gibraltar ●

333

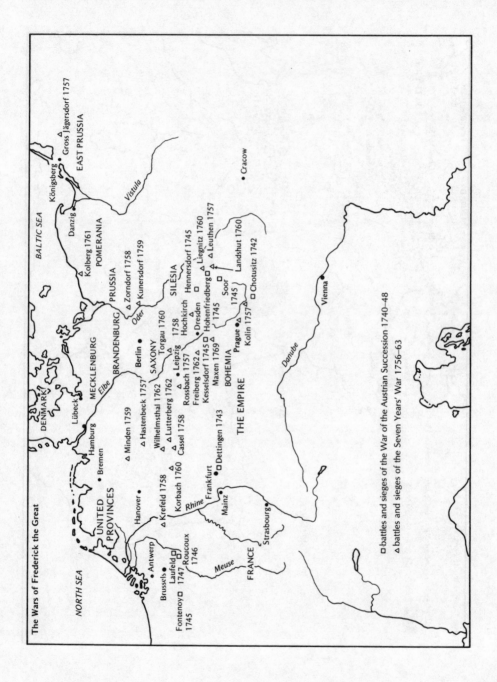

The Wars of Frederick the Great

NORTH SEA

BALTIC SEA

DENMARK

Lübeck ·

Hamburg ·

Bremen ·

Hanover ·

UNITED PROVINCES

Antwerp ·

Brussels ·

Fontenoy □ 1745

Laufeld □ 1747

Roucoux □ 1746

FRANCE

Strasbourg ·

Mainz ·

Frankfurt ·

Rhine

Meuse

△ Krefeld 1758

△ Korbach 1760

□ Dettingen 1743

△ Minden 1759

△ Hastenbeck 1757

Wilhelmsthal 1762 △

Lutterberg 1762 △

Cassel 1758 △

MECKLENBURG

Elbe

BRANDENBURG

Berlin ·

SAXONY

Torgau 1760 △

Leipzig △

Dresden □

Freiberg 1762 △

Rossbach 1757 △

Kesselsdorf 1745 □

Maxen 1769 □

BOHEMIA

Prague ● △

Kolin 1757 △

THE EMPIRE

POMERANIA

Kolberg 1761 △

Danzig ·

Königsberg ·

EAST PRUSSIA

Gross Jägersdorf 1757 △

Vistula

PRUSSIA

Oder

△ Zorndorf 1758

△ Kunersdorf 1759

SILESIA

Hennersdorf 1745 △

△ Liegnitz 1760

Hohenfriedberg 1745 □

Hochkirch □

1758

Soor
1745 △

Landshut 1760 △

△ Leuthen 1757

□ Chotusitz 1742

Cracow ·

Danube

Vienna ·

□ battles and sieges of the War of the Austrian Succession 1740–48

△ battles and sieges of the Seven Years' War 1756–63

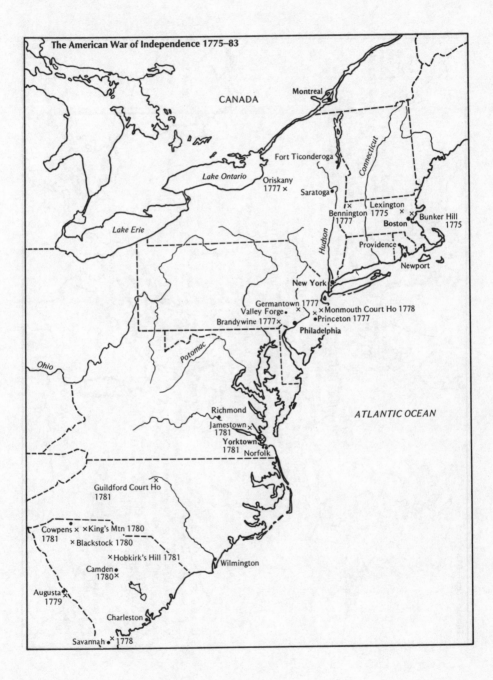

The American War of Independence 1775–83

CANADA

Montreal

Fort Ticonderoga

Lake Ontario

Oriskany 1777 ×

Saratoga

Connecticut

Lexington

Bennington 1775
1777

× Bunker Hill 1775

Boston

Lake Erie

Providence

Newport

Hudson

New York

Ohio

Germantown 1777

Valley Forge ×Monmouth Court Ho 1778

Brandywine 1777×

Princeton 1777

Philadelphia

Potomac

Richmond

ATLANTIC OCEAN

Jamestown ×
1781

Yorktown
1781

Norfolk

Guildford Court Ho
1781

Cowpens × ×King's Mtn 1780
1781

× Blackstock 1780

×Hobkirk's Hill 1781

Camden
1780×

Wilmington

Augusta×
1779

Charleston

Savannah ●×1778

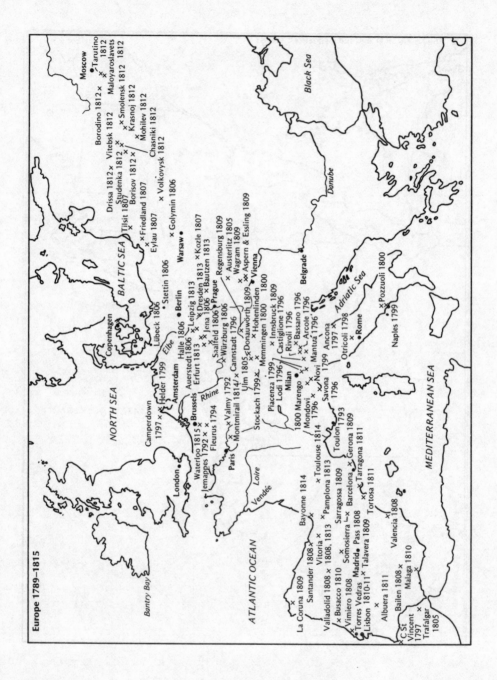

Europe 1789–1815

Moscow ● Tarutino 1812
×Maloyaroslavets 1812
Borodino 1812 × Vitebsk 1812 × ×Smolensk 1812
Studenka 1812 × ×Krasnoj 1812
Drissa 1812 × Borisov 1812 × Mohilev 1812
Tilsit 1807 × Chasniki 1812
× ×Friedland 1807 × Volkovysk 1812
Eylau 1807 × Golymin 1806

Black Sea

Danube

BALTIC SEA
Copenhagen
Lübeck 1806
Stettin 1806 ● Berlin ● Warsaw
Halle 1806 × Leipzig 1813
Auersted 1806 × ×Dresden 1813 ×Kozle 1807
Erfurt 1813 × × Bautzen 1813
× × ×Jena 1806 Prague
Saalfeld 1806 × Würzburg 1806
Regensburg 1809
× Austerlitz 1805
× Wagram 1809
× ×Aspern & Essling 1809
Donauwörth 1809 × Vienna
Ulm 1805 × ×Hohenlinden
Cannstadt 1796 Memmingen 1800 1800
× Innsbruck 1809

NORTH SEA
Camperdown
1797 × Helder 1799 ● Amsterdam
× London
Waterloo 1815 × ● Brussels
Jemappes 1792 × ×
Fleurus 1794
× Valmy 1792
Montmirail 1814 × × Cannstadt 1796
Paris × Stockach 1799

Elbe
Rhine

Loire
Vendée

Castiglione 1796
Piacenza 1799 × Rivoli 1796
Lodi 1796 × ×Bassano 1796
Milan × ×Arcole 1796
1800 Marengo × ×Mantua 1796
Mondovi × Novi 1799 Ancona
Savona 1799 × 1797 ×
1796 Orricoli 1798 ● Rome
Toulon 1793
× Toulouse 1814 × Pamplona 1813
Sarragossa 1809
Barcelona ×—× Gerona 1809
×Tarragona 1811
× Tortosa 1811

Adriatic Sea
Belgrade

Pozzuoli 1800
×
Naples 1799

Bayonne 1814
×
La Coruna 1809
Santander 1808 ×
Vitoria × 1808, 1813
Valladolid 1808 × Busacco 1810
×Somosierra Pass 1808
Vimiero 1808 × Madrid ● ×Talavera 1809
× Torres Vedras
Lisbon 1810-11 ×
Albuera 1811
×

MEDITERRANEAN SEA

Valencia 1808
×
Bailen 1808 × ×Malaga 1810
×
C St
Vincent
1797 ×
Trafalgar
1805

ATLANTIC OCEAN
Bantry Bay

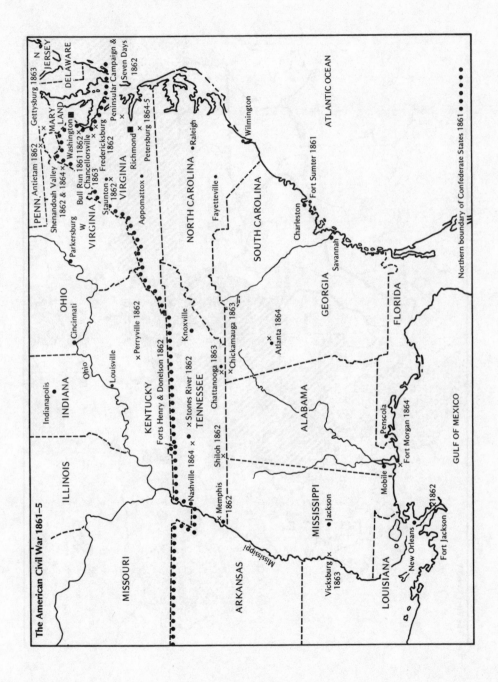

The American Civil War 1861–5

PENN

N
JERSEY

DELAWARE

MARY
LAND

Antietam 1862 ×
Gettysburg 1863 ×

Washington ■
Bull Run 1861 1862 ×
1862 & 1864 × Chancellorsville
Shenandoah Valley 1863
Parkersburg W × Fredericksburg
1862
Staunton × 1862
VIRGINIA Richmond ■

Peninsular Campaign &
Seven Days
1862

VIRGINIA × Appomattox × Petersburg 1864-5

NORTH CAROLINA ● Raleigh

Fayetteville ●

SOUTH CAROLINA

Wilmington ●

Charleston ×

Fort Sumter 1861

ATLANTIC OCEAN

OHIO

Cincinnati ●

Ohio

Louisville ●

KENTUCKY

× Perryville 1862

× Knoxville
Forts Henry & Donelson 1862
× Stones River 1862

Chattanooga 1863 ×
× Chickamauga 1863

GEORGIA

Savannah ●

FLORIDA

Indianapolis ●

INDIANA

ILLINOIS

TENNESSEE

Nashville 1864 ×
Shiloh 1862
× Memphis
1862

Atlanta 1864 ×

ALABAMA

MISSISSIPPI

Jackson ●

Pensola ●

Fort Morgan 1864

Mobile ×

GULF OF MEXICO

MISSOURI

Mississippi

ARKANSAS

Vicksburg
1863 ×

LOUISIANA

New Orleans ●

Fort Jackson

× 1862

● ● ● ● ● Northern boundary of Confederate States 1861

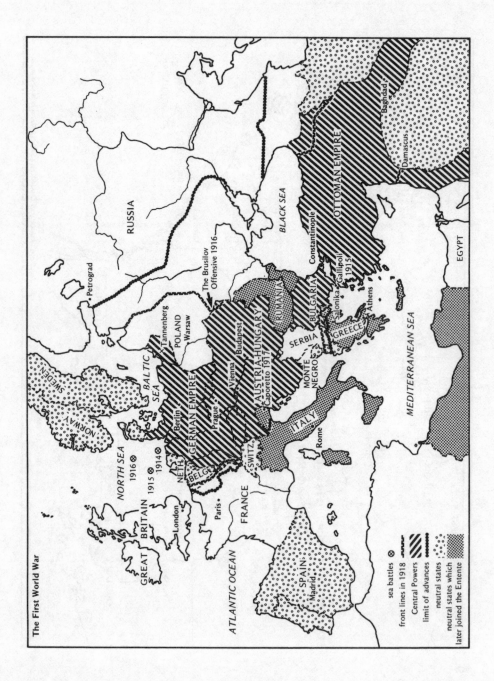

The First World War

RUSSIA

Petrograd

BLACK SEA

OTTOMAN EMPIRE

Baghdad

Damascus

Constantinople

The Brusilov
Offensive 1916

Gallipoli
1915

Salonika

Athens

EGYPT

MEDITERRANEAN SEA

SWEDEN

NORWAY

BALTIC
SEA

Tannenberg

POLAND

Warsaw

RUMANIA

BULGARIA

GREECE

NORTH SEA

1916 ⊗

1915 ⊗ 1914 ⊗

Berlin

GERMAN EMPIRE

Prague

Vienna

Budapest

AUSTRIA-HUNGARY

SERBIA

MONTE
NEGRO

Caporetto 1917

ITALY

Rome

NETH.

BELG.

SWITZ.

GREAT
BRITAIN

London

Paris

FRANCE

ATLANTIC OCEAN

SPAIN

Madrid

⊗ sea battles

━ front lines in 1918

▨ Central Powers

••• limit of advances

⫶ neutral states which

▦ later joined the Entente

neutral states

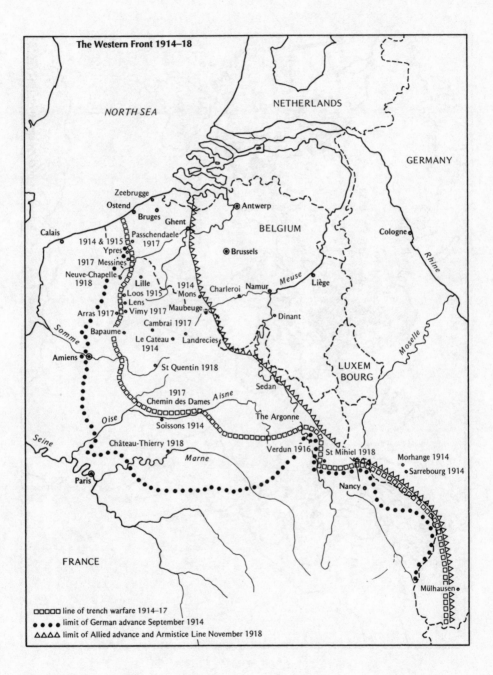

The Western Front 1914–18

NORTH SEA

NETHERLANDS

GERMANY

BELGIUM

Zeebrugge
Ostend
Bruges
Ghent
Antwerp
Cologne

Calais

1914 & 1915
Ypres
Passchendaele
1917
Brussels
Rhine

1917 Messines
Neuve-Chapelle
1918
Lille
Loos 1915
Lens
Arras 1917
Vimy 1917
1914
Mons
Charleroi
Namur
Liège
Meuse

Maubeuge
Cambrai 1917
Dinant

Bapaume
Somme
Le Cateau
1914
Landrecies

Amiens
St Quentin 1918

LUXEM
BOURG

1917
Chemin des Dames
Aisne
Sedan

Oise
Soissons 1914
The Argonne

Seine
Château-Thierry 1918
Marne
Verdun 1916
St Mihiel 1918
Morhange 1914
Sarrebourg 1914

Paris
Nancy
Moselle

FRANCE

Mülhausen

ㅁㅁㅁㅁㅁ line of trench warfare 1914–17
●●●● limit of German advance September 1914
△△△△ limit of Allied advance and Armistice Line November 1918

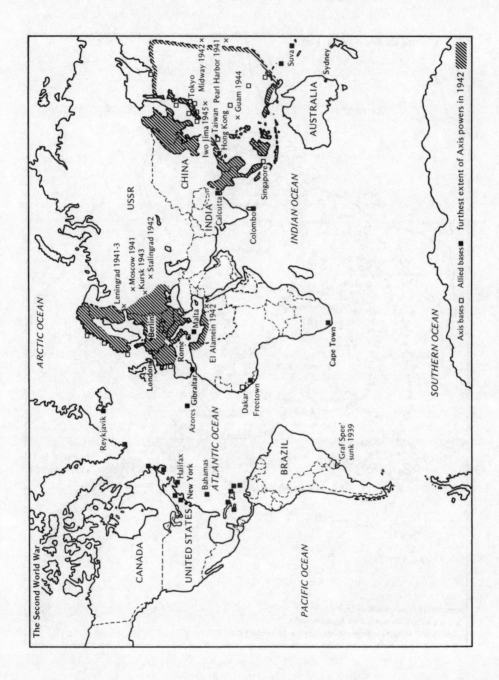